Professional Stage

Module F

Financial Reporting Environment

Revision Series

1773/F00

British Library Cataloguing-in-Publication Data

A catalogue record for this book is available from the British Library.

Published by AT Foulks Lynch Ltd
Number 4
The Griffin Centre
Staines Road
Feltham
Middlesex
TW14 0HS

ISBN 0 7483 4177 3

© AT Foulks Lynch Ltd, 2000

Acknowledgements

The past ACCA examination questions are the copyright of the Association of Chartered Certified Accountants. The answers to the questions from June 1994 onwards are the answers produced by the examiners themselves and are the copyright of the Association of Chartered Certified Accountants. The answers to the questions prior to June 1994 have been produced by AT Foulks Lynch Ltd.

We are grateful to the Chartered Institute of Management Accountants and the Institute of Chartered Accountants in England and Wales for permission to reproduce past examination questions. The answers have been prepared by AT Foulks Lynch Ltd.

CONTENTS

Question number		*Questions Page*	*Answers Page*
	THE ACCOUNTANT AS PROFESSIONAL		
	International issues		
1	CIC plc *(J91)*	1	15

Cash flow statements

Additional reports and share valuation

ACCOUNTING FOR RECONSTRUCTIONS, MERGERS AND COMBINATIONS

ANALYSING AND APPRAISING FINANCIAL AND RELATED INFORMATION

Note that the ACCA changes examiners from time to time and that there was a new examiner for Paper 13 from June 1997. However, we ensure that the answers included here are those written by the original examiner who set the questions.

PREFACE

The new edition of the ACCA Revision Series, published for the June and December 2000 examinations, contains a wealth of features to make your prospects of passing the exams even brighter.

Examiner Plus

This book contains all the new syllabus examinations from June 1994 up to and including December 1999 plus the examiner's official answers. All the exams from June 1994 to December 1999 are set out in chronological order in this book.

We have cross referenced all these questions to their topic headings in the contents pages so you can see at a glance what questions have been set on each syllabus area to date, topic by topic.

The inclusion of these questions and answers really does give students an unparalleled view of the way the new syllabus examinations are set and, even more importantly, a tremendous insight into the mind of the Examiner. The Examiner's answers are in some cases fairly lengthy and whilst the Examiner would not necessarily expect you to include all the points that his answers include, they do nevertheless give you an excellent insight into the sorts of things that the Examiner is looking for and will help you produce answers in line with the Examiner's thinking.

Key Features

Step by Step Answer Plans and *'Did you answer the question?'* checkpoints are fully explained on the following two pages.

Tutorial Notes

In some situations the examiner's official answers benefit from a little extra explanation when they are to be used as a learning aid. Where appropriate, we have incorporated extra workings or explanatory notes, so that you derive the maximum benefit from these answers in preparation for your own exam.

Topic Index

The topics covered in all the answers have been indexed. This means that you can easily access an answer relating to any topic which you want to consider by use of the index as well as by reference to the contents page at the front of the book.

The Revision Series also contains the following features:

- Practice questions and answers - a total bank of around 80 questions and answers

- An analysis of the new syllabus exams from June 1994 to December 1999

- Update notes to bring you up to date for new examinable documents and any changes to legislation as at 1st December 1999.

- The syllabus and format of the examination

- General Revision Guidance

- Examination Technique - an essential guide to ensure that you approach the examinations correctly

- Key Revision Topics

- Formulae and tables where appropriate

HOW TO USE THE ANSWER PLANS AND 'DID YOU ANSWER THE QUESTION?' CHECKPOINTS

STEP BY STEP ANSWER PLANS

A key feature in this year's Revision Series is the Step by Step Answer Plans, produced for all new syllabus exam questions from June 1995 to June 1999.

Students are always being told to plan their answers and this feature gives you positive assistance by showing you how you should plan your answer and the type of plan that you should produce before you attempt the question.

Of course, in the exam, your answer Plan can be less fully written than ours because you are writing it for yourself. We are producing an answer plan which communicates the details to you the student and therefore is of necessity much fuller. However, all the detail is there, written in a way which shows you the lines along which you should be thinking in order to produce the answer plan.

You will notice that the Answer Plans start and finish with the exhortation that you must make sure that you have read the question and that you are answering it correctly. Each time you write down the next step in the Answer Plan, you must ask yourself - 'Why am I including this step?' 'Is it relevant?' 'Is this what the Examiner has asked me to do and expected me to do?'

Help with the answer

In addition, if you really do get stuck with the question and cannot see how to approach it, you may find it helpful to turn to the answer page, **cover up the answer itself!,** and start to read the Answer Plan. This may trigger your memory such that you can then return to the question itself and gain all the benefit of doing the question properly without reference to the answer itself.

Practice makes perfect

Like all elements of examination technique the time to learn how to plan your answers is not in the examination itself. You have to practise them now - every time you produce an answer - so that when you come to the examination itself these answer plans will be second nature.

It is probably a good idea to sketch out your answer plans in the way we have produced them here (but remember they can be briefer) and then compare them swiftly to our Answer Plan at the back of the book (don't look at the answer itself at this stage!).

This may indicate that you have completely missed the point of the question or it might indicate one or two other areas that you might wish to explore.

Then, without having yet looked at the answer itself, start writing your answer proper and then compare that with the examiner's own answer.

'DID YOU ANSWER THE QUESTION?' CHECKPOINTS

This is another feature included in this year's edition of the Revision Series. They are included in the new syllabus exam answers from June 1995 to June 1999.

At various points of the answers, you will come across a box headed **'Did you answer the question'**, followed by a brief note which shows you how the printed answer is answering the question and encourages you to make sure that your own answer has not wandered off the point or missed the point of the question completely.

This is an invaluable feature and it is a discipline you must develop as you practise answering questions. It is an area of examination technique that you must practise and practise again and again until it becomes second nature. How often do we read in an Examiner's report that candidates did not answer the question the Examiner had set but had simply answered the question that they wanted him to set or simply wandered off the point altogether? You must make sure that your answers do not fall into that particular trap and that they do rigorously follow the questions set.

A good way of practising this aspect of examination technique is to imagine an empty box headed up 'Did you answer the question?' at the end of the paragraph or paragraphs you are about to write on a particular topic. Try and imagine what you are going to write in that box; what are you going to say in that box which justifies the two or three paragraphs that you are about to write. If you can't imagine what you are going to put in that box, or when you imagine it you find that you are struggling to relate the next few paragraphs to the question, then think very hard before you start writing those paragraphs. Are they completely relevant? Why are you writing them? How are they relevant to the question?

You will find this 'imagining the box' a very useful way of focusing your mind on what you are writing and its relevance to the question.

SUMMARY

Use the two techniques together. They will help you to produce planned answers and they will help you make sure that your answers are focused very fully and carefully on the question the Examiner has actually set.

1 EXAMINATION FORMAT AND SYLLABUS

FORMAT OF THE EXAMINATION

		Number of marks
Section A:	1 compulsory question of 30 marks	30
Section B:	2 (out of 3) questions of 25 marks each	50
Section C:	1 (out of 2) questions of 20 marks each	20
		100

Section A will cover group accounts and other associated topics such as reconstructions. Section B will include detailed questions on the more complex accounting standards, exposure drafts and discussion documents. Section C will include questions concentrating on current issues and controversies in auditing.

Introduction

This Paper builds upon the financial accounting knowledge gained in the Papers 1, 6 and 10. Coverage of the topics will make reference to their audit implications.

(1)   THE ACCOUNTANT AS A PROFESSIONAL

    (a)   Interpretation and application of all extant SSAPs and FRSs.

    (b)   Critically appraising, evaluating proposed changes and promoting changes in

        (i)   accounting theories and principles

        (ii)   concepts

        (iii)   Accounting Standards

        (iv)   Financial Reporting Standards

        (v)   Financial Reporting Exposure Drafts

        (vi)   Discussion Drafts

        (vii)   guidelines

        (viii) major pronouncements of the Urgent Issues Task Force and the Review Panel

        (ix)   accounting aspects of company law.

    (c)   Monitoring and evaluating

        (i)   international issues
        (ii)   ethical issues.

(2)   PREPARING FINANCIAL STATEMENTS AND REPORTS

(a)   Preparation of financial statements and reports under conditions of stable or changing prices.

(b)   Groups of companies

   (i)   explaining statutory and professional requirements relating to the preparation for publication of consolidated accounts for groups and the audit thereof

   (ii)   accounting for the following organisational situations

   • foreign subsidiary undertaking
   • mixed and vertical groups.

(c)   The preparation of reports for a variety of users including

   (i)   shareholders relating to offers for sale, rights issues, profit forecasts

   (ii)   lenders to assist in decisions relating to company loan obligations

   (iii)   employees

   (iv)   assessing the valuation of shares in unquoted companies for balance sheet purposes

   (v)   calculating and appraising the impact on profit reporting and balance sheet of the available methods of valuation.

(3)   ACCOUNTING FOR RECONSTRUCTIONS, MERGERS AND COMBINATIONS

(a)   Accounting for changes in organisational structures

   (i)   single companies

   • reconstruction
   • capital reorganisations
   • amalgamations and absorptions

   (ii)   groups

   • changes of parent company interest.

(b)   Explaining the major features of reconstructions, mergers and take-overs, their principal aspects and the legal and audit consequences in relation to

   (i)   control of mergers and the public interest
   (ii)   regulation of take-overs; statutory procedures
   (iii)   obligations on directors
   (iv)   minority rights.

(c)   Explaining the major features of dissolution, its principal aspects and the legal consequences in relation to

   (i)   administrative receivership
   (ii)   voluntary winding up
   (iii)   compulsory winding up.

(4)   **ANALYSING AND APPRAISING FINANCIAL AND RELATED INFORMATION**

The analysis and appraisal of implications of financial and related information for accounting purposes and for the auditor's analytical review to include

(a)   Evaluating internal consistency and validity of the information collected/produced for the accounts.

(b)   Identifying matters for further interpretation in the information produced (eg, by comparing it to other information such as prior years, budgets/targets, industry norms, state of the economy).

(c)   Interpreting and analysing accounts and statements (eg, by ratio analysis) for indications of aspects of business performance such as value for money, quality, long-term solvency and stability, short-term solvency and liquidity, profitability, efficiency, growth, failure prediction using, for example

     (i)   inter-temporal analysis
     (ii)   intra and inter-firm comparisons
     (iii)   multi-variate analysis
     (iv)   trend analysis.

(d)   Assessing the impact of price level changes on the analysis.

(e)   Assessing informational weaknesses/limitations of statements and analyses.

(f)   Presenting financial and related information and analysis in reports taking account of

     (i)   sources of information for the purpose of comparisons, such as financial statements for previous periods, industry norms

     (ii)   background to the organisation (eg, market, sales, profits, capital investment, management structure, employees and industrial relations)

     (iii)   future trends affecting the organisation (national and international)

     (iv)   types and relevance of different ratios and trends

     (v)   levels of ratios expected for the organisation/sector.

(5)   **CURRENT ISSUES AND CONTROVERSIES**

(a)   The evaluation of current issues and controversies relating to auditing, including audit expectations, the regulation of audits.

(b)   The monitoring and evaluation of international issues affecting auditing including EC developments.

(c)   Monitoring developments in auditing theories and their implications for the profession.

2 ANALYSIS OF PAST PAPERS

Topics	J94	D94	J95	D95	J96	D96	J97	D97	J98	D98	J99	D99
Foreign currency translation	1 □				1 □			2 ○	1 □			
Consolidated financial statements	1 □		1 □	1 □	1 □	1 □ 5 ○	1 □ 3 ● 4 ●	3 ○	1 □	1 □	1 □ 3 ○	1 □
Reconstructions and reorganisations	2 □		3 ○	3 ○	4 ○	4 ○				3 ○		
Inflation accounting	3 □									2 ○		
Interpretation of financial statements	3 ■	3 □	2 □	2 □	2 □	2 □	2 ■		2 ○			
Application of accounting standards and accounting principles	4 □	4 □				5 ○	3 ○	2 □ 4 ○	3 ○ 4 ●	4 ○		4 ○
FRS 5				4 ○					3 ○			
Tangible fixed assets	3 □									4 ●		
SSAP 9		2 □										
SSAP 15		2 □				3 ○		4 ○				
SSAP 24			4 ○				4 ○					
The cash flow statement		1 □							1 □			
Financial instruments												3 ○
International issues			5 ○				2 ■					
Distributable profits					3 ○							
Ethical issues					5 ○			5 ○	5 ○	6 ○		6 ○
Intangible assets							3 ○				1 ■	
Related party disclosures							5 ○					2 ○
Segmental reporting											2 ○	
Earnings per share											4 ○	
Liability of auditors								6 ○				
Share valuation										4 ○		
Current issues in auditing									6 ○	5 ○	5 ○ 6 ○	5 ○

Key

The number refers to the number of the question where this topic was examined in the exam.

□   This topic formed the whole or a substantial part of a compulsory question.

■   This topic formed a non-substantial part of a compulsory question.

○   This topic formed the whole or a substantial part of an optional question.

●   This topic formed a non-substantial part of an optional question.

3 GENERAL REVISION GUIDANCE

PLANNING YOUR REVISION

What is revision?

Revision is the process by which you remind yourself of the material you have studied during your course, clarify any problem areas and bring your knowledge to a state where you can retrieve it and present it in a way that will satisfy the Examiners.

Revision is not a substitute for hard work earlier in the course. The syllabus for this paper is too large to be hastily 'crammed' a week or so before the examination. You should think of your revision as the final stage in your study of any topic. It can only be effective if you have already completed earlier stages.

Ideally, you should begin your revision shortly after you begin an examination course. At the end of every week and at the end of every month, you should review the topics you have covered. If you constantly consolidate your work and integrate revision into your normal pattern of study, you should find that the final period of revision - and the examination itself - are much less daunting.

If you are reading this revision text while you are still working through your course, we strongly suggest that you begin now to review the earlier work you did for this paper. Remember, the more times you return to a topic, the more confident you will become with it.

The main purpose of this book, however, is to help you to make the best use of the last few weeks before the examination. In this section we offer some suggestions for effective planning of your final revision and discuss some revision techniques which you may find helpful.

Planning your time

Most candidates find themselves in the position where they have less time than they would like to revise, particularly if they are taking several papers at one diet. The majority of people must balance their study with conflicting demands from work, family or other commitments.

It is impossible to give hard and fast rules about the amount of revision you should do. You should aim to start your final revision at least four weeks before your examination. If you finish your course work earlier than this, you would be well advised to take full advantage of the extra time available to you. The number of hours you spend revising each week will depend on many factors, including the number of papers you are sitting. You should probably aim to do a minimum of about six to eight hours a week for each paper.

In order to make best use of the revision time that you have, it is worth spending a little of it at the planning stage. We suggest that you begin by asking yourself two questions:

- How much time do I have available for revision?
- What do I need to cover during my revision?

Once you have answered these questions, you should be able to draw up a detailed timetable. We will now consider these questions in more detail.

How much time do I have available for revision?

Many people find it helpful to work out a regular weekly pattern for their revision. We suggest you use the time planning chart provided to do this. Your aim should be to construct a timetable that is sustainable over a period of several weeks.

Time planning chart

	Monday	Tuesday	Wednesday	Thursday	Friday	Saturday	Sunday
00.00							
01.00							
02.00							
03.00							
04.00							
05.00							
06.00							
07.00							
08.00							
09.00							
10.00							
11.00							
12.00							
13.00							
14.00							
15.00							
16.00							
17.00							
18.00							
19.00							
20.00							
21.00							
22.00							
23.00							

1   First, block out all the time that is **definitely unavailable** for revision. This will include the hours when you normally sleep, the time you are at work and any other regular and clear commitments.

2   Think about **other people's claims on your time**. If you have a family, or friends whom you see regularly, you may want to discuss your plans with them. People are likely to be flexible in the demands they make on you in the run-up to your examinations, especially if they are aware that you have considered their needs as well as your own. If you consult the individuals who are affected by your plans, you may find that they are surprisingly supportive, instead of being resentful of the extra time you are spending studying.

3   Next, give some thought to the times of day when you **work most effectively**. This differs very much from individual to individual. Some people can concentrate first thing in the morning. Others work best in the early evening, or last thing at night. Some people find their day-to-day work so demanding that they are unable to do anything extra during the week, but must concentrate their study time at weekends. Mark the times when you feel you could do your best work on the

timetable. It is extremely important to acknowledge your personal preferences here. If you ignore them, you may devise a timetable that is completely unrealistic and which you will not be able to adhere to.

4   Consider your **other commitments**. Everybody has certain tasks, from doing the washing to walking the dog, that must be performed on a regular basis. These tasks may not have to be done at a particular time, but you should take them into consideration when planning your schedule. You may be able to find more convenient times to get these jobs done, or be able to persuade other people to help you with them.

5   Now mark some time for **relaxation**. If your timetable is to be sustainable, it must include some time for you to build up your reserves. If your normal week does not include any regular physical activity, make sure that you include some in your revision timetable. A couple of hours spent in a sports centre or swimming pool each week will probably enhance your ability to concentrate.

6   Your timetable should now be taking shape. You can probably see obvious study sessions emerging. It is not advisable to work for too long at any one session. Most people find that they can only really concentrate for one or two hours at a time. If your study sessions are longer than this, you should split them up.

What do I need to cover during my revision?

Most candidates are more confident about some parts of the syllabus than others. Before you begin your revision, it is important to have an overview of where your strengths and weaknesses lie.

One way to do this is to take a sheet of paper and divide it into three columns. Mark the columns:

OK Marginal Not OK

or use similar headings to indicate how confident you are with a topic. Then go through the syllabus (reprinted in Section 1) and list the topics under the appropriate headings. Alternatively, you could use the list of key topics in Section 5 of this book to compile your overview. You might also find it useful to skim through the introductions or summaries to the textbook or workbooks you have used in your course. These should remind you of parts of the course that you found particularly easy or difficult at the time. You could also use some of the exercises and questions in the workbooks or textbooks, or some of the questions in this book, as a diagnostic aid to discover the areas where you need to work hardest.

It is also important to be aware which areas of the syllabus are so central to the subject that they are likely to be examined in every diet, and which are more obscure, and not likely to come up so frequently. Your textbooks, workbooks and lecture notes will help you here, and section 2 of this book contains an analysis of past papers. Remember, the Examiner will be looking for broad coverage of the syllabus. There is no point in knowing one or two topics in exhaustive detail if you do so at the expense of the rest of the course.

Writing your revision timetable

You now have the information you need to write your timetable. You know how many weeks you have available, and the approximate amount of time that is available in each week.

You should stop all serious revision 48 hours before your examination. After this point, you may want to look back at your notes to refresh your memory, but you should not attempt to revise any new topics. A clear and rested brain is worth more than any extra facts you could memorise in this period.

Make one copy of this chart for each week you have available for revision.

Using your time planning chart, write in the times of your various study sessions during the week.

In the lower part of the chart, write in the topics that you will cover in each of these sessions.

Example of a revision timetable

Revision timetable Week beginning:	Monday	Tuesday	Wednesday	Thursday	Friday	Saturday	Sunday
Study sessions							
Topics							

Some revision techniques

There should be two elements in your revision. You must **look back** to the work you have covered in the course and **look forward** to the examination. The techniques you use should reflect these two aspects of revision.

Revision should not be boring. It is useful to try a variety of techniques. You probably already have some revision techniques of your own and you may also like to try some of the techniques suggested here, if they are new to you. However, don't waste time with methods of revision which are not effective for you.

- Go through your lecture notes, textbook or workbooks and use a highlighter pen to mark important points.

- Produce a new set of summarised notes. This can be a useful way of re-absorbing information, but you must be careful to keep your notes concise, or you may find that you are simply reproducing work you have done before. It is helpful to use a different format for your notes.

- Make a collection of key words which remind you of the essential concepts of a topic.

- Reduce your notes to a set of key facts and definitions which you must memorise. Write them on cards which you can keep with you all the time.

- When you come across areas which you were unsure about first time around, rework relevant questions in your course materials, then study the answers in great detail.

- If there are isolated topics which you feel are completely beyond you, identify exactly what it is that you cannot understand and find someone (such as a lecturer or recent graduate) who can explain these points to you.

- Practise as many exam standard questions as you can. The best way to do this is to work to time, under exam conditions. You should always resist looking at the answer until you have finished.

- If you have come to rely on a word processor in your day-to-day work, you may have got out of the habit of writing at speed. It is well worth reviving this skill before you sit down in the examination hall: it is something you will need.

- If you have a plentiful supply of relevant questions, you could use them to practise planning answers, and then compare your notes with the answers provided. This is not a substitute for writing full answers, but can be helpful additional practice.

- Go back to questions you have already worked on during the course. This time, complete them under exam conditions, paying special attention to the layout and organisation of your answers. Then compare them in detail with the suggested answers and think about the ways in which your answer differs. This is a useful way of 'fine tuning' your technique.

- During your revision period, do make a conscious effort to identify situations which illustrate concepts and ideas that may arise in the examination. These situations could come from your own work, or from reading the business pages of the quality press. This technique will give you a new perspective on your studies and could also provide material which you can use in the examination.

4 EXAMINATION TECHNIQUES

THE EXAMINATION

This section is divided into two parts. The first part considers the practicalities of sitting the examination. If you have taken other ACCA examinations recently, you may find that everything here is familiar to you. The second part discusses some examination techniques which you may find useful.

The practicalities

What to take with you

You should make sure that you have:

- your ACCA registration card
- your ACCA registration docket.

You may also take to your desk:

- pens and pencils
- a ruler and slide rule
- a calculator
- charting template and geometrical instruments
- eraser and correction fluid.

You are not allowed to take rough paper into the examination.

If you take any last-minute notes with you to the examination hall, make sure these are not on your person. You should keep notes or books in your bag or briefcase, which you will be asked to leave at the side of the examination hall.

Although most examination halls will have a clock, it is advisable to wear a watch, just in case your view is obscured.

If your calculator is solar-powered, make sure it works in artificial light. Some examination halls are not particularly well-lit. If you use a battery-powered calculator, take some spare batteries with you. For obvious reasons, you may not use a calculator which has a graphic/word display memory. Calculators with printout facilities are not allowed because they could disturb other candidates

Getting there

You should arrange to arrive at the examination hall at least half an hour before the examination is due to start. If the hall is a large one, the invigilator will start filling the hall half an hour before the starting time.

Make absolutely sure that you know how to get to the examination hall and how long it will take you. Check on parking or public transport. Leave yourself enough time so that you will not be anxious if the journey takes a little longer than you anticipated. Many people like to make a practice trip the day before their first examination.

At the examination hall

Examination halls differ greatly in size. Some only hold about ten candidates. Others can sit many hundreds of people. You may find that more than one examination is being taken at the hall at the same time, so don't panic if you hear people discussing a completely different subject from the one you have revised.

While you are waiting to go in, don't be put off by other people talking about how well, or badly, they have prepared for the examination.

You will be told when to come in to the examination hall. The desks are numbered. (Your number will be on your examination docket.) You will be asked to leave any bags at the side of the hall.

Inside the hall, the atmosphere will be extremely formal. The invigilator has certain things which he or she must tell candidates, often using a particular form of words. Listen carefully, in case there are any unexpected changes to the arrangements.

On your desk you will see a question paper and an answer booklet in which to write your answers. You will be told when to turn over the paper.

During the examination

You will have to leave your examination paper and answer booklet in the hall at the end of the examination. It is quite acceptable to write on your examination paper if it helps you to think about the questions. However, all workings should be in your answers. You may write any plans and notes in your answer booklet, as long as you cross them out afterwards.

If you require a new answer booklet, put your hand up and a supervisor will come and bring you one.

At various times during the examination, you will be told how much time you have left.

You should not need to leave the examination hall until the examination is finished. Put up your hand if you need to go to the toilet, and a supervisor will accompany you. If you feel unwell, put up your hand, and someone will come to your assistance. If you simply get up and walk out of the hall, you will not be allowed to reenter.

Before you finish, you must fill in the required information on the front of your answer booklet.

Examination techniques

Tackling Paper 13

The examination will include 6 questions. The format of this paper has changed with effect from December 1997. The paper is in three sections. Section A consists of one compulsory question of 30 marks, which will cover group accounts and related topics. Section B contains 3 questions of 25 marks each, of which you will have to answer 2 questions only. These questions will cover the remainder of the financial reporting part of the syllabus. Section C contains 2 questions of 20 marks each, of which you will have to answer one question only. These questions will cover current issues and controversies in auditing.

This paper will ask you to demonstrate the skills expected at the professional stage. You will have to exercise narrative and technical skills and use your judgement to present reasoned conclusions. You will also be expected to draw on and integrate your knowledge from earlier papers.

The Examiner will be looking for evidence that you can apply your knowledge and present it persuasively and accurately.

Your general strategy

You should spend the first ten minutes of the examination reading the paper. Where you have a choice of question, decide which questions you will do. You must divide the time you spend on questions in proportion to the marks on offer. Don't be tempted to spend more time on a question you know a lot about, or one which you find particularly difficult. If a question has more than one part, you must complete each part.

On every question, the first marks are the easiest to gain. Even if things go wrong with your timing and you don't have time to complete a question properly, you will probably gain some marks by making a start.

Spend the last five minutes reading through your answers and making any additions or corrections.

You may answer written questions in any order you like. Some people start with their best question, to help them relax. Another strategy is to begin with your second best question, so that you are working even more effectively when you reach the question you are most confident about.

Once you have embarked on a question, you should try to stay with it, and not let your mind stray to other questions on the paper. You can only concentrate on one thing at once. However, if you get completely stuck with a question, leave space in your answer book and return to it later.

Answering the question

All Examiners say that the most frequent reason for failure in examinations, apart from basic lack of knowledge, is candidates' unwillingness to answer the question that the Examiner has asked. A great many people include every scrap of knowledge they have on a topic, just in case it is relevant. Stick to the question and tailor your answer to what you are asked. Pay particular attention to the verbs in the question.

You should be particularly wary if you come across a question which appears to be almost identical to one which you have practised during your revision. It probably isn't! Wishful thinking makes many people see the question they would like to see on the paper, not the one that is actually there. Read a question at least twice before you begin your answer. Underline key words on the question paper, if it helps focus your mind on what is required.

If you don't understand what a question is asking, state your assumptions. Even if you do not answer in precisely the way the Examiner hoped, you may be given some credit, if your assumptions are reasonable.

Presentation

You should do everything you can to make things easy for the marker. Although you will not be marked on your handwriting, the marker will find it easier to identify the points you have made if your answers are legible. The same applies to spelling and grammar. Use blue or black ink. The marker will be using red or green.

Use the margin to clearly identify which question, or part of a question, you are answering.

Start each answer on a new page. The order in which you answer the questions does not matter, but if a question has several parts, these parts should appear in the correct order in your answer book.

If there is the slightest doubt when an answer continues on another page, indicate to the marker that he or she must turn over. It is irritating for a marker to think he or she has reached the end of an answer, only to turn the page and find that the answer continues.

Use columnar layouts for computations. This will help you to avoid mistakes, and is easier to follow.

Use headings and numbered sentences if they help to show the structure of your answer. However, don't write your answers in one-word note form.

It is a good idea to make a rough plan of an answer before you begin to write. Do this in your answer booklet, but make sure you cross it out neatly afterwards. The marker needs to be clear whether he or she is looking at your rough notes, or the answer itself.

Computations

Before you begin a computation, you may find it helpful to jot down the stages you will go through. Cross out these notes afterwards.

It is essential to include all your workings and to indicate where they fit in to your answer. It is important that the marker can see where you got the figures in your answer from. Even if you make mistakes in your computations, you will be given credit for using a principle correctly, if it is clear from your workings and the structure of your answer.

If you spot an arithmetical error which has implications for figures later in your answer, it may not be worth spending a lot of time reworking your computation.

If you are asked to comment or make recommendations on a computation, you must do so. There are important marks to be gained here. Even if your computation contains mistakes, you may still gain marks if your reasoning is correct.

Use the layouts which you see in the answers given in this booklet and in model answers. A clear layout will help you avoid errors and will impress the marker.

Essay questions

You must plan an essay before you start writing. One technique is to quickly jot down any ideas which you think are relevant. Re-read the question and cross out any points in your notes which are not relevant. Then number your points. Remember to cross out your plan afterwards.

Your essay should have a clear structure. It should contain a brief introduction, a main section and a conclusion. Don't waste time by restating the question at the start of your essay.

Break your essay up into paragraphs. Use sub-headings and numbered sentences if they help show the structure of your answer.

Be concise. It is better to write a little about a lot of different points than a great deal about one or two points.

The Examiner will be looking for evidence that you have understood the syllabus and can apply your knowledge in new situations. You will also be expected to give opinions and make judgements. These should be based on reasoned and logical arguments.

Reports, memos and other documents

Some questions ask you to present your answer in the form of a report or a memo or other document. It is important that you use the correct format - there are easy marks to be gained here. Adopt the format used in sample questions, or use the format you are familiar with in your day-to-day work, as long as it contains all the essential elements.

You should also consider the audience for any document you are writing. How much do they know about the subject? What kind of information and recommendations are required? The Examiner will be looking for evidence that you can present your ideas in an appropriate form.

5 KEY REVISION TOPICS

The aim of this section is to provide you with a checklist of key information relating to this paper. You should use it as a reminder of topics to be revised rather than as a summary of all you need to know. Aim to revise as many topics as possible because many of the questions in the exam draw on material from more than one section of the syllabus. You will get more out of this section if you read through Section 3, *General Revision Guidance* first.

In this section we will briefly go over the syllabus, pointing out key points that you should remember in order to jog your memory.

1 THE FINANCIAL REPORTING ENVIRONMENT

You must be familiar with:

- the role of: company legislation, the Stock Exchange, the Financial Reporting Council (FRC), the Accounting Standards Board (ASB), the Financial Reporting Review Panel (FRRP), the Urgent Issues Task Force (UITF) and EU Directives

- the benefits of a conceptual framework

- the ASB's Draft Statement of Principles

Refer to Chapter 1 of the Lynchpin.

2 INTERNATIONAL ISSUES

You must be familiar with:

- barriers to international harmonisation and advantages of closer harmonisation

- current progress on harmonisation

- the role of the IASC and the impact of IASs on UK accounting practice

You must be able to:

- identify major differences between UK accounts and overseas accounts

- restate overseas accounts in line with UK accounting policies

Refer to Chapter 2 of the Lynchpin and attempt questions 1, 25 and 47 of this book.

3 TANGIBLE FIXED ASSETS

You must be familiar with:

- alternative definitions of assets

- regulatory requirements on cost and value

- requirements of current accounting standards (SSAP 19, FRS 11 and FRS 15)

Refer to Chapter 3 of the Lynchpin and attempt questions 16 and 66 of this book.

4   INTANGIBLE FIXED ASSETS

You must be familiar with:

- problems of defining, recognising, valuing and depreciating intangibles

- the effect of alternative treatments on performance ratios

- requirements of company legislation and current accounting standards (SSAP 13 and FRS 10)

Refer to Chapter 4 of the Lynchpin and attempt question 48 of this book.

5   STOCKS AND LONG TERM CONTRACTS

You must be familiar with:

- SSAP 9 and Companies Act requirements

- problem areas on long term contracts

Refer to Chapter 5 of the Lynchpin and attempt question 18 of this book.

6   TAX IN COMPANY ACCOUNTS

You must be familiar with:

- requirements of current accounting standards (SSAPs 5, 8 and 15) and recent proposals regarding current taxation (FRED 18)

- alternative methods and bases of providing for deferred tax

- reasons why SSAP 15 has been criticised and the ASB's recent proposals (FRED 19)

Refer to Chapter 6 of the Lynchpin and attempt questions 2, 33 and 54 of this book.

7   ACCOUNTING FOR PENSION COSTS

You must be familiar with:

- the difference between defined benefit and defined contribution schemes

- the accounting and disclosure requirements of SSAP 24

- recent ASB proposals (FRED 20)

Refer to Chapter 7 of the Lynchpin and attempt questions 24 and 44 of this book.

8   REPORTING THE SUBSTANCE OF TRANSACTIONS

You must be familiar with:

- the perceived benefits of off balance sheet finance

- common forms of off balance sheet finance

- accounting and disclosure requirements of FRS 5

- accounting and disclosure requirements of FRS 12

Refer to Chapter 8 of the Lynchpin and attempt questions 4, 29 and 45 of this book.

9   LEASING CONTRACTS

You must be familiar with:

- the difference between an operating lease and a finance lease

- accounting and disclosure requirements of SSAP 21 (lessee's and lessor's accounts)

Refer to Chapter 9 of the Lynchpin and attempt question 59 of this book.

10   REPORTING FINANCIAL PERFORMANCE

You must be familiar with:

- accounting and disclosure requirements of current standards (FRSs 3 and 14)

Refer to Chapter 10 of the Lynchpin and attempt all the remaining questions listed under the heading 'Reporting financial performance' on the contents pages at the front of this book.

11   REALISED AND LEGALLY DISTRIBUTABLE PROFIT

You must be familiar with:

- the definitions of realised profits and distributable profits

- the extent to which SSAPs/FRSs affect realised profits

Refer to Chapter 11 of the Lynchpin and attempt questions 5 and 28 of this book.

12   ACCOUNTING FOR THE EFFECTS OF CHANGING PRICES

You must be familiar with:

- the deficiencies of historic cost accounts and the reasons why historic cost accounts still prevail

- capital maintenance concepts: operating/physical, financial, real terms

- the strengths and weaknesses of CPP and CCA accounting

You must be able to:

- calculate and explain gains and losses caused by the impact of general inflation

- restate a historical cost profit and loss account for RPI movements

- apply the CPP model and calculate the main CCA adjustments

Refer to Chapter 12 of the Lynchpin and attempt all the questions listed under the heading 'Accounting for the effects of changing prices' on the contents pages at the front of this book.

13   CONSOLIDATED ACCOUNTS - SIMPLE GROUPS

You must be familiar with:

- basic consolidation techniques (including intra-group items)

- Companies Act and FRS 2 definitions

- exemption and exclusion requirements (Companies Act and FRS 2)

Refer to Chapter 13 of the Lynchpin and attempt question 7 of this book.

14   CONSOLIDATED ACCOUNTS - MORE COMPLEX GROUPS

You must be familiar with different possible structures of a group (horizontal, vertical, mixed).

You must be able to prepare group financial statements using acquisition accounting involving sub-subsidiaries.

Refer to Chapter 14 of the Lynchpin and attempt question 21 of this book.

15   CONSOLIDATED ACCOUNTS - CHANGES IN A GROUP

You must be able to deal with the following in the context of consolidated financial statements:

- piecemeal acquisitions

- subsequent bonus issues/capital reductions

- disposals (including the correct treatment of goodwill and the requirements of FRS 3)

- demergers

You must also understand the reasons why a company may demerge some of its subsidiaries.

Refer to Chapter 15 of the Lynchpin and attempt questions 21, 41, 46 and 63 of this book.

16   CONSOLIDATED ACCOUNTS - MERGERS AND ACQUISITIONS

You must be familiar with:

- the different methods which could be used to prepare group accounts (acquisition, merger, proportional consolidation)

- the merger method and how it differs from the acquisition method

- the requirements of the Companies Act and FRS 6 (criteria for merger accounting)

- recent proposals (Discussion Paper 'Business Combinations')

- the requirements of FRS 7 (fair values)

You must be able to:

- prepare a simple set of consolidated accounts using the merger method

- apply FRS 7 in given situations

Refer to Chapter 16 of the Lynchpin and attempt question 39 of this book.

17   ASSOCIATED COMPANIES

You must be familiar with:

- the equity method of accounting

- the difference between the equity method and proportional consolidation

- the requirements of the Companies Act and FRS 9 in relation to associates and joint ventures

- **the benefits and weaknesses of equity accounting**

Refer to Chapter 17 of the Lynchpin and attempt questions 7, 36, 40, 69 and 71 of this book.

18   OVERSEAS TRANSACTIONS

You must be familiar with:

- the difference between the temporal and the closing rate methods

- the arguments for each method

- the requirements of the Companies Act and SSAP 20

- hedging

- the weaknesses of SSAP 20

You must be able to apply both the temporal and the closing rate method to translate the financial statements of an overseas subsidiary and an overseas branch.

Refer to Chapter 18 of the Lynchpin and attempt all the questions listed under the heading 'Overseas transactions' on the contents pages at the front of this book.

19 CASH FLOW STATEMENTS

You must be familiar with:

- the requirements of FRS 1 (Revised)

- the strengths and weaknesses of FRS 1 (Revised)

You must be able to prepare a cash flow statement for a group, including the following:

- an acquisition or disposal during the year

- an overseas subsidiary

- an associate or joint venture, applying the requirements of FRS 9

Refer to Chapter 19 of the Lynchpin and attempt all the questions listed under the heading 'Cash flow statements' on the contents pages at the front of this book.

20 THE PREPARATION OF ADDITIONAL REPORTS

You must be familiar with:

- the requirements of the Companies Act and SSAP 25 on segmental reporting

- areas in which SSAP 25 is too vague and flexible

You must be able to prepare:

- a segmental report

- other reports offering guidance/advice to investors, lenders and employees

Refer to Chapter 20 of the Lynchpin.

21 SHARE VALUATION

You must be familiar with:

- the different methods of valuing shares in an unquoted company

- the situations in which each method may be appropriate

- the reasons why a company may wish to purchase its own shares

Refer to Chapter 21 of the Lynchpin and attempt all the questions listed under the heading 'Additional reports and share valuation' on the contents pages at the front of this book.

22 CHANGES IN ORGANISATIONAL STRUCTURE

You must be familiar with:

- the legal requirements relating to capital reductions and reorganisations

- the legal requirements relating to the redemption and purchase of own shares

- the circumstances when a capital redemption or reorganisation scheme is recommended

You must be able to prepare financial statements in accordance with a given scheme.

Refer to Chapter 22 of the Lynchpin.

23   RECONSTRUCTIONS, MERGERS AND TAKEOVERS

You must be familiar with:

- the legal requirements relating to dissolution and liquidation

- takeovers and mergers in the public interest (including obligations on directors during takeover bids and ways in which the rights of the minority are protected)

Refer to Chapter 23 of the Lynchpin and attempt all the questions listed under the heading 'Accounting for reconstructions, mergers and combinations' on the contents pages at the front of this book.

24   FINANCIAL ANALYSIS - RATIO ANALYSIS

You must be familiar with:

- the demand for financial analysis and the sources of information

- the relationship between the market price of a share and its EPS

- causes of changes in profitability

- problems of defining profit and net assets

- importance of maintaining a healthy liquid position

- causes of changes in liquidity

- implications of high or low gearing

- how GAAP affects the gearing of an individual company

- the difficulty in assessing the gearing of a group

Refer to Chapter 24 of the Lynchpin.

25   FINANCIAL ANALYSIS - ADDITIONAL STATEMENTS

You must be familiar with:

- the interpretation of current value accounts

- use of cash flow statements in interpretation (including advantages and disadvantages)

- the nature and value of information from other internal reports (e.g. value added statement, employee reports, non-financial information)

- nature and value of information from external sources (e.g. stockbrokers' circulars, press comment)

Refer to Chapter 25 of the Lynchpin.

26   CORPORATE FAILURE PREDICTION

You must be familiar with:

- the major causes of insolvency

- the use of multi-variate analysis to predict corporate failure

- the information provided in a statement of affairs

Refer to Chapter 26 of the Lynchpin.

27   LIMITATIONS OF RATIO ANALYSIS

You must be familiar with:

- the effect of inflation, different accounting policies, seasonal trading and window dressing upon financial statements and ratios

- Companies Act, Stock Exchange and FRS 8 requirements on related party transactions and disclosures

Refer to Chapter 27 of the Lynchpin.

28   FINANCIAL INSTRUMENTS

You must be familiar with:

- the requirements of FRS 4

- the problems of accounting for derivatives and financial instruments

- the disclosure requirements of FRS 13

Refer to Chapter 28 of the Lynchpin. Now attempt all the questions listed under the heading 'Analysing and appraising financial and related information' on the contents pages at the front of this book.

29   CURRENT ISSUES AND CONTROVERSIES

You must be familiar with:

- the financial reporting standard for smaller entities (FRSSE)

- current issues in auditing (e.g. legal liability, independence, international harmonisation)

- corporate governance issues (including the 'Cadbury Report')

Refer to Chapter 29 of the Lynchpin and attempt all the questions listed under the heading 'Current issues and controversies in auditing' on the contents pages at the front of this book.

6 UPDATES

INTRODUCTION

Examinable documents

Every six months (on 1 June and 1 December) the ACCA publish a list of 'examinable documents' which form the basis of the legislation and accounting regulations that will be examinable at the following diet.

The ACCA Official Textbooks published in July 1999 were fully up-to-date for these examinable documents published by the Association on 1 June 1999 and this section gives details of additional examinable documents listed by the ACCA at 1 December 1999.

Students are reminded that they should also read the ACCA Students' Newsletter. This is particularly important for students sitting Paper 13, because FREDs and Discussion Papers will be examined on the basis of articles published in the Newsletter.

The following technical developments are discussed in this section:

1   FRED 18: Current taxation
2   FRED 19: Deferred tax
3   FRED 20: Retirement benefits
4   Discussion Paper: Reporting financial performance
5   Updating notes for December 2000 students

FRED 18: CURRENT TAXATION

Background

During the last two years there have been many changes to the UK tax system. From July 1997, most companies and pension schemes were no longer able to reclaim tax credits on dividends received. Advance Corporation Tax (ACT) was abolished in April 1999. As a result, much of SSAP 8 *The treatment of taxation under the imputation system in the accounts of companies* has become obsolete.

FRED 18 was issued in June 1999. Its main proposals were non-controversial and it was adopted as an FRS in December 1999. However, for the June 2000 examination, FRED 18 remains examinable. FRS 16, which replaces it, is discussed below, but is not examinable until December 2000. It will replace SSAP 8. FRED 18 does not cover deferred tax, which is being addressed as a separate project (see below).

Main proposals

The main changes proposed from SSAP 8 are described below.

Dividends receivable

Dividends receivable should be recognised in the profit and loss account at the amount received or receivable without 'grossing up' for the related tax credit. (Under SSAP 8, dividends receivable included the tax credit, which was also recognised and disclosed as part of the tax charge for the period.)

Dividends receivable (and interest receivable) subject to a withholding tax should be recognised before the deduction of any withholding tax. The effect of any withholding tax suffered should be included as part of the tax charge. (This is similar to the treatment of tax credits under SSAP 8.) SSAP 8 did not consider withholding tax.

Definitions:

- A **tax credit** is the credit attributable to the recipient of a dividend under UK tax legislation because the dividend received is paid out of income that has already been subject to tax in the company that earned it.

- **Withholding tax** is tax deducted from dividends received or other income, paid to the tax authorities wholly on behalf of the recipient.

Other proposed changes

- Tax relating to gains or losses recognised in the Statement of total recognised gains and losses (STRGL) should also be recognised in the STRGL.

- Income and expenses subject to non-standard rates of tax should be included in the pre-tax results on the basis of the amounts actually receivable or payable (this is currently required by UITF Abstract 16).

FRED 19: DEFERRED TAX

Background

FRED 19 has been developed from proposals in the ASB's 1995 Discussion Paper *Accounting for tax*. If its proposals are adopted it will replace SSAP 15 *Accounting for deferred tax*.

SSAP 15 has been coming under increasing criticism, mainly because of problems arising from the fact that it requires deferred tax to be accounted for using the partial provision method:

- SSAP 15 was originally issued at a time when generous capital allowances and high inflation meant that many entities had a 'core' of timing differences that would never reverse and therefore partial provision reflected economic reality. Since then, conditions have changed, and there is now a far greater likelihood that timing differences will reverse.

- Partial provision is subjective and dependent on management intentions. It is potentially complicated to apply because it involves predicting future events, such as changes in the taxation system, capital expenditure and the useful economic lives of assets.

- It takes into account future transactions. This is inconsistent with the ASB's draft Statement of Principles (a liability can only exist as a result of a past transaction).

There are other problems:

- There are inconsistencies within the SSAP. Full provision is required for timing differences in respect of post-retirement benefits, but partial provision is required for all other timing differences.

- There are inconsistencies in the application of partial provision (eg, some entities provide deferred tax on fair value adjustments on acquisition while some do not). There is evidence that some entities make full provision on grounds of simplicity and this reduces the comparability of financial statements.

Arguably the most important reason for developing a new accounting standard is that partial provision is now inconsistent with international practice. Almost all other major standard setters (including the FASB and the IASC) now require full provision.

Full provision

FRED 19 proposes that full provision should be made for all deferred tax assets and liabilities arising from timing differences.

However, deferred tax assets or liabilities only arise if the transactions or events that increase or decrease future tax charges have occurred by the balance sheet date. This means that deferred tax is recognised on timing differences arising from:

- accelerated capital allowances;
- accruals for pension costs that will be deductible for tax purposes only when paid;
- elimination of unrealised intra group profits on consolidation;
- unrelieved tax losses; and
- other sources of short term timing differences.

Deferred tax is not recognised on timing differences arising:

- on gains on revaluing assets, unless the entity has entered into a binding agreement to sell the asset;
- following the sale of assets, on gains that have been rolled over onto replacement assets;
- on unremitted earnings of subsidiaries, associates and joint ventures.

Deferred tax assets are recognised only to the extent that, on the basis of all available evidence, it is believed to be more likely than not that they will be recovered.

The principle behind the above rules is that deferred tax is only provided where it represents an asset or a liability in its own right (this is called the incremental liability approach). For example, if an entity has capital allowances in excess of depreciation it has an obligation to pay more tax in future. It cannot avoid this obligation. In contrast, if an entity revalues a fixed asset, it will not have an obligation to pay more tax unless it enters into a binding agreement to sell the asset.

Other proposals

- Deferred tax attributable to gains or losses recognised in the Statement of total recognised gains and losses (STRGL) should also be recognised in the STRGL.

- Deferred tax should be measured at the average tax rates that are expected to apply in the periods in which the timing differences are expected to reverse, based on tax rates and laws that have been enacted or substantively enacted by the balance sheet date. SSAP 15 also requires deferred tax to be measured at the rate at which it is estimated that tax will be paid when the timing differences reverse (the liability method) but does not stipulate that enacted rates must be used.

- Deferred tax assets and liabilities should be discounted if:

  - the timing differences on which they are based have been measured by reference to undiscounted cash flows; and

  - the effect of discounting is material.

  In most cases, full provision will increase liabilities and reduce earnings. Discounting deferred tax liabilities should mitigate the effects of full provision.

Presentation and disclosure

FRED 19 includes a number of proposals, of which the most important are:

- Deferred tax assets and liabilities should be separately disclosed on the face of the balance sheet if the amounts are so material in the context of the total net current assets or net assets that readers might misinterpret the accounts otherwise.

- Information should be disclosed about factors affecting current and future tax charges. This should include a reconciliation of the current tax charge for the period to the profit before tax on ordinary activities multiplied by the standard rate of corporation tax.

Comments

Most respondents to the ASB's earlier Discussion Paper favoured the retention of partial provision. Full provision is likely to be unpopular with preparers of accounts because it will weaken the balance sheet and reduce the amount available for dividends.

The ASB has admitted that it is not wholly convinced by the arguments for the full provision method. Nevertheless, it does not believe that this is one of the areas where a good case can be made for standing up against international opinion. It believes that continuing with the partial provision method would damage the credibility of UK financial reporting.

Although the ASB has accepted the need for full provision, it has not adopted the same approach as the IASC. Unlike FRED 19, IAS 12 *Income Taxes* requires deferred tax to be provided on revaluation gains and retained profits of associates and joint ventures.

FRED 20: RETIREMENT BENEFITS

Background

FRED 20 covers pensions and other forms of retirement benefit, eg, the provision of post-employment medical care. It has been developed from proposals in the ASB's 1998 Discussion Paper *Aspects of accounting for pension costs* and will eventually replace SSAP 24 *Accounting for pension costs* if its proposals are adopted.

The ASB's earlier work has highlighted problems relating to SSAP 24:

- Too many options are permitted, leading to inconsistency between companies. This also provides companies with flexibility to adjust results on a short term basis.

- Its disclosure requirements are insufficient to explain the pension cost and related amounts in the balance sheet.

Valuing pension scheme assets

There are two main methods of valuing pension scheme assets:

- the actuarial method; and
- the market value method.

SSAP 24 requires the use of the actuarial method, but IAS 19 *Employee benefits* requires the use of market values to measure pension scheme assets, on the grounds that these give the most objective and comparable information. Most other major standard setters also require the use of market values.

The proposals below affect defined benefit schemes. Accounting for defined contribution schemes will not change.

Measurement of scheme assets and liabilities

FRED 20 proposes that:

- scheme assets should be measured at fair value (instead of on an actuarial basis); and
- scheme liabilities should be measured on a discounted basis (approximating to fair value) using the projected unit method.

In theory, scheme liabilities should also be valued at fair value, but this is not possible as there is no active market for most defined benefit scheme liabilities. Fair value must therefore be estimated using actuarial techniques.

Scheme liabilities should be discounted at a rate that reflects the time value of money and the characteristics of the liability (this is assumed to be the current rate of return on an AA corporate bond of equivalent currency and term to the scheme liability).

Recognition in the balance sheet

These proposals also represent a major change from SSAP 24.

- A surplus in a defined benefit scheme should be recognised as an asset to the extent that the employer is able to recover the surplus (eg, through reduced contributions and refunds).

- A deficit should be recognised as a liability to the extent of the employer's legal or constructive obligation to fund it.

- Contributions overpaid or underpaid should be disclosed as debtors or creditors due within one year.

- The remaining defined benefit asset or liability (net of deferred tax) should be presented separately on the face of the balance sheet after other net assets.

  Example (from the Appendix to FRED 20):

	20X1 £m	20X0 £m
Net assets excluding pension asset	700	650
Net pension asset	335	143
Net assets including pension asset	1,035	793

This approach contrasts with that of SSAP 24. Under SSAP 24, where actuarial gains and losses are recognised over the future service lives of employees, the amount recognised in the balance sheet does not represent the surplus or deficit of the scheme. Instead it represents the difference between the contributions paid and the amount recognised in the profit and loss account as a result of the 'spreading' approach.

Recognition in the performance statements

The change in the defined benefit asset or liability in the period (other than that arising from contributions paid) is analysed into its components:

- Current service cost is recognised in the profit and loss account as part of operating results.

- The interest cost and the expected return on assets are recognised in the profit and loss account as a net figure adjacent to interest.

- Actuarial gains and losses are recognised immediately in the Statement of total recognised gains and losses (STRGL). (These are treated in a similar way to revaluation gains and losses.)

Disclosure

FRED 20 proposes extensive disclosures of which the main ones are as follows:

- the main assumptions underlying the scheme
- an analysis of scheme assets into broad classes and the expected rate of return on each class
- an analysis of the amounts included:
  - (a)   within operating profit;
  - (b)   as a financial item adjacent to interest; and
  - (c)   within the statement of total recognised gains and losses.
- a five year history of:
  - (a)   the difference between expected and actual return on assets;
  - (b)   experience gains and losses on scheme liabilities; and
  - (c)   the total actuarial gain or loss.
- an analysis of the movement in the surplus/deficit in the scheme over the period
- a reconciliation of the surplus/deficit to the balance sheet asset/liability.

Comment

The ASB (and most respondents to its earlier 1995 Discussion Paper) did not initially favour the market value approach. It was feared that this might lead to volatile results. However, following the issue of IAS 19 the ASB concluded that the UK must move into line with international practice.

One major difference between FRED 20 and IAS 19 is that FRED 20 proposes that actuarial gains and losses should be recognised immediately in the statement of total recognised gains and losses rather than in the profit and loss account. This means that the problem of volatile results should be avoided.

DISCUSSION PAPER: REPORTING FINANCIAL PERFORMANCE

Background

This Discussion Paper has been developed by the 'G4+1' group of standard setters and in the UK its proposals will almost certainly lead to a revision of FRS 3.

The ASB believes that a review of FRS 3 is necessary for the following reasons:

- Its recent and current projects on derivatives, impairment and pensions have highlighted the need to reconsider the purpose of the statement of total recognised gains and losses (STRGL). When fixed assets, financial instruments or pension scheme assets and liabilities change in value some gains and losses arise that could in theory be reported in either the profit and loss account or in the STRGL.

- There is also some evidence that users and preparers of accounts are confused by the existence of two performance statements. Therefore they concentrate on the profit and loss account and largely ignore the STRGL.

New statement of performance

The central proposal of the Discussion Paper is that there should be a single performance statement with three main components:

- Results of operating (or trading) activities
- Results of financing and other treasury activities
- Other gains and losses

The Discussion Paper includes an illustration of how a 'typical' performance statement might appear:

STATEMENT OF FINANCIAL PERFORMANCE

	£'000	£'000
Operating (trading) activities		
Revenues		775
Cost of sales		(620)
Other expenses		(104)
		——
Operating income		51
Financing and other treasury activities		
Interest on debt	(26)	
Gains and losses on financial instruments	8	
	——	
Financing income		(18)
		——
Operating and financing income before taxation		33
Taxation on income		(12)
Operating and financing income after taxation		21
Other gains and losses		
Profit on disposal of discontinued operations	3	
Profit on sale of properties in continuing operations	6	
Revaluation of long-term assets	4	
Exchange translation differences on foreign currency net investments	(2)	
	——	
Other gains and losses before taxation	11	
Taxation on other gains and losses	(4)	
	——	
Other gains and losses after taxation		7
		——
Total [Increase (decrease) in equity other than from contributions by or distributions to owners]		28
		——

Broadly speaking, items that currently appear in the profit and loss account would be shown under operating activities or financing and other treasury activities, while items that currently appear in the STRGL would be shown under 'other gains and losses'.

The main principle behind the statement of financial performance is that items with similar characteristics are grouped together.

Exceptional items

The Discussion Paper proposes changes to the way in which exceptional items are disclosed. At present, FRS 3 requires three types of exceptional item to be separately disclosed on the face of the profit and loss account below operating profit. These would still be disclosed on the face of the statement, but in different positions:

- Profits and losses on sale or termination of an operation in 'other gains and losses'.
- Profits and losses on disposal of fixed assets in 'other gains and losses'.
- Costs of a fundamental reorganisation or restructuring in 'operating activities'.

Other proposed changes to FRS 3

- Some entities voluntarily disclose 'pre exceptional results'. This would remain optional, but where they are disclosed, details of pre exceptional results, exceptional items and post exceptional results would be required for each of the past (say) five years.

- **All** material errors would require correction by prior period adjustment (FRS 3 permits prior period adjustments only where there have been fundamental errors).

Most other requirements of FRS 3 would remain unchanged.

Dividends paid and proposed

The ASB believes that dividends paid are an appropriation of profit, not part of financial performance and proposes that they should no longer be disclosed in the statement of financial performance but as part of changes in equity. Legal issues will have to be addressed as the Companies Act 1985 requires that dividends paid and proposed are disclosed on the face of the profit and loss account as a deduction from profit.

UPDATING NOTES FOR DECEMBER 2000 STUDENTS

For students taking the December 2000 exam, the cut-off date for examinable material is 1 June 2000. As at the time of writing (January 2000), several new documents have already been issued in December 1999, described below. You should read the Students' Newsletter and the accountancy press carefully, to identify any further documents that might be issued before 1 June 2000.

These notes describe:

(i)   FRS 16 'Current tax'
(ii)   Statement of principles for financial reporting
(iii)   Financial Reporting Standard for Smaller Entities (FRSSE)
(iv)   FRED 21 ' Accounting policies'
(v)   Discussion paper 'Leases: implementation of a new approach'

(i)   FRS 16 ' Current tax'

This short uncontroversial FRS implements the proposals of FRED 18 with few changes. Incoming dividends are now recognised at the amount receivable, without being grossed up for tax credits. Dividends are also now to be recognised at an amount including any withholding taxes (SSAP 8 was silent on this matter).

(ii)   Statement of principles for financial reporting

The final version of the Statement of Principles has finally been issued, based largely on the revised ED issued in March 1999. The same eight chapter headings are used in both documents. There are minor changes in wording, but the sense is essentially unchanged from the March 1999 draft.

(iii)   Financial Reporting Standard for Smaller Entities

The new version of the FRSSE is a routine updating, incorporating new FRSs and UITF Abstracts. FRS 12, FRS 14 and FRS 15 replace SSAP 18, SSAP 3 and SSAP 12, but there are no major changes to the logic of the standard.

(iv)   FRED 21 'Accounting policies'

Now that the Statement of Principles has been issued in its final form the ASB believe that certain sections of the Statement have a different emphasis to SSAP 2, thus a proposed replacement to SSAP 2 is called for which is consistent with the Statement of Principles. The familiar SSAP 2 concepts of going concern, accruals, consistency and prudence are no longer singled out as fundamental accounting concepts. Instead, entities should choose their accounting policies against the objectives identified in Chapter 3 of the statement of Principles (relevance, reliability, comparability and understandability), and should disclose the particular policies followed.

(v)   Discussion paper 'Leases: implementation of a new approach'

This discussion paper presents a Position Paper which has been developed by the G4+1 group of accounting standard-setters. Internationally there is disquiet that the currently required distinction between operating leases and finance leases is arbitrary and unsatisfactory. If an entity has use of an item under an operating lease, does this not fall within the definition of an asset in the Statement of Principles, so should be shown on the balance sheet. It is therefore proposed to replace SSAP 21 with a standard applying the same accounting treatment to all leases. At the beginning of a lease term, the fair value of the rights and obligations that are conveyed by the lease should be recognised by the lessee as assets and liabilities. This is clearly controversial, and it may be some time before a FRED along these lines is issued.

7 PRACTICE QUESTIONS

---

1 CIC PLC

CIC plc is a multinational chemical company that is registered in the United Kingdom and quoted on the London Stock Exchange.

The company is a member of an inter-company comparison scheme for companies that operate in the United Kingdom and it receives an annual comparison report including information such as returns on capital employed, returns on investment, asset utilisation and liquidity. The information relates to CIC plc and 32 other chemical companies that operate in the United Kingdom market. However, the directors are not finding the report as useful as they wished because CIC plc has over 90% of the United Kingdom market and the other 32 companies are United Kingdom registered marketing subsidiaries of major multinational companies which are based in other countries such as America, France, Germany, Italy, Japan and South America.

They have requested the accountant to produce an inter-company comparison report based on the statements of the other multinational companies rather than on the financial statements of the marketing subsidiaries and also to advise them of any problems that may arise in extracting and interpreting ratios from the consolidated financial statements of foreign multinational competitors.

You are required:

(a)   to draft a memorandum to the directors to explain the problems that may arise in:

     (i)   collecting the relevant data;
     (ii)   interpreting the data when it has been prepared to satisfy different disclosure requirements;
     (iii)   interpreting the data when there may be differing attitudes to financing and risk;
     (iv)   interpreting the data when there may have been differing user requirements.

(10 marks)

(b)   to discuss the extent to which you consider that the harmonisation of accounting disclosure requirements will reduce the problems. **(10 marks)**

(Total: 20 marks)
(ACCA June 91)

---

2 ORCHAOS PLC

The draft accounts of Orchaos plc have been prepared as at 31 December 19X2 and showed a profit of £28m.

The fixed assets had a net book value of £138.6m and consisted of offices, new plant and equipment. The offices had been acquired on 1 January 19X2 under a 20 year lease for £30m. The new plant had been acquired on 1 January 19X2 for £10m and the company had received a government grant of £2.5m which it has credited to the plant fixed asset account. The equipment had been acquired in earlier years at a cost of £130m and had a written-down value of £102.9m at 31 December 19X2. The company planned to undertake substantial further investment in fixed assets in 19X7.

Capital allowances of £35.4m have been allowed. The offices did not qualify for any tax allowances. The new plant had an estimated useful life of 25 years and qualified for a 25% writing-down allowance on the net cost.

The company prepared the following estimates for the four years ended 31 December 19X6:

Year ended 31 December	Depreciation £m	Capital allowances £m
19X3	11.0	18.92
19X4	19.8	12.32
19X5	19.8	10.12
19X6	17.6	14.84

Assume a corporation tax rate of 35%.

Required

(a)   Explain

(i)   the extent to which tax deferred or accelerated by the effect of timing differences should be accounted for; and

(ii)   the procedure for determining the amount to be quantified.   **(6 marks)**

(b)   (i)   Prepare the balance sheet entry for Orchaos plc as at 31 December 19X2 for deferred taxation to comply with the provisions of SSAP 15 'Accounting for Deferred Tax'.

(ii)   Explain the effect on the deferred tax computation for Orchaos plc as at 31 December 19X2 if the company has suffered its first loss following a year in which it had incurred substantial costs in relocating with the result that the accounts showed a loss adjusted for tax purposes of £28m.   **(14 marks)**

(c)   Assuming that the new plant attracted a 25% writing-down allowance on the full cost of £10m:

(i)   Explain how this would affect the calculation of deferred tax; and
(ii)   Calculate the tax effect of the timing difference as at 31 December 19X2.   **(4 marks)**

(d)   Critically discuss the statement that SSAP 15 Deferred Taxation does not necessarily result in the accounts of different companies in the same industry being comparable.   **(6 marks)**

                    (Total: 30 marks)
                    (ACCA June 93)

---

3   BRACHOL PLC

Brachol plc is preparing its accounts for the year ended 30 November 19X2.

The following information is available from the previous year's balance sheet:

At 30 November 19X1 there were credit balances on the share premium account of £2,025,000, the revaluation reserve of £4,050,000 and the profit and loss account of £2,700,000.

During 19X2 the following transactions occurred:

(a)   One million shares of £1 each were issued in exchange for net assets that had a fair value of £3,755,000.

(b) A factory property that had been revalued from £500,000 to £1,310,000 in 19X0 was sold for £2,525,000.

(c) A fixed asset investment was revalued from £1,305,000 to £900,000.

(d) There was a currency translation loss of £270,000 arising on foreign currency net investments.

(e) A warehouse property was revalued from £1,000,000 to £1,540,000.

A prior period adjustment of £1,350,000 was required which had arisen from a change in accounting policy that had overstated the previous year's profit.

The profit and loss account for the year ended 30 November 19X2 showed a profit attributable to members of the company of £810,000 and a dividend of £675,000.

Required

(a) (i) Draft a note showing the movements on reserves as at 30 November 19X2.

(ii) Draft a statement of total recognised gains and losses to show the net deduction from or addition to net assets as at 30 November 19X2. **(6 marks)**

(b) Explain briefly

(i) the purpose of the statement of total recognised gains and losses; and

(ii) the extent to which a user of the accounts will be better able to make decisions by referring to a statement of total recognised gains and losses rather than the statement of movements on reserves that is produced to comply with the Companies Act 1985. **(7 marks)**

(c) Explain briefly

(i) the nature of the adjustments that would be required to reconcile the profit on ordinary activities before tax to the historical cost profit.

(ii) the possible use that can be made of such information by a potential investor. **(7 marks)**
(Total: 20 marks)
(ACCA June 93)

---

4   ROWSLEY PLC

Rowsley plc is a diverse group with many subsidiaries. The group is proud of its reputation as a 'caring' organisation and has adopted various ethical policies towards its employees and the wider community in which it operates. As part of its Annual Report, the group publishes details of its environmental policies, which include setting performance targets for activities such as recycling, controlling emissions of noxious substances and limiting use of non-renewable resources.

The finance director is reviewing the accounting treatment of various items prior to the signing of the accounts for the year ended 31 March 19X9. All four items are material in the context of the accounts as a whole. The accounts are to be approved by the directors on 30 June 19X9.

(1) On 15 February 19X9 the board of Rowsley plc decided to close down a large factory in Derby. The board is trying to draw up a plan to manage the effects of the reorganisation, and it is envisaged that production will be transferred to other factories, mainly in Wales. The factory will be closed on 31 August 19X9, but at 31 March this decision had not yet been announced to the employees or to any other interested parties. Costs of the reorganisation have been estimated at £45 million. **(6 marks)**

(2) During December 19X8 one of the subsidiary companies moved from Buckingham to Sunderland in order to take advantage of regional development grants. It holds its main premises in Buckingham under an operating lease, which runs until 31 March 19Y1. Annual rentals under the lease are £10 million. The company is unable to cancel the lease, but it has let some of the premises to a charitable organisation at a nominal rent. The company is attempting to rent the remainder of the premises at a commercial rent, but the directors have been advised that the chances of achieving this are less than 50%. **(6 marks)**

(3) During the year to 31 March 19X9, a customer started legal proceedings against the group, claiming that one of the food products that it manufactures had caused several members of his family to become seriously ill. The group's lawyers have advised that this action will probably not succeed. **(3 marks)**

(4) The group has an overseas subsidiary that is involved in mining precious metals. These activities cause significant damage to the environment, including deforestation. The company expects to abandon the mine in eight years time. The mine is situated in a country where there is no environmental legislation obliging companies to rectify environmental damage and it is very unlikely that any such legislation will be enacted within the next eight years. It has been estimated that the cost of cleaning the site and re-planting the trees will be £25 million if the re-planting were successful at the first attempt, but it will probably be necessary to make a further attempt, which will increase the cost by a further £5 million. **(5 marks)**

Required:

Explain how each of the items (1) to (4) above should be treated in the consolidated accounts for the year ended 31 March 19X9. **(Total: 20 marks)**

---

5   OMEGA

The balance sheet of Omega as at 30 September 19X5 contained the following balances and notes:

		£'000
Share capital		10,000
Reserves:		
Share premium	Note 1	1,000
Revaluation reserve	Note 2	1,780
Other reserves:		
Merger reserve	Note 3	550
Profit and loss account - 19X5	Note 4	1,940
Profit and loss account b/d		(200)
Capital and reserves		15,070
Liabilities		15,070
Total assets		30,140

Note 1 The share premium arose on the issue of shares on 1 October 19X2.

Note 2 The revaluation reserve arose as a result of a revaluation of certain of the fixed assets on 1 October 19X4. It comprises a gain of £2,000,000 on the revaluation of plant and machinery, which is the balance remaining after the transfer to the profit and loss account of £200,000 representing the depreciation on the revaluation surplus; and a loss of £220,000 arising from the revaluation of office premises. The directors propose to revalue the remaining fixed assets which currently appear at historic cost in a subsequent financial year.

Note 3 The merger reserve represented the premium of £550,000 on shares issued on the acquisition on 1 October 19X4 of a subsidiary, Alpha plc in accordance with the merger provisions of the CA85.

Note 4 The profit and loss account balance is the balance after:

(i) creating a provision of £1,200,000 representing an impairment in the value of a subsidiary, Gamma plc.

(ii) the transfer of the £200,000 mentioned in *Note 2* from the revaluation reserve to the profit and loss account representing the amount by which the total depreciation charge for the year exceeded the amount that would have been provided if the plant had not been revalued.

(iii) crediting an exchange gain of £38,000 that arose on the translation of a long-term loan taken out in French francs on 1 October 19X4. The loan was taken out to use in the United Kingdom because the interest rate was favourable at the date the loan was raised.

You are required:

(a) to calculate the amount of distributable profit for Omega on the basis that it is:

    (i) a public company
    (ii) an investment company. **(10 marks)**

(b) to explain briefly:

    (i) the disclosure requirements relating to distributable profits in a single company and group context

    (ii) the effect on the distributable profits of the parent company if the group has sufficient distributable profits in aggregate to make a distribution to the parent company's shareholders but the parent company itself has insufficient distributable profits

    (iii) the effect on the distributable profits of the parent company if the holding company has sold one subsidiary company to another subsidiary for a consideration that exceeds the carrying value of the investment in the holding company's accounts

    (iv) the effect on the distributable profits of the parent company if a subsidiary company which has a coterminous accounting period declares a dividend after the end of the parent company's year end. **(10 marks)**
(Total: 20 marks)
(ACCA Dec 92)

---

6   CHANGELING PLC

An assistant accountant of Changeling plc has been requested to prepare a profit and loss account using the CPP model for the year ended 31 March 19X3. He has calculated the net operating profit for the year and the remaining entries are yet to be completed.

The profit and loss accounts for the year ended 31 March 19X3 are set out below, comprising the historic cost profit and loss account and partially completed CPP profit and loss account.

	Historic cost £'000	Index factor	CPP units as at 31.3.X3 000
Sales	6,500	2,000/1,875	6,933
Opening stock	700	2,000/1,700	824
Purchases	4,250	2,000/1,875	4,533
	4,950		5,357
Closing stock	(900)	2,000/1,937	(929)
	4,050		4,428
Gross profit	2,450		2,505
Expenses	1,150	2,000/1,875	1,227
Depreciation:			
Original equipment	500	2,000/1,025	976
New equipment	50	2,000/1,813	55
Net Operating profit	750		247
Tax	338		
Profit (loss) after tax	412		
Gain(loss) on net monetary assets	-		
Gain(loss) on long-term loans	-		
Net profit (loss) for year	412		
Dividends	187		
Retained profit (loss) for year	225		
Retained profit brought forward	750		
Retained profit carried forward	975		

The balance sheets as at 31 March 19X2 and 19X3 are set out below.

	Historic cost £'000	Index factor	CPP units as at 31.3.X2 000	Index factor	CPP units as at 31.3.X3 000
Capital	2,500	1,750/950	4,605	2,000/1,750	5,263
Retained profit	750		1,142		1,305
	3,250		5,747		6,568
Fixed assets					
Equipment	5,000	1,750/1,025	8,537	2,000/1,750	9,757
Depreciation	(1,500)	1,750/1,025	(2,561)	2,000/1,750	(2,927)

Current assets

Stock	700	$\frac{1,750}{1,700}$	721	$\frac{2,000}{1,750}$	824
Debtors	1,050	–	1,050	$\frac{2,000}{1,750}$	1,200

Current liabilities

Trade creditors	(875)	–	(875)	$\frac{2,000}{1,750}$	(1,000)

Non-current liabilities

Loan	(1,125)	–	(1,125)	$\frac{2,000}{1,750}$	(1,286)
	3,250		5,747		6,568

Balance sheet as at 31 March 19X3:

	Historic cost £'000	Index factor	CPP units as at 31.3.X3 000
Capital	2,500	$\frac{2,000}{950}$	5,263
Retained profit	975	–	1,142
	3,475		6,405
Fixed assets			
Equipment	5,000	$\frac{2,000}{1,025}$	9,757
Depreciation	(2,000)	$\frac{2,000}{1,025}$	(3,903)
New equipment	500	$\frac{2,000}{1,813}$	552
Depreciation	(50)	$\frac{2,000}{1,813}$	(55)
Current assets			
Stock	900	$\frac{2,000}{1,938}$	929
Debtors	1,150	–	1,150
Current liabilities			
Trade creditors	(400)	–	(400)
Non-current liabilities			
Loan	(1,625)	–	(1,625)
	3,475		6,405

Assume that inflation index increased evenly through the year ended 31 March 19X3; the tax and dividends were paid on 31 March 19X3, and that the loan was raised at the same time that the additional fixed assets were acquired.

You are required:

(a)   to calculate the retained profit (loss) for the year using the CPP model for the year ended 31 March 19X3.   **(5 marks)**

(b)   to explain what the method of indexing is attempting to deal with and discuss the process from the viewpoint of both the entity and the proprietors.   **(5 marks)**

(c)   to write a brief report to the principal shareholder of Changeling Ltd who holds 20% of the issued share capital on the management of the company commenting on profitability, liquidity and financial structure.   **(10 marks)**

(Total: 20 marks)
(ACCA 1994 Pilot Paper)

---

7   FSR GROUP

The FSR Group consists of the holding company FSR plc and two subsidiary companies, GBH plc and Short plc. FSR plc had acquired 75% of the ordinary shares in GBH plc and 80% of the ordinary shares in Short plc on 1 December 19X2. The ordinary shares in Short plc are held exclusively with a view to subsequent resale; the ordinary shares in GBH plc are held on a long-term basis. FSR plc prepares its accounts to 30 November each year.

A trainee accountant working on the consolidation for the year ended 30 November 19X3 has proposed the following adjustments.

(i)   Treatment of profit arising from intra-group sales

During October 19X3 GBH plc sold goods costing it £200,000 to FSR plc for £220,000. All of the goods were in stock as at 30 November 19X3.

Proposed to reduce the stock and consolidated profit and loss account by £15,000.

During September 19X3 FSR plc sold goods costing £60,000 to GBH plc for £72,000. All of the goods were in stock as at 30 November 19X3.

Proposed to reduce the stock and consolidated profit and loss account by £12,000.

(ii)   Treatment of goodwill arising on acquisition of GBH plc

The 75% shareholding in GBH plc was acquired on 1 December 19X2 for £3,000,000 when the fair value of the total net assets in GBH plc was estimated to be £3,000,000.

Proposed to apply the entity concept and credit the minority interest with £250,000 and record the goodwill at 1 December 19X2 at £1,000,000. In accordance with group policy, this goodwill was to be written off over five years. The charge in the 19X3 accounts was to be £200,000.

(iii)   Treatment of profit arising from sale by Short plc

Short plc sold goods costing £100,000 to FSR plc for £110,000 on 31 August 19X3. All of the goods were in stock as at 30 November 19X3.

Proposed to reduce the stock and the consolidated profit and loss account by £8,000.

Required

(a)   Describe the accounting treatment required in the consolidated accounts of the FSR Group as at 30 November 19X3 of the investment in Short plc

(i)   to comply with the Companies Act 1985
(ii)   to comply with Financial Reporting Standards with a brief explanation as to why this differs from the provisions of the Companies Act 1985.   **(5 marks)**

(b)   Inform the trainee accountant whether the proposed consolidation adjustments in (i) to (iii) above comply with accounting standards.   State any additional information which could affect the accounting treatment.   **(9 marks)**

(c)   Explain briefly the reasons for the accounting treatment recommended for (i) to (iii) above.
          (6 marks)
          (Total: 20 marks)
          (ACCA Dec 93)

8	BULL PLC

Bull plc is a company that trades in the United Kingdom manufacturing drugs for animals. Dog Inc has been a wholly owned foreign subsidiary of Bull plc since incorporation carrying on business as a buyer of soya oil which it sells to Bull plc for use as a raw material in its drugs.

Dog Inc has prepared a draft profit and loss account for the year ended 31 October 19X3 and a balance sheet as at that date in dollars ($) as follows:

Profit and loss account for the year ended 31 October 19X3

	$'000	$'000
Sales		3,750
Cost of sales		
Stock at 1.11.X2	115	
Purchases	3,000	
	3,115	
Stock at 31.10.X3	120	
		2,995
Gross profit		755
Administration expenses	100	
Handling charges	200	
Depreciation	150	
		450
Profit before tax		305
Tax		150
Profit after tax		155

Balance sheet as at 31 October 19X3

	$'000	$'000
Fixed assets		
Plant and equipment	1,800	
Less aggregate depreciation	750	
		1,050
Current assets		
Stock	120	
Debtors	80	
Bank	350	
	550	
Current liabilities		
Creditors	175	
Net current assets		375
		1,425
Ordinary share capital		375
Profit and loss account		1,050
		1,425

Additional information is available relating to exchange rates and depreciation:

Exchange rates have been as follows:

	$ to £
At date of incorporation	3.6
At date of acquisition of fixed assets on 1.11.W8	2.2
On 1.11.X2	1.8
On 31.10.X3	1.1
Average rate for financial year ended 31.10.X3	1.5
At date of purchase of stock at beginning of year	1.8
At date of purchase of stock at end of year	1.1

Depreciation is charged on a straight-line basis on cost. No fixed assets have been acquired since 19W8.

Required

(a)   (i)   Explain the factors that needed to be taken into account when selecting the appropriate method for translating the financial statements of a foreign subsidiary for consolidation purposes; and

       (ii)   Advise the management on the method that is appropriate for translating the financial statements of Dog Inc in accordance with the provisions of SSAP 20 'Foreign Currency Translation'. **(6 marks)**

(b)   On the assumption that the temporal method is appropriate:

       Translate the profit and loss account and balance sheet of Dog Inc for consolidation purposes using the temporal method. Show all workings clearly. **(10 marks)**

(c)   On the assumption that the closing rate method is appropriate:

   (i)   Reconcile the sterling profit and loss balance of Dog Inc as at 1 November 19X32 with the sterling profit and loss balance as at 31 October 19X3 using the closing rate of exchange to translate the profit and loss account.

   (ii)   Calculate the explain how the difference between the retained profit using the closing rate and the retained profit using the average rate of exchange for the profit and loss account would be recorded. **(10 marks)**

(d)   Assuming that Bull plc borrowed $750,000 on 1 November 19X2 to provide a hedge against the investment, explain the treatment of any gain/loss arising on translating the loan using the closing rate method in the company-only profit and loss account for the year ended 31 October 19X3 and balance sheet as at that date of Bull plc. **(4 marks)**

(Total: 30 marks)
(ACCA Dec 93)

---

9   LOOK AHEAD & CO

Look Ahead & Co were instructed to value as at 31 December 19X2 a minority holding of 10,000 25p shares in Arbor Ltd held by D Dodd who is considering disposing of his shareholding.

Arbor Ltd is a private company with an issued share capital of £125,000. The shareholdings are as follows:

Shareholder	*Shareholding*
A Arny	61,250
B Brady	30,000
D Brady	20,000
E Brady	11,250
D Dodd	2,500

The following are extracts from the profit and loss accounts of Arbor Ltd for the four years ended 31 December 19X2:

	19W9	*19X0*	*19X1*	*19X2*
	£'000	*£'000*	*£'000*	*£'000*
Sales	4,200	5,600	8,470	11,700
Cost of sales	1,825	2,920	5,205	7,810
Gross profit	2,375	2,680	3,265	3,890
Administration expenses	900	1,000	1,200	1,400
Distribution costs	1,345	1,500	1,800	2,100
Profit before tax	130	180	265	390
Taxation	40	60	90	136
Profit after tax	90	120	175	254
Ordinary dividend	21.6	22.7	23.8	25.0

The following additional information is available:

The gross dividend yields on quoted companies operating in the same sector were 12% and the firm estimated that this yield should be increased to 18% to allow for lack of marketability.

Assume tax credits are available at $\frac{1}{3}$ of net dividends paid.

Required

(a)   Discuss the relevance of dividends in the valuation of D Dodd's shareholding on the assumption that it is sold to his son W Dodd. Illustrate your answer from the data given in the question.

(4 marks)

(b)   Explain briefly the factors that the firm would take into account when:

   (i)   estimating the future net dividends
   (ii)   estimating the investor's required gross yield.   **(8 marks)**

(c)   Explain how the approach adopted by the firm when valuing a minority interest might be influenced by the size of the shareholding or its relative importance to the other shareholdings.   **(8 marks)**

(Total: 20 marks)

(ACCA June 93)

---

10   HARTINGTON PLC

Hartington plc is a manufacturing company which is listed on the London Stock Exchange. During recent years the company's operations have expanded rapidly and this expansion has chiefly been financed by loans from third parties.

During the year ended 30 June 19X7 the company entered into the following transactions:

(1)   On 1 July 19X6 it obtained an index linked loan of £2 million on which interest of 5% is paid annually. The loan is repayable on 30 June 19X9 and the amount to be repaid is the principal amount multiplied by an index. This index stood at 105 on 1 July 19X6 and at 110 on 30 June 19X7.

(2)   On 1 July 19X6 it issued £5 million zero coupon bonds. The bonds are redeemable at £8,051,000 on 30 June 19Y1. This represents the only payment to the holders of the bonds.

   Discount table extract: Present value of £1 to be received after *t* years:

Number of years	*Interest rate per year*		
	8%	*10%*	*12%*
1	0.926	0.909	0.893
2	0.857	0.826	0.797
3	0.794	0.751	0.712
4	0.735	0.683	0.636
5	0.681	0.621	0.567

Required:

(a)   Explain why it became necessary to develop a financial reporting standard on derivatives and other financial instruments.   **(10 marks)**

(b)   Explain how the loans (1) and (2) above should be treated in the financial statements of Hartington plc for the year ended 30 June 19X7.   **(4 marks)**

(c)   Show how the loans should be disclosed in the notes to the balance sheet of Hartington plc for the year ended 30 June 19X7. (Note: you are NOT required to produce a narrative explanation of the role of financial instruments during the period.)   **(6 marks)**

(Total 20: marks)

11	**PROFESSIONAL ETHICS**

Section 2 of the Association's Members' Handbook on 'Rules of Professional Conduct' includes a section on professional independence, and within the section there is a part concerned with conflicts of interest.

You have been asked by the partner in charge of your firm for your advice on the following matters relating to clients of your firm which may create a conflict of interest.

(a)   You are the auditor of Sherwood Wholesalers Ltd and you prepare the accounts of Wollaton Engineering, an unincorporated business. Wollaton Engineering is a small business and its only accounting records are an analysed cash book and copies of sales and purchase invoices.

It appears from your preparation of the business's accounts that Sherwood Wholesalers has not paid one of Wollaton's invoices for about £10,000, but the chairman of Sherwood Wholesalers has told the proprietor of Wollaton that this invoice has been paid. The proprietor of Wollaton Engineering has asked you to carry out further investigations:

(i)   to confirm the invoice has not been paid, by producing a schedule of sales invoices to Sherwood and cash received; and

(ii)   to act on Wollaton's behalf over the dispute with Sherwood.

The proprietor of Wollaton Engineering has said that there are no staff in Wollaton's business who are capable of carrying out this work, and you are the only person who can help him.

You are required to consider the above situation and decide the action you should take

(i)   in relation to the request by the proprietor of Wollaton Engineering, whether you should

(1)   provide confirmation of whether the invoice has not been paid, by producing a schedule of sales invoices to Sherwood and cash received;

(2)   act on Wollaton's behalf over the dispute with Sherwood;

(ii)   Assuming that you decide to provide some help to Wollaton, you are required to consider

(1)   whether you should look at Sherwood's accounting records over this matter

(2)   whether you should act on Sherwood's behalf, if asked to do so by the company's chairman.

(5 marks)

(b)   You are carrying out the audit of Mapperley Engineering Ltd and one of its largest customers, Hucknall Distributors Ltd, is an audit client of your firm. You are aware, from your dealings with Hucknall Distributors, that it is experiencing serious going concern problems. You have discussed the large debt of Hucknall Distributors on Mapperley Engineering's sales ledger and suggested its recovery may be doubtful because of its age, but the directors of Mapperley do not consider a provision for this debt is required. In these discussions you have not disclosed to Mapperley's directors or employees that you are aware of Hucknall's going concern problems.

If Hucknall Distributors is liquidated, none of the amount outstanding to Mapperley Engineering will be repaid. The effect of this bad debt will be material in Mapperley Engineering's accounts, and there is a risk that Mapperley Engineering may no longer be a going concern.

You are required:

(i)   to describe the extent to which you will tell the directors of Mapperley Engineering that Hucknall Distributors is experiencing going concern problems;

(ii)   to describe the investigations you will carry out and the matters you will bring to the notice of the directors of Mapperley Engineering to persuade them to make a provision for Hucknall Distributors' debt;

(iii)   Assuming that the directors of Mapperley Engineering are not prepared to provide for the doubtful debt relating to Hucknall Distributors, describe the factors you would take into account and your decision on the form of your audit report;

(8 marks)

(c)   In the case of part (b) above, assume that you have made no reference to the doubtful debt in your audit report on Mapperley Engineering, and Hucknall Distributors goes into liquidation within a month of your signing your audit report and Hucknall's year end debt proves to be irrecoverable.

You are required to describe the parties who may have a good chance of successfully suing you over giving an incorrect audit opinion. Your answer should cite any relevant cases and statutes relating to auditors' liability for negligence.

(7 marks)
(Total: 20 marks)
(ACCA Dec 91)

---

12   EXPECTATION GAP

The following statement has been made about the 'audit expectation gap' and the means of solving the problem.

'Following the *Caparo* decision, auditors of large companies have no responsibility to ensure that the accounts they audit are accurate, and they are not required to detect and report on error and fraud.

Recent failures of companies and major frauds in financial institutions and pension funds indicate serious weaknesses in the quality of audits. What is required is that auditors should have responsibility:

(a)   to a larger range of parties than those decided in the *Caparo* case   **(7 marks)**

(b)   for detecting and reporting all error and fraud, and   **(5 marks)**

(c)   for institutions holding and investing client's money, and pension funds, auditors should be present at all times to ensure that no loss arises from investing these funds and that fraud is prevented.

(8 marks)

If necessary, there should be changes in legislation to implement these proposals.'

You are required to discuss this statement, particularly the matters noted in parts (a) to (c). Your answer should consider the practicality of implementing these proposals, and, if you believe they are impractical, you should make proposals which should be acceptable to both the general public and auditors.

(Total: 20 marks)
(ACCA June 93)

8 ANSWERS TO PRACTICE QUESTIONS

1	CIC PLC

(Tutorial notes:

(1)   A question that can be answered from general accounting knowledge, although knowledge of foreign financial statements would obviously be of help.

(2)   Use the four requirements of part (a) to structure your memorandum to the directors.

(3)   For part (b) concentrate on the role of the European Community and the International Accounting Standards Committee. General comments on knowledge of different accounting practices is essential to an appreciation of the effect of such differences.*)

(a)   To: The Directors   Date: X-X-XX
       From: A.N. Accountant
       Subject: **Analysing foreign financial statements**

In order that we can assess the financial performance and position of our group on an international scale, it is necessary to attempt to analyse financial statements produced by comparable multinational groups in other countries. Such statements will usually have been produced for 'home market' users and follow national accounting regulations. Such users and regulations will often be different from the user orientation that is reflected in UK financial statements produced within the UK regulatory framework. Such differences will present problems and the most important are set out below.

Data accessibility

Some countries do not require companies to publish their accounts, and in others that do, the level of accessibility is not as high as it is in the US and the UK.

Timeliness of information

Countries vary in the delay between the end of the accounting period and the date the financial statements are made available publicly eg, UK usually around six months, US usually around ninety days. (Note that for some countries there is a considerable delay in producing accounts in the English language.)

Language and terminology barriers

Language is often the major barrier which must initially be overcome and, even when it has been, there are terminology problems. If the foreign enterprises do produce English versions, they may still use terms not easily understood in the UK and some of the important information content of the financial statements may be lost in the translation.

Currency translation

This will probably involve using arbitrary exchange rates. The use of such rates may result in a loss of the relative values of items in the accounts.

Statement formats

These tend not to be too vital after the initial 'shock' of seeing statements in 'foreign' formats. This problem will be most apparent outside the EU where the Fourth Directive standard formats do not apply.

Disclosure requirements

These will be dependent on the main user target. In some countries disclosure will be less than in the UK, making interpretation and analysis very difficult.

Accounting principles

Comparison of companies on an international scale suffers from the same problem as comparisons on a national scale - unless the accounts are prepared on the same accounting principles, direct comparisons are inappropriate. Reconciliations and/or adjustments to allow for the use of different accounting principles must be made.

Environment

The environment in which financial statements are prepared will differ from country to country. Allowances must be made for cultural differences towards risk, creditor protection, secrecy and finance methods. Such differences will often present barriers which cannot be overcome.

(b)   The type of analysis and interpretation being suggested for CIC plc is typical of the investigative work that most large multinational companies (MNCs) will have to undertake. The globalisation of capital markets and the internationalisation of business have resulted in MNCs having to assess, through published financial statements, the financial strengths and weaknesses of their overseas competitors.

Within many countries, including the UK, efforts are made to standardise the type and extent of disclosures in financial statements, particularly where there is more than one accounting basis. The need to have knowledge of the particular policies chosen and the effect that such a choice has on financial performance and position is fairly obvious. Without such meaningful information comparisons cannot be made. However, on an international scale it is more realistic to discuss the harmonisation of such disclosures rather than the standardisation that can be discussed on a national scale.

Within the European Union the company law directives relevant to accounting, mainly the Fourth Directive (for individual companies) and the Seventh Directive (for groups), have resulted in a greater degree of harmony on the financial reporting by companies in member states. The directives have improved the format, terminology and disclosures in financial statements, making it easier (but not necessarily easy) for an analyst to appreciate the contents of, say, a French or German company's accounts. In both these countries, for example, the Seventh Directive has radically changed, and hopefully improved, the consolidated accounts produced. The directive was based on UK standard practices and the consolidated accounts produced in France and Germany are therefore fairly easy to follow, and differences from UK practices are apparent from the disclosures given in such accounts. Without such a harmonisation process these comparisons and appreciations would have been very difficult.

On a global, rather than European, scale the work of the International Accounting Standards Committee must be considered. This committee, while only having thirteen countries represented on its main board, has about one hundred members from all over the world. Its own standards have been adopted by some countries, making disclosure requirements in those countries directly comparable and, while not being adopted by other countries eg, the UK, their content is considered to be persuasive when national standards are developed. Thus the IASC is helping to bring closer the variety of accounting disclosure requirements that currently exist around the world. Such developments must be considered to be to the advantage of those attempting to make inter-company comparisons across national boundaries.

In addition to the formal efforts of the EU and the IASC, the requirements of the major capital markets around the world must be considered. Large companies will attempt to source finance overseas and the requirements of the 'foreign' capital market will result in the 'import' of foreign disclosure requirements. Stock exchanges are very keen to ensure that information is available to investors for the operation of an efficient market, and will therefore promote the type of disclosures that analysts will find very useful in analysing and interpreting a set of accounts.

2   ORCHAOS PLC

(a)   (i)   Deferred tax should be accounted for to the extent that it is probable that a liability or asset will crystallise.

(ii)   Crystallisation

The assessment of whether a liability or asset will crystallise is based upon reasonable assumptions relating to financial plans or projections covering a period of years sufficient to enable an assessment to be made of the likely pattern of future tax liabilities.

If these financial plans are not fully developed or subject to a high degree of uncertainty, a prudent view should be taken. However, there is no minimum period of years specified by standard and in practice there may well be increasing uncertainty beyond say the next two years. In such cases, the procedure is to look for a pattern of originating or timing differences eg, plans for continuing expansion, cyclical capital expenditure.

Given the uncertainty, the plans need to be reviewed each year to assess how closely the actual capital flows have followed the plans for the year eg, a material difference might cause future years to be substantially revised; to take the current liquidity position into account eg, a growth in output might have created a larger than expected need for working capital which might impact on planned future capital expenditure; and to take external changes into account eg, closures or restriction of capital expenditure in response to recession with a fall in demand or credit squeeze with a fall in the availability of finance.

Debit balances

Deferred tax net debit balances should not be carried forward as assets, except to the extent that they are expected to be recoverable without replacement by equivalent debit balances.

(b)   (i)   Prepare the balance sheet entry for Orchaos plc as at 31 December 19X2 for deferred taxation to comply with the provisions of SSAP 15 'Accounting for Deferred Tax'.

Capital allowance timing differences:

The cost of the offices does not qualify for tax allowances and the depreciation of £1.5m on the offices needs to be deducted from the total depreciation charge for deferred tax purposes.

The relevant amounts are:

Year ended 31 December	Depreciation £m	Capital allowances £m	Timing differences £m	Net cumulative £m
19X3	11.0 – 1.5 = 9.5	18.92	9.42 originating	9.42
19X4	19.8 – 1.5 = 18.3	12.32	5.98 reversing	3.44
19X5	19.8 – 1.5 = 18.3	10.12	8.18 reversing	(4.74)
19X6	17.6 – 1.5 = 16.1	14.84	1.26 reversing	(6.00)

The net cumulative timing differences need to be calculated for the future periods as follows:

Year ended 31 December	Timing differences £m	Net cumulative timing differences £m
19X3	9.42 originating	9.42
19X4	5.98 reversing	3.44
19X5	8.18 reversing	(4.74)
19X6	1.26 reversing	(6.00)

Orchaos plc should provide deferred tax on the maximum potential liability of £6m arising in 19X6 at 35% ie, £2.1m.

The balance sheet amount of £2.1m will be included under the heading 'Taxation, including deferred tax' with a note as follows:

Deferred taxation accounted for in the balance sheet

Timing differences on UK capital allowances and depreciation £2.1m

The £2.1m is based on a partial provision approach. In addition there will be a note of the amount not provided for the full potential credit provision. The full provision would be 35% of £8m [Capital allowances of £35.4m – Aggregate depreciation (£28.9m W1 less depreciation on the offices £1.5m) £27.4m].

WORKINGS

(W1)   Aggregate depreciation at 31 December 19X2

	Offices £m	Plant £m	Equipment £m	Total £m
Cost	30.0	7.5	130.0	167.5
Aggregate depreciation	1.5	0.3	27.1	28.9
Net book value at 31.12.X2	28.5	7.2	102.9	138.6

Deferred taxation not accounted for in the balance sheet

UK capital allowances utilised in excess of depreciation charged
  (£2.8m – £2.1m)   £0.7m

(ii)   Discuss the effect on the deferred tax computation for Orchaos plc as at 31 December 19X2 if the company had suffered its first loss following a year in which it had incurred substantial costs in relocating with the result that the accounts showed a loss of £28m.

Deferred asset arising from the taxable losses:

The loss of £28m gives rise to a deferred asset of £9.8m.

There is then the question of whether this can be debited to the deferred tax account and recognised in the balance sheet. This requires an assessment of the recoverability of the tax.

Information will be required that (a) there is a history of profitability with any previous losses having been fully recovered and (b) there must be assurance, beyond a reasonable doubt, that future taxable profits will be sufficient to offset the loss during the period of time permitted for such carry forward.

There is information given in the question that there is a history of profitability. There is no information given as to future trading profits/losses. A deferred asset cannot be created until this estimate of future trading results has been established.

If the company satisfies the recoverability test, the deferred tax account will be debited with the £9.8m arising from the losses resulting in a debit balance of £7.7m which will be classified under 'prepayments and accrued income' in the balance sheet.

(c)   (i)   Capital grants are recognised in the profit and loss account over the estimated useful life of the asset by either crediting the grant to the fixed asset account and charging depreciation on the net sum or by crediting the grant to a deferred credit account and transferring pro-rata over the life of the asset. In the case of Orchaos plc, the grant has been credited to the plant asset account. Consequently, if the capital allowance is on the full cost of £10m, the asset should be grossed up for the purpose of computing the timing differences on which the deferred tax calculation is based.

The grant is a permanent difference and it should be spread over the life of the asset because the tax effect of permanent differences should be recognised in the period in which the item giving rise to the difference is dealt with in the financial statements ie, the grant is spread over the life of the asset and the tax benefit should be dealt with in the same way.

(ii)   The amount of deferred tax calculated would be as follows:

	£m
Cost	10.0
Less grant	-
	10.0
Less depreciation	0.4
Net book value at 31.12.X2	9.6
Cost for tax purposes	10.0
Less writing-down allowance	2.5
Tax written-down value at 31.12.X2	7.5
Timing difference	2.1
Tax effect at 35%	0.735

If the asset is not grossed up the calculation would be as follows:

	£m
Cost	10.0
Less grant	2.5
	7.5
Less depreciation	0.3
Net book value at 31.12.X2	7.2
Cost for tax purposes	10.0
Less writing-down allowance	2.5
Tax written-down value at 31.12.X2	7.5
Timing difference	0.3
Tax effect at 35%	0.105

Not grossing up is to take the whole effect of the permanent difference to the profit and loss account in the first year.

(d)   Critically discuss the statement that SSAP 15 Deferred Taxation does not necessarily result in the accounts of different companies in the same industry being comparable.

There are a number of areas in which the application of the SSAP could give rise to different amounts being calculated for deferred tax although the circumstances might be similar. We will comment on two such areas, namely, assessment of forecasts and revaluations.

Assessment of forecasts

There is the difficulty that any provision is dependent upon an assessment of the accuracy of the future and this depends on the individual making the forecast. As a result, consistency of treatment between companies is unlikely.

The treatment of revaluations

The standard is unsatisfactory in that the standard lacks clarity over the appropriate treatment which means that it is a matter for each individual company as to whether or not to make a provision for a forecast tax liability depending on a decision as to the possible sale or scrapping of the fixed assets eg, it is extremely easy for the management to revalue but profess an intention not to sell any of the revalued assets thereby avoiding the need for any provision.

3   BRACHOL PLC

(a)   (i)   The statement of movements on reserves can be produced in different formats. The following is a common layout:

Reserves	Share premium account £'000	Revaluation reserve £'000	Profit and loss account £'000	Total £'000
At beginning of year as previously stated	2,025	4,050	2,700	8,775
Prior period adjustment			(1,350)	(1,350)
Restated at 1.12.X1	2,025	4,050	1,350	7,425
Premium on issue	2,755			2,755
Transfer from profit and loss account			135	135
Transfer of realised profits		(810)	810	
Decrease in value of investments		(405)		(405)
Currency translation difference			(270)	(270)
Surplus on property revaluation		540		540
	4,780	3,375	2,025	10,180

(ii)   Statement of total recognised gains and losses

The format follows that used in FRS 3 and would be as follows:

	19X2 £'000
Profit attributable to members of the company	810
Unrealised surplus on revaluation of warehouse	540
Unrealised loss on investments	(405)
Total gains and losses for year before currency adjustment	945
Currency translation difference	(270)
Total recognised gains and losses for the year	675
Dividends	675
Total recognised gains and losses for year after dividends	0
Prior year adjustment	(1,350)
Net (deduction from) addition to net assets	(1,350)

(b) (i) The purpose of the statement of total recognised gains and losses

The statement is designed to highlight changes that have been recognised in the financial statements other than those resulting from capital payments or repayments.

If the company were to follow the historic cost convention and operate in its own currency, the balance on the profit and loss account for the year would represent the movement in net assets. However, the use of historic cost convention modified by the revaluation of fixed assets or the use of alternative accounting rules will give rise to unrealised movements that do not currently go through the profit and loss account. The statement will contain these unrealised adjustments to the net assets.

Clearly, it will not contain contra movements between different reserves nor will it contain the realisation of gains that have been recognised in previous periods as these will also be contra movements between reserves.

(ii) The extent to which a user of the accounts will be better able to make decisions by referring to a statement of total recognised gains and losses rather than the statement of movements on reserves that is produced to comply with the Companies Act 1985.

The statement of movement on reserves produced in (a) above shows that there was a change in net assets of £1,405,000 (£10,180,000 - £8,775,000). This change arose from:

	£'000
Premium on issue of new shares	2,755
Retained profit for 19X2 applying realisation concept	135
Revaluation movements (£540,000 - £405,000)	135
Currency translation movements	(270)
Prior period adjustment	(1,350)
	1,405

This is substantially the same information that appears in the statement of total gains and losses with the exception of the dividend distribution.

Why should there be a need for another statement described by FRS 3 as a primary statement when it is a re-arranged statement of movement on reserves?

One explanation might be that the statement of movement on reserves has not a regulatory or mandatory format so that it is clear that the movements contained in the statement are not presented in a uniform format and are not well understood by the user.

The efforts to improve the presentation of information in the accounts are designed to produce decision useful information. By advocating additional primary statements the ASB might be setting the scene for further primary statements that could be used to accommodate future developments eg, value statements with a reconciliation to the historical cost profit.

(c) (i) The nature of the adjustments that would be required to reconcile the profit on ordinary activities before tax to the historical cost profit.

The differences will arise from the modification of the historical cost concept in the preparation of financial statements. This can occur

- when fixed assets that have been revalued are depreciated under FRS 15 and the carrying value is depreciated;

- when there is a realisation of fixed asset revaluation gains of previous years.

(ii) There have been criticisms that because there is no mandatory requirement for companies to follow a uniform procedure in the treatment of revaluations either with regard to timing or method of revaluing it is impossible to carry out effective inter-company comparisons or inter-period comparisons. The inter-company comparisons are impeded because the depreciation charges and realised gains on disposal are influenced by management decision in the individual companies and we have seen examples such as Pilkington where the company has refrained from revaluation because of the impact on its future profits which could, in the directors' view, put it at an apparent disadvantage when compared to other companies that had not revalued. The inter-period comparisons are impeded because the depreciation charges and realised gains on disposal of fixed assets can vary from period to period depending on management decision.

4   ROWSLEY PLC

In all four cases, the key issue is whether or not a provision should be recognised. Under FRS 12 *Provisions, contingent liabilities and contingent assets*, a provision should only be recognised when:

(a)   there is a present obligation as a result of a past event; and

(b)   it is probable that a transfer of economic benefits will be required to settle the obligation; and

(c)   a reliable estimate can be made of the amount of the obligation.

Factory closure

As the factory closure changes the way in which the business is conducted (it involves the relocation of business activities from one part of the country to another) it appears to fall within the FRS 12 definition of a restructuring.

The key issue here is whether the group has an obligation to incur expenditure in connection with the restructuring. There is clearly no legal obligation, but there may be a constructive obligation. FRS 12 states that a constructive obligation only exists if the group has created valid expectations in other parties, such as employees, customers and suppliers, that the restructuring will actually be carried out. As the group is still drawing up a formal plan for the restructuring and no announcements have been made to any of the parties affected, there cannot be an obligation to restructure. A board decision alone is not sufficient. Therefore no provision should be made.

If the group starts to implement the restructuring or makes announcements to those affected before the accounts are approved by the directors it may be necessary to disclose the details in the financial statements as required by SSAP 17 *Accounting for post balance sheet events*. This will be the case if the restructuring is of such importance that non-disclosure would affect the ability of the users of the financial statements to reach a proper understanding of the group's financial position.

Operating lease

The lease contract appears to be an onerous contract as defined by FRS 12 (ie, the unavoidable costs of meeting the obligations under it exceed the economic benefits expected to be received under it).

Because the company has signed the lease contract there is a clear legal obligation and the company will have to transfer economic benefits (pay the lease rentals) in settlement. Therefore the group should recognise a provision for the remaining lease payments. The group may recognise a corresponding asset in relation to the nominal rentals currently being received, if these are virtually certain to continue. (In practice, it is unlikely that this amount is material). As the chances of renting the premises at a commercial rent are less than 50%, no further potential rent receivable may be taken into account.

The financial statements should disclose the carrying amount at the balance sheet date, a description of the nature of the obligation and the expected timing of the lease payments and the amount of any expected rentals receivable from sub-letting. If an asset is recognised in respect of any rentals receivable, this should also be disclosed.

Legal proceedings

It is unlikely that the group has a present obligation to compensate the customer and therefore no provision should be recognised. However, there is a contingent liability. Unless the possibility of a transfer of economic benefits is remote, the financial statements should disclose a brief description of the nature of the contingent liability, an estimate of its financial effect and an indication of the uncertainties relating to the amount or timing of any outflow.

Environmental damage

It is clear that there is no legal obligation to rectify the damage. However, through its published policies, the group has created expectations on the part of those affected that it will take action to do so. There is therefore a constructive obligation to rectify the damage and a transfer of economic benefits is probable.

The group must recognise a provision for the best estimate of the cost. As the most likely outcome is that more than one attempt at re-planting will be needed, the full amount of £30 million should be provided. The expenditure will take place some time in the future, and so the provision should be discounted at a pre-tax rate that reflects current market assessments of the time value of money and the risks specific to the liability.

The financial statements should disclose the carrying amount at the balance sheet date, a description of the nature of the obligation and the expected timing of the expenditure. The financial statements should also give an indication of the uncertainties about the amount and timing of the expenditure.

---

5   OMEGA

(Tutorial note: although part (a) requires only a calculation, it is sensible to include a short justification as to why you have treated certain items as realised or unrealised.

This is particularly relevant as for some of the points the distinction between realised and unrealised is not clear cut.*)*

(a)   (i)   **Rules for all companies**

Realised profits less realised losses

	£'000
Per profit and loss account (1,940 – 200)	1,740
Revaluation deficit *(note 1)*	(220)
Exchange gain *(note 2)*	(38)
	1,482

Notes:

(1)   Deficit arose on piecemeal revaluation of fixed assets and the directors have not 'considered' the value of the assets. Therefore realised loss.

(2)   SSAP 20 states that the gain arising on a long term monetary item is unrealised.

Further rule for plc

Maintain share capital and undistributable reserves ie, deduct excess of unrealised losses over unrealised profits.

There are no unrealised losses.

Therefore distributable profits are   £1,482,000

(ii)   **Exclude capital profits from net realised profits**

There are no realised capital profits

Distributable profits are   £1,482,000

---

or Asset ratio test

Realised revenue profits less revenue losses

	£'000
Distributable profits as per private company rules	1,482
Add back realised capital loss (offices)	220
Distribution	1,702

Subject to assets exceeding 150% of liabilities

Assets per balance sheet	30,140
Liabilities 15,070 × 1.5	22,605
Excess	7,535

Therefore distributable profits are £1,702,000

(b)   (i)   There is no statutory requirement that requires a company to identify the division between distributable and non-distributable reserves. However, in practice, some companies do include a statement with the reserve movements.

                The calculation of distributable profits only relates to an individual company and not to a group. Where consolidated accounts are presented, the relevant distributable profits will be the parent company's realised profits.

    (ii)   This situation mainly arises where the subsidiary companies have not paid dividends to the parent company. As the rules of distribution only apply in an individual context, the subsidiaries will have to declare a dividend which then becomes additional distributable profit to the parent company.

    (iii)   If the sale is at arm's length and is supported by appropriate documentation, then the surplus on sale would appear to be realised. The fact that the transaction has taken place between companies in the same group need not prevent the profit on the transaction being realised, and therefore distributable. If the transaction is artificial it may be unlawful to make a distribution from the resulting profit. If the arrangement were to have been made through inter-company arrangements, it might be argued that the profit had not been realised.

    (iv)   If the dividends receivable from a subsidiary are accrued in the parent company's accounts, the dividend would be regarded as realised even if declared after the parent company's year end whether paid or passed through a current account.

6   CHANGELING PLC

(Tutorial notes:

(a)   Part (a) requires the calculation of the gains and losses on monetary items. Include in the calculation all items which appear in the profit and loss account which affect monetary working capital.

(b)   Note that part (b) breaks down into three elements (use this breakdown to construct your answer).

        (i)   objective of indexing
        (ii)   entity viewpoint of indexing process
        (iii)   proprietors' viewpoint of indexing process

(c)   Report format should be used for part (c) (this will gain you marks), with the report covering **all** three aspects of analysis; profitability, liquidity and gearing (financial structure).

        Do not produce an extensive list of ratios.*)

(a)   **Extract from profit and loss account for the year ended 31 March 19X3**

	£'000		CPP units '000
Net operating profit	750	given	247
Tax	(338)	-	(338)
Profit/(loss) after tax	412		(91)
Gain/(loss) on net monetary assets		working	(98)
Gain/(loss) on long-term loans		working	213
Net profit/(loss) for year	412		24
Dividends	(187)	-	(187)
Retained profit/(loss) for the year	225		(163)
Brought forward	750	given	1,305
Carried forward	975		1,142

(Tutorial note: The transaction date for tax and dividends is the last day of the accounting period and therefore there is no index adjustment.*)*

WORKINGS

Gain/(loss) on net monetary assets

	£'000	Index	CPP units 000
Opening net monetary assets:			
Debtors	1,050		
Creditors	(875)		
	175	$\dfrac{2,000}{1,750}$	200
Increase in net monetary assets:			
Sales	6,500	$\dfrac{2,000}{1,875}$	6,933
Decrease in net monetary assets:			
Purchases	(4,250)	$\dfrac{2,000}{1,875}$	(4,533)
Expenses	(1,150)	$\dfrac{2,000}{1,875}$	(1,227)
Tax	(338)	-	(338)
Dividends	(187)	-	(187)
(Debtors 1,150, Creditors 400)	750		848

Loss in purchasing power = £750 – £C848 = £C98.

Gain/(loss) on long-term loans

Opening balance	1,125	$\dfrac{2,000}{1,750}$	1,286
Increase in loan	500	$\dfrac{2,000}{1,813}$ (As per equipment purchased with loan)	552
Closing balance	1,625		1,838

Gain in purchasing power = £1,625 – £C1,838 = £C213.

(b)   The indexing used in the current purchasing power method of accounting for price level changes is attempting to measure the profit or loss for a period in terms of the increase or decrease in the current purchasing power of shareholders' funds. The use of indexing results in profits or losses being stated after allowing for the declining purchasing power of money due to price inflation. When applied to Historic Cost Accounting the indexing results in CPP accounts that reflect adjustments to income and capital values to allow for the general rate of price inflation.

CPP attempts to maintain the shareholders' capital in terms of its general or consumer purchasing power. However, this proprietorship concept will only be of relevance to the company's owners (proprietors) if the general index used reflects their own consumption pattern which in most cases it will not. The CPP accounts will not therefore automatically be of relevance to the proprietors.

Indexing may be of use to the entity because it does result in the recognition of gains and losses on monetary items in periods of changing prices and does provide financial statements in which all the items are expressed in constant units. However, the indexing will not result in values of individual assets which will be of relevance. A replacement cost or mixed value system needs to be applied to achieve a real terms asset value which may be of relevance.

(c)   To: Principal shareholder   Date: X-X-XX
      From: An accountant
      Subject: Financial statement analysis

Attached is a set of financial statements for Changeling plc for the year to 31 March 19X3. This set includes accounts expressed in purely historic cost terms and accounts that have been adjusted to allow for the effect of general price inflation on the historic cost figures. At present no details of other companies are available for an inter-company analysis. This analysis is therefore based on the concepts - Historic Cost and Current Purchasing Power, and emphasises the level of profitability, liquidity and financial structure reflected in these two sets of accounts.

Profitability

The return (operating profit before tax) achieved on the capital employed (share capital plus retained profit) for the year is 21.7% according to the historic cost figures. However, this return is reduced to a mere 3.9% when adjustments are made to the measure of profit and capital for the effects of inflation.

The level of gross profit achieved on the sales for the period is 37.7% based on historic cost figures, with price inflation adjustments resulting in only a minor decrease to 36.1%. However, there is a dramatic decrease in the level of the profit available for distribution (as dividends) from the £412,000 shown in the historic cost accounts to only £24,000 in the inflation adjusted CPP accounts. The dividend of £187,000 is therefore not covered by profits measured in current purchasing power terms. It may be useful to find out if this is normal for companies similar to Changeling plc.

Liquidity

The company does not appear to have any short-term liquidity problems. The debtors are nearly 3 times the creditors at the end of the year but the company must remember that holding monetary assets in periods of changing prices results in a loss in purchasing power as reflected in the profit and loss account using CPP units ie, £98,000 loss on net monetary assets.

Financial structure

The historic cost accounts show that loans constituted nearly 26% $\left(\dfrac{1,125,000}{3,250,000 + 1,125,000} \right)$ of the long-term funds at the end of 19X2 and this had increased to nearly 32% $\left(\dfrac{1,625,000}{3,475,000 + 1,625,000} \right)$ by the end of 19X3. This may indicate an unfavourable trend but it is necessary to investigate the financial structure of other similar companies before such a conclusion can be reached.

The CPP figures also show a similar trend moving from over 16% $\left(\dfrac{1,286,000}{6,568,000 + 1,286,000} \right)$ at the end of 19X2 to over 20% $\left(\dfrac{1,625,000}{6,405,000 + 1,625,000} \right)$ by the end of 19X3. The CPP profit and loss account does reflect the benefit of holding fixed repayment loans in periods of increasing general price levels ie, the £213,000 gain on the long-term loan.

---

7   FSR GROUP

(a)   (i)   The Companies Act contains permissive exclusions and a required exclusion. One of the permissive exclusions in S229 is where the parent company interest is exclusively with a view to subsequent resale and the undertaking has not previously been included in consolidated group accounts by the parent company.

Depending on the parent company's choice, the investment might be dealt with by consolidation or by treating it as a current asset valued at the lower of cost and net realisable value.

(ii)   FRS 2 'Accounting for Subsidiary Undertakings' issued by the ASB in 1992 recognises that the Act permits exclusion if the group's interest is held exclusively with a view to a subsequent resale but goes further by requiring exclusion in para 25b.

FRS 2 para 29 stipulates that subsidiaries excluded from consolidation because they are held for resale are to be included as current assets at the lower of cost and net realisable value.

The reasoning followed by the ASB FRS 2 para 79b in requiring the subsidiary to be treated as an investment in the consolidated accounts was that such an undertaking did not form part of the continuing activities of the group and the control was not used to deploy the underlying assets and liabilities of the subsidiary as part of the continuing group's activities for the benefit of the parent company. The valuation at the lower of cost and net realisable value recognises the temporary nature of the parent company's interest.

(b)   (i)   FRS 2 para 39 requires the elimination of profits relating to intra-group transactions by setting against the interests held by the group and the minority interest in respective proportion to their holdings in the undertaking whose individual financial statements recorded the eliminated profits.

This means that the stock sold by GBH plc must be reduced to a cost figure of £200,000 and the minority interest will be reduced by £5,000.

The elimination of £12,000 on the stock sold by FSR plc was correctly treated.

(ii)   FRS 2 para 38 provides that the assets and liabilities of a subsidiary undertaking should be attributable to the minority on the same basis as those attributable to the interests held by the parent. However, goodwill arising on acquisition should only be recognised with respect to the part of the subsidiary undertaking that is attributable to the interest held by the parent and its other subsidiary undertakings. No goodwill should be attributed to the minority.

(iii)   The profit on the sale by Short plc need not be eliminated because Short plc is not to be consolidated under the exclusion provision of FRS 2 para 25b if it is assumed that the investment in Short plc is an interest held exclusively with a view to a subsequent resale.

That means obtaining additional information that a purchaser has been identified or is being sought; that there is a reasonable expectation that the investment will be disposed of within approximately one year of its date of acquisition; and Short plc has not previously been consolidated by FSR.

This means ascertaining the date of acquisition and intended disposal and whether Short plc has been previously consolidated.

The situation would be different if the non-consolidation arose because the subsidiary was excluded on the basis of its different activities in that elimination would be required.

(c)   (i)   The reason for the elimination of the £20,000 from the stock held by FSR plc is that the accounts are presented from a group perspective as a single entity. No increase or decrease has occurred in the group's net assets as a result of the transfer of stock from GBH plc to FSR plc. In addition transactions between undertakings included within the consolidation are wholly within the control of the parent company, even though they may not be wholly owned.

The profit has been realised as far as the minority interest are concerned and will properly appear in the accounts of GBH plc but the transaction has not changed the net assets under the parent's control.

(ii)   The reasoning is that the effect of the existence of minority interests on the returns to investors in the parent undertaking is best reflected by presenting the net identifiable assets attributable to minority interests on the same basis as those attributable to group interests.

The goodwill treatment on an entity basis requires the extrapolation of an amount for goodwill attributable to the whole entity. The Explanatory Notes para 82 states that the resulting figure is however hypothetical because the minority is not a party to the transaction by which the subsidiary is acquired.

In addition the goodwill might be a valuation attaching to the obtaining of control rather than a pro rata value attaching to each share in the subsidiary company.

(iii)   The Explanatory Notes to FRS 2 state that profit arising on a sale effected by a subsidiary undertaking excluded on the basis that it is held exclusively with a view to sale need not be eliminated.

It then goes on to say that it is, however, important to consider whether it is prudent to record any profits arising from transactions in these circumstances.

How can a judgement be made as to whether it is prudent? The implication is that the ASB wish to raise a flag that although the profit need not normally be eliminated there may be circumstances where this should happen. If the transactions were presented in a manner that led to a reader misinterpreting the consolidated accounts they would presumably be regarded as failing to satisfy the true and fair test. The implication in the Explanatory Notes to FRS 2 is that there should be vigilance to possible risks eg, 'The Qualitative Characteristics of Financial Information' para 2.20 ... the exercise of prudence results in a degree of caution under conditions of uncertainty.

8   BULL PLC

(a)   (i)   The question requires a knowledge of the considerations that influence the choice of translation method; an understanding of dominant currency; an ability to apply the criteria of the standard to the particular circumstances given.

Choice of translation method

The standard requires that the method to be used for translating the financial statements of a foreign enterprise should reflect the financial and other operational relationship which exists between the holding company and its foreign enterprise: SSAP 20 para 13. In most cases this means that the consolidated accounts will be prepared using the closing rate/net investment method. However, the temporal method is to be used where the trade of the foreign enterprise is more dependent on the economic environment of the investing company's currency than that of its own reporting currency.

Dominant currency

The determination of the dominant currency requires other factors to be taken into account SSAP 20 para 23 including:

- The extent to which the cash flows of the enterprise have a direct impact upon those of the investing company eg, whether there is a regular and frequent movement of cash between the holding company and the foreign enterprise.

- The extent to which the functioning of the enterprise is dependent directly upon the investing company eg, whether management is based locally.

- The currency in which the majority of the trading transactions are denominated eg, whether invoicing and payment of expenses are in the foreign currency.

- The major currency to which the operation is exposed eg, whether the company is dependent on local financing.

Examples of situations where the temporal method may be appropriate are:

- Where enterprise acts as a selling agency for holding company products.
- Where enterprise supplies raw materials for inclusion in the holding company products.
- Where the enterprise is located overseas for tax purposes.

Application to facts given in the question

(ii)   Advising management

The question states that Dog Inc supplies soya oil to be used as a raw material in the drugs manufactured by Bull plc. This indicates that the appropriate method is the temporal method under the example listed above.

(b)   Translate the profit and loss account and balance sheet of Dog Inc for consolidation purposes using the temporal method.

The first stage is to establish the equity interest at 1 November 19X2 as follows:

	$'000	Exchange rate	£
Fixed assets			
Plant and equipment			
Cost	1,800	2.2	818,182
Aggregate depreciation	600	2.2	272,727
	1,200	2.2	545,455
Current assets			
Stock	115	1.8	63,889
Net monetary assets (balance)	(45)	1.8	(25,000)
	1,270		584,344

Ordinary share capital	375	3.6	104,167
Profit and loss account	895	balance	480,177
	1,270		584,344

The second stage is to translate the balance sheet as at 31 October 19X3 as follows:

	$'000	Exchange rate	£
Fixed assets			
Plant and equipment			
Cost	1,800	2.2	818,182
Aggregate depreciation	750	2.2	340,909
	1,050	2.2	477,273
Current assets			
Stock	120	1.1	109,091
Net monetary assets (balance)	255	1.1	231,818
	1,425		818,182
Ordinary share capital	375	3.6	104,167
Profit and loss account	1,050	balance	714,015
	1,425		818,182

The third stage is to translate the profit and loss account excluding the exchange difference as follows:

Profit and loss account for the year ended 31 October 19X3

	$'000	$'000	Exchange rate	£
Sales		3,750	1.5	2,500,000
Cost of sales				
Stock at 1.11.X2	115		1.8	63,889
Purchases	3,000		1.5	2,000,000
	3,115			2,063,889
Stock at 31.10.X3	120		1.1	109,091
		2,995		1,954,798
Gross profit		755		545,202
Administration expenses	100		1.5	66,667
Handling charges	200		1.5	133,333
Depreciation	150		2.2	68,182
	—	450		
Profit before tax		305		277,020
Tax		150	1.5	100,000
Profit after tax		155		177,020

The fourth stage is to identify the exchange difference as follows:

	£
Profit and loss as at 1.11.X2	480,177
Add retained profits	177,020
	657,197
Less profit and loss as at 31.10.X3	714,015
Exchange gain	56,818

The profit before tax is revised:

	£
Profit pre-exchange loss	277,020
Exchange gain	56,818
Profit before tax	333,838
Less: Tax	100,000
Profit after tax	233,838

(c)　(i)　There is an exchange gain of £448,990 calculated as follows:

	$'000
Net assets at 1.11.X2	1,270

	£
At rate at 1.11.X2 [1,270,000/1.8]	705,555
At rate at 31.10.X2 [1,270,000/1.1]	1,154,545
Exchange gain	448,990

The exchange gain will be recorded as movement on reserves. If exchange differences were introduced into the profit and loss account, the results from trading operations, as shown in the local currency financial statements would be distorted.

The question requires a further analysis to quantify the profit for the year and the opening and closing profit and loss account balance in the balance sheet.

First, establish the profit and loss account balance as at 1 November 19X2 as follows:

	$'000	Exchange rate	£
Net assets	1,270	1.8	705,556
Ordinary share capital	375	3.6	104,167
Profit and loss account	895	balance	601,389
	1,270		705,556

Second, establish the profit and loss account balance as at 31 October 19X3.

	$'000	*Exchange rate*	£
Net assets	1,425	1.1	1,295,455

Third, translate the profit for the year ended 31 October 19X3 at the closing rate:

$155,000/1.1 = £140,909

Finally, reconcile the profit and loss account balances as follows:

	£
Profit and loss account as at 31.10.X2	601,389
Add: Profit for the year	140,909
	742,298
Add: The exchange gain	448,990
Profit and loss account as at 31.10.X3	1,191,288

(ii)   The profit for the year using the average rate of exchange would be $155,000/1.5 = £103,333.

The difference of £37,576 [£140,909-£103,333] would be recorded as a movement on reserves.

(d)   This requires an understanding of the effect of financing foreign equity investments by borrowings on the company-only accounts.

In the company-only accounts, there will be a gain on the investment and a loss on the loan. These are calculated as follows:

	£
Investment in Dog Inc	
1.11.X2 $375,000 at 1.8 =	208,333
31.10.X3 $375,000 at 1.1 =	340,909
Exchange gain	132,576
Loan	
1.11.X2 $750,000 at 1.8 =	416,667
31.10.X3 $750,000 at 1.1 =	681,818
Exchange loss	265,151

The exchange gain on the investment would be set against the exchange loss on the loan and the net difference of £132,575 would be debited to the profit and loss account.

9   LOOK AHEAD & CO

(a)   Discuss the relevance of dividends in the valuation of D Dodd's shareholding on the assumption that it is sold to his son W Dodd illustrating your answer from the data given in the question.

There is a problem for the valuer in that the dividend policy is outside the control of the shareholder wishing to sell his shares and, because the company is a private company, there is not the same pressure on the directors to maintain a consistent dividend policy or, indeed, to even pay a dividend.

This means that there is uncertainty. At one extreme the valuer could value the shares at nil because there is the possibility of no dividends being declared in future years; at the other extreme the valuer could value the shares on an earnings basis in the hope that the earnings will be fully distributed in future years.

In between these two extremes the valuer could make a valuation based on the probability of the level of dividends.

A prudent approach might be to assume that the current dividend will be maintained. If this were to be assumed the valuation of the shares would be £3,703.70. This is calculated as follows:

The valuation of each share would be based on the gross dividend of 6.67p per share to produce a valuation of 37.04p per share. (5p/75 × 100/.18 = 37.04p per 25p share).

The 10,000 shareholding would be valued at £3,703.70.

This method is referred to in 'Valuation of Unquoted Securities' by C G Glover as the initial yield method. It is simple to use and has a wide following in practice.

An inappropriate choice of comparator company would clearly be misleading but it should be recognised that the use of sector averages published in the FT Actuaries Share Index can be even more misleading because the prices arising from dealings by institutional investors often reflect short-term political and economic circumstances whereas the investor in a private company may be looking for long-term considerations.

This method does not take account of a possible range of dividends and required rates of return. It is a normal practice for a valuer to produce a table of values to indicate to a client for negotiation purposes the range of possible values. For example, the following table could be produced on the assumption that the future net dividend would be between 5p and 7p; that the investor's required gross rate of return would be between 16% and 22%; and that the rate of tax was 25%.

Dividend		Investor's required rate of return			
Net	Gross	16%	18%	20%	22%
5p	6.67p	41.7	37.1	33.4	30.1
6p	8.00p	50.0	44.4	40.0	36.4
7p	9.33p	58.1	51.8	46.7	42.4

This is simplistic but the table indicates that from the estimated dividends and required rate of return a share price can be derived that lies between 30.1p and 58.1p. It indicates the sensitivity of the share price to a variation in the assumption of dividend per share and required rate of return. In relation to the shares being considered, that indicates an offer of between £3,010 and £5,810.

The tabular method is attempting to allow for a growth in the dividend by setting out three levels of dividend. An alternative approach that features in the academic texts is to estimate the rate of growth. In the present example, it is clear that there has been a consistent dividend policy.

The directors have followed a policy of increasing the dividends at the rate of 5% per year. The dividend cover has varied between 4 and 10 indicating a policy of maintaining dividend growth rather than maintaining the dividend cover and relating the dividend directly to the earnings of the year in which the dividend is paid.

Applying the growth formula, the value of a share would be:

$$\frac{\text{Gross dividend} \times \text{growth rate}}{\text{Required rate of return - growth rate}} = \frac{(5p/75 \times 100) \times 1.05}{18-5}$$

$$= 53.85p$$

The 10,000 shares would have a value of £5,384.62.

On the data given in the question, there is a clear dividend policy and a valuation could be based on that. The earnings are not relevant unless there is some indication that they will fail to support the dividend or some indication that the dividend policy will change to reflect the earnings growth eg, following a flotation on the AIM.

(b)   (i)   Explain briefly the factors that the firm would take into account when estimating the future net dividends.

In order to estimate the likely range of future dividends, the firm needs to evaluate the directors' dividend policy.

In Arbor Ltd there has been a consistent policy of increasing the dividend per share by 5% per annum. The future dividends can be related to that policy assuming that there are no contra-indications such as liquidity pressures or expansion plans that could affect the maintenance of the existing policy. There is less need to consider the future rate of increase in the profits.

However, if the directors appear to have adopted an identifiable dividend cover policy, then efforts should be made to determine the future profitability and to apply the historic dividend cover rate to the forecast profits.

If the directors have a restrictive attitude towards paying dividends, this might result in the payment of a constant amount regardless of earnings growth or even in the payment of no dividends with profits taken as directors' remuneration or ploughed back into the business.

Where there is no discernible pattern, this could have an impact on the investor's required rate of return.

(ii)   Explain briefly the factors that the firm would take into account when making an initial estimate of the investor's required gross yield.

The rate of return on a security has to take account of:

(1)   forgoing the pure or risk-free rate of interest;
(2)   bearing the risk of equity investment;
(3)   suffering any lack of marketability; and
(4)   possible changes in the marketability.

The firm usually considers three main sources of information.

(1)   in order to assess the risk-free rate of interest

The current market statistics of average gross interest yields to redemption of British government stocks together with the gross returns available from local authority loans and building societies, will give a fairly reliable guide to the interest rates prevailing at the date of the valuation.

These rates of return after deducting the investor's top rate of tax and after deducting the rate of inflation will indicate the real return obtainable by the investor.

(2)   in order to assess the premium for equity investment

The second source of information is the current market statistics of gross dividend yields on minority holdings of equity shares that are quoted. The market will have taken business risk arising from the nature of the company's operations and financial structure into account in arriving at a price.

However, it is often difficult to identify a company whose business, trading record and financial structure are similar to the company whose shares are being valued and an adjustment might be needed to take account of any material differences.

Adjustment for differing operating conditions is subjective. It will involve a consideration of a number of factors. For example, it could involve comparing the workforce if the target has a new workforce and the comparator has a long established, experienced workforce; or comparing the products/services; or the pricing structures; or the tangible assets eg, the target might have new fixed assets and the comparator heavily depreciated ones.

Adjustment for different capital structures is also subjective. It may involve a consideration of present gearing levels and also future changes eg, arising from changes in the working capital requirements.

(3)   in order to assess a premium for lack of marketability

An adjustment is required for the lack of marketability. This is a subjective adjustment. It will be influenced by the valuer's knowledge of the market in unquoted minority shares that prevails at the date of the valuation.

(4)   Possible changes in the lack of marketability

If there is any indication that the minority interest will become more marketable then the premium for this risk will be reduced.

For example there may be some indication of an exit route other than by sale within the existing articles and memorandum of association eg, flotation or take-over.

(c)   Explain how the approach adopted by the firm when valuing a minority interest might be influenced by the size of the shareholding or its relative importance to the other shareholdings.

The firm will need to consider the ownership of other shares before and after the transaction and the effect that this has on the control and management of the company assuming that the shares passed into the ownership of one or more of the other shareholders. It is important to consider the powers attaching to the shares.

The powers attaching to degree of ownership

With a holding that exceeds 10% a shareholder has the power to prevent a complete take-over by another company (Companies Act 1985 Ss428-430) that might have sought to enforce a compulsory acquisition of the minority that has not accepted the offer.

With a holding that exceeds 25% the minority shareholder has the power to block a special resolution such as that required to change the objects of the company (Companies Act 1985 s.4) without recourse to the court as a dissenting minority.

With a holding that exceeds 25% the minority shareholder has the power to block extraordinary resolutions such as that required to wind up a company voluntarily when because of its liabilities it cannot continue to trade: IA 1986 s.84.

With a holding that exceeds 50% the shareholder is able to control the constitution of the board of directors and the dividend distribution policy of the company.

This effect of the above considerations is that there may be a special buyer to whom the shares have a value that is greater than that based on dividend yields. The special buyer might be acting to achieve a positive effect eg, to control dividend distribution policy or to achieve a negative effect eg, to frustrate control being achieved by a single person.

Powers attaching to existing shareholding

In the present situation the shares are held so that no single shareholder can pass ordinary resolutions but A Arny is able to prevent a special or extraordinary resolution being passed eg,

Shareholder	Shareholding	% holding
A Arny	61,250	49%
B Brady	30,000	24%
D Brady	20,000	16%
E Brady	11,250	9%
D Dodd	2,500	2%

Existence of special buyer(s) in Arbor Ltd

In the present situation, where there are shareholdings on the margins of 10%, 25% and 50% there are clearly potential special buyers.

The sale to A Arny would allow A Arny to control the company and the dividend distribution policy. This could have an effect on the value of the other minority shareholdings if he were to change the dividend policy from its present pattern of 5% increase each year. If there were any likelihood of this then the other shareholders would consider a premium to protect the valuation based on the dividend growth model.

The sale to B Brady would allow him to prevent the passing of a special or extraordinary resolution.

The sale to any of the Bradys would allow them, acting in concert, to control the company.

The effect of a special buyer on the share valuation method

The point that needs to be considered is whether the existence of a special buyer has an implication for the share valuation method that is applied.

For example, should the shareholding being sold be valued on an earnings basis rather than on a dividend basis.

If an earnings basis is applicable, then a profit forecast and earnings yield approach would be followed.

This could be significant in the case of Arbor Ltd because the growth of earnings has been at a substantially greater rate of approximately 40% than the 5% growth in the dividends distributed.

10   HARTINGTON PLC

(a)   **Why a financial reporting standard was needed**

In recent years, large companies have made increasing use of a wide range of complex financial instruments. These have included traditional primary financial instruments (for example, shares and debentures), and derivative financial instruments. A derivative financial instrument is a financial instrument that derives its value from the price or rate of some underlying item, such as interest rates, exchange rates and stock market and other indices. Derivatives include futures, options, forward contracts, interest rate swaps and currency swaps.

The Companies Act and FRS 4 *Capital Instruments* already require entities to provide some information about their use of financial instruments, in particular, about the maturity of debt and the interest rate terms of indebtedness. However, the ASB believed that these disclosures were inadequate where derivatives were used. This is because the use of derivatives poses particular problems:

(a)   Many derivatives have no cost. This means that they may represent substantial assets and liabilities of the company and yet they might not appear in the balance sheet.

(b)   Gains and losses are normally not recorded until cash is exchanged. Because gains and losses can be easily realised, management may be able to choose when to report gains and losses on realisation.

(c)   Because the value of a derivative depends on the value of underlying items it can change very rapidly, thus exposing an entity to the risk of large profits or losses. Derivatives can rapidly transform the position, performance and risk profile of an entity, yet the financial statements often contained little or no information about the impact of derivatives on the risks faced by an entity.

There have been a number of well publicised financial disasters involving derivatives and these have highlighted the inadequacies of traditional accounting practices, including disclosure, in this area.

A further reason why the ASB wished to undertake work on derivatives is that the increasing globalisation of financial markets has meant that derivatives and other financial instruments have become a topic of international concern. The ASB wishes to be able to make an effective contribution to the international debate.

The ASB decided to address the disclosure issues as a priority, so that users of the financial statements would have information about the main aspects of the entity's risk profile and an understanding of how this risk profile is being managed.

A further financial reporting standard on the measurement of financial instruments is currently being developed.

(b)   **Index linked loan**

The loan will be included in the balance sheet at a value of £2,095,238 (2,000,000 × 110/105) and the change in value is treated as an additional finance cost in accordance with the requirements of FRS 4 which states that finance costs contingent on uncertain events should be recognised only once the events have occurred. Total finance costs are £195,238 and consist of interest paid of £100,000 (2,000,000 × 5%) plus the change in value of the principal amount.

Zero coupon bonds

Although no interest is paid during the term of the bonds, there is a finance charge which represents the difference between the issue proceeds and the amount to be paid on redemption. FRS 4 requires that this is allocated to periods over the term of the debt at a constant rate on the carrying amount. The effective rate of interest on the bonds is 10% and therefore they will be included in the balance sheet at £5,500,000. The finance cost of £500,000 is charged to the profit and loss account.

(c)   **Notes to the financial statements: extracts**

	£'000
Creditors: Amounts falling due after more than one year:	
Debenture loans	5,500
Bank loans and overdrafts	2,095
	7,595

On 1 July 19X6 the company issued zero coupon bonds of £5,000,000. The total consideration received for this issue amounted to £5,000,000.

	£'000
Interest rate profile:	
Fixed rate financial liabilities	5,500
Floating rate financial liabilities	2,095
	7,595

All liabilities are denominated in sterling. The weighted average interest rate for the fixed rate financial liabilities is 10%. The floating rate financial liabilities comprise a bank loan that bears interest at rates based on an index.

Maturity of financial liabilities

The maturity profile of the group's financial liabilities at 30 June 19X7 was as follows:

	£'000
In more than one year, but not more than two years	2,095
In more than two years, but not more than five years	5,500
	7,595

In addition to the disclosures above, the aggregate fair values of the long term borrowings should also be disclosed.

WORKING

Interest rate on zero coupon bonds: $\dfrac{5,000}{8,051} = 0.621$, which is the discount factor for five years at 10%.

---

11   PROFESSIONAL ETHICS

(Tutorial note: a good question on the problems of the application of professional ethics. You would fare best here by

(a)   not taking an overly dogmatic approach on the assumption that there is a 'right' answer

(b)   'considering' ie, discussing, the situations presented by the question from various angles, which is what the question asks for

(c)   'biting the bullet' and coming to a decision - again, as the question required. This does involve stating assumptions, however, and you should not be afraid of doing so where this is required.*)*

(a)   (i)   The statement on professional independence states that conflicts of interest should be avoided. Thus it is undesirable to act for two clients in dispute with one another. However, where such undesirable situations cannot be avoided, it is necessary for the member to explain the situation in full to both parties, without, of course, divulging confidential information about the other client's affairs. 'Ideally' then we should disengage from both parties. Given that this will be both commercially and ethically disadvantageous to both us and our clients (it is inappropriate to 'abandon' a client in difficulties without good cause) we will probably not do so. If we decide to proceed with preparing a schedule of sales invoices and cash for Wollaton we will ipso facto be acting on Wollaton's behalf in respect of the dispute and that fact must be communicated to Sherwood Ltd with the highly likely effect of losing its audit.

(ii)   In the unlikely situation of us acting for Wollaton and retaining Sherwood's audit, it would be wholly inappropriate to use knowledge of Sherwood's accounting records as this would be a breach of our duty of confidentiality in relation to Sherwood quite apart from contravening the laws of natural justice. This would in practice necessitate a complete separation of the teams working on the two clients for obvious reasons. Equally it would be wholly inappropriate to act for both clients in respect of the same dispute and so a request to act on behalf of Sherwood after we had agreed to act on behalf of Wollaton must be declined.

(b)   (i)   The statements on confidentiality as applied to these circumstances mean that we may not divulge anything to Mapperley Ltd about Hucknall Ltd.

(ii)   (1)   Analytical review of the ageing of Hucknall Ltd's debt should provide some evidence to the directors of the doubtfulness of the debt.

(2)   Press comments might be brought to the attention of the directors, indicating loss of orders, lay-offs, etc if they exist.

(3)   We should consider circularising the debt (with Mapperley Ltd's permission) - problems in eliciting a reply might give rise to suspicions by directors.

(4)   We should ensure that systems in relation to credit control are adequate. We should voice general concern if it appears that Hucknall Ltd has had extensive credit extended to it beyond what is warranted or recommended by credit reference agencies. Firms commonly do this, fearing that they will lose a valued customer if credit is refused.

(5)   Any 'unusual' circumstances - round sum payments, irregular payments should be brought to the attention of directors.

It may well be difficult to follow the above procedures without giving the impression to directors that something is 'wrong', especially as they may well know that we are also auditors of Hucknall Ltd.

(iii)   In deciding whether to qualify we would consider the following

(1)   The degree to which we are confident that Hucknall Ltd is not a going concern.

(2)   The degree to which we can support our opinion that the debt should be provided for from Mapperley Ltd's records alone.

(3)   The possibility of delaying our report that would allow Hucknall Ltd to go into formal liquidation and thus provide publicly available information on the status of the debt.

The qualification would be an 'except for' or an 'adverse' opinion (depending on the amounts involved) if we were certain that the debt should be provided for and could produce evidence to support this opinion.

If we are uncertain about the debt, then in SAS600 terminology we have an 'inherent uncertainty' ie, an uncertainty whose resolution is dependent upon certain future events outside the control of the reporting entity's directors at the date the financial statements are approved.

As the debt is 'large', its potential impact is so great that the inherent uncertainty is probably a 'fundamental uncertainty'. A fundamental uncertainty requires disclosure in the financial statements. If the directors include a note in the financial statements, the audit report should include an explanatory paragraph referring to the uncertainty. The report would not be qualified.

If there is no disclosure by the directors, we would issue an 'except for' or 'disclaimer' opinion depending on the amounts involved.

(c)   (i)   We will be liable in the tort of negligence to third parties who rely on our report where

(1)   we owe a duty of care to the third party and
(2)   where that duty is breached and
(3)   where loss has been suffered by the third party as a direct result of the breach.

We will owe a duty of care where we are sufficiently 'proximate' to the third party, where the third party's reliance on the audited financial statements is foreseeable and where it is equitable that we should be liable to that party. In practical terms this means that we will probably have to have known who the third party was (or at least known that the party was a member of a small class, eg rival takeover bidders or possibly creditors, as in this case) at the time we signed the audit report, and that the third party would be likely to rely on our report in making a decision. If Mapperley Ltd can show that we knew that it was relying on our audit report for the purposes of its extending credit to Hucknall Ltd, we will owe it a duty of care. Mapperley will then have to show that we breached our duty and that its loss was a direct result. If our audit was conducted in accordance with Auditing Standards, it is unlikely that we will be found to be negligent.

In **Caparo Industries v Dickman & Others (1989)** the House of Lords held that no duty of care is owed by auditors to individual shareholders or potential shareholders as there is a lack of sufficient proximity between the parties in the case of public companies where share ownership changes daily. Also it would be inequitable to make auditors liable to such an indeterminate class of people. The facts with Mapperley Ltd are different in that we are dealing with creditors and not shareholders and the fact that both companies are private and not public. If either Mapperley or any other third party can show that the elements for the tort of negligence are present, they may have a chance of successfully suing us.

(ii)   We are bound in contract to Hucknall Ltd in respect of our audit report. If it can show that we have breached our contractual duty and that it has thereby suffered loss, it may be able to sue us in contract but this would seem unlikely.

(iii)   Statute only provides that we may not limit our liability in contract. It is possible that the EEC Fifth Directive may in future render auditors statutorily liable to third parties.

12   EXPECTATION GAP

(a)   The *Caparo* decision limits the parties who may successfully sue the auditor for negligence to the company and shareholders as a body. No other party is entitled to damages if there are material errors in the accounts. Essentially, it appears that the decision is based on the fact that only persons who have a contractual relationship with the auditor can make a successful claim (ie, those who have paid a fee to the auditor). In some respects this decision is reasonable, as it seems unfair that a third party should be able to successfully sue an auditor for damages when he has paid nothing towards the cost of the audit. However, the *Caparo* decision does appear to have reduced the credibility of the audit report and hence audited accounts.

In almost all circumstances, a set of accounts should have the same meaning to the company, existing shareholders and third parties, so I believe it is unreasonable for auditors to argue that an error in the accounts could be material to third parties but not material to shareholders or the company's management. Also, if third parties believe audited accounts may not be accurate, this can affect decisions by potential investors and banks who lend money to companies. The long-term effect is likely to be that investors will be less willing to purchase shares of companies, which will result in a fall in share prices and companies having increasing difficulty in raising new funds. Also, banks and individuals will be less willing to lend money to companies. Thus, I come to the conclusion that it is probably unreasonable that auditors should be liable for negligence to a wider range of third parties. However, it is desirable that accounts of companies should be accurate to ensure that third parties will be encouraged to buy shares and lend money to businesses. Unless auditors are liable to third parties for negligence, it appears that the credibility of audited accounts will continue to be eroded. There appear to be a number of solutions to this problem, including:

(i)   Companies could pay an additional fee to the auditor, so that the auditor's liability includes potential shareholders and creditors. However, it may be difficult for the third party to make a successful claim against the auditor, as no consideration has passed between the third party and the auditor.

(ii)   The third party could pay a fee to the auditor to confirm the accounts are correct.

(iii)   There could be a change in the law so that certain third parties are included.

Ideally, option (i) appears to be the optimum solution provided auditors are prepared to accept this additional potential liability. Option (ii) could be expensive for the third party if the investment or loan is small. However, it does have the advantage that the auditor would be aware of the parties to whom he will be responsible if a case of negligence arises. Option (iii) is likely to be inflexible and may include third parties the company and its shareholders do not wish to protect. For instance, in a family controlled business where there is no intention to sell the business, it would be a waste of money for the company to protect potential investors.

(b)   The statement in the question that the auditor has no duty to detect and report on error and fraud is incorrect. SAS 110 on the auditor's responsibility in relation to fraud and error says that the auditor should 'design audit procedures so as to have a reasonable expectation of detecting misstatements arising from fraud or error which are material to the financial statements'. So, the auditor is not responsible for detecting immaterial errors or fraud. It appears that he is responsible for detecting material errors and fraud. However, if a set of accounts is subsequently shown to have material errors or fraud, the auditor may use as defence against the allegation that the fraud or error was deliberately hidden by the company's management, and it would be unreasonable to expect the auditor to detect it using normal audit procedures.

I believe that auditor's current responsibilities in relation to error and fraud are reasonable for both the auditor and the general public. It would be unreasonable to ask the auditor to detect all errors and fraud (including immaterial ones), as it would increase the cost of the audit substantially, and the final result will probably not be cost effective (ie, the increased audit cost of detecting error and fraud will be greater than the value of errors and fraud detected). Also, uncertainties in relation to error and fraud are difficult to deal with. For instance, can an auditor be certain that all expense claims by employees are correct? There may be insufficient evidence to confirm or refute these claims.

However, if the auditor is only responsible for detecting material error and fraud, this enables him to ignore immaterial items and it does not require him to report on small errors and fraud. So, the auditor performs a more cost effective audit. For investors, I would argue that they are only interested in material error and fraud, so the current situation satisfies them as well.

(c)   In the UK, most institutions who hold clients' money and invest money for them are covered by the Financial Services Act 1986. This places additional responsibilities on the auditor, and it allows the auditor to report to the regulator of the responsible body if there are any breaches in the regulations - the Financial Services Act allows the auditor to report in this way, without being liable to the client for breach of confidence. Also, the auditor has to make an annual report to the regulator of a firm's investment business. A further requirement of the Financial Services Act is that the auditor has to consider the systems of internal control in the business and make a statement in his report on these controls. Solicitors and estate agents are covered by rules of their professional body over holding clients' money, and the client accounts have to be audited by a registered auditor.

So, for investment businesses there is a more onerous audit requirement than for companies.

Most company pension funds are not covered by the Financial Services Act, but if the pension fund receives investment advice (which is probable), the body giving this advice is required to comply with the Financial Services Act.

It can be seen from the discussion above, that institutions holding clients' moneys are more tightly controlled than other businesses, which are solely covered by the Companies Acts. These additional controls are designed to reduce the risk of misappropriation of clients' funds. The question says that the auditor should ensure that no loss arises from investing clients' funds. I believe this requirement is unreasonable, as many investments involve risk, with a chance that the value of investments will decrease as well as increase (eg, in 1991 the index of the share prices of the largest 100 firms in the UK (ie, FTSE) fell by 13%). If there was a requirement for no loss, all investment businesses would have to make very safe investments (eg, in government fixed interest securities), and this would not satisfy the requirements of many investors.

So, it is unreasonable to ask the auditor to ensure that no loss occurs on investments held by a financial institution. However, there does appear to be a need for the auditor to ensure that funds are invested in accordance with the wishes of the investors, that unauthorised investments are not made and there is no fraudulent misappropriation of these funds, or investment in funds with a view to committing a fraud. Fraudulent misappropriation of funds may be relatively easy to detect, but detecting investment in funds with a view to committing a fraud is more difficult to detect. For instance, the business may invest in a company (X Ltd) which is owned by one of the directors of the investment company and X Ltd is used to finance an expensive life-style for the director. It may be difficult to detect who runs X Ltd and whether it is likely to be a profitable investment. A possible solution to this problem is to ensure that the investment trust only invests in certain types of business (eg, companies quoted on the Stock Exchange) and that surplus funds are invested securely (eg, in either a UK clearing bank deposit account or government securities).

With some recent major frauds, such as Barlow Clowes, and the alleged misappropriation of funds from the Mirror Group Newspapers pension fund, it may appear that the only solution is that the auditor should be present at all times to check all investment transactions. However, it would be expensive for the auditor to be permanently present to check transactions, and many people would argue that it would interfere with the running of the business. The main problems with these businesses was a weakness in the system of internal control due to a dominant chief executive. With Barlow Clowes, it appears that although the investors believed the company was investing in government fixed interest securities, there was a clause which allowed the company to make any other investment. Barlow Clowes used this clause to make 'other investments' which were then used to fund the extravagant life-style of the proprietor of the business. The solution to this problem is to prohibit 'get out clauses' which allow investment in any other activity. This could be controlled by the regulator of the investment business rejecting registration from companies with 'get out clauses'. Then the auditor will be able to report to the regulator if the company is not complying with its investment rules. Most of the Barlow Clowes fraud took place before the Financial Services Act came into force, so it could be argued that it would have been detected earlier if the Act had been in force during all of Barlow Clowes existence.

With the Mirror Group Newspapers pension fund, Robert Maxwell was the chairman of the trustees of the pension fund, and he owned the company which dealt with the pension fund's investments. There is a problem of who should be the chairman of the trustees of a pension fund, and whether the employees or the company should have a majority of the trustees. As a pension fund is for the benefit of the employees, and is legally separate from the company, I believe the employees should be the majority of the trustees and one of their number should be chairman of the trustees. However, it could be argued that the company makes significant contributions to the pension fund (usually more than the employees) and the company is usually required to fund any deficiency in the pension fund assets. These reasons could justify the company having the majority of trustees. My view is that the pension fund should be seen to be independent of the company and that the majority of the trustees should be employees (rather than representatives of the company). An alternative would be to have an independent trustee who has a casting vote in the case of a dispute between the employees and the company's representatives.

On investment by the pension fund, there are limits over the amount of the pension fund assets which can be invested in the company. These limits could be further tightened. The major problem with the Mirror Group Newspaper pension fund appears to be that the investment adviser was owned by Robert Maxwell, and that it invested in private companies owned by Robert Maxwell. Also, it provided loans and guaranteed loans to companies controlled by Robert Maxwell. I believe that there should be legislation to limit investment by pension funds in companies owned by directors of the company. An alternative is to authorise certain companies to advise on investment by pension funds (similar to authorisation under the Financial Services Act), and to disqualify an investment advisor which has any connection with the company or its pension fund. By 'connected' I mean that none of the major shareholders or directors of the investment adviser should be directors of the company or trustees of the pension fund.

So, I believe the employees should be a majority of the trustees of a pension fund, and pension fund advisors should be independent of the company and the pension fund. This new requirement for independence of pension fund advisors will probably require statutory backing.

The solution to many of the problems with investment companies and pension funds is that there should be a proper system of internal control in these organisations. With both Barlow Clowes and the Maxwell pension funds there was a dominant individual who prevented the operation of effective internal controls. I believe the auditor should report if controls are effective and report to a supervisory body if they are ineffective. Legislation may need to be introduced to take action against investment companies and pension funds where controls are not effective (eg, by an independent body taking over the control of these organisations). I do not believe that requiring the auditor to be present at all times is an effective way of overcoming these problems.

9 NEW SYLLABUS EXAMINATIONS

ALL FOUR questions are compulsory and MUST be attempted

13 (Question 1 of examination)

Rowen plc was formed in 1975 to manufacture executive toys. The directors decided to expand their exports and on 1 January 1989 it acquired investments in an American company, Overseas Inc and a French company, Europe SA, which were to act as selling agencies for the company's products.

The investments consisted of 800,000 shares of US$10 each in Overseas Inc when its reserves were US$25m and of 2,250,000 shares of FF20 each in Europe SA when its reserves were FF230m. At the dates of acquisition, the book values were the same as the fair values.

The directors have instructed their accountant to prepare draft consolidated accounts as at 31 December 1993 on the basis that Overseas Inc is a subsidiary undertaking due to the fact that they exercise a dominant influence; and that Europe SA is a participating interest but not an associated undertaking.

The balance sheets as at 31 December 1993 were as follows:

	Rowen £m	Overseas US$m	Europe FFm
Fixed assets			
Tangible assets	669	458	4,231
Investment in Overseas Inc	12		
Investment in Europe SA	10		
Current assets			
Stocks	675	44	404
Cash	46	113	1,038
Current liabilities			
Creditors	(490)	(31)	(288)
Creditors falling due after more than one year			
Loan	(370)	(103)	(954)
	552	481	4,431
Capital and reserves			
Share capital	185	20	180
Profit and loss account	367	461	4,251
	552	481	4,431

The profit and loss accounts for the year ended 31 December 1993 are as follows:

	Rowen £m	Overseas US$m	Europe FFm
Turnover	2,784	1,150	10,615
Cost of sales	1,822	775	7,154
Gross profit	962	375	3,461

Distribution costs	392	90	831
Administrative expenses	370	30	278
Depreciation	35	24	230
Dividend from Overseas Inc	(12)		
Dividend from Europe SA	(11)		
Profit before tax	188	231	2,122
Tax	93	90	831
Profit after tax	95	141	1,291
Dividends paid 31.7.93	37	51	440
Retained profit	58	90	851

Further information

(1)   The fixed assets in both Overseas Inc and Europe SA were acquired on 1 January 1985. They are stated at cost less depreciation and there have been no acquisitions or disposals during the year.

(2)   Stocks

	31 December 1992		31 December 1993	
	Stock	Exchange rate at purchase date	Stock	Exchange rate at purchase date
Overseas US$m	57	2.0	44	1.6
Europe FFm	523	11.5	404	8.5

(3)   Exchange rates have been as follows:

	US$ = £1	FF = £1
1 January 1985	2.4	12.0
1 January 1989	2.0	12.5
31 December 1992	1.8	11.0
Average for 1993	1.7	10.0
31 July 1993	1.7	10.0
31 December 1993	1.5	8.0

(4)   Rowen plc policy is to write off goodwill over ten years.

(5)   The foreign exchange translation of the foreign subsidiary is to be on the basis that the functional currency of the American operation is sterling.

(6)   There has been no change in the share capital of Overseas Inc or Europe SA since the date of acquisition.

Required

(a)   Prepare a draft consolidated profit and loss account for the Rowen Group for the year ended 31 December 1993 and a draft consolidated balance sheet as at that date.   **(15 marks)**

(b)   (i)   Calculate the effect on the consolidated profit and loss account for the year ended 31 December 1993 if the investment in Europe SA is classified as an associated interest.

         (ii)   Calculate the carrying value of the investment in the consolidated balance sheet as at 31 December 1993.

                                                                                          (6 marks)

(c)   [Not reproduced as this part of the question is no longer within the syllabus.]   **(9 marks)**
                                                                                    (Total: 30 marks)

14 (Question 2 of examination)

Aztec plc was incorporated in 1968 as an importer of silver artefacts from South America which it customised for the UK market. The company had sold its products in the luxury market and traded profitably until 1989. Since that date it has suffered continuous losses which have resulted in a negative balance on the profit and loss account. The balance sheet as at 31 December 1993 showed the following:

	£
Share capital and reserves	
Ordinary shares of £1 each	675,000
7% Preference shares of £1 each	135,000
Profit and loss account	(573,000)
Net capital employed	237,000
Fixed assets	
Leasehold premises	397,000
Vehicles and equipment	105,000
Machinery	250,000
Current assets	
Stock	295,000
Debtors	120,000
Current liabilities	
Suppliers	(288,000)
Wages, VAT and PAYE	(80,000)
Hire-purchase liability on vehicles/equipment	(20,000)
Bank overdraft (secured by a fixed charge over the machinery)	(112,000)
Non-current liabilities	
Hire-purchase liability on vehicles and equipment	(25,000)
11% Debentures (secured by a floating charge)	(405,000)
Net assets	237,000

Since 1989 the company has been developing an export market for its products in Europe and the directors forecast that the company will return to profit in 1994. They expect profits before tax and debenture interest to be in the range of £70,000 to £140,000 per annum over the next three years. As a result of developing the export market, they expect that the company will require warehouse premises on the continent in 1996 at a forecast cost of £250,000.

However, the directors are concerned that even if the company achieves a profit of £70,000 per year it will be a number of years before a dividend could be distributed to the ordinary shareholders and it would be difficult to raise fresh funds from the shareholders in 1996 if there were to be little prospect of a dividend until the year 2000.

The directors have been considering various possible courses of action available under the Companies Act 1985 and the Insolvency Act 1986 and have had initial discussions with their auditors.

As a result of these discussions it was agreed that the finance director would produce a draft proposal for reorganisation; the auditors would let the finance director have their comments on the draft proposal: and the finance director would then submit a proposal to the board of directors for their consideration.

The following additional information was obtained by the finance director concerning the assets and liabilities at 31 December 1993 and estimated costs of liquidating or reorganising:

(a)   Fair values and liquidation values of assets were:

	Fair values on a going concern basis £	Liquidation values on a forced sale basis £
Leasehold premises	360,000	100,000
Vehicles and equipment	85,000	35,000
Machinery	225,000	122,000
Current assets		
Stock	285,000	150,000
Debtors	110,000	100,000

(b)   Preference dividends are four years in arrears.

(c)   Wages, VAT and PAYE would be preferential creditors in a liquidation.

(d)   The costs of liquidating Aztec plc were estimated at £55,000.

(e)   The costs of reorganisation were estimated at £40,000; these would be paid by Aztec (Europe) plc and treated as part of the purchase consideration.

The finance director prepared the following draft proposal:

(i)   A new company was to be formed Aztec (Europe) plc with a share capital of £270,000 in 10p shares to acquire the assets and liabilities of Aztec plc as at 31 December 1993.

(ii)   The ordinary shareholders were to receive less than 25% of the ordinary shares in Aztec (Europe) plc so that the existing preference shareholders and debenture holders each had a significant interest and acting together had control of the new company.

(iii)   The arrears of preference dividends were to be cancelled.

(iv)   The new company was to issue:

–   900,000 ordinary shares and £70,000 of 13% debentures to the existing preference shareholders

–   1,200,000 ordinary shares and £200,000 of 13% debentures to the existing 11% debenture holders

–   600,000 ordinary shares to the existing ordinary shareholders.

(v)   The variation of the rights of the shareholders and creditors was to be effected under S425 of the Companies Act 1985 which requires that the scheme should be approved by a majority in number and 75% in value of each class of shareholders, by a majority in number and 75% in value of each class of creditor affected and by the court.

(vi)   The transfer of the assets to Aztec (Europe) plc was to be effected under S427 of the Companies Act 1985 which would ensure that the court dealt with the transfer of the assets and liabilities and the dissolution of Aztec plc to avoid the costs of winding up that company.

Assume a corporation tax rate of 35% and an income tax rate of 25%.

Required

(a)   Assuming that the necessary approvals have been obtained for assets and liabilities to be transferred on the proposed terms on 31 December 1993:

(i)   prepare journal entries to close the books of Aztec plc; and

(ii)   prepare the balance sheet of Aztec (Europe) plc after the transfer of assets and liabilities.

(10 marks)

(b)   Draft a memo to the finance director commenting on his draft proposals for a scheme of capital reduction and reorganisation.
(16 marks)

(c)   Advise the directors as to the course of action they should take in order to be able to proceed with their plans for reorganisation if they learn that a creditor has obtained a judgement against the company and is considering seeking a compulsory winding-up order.

(4 marks)
(Total: 30 marks)

---

15   (Question 3 of examination)

Air Fare plc is the subsidiary of an American parent company. It had been incorporated in the United Kingdom in 1985 to provide in-flight packed meals for American airlines on return flights from the United Kingdom.

The fixed assets in the annual accounts have been carried at cost less depreciation but the directors have been considering the production of supplementary statements that are based on current values and show a profit after maintaining the operating capital and also a profit that encompassed gains on holding assets to the extent that these were real gains after allowing for general/average inflation.

The following information (1) to (6) was available when preparing the supplementary statements for the year ended 31 December 1993.

(1)   Draft profit and loss account for the year ended 31 December 1993 prepared under the historic cost convention.

	£'000
Sales	11,441
Cost of sales	10,292
	1,149
Loan interest	625
	524
Tax	124
	400
Less: Proposed dividend	100
	300

(2)   The current cost values of the net assets representing shareholders' funds was £25m at 1 January 1993.

(3)   Freehold premises had cost £8m in 1985 and were being depreciated over 40 years which was the group policy specified by the American parent. The current gross replacement cost was £14m at 31 December 1993 and £13.8m at 1 January 1993.

Equipment had cost £12m in 1991 and was being depreciated over 15 years. The gross replacement cost was £12.6m at 31 December 1993 and £12.5m at 1 January 1993.

(4)   The cost of sales had increased by £412,000 during the year due to price increases. The costs and price increases occurred evenly during the year.

(5)   The retail price index had risen by 3% during the year.

(6)   Stock at the beginning of the year was £660,000 at cost and £670,000 at current replacement cost and stock at the end of the year was £750,000 at cost and £795,000 at current replacement cost.

The following information relates to a consideration not to provide for depreciation on the freehold property.

The freehold property consisted of the premises where the meals were prepared and packed. When the directors were reviewing the information prepared for the current value supplementary statements, they noted that the current value of the freehold property exceeded the book value and decided that it was appropriate not to provide for depreciation.

The chief accountant advised them that it was probable that the auditor would qualify the accounts if depreciation were not provided in accordance with the provisions of FRS 15 *Tangible fixed assets*.

The directors had been discussing the problem over lunch at the local hotel and were surprised when the owner of the hotel informed them that the auditor of the company that owned the hotel had not required depreciation to be provided on the hotel premises. Further enquiry by the directors established that there were a number of companies that were not providing depreciation on freehold properties from a range of industries that included hotels, retail shops and banks. They even discovered that the Financial Reporting Review Panel had accepted one company's policy on non-depreciation of freehold buildings in respect of the accounts of Forte plc. They had therefore formed the view that non-depreciation was acceptable provided the auditors were offered and accepted the company's reasons.

They accordingly requested the chief accountant to prepare a brief report for the board of reasons to support a decision by the company to adopt an accounting policy of non-depreciation which they could subsequently discuss with the auditors.

Required

(a)   (i)   Prepare a profit and loss account that shows a result after maintaining the operating capital and also a result that encompasses the gains for the year on holding assets to the extent that these are real gains after allowing for inflation.

     (ii)   Write a brief memo to the directors explaining the results disclosed in the profit and loss account prepared in (i).   **(10 marks)**

(b)   As chief accountant, prepare a brief report for the board giving reasons to support a decision by the company to adopt an accounting policy of non-depreciation of the freehold property.

(10 marks)
(Total: 20 marks)

---

16   (Question 4 of examination)

Industrial Estates plc is a company that was formed in 1962 to build and sell industrial units. Its share capital and reserves totalled £500m at 31 December 1992.

During the three years 1990/1992, sales turnover fell as a result of financial lending institutions restricting the amount they were prepared to lend to prospective purchasers to 60% of the sales price of an industrial unit.

In 1993 the company was building standard units to be sold for £1,250,000 each and in order to overcome the decline in sales it introduced a new scheme which was to be offered as an option to outright purchase whereby:

(i)   the company transferred the legal ownership of an industrial unit on payment by the purchaser of £750,000 being 60% of the sales price;

(ii)   the purchaser gave a second charge over the industrial unit as security for the amount outstanding of £500,000 being 40% of the sales price;

(iii)   the purchaser paid no annual interest on the £500,000 but, in the event of a re-sale to a third party, would pay the company 40% of the market value as at the date of the re-sale in full settlement of the amount outstanding; and

(iv)   the company agreed to repurchase the unit in the event that the purchaser ceased trading on payment of the market price as at the date of cessation less the £500,000 balance unpaid.

The following information was available at 31 December 1993:

(a) Industrial units under construction

There were three units which were each 75% complete. At the commencement of building, the estimated total construction cost had been £1,000,000 per unit. The costs incurred on two of the units was in accordance with the original estimate but additional costs of £300,000 had been incurred on the third unit as a result of defective workmanship.

Reservation deposits of £50,000 had been received on each of these units from potential purchasers interested in an outright purchase for £1,250,000 per unit but no formal sales contracts had been entered into by 31 December 1993.

The directors are proposing to show these units at cost plus attributable profit in the balance sheet.

(b) Industrial units sold under the new scheme on payment of 60% of the selling price

Five units had been built in 1993. The total cost of each unit had been £1,000,000 and the selling price £1,250,000. The sales contracts required a payment of 60% on signing the contract and a charge for the remaining 40%.

(c) A further unit had been sold under the new scheme at the standard selling price of £1,250,000 and payment of £750,000. Later in the year the company repurchased the unit at an agreed repurchase price of £1,350,000. This unit was unsold at the year end.

Required

(a) Explain how the industrial units under construction should be treated in the balance sheet. Show workings to support the entry or entries. **(5 marks)**

(b) As the chief accountant, write a memo to explain to your assistant how you are proposing to treat the five industrial units which have been sold under the new scheme in the profit and loss account and balance sheet for the year ended 31 December 1993.

Assume that the transactions are to be treated in accordance with the legal position.

(5 marks)

(c) Draft journal entries to record the accounting treatment of the unit repurchased during the year.

(4 marks)

(d) The auditors, Messrs Uptodate & Co, ascertained on reading the agreement relating to the new scheme that the conditions relating to repurchase were not as the company had stated in the information given in the question.

The actual terms were that on a repurchase the company would pay the original purchaser 60% of the market value.

As auditors, write a letter to the chief accountant, explaining the effect of this on the treatment of the five units built and sold in 1993 in the profit and loss account and balance sheet of Industrial Estates plc as at 31 December 1993. **(6 marks)**

(Total: 20 marks)

EXAMINER'S COMMENTS

Question 1: examined candidates' technical competence to produce financial statements and their understanding of the audit implications.

This question was generally well answered.

Part (a) required the candidates to prepare consolidated accounts for a UK company that had investments in a US and French company. The investment in the US company was a 40% interest but a dominant influence meant that it needed to be consolidated using the temporal method. A number of candidates used the closing rate method and appropriate credit was allowed for this.

A number of candidates omitted any mention of the minority interest; perhaps this was because the company held less than 50% of the equity.

Good candidates identified an exchange difference and included it within the profit and loss account; a significant number of candidates failed to identify, quantify or include an exchange difference.

The investment in the French company was a 25% interest that the company did *not* want to treat as an associated undertaking; some candidates interpreted this to mean that company was a subsidiary. Where candidates did treat the investment as a subsidiary in part (a) of the question, marks were awarded for answers that followed this treatment through into part (c)(ii) when considering the required verification.

Part (b) required candidates to calculate the effect on the consolidated profit and loss account and balance sheet if the investment in Europe were classified as an associate. This was generally well done. A number of candidates wrote off a goodwill figure for which credit was given.

Part (c)(i) required an explanation as to how the auditor would verify that Overseas was a subsidiary undertaking. This was generally well answered.

Part (c)(ii) required an explanation as to how the auditor would verify the accounting treatment of Europe SA. Some candidates failed to gain marks because they did not answer the question set; they stated the accounting treatment without explaining how the auditor would verify it. For example, frequent reference was made to dominant influence and participating interest but without any explanation as to how these would be verified.

Question 2: examined the technical ability to prepare closing journal entries for the old company; the balance sheet of the new company; an evaluation of the scheme of reorganisation and how to deal with a creditor who is petitioning for a winding up order.

Part (a) of the question posed the case of a plc with accumulated losses from declining markets since 1989, but with the expectation of better prospects ahead from new markets in Europe, and a projected profit range that would allow dividends to be restored to equity shareholders, but with capital expenditure needs. The company would clearly benefit from restructuring and the Financial Director has formulated a plan.

Part (a)(i) was generally well answered with a good answer effecting a series of debits and credits via the journal to record the key items such as the treatment of the purchase consideration and closure of the existing members' accounts. Weaker candidates produced confused answers, eg, some treated it as an internal reconstruction and produced profit and loss calculations for each asset based on fair values.

Part (a)(ii) was generally well answered although the majority of candidates omitted the goodwill figure from the balance sheet.

Part (b) required an appraisal of the scheme that was being proposed by the company for fairness to all parties with regard to income and capital.

Good answers considered the capital and income entitlements of stakeholders under existing and revised structures with supplementary information on the position in liquidation and use of the projected profits range given. The good answers also evaluated the results and commented on the benefits/defects of the scheme from each viewpoint and commented on the viability of the new company from a gearing, liquidity and other viewpoint. Weaker answers failed to support their narrative comments with capital or income effect data from the question or concentrated on only one aspect of the scheme, eg, the position of the creditors.

Part (c) required candidates to advise on the appropriate insolvency action where a creditor threatened to petition for compulsory winding up. Few candidates referred to Administration but marks were awarded for other valid points raised of a more general nature such as the risk of receiving nothing if they persisted with their application because a Receiver would be appointed by the secured creditor.

Question 3: examined candidates' ability to produce profit figures in accordance with the Handbook, Accounting for the Effects of Changing Prices, and to discuss the accounting policy of non-depreciation of freehold property.

This question was generally badly answered. There appeared to be a little knowledge of CPP and CCA but not of the provisions of the Handbook. There was confusion over what was realised and what was unrealised, eg, the unrealised holding gain on stock was frequently correctly calculated but then treated as a Cost of Sales Adjustment.

The depreciation adjustment was frequently calculated on end of year values and credit was given for this. Credit was also given for the backlog depreciation approach.

Part (a)(ii) required candidates to discuss the revised data in the profit and loss account. This did not relate to their own profit and loss account but marks were awarded for substantive points such as the effect on the dividend decision and for other valid points such as a comment on operating capital maintenance and unrealised holding gains. Part (b) required candidates to prepare a report to the directors who were considering non-depreciation of the freehold property. Good answers included points such as the effect of regular maintenance; total write off can result in the asset failing to appear on the balance sheet which is not true and fair; and implication of the American company's accounting policies.

Question 4: examined the application of accounting standards and exposure drafts.

Part (a) required candidates to determine the classification of construction work and to produce the balance sheet entries.

Few candidates identified the correct accounting treatment of work-in-progress to be valued at the lower of cost or net realisable value and of these many candidates valued all three units at cost. A number wrongly concluded that it was a long-term contract. Credit was given for the balance sheet entries if consistent with their classification.

Part (b) required the candidates to explain the accounting treatment in accordance with the legal position. This was generally well answered and credit was given for answers in either narrative or account entry form as many attempted to answer by the use of figures rather than a clear explanation. Good candidates correctly identified the treatment of the 40% unpaid.

Answers to part (c) which required journal entries to record the accounting entries for the repurchased unit were mixed.

Part (d) required a consideration of substance over form. This was generally poorly answered. Marks were awarded for other points discussed such as a consideration of a contingent liability.

ANSWERS TO JUNE 1994 EXAMINATION

13   (Answer 1 of examination)

(a)

**Consolidated profit and loss account of the Rowen Group
for the year ended 31 December 1993**

	Rowen £m	Overseas £m	Consolidated £m
Turnover	2,784	676.5	3,460.5
Cost of sales	1,822	449.2	2,271.2
Gross profit	962	227.3	1,189.3
Distribution costs	392	53.0	445.0
Administrative expenses	370	17.7	387.7
Depreciation and amortisation	35	12.0	47.3
Dividends received	(23)		(11.0)
Exchange differences		6.5	6.5
Profit before tax	188	138.1	313.8
Tax	93	53.0	146.0
Profit after tax	95	85.1	167.8
Minority interests		60% of 85.1	51.0
			116.8
Dividends paid			37.0
			79.8

Consolidated balance sheet as at 31 December 1993

	Rowen £m	Overseas £m	Consolidated £m
Fixed assets			
Intangible assets: goodwill			1.5
Tangible assets	669	229.0	898.0
Investment in Europe	10		10.0
Current assets			
Stock	675	27.5	702.5
Cash	46	75.3	121.3
Current liabilities			
Trade creditors	(490)	20.7	(510.7)
Creditors due after more than one year			
Loans	(370)	68.7	(438.7)
			783.9
Capital and reserves			
Share capital			185.0
Profit and loss account			453.5
Minority interest (60% of 242.4)			145.4
			783.9

Statement of group reserves for the year ended 31 December 1993

Profit and loss account at 31 December 1992	373.7
Retained profit for the year	79.8
Profit and loss account at 31 December 1993	453.5

WORKINGS

(W1)   Goodwill to be recognised on Overseas Inc acquisition

		US$m	£m
Cost			12
Less:	Share of net assets acquired		
	Share capital	20	
	Profit and loss account	25	
		45	
Translated at $2 × 40%			9
Goodwill			3

∴ annual amortisation charge = £0.3m.

(W2)   Translation of Overseas Inc balance sheet at 31 December 1993

	Overseas US$m	Exchange rate	£m
Fixed assets			
Tangible assets	458	2.0	229.0
Current assets			
Stocks	44	1.6	27.5
Cash	113	1.5	75.3
Current liabilities			
Creditors	(31)	1.5	(20.7)
Creditors falling due after more than one year			
Loan	(103)	1.5	(68.7)
	481		242.4
Capital and reserves			
Share capital	20	2.0	10.0
Pre-acquisition profit	25	2.0	12.5
Post-acquisition profit	436	Balance	219.9
	481		242.4

(W3)   Group reserves at 31 December 1993

	£m
Rowen plc	367.0
Overseas Inc (40% of 219.9)	88.0
	455.0
Less goodwill amortised to date	(1.5)
	453.5

(W4)   Translation of the profit and loss account of Overseas Inc for the year ended 31 December 1993

The profit and loss accounts for the year ended 31 December 1993 are as follows:

	Overseas US$m	Rate	£m	£m
Turnover	1,150	1.7		676.5
Opening stock	57	2.0	28.5	
Purchases	762	1.7	448.2	
Closing stock	(44)	1.6	(27.5)	
Cost of sales	775			449.2
Gross profit	375			227.3
Distribution costs	90	1.7	53.0	
Admin. expenses	30	1.7	17.7	
Depreciation	24	2.0	12.0	
				82.7
Exchange differences				6.5
Profit before tax	231			138.1
Tax	90	1.7		53.0
Profit after tax	141			85.1
Dividends paid 31.7.93	51	1.7		30.0
Retained profit	90			55.1
Profit and loss a/c b/f (W5)	346			164.8
Profit and loss a/c c/f (W2)	436			219.9

(W5)   (a)   Calculating net assets/liabilities at 31 December 1992 in US$

		US$m
Share capital		20
Pre-acquisition profit		25
Post-acquisition profit (436 – 90)		346
		391
Less: Fixed assets (458 + 24)	482	
Stock	57	
		539
Net monetary liabilities		148

(b)   Calculate the opening post-acquisition profit and loss account balance

	US$m	Rate	£m
Fixed assets	482	2.0	241.0
Stock	57	2.0	28.5
Net monetary liabilities	(148)	1.8	(82.2)
			187.3

Less: Share capital	20	2.0	(10.0)
Pre-acquisition profit	25	2.0	(12.5)
Post-acquisition profit			
(436 – 90)	346		164.8

(W6)   Group reserves at 31 December 1992

Rowen plc	(367-58)	309.0
Overseas Inc	[40% of 164.8]	65.9
		374.9
Less: Goodwill amortised to date		1.2
		373.7

(W7)   Exchange difference carried to profit and loss account

On opening net monetary liabilities of US$148m

Translated at US$1.5 exchange rate at 31.12.93	(98.7)	
Translated at US$1.8 exchange rate at 31.12.92	82.2	
		(16.5)

On profit and loss items expressed at average rate

	US$m	
Balance retained	90.0	
Stock change	13.0	
Depreciation	24.0	
	127.0	
Translated at US$1.5 rate at 31.12.93	84.7	
Translated at US$1.7 rate at average	(74.7)	
		10.0
Exchange loss		(6.5)

(b)   (i)   The profit and loss account for the year ended 31 December 1993 will be translated using the closing rate to arrive at the profit before tax; tax and profit after tax figures.

	Europe FFm	Exchange rate	Included in the consolidation £m
Turnover	10,615		
Cost of sales	7,154		
Gross profit	3,461		
Distribution costs	831		
Administrative expenses	278		
Depreciation	230		
Profit before tax	2,122	8.0	265.3
Tax	831	8.0	103.9
Profit after tax	1,291	8.0	161.4
Dividends paid 31.7.93	440		
Retained profit	851		

		£m
Profit before tax per draft consolidated accounts		313.8
Less: Dividends received from Europe SA		11.0
Amortisation charge (W)		0.2
		302.6
Add: 25% share of associated undertaking's profit		
(25% of 265.3)		66.3
Amended profit before tax		368.9
Tax per consolidated accounts	146.0	
Add 25% of Europe's tax	26.0	
		172.0
Amended profit after tax		196.9

(ii)   Carrying value of investment in Europe if treated as an associated undertaking

	£m
Share of net assets	
$25\% \times \dfrac{FF4,431m}{8}$	138.5
Premium on acquisition (W)	0.9
	139.4

Working

Goodwill arising on acquiring 25% of Europe SA

	FFm	£m
Cost		10.0
Net assets acquired		
Share capital	180	
Reserves	230	
	410	
$25\% \times \dfrac{410}{12.5}$		8.2
		1.8

∴ annual amortisation charge = £0.2m.

After 5 years the NBV of goodwill = $\dfrac{5}{10} \times$ £1.8m = £0.9m.

---

14   (Answer 2 of examination)

(a)   (i)   **Journal entries to close books of Aztec plc**

	Dr £	Cr £
Capital reduction and reorganisation a/c	1,167,000	
To leasehold premises		397,000
Vehicles and equipment		105,000
Machinery		250,000
Stock		295,000
Debtors		120,000
Transferring assets		

	Dr £	Cr £
Hire-purchase liability	25,000	
Suppliers	288,000	
Wages, VAT and PAYE	80,000	
Hire-purchase liability	20,000	
Bank overdraft	112,000	
To capital reduction and reorganisation a/c		525,000

Transferring liabilities

	Dr £	Cr £
Aztec (Europe) plc	540,000	
To capital reduction and reorganisation a/c		540,000

Liability for the agreed purchase consideration

	Dr £	Cr £
Shares in Aztec (Europe) plc	270,000	
13% Debentures in Aztec (Europe) plc	270,000	
To Aztec (Europe) plc		540,000

Settlement of the agreed purchase consideration

	Dr £	Cr £
Ordinary shareholders	60,000	
Preference shareholders	160,000	
11 % Debenture holders	320,000	
To shares in Aztec (Europe) plc		270,000
13% Debentures in Aztec (Europe) plc		270,000

Distribution of the purchase consideration

	Dr £	Cr £
Capital reduction and reorganisation a/c		102,000
Ordinary shareholders	42,000	
Preference shareholders		25,000
11 % Debenture holders	85,000	

Closing the share and loan accounts

(ii)   **For information only**

Journal entries to open books of Aztec (Europe) plc

	Dr £	Cr £
Leasehold premises	360,000	
Vehicles and equipment	85,000	
Machinery	225,000	
Stock	285,000	
Debtors	110,000	
Hire-purchase liability		25,000
Suppliers		288,000
Wages, VAT and PAYE		80,000
Hire-purchase liability		20,000
Bank overdraft		112,000
Aztec plc		580,000
Goodwill	40,000	

Introducing assets and liabilities

	Dr £	Cr £
Aztec plc	580,000	
Ordinary shares		270,000
13% Debentures		270,000
Cost of reorganisation		40,000

Settlement of the purchase consideration

	Dr £	Cr £
Costs of reorganisation	40,000	
Bank		40,000

Payment of reorganisation costs

Balance sheet of Aztec (Europe) plc as at 31 December 1993
(following the transfer of assets and liabilities)

	£	£
Ordinary shares of 10p each		270,000
Fixed assets		
Intangible fixed assets		40,000
Tangible fixed assets		
Leasehold premises	360,000	
Vehicles and equipment	85,000	
Machinery	225,000	
		670,000
Current assets		
Stock	285,000	
Debtors	110,000	
		395,000
Current liabilities		
Hire-purchase liability	25,000	
Suppliers	288,000	
Wages, VAT and PAYE	80,000	
Hire-purchase liability	20,000	
Bank overdraft	152,000	
		(565,000)
Non-current liabilities		
13% Debentures		(270,000)
		270,000

(Tutorial note: The examiner has included the non-current portion of the HP liability in current liabilities, presumably for reasons of prudence.*)*

(b)   **M E M O R A N D U M**

To: Finance Director

From: Auditors

Re: Draft proposals for scheme of capital reduction and reorganisation of Aztec plc as at 31 December 1993

Thank you for a copy of the draft scheme.

We are in agreement that the proposal to proceed under the provisions of Ss425 – 427 of the Companies Act 1985 is an appropriate course to follow.

In our view, one of the key considerations for the court and the various parties whose rights are being varied is whether the scheme is fair to all parties.

We have therefore reviewed how the scheme will affect the rights of the ordinary shareholders, the preference shareholders and the debenture holders with regard to their entitlement to capital repayment and to interest/dividends.

Entitlement to capital repayment

The rights of the shareholders and debenture holders assuming different values are as follows:

	Existing book values Note 1 £	*Fair values Note 2* £	*Forced sale values Note 3* £	*Draft proposed scheme Note 4* £
Ordinary shareholders	102,000	–	–	60,000
Preference shareholders	135,000	135,000	–	160,000
Debenture holders	405,000	405,000	280,000	320,000

Note 1: Ordinary shareholders have an asset backing of 15p per £1 share using book values as shown in the balance sheet.

Note 2: Ordinary shareholders have a nil asset backing if fair values are substituted for the book values shown in the balance sheet.

Note 3: Values under forced sale are calculated as follows:

	£	£
Machinery		122,000
Less: Bank charge		(112,000)
		10,000
Vehicles and equipment	35,000	
Less: Hire-purchase creditors	45,000	
		–
Premises		100,000
Stock		150,000
Debtors		100,000
		360,000
Less: Liquidation costs		(55,000)
		305,000
Less: Preferential creditors (wages, VAT and PAYE)		(80,000)
Available for floating charge		225,000

(*Tutorial note:* it would be acceptable to use £225,000 as the figure for forced sale values available to the debenture holders.)

Note 4: Whilst recognising that it is proposed to offer the debenture holders a 44% shareholding in the new company, it would appear from the above that the debenture holders are not being fairly treated in relation to the shareholders from the capital entitlement viewpoint. This will undoubtedly be raised by the debenture holders and require amendment if it is to obtain the approval of the court.

It is particularly relevant because the debenture holders would from the figures produced, be in a better position by exercising their right to appoint an administrative receiver.

Income entitlement – 1994 – 1996

	Rights in Aztec plc £	*Rights in Aztec plc assuming a pre-tax profit* £70,000 £	£140,000 £
Ordinary shareholders	–	6,721	20,203
Preference shareholders	–	19,183	39,404
Debenture holders – gross	44,550	39,443	66,405

Calculating income in Aztec plc at two levels of profit without reorganisation and capital reduction:

	£	£
Profit before tax	70,000	140,000
Less: Debenture interest	44,550	44,550
	25,450	95,450
Tax at 35%	8,908	33,408
Profit after tax	16,542	62,042

Years to eliminate debit balance	35 years	9 years

For comparison purposes let us assume that there is a distribution without making good the debit balance:

	£	£
Profit after tax	16,542	62,042
Preference dividend	9,450	9,450
Available for ordinary shareholders	7,092	52,592

	Rights in Aztec plc assuming a pre-tax profit £70,000 £	£140,000 £
Ordinary shareholders – gross	9,456	70,123
Preference shareholders – gross	12,600	12,600
Debenture holders – gross	44,550	44,550

Calculating the income in Aztec (Europe) plc at two levels of profit:

	£	£
Profit before tax	70,000	140,000
Less: Debenture interest	35,100	35,100
	34,900	104,900
Tax at 35%	12,215	36,715
	22,685	68,185

Assuming all profit is distributed:

Dividend per share	£0.84	£2.53

Income for debenture holders:

	£	£
Debenture interest (gross)	26,000	26,000
1,200,000 shares	10,082	30,304
	36,082	56,304

Income for preference shareholders:

	£	£
Debenture interest (gross)	9,100	9,100
900,000 shares	7,562	22,728
	16,662	31,828

Income for ordinary shareholders:

	£	£
600,000 shares	5,041	15,152

The above indicates that the debenture holders will receive less than their current income entitlement at the £70,000 level of pre-tax profits whereas the preference shareholders will receive more income at that level than might be considered equitable.

With regard to the three parties:

The scheme is unfair to the debenture holders in respect of both the capital and income entitlement and should be revised.

The scheme is unfair in that the ordinary shareholders who would have lost everything in a liquidation are credited with capital of £60,000 to retain a 22% interest in the net assets.

Comments on the balance sheet of Aztec (Europe) plc

The balance sheet shows that there are continuing problems in that the new company has negative current assets which makes the company unattractive to trade creditors. In addition there is very high gearing and there have been no proposals for raising further capital with the result that the company will see its overdraft standing at a higher figure than the closing balance in the old company due to reorganisation costs, and no funds to purchase the continental warehouse referred to in the question.

(c) The objective is to ensure that the company has time to organise its affairs to maximise the benefit to all parties.

There is provision under the Insolvency Act 1986 to apply to the court for an Administration Order.

This type of order is intended to give a company breathing space to sort out its affairs. The court before making an order has to be satisfied, firstly, that the company is, or is likely to become, unable to pay its debts and, secondly, that the making of an order would be likely to achieve one or more of the following purposes;

–   the survival of the company, or at least part of its business, as a going concern
–   the approval of a voluntary arrangement
–   a more advantageous realisation of assets than would be achieved in a liquidation
–   the sanctioning of a scheme of arrangement under the Companies Act 1985.

The administrator will become responsible for preparing proposals to put before a meeting of the company's creditors. In the present case that proposals would be a revision of the proposals that the finance director has drafted and it would appear reasonable to assume that there is a reasonable basis, subject to our comments concerning the fairness of the proposals, for obtaining approval of a revised scheme.

15   (Answer 3 of examination)

(a)   (i)   **Profit and loss account for the year ended 31 December 1993**

		£'000	£'000
Sales			11,441
Cost of sales		10,292	
Cost of sales adjustment		412	
Depreciation adjustment			
Freehold property	£6.0m/40 years	150	
Equipment	£0.60m/15 years	40	
			10,894
Current cost operating profit			547
Less: Interest			625
Current cost profit (loss) before tax			(78)
Tax			(124)
Current cost profit (loss) after tax			(202)
Add: Realised holding gains			
Cost of sales adjustment		412	
Depreciation adjustment		190	
		602	
Unrealised holding gains			

	1.1.93	*31.12.93*		
Stock	£45,000 –	£10,000	35	
Freehold premises	(£14m –	13.8) × 32/40	160	
Equipment	(£12.6m – 12.5m) × 13/15		87	
			282	

		£'000
Less: Depreciation adjustment previously recognised as unrealised		(190)
Total holding gains		694
Total gains		492
Less: Inflation adjustment to shareholder's funds		
3% of £25m		(750)
Total real loss		(258)
Dividend		(100)
		(358)

Note the depreciation adjustment could have been based on average current values for the year, the result would not have been materially different from the depreciation adjustment based on the year end current value.

(ii)   The company achieved a current cost operating profit of £547,000 after deducting the realised holding gains on the stock and fixed assets ie, £547,000 after maintaining the operating capacity of the company and ignoring the MWCA. The historic cost gross profit of £1,149,000 has been reduced by the realised holding gains of £602,000.

The holding gains which are stated in money terms and calculated by reference to the specific price changes of the assets are reduced by the general inflation adjustment to the opening shareholders' funds stated at current cost representing a charge for general inflation. The result is a total real loss before dividends of £258,000. This implies that the declaration of the proposed dividend of £100,000 is imprudent.

(b)   **Report to Directors of Air Fare plc**   **Dated:**

Re: Non-depreciation of freehold property

I have reviewed the circumstances in which other companies have not made a property depreciation charge in the profit and loss account. It would appear that they have rarely been able to make a case for exemption from the provisions of FRS 15 *Tangible fixed assets* with the exception of property companies who are subject to the provisions of SSAP 19.

In my view we need to present a case that the amount is immaterial and that the original decision to depreciate was a passive decision rather than an active assessment of the life and residual value of the freehold properties. My draft of the points to raise are set out below.

There have been references made to the Financial Reporting Review Panel in respect of non-compliance and they have made decisions both for and against such a practice.

In my view it will be important for the company to be able to show that it has substance for such a decision.

Draft points to be raised in support of non-depreciation

The following points are raised for your consideration with the auditors.

(1)   *Materiality of current charge*

The profit before tax for the year ended 31 December 1993 was £524,000. This figure was arrived at after making a depreciation charge for the year of £200,000 on the freehold property. The amount is therefore material. Even if the charge were immaterial in relation to the profit and loss account, the accumulated figure would probably not be immaterial and the user of the accounts would have lost the benefit of this piece of information.

Users of the accounts tend to refer to the relationship between the balance outstanding and the cost to assess the extent to which the life of the asset has been exhausted and at what point they are likely to need to be replaced.

(2)   *Basis of current rate of depreciation*

The company has been depreciating its freehold properties using a rate of 2.5% straight line.

I would like to emphasise that this was not a thought through decision on the part of the company in as much as it reflected the group policy of the American parent company.

We certainly did not base it on an estimate of the life of the building and the residual value at the date of purchase.

In our view the assumptions underlying the choice of rate of depreciation need to be defined. I won't say redefined because, as I have mentioned, they were never actually defined by our company's management.

(3)   *Determining a true and fair charge*

To arrive at a true and fair charge, I think we should recognise that the buildings are subject to Health and Safety and Public Health inspections because we are preparing food. This means that the company is required to maintain the premises in a continual state of sound repair.

In the directors' view this means that the life of the premises is so long and residual value, based on prices prevailing at the time of acquisition, so large that depreciation is insignificant.

We should, however, note that FRS 15 states that subsequent expenditure that maintains or enhances an asset does not negate the need to charge depreciation.

(4)   *Impairment*

The directors undertake to charge any impairment in the value of the premises to the profit and loss account as appropriate. Indeed, FRS 15 requires that the premises are reviewed for impairment when no depreciation charge is made on the grounds that the charge is immaterial.

(5)   *Costs incurred on maintenance*

The maintenance and repair costs have been separately recorded each year and I will prepare a schedule of these on an annual basis if you consider that to be relevant.

Could you please consider the points raised and let me know how you would like to take this forward.

(Tutorial Note: At the time that this question was originally set, FRS 15 had not yet been issued and the answer has been amended slightly to reflect this development.

One of the arguments against depreciating the premises (ie, that they are maintained to such a high standard that their useful economic life is very long) has become much less valid since the issue of FRS 15. However, although the ASB has attempted to discourage non-depreciation, it has not actually prohibited it.*)*

---

16   (Answer 4 of examination)

(a)   The information in the question is that the units under construction are not subject to a legal contract of sale as at the date of the balance sheet. It is therefore inappropriate to treat them as long-term contracts.

The correct accounting treatment is to classify them as work in progress and show them in the balance sheet at the lower of cost or net realisable value.

The balance sheet figure would be £2,500,000 made up as follows:

(i)   **Two units at cost**

	£
Two units at cost 2 × 75% of £1,000,000	1,500,000

(ii)   **One unit at NRV**

Third unit on which additional costs were incurred:

	£	£
Cost incurred to date		
Per budget		750,000
Additional		300,000
		1,050,000
Selling price	1,250,000	
Less: Cost to complete	250,000	
	1,000,000	

Carrying value lower of cost and NRV	1,000,000
Written off	50,000
Balance sheet entry:	
Work in progress at lower of cost and NRV	£2,500,000

In the absence of a contract of sale it is unacceptable to bring attributable profit into account. There is no legal contract and the partly completed units should be shown at the lower of cost and net realisable value. The deposits of £50,000 will be shown as current liabilities.

(b)   **M E M O R A N D U M**

From:	Chief Accountant
To:	Assistant Accountant
Re:	Treatment of sales effected under our new scheme.

This year we will need to decide on the effect of the new scheme on our year end accounts.

I have set out my views and indicated a proposed treatment. We will clearly need to have discussions with the auditors but before that could you please review the following and let me have your comments.

I don't see any particular problem with the figures for the profit and loss account or balance sheet here.

(i)   **The sales turnover figure**

The legal position is quite clear. The company has sold its entire interest and retained a charge to cover 40% of the sales proceeds. I think we can happily record the full selling price as sales turnover.

(ii)   **The treatment of the 40% unpaid**

We will show this balance as a debtor in the accounts under amounts falling due after more than one year. There is no interest or rental income arising so there will be no profit and loss account entries.

There is the question of the effect of UITF 4 to which we will need to give some thought. We will need to comply with the provisions of UITF 4 (covered in a Technical Department Student Newsletter article) with regard to the way we disclose the debtor.

As I read it, UITF 4 requires that in applying the Companies Legislation requirement to distinguish between debtors due within one year and in more than one year, it will usually be sufficient to disclose the size of debtors due after more than one year in the notes to the accounts. However, we might fall foul of the provision that where the amount of a debtor due after more than one year is particularly material it should be disclosed on the face of the balance sheet as leaving such information as a note may mislead users.

My own view is that the debtor figure is not material in relation to the total assets and we need only make a reference in the notes to the accounts.

Again, could we discuss this before we meet the auditors.

(c)   Journal entries to record the unit repurchased during the year would be as follows:

	Dr	*Cr*
	£	£
Sales	1,250,000	
Stock	1,100,000	
Debtors		850,000

Debtors	1,350,000
Cost of sales	1,000,000
Cash	850,000

Note: the entries recording the original sale are reversed. The cash payment to the debtor of £1,350,000 – the outstanding amount of £500,000 is recorded with a resulting debit balance transferred to the stock carrying figure.

(d)   Dear   Date

Re: Industrial Estates plc

Accounts for year ended 31 December 1993

We have been reviewing the documentation relating to the new sales scheme introduced by your company and noted that the terms of repurchasing units are that your company undertakes to pay the original purchaser 60% of the market value as at the date of repurchase.

This means that your company is entitled to share in the increase in value of the property and is subject to the risks of a fall in its value. Because of this, our view is that the transactions fall within the scope of FRS 5 *Reporting the substance of transactions* and the company should report in accordance with the commercial substance of the transactions.

Our view is that accounting for the transactions in accordance with their legal form would not give a true and fair view because the commercial substance is so different from the legal form that no amount of notes could correct the potentially misleading impression given by accounts prepared in accordance with the legal form.

It would be necessary to apply the provisions of UITF 7 in these circumstances. This would mean providing a statement of the treatment that the Companies Act would normally require and a description of the treatment actually adopted: a statement as to why the treatment prescribed would not give a true and fair view and a description of how the position shown in the accounts is different as a result of the departure with a quantification if necessary.

We set out below our view of the effect on the profit and loss account and balance sheet.

The effect on the profit and loss account

The company should treat the initial transaction as the sale of a 60% interest.

This means that the sales would be recorded at £750,000 per unit sold rather than at the existing figure of £1,250,000 per unit.

The cost of sales will be recorded at £600,000 per unit being 60% of total cost per unit.

The 40% interest will not affect the profit and loss account until it is sold when there will be a profit or loss on disposal.

The effect on the balance sheet

The 40% interest will be treated as a fixed asset or work in progress depending on the circumstances and carried at £400,000 per unit. The buildings element will need to be depreciated in accordance with the provisions of FRS 15.

On a sale of the 40% interest the profit or loss calculated in relation to the depreciated cost amount will be taken to the profit and loss account.

We will also need to ensure that the transfer value from current asset to fixed asset complies with UITF 5 which provides that where an asset is transferred from current to fixed assets the current asset rules should apply up to the date of transfer and the transfer should be made at the lower of cost or net realisable value. In the present situation, the net realisable value exceeds cost, and the fixed asset will therefore be transferred at £400,000 per unit.

We must express our concern that representations made to us in respect of the new terms of sale were materially inaccurate. Given the reliance that might be made on such representations and the effect of additional audit work on the audit fee, it is clearly a matter of material concern. We will therefore need to review other representations that the officers of the company have made during the current audit.

We look forward to discussing the immediate matter under consideration and the wider implication for representations at our next meeting.

Yours sincerely

Messrs Uptodate & Co

*(**Tutorial note:** the syllabus has changed since this question was originally set. As 'managing the audit' is no longer within the syllabus for Paper 13, part (d) would probably now simply ask for an explanation of the effect of the different condition, rather than presenting the new information as a consequence of the audit. Therefore the last two paragraphs of the answer would no longer be relevant.)*

DECEMBER 1994 QUESTIONS

ALL FOUR questions are compulsory and MUST be attempted

17 (Question 1 of examination)

Carver plc is a listed company incorporated in 1958 to produce models carved from wood. In 1975 it acquired a 100% interest in a wood importing company, Olio Ltd; in 1989 it acquired a 40% interest in a competitor, Multi-products Ltd; and on 1 October 1993 it acquired a 75% interest in Good Display Ltd. It is planning to make a number of additional acquisitions during the next three years.

The draft consolidated accounts for the Carver Group are as follows:

Draft consolidated profit and loss account for the year ended 30 September 1994

	£'000	£'000
Operating profit		1,475
Share of profits of associated undertakings		495
Income from fixed asset investment		155
Interest payable		(150)
Profit on ordinary activities before taxation		1,975
Tax on profit on ordinary activities		
Corporation tax	391	
Deferred taxation	104	
Tax attributable to income of associated undertakings	145	
		(640)
Profit on ordinary activities after taxation		1,335
Minority interests		(100)
Profit for the financial year		1,235
Dividends paid and proposed		(400)
Retained profit for the year		835

Draft consolidated balance sheet as at 30 September

	1993		1994	
	£'000	£'000	£'000	£'000
Fixed assets				
Intangible assets: goodwill				90
Tangible assets				
Buildings at net book value		2,200		2,075
Machinery				
Cost	1,400		3,000	
Aggregate depreciation	(1,100)		(1,200)	
Net book value		300		1,800
		2,500		3,965
Investments in associated undertaking		1,000		1,100
Fixed asset investments		410		410
Current assets				
Stocks		1,000		1,975
Trade debtors		1,275		1,850
Cash		1,820		4,515
		4,095		8,340

Creditors: Amounts falling due within one year		
Trade creditors	280	500
Obligations under finance leases	200	240
Corporation tax	217	462
Dividends	200	300
Accrued interest and finance charges	30	40
	927	1,542

Net current assets	3,168	6,798
Total assets less current liabilities	7,078	12,273
Creditors: Amounts falling due after more than one year		
Obligations under finance leases	170	710
Loans	500	1,460
Provisions for liabilities		
Deferred taxation	13	30
Net assets	6,395	10,073

Capital and reserves		
Called up share capital in 25p shares	2,000	3,940
Share premium account	2,095	2,883
Profit and loss account	2,300	3,135
Total shareholders' equity	6,395	9,958
Minority interest	–	115
Net assets	6,395	10,073

Note 1: There had been no acquisitions or disposals of buildings during the year.

Machinery costing £500,000 was sold for £500,000 resulting in a profit of £100,000. New machinery was acquired in 1994 including additions of £850,000 acquired under finance leases.

Note 2: Information relating to the acquisition of Good Display Ltd.

	£'000
Machinery	165
Stocks	32
Trade debtors	28
Cash	112
Less: Trade creditors	(68)
Corporation tax	(17)
	252
Less: Minority interest	(63)
	189
Goodwill	100
	289

	£'000
880,000 shares issued as part consideration	275
Balance of consideration paid in cash	14
	289

Goodwill arising on this acquisition is capitalised and amortised through the profit and loss account over its useful economic life. The amortisation charge for the year was £10,000.

Note 3: Loans were issued at a discount in 1994 and the carrying amount of the loans at 30 September 1994 included £40,000 representing the finance cost attributable to the discount and allocated in respect of the current reporting period.

Required

(a)   Prepare a consolidated cash flow statement for the Carver Group for the year ended 30 September 1994 with supporting notes for:

    (i)   Reconciliation of operating profit to net cash flow from operating activities.
    (ii)   Reconciliation of net cash flow to movement in net debt.
    (iii)   Analysis of changes in net debt.

                                                                                        (20 marks)

(b)   Explain and illustrate any adjustments that you consider the company should make to the cash flow statement prepared in (a) above to take account of the following information:

    (i)   Carver plc had constructed a laser cutter which is included in the machinery cost figure at £73,000.

             The costs comprise:

	£'000
Materials	50
Labour	12
Overheads	6
Interest capitalised	5
	73

    (ii)   The cash figures comprised the following:

	1.10.93 £'000	30.9.94 £'000
Cash in hand	10	15
Bank overdrafts	(770)	(65)
Bank	1,080	1,890
10% Treasury Stock 1993	1,500	–
Bank deposits	–	1,125
Gas 3% 1990–1995	–	1,550
	1,820	4,515

             The 10% Treasury Stock 1993 was acquired on 1 September 1993 and redeemed on 31 October 1993.

             The bank deposits were made on 1 January 1994 for a 12 month term.

             The Gas 3% was acquired on 1 June 1994 and the company proposes to realise this investment on 30 November 1994.   **(5 marks)**

(c)   [Not reproduced as this part of the question is no longer within the syllabus.]   **(5 marks)**
                                                                                        (Total: 30 marks)

18 (Question 2 of examination)

Osmosis plc carries on business as a manufacturer and installer of wind turbines. The company's accounting staff are currently calculating the amounts for long-term contracts and deferred taxation for inclusion in the draft accounts being prepared for the year ended 30 November 1994.

Long-term contracts

The company has three contracts not completed at the year end. These are for the manufacture and installation of wind turbines at Ascot, Bude and Cowes. The following information is available:

Ascot and Cowes contracts

	Ascot contract	Cowes contract
Contract commenced	1.12.93	1.7.94
	£'000	£'000
Fixed contract price	1,350	2,275.0
Payments on account	729	520.0
Costs incurred to date	675	577.2
Estimated cost to complete	405	1,731.6
Estimated per cent of work completed	60%	25%

It is company policy to match the cost of sales to turnover to date to give a profit in proportion to the turnover.

Bude contract

Contract commenced 1.12.92

Information relating to	1992–93	1993–94 Cumulative
	£'000	£'000
Payments on account	1,581	3,442.5
Costs incurred to date	1,428	2,652.0
Costs relating to work invoiced	1,428	2,550.0
Sales value of work done and invoiced	1,530	3,315.0

There was no expectation of any foreseeable loss on the Bude contract which was due to be completed in 1995.

Deferred taxation

Osmosis plc had been highly profitable and expanding its fixed asset base annually. At 30 November 1994 the net book value in the balance sheet exceeded the tax written-down values by £1,200,000 and the company has not provided for deferred tax. The pattern of capital expenditure is likely to be more irregular in the future and the following forecast has been prepared:

	Capital allowances £'000	Depreciation £'000
1994/95	2,560	2,240
1995/96	2,800	2,560
1996/97	1,760	2,672

The corporation tax rate for 1993/94 is 33%. Assume that it has been announced that the rates for future years are to increase to 35%.

Required

(a)   (i)   Calculate the amounts that would appear in the balance sheet from the three contracts in accordance with the provisions of SSAP 9 *Stocks and long-term contracts*.   **(12 marks)**

(ii)   Calculate the charge or credit for deferred tax that will appear in the profit and loss account for the years ended 30 November 1994 and 1995.

Calculate the amounts that will appear in the deferred tax account in the balance sheets as at those dates.

Draft an appropriate note to the profit and loss accounts in accordance with the provisions of SSAP 15 *Accounting for deferred tax*.   **(8 marks)**

(b)   (i)   Explain the effect on the accounts if the auditor obtained two items of information that had not been available to the chief accountant when the contracts were being evaluated.

The first item of information related to the cost of materials. As a result of a creditor circularisation on 15 December 1994 a supplier has advised that, under the terms of their contract, the cost of materials supplied to Osmosis plc since 1 November 1994 are to be increased. This increase is because the supplier's own costs have risen by more than 10% thereby bringing into effect a price increase clause. It is estimated that the materials for the Ascot contract will increase by £67,500 of which amount £5,000 relates to goods supplied to the company prior to 30 November 1994. This increase in the cost of materials does not affect the Cowes and Bude contracts. The supplier had not been aware of the increase in his own costs until dealing with and responding to the circularisation letter.

The second item of information related to labour costs. A wages agreement authorised by the company on 1 December 1994 resulted in labour costs becoming £25,000 more than originally estimated.   **(4 marks)**

(ii)   [Not reproduced as this part of the question is no longer within the syllabus.]   **(2 marks)**

(c)   The directors are proposing not to provide for deferred taxation in the 1993/94 accounts on the basis that the company expects to make trading losses of £1,120,000 in 1994/95 before returning to profits. The audit manager has reported to the audit partner that from his initial discussions with the directors it would appear that they are firmly committed to the treatment they are proposing.

Write a brief memo giving the auditor's response to the directors' proposal.   **(4 marks)**
(Total: 30 marks)

---

19   (Question 3 of examination)

Heavy Goods plc carries on business as a manufacturer of tractors. In 1994 the company was looking for acquisitions and carrying out investigations into a number of possible targets. One of these was a competitor, Modern Tractors plc.

The company's acquisition strategy was to acquire companies that were vulnerable to a takeover and in which there was an opportunity to improve asset management and profitability.

The chief accountant of Heavy Goods plc has instructed his assistant to calculate ratios from the financial statements of Modern Tractors plc for the past three years and to prepare a report based on these ratios and the industry average ratios that have been provided by the trade association. The ratios prepared by the assistant accountant and the industry averages for 1994 are set out below:

Required

(a)   Assuming the role of the Chief Accountant, draft a brief report to be submitted to the managing director based on the ratios of Modern Tractors plc for 1992–94 and the industry averages for 1994.

(12 marks)

(b)   Draft a brief memo to management explaining:

     (i)   in general terms why the comparison of the 1994 ratios with the ratios of previous years and other companies might be misleading; and   **(3 marks)**

     (ii)   how specific ratios might be affected and the possible implications for the evaluation of the report.

         (5 marks)
         (Total: 20 marks)
         (ACCA Dec 94)

		1992	*1993*	*1994*	*Industry average 1994*
Sales growth	%	30.00	40.00	9.52	8.25
Sales/total assets		1.83	2.05	1.60	2.43
Sales/net fixed assets		2.94	3.59	2.74	16.85
Sales/working capital		−21.43	−140.00	38.33	10.81
Sales/debtors		37.50	70.00	92.00	16.00
Gross profit/sales	%	18.67	22.62	19.57	23.92
Profit before tax/sales	%	8.00	17.62	11.74	4.06
Profit before interest/interest		6.45	26.57	14.50	4.95
Profit after tax/total assets	%	9.76	27.80	13.24	8.97
Profit after tax/equity	%	57.14	75.00	39.58	28.90
Net fixed assets/total assets	%	62.20	57.07	58.54	19.12
Net fixed assets/equity		3.64	1.54	1.75	0.58
Equity/total assets	%	18.29	37.07	33.45	32.96
Total liabilities/total assets	%	81.71	62.93	66.55	69.00
Total liabilities/equity		4.47	1.70	1.99	2.40
Long-term debt/total assets	%	36.59	18.54	29.27	19.00
Current liabilities/total assets	%	45.12	44.39	37.28	50.00
Current assets/current liabilities		0.84	0.97	1.11	1.63
(Current assets − Stock)/Current liabilities		0.43	0.54	0.72	0.58
Stock/total assets	%	17.07	18.54	14.63	41.90
Cost of sales/stock		8.71	8.55	8.81	4.29
Cost of sales/creditors		6.10	6.25	6.17	12.87
Debtors/total assets	%	4.88	2.93	1.70	18.40
Cash/total assets	%	15.85	21.46	25.08	9.60

Note

Total assets = Fixed assets at net book value + Current assets
Net fixed assets = Fixed assets at net book value.

---

20   (Question 4 of examination)

[This question has not been reproduced as it is no longer valid following technical developments.]

EXAMINER'S COMMENTS

Question 1: Part (a) examined the preparation of a consolidated cash flow statement in FRS 1 format for a group where there was an acquisition during the year, income from a participating undertaking with a 40% interest, disposal of fixed assets and loan stock issued at a discount. Part (b)(i) examined the understanding and treatment of capitalised interest in the cash flow statement. Part (b)(ii) examined the understanding and treatment of cash equivalents. Part (c) examined the possibility of the auditor's independence being impaired.

Part (a) was generally well done. Common errors were confusion as to where to include items which were correctly calculated within the workings in the cash flow statement itself; failure to treat the discount; miscalculation of the dividend received from the fixed asset investment and the depreciation; adding profit on sale; failure to adjust for the assets and liabilities assumed on the acquisition of the subsidiary; omission of items, eg, share premium element in the Financing section.

Part (b)(i) was generally poorly answered. Weaker answers either produced a rationale for capitalising interest without relating it to the cash flow implication or concluded that the interest element had not been paid and therefore had no cash flow effect.

Answers to part (b)(ii) were mixed. Weaker answers identified all items as cash equivalents or classified them correctly but then failed to illustrate the effect on the cash flow.

Question 2: Part (a)(i) tested the preparation of balance sheet extracts for three contracts involving a range of situations, eg, fixed contract price, price at valuation, losses, provisions, cumulative data. Part (a)(ii) tested the preparation of the balance sheet extracts for deferred tax where there was a known change of tax rate. Part (b)(i) tested the application of SSAP 17 *Post Balance Sheet Events* to given situations whereby a post balance sheet event can adjust an estimate of future costs which affect the current year. Part (b)(ii) tested the understanding of audit procedures required to determine the existence of other post balance sheet events.

Part (a)(i) was generally well answered with a reasonable performance from most candidates. Weaker answers spent time on elaborate workings to calculate the profit on each contract and failed to extract and classify items from their workings.

Performance on part (a)(ii) was mixed. The topic appeared to be either well understood with high marks or very poorly understood with marks only gained from understanding general principles. Weaker answers calculated a full provision each year using the incorrect tax rate.

Answers to part (b)(i) were mixed. Good answers identified the need to apply SSAP 17 and explained the need for adjustment including the effect on profit, costs and losses. Weaker answers simply stated that labour cost change was immaterial and made little attempt to go any further even to the extent of ignoring the SSAP 17 implications.

Part (c) was reasonably well answered with the majority of candidates achieving a pass mark. Weaker answers omitted to consider the effect of losses on deferred taxation or appreciating that the problem was anticipating the loss.

Question 3: Part (a) examined the ability to prepare a report to the managing director of an acquisitive company on a target company's vulnerability to takeover based on a detailed summary of ratios for the past three years together with the industry averages with particular reference to asset management and profitability. Part (b)(i) tested the understanding of factors that could make ratio comparisons misleading and the ability to convey this to management. Part (b)(ii) tested the ability to relate the possible defects to specific ratios that had been included within their report to the managing director in (a) with an explanation to management so that they could consider how this might affect their evaluation.

There were a lot of average answers to part (a). Answers were usually generally with a report concluding that Modern Tractors was a healthy company and should be taken over. Too many answers simply commented that a ratio had increased or decreased with no clear conclusion. A general weakness was the failure to address the question set which was to comment on strengths/weaknesses in the areas of asset management and profitability from an acquirer's perspective. In addition greater attention needs to be given to the preparation of reports.

Part (b)(i) was generally quite well answered with explanations of the effect of inflation, different accounting policies, different capital and asset structures and window dressing. However, there was a certain confusion among weaker candidates who offered explanations of different performance as reasons for non-comparability.

Part (b)(ii) was poorly answered. Good answers considered how a defect could have affected the two key aspects of asset management and profitability that were the focus for the report in part (a). However, surprisingly few candidates produced the quality of performance that they had shown in (b)(i) with the weaker answers failing to relate the defects of specific ratios.

Question 4: Comments not reproduced as the question is no longer valid following technical developments.

ANSWERS TO DECEMBER 1994 EXAMINATION

17   (Answer 1 of examination)

(*Note:* this question and answer have been amended to reflect the changes introduced by FRS 1 (Revised), which was issued in October 1996, and other technical developments including the issue of FRS 10 and the abolition of ACT).

(a)   **Consolidated cash flow statement for the year ended 30 September 1994**

		£'000	£'000
Operating activities	Note 1		
Net cash inflow from operating activities			372
Dividends received from associates	W5		250
Returns on investments and servicing of finance			
Interest paid (150 + 30 − 40) − 40 discount		(100)	
Dividends received from fixed asset investments		155	
Dividends paid to minority interest	W6	(48)	
Net cash from returns on investments and servicing of debt			7
Taxation			
UK corporation tax paid	W7		(250)
Capital expenditure			
Purchase of tangible fixed assets			
Machinery	W8	(1,085)	
Sale of tangible fixed assets			
Machinery		500	(585)
Acquisitions and disposals			
Purchase of subsidiary undertaking	W9	98	
			98
Equity dividends paid (400 + 200 − 300)			(300)
Financing			
Issue of ordinary share capital	W10	2,453	
Issue of loan stock	W11	920	
Capital payments under leases	W12	(270)	
Net cash inflow from financing			3,103
Increase in cash			2,695

Notes to cash flow statement

1   *Reconciliation of operating profit to net cash flow from operating activities*

	£'000	
Operating profit	1,475	
Depreciation charges	335	W1
Profit on sale of machinery	(100)	
Increase in stocks	(943)	W2
Increase in trade debtors	(547)	W3
Increase in trade creditors	152	W4
Net cash inflow from operating activities	372	

2   *Reconciliation of net cash flow to movement in net funds (Note 3)*

	£'000
Increase in cash in the period	2,695
Cash outflow from lease financing	270
Cash inflow from issue of loan stock	(920)
Change in net funds resulting from cash flows	2,045
Accrued interest on loan	(40)
New finance leases	(850)
Movement in net funds in the period	1,155
Net funds at 1 October 1993	950
Net funds at 30 September 1994	2,105

3   *Analysis of changes in net funds*

	At 1 Oct 1993 £'000	*Cash flows* £'000	*Other changes* £'000	*At 30 Sept 1994* £'000
Cash at bank and in hand	1,820	2,695		4,515
Loans	(500)	(920)	(40)	(1,460)
Obligations under finance leases	(370)	270	(850)	(950)
Total	950	2,045	(890)	2,105

Workings

(1)   *Depreciation charges*

	£'000	£'000
Buildings		125
Machinery		
Closing aggregate amount	1,200	
Less opening aggregate amount	(1,100)	
	100	
Add depreciation on disposal	100	
		200
		325
Add: Amortisation of goodwill		10
		335

(2)   *Stock*

	£'000	£'000
Closing balance		1,975
Less:		
Opening balance	1,000	
Arising from the acquisition	32	
		(1,032)
Cash outflow		943

(3)   *Trade debtors*

		£'000	£'000
Closing balance			1,850
Less:	Opening balance	1,275	
	Arising from the acquisition	28	
			(1,303)
Cash outflow			547

(4)   *Trade creditors*

		£'000	£'000
Closing balance			500
Less:	Opening balance	280	
	Arising from the acquisition	68	
			(348)
Cash inflow			152

(5)   *Dividends received from associate*

	£'000	£'000
Opening balance		1,000
Add share of profit	495	
Less tax	(145)	
		350
		1,350
Closing balance		(1,100)
Cash inflow		250

(6)   *Minority*

	£'000
Opening balance	–
Add profit for year	100
Add arising from acquisition	63
	163
Less closing balance	(115)
Cash outflow	48

(7)   *Tax*

	£'000
Opening balances	
Corporation tax	217
Deferred tax	13
Transfer from profit and loss account	495
Closing balances	
Corporation tax	(462)
Deferred tax	(30)
	233
Acquisition tax	17
Cash outflow	250

(8)   *Investment in machinery*

		£'000
Cost at 30.9.94		3,000
Less cost at 1.10.93		(1,400)
		1,600
Add disposal		500
		2,100
Less:	Arising from acquisition	(165)
	Leased	(850)
Cash outflow		1,085

(9)   *Cash*

	£'000
Cash acquired from acquisition	112
Less cash consideration	(14)
Cash inflow	98

(10)   *Shares*

		£'000
Closing balance		
	Shares	3,940
	Premium	2,883
		6,823
Less: Opening balance		
	Shares	(2,000)
	Premium	(2,095)
Non-cash consideration		
	Shares	(220)
	Premium	(55)
Cash inflow		2,453

(11)   *Loans*

	£'000
Closing balance	1,460
Less: Opening balance	(500)
	960
Less increase – finance cost	(40)
Cash inflow	920

(12)   *Lease – capital payments*

	£'000
Opening balances (200 + 170)	370
Add new lease commitment	850
	1,220
Less closing balances (240 + 710)	(950)
Cash outflow	270

(b)   (i)   **The treatment of capitalised interest**

FRS 1 requires capitalised interest to be shown within the interest paid heading in the Returns on Investments and Servicing of Finance section of the cash flow statement.

The effect of this will be to increase the interest paid from £140,000 to £145,000. The purchase of tangible fixed assets will be reduced by the same amount from £1,085,000 to £1,080,000.

(Tutorial note: interest paid in the cash flow statement is net of the discount; the figure shown will increase from £100,000 to £105,000.)

(ii)   **The treatment of cash and cash equivalents**

We have noted that the cash figures comprised the following:

	1.10.93 £'000	30.9.94 £'000
Cash in hand	10	15
Bank overdrafts	(770)	(65)
Bank	1,080	1,890
10% Treasury Stock 1993	1,500	–
Bank deposits	–	1,125
Gas 3% 1990–1995	–	1,550
	1,820	4,515

FRS 1 (revised) converts the cash flow statement into a statement of movements in pure cash only. What used to be called 'cash equivalents' are now dealt with in the statement under a separate heading 'Management of liquid resources'.

The cash in hand, bank overdrafts and bank figures comprise the balance of cash. The other three components of the cash figure satisfy the FRS 1 (revised) definition of liquid resources, so the cash flow statement for the year ended 30 September 1994 would show cash received from the sale of the Treasury Stock and cash paid to acquire the deposits and the Gas Stock in the 'Management of liquid resources' section.

---

18   (Answer 2 of examination)

(a)   (i)   **Contracts - balance sheet extract**

		£'000
Stock – long-term contract work in progress	W1	27
Debtors – amounts recoverable on contracts	W2, W3	129.75
Creditors – payments on account	W4	25.5
Provision for losses on long-term contracts	W5	25.35

Workings – Ascot contract

Turnover recognised was 60% of the contract price ie, £810,000.

Work in progress

	£'000
Costs to date	675
Cost of sales (60% of £675,000 + £405,000)	(648)
Stock – long-term contract balance	27 W1

Debtors

	£'000
Turnover recognised (60% of £1,350,000)	810
Less payments on account	(729)
Amounts recoverable on contract	81 W2

Workings – Cowes contract

Turnover recognised was 25% of the contract price ie, £568,750.

Debtors

	£'000
Turnover recognised (25% of £2,275,000)	568.75
Less cumulative payments on account	(520.00)
Amounts recoverable on contract	48.75 W3

Provision for future losses

	£'000
Turnover recognised	568.75
Less costs incurred	(577.20)
Loss	(8.45)

	£'000
Foreseeable loss	33.80
Less loss in trading account	(8.45)
Provision for losses on long-term contracts	25.35 W5

Workings – Bude contract

Creditors

	£'000
Payment on account (£3,442,500 – £3,315,000)	127.5
Less: Long-term contracts work in progress (£2,652,000 – £2,550,000)	(102.0)
Payments on account	25.5 W4

(ii) **Deferred taxation**

SSAP 15 requires deferred tax provisions to be calculated at the rate at which tax is likely to be paid. Usually the current rate is used as the best estimate but, as the change is known in advance, the new rate of 35% should be used in the calculation.

1993/94

The profit and loss account charge will be £123,200 and the deferred tax account in the balance sheet will show a credit balance of £123,200.

1994/95

The profit and loss account charge will be £112,000 and the deferred tax account in the balance sheet will show a credit balance of £235,200.

Workings – deferred taxation

	Capital allowances £'000	Depreciation £'000	Timing differences originating £'000	Timing differences reversing £'000	Cumulative £'000
1994/95	2,560	2,240	320		320
1995/96	2,800	2,560	240		560
1996/97	1,760	2,672		912	(352)

The deferred taxation account balance will be:

	£'000		£'000
30.11.94	352 × 35%	=	123.2
30.11.95	672 × 35%	=	235.2
30.11.96	912 × 35%	=	319.2
30.11.97	0 × 35%	=	0

The profit and loss charge will be:

	£'000
1993/94	123.2
1994/95	112.0
1995/96	84.0
1996/97	(319.2)

Note to the profit and loss account

1993/94 profit and loss account

The amount of deferred taxation not provided, arising on capital allowances computed at 35% was £296,800.

1994/95 profit and loss account

The amount of deferred taxation not provided, arising on capital allowances computed at 35% was £296,800.

Workings – supporting the note to profit and loss account

1993/94

	£'000
Total potential deferred tax at 30.11.94 (£1,200,000 × 35%)	420.0
Less deferred tax charge	123.2
Not provided	296.8

1994/95

	£'000
Total potential deferred tax at 30.11.95 [(£1,200,000 + £320,000) × 35%]	532.0
Less deferred tax balance	235.2
Not provided	296.8

(b)　(i)　**Material cost increase**

The information relating to the materials falls within the provisions of SSAP 17 *Accounting for post balance sheet events*. The standard states in respect of stock and work in progress that it is an adjusting event when there is the receipt of evidence that the previous estimate of accrued profit on a long-term contract was materially inaccurate.

The increased cost of materials is 17% of the estimated cost to complete and 25% of the expected profit on the contract. It is therefore a material amount and will fall to be adjusted under SSAP 17.

The cost of sales will be increased from 60% of £1,080,000 to 60% of £1,147,500, an increase of £40,500. The stocks – long-term contracts amount of £27,000 will be eliminated and in addition there will be a provision of £13,500 because the cost of sales matched to the turnover exceeds the actual costs incurred of £675,000 by this amount. Application of the company policy for the recognition of turnover and matching cost of sales requires this treatment.

It could be argued that the amount of £5,000 applicable to goods supplied to the company prior to the year end should be regarded as an accounting error. In which case, the costs would be increased to £680,000 and the provision reduced to £8,500. The cost of sales would remain at the amended figure of £688,500.

Labour cost increase

As for the materials, the information relating to the labour costs falls within the provisions of SSAP 17 *Accounting for post balance sheet events* which states that it is an adjusting event when there is the receipt of evidence that the previous estimate of accrued profit on a long-term contract was materially inaccurate.

There is no exact definition of materiality. The approach used in this answer is to regard the effect on the profit/loss for the year as being a final review consideration and to decide on materiality in relation to the Ascot contract. The labour cost is more than 5% but less than 10% of the original estimate of profit ie, £270,000 which could be reasonably acceptable as within the range for the auditor to exercise his professional judgement in deciding whether it is material or not. However, the adjustment required to reflect the increase in the cost of materials means that in this particular case the labour increase exceeds 10% and would be treated as an adjusting event. The provision of £13,500 created by the previous item/adjustment would need to be increased by £15,000 (ie, 60% of the increased labour cost of £25,000).

(c)

MEMORANDUM

To: Directors of Osmosis plc   **Dated:**

Re: Proposed treatment of future losses in relation to deferred tax.

The treatment you are proposing of the future trading losses of £1,120,000 in relation to deferred tax provisioning has been raised as an audit point by our audit manager.

Because we recognise that there are differences of opinion within the profession over the topic, we are writing briefly to set out our firm's position.

There has been a great deal of debate about the treatment of trading losses foreseen in the future when assessing the level of deferred tax to be provided with two proposed treatments.

Those supporting the treatment you are proposing argue that the loss when incurred will reduce the amount of tax payable and under the partial provision rules would say that the liability should not exceed the amount that will be paid.

However, our view is that the deferred tax cannot be reduced by a trading loss that has not yet been incurred and which has not yet been accounted for and that it is not the function of deferred tax to anticipate the effects of future trading results, only to account for the impact of timing differences which have affected trading results reported to date. We recognise that trading losses can be carried back (three years) and this would also be taken into account.

It seems to us that part of the confusion arises because SSAP 15 states that a loss for tax purposes which is available to relieve future profits from tax constitutes a timing difference. This is true in respect of current and past trading losses but to recognise the effect of future losses but not otherwise to provide for them in the financial statements would have the effect of creating a timing difference where none had previously existed.

Consequently, we believe that the company should not take the forecast trading loss into account when assessing the reversing timing differences.

In our view the effect of this disagreement is not such that the financial statements as a whole would be misleading but, if the company continued with its proposed treatment, we would feel ourselves required to qualify our audit report with an 'Except for . . .' qualification.

Given the general uncertainty surrounding the topic, we would be pleased to meet to discuss the matter further if you think this to be helpful.

(Tutorial note: The syllabus has changed since this question was originally set. As a result, parts (b)(i) and (c) would probably now be worded differently, with the examiner simply asking candidates to consider the effects of the findings and proposed treatments without reference to the audit. As a result, references to the audit report in part (c) would no longer be required.*)*

19   (Answer 3 of examination)

(a)   **To:**   Managing Director   **Dated:** 1 December 1994

        From: Chief Accountant

        Re: Report on performance of Modern Tractors plc based on ratios for 1992-94 and Industry Averages for
                     1994.

In this report I propose to comment on five aspects of the company's performance, namely, liquidity, asset utilisation, interest cover, capital gearing and profitability based on the inter-period ratios for 1992-94 and the inter-company ratios for 1994.

Liquidity

The liquidity ratios ie, current and quick ratios have increased in each of the past three years. However, compared to the industry average they are giving apparently conflicting signals with the current ratio being below and the quick ratio being above the industry average. This would appear to arise from the company's relatively lower stock holding and relatively higher debtors/cash holding confirmed by the stock turnover ratio and the stock/total assets figures.

Liquidity has progressively improved with less dependence on realising stock to meet short-term liabilities to the point where its quick ratio is higher than that for the industry.

The company is cash rich and not vulnerable in this area which is confirmed by the cash/total assets ratio.

Asset utilisation

To assist with the evaluation of the company's asset utilisation, 'Turnover' ratios have been calculated.

Starting with the sales to total assets ratio, this has fluctuated over the past three years and is currently lower at 1.6 than the industry average of 2.43.

This could indicate that the company is less efficient at generating sales with the economic resources available to it.

However, a more detailed analysis is required of the constituents of the total asset figure. For example they may include investments that are not generating sales but do provide investment income which might well fluctuate between years.

The turnover of each class of asset has been calculated to identify any that exceeds the industry average. This has been done for each class of asset, starting with the fixed asset and working capital turnover rates.

Fixed asset turnover

In 1994, the company is only generating £2.74 per £ of net fixed asset whereas the industry is on average generating £16.85 per £ of fixed asset. There can be a number of explanations. For example, it could reflect adversely on the management of Modern Tractors or it could indicate a capital investment programme geared up to continuing sales growth. This will require further evaluation.

Working capital turnover

The company's turnover rate of 38.33 is much higher than the industry average of 10.81. A review of the constituent ratios will indicate which item(s) within the current assets/current liabilities is responsible for the difference.

The report considers each constituent in turn.

Stock turnover

The company is turning over its stock at more than twice the average industry rate. This might be due to higher sales or to lower stock holdings. This therefore needs to be investigated in the context of the balance sheet which shows that the company's stock represents only 14.63% of total assets as opposed to the 41.90% for the industry.

This requires further enquiry to identify any downside eg, a low stock holding might be associated with stockouts and lost sales.

In many acquisitions there is an immediate advantage available to the acquirer by improving stock control – this would not appear to be available to us in this case.

Debtors turnover

The ratio for Modern Tractors is substantially higher than the industry average. We need to assess the significance of the amount and one indication is that debtors represent only 1.70% of the total assets as opposed to the industry average of 18.40%. The difference might be due to an efficient debtors ledger operation but the difference is so great that it is more likely to reflect a difference in policy eg, Modern Tractors factors its debtors ledger with only four days sales appearing as debtors. The industry average is also low at 23 days and would indicate that factoring is an industry practice.

Cash

The cash to total assets at 25.08% is high and might support the view that the debtors are being factored.

Creditors turnover

The company is taking twice as long to pay its creditors than the industry average. However, the balance sheet ratio, current liabilities to total assets, indicates that even so the company is less reliant on short-term credit than the industry.

From the above, we can see that the company is significantly different from the industry average on all of the turnover ratios we have examined. Management should investigate this further to assess whether there is a problem eg, consider if the mix of fixed assets is appropriate; consider if there is a likelihood of a stock-out; consider the make-up of the working capital. If there is no problem then it could be determined whether company policy is significantly different from competitors and whether the industry comparisons are not valid comparators.

Interest cover

The company's cover is almost three times that of the industry average. This indicates that the company is well able to service the existing debt and that it could expand this form of financing if it required additional capital.

Gearing

The company's long-term debt to total assets is 29.27% which is higher than the industry average of 19%. Modern Tractors has a higher dependence on long-term debt (gearing), but a lower level of short-term financing (current liabilities), overall debt is at a similar level to the industry average.

At the same time, although there is a higher level of long-term debt, the interest cover is substantially higher than the industry average as mentioned above. Information is also required on rates of interest as the company might have renegotiated its loans or obtained additional finance at a lower rate than the rest of the industry is paying. It is noted that the interest cover in 1993 was 26 times and further information would be required to assess the extent to which this is the result of differences in the interest charge rather than in the profit available to cover the interest.

The debt equity ratio can be calculated from the ratios given in the question, as follows:

(Long-term debt/Total assets) / (Equity/Total assets)

which produces debt equity percentages as follows:

			Industry
1992	*1993*	*1994*	*average*
200%	50%	87%	58%

The 1994 debt equity ratio for the company is higher than the industry average but this does not pose a problem for servicing the debt.

Profitability

The gross profit at 19.57% is a little lower than the industry. However, the initial thought is that its pricing is similar to that of the industry and its manufacturing costs are similar.

At an operating level, the company has an operating profit percentage that is more than twice the industry average. This may be due to one factor or a combination of factors eg, lower operating expenses, lower interest costs, other income as mentioned above.

The company's profit after tax to total assets is 48% higher than the industry's average and its return on equity 37% higher. Assuming that there is scope to increase the financial leverage, the return on equity could be significantly improved.

Conclusion

The company appears to have increased its fixed asset base in 1994 following two years of substantial sales growth in 1992 and 1993. It has not maintained the same level of growth and it would be helpful to obtain forecasts for the following three years.

The make-up of the fixed assets has not been given. Information is required about this with a view to considering an improvement in their utilisation.

The gross profit margin has remained at about the same level. However, there has been a fluctuation in the profit before tax figure. Further information is required to ascertain the reason for this. It is possible that there has been fluctuations in other income eg, arising from the disposal of investments. This will need to be taken into account when assessing future maintainable profits.

The company appears to be financially sound with cash increasing to 25.08% of total assets by 1994 compared to the industry average of 9.6%.

Considering the financial structure of the company, there appears to be scope for increasing the amounts borrowed without endangering the capacity to service the loans. This could lead to a significant improvement in the return on equity and share price if the funds could be used as effectively as at present within the business. However, this method of increasing the return on equity brings with it an increase in the financial risk.

The company appears to be poised for growth with new fixed assets and a high level of cash. This might be an opportune moment to initiate an approach – before this sound base is translated into sustained profit growth.

(b)   **Memo to management**   **Dated**

(i)   **Re: Limitations of inter-period and inter-company comparisons**

The following is a brief comment to bring out the fact that there are limitations which may make the interpretation of inter-period and inter-firm comparative ratios difficult to accurately evaluate.

These include:

–　The data might need to be adjusted for inflation if valid comparisons are to be made over time. Some companies achieve this by adjusting their five-and ten-year summaries to take inflation into account.

–　The financial statements might have been prepared using different accounting policies eg, choice of fixed asset depreciation and stock valuation policies.

–　Accounts may be made up to a different date which can significantly affect ratios if the business is seasonal eg, before or after the start of the new season's models.

–　Traditional analysis tends to focus on profitability. Greater attention is needed to be paid to assessing liquidity and the capacity to adapt by reference to the cash flow statement.

–　Informal typologies of ratios have been long established and certain ratios have come to be accepted as suitable indicators of each characteristic of firm performance to be investigated. This in itself can limit the investigation and care is required to explore beyond the conventional ratios. For example, productivity ratios could be extremely important in an industry such as tractor manufacture. Appropriate ratios could include average sales per employee, operating profit per employee, capital employed per employee and stock and work in progress per employee.

–　The balance sheet is prepared at a single point in time. This means that it is possible to practise window dressing eg, by selecting a year end date when stocks are low, dispatching stock which may not have been as carefully inspected as normal in order to improve the current year's sales and stock levels.

–　The industry average does not indicate the distribution of results around the average. It would be helpful to also have quartile and decile figures.

(ii)   **Specific comments**

Liquidity ratios

The liquidity ratios appearing in the inter-firm comparison scheme are not strictly measures of liquidity as there is no indication of the timing of their conversion into cash. The assumption behind the quick and current ratios is that the current assets will be converted into cash sufficiently readily to meet the liabilities on their due dates.

The liquidity ratios are at one particular point in time. Other companies might have taken steps to produce liquidity ratios that are not representative of their normal ratios that exist throughout the year. For example, levels of stock might be changed – this might be achieved by simply delaying purchases or by unacceptable techniques such as selling stock to associated companies and reversing the transaction after the year end; creditors might be paid early and overdrafts reviewed by negotiating term loans with the bank to remove them from the classification of being payable within one year. Some of these practices are perfectly acceptable commercially and by the auditors eg, restricting purchases; others are window dressing and would be objected to by the auditors if they were to become aware that they had occurred eg, sale to and buy back from an associated company by a subsidiary – in practice however they might not be readily detected.

Asset utilisation

Turnover ratios can be affected if the sales trend is different from previous years in either our own or other companies. For example, if the sales were skewed towards the end of the year, the debtor turnover would be lower than in previous years or in other companies not having the same pattern. Such a skewing could result from market conditions, eg, the economy picking-up or from internal decisions eg, commercial decisions to promote heavily or window dressing decisions to ship out uninspected goods to contractees although aware that there will be heavy returns due to warranty claims for defective work after the year end.

They can also be affected by the choice of accounting policies eg, Modern Tractors plc might revalue its fixed assets and competitors leave their fixed assets at depreciated cost which could result in significant differences in fixed asset turnover ratios.

They can also be affected by commercial changes that are being put in place but not yet effective eg, building factory space, acquiring machinery, introducing robotics which will come into operation in 1995 or later.

Questions that need answering in relation to the fixed asset turnover ratios include the following:

– Are other companies using older written-down equipment?

– Are any of the companies leasing?

– When were the new fixed assets acquired by Modern Tractors?

– Were they acquired late in the year?

– Is Modern Tractors still commissioning its fixed assets?

– What is the make-up of fixed assets in Modern Tractors and in the industry?

– Is there a different mix eg, properties that will produce a capital rather than revenue profit?

The stock level of Modern Tractors is lower than the industry average. This might indicate that the company has stock financing arranged and there might be recourse liabilities that need to be taken into account.

Gearing

This could be affected by a number of factors. For example, the choice of accounting policies such as a decision to revalue fixed assets would affect the debt/equity ratio by increasing the equity amount and so improving the ratio; a decision to re-negotiate an overdraft to a term loan would increase the debt/equity ratio and improve the quick ratio, a policy of borrowing rather than relying on short-term credit will increase gearing.

There might be different pressures on the management of different companies to influence the gearing percentages eg, a company that is likely to breach loan covenants relating to acceptable debt/equity levels might resort to commercial or artificial measures to contain or reduce the debt/equity relationship that appears in the year end financial accounts. For example, there might be an increase in the use of leasing with lessor companies structuring the agreement to fall outside the finance lease classification. A detailed reading of the financial statements and the notes to the accounts will give indications of the existence of such arrangements and changes in company practice.

Profitability

Sales growth per cent is based on historic transaction data. They indicate that the company has achieved growth in each of the past three years. However, this should be adjusted for inflation if one is to be able to identify whether there has been a growth in the sales volume. It is possible that adjusted for inflation the company's sales have actually fallen in volume terms.

Gross profit per cent could be affected by changes in the choice of accounting policies eg, the choice of depreciation method; or by technical manipulation eg, structuring leasing agreements so that they become classified as operating leases with no depreciation charged in the cost of sales.

Net profit could be affected by company attitudes to provisioning and releasing deferred income into the profit and loss account eg, debtor provisioning and decisions on releasing grants into the current year's profit.

Conclusion

The comparative ratios are a useful initial indicator. They identify symptoms not causes. Causes require further enquiry but they do provide useful signposts. For example, there is a clear need for us to consider the causes of the differences in the relative fixed asset levels (which are higher) and stock levels (which are lower) and the apparent debtor factoring.

I would be pleased to produce a follow up report on dealing with any questions that you raise on the basis of this initial report.

---

20   (Answer 4 of examination)

[This answer has not been reproduced as it is no longer valid due to technical developments.]

JUNE 1995 QUESTIONS

Section A – BOTH questions are compulsory and MUST be attempted

21   (Question 1 of examination)

The Exotic Group carries on business as a distributor of warehouse equipment and importer of fruit into the United Kingdom. Exotic plc was incorporated in 1975 to distribute warehouse equipment. It diversified its activities during the 1980s to include the import and distribution of fruit, and expanded its operations by the acquisition of shares in Madeira plc in 1979, in Melon plc in 1989 and in Kiwi plc in 1991.

Accounts for all companies are made up to 31 December.

The draft profit and loss accounts for Exotic plc, Melon plc and Kiwi plc for the year ended 31 December 1994 are as follows:

	Exotic plc £'000	Melon plc £'000	Kiwi plc £'000
Turnover	45,600	24,700	22,800
Cost of sales	(18,050)	(5,463)	(5,320)
Gross profit	27,550	19,237	17,480
Distribution costs	(3,325)	(2,137)	(1,900)
Administrative expenses	(3,475)	(950)	(1,900)
Operating profit	20,750	16,150	13,680
Interest paid	(325)		
Profit before tax	20,425	16,150	13,680
Tax on profit on ordinary activities	(8,300)	(5,390)	(4,241)
Profit on ordinary activities after tax	12,125	10,760	9,439
Dividends – proposed	(9,500)		
Retained profit for year	2,625	10,760	9,439
Retained profit brought forward	20,013	13,315	10,459
Retained profit carried forward	22,638	24,075	19,898

The draft balance sheets as at 31 December 1994 are as follows:

	Exotic plc £'000	Melon plc £'000	Kiwi plc £'000
Fixed assets (NBV)	35,483	24,273	13,063
Investments			
Shares in Melon plc	6,650		
Shares in Kiwi plc		3,800	
Current assets	1,568	9,025	8,883
Current liabilities	(13,063)	(10,023)	(48)
	30,638	27,075	21,898
Share capital and reserves			
Ordinary £1 shares	8,000	3,000	2,000
Profit and loss account	22,638	24,075	19,898
	30,638	27,075	21,898

The following information is available relating to Exotic plc, Melon plc and Kiwi plc:

(1) On 1 January 1989 Exotic plc acquired 2,700,000 £1 ordinary shares in Melon plc for £6,650,000 at which date there was a credit balance on the profit and loss account of Melon plc of £1,425,000. No shares have been issued by Melon plc since Exotic plc acquired its interest.

(2) On 1 January 1991 Melon plc acquired 1,600,000 £1 ordinary shares in Kiwi plc for £3,800,000 at which date there was a credit balance on the profit and loss account of Kiwi plc of £950,000. No shares have been issued by Kiwi plc since Melon plc acquired its interest.

(3) During 1994, Kiwi plc had made inter-company sales to Melon plc of £480,000 making a profit of 25% on cost and £75,000 of these goods were in stock at 31 December 1994.

(4) During 1994, Melon plc had made inter-company sales to Exotic plc of £260,000 making a profit of 33^{1}/3% on cost and £60,000 of these goods were in stock at 31 December 1994.

(5) On 1 November 1994 Exotic plc sold warehouse equipment to Melon plc for £240,000 from stock. Melon plc has included this equipment in its fixed assets. The equipment had been purchased on credit by Exotic plc for £200,000 in October 1994 and this amount is included in its current liabilities as at 31 December 1994.

(6) Melon plc charges depreciation on its warehouse equipment at 20% on cost. It is company policy to charge a full year's depreciation in the year of acquisition to be included in the cost of sales.

(7) It is group policy to capitalise and amortise all goodwill through the profit and loss account over three years from the date of acquisition.

The following information is available relating to Madeira plc:

(1) In 1979 Madeira plc was incorporated as a wholly owned subsidiary of Exotic plc to carry on business importing bananas from Madeira to the United Kingdom. Increased competition from growers in other world markets has resulted in recurring trade losses.

(2) In 1991 the directors of the parent company arranged for all warehousing and distribution for Madeira plc to be physically handled by Melon plc. Madeira plc retained its office accommodation.

(3) In the financial year ended 31 December 1992 Exotic plc wrote off its investment in Madeira plc in its accounts.

(4) In 1993 Exotic plc decided to discontinue the trade carried on in Madeira plc's name as early as possible in 1994. However, due to protracted negotiations with employees, the termination was not completed until November 1994.

(5) The following data relates to Madeira plc in 1994:

	£'000
Turnover	2,000
Cost of sales	(2,682)
Distribution costs	(18)
Administrative expenses	(100)
Redundancy costs	(427)
Profit on sale of fixed assets	115
Loss on sale of net current assets	(36)

Required

(a) Excluding Madeira plc:

(i) prepare a consolidated profit and loss account, including brought forward reserves, for the Exotic Group for the year ended 31 December 1994; and **(12 marks)**

(ii) prepare a consolidated balance sheet as at that date. **(9 marks)**

(b)   Show the accounting treatment for Madeira plc in the consolidated profit and loss account of the Exotic Group for the year ended 31 December 1994 in accordance with FRS 3 on the assumption that there has been a discontinuance and that a provision of £500,000 had been created in 1993 in expectation of trading losses.

(3 marks)

(c)   [Not reproduced as this part of the question is no longer within the syllabus.]   **(6 marks)**
(Total 30 marks)

---

22   (Question 2 of examination)

Lewes Holdings plc is an international group whose principal activities are the manufacture of air-conditioning systems, the supply of packaging products and automated manufacturing systems. The draft consolidated financial statements for the year ended 31 December 1994 together with supporting extracts are set out below.

Consolidated profit and loss account of the Lewes Group for the year ended 31 December

	£m	1994 £m	1993 £m
Turnover (Note 1)			
Continuing operations		2,928.6	1,966.3
Acquisitions		453.2	–
		3,381.8	1,966.3
Operating costs		(3,168.7)	(1,843.7)
Operating profit			
Continuing operations	183.2		
Acquisitions	29.9		
		213.1	122.6
Costs of restructuring UK subsidiaries		(18.9)	–
Profit on ordinary activities before interest		194.2	122.6
Income from associated undertakings		6.0	4.6
Interest		(23.9)	(5.6)
Profit on ordinary activities before tax		176.3	121.6
Tax on profit on ordinary activities		(42.4)	(25.4)
Profit on ordinary activities after tax		133.9	96.2
Dividends			
On preference shares		(4.2)	(4.2)
On ordinary shares		(61.1)	(35.0)
Retained profit transferred to reserves		68.6	57.0
EPS		16p	14p

Consolidated balance sheet of the Lewes Group as at 31 December

	1994 £m	1993 £m
Fixed assets		
Intangible assets	252.5	0.5
Tangible assets	438.5	277.0
Investments		
Associate	6.7	1.3
Other listed investments	7.4	0.5
	705.1	279.3

Current assets		
Stocks	259.8	129.5
Debtors	966.9	574.7
Investments	31.6	28.5
Cash at bank	165.1	108.7
	1,423.4	841.4
Creditors: Amounts falling due within one year	(1,186.2)	(691.4)
Net current assets	237.2	150.0
Total assets less current liabilities	942.3	429.3
Creditors: Amounts falling due after more than one year	(212.4)	(97.3)
Provisions for liabilities and charges	(36.5)	(6.8)
	693.4	325.2
Capital and reserves		
Called up share capital		
Ordinary shares (20p each)	172.7	148.0
9% Preference shares (£1 each)	47.0	47.0
Share premium account	9.9	9.2
Revaluation reserve	33.5	27.0
Other reserve – distributable	43.9	43.9
Merger reserve	247.4	–
Capital redemption reserve	0.6	0.6
Profit and loss account (Note 2)	138.4	49.5
	693.4	325.2

Notes

(1)   *Group turnover and profit on ordinary activities before tax*

(a)   Analysis by geographical area by destination

	1994		1993	
	Turnover £m	Profit £m	Turnover £m	Profit £m
United Kingdom	1,892.3	133.3	1,191.5	137.5
Continental Europe	260.8	21.4	201.9	15.4
North America				
USA	1,002.2	36.9	396.2	(15.3)
Canada	160.1	6.8	121.3	(3.9)
Other areas	66.4	3.5	55.4	3.1
	3,381.8	201.9	1,966.3	136.8
Central items, including interest and investment income		(25.6)		(15.2)
	3,381.8	176.3	1,966.3	121.6

(b)   Analysis by class of business

	1994		1993	
	Turnover £m	Profit £m	Turnover £m	Profit £m
Manufacturing	1,041.4	65.5	533.4	60.1
Distribution	489.0	51.0	268.5	34.7

Automated manufacturing systems				
UK and Europe	889.2	48.3	666.7	56.3
North America	962.2	37.1	497.7	(14.3)
	3,381.8	201.9	1,966.3	136.8
Central items, including interest and investment income		(25.6)		(15.2)
	3,381.8	176.3	1,966.3	121.6

(2)   *Profit and loss account*

	£m
Opening balance	49.5
Retained profit for year	68.6
Foreign exchange adjustments	20.3
Profit and loss account	138.4

(3)   *Goodwill*

Goodwill arose on the acquisitions in the year as follows:

	£m
Fair value of consideration	385.4
Fair value of assets (Note 4)	(133.6)
Total goodwill	251.8

(4)   *Values of assets and liabilities of companies acquired on 1 January 1994*

	£m
Fixed assets	
Intangible assets	0.3
Tangible assets	92.5
	92.8
Current assets	
Stocks	117.8
Debtors	197.0
Cash at bank	23.8
	338.6
Creditors: Amounts falling due within one year	
Bank overdrafts	(35.6)
Other creditors	(245.7)
Net current assets	57.3
Total assets less current liabilities	150.1
Creditors: Amounts falling due after more than one year	(11.4)
Provisions for liabilities and charges	(5.1)
	133.6

Note that no acquisitions in 1994 have been merger accounted.

Required:

(a) (i) Explain briefly the principal aim of the financial review section of an operating and financial review prepared in accordance with the ASB Statement *Operating and financial review*.

(ii) Explain briefly the matters that should be considered when discussing capital structure and treasury policy.

(5 marks)

(b) (i) Draft a brief report for an existing shareholder who was concerned that earnings per share in 1994 had risen by only 14% although turnover had increased by more than 70% and who is considering whether to sell his shareholding in Lewes plc.

(ii) State any additional information arising from a review of the information given in the question that would assist the investor in making a hold or sell decision.

(18 marks)

(c) [Not reproduced as this part of the question is no longer within the syllabus.]

(7 marks)

(Total 30 marks)

Section B – TWO questions ONLY to be attempted

---

23   (Question 3 of examination)

Strained plc supplies office equipment. It has expanded rapidly and its working capital has been under increasing pressure. An extract from the balance sheet as at 31 March 1994 appeared as follows:

	£m
Ordinary shares	4.95
Share premium	5.50
Profit and loss account	4.40
Loans repayable 1.4.96	13.75
Net current liabilities	5.50

In order to obtain funds the company has entered into the following transactions:

(a) On 1 April 1994 the company issued £2,000,000 7% redeemable preference shares at a premium of 20p per share paying issue costs of £100,000. The shares are redeemable on 31 March 2004 for £1.25 per share.

(b) On 1 April 1994 the company borrowed £5m under an agreement to pay interest of 7% on 31 March 1995, 10% on 31 March 1996 and a final payment of interest and capital totalling £5,514,000 on 31 March 1997.

(c) On 1 April 1994 the company entered into an agreement to sell its vehicles to SFC Finance plc for £10m and to lease the vehicles back on an operating lease for four years at £1m per year, payable in arrears. At the date of the agreement the net book value of the vehicles was £8m and their fair value was £8.5m. Assume an interest rate of 10%.

Annuity table extract: Present value of £1 per year for each of t years $= 1/r - 1/[r(1+r)^t]$

Number of years	*Interest rate per year*		
	8%	*10%*	*12%*
1	0.926	0.909	0.893
2	1.783	1.736	1.713
3	2.577	2.487	2.402
4	3.312	3.170	3.037
5	3.993	3.791	3.605

(d) On 1 March 1995 the company entered into a factor arrangement with Blue Factors plc whereby Blue Factors plc administered the company's sales ledger. During March 1995 Blue Factors plc made payments to Strained plc of £45m which represented 90% of the debtors as at 31 March 1995. Strained plc have eliminated the debtors from the balance sheet and show Blue Factors plc as a debtor for £1m representing the balance of the total debtors for which Strained plc had not received cash.

Required

(a)   (i)   Prepare an analysis of shareholders' funds immediately following the issue of the redeemable preference shares with an explanation for the treatment of each of the items included within the shareholders' funds.

       (ii)   Calculate the *total* finance cost of the redeemable preference shares and explain how this would be allocated to accounting periods in the company's profit and loss account.   **(6 marks)**

       (Note: You are not required to calculate each year's profit and loss account charge.)

(b)   Calculate the carrying amount of the loan of £5m in the balance sheets as at 31 March 1995 and 1996 assuming that the overall effective rate of interest was 9% and explain the reasoning for the proposed accounting treatment.   **(5 marks)**

(c)   Calculate the profit and loss account and balance sheet entries arising from the vehicle sale and leasing transaction for the year ended 31 March 1995 and explain the reasoning for the entries.

       (5 marks)

(d)   Give details of any further information that you would require in order to be able to advise the directors of Strained plc whether the proposed treatment of the transaction with Blue Factors plc is acceptable.   **(4 marks)**
       (Total 20 marks)

---

24   (Question 4 of examination)

The Pensoft Group operates a defined benefit pension scheme for its employees in the UK, the Pensoft Pension Scheme, whereby contributions are charged to the profit and loss account so as to spread the costs of pensions over employees' working lives with the employer. Contributions are determined by a qualified actuary on the basis of triennial valuations.

The group makes up its accounts to 31 December and the following information is available at 31 December 1994 relating to the scheme:

Pensoft plc made a contribution of £9m to the Pensoft Pension Scheme fund in 1993.

In 1994 the triennial actuarial valuation of the fund's assets exceeded the valuation of the fund's liabilities, by £9m based on the assumption that the average remaining service life of employees was eight years. As a result, the company has been advised that it can either take a one year contribution holiday in 1994 or reduce its contributions by £3m from 1994 to 1996.

Required

(a)   Explain the problems in accounting for a defined benefit scheme.   **(5 marks)**

(b)   Calculate the charge to the profit and loss account and the balance sheet entries for the two years ending 31 December 1994 and 1995 on the assumption that Pensoft plc:

       (i)   takes a contribution holiday;
       (ii)   makes reduced contributions for three years.

       (Ignore discounting.)   **(6 marks)**

(c)   Comment, with reasons, on the acceptability of the proposed accounting treatment of the following:

       It is established in connection with the £9m surplus that £6m of that figure arose from a significant reduction in the number of employees.

       Pensoft plc proposes to make reduced contributions as in (b)(ii) above and to treat both the £6m and balance of £3m in the same way.   **(3 marks)**

(d)   [Not reproduced as this part of the question is no longer within the syllabus.]   **(6 marks)**
       (Total 20 marks)

25 (Question 5 of examination)

(a) Discuss the potential benefits of greater harmonisation of international accounting policies and disclosure requirements, and comment on the obstacles hindering its progress.

(6 marks)

(b) (i) Explain why you think each of the adjustments has been made in the statement for Stateside plc reconciling UK to US GAAP as at 31 May 1995:

Income statement adjustments

	£m
Net profit per UK GAAP	100
US GAAP Adjustments (assumed net of tax)	
Capitalised interest amortised	(5)
Deferred tax	(40)
Elimination of results prior to merger	(150)
Acquisition accounting – additional depreciation and amortisation of goodwill	(200)
Estimated reported loss as adjusted to accord with US GAAP	(295)

(ii) Explain whether the equity as reported per UK GAAP will be increased or decreased when reconciled to the equity as adjusted to accord with US GAAP for the items in (b)(i).

(iii) Explain the effect on the equity of a proposed final dividend which under US GAAP has to be included in the year in which the directors propose to pay the dividends. **(9 marks)**

(c) Assuming that the fixed assets were revalued from £20m to £30m on 1 June 1993 at which date they had a remaining life of 10 years and disposed of for £40m on 31 May 1995.

(i) Show the accounting treatment in the accounts for 1994 and 1995 of the revaluation and disposal of fixed assets in accordance with FRS 3 (note that a full year's depreciation is charged in 1994 and 1995); and

(ii) Explain the reasons why the ASB required such accounting treatment. **(5 marks)**

(Total 20 marks)

ANSWERS TO JUNE 1995 EXAMINATION

21   (Answer 1 of examination)

Examiner's comments and marking guide

Question 1: tested technical competence in preparing and presenting consolidated financial statements for financial reporting purposes applying legal and professional requirements relating to form and content; applying appropriate standards eg, FRS 2 and FRS 3; clarifying information on the client entity which would be needed in identifying their regulatory obligations. The vertical group consolidation gained high marks for any well prepared student. A number of candidates who were clearly familiar with the general consolidation process were less able to deal with the sub-subsidiary aspect of the question. Part 1(a)(i) and (ii) examined the preparation of a Consolidated Profit and Loss Account and Balance Sheet for a UK group with a parent and two subsidiaries with a direct and an indirect holding including adjustments for the elimination of inter-company sales of stock and fixed assets, unrealised profit in stock and fixed assets, depreciation and minority interest.

Good answers supported these accounts with appropriate workings in columnar, double entry or written format.

Major defects were the incorrect elimination of inter-company items; errors in calculating the goodwill for Kiwi with many ignoring the fact that it was an indirect interest; omission or miscalculation of the minority interest in the Consolidated Profit and Loss Account, eg, including the balance sheet amounts calculating minority based on the retained profits carried forward or profit before tax. A small number included Madeira in the main consolidation but although this took up time it did not affect marks awarded.

Part 1 (b) examined the accounting treatment for discontinued businesses in accordance with FRS 3. There were many good answers. Weaker answers still treated the discontinuance as an extraordinary item.

Good answers referred to FRS 3 and stated the key conditions for discontinuance treatment but few referred to the results of Madeira plc to any extent.

		Available marks	*Rubric marks*
(a)	Consolidated profit and loss account	14	
	Consolidated balance sheet	10	21
(b)	Discontinued schedule	4	3
(c)	Audit points	8	6
		36	30

Step by step answer plan

Step 1   Read the question again and make sure that you focus on precisely what is required. The first question on the paper almost invariably examines some aspect of group accounts. The important clues are in the additional information. Points (1) and (2) reveal that this is a complex group and points (3) to (5) describe intra-group transactions. There is also a further subsidiary which may qualify as a discontinued operation.

Read the requirement carefully. Part (a) concerns the main group; part (b) concerns the discontinued operation.

Step 2   Establish the group structure.

Step 3   Calculate the adjustments for the intra-group transactions (workings (a) to (d)). This will enable you to complete most of the profit and loss account.

Step 4   Set up a columnar working for the profit and loss account and complete it as far as profit after tax.

Step 5   Calculate minority interest (e) and retained profits brought forward (f). Then complete the profit and loss account.

Step 6   Do the main consolidation workings: goodwill (g); and minority interest (i).

Step 7   Calculate liabilities (h) and complete the top half of the balance sheet.

Step 8   Calculate retained profits carried forward (TN1) and complete the bottom half of the balance sheet.

Step 9   Re-read part (b) of the question and then complete it.

Items not required by the Examiner for this question: inclusion of Madeira (the discontinued operation) in the consolidation in part (a).

The examiner's answer

(a)   (i)   **Consolidated profit and loss account of the Exotic Group**
for the year ended 31 December 1994

	£'000	£'000
Turnover		92,120
Cost of sales		(27,915)
Gross profit		64,205
Distribution costs		(7,362)
Administrative expenses		(6,325)
Operating profit		50,518
Interest		(325)
Profit on ordinary activities before tax		50,193
Taxation		(17,931)
Profit on ordinary activities after tax		32,262
Minority interest		(3,714)
Profit available for distribution		28,548
Dividends proposed		(9,500)
Retained profit for the year		19,048
Retained profits brought forward		
Exotic plc	20,013	
Melon plc	10,701	
Kiwi plc	6,846	
		37,560
		56,608

(ii)   **Consolidated balance sheet for the Exotic Group as at 31 December 1994**

	£'000
Fixed assets	72,787
Current assets	19,446
Current liabilities	(23,134)
Minority interest	(8,454)
	60,645

Share capital and reserves	
Ordinary shares	8,000
Profit and loss account	
(56,608,000 – 2,667,000 – 1,296,000)	52,645
	60,645

WORKINGS FOR CONSOLIDATED PROFIT AND LOSS ACCOUNT

	Exotic plc £'000	Melon plc £'000	Kiwi plc £'000		(Dr)/Cr £'000	CPL £'000
Turnover	45,600	24,700	22,800	(a)	(740)	
				(c)	(240)	92,120
Cost of sales	(18,050)	(5,463)	(5,320)	(a)	740	
				(c)	200	(27,893)
Provision/stock		(15)	(15)	(b)		(30)
Depreciation adjustment		8		(d)		8
Gross profit	27,510	19,230	17,465			64,205
Distribution costs	3,325	2,137	1,900			(7,362)
Administrative expenses	3,475	950	1,900			(6,325)
Operating profit	20,710	16,143	13,665			50,518
Interest paid	325					(325)
Profit before tax	20,385	16,143	13,665			50,193
Tax on profit on ordinary activities	8,300	5,390	4,241			(17,931)
Profit on ordinary activities after tax	12,085	10,753	9,424			32,262
Minority interest			[10% + 28%]	(e)	3,714	(3,714)
						28,548
Dividends – proposed	9,500					(9,500)
Retained profit for year	2,585	10,753	9,424			19,048
Retained profit brought forward	20,013	13,315	10,459	(f)		37,560
Retained profit carried forward	22,598	24,068	19,883			56,608

(a)   **Elimination of inter-company sales from turnover and cost of sales**

	£'000
Kiwi	480
Melon	260
	740

(b)   **Elimination of unrealised profit on stock**

	£'000
Kiwi 20% of £75,000	15
Melon 25% of £60,000	15
	30

(c)   **Elimination of unrealised profit on fixed asset**

	£'000
Sale price to Melon plc	240
Cost price to Exotic plc	(200)
Unrealised profit	40

(d)   **Adjust for depreciation on inter-company fixed asset sale**

	£'000
20% of sales price	48
20% of cost price	(40)
Excess depreciation	8

(e)   **Minority interest**

	£'000
Melon 10% of £10,753,000	1,075
Kiwi 28% of £9,424,000	2,639
	3,714

(f)   **Profit and loss account balance brought forward**

	£'000
Exotic plc	20,013
Melon plc 90% of (13,315,000 – 1,425,000)	10,701
Kiwi plc 90% of 80% of (10,459,000 – 950,000)	6,846
	37,560

WORKINGS FOR CONSOLIDATED BALANCE SHEET

	Exotic plc £'000	Melon plc £'000	Kiwi plc £'000		(Dr)/Cr £'000	CBS £'000
Fixed assets (NBV)	35,483	24,273	13,063	(c)	(40)	
				(d)	8	72,787
Investments						
Shares in Melon plc	6,650			(g)		2,667
Shares in Kiwi plc		3,800		(g)		1,296
Current assets	1,568	9,025	8,883	(b)	(30)	19,446
Current liabilities	13,063	10,023	48	(h)	(9,500)	(13,634)
Exotic plc dividend				(h)		(9,500)
Minority interest				(i)		(8,454)
	30,638	27,075	21,898			64,608
Share capital and reserves						
Ordinary shares	8,000	3,000	2,000			8,000
Profit and loss account	22,638	24,075	19,898			56,608
	30,638	27,075	21,898			64,608

(g)   **Goodwill on acquisition**

Melon plc investment in Kiwi plc

(*Note:* Exotic's indirect investment in Kiwi plc is 90% × 80% = 72% minority interest is 28%.)

	£'000	£'000
Investment 90% of £3,800,000		3,420
Less: Shares (72% of £2,000,000)	1,440	
Preacquisition reserves (72% of £950,000)	684	
		2,124
Goodwill		1,296

Exotic plc investment in Melon plc

	£'000	£'000
Investment		6,650
Less: Shares (90% of £3,000,000)	2,700	
Preacquisition reserves (90% of £1,425,000)	1,283	
		3,983
Goodwill		2,667

	£'000
Goodwill – Melon in Kiwi	1,296
Goodwill – Exotic in Melon	2,667
	3,963

(h)   **Current liabilities**

	£'000	£'000	£'000	£'000
Current liabilities	13,063	10,023	48	
Less: Dividends	9,500			
	3,563	10,023	48	
Total				13,634
Dividends				9,500

(i)   **Minority interest**

In Kiwi plc (28%)

	£'000
Ordinary share capital 28% of £2,000,000	560
Reserves 28% of (19,898,000 –15,000)	5,567
	6,127
Less: Cost of investment 10% of £3,800,000	(380)
	5,747

In Melon plc (10%)

	£'000
Ordinary share capital 10% of £3,000,000	300
Reserves 10% of (24,075,000 + 8,000 – 15,000)	2,407
	2,707
Total minority interest (5,747,000 + 2,707,000) =	8,454

(b) **Madeira plc**

The results will appear under discontinued operations.

The entries will be as follows:

	Discontinued operations £'000
Turnover	2,000
Cost of sales	(2,682)
Less: 1993 provision	500
Gross loss	(182)
Operating expenses	(118)
Operating loss	(300)
Loss on termination of discontinued operations	(348)
Loss on ordinary activities before tax	(648)

Applying the FRS 3 Example 1 format, the results would appear as follows:

	£'000
Turnover	2,000
Operating loss	
Discontinued operations	(800)
Less 1993 provision	500
	(300)
Loss on termination of discontinued operations	(348)
Loss on ordinary activities before tax	(648)

Did you answer the question?

The requirement was to show how Madeira would appear in the financial statements. This answer shows both the accounting entries in the profit and loss account and the actual presentation required by FRS 3 Example Format 1. It would also have been possible to use Example Format 2.

Tutorial note

The Examiner's answer calculates retained profit carried forward in three stages: retained profit brought forward, plus retained profit for the year, less goodwill. It is possible to 'prove' the calculation as follows:

	£'000	£'000
Exotic plc (22,638 – 40)		22,598
Melon plc: At the year-end (24,075 – 15 + 8)	24,068	
At acquisition	(1,425)	
Group share (90%)	22,643	20,379
Kiwi plc: At the year-end (19,898 – 15)	19,883	
At acquisition	(950)	
Group share (72%)	18,933	13,631
		56,608
Less: goodwill (fully amortised) (2,667 + 1,296)		(3,963)
		52,645

---

22 (Answer 2 of examination)

Examiner's comments and marking guide

Question 2: tested technical knowledge of regulatory pronouncements; interpreting and analysing accounts and supporting data for indications of aspects of business performance; drawing appropriate inferences and conclusions; developing proposals based on analysis; presenting a report taking into account the needs and wishes of the client identifying any adverse implications of the financial position or aspects of performance which have a wider implication when assessing inherent audit risk.

Overall, the report writing was generally at a lower level than the technical competence shown in question 1. Performance was only average mainly because candidates failed to devise an answer plan and failed to spend some time evaluating the given information – this would have greatly improved the quality and relevance of their answers. In general, there was too little structure to the reports and too much random comment. There were of course some excellent answers which demonstrated, often quite briefly and concisely, an understanding of the information and its relevance. Report writing is a competence that is at the core of the syllabus and candidates should continue to develop their skills in this area.

Part (a) examined awareness of the Operating and Financial Review (OFR) and the type of information that would be available to a report writer in addition to the profit and loss account and balance sheet.

Part (a)(i) required a brief explanation of the aims of OFRs financial review section.

This was poorly answered with candidates either having no knowledge of the OFR or some knowledge but relating their answer to the OFR in general rather than the Financial Review section; or confused it with the ASB's Statement of Principles or with other FREDs and standards; or confused it with audit analytical review.

Part (a)(ii) was poorly answered with many candidates basing their answers on a general knowledge of capital structures and gearing.

Part (b) required candidates to prepare a brief report on the performance and condition of an international group for the benefit of a concerned shareholder who has focused on the considerable disparity between the percentage increase in turnover and in EPS between the current and previous year.

The group had three core activities operating in three geographical locations in the UK, the US and Europe; it had undergone considerable change during the year under review through acquisition and internal restructuring. The

---

information provided consisted of the draft consolidated profit and loss account and balance sheet with supporting notes on segments, exchange adjustments, goodwill and asset/liability values of companies acquired.

Good answers refuted the suggestion that change in turnover must always result in a similar change in EPS and showed the components of the EPS calculation; pinpointed the principal causes of the lack of correlation for 1993 and 1994 in so far as the data allowed; summarised the operating performance and financial condition and changes therein of the group for the current year and compared with the previous year in the light of significant changes during 1994; focused on significant areas of profitability which impacted directly on the Turnover/EPS problem, the capital structure exchanges and consequences and liquidity/solvency factors.

Weaker candidates showed poor interpretational skills making inadequate use of the specific data contained in the question and producing unstructured, almost incoherent, narrative that focused on a few points which were repeated and recycled without conclusion; or lists of ratios unsupported by a structured report and ignoring the need to consider the Turnover/EPS concern; or were too brief; or in part (b)(ii) produced additional inferences rather than identified additional information.

			Available marks	Rubric marks
(a)	(i)	OFR aim	3	
	(ii)	Discussion - 1 per point	4	5
(b)	(i)	Report	14	
	(ii)	Additional information	6	18
(c)		Assess audit risk	9	7
			36	30

Step by step answer plan

Step 1 Read the question again and make sure that you focus on precisely what is required. There is a lot of information, so it is particularly important to look at the requirements. Although the bulk of the available marks are for 'interpretation', the question is asking you to do very specific things.

Step 2 Approach part (a) (i) by writing short paragraphs. Note that the key requirement words are *explain briefly*.

Step 3 Answer part (a) (ii) by writing short paragraphs on capital structure and treasury policy in turn. Again, the requirement is *explain briefly*.

Step 4 Start part (b) (i) by looking at the information in the question and by calculating a selection of ratios.

Step 5 Write the report. First interpret the general picture and then move to the specific items affecting profitability: new acquisitions, restructuring, capital gearing. Finally explain the significance of the segmental information.

Step 6 Answer part (b) (ii) by stating and explaining additional information required in respect of new acquisitions and liquidity in turn.

Step 7 Write a conclusion.

Items not required by the Examiner for this question:

- general discussion of the Operating and Financial Review;
- discussion of the Statement of Principles.

The examiner's answer

(a) (i) The principal aim of the financial review section is to explain to the user of the annual report the capital structure of the business, its treasury policy and the dynamics of its financial position – its sources of liquidity and their application, including the implications of the financing arising from its capital expenditure plans.

The discussion should concentrate on matters of significance to the position of the business as a whole. It should be a narrative commentary supported by figures where these assist understanding of the policies and their effect in practice.

(ii)   Specific matters that should be addressed when discussing capital structure and treasury policy include:

Discuss the capital structure in terms of maturity profile of debt, type of capital instruments used, currency, and interest rate structure including comments on relevant ratios such as interest cover and debt/equity ratios.

The *policies* and *objectives* covering the management of the maturity profile of borrowings, exchange rate and interest rate risk and the implementation of such policies in the period under review in terms of:

–   the manner in which the treasury activities are controlled;

–   the use of financial instruments for hedging purposes;

–   the extent to which foreign currency net investments are hedged by currency borrowings and other hedging instruments;

–   the currencies in which borrowings are made and in which cash and cash equivalents are held;

–   the extent to which borrowings are at fixed interest rates;

–   the purpose and effect of major financing transactions undertaken up to the date of approval of the financial statements;

–   the effect of interest costs on profits and the potential impact of interest rate changes.

Did you answer the question?

This part of the answer is taken almost directly from the Operating and Financial Review itself. However, notice that it does meet the requirement. Only 5 marks are available for part (a), so clearly the Examiner is not expecting a lot of detail.

(b)   (i)   **Report to an existing shareholder**

To:

From:

Re: Performance of the Lewes Group   Date: 15 June 1995

In accordance with your instructions we have reviewed the consolidated profit and loss account and balance sheet of the Lewes Group as at 31 December 1994 and certain supporting notes in relation to your concern that a substantial increase in turnover was not reflected in the earnings per share for 1994.

Did you answer the question?

This introductory paragraph is important because it indicates that the answer is in report format.

Profitability

Although the profit on ordinary activities has increased by 45% from £121,600,000 to £176,300,000 in 1994, the percentage of profit on ordinary activities to turnover has actually fallen from 6.2% in 1993 (121.6/1,966.3 × 100) to 5.2% in 1994 (176.3/3,381.8 × 100).

A key question is whether it is because the operations of the group have become less profitable that the above ratio fell. The fall therefore needs to be evaluated taking account of the changes that have occurred during 1994 ie, the acquisitions, the restructuring costs and increased gearing.

The operating profit to turnover percentage has improved slightly from 6.2% in 1993 (122.6/1,966.3 × 100) to 6.3% in 1994 (213.1/3,381.8 × 100) indicating that, at the group level, operating does not appear to have become less efficient or to have suffered from cost increases that it could not pass on to customers.

Did you answer the question?

Notice that the answer immediately addresses the specific concern of the reader; the fall in profitability relative to the increase in turnover. All the ratios calculated relate to profitability in some way.

We then considered the impact of new acquisitions, restructuring costs and increased gearing on the profit before tax percentage.

New acquisition

The turnover and operating costs of the new acquisitions have been given so that we can calculate the impact on the operating profit percentage. From these we see that the new business is producing an operating profit slightly higher than the consolidated business ie, 6.6% (29.9/453.2 × 100), however this has had no significant effect on the group's overall results.

Restructuring costs

Exceptional costs of £18.9m have been incurred in 1994. Prior to FRS 3 these might well have been disclosed as extraordinary and not had an impact on the earnings per share figure. However, they are now classified as exceptional and an EPS figure is required to be disclosed after deducting such costs. However, in recognition of the fact that they are non-recurring, a number of companies disclose two EPS figures – one in accordance with FRS 3 and a further company defined figure that would exclude such exceptional items.

The EPS figure adjusted for restructuring costs is 18.3p [16 × ((133.9 − 4.2) + 18.9)/129.7]. This shows an increase of 31% over the 1993 figure.

Did you answer the question?

Notice that very few ratios are presented, but that they are all relevant to the central concern of the reader. Notice also that one of them is an alternative measure of EPS. This is particularly appropriate because the draft profit and loss account shows the information required under FRS 3 and because the reader is specifically concerned with EPS.

Capital gearing

The amounts falling due after more than one year have increased from £97.3m in 1993 to £212.4m in 1994. There is a consequent increase in the interest charged from £5.6m in 1993 to £23.9m in 1994. The percentage increase in the interest far exceeds the change in the level of debt at the respective year ends which may indicate that the debt has increased from a low level at the beginning of 1993 and/or the interest rates have increased. Also some of the interest may relate to a seasonal overdraft that does not appear in the year end balance sheet.

When preference share capital is included in the debt figure, the debt to equity ratio was 52% in 1993 [(97.3 + 47.0)/(325.2 − 47.0) × 100] falling to 40% in 1994 [(212.4 + 47.0)/(693.4 − 47.0) × 100].

The effect of the increased borrowings has been to increase the interest charge but, because the ROCE is greater than the rate of interest, the earnings available for distribution in 1994 have increased and the change has been to the advantage of the equity shareholders.

The above comments are based on the consolidated profit and loss account and balance sheet. Any decision on realising your investment should also take into account future prospects. In assessing these, the segmental information can be helpful.

> **Did you answer the question?**
>
> Notice that gearing is only covered because of its effect on profit. The answer does not discuss gearing in terms of liquidity or solvency.

The significance of the segmental information

The geographical analysis shows that the group is diversifying into overseas markets. In 1994 56% of the turnover arose in the UK and 30% in the USA which is a material change from the position in 1993 when 60% of the turnover was from the UK and 20% from the USA.

The profit percentage on UK sales has fallen from 11.5% in 1993 (137.5/1,191.5 × 100) to 7% in 1994 (133.3/1,892.3 × 100). There could be a number of possible reasons for this change of 4.5% eg, the exceptional restructuring cost of £18.9m related to UK subsidiaries.

Also, the increase in the UK turnover by 59% [(1,892.3 − 1,191.5)/1,191.5] might be related to the fall in profitability eg, a conscious decision to reduce margins stimulated demand.

The profit percentage on US sales has improved from a loss in 1993 of 4% to a profit of 4% in 1994. The majority of the US turnover was derived from automated manufacturing systems and the profit per cent on these appears to be lower in the US at 4% than in UK and Europe where it is 5%.

The segmental analysis indicates that the group has diversified geographically and in classes of business with entry into the US market and that it has successfully addressed the losses that were occurring in the US in 1993.

However, it is important to note that despite the decline in UK profitability and the improvement in the US profitability, the UK operations are still more profitable than the US operations.

> **Did you answer the question?**
>
> The fact that a segmental report has been included in the question is a fairly clear indication that the answer must use that information.

(ii)   **Additional information**

The following additional information would be helpful in considering whether to hold or sell the investment in Lewes plc.

(1)   *New acquisitions*

The net assets acquired (other than goodwill) indicate that the group has acquired net assets that represent 40% of the pre-acquisition net assets (133.6/325.2 × 100). For certain individual classes of asset it represents a significant addition in relation to its pre-acquisition size eg, the acquired stock of £117.8m was 90% of the 1993 group stock figure at 31 December 1993.

An important consideration is the relative size of the goodwill as this alone represents 77% of the pre-acquisition net assets (251.8/325.2 × 100) which raises the question as to the extent to which this represents a payment to gain control rather than a valuable asset that would result in the generation of future profits. In this context, it would be useful to review the financial statements of the acquired business for prior years to identify trends in turnover, product mix and profits and to ascertain from the management of Lewes plc the reason for the acquisition.

Restructuring costs were incurred in 1994 which reduced the EPS for that year. The likelihood and extent of restructuring costs arising from the new acquisition might have a similar depressing effect on future years. Conversely restructuring may be complete and future earnings may be increased by the absence of such costs.

Goodwill of £251.8m has been capitalised and is now included in intangible fixed assets. This means that profit on ordinary activities will be reduced in future years as a result of amortisation charges. The useful economic life of the goodwill is not known and therefore it is difficult to quantify the effect on profit, but the amortisation charge might be approximately £25m per annum (10% of the goodwill). The effect on profit in future years will depend on any increase in future profits arising from the acquisition. The return from the acquisition (29.9/133.6 or 385.4) is much lower than the overall ROCE, and is thus depressing profitability, however, this may be partly due to the fact that under acquisition accounting the 1994 results may not include a full year's profit from the acquired company(ies) ie, they would only include post-acquisition profits.

(2)　　*Liquidity*

At the working capital level, the current ratio has remained at 1.2:1 in 1993 and 1994 and the acid-test ratio has remained at approximately 1:1.

However, at the financing level, the long-term liability has more than doubled and there are issued preference shares.

Further information is required as to the maturity dates of the loans, the redemption terms for the preference shares (if any) and any capital commitments for fixed assets.

The significance for the investor is that Lewes plc might be looking to making a rights issue in the near future if operating cash flows are not sufficient to meet any investment or financing outflows.

Did you answer the question?

Notice the way in which part (ii) of the answer considers not only what has happened, but what may happen in the future. This is important because the hold or sell decision is concerned with future earnings. Again, liquidity is only covered because of its possible implications for future earnings.

Conclusion

On the information provided, the Lewes Group is expanding and diversifying internationally and by class of business. The group is expanding its automated manufacturing systems business with an increase of 60% in turnover [((889.2 + 962.2) – (666.7 + 497.7))/(666.7 + 497.7)]. This produced a slightly lower rate of profit but there appears to be an increasing market. Previous losses in North America have been eliminated and the group has made significant acquisitions in 1994. In deciding whether to hold or sell, much will depend upon the investor's assessment of the management skills of the Lewes management in integrating the new acquisitions and improving profit levels.

In addition, the investor would take into account the possibility that there might be an early need for a rights issue.

Did you answer the question?

Given that the answer must be in report form, the conclusion is essential. Notice that it develops from the main part of the answer, rather than introducing new points at this stage.

(Tutorial Notes:

This question and answer have been amended slightly to reflect the changes to the accounting treatment of goodwill introduced by FRS 10 'Goodwill and intangible assets'.

The Examiner's Answer discusses the return from the acquisition compared to overall ROCE. In practice, there are several possible calculations:

	Acquisition	Group 1994	Group 1993
$\dfrac{\text{Operating profit}}{\text{Capital employed}}$	$\dfrac{29.9}{150.1} = 19.9\%$	$\dfrac{213.1}{942.3} = 22.6\%$	$\dfrac{122.6}{429.3} = 28.6\%$
$\dfrac{\text{Operating profit}}{\text{Net assets employed}}$	$\dfrac{29.9}{133.6} = 22.4\%$	$\dfrac{213.1}{693.4} = 30.7\%$	$\dfrac{122.6}{325.2} = 37.7\%$
$\dfrac{\text{Operating profit}}{\text{Net assets employed}}$	$\dfrac{29.9}{385.4} = 7.7\%$	$\dfrac{213.1}{693.4} = 30.7\%$	$\dfrac{122.6}{325.2} = 37.7\%$

(taking into account the effect of the goodwill)

The Examiner's Answer uses the second and third calculations, which are not based on conventional ROCE, but provided that like is compared with like, all these calculations illustrate the point being made and all are acceptable in the context of this question.)

23   (Answer 3 of examination)

Examiner's comments and marking guide

Question 3: part (a) examined FRS 4 requirements for the analysis of shareholders' funds between amounts attributable to Equity and Non-equity interests with appropriate treatment of the issue costs and the finance costs.

This part was not well answered. Common mistakes were to analyse the shareholders' funds between prior to and after the issue of the preference shares; inability to determine the net costs of redemption; overlooking the dividend.

Part (b) examined the candidates' ability to account for a loan in accordance with the requirements of FRS 4 in a situation where the terms of raising it provided for varying rates during its three years term.

Many candidates gained high marks for correct calculation and it seems that candidates have been tutored mainly on the treatment of debt with insufficient consideration given to the treatment of non-equity shares required in (a) above. Few gave reasoning for the accounting entries. A common error was the time wasted by candidates who carried on to show how the relevant transactions were to be recorded in the third year.

Part (c) examined the calculation of profit and loss account and balance sheet entries for a sale and lease back transaction under pre and post FRS 5 requirements.

This was poorly answered with a number of candidates refusing to accept that the leaseback was an operating lease and spending time debating the nature of the lease. Balance sheet entries were not attempted in the weaker answers and there was a lack of explanation.

Part (d) examined candidates' understanding of FRS 5 when related to a factoring arrangement.

This was generally well answered and many candidates made the point that the accounting has to be in accordance with the substance of the arrangement rather than its legal form and identified the treatments required under FRS 5 within alternative scenarios. The information required for determining the appropriate accounting treatment was well identified.

			Available marks	*Rubric marks*
(a)	(i)	1 mark per calculation and comment	3	
	(ii)	Calculate	2	
		Explain	3	6
(b)		1995 carrying amount	3	
		1996 carrying amount	3	5

(c)	P & L and balance sheet	4	
	Explanation	2	5
(d)	Further details	5	4
		——	——
		25	20
		——	——

Step by step answer plan

Step 1 Read the question again and make sure that you focus on precisely what is required. The references to capital instruments, sale and repurchase agreements and factoring arrangements in the scenario should tell you that this is a question about FRS 4 and FRS 5. There are four distinct parts, each relating to one of the four transactions described in the scenario. It is important to allocate your time properly. Part (a) should take about 10 minutes, parts (b) and (c) about 8 minutes each and part (d) about 7 minutes.

Step 2 Start part (a) (i) by writing a brief paragraph explaining the requirements of FRS 4 paragraphs 40 and 41. Then calculate share capital and share premium on the issue of the preference shares and prepare the analysis of shareholders' funds.

Step 3 Answer part (a) (ii) by calculating the total finance cost. Briefly explain how FRS 4 requires this to be allocated to accounting periods.

Step 4 Answer part (b) by calculating the interest charges and cash flows on the loan over its life. This will give you the carrying amounts at each of the two dates. Then briefly explain the reasoning behind your calculations.

Step 5 Read the scenario for part (c) again and determine the substance of the transaction. This will enable you to draw up and explain the profit and loss account and balance sheet entries.

Step 6 Read the scenario for part (d) again. Then analyse the transaction in terms of alternative views of its substance. Explain each of the risks of ownership and the information which would enable you to determine where they lie.

Not required by the Examiner for this question:

- calculation of the annual profit and loss account charge in part (a);
- discussion as to whether the lease in part (c) is a finance lease;
- general discussion of FRS 4 and FRS 5 without reference to the transactions described.

The examiner's answer

(a) (i) FRS 4 para 40 requires shareholders' funds to be analysed between the amount attributable to equity interests and the amount attributable to non-equity interests. The amount of shareholders' funds attributable to equity interests is the difference between total shareholders' funds and the total amount attributable to non-equity interests. Para 41 states that immediately after the issue of a non-equity instrument the amount of non-equity shareholders' funds attributable to it should be the net proceeds of the issue.

This is achieved by a two column analysis for equity and non-equity and inclusion of the premium as follows:

	Equity shareholders' interest £m	Non-equity shareholders' interest £m	Total £m
Share capital	4.95	2.0	6.95
Share premium	5.50	0.3 [0.4 – 0.1]	5.80
Profit and loss account	4.40		4.40
	——	——	——
	14.85	2.3	17.15
	——	——	——

(ii)   The finance cost of the non-equity shares is calculated as follows:

	£
Redeemable amount	2,500,000
Dividends (7% of £2,000,000) for 10 years	1,400,000
	3,900,000
Less: Net proceeds	2,300,000
Total finance cost	1,600,000

This amount will be shown as an appropriation of the company's profit and loss account at a constant rate based on the carrying amount of the preference shares.

(b)   The carrying amounts are

	£'000
31.3.95	5,100
31.3.96	5,059

They are calculated as follows:

Loan £'000	Overall effective rate interest 9% £'000	Cash paid £'000	Carrying amount £'000
5,000	450	350	5,100
5,100	459	500	5,059
5,059	455	5,514	–

The reasoning for the treatment is that the stated rate of interest does not reflect the true economic cost of borrowing in any period during the time the loan is outstanding, since low rates of interest in one period are compensated for by higher rates in another.

The payments required by the debt should be apportioned between a finance charge for any accounting period at a constant rate on the outstanding obligation and a reduction of the carrying amount. The effect of this accounting on a stepped interest loan is that an overall effective interest cost will be charged in each accounting period; an accrual will be made in addition to the cash payments in earlier periods and will reverse, partially offsetting the higher cash payments, in later periods.

Did you answer the question?

Notice that this answer does not discuss the treatment of finance costs in general. It refers to the actual transaction in the scenario.

(c)   The transaction falls within the provisions of para 47(c) of SSAP 21 *Accounting for leases and hire-purchase contracts*. However, the provisions of FRS 5 also require to be taken into account and the substance of the transaction considered.

Profit and loss entries

The company will recognise a profit on the sale of £500,000 which is equal to the fair value of £8.5m less the carrying value of £8m at the date of sale.

Prior to the issue of FRS 5, the excess of the sale price over the fair value was not regarded as a realised profit and arose because the operating lease rentals in future years were deemed also to be above fair value. The excess was therefore deferred and amortised over the period of the lease term with the net annual operating rental charged in the profit and loss account being reduced to £625,000 [£1m – (£1.5m/4)].

However, the substance would appear to be that the company has received a loan of £1,500,000 for four years on which interest will be paid. The annual payment of £1,000,000 would consequently need to be divided into three elements, namely, the capital repayment of the loan, the interest element and the operating lease payment. The profit and loss account entries will be:

	£
Interest	150,000
Operating lease payment £1,000,000 – (£1,500,000/3.170)]	526,814

Note: 3.170 is the four year annuity factor at 10%.

Balance sheet entries

The vehicles will no longer appear in the balance sheet as an asset. Prior to FRS 5 there would have been a deferred gain of £1.5m as at 1 April 1994 which would have been reduced by £375,000 per annum as it was amortised.

Under FRS 5, there will be a loan account showing the balance of the £1,500,000 as at 31 March 1995 as follows:

	£
Loan account [£1,500,000 + 150,000 – 473,186]	1,176,814

(d) The question that needs to be addressed is whether the transaction is really a sale in substance or whether it is simply a borrowing transaction with the trade debtors being used as collateral and the £4m retained by Blue Factors plc being in substance an interest charge. The overall terms of the agreement would need to be examined in aggregate. The focus is on the risks of ownership.

The two main risks associated with trade debtors are the risk of slow payment which gives rise to a finance cost and the risk of non-payment.

Risk of non-payment

The risk of non-payment is regarded as remaining with the seller if one of the terms of the agreement is that unpaid debts are sold back to the seller. In such a case the transaction is regarded as a financing transaction; the amount received from Blue Factors plc will be shown as a loan; any amounts expected under a recourse agreement will be disclosed within provisions.

Risk of slow payment

This will depend on whether the factor has assumed any substantial risk of slow payment of the debts. For example, the discount charged by the factor will normally be estimated at a rate of interest related to the time between payment to Strained plc and collection by Blue Factors plc from the debtors. If the actual time for the debtors to be collected can substantially exceed the expected time without cost to Strained plc then it may be assumed that the risk lies with the factor and there has been a sale. Otherwise it will be treated as a finance arrangement.

Did you answer the question?

Notice the way in which this answer approaches the problem. It states the alternative views of the transaction and then analyses it in terms of the main risks of ownership. We need information that will tell us which party bears those risks. Notice also that the answer refers to the specific transaction by using the names of the two companies.

---

24 (Answer 4 of examination)

Examiner's comments and marking guide

Question 4: part (a) examined candidates' understanding of the difference between a defined benefit and defined contribution pension contributions pension scheme.

This part was reasonably well attempted and most candidates could identify the schemes and outline some of the problem areas emphasising the difficulties in making assumptions, particularly in dealing with employees' earnings.

Part (b) examined the ability to prepare profit and loss accounts and balance sheet entries where triennial valuation shows a surplus and alternatives of a contribution holiday or reduced payments are envisaged. This part was an all or nothing situation. Candidates either knew the correct entries and gained high marks or did not and failed to gain many marks. A common error was to confuse the cash fund payment with the charge to the profit and loss account.

Part (c) required a comment on proposal to treat reduced contributions resulting from a reduction in the number of employees in the same way as a normal triennial adjustment by spreading the benefit over the remaining service lives of the employees.

Good answers commented on the need to recognise in the current year as it relates to employees who have left and the basis of remaining employees is not relevant. Marks were polarised as in part (b).

			Available marks	*Rubric marks*
(a)		1 per point	6	5
(b)		1 per point	7	6
(c)		1 per point	4	3
(d)	(i)	1 per point	4	
	(ii)	1 per point	4	6
			25	20

Step by step answer plan

Step 1 Read the question again and make sure that you focus on precisely what is required.

Step 2 The key requirement words in part (a) are *explain the problems*. Answer part (a) by briefly explaining the general nature of a defined benefit scheme and then move on to explain why this causes problems. Remember that only 5 marks/8 minutes are available for this part of the question.

Step 3 Start part (b) (i) by calculating the total contributions paid during the average remaining service life of the employees. This will enable you to calculate the profit and loss account charges and the balance sheet entries.

Step 4 Repeat Step 3 for part (b) (ii).

Step 5 Re-read the scenario and requirement in part (c) and then write your answer.

The examiner's answer

(a)   A defined benefit scheme is one in which the benefits to be paid on retirement are set out and the company is required to make contributions of sufficient amount to fund this liability. In the UK SSAP 24 has been formulated on the basis that neither the pension liability nor the fund asset should appear on the balance sheet. This is on the assumption that the liability, from a company reporting point of view, has been effectively discharged by the annual contributions to a pension fund.

> **Did you answer the question?**
>
> The answer starts by explaining the nature of defined benefit schemes. This is necessary in order to explain the problems of accounting for them.

Accounting for a defined benefit pension scheme has been described 'as one of the most difficult challenges for the employer companies in the whole field of financial reporting'.

The reasons for this are that:

−   the amounts involved are large;

– there is a long timescale between making contributions to build up the assets of a fund and meeting the pension liabilities;

– the process of estimation is complex and involves many uncertainties for which assumptions have to be made.

The principal assumptions involve estimating percentages for items such as the following:

	Estimate (for example)
Rate of return on new investment	9.5%
Earnings increase	7.0%
Pensions increase	5.0%
Growth of dividends	5.0%

The funding plan and pensions charge in the profit and loss account are both affected by these assumptions. For example, if the rate of return on new investments were assumed to be a lower figure than 9.5% or earnings increase higher than 7.0% then the funding requirement would be greater.

The accounting regulations attempt to smooth the impact on profits by spreading fluctuations that arise when the actuarial assumptions are varied at the triennial valuations.

This means that surpluses and deficits are spread over a number of years unless there are circumstances where it is inappropriate to carry a surplus or deficit forward eg, where it arises from a significant reduction in staff due to redundancies.

The pension cost used to be simply the amount of the contribution that an employer company paid into a scheme. Under current regulations however the pension expense for a defined benefit scheme is derived directly from actuarial valuations of the scheme and accounting regulations have been framed so as to attempt to avoid wide fluctuations in the amount of the annual charge by requiring changes in valuation to be recognised gradually by amortising them over a number of years, in theory, the remaining working lives of the employees.

Did you answer the question?

The remainder of the answer explains the reasons why the annual funding may fluctuate. This leads us to the fundamental problem; accounting for the fluctuations and applying the accruals concept, as required by SSAP 24.

(b)　　(i)　　**Accounting entries**

Profit and loss entries for 1994 and 1995

These are calculated as follows:

Number of years	Contribution £m	Total £m
1	0	0
7	9	63
		——
		63
		——

Charge for 1994 and 1995 will be £7.88m ie,(£63m/8).

Alternatively, this can be calculated as follows:

$$\text{Regular cost} - \frac{\text{Surplus}}{\text{Remaining service lives}} = £9m - \frac{£9m}{8} = £7.88m$$

Balance sheet entries

Year ended

31 December 1994	Provision £7.88m with no cash fund payment
31 December 1995	Provision £6.76m

The 1994 provision is reduced by the difference between the fund payment and the profit and loss charge ie, [£7.88 – (£9m – 7.88)].

(ii)   *Profit and loss entries for 1994 and 1995*

Number of years	Contribution £m	Total £m
3	6	18
5	9	45
		___
		63
		___

Charge for 1994 and 1995 will be £7.88m ie, (£63m/8).

Balance sheet entries

Year ended

31 December 1994	Provision £1.88m
	Being charge of £7.88m – fund payment of £6m
31 December 1995	Provision £3.76m
	Being charge of £7.88m – fund payment of £6m cumulative.

(c)   The company's proposed treatment is unacceptable. The reason for this is that SSAP 24 has been revised following the issue of FRS 3 and now states that:

'Where a significant reduction in the number of employees is related to the sale or termination of an operation, the associated pension cost or credit should be recognised immediately to the extent that it is necessary to comply with the requirements of FRS 3 para 18. In all other cases where there is a significant reduction in employees, the reduction of contributions should be recognised as it occurs.'

The reason for the differentiation is that it makes little economic sense to spread the surplus over the working lives of the employees who remain when the surplus relates to those who have left. Instead it would be available to set against provisions for costs of termination.

Did you answer the question?

Only 3 marks (about 5 minutes) are available for this part of the question. Therefore the Examiner is not expecting a lot of detail. Notice, however, that the answer does not only state the requirements of SSAP 24 and FRS 3 but explains the reasoning behind those requirements.

---

25   (Answer 5 of examination)

Examiner's comments and marking guide

Question 5: part (a) required a discussion of the potential benefits of greater harmonisation.

Candidates were well prepared for this topic and this part was generally well answered.

Part (b) examined the reasons for differences in UK and US GAAP and the effect on equity.

A number of candidates did know the differences in treatment in the US and answered this section well. However, it was generally poorly attempted and answers were confused with few attempting to give a reasoned explanation for the increase or decrease in equity.

Part (c) examined the treatment in the reconciliation to US GAAP on reported profit and equity in respect of fixed assets which had been subject to revaluation in the UK accounts.

This part was reasonably answered with the correct identification of the effect on the revaluation reserves, the depreciation in the profit and loss account and profit on disposal. Only a few candidates appreciated the significance of a Statement of Recognised Gains and Losses and the presentation of realised gains which have been recognised in a previous period. Candidates do not yet seem to be familiar with the FRS 3 requirements.

		Available marks	Rubric marks
(a)	Benefits	4	
	Obstacles	4	6
(b)		10	9
(c)		7	5
		25	20

Step by step answer plan

Step 1   Read the question again and make sure that you focus on precisely what is required. At first sight this looks like a question about international harmonisation, but part (c) is about FRS 3 and is completely separate from the rest of the question.

Step 2   Answer part (a) by writing short paragraphs, each paragraph dealing with a particular benefit or obstacle.

Step 3   Approach part (b) (i) by taking each adjustment in turn. Describe the standard UK accounting treatment. This gives you the reason for each adjustment.

Step 4   Approach part (b) (ii) in the same way, using the different accounting treatments identified in part (i).

Step 5   Answer part (b) (iii).

Step 6   Re-read the scenario for part (c). Take each of the two years in turn and briefly describe the effect on each statement/note to answer part (i).

Step 7   Answer part (c) (ii) by considering the benefits to users of financial statements of the approach in FRS 3.

Items not required by the Examiner for this question: requirements of FRS 3 not relating to the scenario in part (c).

The examiner's answer

(a)   There is no definitive answer and credit will be given for valid points raised.

Potential benefits of greater harmonisation include:

(i)   **A user's perspective**

Cross border investment is increasing and it is important that potential investors are not misled by the financial statements. For example, there could be an assumption that the liquidity position of a company that makes a full provision for deferred tax liabilities is worse than that of a company that is only required to provide an amount that is likely to crystallise as a liability.

(ii)   **A preparer's perspective**

There is an increase in the cost of preparing financial statements that need to be adjusted to comply with different national accounting standards.

Obstacles hindering greater harmonisation include:

(i)   **Different legal systems**

Countries vary in the amount of detailed legislation on accounting that has been enacted. In Europe for example this meant that prior to the issue of EC Directives accounting requirements in the UK differed substantially from those in France.

(ii)   **Different capital financing systems**

Types of business organisation and their financing differ internationally and it therefore follows that if financiers and owners differ then the primary users of accounting information will differ. The rule makers in the US and UK regard the existing and potential investors as the primary users. However, there are other ways of financing business and capital provided by banks may be very significant. In Germany and Japan the banks are important owners of companies as well as providers of debt finance. This enables them to appoint directors and they will therefore be able to obtain information other than that which is included in the published annual report.

Where there are fewer outsider shareholders external reporting has been largely for the purposes of government, as tax collectors or controllers of the economy.

(iii)   **Degree to which taxation regulations determine accounting measurements**

In some countries the tax rules are the accounting rules. For example, although depreciation in the UK differs from the capital allowance for tax purposes, in other countries the accounting depreciation is the same as the equivalent of the capital allowance for tax purposes.

(iv)   **Differences in the size and competence of the accounting/auditing profession**

The lack of a substantial body of private investors and public companies in some countries means that the need for and status of the auditors is much smaller than in the US or UK. Also there is an impact on the type of accounting that is or could be practised. Without a strong profession there is a limit to the extent to which national accounting standards can be developed.

(v)   **Environmental/cultural factors**

These include educational standards which can be an important factor in developing countries; political factors where there is central control over the accounting and reporting system and cultural factors where for example cultures that tend towards secrecy are unlikely to adopt full disclosure-based financial reporting practices.

Did you answer the question?

Notice the way in which this answer is structured. There are short paragraphs, each dealing with one benefit or obstacle. The structure makes it easy for the Examiner to appreciate that you have covered a range of points.

(b)   (i)   *Capitalised interest*

Under FRS 15 *Tangible fixed assets* companies have a choice of writing off or capitalising and amortising. Stateside plc appears to have written off interest costs. In the US the interest relating to this fixed asset would be capitalised and amortised with an amortisation charge of £5m.

Deferred tax

In the UK deferred tax will have been provided on a partial provision basis under the liability method. In the US the charge has been increased indicating that a full provision is required with an increased charge to the profit and loss account of £40m.

Merger accounting adjusted to acquisition accounting

There has been a merger during the year which has satisfied UK criteria for treatment as a merger. The adjustment indicates that this has not however satisfied the US criteria. Consequently pre-acquisition profits of £150m are eliminated on reconciliation, together with additional depreciation and amortisation of goodwill of £200m.

(ii) *Capitalised interest*

The equity will be increased by any unamortised balance outstanding.

Deferred tax

The equity will be reduced by the cumulative increase in the charge.

Merger accounting adjusted to acquisition accounting

The equity will be increased by any increase in net assets (most likely) and decreased by any decrease in net assets (unlikely) arising from fair value adjustments. The equity would also be increased by the unamortised amount of any consolidated goodwill that would arise under acquisition accounting.

(iii) **Proposed dividend**

The shareholders' equity will be increased by the amount of the proposed dividend because in the UK dividends are accounted for in the fiscal year to which they relate.

(c) (i) Year to 31.5.94: Statement of total recognised gains and losses

This will disclose the £10m gain

Year to 31.5.94: Profit and loss account

There will be a depreciation charge of £3m based on revalued amount

Year to 31.5.94: Note of historical cost profits and losses

Difference between a historical cost depreciation charge and the actual depreciation charge of the year calculated on the revalued amount   £1m

Year to 31.5.94: Revaluation reserve

A revaluation reserve of £10m will be created via the Statement of total recognised gains and losses and £1m will be transferred to realised profit

Year to 31.5.95: Note of historical cost profits and losses

Realisation of property gains	£8m
Profit and loss account profit [£40m – (£27m – £3m)]	£16m
Working note: Total = £40m – (£20m – £2m – £2m)	£24m
Difference between a historical cost depreciation charge and the actual depreciation charge of the year calculated on the revalued amount	£1m

Year to 31.5.95: Revaluation reserve

There will be a transfer from the revaluation reserve of £9m to realised profits comprising £1m excess depreciation and the £8m shown above.

(ii)   The reasons lie in the ASB's balance sheet approach to the recognition of assets, liabilities, gains and losses.

According to the Statement of Principles, recognition of a gain is triggered where a past event indicates that there has been a measurable change in assets which has not been offset by an equal change in liabilities unless the change relates to a transaction with the entity's owners, in which case a contribution from owners or distribution to owners will be recognised.

Gains which are earned but not realised are recognised in the statement of total recognised gains and loses. Gains which are realised are recognised in the profit and loss account. However, it follows from this approach that gains should not be recognised twice ie, at the point of revaluation and at the point of realisation. Once an asset has been revalued in an entity's balance sheet any subsequent transactions must be based on the balance sheet carrying amount of that asset.

The ASB has taken account of the fact that it is common practice for companies to produce modified historical cost basis and that there is currently no mandatory requirement for regular revaluations by requiring a note of historical cost profits and losses. This note will reconcile the modified profit to the pure historical cost profit where material differences exist.

The ASB stance might be seen to be at odds with the statutory approach of using historical cost accounts to determine capital maintenance and distributable profits. However, the ASB is basing its approach on the view that the income statement should be primarily concerned with the measurement of performance which can be distorted when reported figures are not related to current values. In such cases, there can be over- or under-statement of performance as measured by profits and return on assets.

Did you answer the question?

This answer covers two main reasons for the treatment: the theory behind it as set out in the Statement of Principles; and the benefits to users of the financial statements in terms of additional useful information.

(***Tutorial note:*** This question and answer have been slightly amended to reflect the changes to accounting for goodwill and tangible fixed assets introduced by FRS 10 'Goodwill and intangible assets' and FRS 15 'Tangible fixed assets'.)

DECEMBER 1995 QUESTIONS

Section A – BOTH questions are compulsory and MUST be attempted

26   (Question 1 of examination)

1   At 1 January 1994 Wales plc held 85% of the 141m £1 ordinary shares issued by Miami plc which it had acquired some years ago at a cost of £527m when the reserves of Miami plc showed a credit balance of £359m. The fair value of Miami plc's net assets was equal to their book value.

On 1 April 1994 Wales plc acquired 75% of the 300m £1 ordinary shares issued by Scotland plc at a cost of £450m and the whole of the £40m 10% debentures issued by Scotland plc at a cost of £60m.

On 1 July 1994 Wales plc sold shares in Miami plc for £575m leaving it holding a 60% interest.

The profit and loss accounts for the year ended 31 December 1994 are as follows:

	Wales plc £m	Miami plc £m	Scotland plc £m
Turnover	8,000	6,000	1,000
Cost of goods sold	(5,000)	(4,112)	(700)
Gross profit	3,000	1,888	300
Administrative expenses	(660)	(530)	(100)
Distribution costs	(1,427)	(1,001)	(80)
Operating profit	913	357	120
Interest paid/payable	(3)		(4)
Interest received from Scotland	4		
Profit on ordinary activities before tax	914	357	116
Tax	(315)	(125)	(36)
Profit on ordinary activities after tax	599	232	80
Dividends	(90)	–	–
Retained profit for the financial year	509	232	80
Profit and loss account b/f	1,000	651	106
Profit and loss account c/f	1,509	883	186

Further information

(1)   The group policy is to write off goodwill over five years, with a full year's charge in the year of acquisition.

(2)   Wales plc has not yet accounted for the sale of shares in Miami plc. Taxation on the gain is to be ignored.

(3)   Scotland plc has made sales of £60m to Wales plc in the period following the acquisition, at cost plus 25%. A quarter of the goods were still in stock at 31 December 1994.

The directors of the Wales Group have requested that the normal level of external audit work be reduced when auditing the new subsidiary, Scotland plc, on the grounds that the company employs an internal audit department.

Required

(a) (i) Prepare a consolidated profit and loss account disclosing the retained profit for the year for the Wales Group for the year ended 31 December 1994.

(ii) Calculate the brought forward and carried forward group reserves.

Work to the nearest £million. **(21 marks)**

(b) [Not reproduced as this part of the question is no longer within the syllabus.] **(6 marks)**

(c) [Not reproduced as this part of the question is no longer within the syllabus.] **(3 marks)**
(Total 30 marks)

27	**(Question 2 of examination)**

2 Bewise plc had carried on business as a furniture retailer since 1954 operating from a number of stores under short-term annual rental leases. In 1992 the company extended its product range to include domestic electrical goods. Each store was regarded as a separate profit centre and had authority to agree its own credit terms with customers including the amount of deposit required and the length of the repayment period.

In order to improve the sales per square metre of stores area, it was company policy that all store managers were paid a basic salary plus a commission based on sales.

The profit and loss accounts and balance sheets for the four years ended 31 December 1995 were as follows (note 1995's figures are a forecast):

Profit and loss accounts for the years ended 31 December

	1992	1993	1994	1995 Forecast
	£m	£m	£m	£m
Turnover	1,706	1,867	2,233	2,512
Cost of sales	(1,138)	(1,257)	(1,519)	(1,731)
Gross profit	568	610	714	781
Administrative expenses	(140)	(163)	(166)	(177)
Selling/distribution costs	(338)	(378)	(461)	(534)
Depreciation	(13)	(14)	(16)	(18)
	77	55	71	52
Investment income	2	2	2	2
Interest paid	(28)	(24)	(30)	(107)
Bad debts			(27)	(28)
Finance income from credit sales	42	45	66	101
Profit before tax	93	78	82	20
Tax	(43)	(35)	(34)	(4)
Profit after tax	50	43	48	16
Dividends	(28)	(28)	(28)	(28)
Profit/(loss) retained	22	15	20	(12)
EPS	59p	51p	56p	19p

Balance sheets as at 31 December

	1992		1993		1994		1995	
	£m	£m	£m	£m	£m	£m	£m	£m
Fixed assets		82		104		123		136
Investments		32		43		49		59
Stock	351		404		540		609	
Debtors	483		551		633		730	
Cash	47		67		41		63	
		881		1,022		1,214		1,402
		995		1,169		1,386		1,597
Share capital	85		85		85		85	
Reserves	277		292		312		300	
		362		377		397		385
Long-term loans – repayment date 2010		62		194		194		323
Creditors	239		277		269		278	
Liability to company's bank								
Short-term loans	135		135		324		324	
Overdraft (unsecured)	197		186		202		287	
		571		598		795		889
		995		1,169		1,386		1,597

The company had an agreed overdraft limit of £240m which was to be reviewed at 31 December 1995.

Required

(a) Prepare, as independent accountants, a report to the bank on 30 June 1995 to assist it in making a decision relating to a requested increase in short-term loans to Bewise plc. The report is to be supported by appropriate financial data. **(20 marks)**

(b) [Not reproduced as this part of the question is no longer within the syllabus.] **(4 marks)**

(c) [Not reproduced as this part of the question is no longer within the syllabus.] **(6 marks)**
(Total 30 marks)

Section B – TWO questions ONLY to be attempted

28   (Question 3 of examination)

3   Capital plc carried on business in four product segments, namely aircraft design, hairdressing salons, import agencies and beauty products. The directors are now considering the dividend policy and the future capital structure of the company. The draft accounts of Capital plc as at 30 November 1995 showed the following share capital and reserves:

Share capital		£m	
Ordinary shares of £1 each	Note 1	500	1·60
8% Redeemable preference shares of £1 each	Note 2	50	PAR.

Reserves – all credit balances		
Share premium		63
Capital redemption reserve		10
Fixed asset revaluation reserve	Note 3	43
Profit and loss account	Note 4	775

Notes

(1)   The market value of ordinary shares as at 30 November 1995 was £1.60.

(2)   The redeemable preference shares were issued in 1985. They are redeemable at par.

(3)   A revaluation reserve of £45m was created on 1 December 1994 on the revaluation of some of the buildings. A debit of £2m was made to the reserve in 1995 arising from a permanent fall in value on the revaluation of certain computer equipment.

(4)   The profit and loss account of Capital plc for the year ended 30 November 1995 contained the following items:

(i)   Exchange gain on a long-term German mark loan taken out
on 1 December 1994   £6m

(ii)   Depreciation based on historic cost of fixed assets   £68m

Additional depreciation based on revalued amount of fixed assets   £13m

(iii)   Development costs for the year written off   £22m

(iv)   Profit attributed to long-term contracts in beauty products   £9m

At their next meeting the directors will be considering proposals for:

(a)   the purchase 'off market' at £1.50 per share of 30% of the issued ordinary shares of Capital plc which are currently held by Venture plc, a venture capital company. The directors consider that the shares are substantially undervalued and that the company should purchase the shares and hold them as an investment classified under 'own shares' in the balance sheet;

(b)   the redemption of the preference shares;

(c)   the distribution to the shareholders of Capital plc of shares in Kind plc, which have been held as an investment (the investment appears at cost, £15m, in the balance sheet and the directors estimate that it has a market value of £24m at 30 November 1995);

(d)   a bonus issue of one ordinary share for every 20 ordinary shares held; and

(e)   the amount of the final dividend to recommend for 1995.

The finance director has been requested to present a report in relation to these proposals.

Required

(a)   (i)   Advise the board on its proposed procedure for purchasing the issued shares in Capital plc held by Venture plc and on its intention to hold these as an investment.

(ii)   Draft the journal entries to record the purchase transaction assuming that the board acts in accordance with the requirements of the Companies Act 1985.   **(4 marks)**

(b)   (i)   Explain the definition of distributable profits in a public company (ignore the rules relating to investment companies).

(ii)   Identify which of the proposals (a) to (e) above would be classified as a distribution.

(iii)   Describe the accounting treatment of proposal (c), distribution of shares held as an investment in Kind plc.   **(5 marks)**

(c)   Calculate the distributable profits as at 30 November 1995 on the assumption that the company had redeemed the preference shares and made the bonus issue but delayed action on the purchase of own shares and the distribution of the shares in Kind plc until 1996. Explain clearly your treatment of each item mentioned in the reserves.   **(11 marks)**
                                                                                                        (Total 20 marks)

29	**(Question 4 of examination)**

4   Required:

(a) (i)   Explain briefly the objective of FRS 5 *Reporting the substance of transactions*.

(ii)   Explain the criteria for ceasing to recognise an asset and give an illustration of the application of each.   **(5 marks)**

(b) Explain the appropriate accounting treatment for the following transactions and the entries that would appear in the balance sheet as at 31 October 1995 for transaction (i) and in the profit and loss account for the year ended 31 October 1995 and balance sheet as at 31 October 1995 for transactions (ii) (iii) and (iv).

(i)   Timber Products plc supplied large industrial and commercial customers direct on three month credit terms. On 1 November 1994 it entered into an agreement with Ready Support plc whereby it transferred title to the debtors to that company subject to a reduction for bad debts based on Timber Products plc's past experience and in return received an immediate payment of 90% of the net debtor total plus rights to a future sum the amount of which depended on whether and when the debtors paid. Ready Support plc had the right of recourse against Timber Products plc for any additional losses up to an agreed maximum amount.

The position at the year end, 31 October 1995, was that title had been transferred to debtors with an invoice value of £15m less a bad debt provision of £600,000 and Timber Products plc was subject under the agreement to a maximum potential debit of £200,000 to cover losses.

(ii)   Timber Products plc imports unseasoned hardwood and keeps it for five years under controlled conditions prior to manufacturing high quality furniture. In the year ended 31 October 1995 it imported unseasoned timber at a cost of £40m. It contracted to sell the whole amount for £40m and to buy it back in five years time for £56.10m.

(iii) Timber Products plc manufactures and supplies retailers with furniture on a consignment basis such that either party can require the return of the furniture to the manufacturer within a period of six months from delivery. The retailers are required to pay a monthly charge for the facility to display the furniture. The manufacturer uses this monthly charge to pay for insurance cover and carriage costs. At the end of six months the retailer is required to pay Timber Products plc the trade price as at the date of delivery. No retailers have yet sent any goods back to Timber Products plc at the end of the six month period.

In the year ended 31 October 1995, Timber Products plc had supplied furniture to retailers at the normal trade price of £10m being cost plus $33\frac{1}{3}$%; received £50,000 in display charges; incurred insurance costs of £15,000 and carriage costs of £10,000; and received £6m from retailers.

(iv)   On 1 December 1994 Timber Products plc sold a factory that it owned in Scotland to Inter plc a wholly owned subsidiary of Offshore Banking plc for £10m. The factory had a book value of £8.5m. Inter plc was financed by a loan of £10m from Offshore Banking plc. Timber Products plc was paid a fee by Inter plc to continue to operate the factory, such fee representing the balance of profit remaining after Inter plc paid its parent company loan interest set at a level that represented current interest rates. If there was an operating loss, then Timber Products plc would be charged a fee that would cover the operating losses and interest payable.

For the year ended 31 October 1995 the fee paid to Timber Products plc amounted to £3m and the loan interest paid by Inter plc amounted to £1.5m.   **(12 marks)**

(c) State what further information you would seek in order to determine the substance of the following transaction:

Timber Products plc has installed computer controlled equipment in its furniture making factory. This has created the need for large extractor fans to remove dust particles. The company has contracted with Extractor-Plus plc for that company to build and install extractor equipment. Timber Products plc will maintain and insure the equipment and make an annual payment to Extractor-Plus plc comprising a fixed quarterly rental and an hourly usage charge.

In the year ended 31 October 1995 Timber Products plc has paid the fixed quarterly rentals totalling £80,000 and hourly charges totalling £120,000.

(3 marks)

(Total 20 marks)

Compound interest table

No. of Years	Interest rate per year				
	5%	6%	7%	8%	9%
1	1.050	1.060	1.070	1.080	1.090
2	1.102	1.124	1.143	1.166	1.188
3	1.158	1.191	1.225	1.260	1.295
4	1.216	1.262	1.311	1.360	1.412
5	1.276	1.338	1.403	1.469	1.539
6	1.340	1.419	1.501	1.587	1.677

---

30   (Question 5 of examination)

---

5   Daxon plc is a listed company that carries on business as a book wholesaler. In the financial year ended 31 October 1995, the growth in sales turnover to £25m has continued to match the rate of inflation; costs have been contained by reducing staff from 96 to 90; the asset turnover rate has been maintained at five times.

The Daxon plc accountant has prepared draft accounts for the year ended 31 October 1995, and included the following directors' responsibilities statement:

'The directors are required by UK company law to prepare financial statements for each financial period which give a true and fair view of the state of affairs of the group as at the end of the financial period and of the profit and loss for that period. In preparing the financial statements, suitable accounting policies have been used and applied consistently, and reasonable and prudent judgements and estimates have been made. Applicable accounting standards have been followed. The directors are also responsible for maintaining adequate accounting records, for safeguarding the assets of the group, and for preventing and detecting fraud and other irregularities.'

On receiving the statement, one of Daxon plc's directors commented that the statement included aspects that he had always assumed were the responsibility of the auditor and complained about the apparent proliferation of irrelevant new rules.

He requested that the accountant should prepare a memo for the board to explain certain of the items.

Required

(a)   Assuming that you are the accountant of Daxon plc, draft a memo to the board of directors explaining:

   (i)   The background to the inclusion in the annual report of a directors' responsibilities statement.   **(6 marks)**

   (ii)   What is meant by true and fair and how the board can determine whether the financial statements give a true and fair view.   **(5 marks)**

   (iii)   What would constitute adequate steps for safeguarding the assets and preventing and detecting fraud.   **(5 marks)**

(b)   Discuss the proposal that Daxon plc should be exempt from the requirement to apply some or all accounting standards on the grounds that it is a relatively small company.   **(4 marks)**

(Total 20 marks)

ANSWERS TO DECEMBER 1995 EXAMINATION

---

26   (Answer 1 of examination)

Examiner's comments and marking guide

Question 1: part (a)(i) required the preparation of the Consolidated Profit and Loss Account in published format for a group of companies comprising a parent and two directly held subsidiaries requiring accounting for an acquisition and a disposal. One of the subsidiaries was acquired during the year; the other was an 85% holding which was reduced to 60% during the year.

Candidates generally performed well.

Candidates missed out on marks for the calculations eg, the unrealised profit on stock and inter-company transactions; incorrect calculation of the profit on disposal; incorrect calculation of the minority interest in Scotland by omitting to adjust for the unrealised profit.

Candidates also failed to earn marks due to errors of principle. These included the omission of the minority interest and profit on disposal from the CPL; the treatment of the 60% holding on a proportional consolidation basis; and accounting for the acquisition by full inclusion of the sales and expenses of the acquired company with no time apportionment (although some credit was given where there was a pre-acquisition adjustment).

Marks could be gained from improved examination technique eg, both a consolidation schedule and a CPL were prepared with the CPL being a fair copy of the total column; entries in the consolidation schedule were not extended; various workings were produced for minority interest, goodwill calculations, unrealised profit without indicating where they would appear in the CPL.

Part (a)(ii) required the calculation of group reserves to link with the group retained profit for the year.

Candidates performed less well on this part and missed out on marks; many of them were unable to calculate a retained profit brought forward figure with a high proportion including an element for the subsidiary acquired during the year and the majority were unable to correctly treat the goodwill on the disposal.

				Marks
(a)	(i)	Consolidated profit and loss account		
		Turnover		1
		Cost of sales		1
		Administrative/Distribution		1
		Part disposal		4
		Interest		2
		Tax		1
		Minority interest		5
		Dividends		1
	(ii)	P and L b/f		3
		P and L c/f		4
				23/21
(b)	Major criteria	1 per item up to	3	
	Explanation	1 per point up to	3	
	Considerations	1 per point	2	
				8/6
(c)	Description	1 per point up to	4/3	
				35/30

Step by step answer plan

Step 1 Read the question again and make sure that you focus on precisely what is required. This is obviously a group accounts question and the opening paragraphs of the scenario reveal that the main complications are a part disposal and a mid-year acquisition. You are also given the group structure and told that the subsidiary does not change status as a result of the part disposal.

Step 2 Calculate the group turnover and cost of sales figures, including the unrealised profit on intra-group trading. Calculate goodwill, including the amortisation charge for the year. Then complete the profit and loss account as far as operating profit.

Step 3 Calculate the profit on disposal. This will enable you to complete the profit and loss account as far as profit on ordinary activities after tax.

Step 4 Calculate minority interest and complete the profit and loss account down to retained profit for the year.

Step 5 Calculate the consolidated profit and loss account brought forward and carried forward to complete your answer.

Items not required by the Examiner for this question:

- notes to the consolidated profit and loss account;
- FRS 3 analysis of acquisitions.

The examiner's answer

(a)   (i)   **Consolidated profit and loss account
            for the year ended 31 December 1994**

	£m
Turnover (W1)	14,690
Cost of goods sold (W1)	(9,580)
Gross profit	5,110
Administration expenses [660 + 530 + 75 + 30 (W5)]	(1,295)
Distribution costs [1,427 + 1,001 + 60]	(2,488)
Operating profit	1,327
Profit on part disposal of shares in subsidiary undertaking (W2)	348
Income from other fixed asset investments Interest payable	(3)
Profit on ordinary activities before tax	1,672
Tax on profit on ordinary activities [315 + 125 + 27]	(467)
Profit on ordinary activities after tax	1,205
Minority interest (W3)	(78)
Profit on ordinary activities attributable to members of Wales Ltd	1,127
Dividends	(90)
Retained profit for the financial year	1,037

(ii)

Consolidated profit and loss account

	£m	£m
Wales	1,000	
Miami 85% × (883m – 232m – 359m)	248	
	1,248	
Less: Goodwill written off – Miami (W4)	(102)	
Consolidated profit and loss b/f		1,146
Retained for year (above)		1,037
Consolidated profit and loss c/f		2,183

Did you answer the question?

Notice the format of part (ii). Although the question did not explicitly ask for a statement of reserves, this is the obvious way to answer the question.

Consolidated profit and loss account c/f

Proof for information only:

	£m
Wales [1,509m – 1m debenture interest]	1,508
Profit on sale of Miami shares (W2)	420
Miami 60% [883m – 359m Pre-acquisition]	314
Scotland 75% [186 – (106 + 20) – 3 Unrealised]	43
	2,285
Less: Goodwill re Miami: (W4)	(72)
Goodwill re Scotland: (W5)	(30)
	2,183

WORKINGS

(W1)   Turnover

	£m
Wales	8,000
Miami	6,000
Scotland	750
	14,750
Less: Elimination	(60)
	14,690

Cost of goods sold

	£m
Wales	5,000
Miami	4,112
Scotland	525
	9,637
Less: Elimination	(57)
	9,580

Turnover elimination

	£m
Scotland turnover eliminated	60
Wales stock – unrealised profit [20% of £15m]	(3)
Cost of sales eliminated	57

(W2)   Profit on sale of shares in Miami plc

	£m
Proceeds	575
Cost of shares [25/85 × 527m]	(155)
Parent company's exceptional item	420

In consolidated profit and loss account:

	£m	£m
Proceeds		575
Net assets of Miami plc		
At 31 December 1994 [883 + 141]	1,024	
Less: Retained profit for six months	(116)	
At 30.6.94	908	
Disposed of 25%		(227)
		348

(*Note:* No adjustment for goodwill is required since all the goodwill relating to Miami plc has already been charged through the consolidated profit and loss account.)

(W3)   Minority interest

	£m
Miami plc	
15% × £232m × 6/12	17
40% × £232m × 6/12	47
	64
Scotland plc	
25% × (60 – 3 unrealised profit)	14
Total	78

(W4)   Goodwill in Miami

	£m
On original purchase:	
Cost	527
Share of net assets (85% × 500m)	(425)
	102

On 60% remaining:

$$\frac{60}{85} \times 102m = £72m$$

All goodwill in Miami is fully amortised by 1994 since the acquisition was made some years ago.

(W5)   Goodwill in Scotland

Ordinary shares

		£m	£m
Cost			450
Less:	Share capital	300	
	Reserves		
	At 1.1.94	106	
	Three months to 31.3.94	20	
		426	
	75% thereof		320
Goodwill			130

(handwritten annotation: "3 Retained profit")

	£m
Debentures	
Cost [60m – 1m]	59
Less: Nominal value	(40)
Premium	19
Total [130 + 19]	149

Amortisation charge for year $= \dfrac{149}{5} = £30m.$

27   (Answer 2 of examination)

Examiner's comments and marking guide

Question 2: part (a) required a report as at 30 June 1995 by independent accountants to Bewise plc's bankers to enable them to respond to a request from the company for an unspecified increase in short-term lending (currently 20% of gross assets) based on three years accounts to 31 December 1994 and forecast accounts to 31 December 1995. The company, a furniture retailer since 1954, diversified into the sale of domestic electrical goods in 1992 and, during the period up to 31 December 1995, it has enjoyed double digit sales growth with each branch operating as a profit centre with absolute freedom to fix sales credit terms with customers, rewarding branch managers with sales commission. The company is highly geared with equity funds contributing a falling percentage of gross assets from 1992 to 1995.

Most candidates produced a reasonably structured report, supported by ratios, summarising the company performance over the four year period in terms of profitability, liquidity, solvency, financing and other contributory factors eg, turnover, specific issues such as sales policy and arriving at a logical conclusion in respect of the request for additional funds.

Again, candidates missed out on marks due to errors of principle in the calculation of the ratios. These included frequently a mis-match between the numerator and denominator in the ROCE; confusion of ROCE and Return on Equity; omitting reserves when calculating gearing.

Marks could be improved from better examination technique eg, preparing a report with an introduction, structured development and conclusion; supplying calculations to support ratios; reducing the excessive number of ratios; improving the comment from simple observations, such as stock turnover has decreased; and making efforts to explain cause or effect.

			Marks
(a)	Structure of report		
	ie, introduction and development		1
	Signficant matters:		
	identification	1 per point up to	6
	development	1 per point up to	6
	Supporting financial data		
	1 per relevant item up to		8
	Recommendation		1
			22/20
(b)	Significant items		
	Identifying	1 per point up to	3
	Developing	1 per point up to	2
			5/4
(c)	Critical aspects		
	Identifying	1 per point up to	4
	Reasons	1 per point up to	4
			8/6
			35/30

Step by step answer plan

Step 1 Read the question again and make sure that you focus on precisely what is required. The focus of this particular 'interpretation' question is liquidity (specifically whether to increase a short term loan). The recipient of the report is the bank.

Step 2 Calculate a selection of ratios covering profitability, liquidity and solvency. Set these out as Appendices to your main report.

Step 3 Calculate cash flow information for the period and set that out as a further Appendix.

Step 4 Draw up headings and a brief introductory paragraph for the report.

Step 5 Write the main body of the report.

Step 6 Draw a conclusion.

Step 7 Now look back at your answer and make sure that it does answer the question as set.

The examiner's answer

(a)   To: Bewise Bank Manager

From:

Date: 30 June 1995

Re: Request for increase in short-term loans by Bewise plc

The following report is submitted in accordance with your instructions following a request by Bewise plc to increase its short-term loans having forecast that its overdraft will exceed its agreed overdraft level of £240m as at 31 December 1995.

The report considers the company's performance in four key areas, namely, turnover rates, profitability, liquidity and solvency and concludes with our recommendation concerning the short-term loan request.

Did you answer the question?

This introductory paragraph shows the marker that the answer is in report format. It also sets out the structure which the report will follow.

Turnover

Sales turnover has increased by 9%, and 20% over the past two years and is forecast to increase by 12% in the current year.

The rates of total asset and debtor turnover have remained reasonably steady over the four year period with the asset turnover remaining at around 1.6 and the debtor turnover at around 3.4 as shown in Appendix A.

The rate of stock turnover based on selling prices, however, has fallen from 4.9 to 4.1 as stock levels have increased. This fall might possibly have partly arisen from the fluctuations in the rate of percentage growth in sales. If the company achieved the same rate of turnover as in 1992, it would reduce its stock by approximately £92m [609 − (2,512 × 351/1,706)].

If based on cost of sales, it would reduce stock by approximately £75m [609 − (1,731 × 351/1,138)].

If the return were calculated as net assets deducting creditors but not the overdraft because of its permanence, the ROCE for 1992 would be 16% (93 + 28)/(85 + 277 + 62 + 135 + 197) and the trend would be similar to that based on gross assets.

Profitability

The return on gross assets has been falling over the four years from 12.2% in 1992 to 8.0% in 1995, although it has remained fairly static in 1994 and 1995.

The return on equity remained fairly constant from 1992 to 1994. However, in 1995 there is forecast to be a dramatic fall in the ratio to 4.2%. We have seen that the rate of asset turnover had remained reasonably steady and that the reason for the declining returns resulted from the fact that the profit after tax had not increased at the same rate as the sales turnover.

Gross profit

The gross profit percentage has fallen steadily from 33.3% in 1992 to 31.1% in 1995.

Finance cost

The finance cost has risen significantly to 11.5% in 1995 from 7.1% in 1992 based on year end figures in the balance sheets. The ratios are set out in Appendix B.

Liquidity

The current and acid-test ratios have remained reasonably steady over the four year period. As set out in Appendix C, the current ratio has remained at 1.5 to 1.7 and the acid-test ratio at 0.8 to 1.0. Both of these ratios are within normally acceptable ranges. However, with HP debtors it is likely that some of the current assets (debtors) are receivable after more than one year and this would affect the current ratio.

Did you answer the question?

Notice that the answer does not only state the results of the ratio calculations, it interprets them (e.g. 'within normally acceptable ranges'). Readers are also directed to the calculations set out in the Appendices.

Solvency

The gearing has increased significantly in every year since 1992.

The debts were 1.1 times the equity in 1992; by 1995 they are forecast to be 2.4 times the equity as set out in Appendix D. This indicates that the increase in working capital to support the increase in the sales turnover of 47% that the company has achieved since 1992, and the increases in fixed assets have been financed almost entirely by external borrowing. This is an important feature when considering the company's request for additional short-term support and it is towards this aspect of the company's operating that we have directed our attention.

With regard to the stocks, it is noted that although they have increased by 74% from the 1992 figure, this has not been matched by a similar increase in the creditors figure which has only increased by 16%.

Other matters that should be noted are that the company has maintained its dividends although the EPS has been declining since 1992 and there appear to be high cash balances and increasing investments at a time when the company has been experiencing solvency problems.

Financing Bewise plc's increased activity

To assess more clearly the impact of the increased level of activity on the cash position of the company we have prepared cash flow data. This shows that the company has had a negative cash flow from operations in each year since 1992 as shown in Appendix E.

Did you answer the question?

This part of the report uses observation as well as ratio calculations.

Conclusion

The company has not financed its expansion from equity or from operating cash flows. Until therefore the company reaches a position where it is generating a positive cash flow from operations, it will continue to need loan capital to support its operations.

In our view the failure to generate positive operating cash flows is a long standing problem. The fact that it has been allowed to continue reflects adversely on the effectiveness of the senior management of the company. There is an indication of lack of effective planning to provide adequate finance to support the growth in the company's activity and also a failure to adequately control the working capital of the company as evidenced by the falling rate of stock turnover.

Our recommendation is therefore that

(i)   the bank should not increase the facility offered to Bewise plc; and

(ii)   the bank should take immediate action to ensure that the company puts into place positive measures to improve its operating performance and control its working capital.

We realise that the latter suggestion might well be dependent upon changes of management at a senior level and for this reason it is our view that representation of the bank's interest on the board of directors is essential. We would be pleased to advise further if you decide to pursue such a policy.

Please advise us if you wish to arrange a meeting to discuss the report or any matters relating to this assignment.

Reporting accountants

Dated:

Did you answer the question?

The conclusion is an essential part of the answer. It sums up the observations made in the earlier part of the report and then makes firm recommendations.

Appendix A – Turnover rates

Asset turnover		1992	[1,706/995]	=	1.7
		1993	[1,867/1,169]	=	1.6
		1994	[2,233/1,386]	=	1.6
	Forecast	1995	[2,512/1,597]	=	1.6

Stock turnover		1992	[1,706/351]	=	4.9
based on sales		1993	[1,867/404]	=	4.6
		1994	[2,233/540]	=	4.1
	Forecast	1995	[2,512/609]	=	4.1
Debtor turnover		1992	[1,706/483]	=	3.5
		1993	[1,867/551]	=	3.4
		1994	[2,233/633]	=	3.5
	Forecast	1995	[2,512/730]	=	3.4

Appendix B – Profitability ratios

Return on gross assets		1992	[(93 + 28)/995]	× 100	=	12.2%
		1993	[(78 + 24)/1,169]	× 100	=	8.7%
		1994	[(82 + 30)/1,386]	× 100	=	8.1%
	Forecast	1995	[(20 + 107)/1,597]	× 100	=	8.0%

In defining this ratio, the bad debts have been treated as an operating expense, the finance income has been assumed to be related to the debtors and, as the debtors have been included in the denominator, it has been included in the profit figure to be consistent. Note that the return on net assets would be 16%, 11.4%, 10% and 9.6% for 1992 to 1995 respectively:

Return on equity		1992	[50/362]	× 100	=	13.8%
		1993	[43/377]	× 100	=	11.4%
		1994	[48/397]	× 100	=	12.1 %
	Forecast	1995	[16/385]	× 100	=	4.2%
Gross profit %		1992	[568/1,706]	× 100	=	33.3%
		1993	[610/1,867]	× 100	=	32.7%
		1994	[714/2,233]	× 100	=	32.0%
	Forecast	1995	[781/2,512]	× 100	=	31.1%
Finance cost %		1992	[28/394]	× 100	=	7.1%
		1993	[24/515]	× 100	=	4.7%
		1994	[30/720]	× 100	=	4.2%
	Forecast	1995	[107/934]	× 100	=	11.5%

Appendix C – Liquidity

Acid-test ratio		1992	[530/571]	=	0.9
		1993	[618/598]	=	1.0
		1994	[674/795]	=	0.8
	Forecast	1995	[793/889]	=	0.9
Current ratio		1992	[881/571]	=	1.5
		1993	[1,022/598]	=	1.7
		1994	[1,214/795]	=	1.5
	Forecast	1995	[1,402/889]	=	1.6

Appendix D – Solvency

Debt/Equity		1992	[394/362]	=	1.1
		1993	[515/377]	=	1.4
		1994	[720/397]	=	1.8
	Forecast	1995	[934/385]	=	2.4

Appendix E – Operating cash flows

		1993	1994	1995
Profit after tax		43	48	16
Depreciation		14	16	18
Creditor increase		38		9
		—	—	—
		95	64	43
Less:	Stock increase	(53)	(136)	(69)
	Debtor increase	(68)	(82)	(97)
	Creditor decrease		(8)	
		—	—	—
	Negative cash flow from operations	(26)	(162)	(123)
		—	—	—

---

28   (Answer 3 of examination)

(**Examiner's comments and marking guide**)

Question 3: this was an unpopular question. There was a polarisation of marks that indicated that some candidates had a good understanding of the topic and others only the vaguest idea.

Part (a) required advice to the Board of Directors on the technical procedure involved in the redemption of shares with supporting journal entries.

This part was moderately answered although a substantial number of candidates considered it appropriate to hold the redeemed shares as an investment and many were unable to complete the journal entries correctly, failing to account for the Capital Redemption Reserve (CRR) or the premium.

Part (b)(i) required an explanation of the definition of distributable profits. Most candidates simply stated that realised profits less losses could be distributed forgetting to mention that it is the accumulated figure that is relevant. Fewer marks were awarded to answers that merely stated that distributable profits are those profits that are distributable.

Part (b)(ii) required candidates to identify which proposal was a distribution. The majority identified the dividend as a distribution but there was no clear understanding of the other items.

Part (b)(iii) required a description of a distribution in kind. This was invariably incomplete. Good answers identified that the investment would be revalued and that the dividend would be the revalued amount. Many recorded the revaluation with no reference to the distribution or the distribution with no reference to the revaluation.

Part (c) required the calculation and explanation of the distributable profits. This was generally not well answered. There was uncertainty as to the treatment eg, development costs and profit on long-term contracts; omission to deduct the CRR transfer; addition of the exchange gain. Candidates failed to score as well as they could if they produced entries without explanations or explanations only without any entries.

			Marks
(a)	Advising on procedure for purchasing shares		2
	Advising on intention to hold as investment		2
	Journal entries		2
			6/4
(b)	Explanation of definition		1
	Classifying	1 per point	3
	Describing accounting treatment	1 per point	2
			6/5
(c)	Bonus issue		1
	Preference share		2
	Share premium		1
	CRR		1
	Revaluation reserve		1
	Profit and loss account		5
	Development costs		1
	Long-term contracts		1
			13/11
			25/20

Step by step answer plan

Step 1 Read the question again and make sure that you focus on precisely what is required. In this case, the requirements hold the clue to the topics being examined: purchase of own shares and distributable profits. The question is in three distinct parts and the requirements are very precise. You should be clear which of the five proposals applies to which requirement.

Step 2 Answer part (a) (i) by describing the procedure for purchasing own shares. Then comment on the specific features of proposal (a). The key requirement word is *advise*.

Step 3 Draw up journal entries to answer part (a) (ii).

Step 4 Answer part (b) (i). Note that the key requirement word is *explain*, so it is not enough just to state the definition.

Step 5 Part (b) (ii) relates to all five proposals. List those which qualify as distributions, with brief explanations where necessary.

Step 6 Answer part (b) (iii) by writing a brief paragraph. The key requirement word is *describe*.

Step 7 Re-read the requirement of part (c) and focus on the assumptions you are asked to make. Proposals (b) and (d) are relevant to this part of the question.

Step 8 Adjust the reserves for the effects of proposals (b) and (d). Then classify the reserves into distributable and non distributable.

Step 9 Draw up a schedule of adjustments to distributable reserves. Consider each of the potential adjustments in points (3) and (4) in turn.

Step 10 For each item, explain why you have or have not included it in your calculation.

Items not required by the Examiner for this question: distributable profits rules for investment companies in part (b) (i).

The examiner's answer

(a)   (i)   **Purchase of own shares**

Procedure for purchase of own shares

Companies may purchase their own shares subject to certain conditions. The principal conditions are that the company has authority in its articles of association, it is not left with only redeemable shares in issue, the shares must be fully paid and there is compliance with the capital maintenance requirements by making a new issue or making a transfer to a capital redemption reserve.

Procedure in relation to Venture plc

A purchase may be made as a market purchase on a recognised investment exchange or as an 'off market' purchase which does not take place on a recognised investment exchange.

However, for an off market purchase it would be necessary for the terms to be authorised by a special resolution. The party whose shares are to be purchased is not permitted to vote.

Holding shares as an investment

When a company purchases its own shares, it must cancel them at the time it purchases them.

There is a sub-heading of own 'own shares' under investments in the balance sheet but, unlike in the USA, it is not permissible for a company to purchase its own shares and hold them as treasury shares until it resells them. Under that particular sub-heading, a company would normally include shares which have been acquired by forfeiture, surrender in lieu of forfeiture or by way of gift.

Even then there is a requirement to dispose of them within three years or cancel them.

> **Did you answer the question?**
>
> Notice the structure of this part of the answer. There is a short paragraph on each aspect of the proposal: purchase of own shares; off market purchase; holding own shares.

(ii)   **Journal entries in accordance with the requirements of the Companies Act 1985**

	£m	£m
Share capital (nominal value of shares purchased)	150	
Cash		150
Premium on redemption (premium on shares redeemed)	75	
Cash		75
Profit and loss account reserve	225	
Capital redemption reserve (nominal value of shares purchased)		150
Premium on redemption		75

(b)   (i)   Distributable profits are defined in the Companies Act S263(3) as the cumulative realised profits so far as not previously distributed or capitalised, less cumulative realised losses not previously written off in a reduction or reorganisation of capital.

The definition is based on considering the cumulative position rather than the profits of a single year. This effectively means that past losses have to be made good before dividends can be paid and unrealised profits cannot be distributed. There is the distinction between revenue and capital profits.

(ii)   The following would be classified as distributions

–   The purchase and cancellation of the company's own shares is a partial distribution with the difference between the issue price and redemption price treated as a distribution.

–   The distribution to the shareholders of Capital plc of the shares in Kind plc.

–   The amount of the final dividend to be recommended for 1995.

(iii)   The distribution of the shares held as an investment is a distribution in kind often referred to as *in specie*. The investment is shown at cost in the balance sheet but for dividend disclosure purposes it is necessary to revalue the investment to its fair value of £24m. The difference between the cost of £15m and market value of £24m is regarded as realised for the purposes of the distribution. The difference of £9m would be credited as an exceptional item of material in the profit and loss account and the dividend would be disclosed as £24m.

(c)   The bonus issue of £25m is a capitalisation issue and will therefore be transferred from a capital non-distributable reserve eg, share premium account and/or capital redemption reserve.

The preference share redemption is not being made out of the proceeds of a new issue and consequently the nominal value of £50m transferred to the capital redemption reserve will be debited to distributable reserves eg, profit and loss account.

The reserves then need to be classified into non-distributable and distributable.

	Either £m	Or £m
Non-distributable reserves		
Share premium (£63m – £25m bonus issue)	38	63
Capital redemption reserve (£10m + £50m transfer)	60	35

By definition these reserves are not distributable.

The remaining reserves need further consideration to separate into realised and unrealised:

	£m
Fixed asset revaluation reserve	43
Add back the computer equipment provision as realised	2
Unrealised capital profit	45

On the basis of the prudence concept a surplus arising from a revaluation of a fixed asset is regarded as unrealised and the Companies Act requires a permanent fall in value to be treated as a realised loss.

Profit and loss account

			£m
Profit per question			775
(i)	Transfer to CRR		(50)
(ii)	Bonus issue		(25)
(iii)	Exchange gain on a long-term German mark loan taken out on 1.12.94		(6)
	The company must treat the whole of this gain as unrealised even though it appears in the profit and loss account per SSAP 20 para 10/11.		
(iv)	Additional depreciation based on revalued amount of fixed assets		13
	The company is required to treat an amount equal to the excess depreciation on the revaluation surplus as a realised profit: S275(2)		
Realised revenue profits			707
Less:	Computer equipment deficit		(2)
Realised profits			705

The following items will not affect the distributable profits:

Development costs of £22m for the year written off. There is no change because if development costs had been shown as an asset in the company's balance sheet, the amount would be treated as a realised revenue loss [S269(1)] unless there are special circumstances that justify the directors deciding not to treat it as a realised revenue loss eg, compliance with SSAP 13.

Profit of £9m attributed to long-term contracts in beauty products segment. There is no change because attributable profit included in accordance with SSAP 9 is regarded as realised.

The distributable profits will be £705m.

Did you answer the question?

This is quite a complicated exercise, but the answer proceeds in a systematic and structured way. It explains the adjustments, then analyses the reserves into distributable and non-distributable, then realised and unrealised. It then adjusts the profit and loss account, explaining the items as part of the schedule. It then covers the items not affecting distributable profits, and lastly, states the figure. This answer meets the requirement for calculations *and* explanations.

(Tutorial note: in practice, the bonus issue would almost certainly be made from the share premium account and the distributable profits would then be £730m.*)*

29   (Answer 4 of examination)

Examiner's comments and marking guide

Question 4: part (a) required a brief explanation of the objectives of FRS 5 and a statement of criteria for derecognition.

This part was reasonably well answered. However, poor examination technique tempted some candidates to write everything they knew about the FRS, the Notes, a summary of the main types of transaction encompassed by the standard - all good material but excessive for the 5 marks that were available; some candidates explained when an asset should be recognised rather than de-recognised.

Part (b) required the accounting treatment for a series of transactions which impacted on the profit and loss account and balance sheet.

Transaction (i) was a factoring of debts which required a linked presentation and provision for potential recourse. This part was quite well answered although the principal weakness was failure to mention linked presentation.

Transaction (ii) was a financing transaction based on a sale and buy-back arrangement which required the recognition of a loan and a stock item in the balance sheet. This part was well answered. The principal error was in the calculation of the interest element with many opting for equal division.

Transaction (iii) involved consignment stock for a six month period with a display charge to cover expenses and payment of the trade price at the date of delivery if held over six months. This part was quite well done and most candidates obtained marks for the calculation although the explanation was often weaker than the calculation. Arguments were accepted for alternative treatments eg, treatment as a sale only if retained after six months.

Transaction (iv) was a sale by the company to its quasi-subsidiary requiring consolidation under FRS 2 with consequential eliminations of inter-company income, expenses, assets and liabilities.

Few candidates identified that this was a quasi-subsidiary company with a need to consolidate. Credit was given for identifying that it was a loan and that the factory should appear as an asset.

Part (c) was mainly approached by candidates as a decision between finance or operating lease and credit was given for this approach.

			Marks	
(a)	Objectives		1	
	Criteria	1 per point	2	
	Illustration	1 per point	2	
			—	
				5/5
(b)	Per transaction		2	
	Accounting treatment described		2	
	Balance sheet		1	
	Profit and loss account		1	
			—	
				16/12
(c)	Further information	1 per point	4	
			—	
				4/3
				——
				25/20

Step by step answer plan

Step 1   Read the question again and make sure that you focus on precisely what is required. The first requirement and the nature of the subsequent scenarios should make it obvious that this is a question about substance over form.

Step 2 Answer part (a) (i). Note that the requirement is to *explain briefly* and that only 5 marks/8 minutes are available for the whole of part (a).

Step 3 Answer part (a) (ii) by briefly explaining and giving examples of the two types of transaction where an asset might cease to be recognised.

Step 4 Re-read the requirement for part (b). Part (b) carries over half the available marks for this question. Note that you are not required to give profit and loss account entries for transaction (i). Assume that all four transactions carry equal marks and allocate your time accordingly.

Step 5 Analyse transaction (i), which is a factoring agreement. This, and the fact that the Examiner is only interested in the balance sheet is a clue that linked presentation may apply here. Determine the substance of the transaction by asking yourself who bears the risks of ownership of the debts. The substance of the transaction determines the accounting treatment. Draw up the balance sheet entries.

Step 6 Approach transactions (ii), (iii) and (iv) in exactly the same way. Determine the substance of the transaction first and then draw up and explain the profit and loss account and balance sheet entries for each.

Step 7 Re-read the requirement for part (c). Explain the two alternative views of the transaction and the information that you would need in order to determine who bears the risks and rewards of ownership.

Items not required by the Examiner for this question: general description of all the requirements of FRS 5; criteria for recognising an asset in part (a) (ii).

The examiner's answer

(a) (i) The objective (FRS 5 para 1) of the FRS *Reporting the substance of transactions* is to ensure that the substance of an entity's transactions is reported in its financial statements. The commercial effect of the entity's transactions, and any resulting assets, liabilities, gains or losses, should be faithfully represented in its financial statements. This will affect the accounting for any arrangement the effect of which is to inappropriately omit assets and liabilities from the balance sheet. It achieves this by requiring financial statements to be prepared reporting the substance rather than the legal form of transactions.

  (ii) The FRS recognises two types of transaction where an asset might cease to be recognised.

    The first is where all significant benefits and risks relating to an asset are transferred. An example is where a car manufacturer supplies parts at listed trade price to a service station customer.

    The second is where not all significant benefits and risks relating to an asset are transferred, but it is necessary to change the description or monetary amount of the original asset or to record a new liability for any obligation assumed. An example is where a car dealer supplies a car subject to a guaranteed residual repurchase price.

(b) (i) **Disclosure using linked presentation**

    The transaction appears to satisfy the criteria set out in FRS 5 for linked presentation in that the finance will be repaid only from the proceeds generated by the specific item it finances and there is no possibility of any claim on the entity being established other than against funds generated by that item and there is no provision whereby the entity may either keep the item on repayment of the finance or reacquire it at any time.

The accounting treatment for linked presentation is as follows:

	£m	£m
Current assets		
Receivables subject to financing arrangements		
Gross receivables		14.40
(After providing £600,000 for bad debts)		
Less: Non-returnable proceeds		
90% of net debtors £14.4m	12.96	
Less potential recourse	0.20	
		(12.76)
		1.64
Current asset: Cash		12.96
Creditors: Recourse under factored debts		0.20

(ii)   **How to determine the substance/whether to include in balance sheet/recognition**

Under FRS 5 the transaction would be regarded as a financing transaction in that Timber Products plc has not transferred the risks and rewards of ownership of the timber. It has in fact borrowed money on the security of the timber. The timber will therefore appear as stock in the balance sheet and the loan will appear as a creditor. Each year there will be an interest element charged to the profit and loss account and added to the liability.

The balance sheet as at 31 October 1995 will show:

	£m
Stock	40.0
Loan payable after more than one year	42.8

Note: The loan is secured by stock of £40m at cost.

The profit and loss account will show:

Interest payable [7% of £40m]	£2.8m

(iii)   **How to determine the substance/whether to include in balance sheet/derecognition**

The problem in this transaction is to determine the substance of the transaction ie, whether or not the 'outstanding' stock of £4m at selling price (£3m cost price), has been sold. If it has this would mean that the stock appears in the balance sheet of the retailers at £4m.

Possibly the principal point that would support recognition of a sale and derecognition of the stock in the balance sheet of Timber Products plc is the fact that the retailers are able to purchase at the trade price as at the date of delivery. If they were required to pay the trade price as at the end of the six month display period then the substance would be that the rewards remained with Timber Products plc and the stock would continue to be recognised by their balance sheet at cost of £3m, or net realisable value if lower.

Thus, the more prudent view, treats the transaction as a genuine sale or return with the manufacturer holding the price for six months.

There is a further point, which is that the retailers could take the opportunity immediately prior to the end of the six months to return all unsold consignment stock. This would support the view that the risk and rewards remained with Timber Products plc.

The decision in this case has to be taken on balance ie, giving weight to those matters that are likely to have a commercial effect in practice. There is no absolute answer. The persuasive factor is probably the date of fixing the price which would support treating the item as sold and therefore derecognised from the Timber Products plc balance sheet.

The accounting entries on that basis would be:

Profit and loss account for the year ended 31 October 1995

Sales	£10m
Cost of sales	£7.5m
Other income	£50,000
Insurance costs	£15,000
Carriage costs	£10,000

Balance sheet as at 31 October 1995

Debtors	£4m

A provision for returns should be made based on past experience.

However, a case could also be made under the prudence concept for the stock to appear on both the manufacturer's and the retailer's balance sheets.

(iv)   **Quasi-subsidiary**

The arrangement with Inter plc has been structured so that it does not meet the legal definition of a subsidiary within the provisions of FRS 2 para 14. However, the commercial effect is no different from that which would result were Inter plc to be a subsidiary of Timber Products plc and under FRS 5 it falls to be treated as a quasi-subsidiary.

Under FRS 5, the factory will appear as an asset in the Timber Products consolidated accounts and it will be reduced to £8.5m being cost to the group and the profit on disposal will be cancelled out; the fee will be cancelled as an intra group transaction; the loan interest will appear at £1.5m in the consolidated profit and loss account; the loan of £10m will appear as a creditor in the consolidated balance sheet.

Did you answer the question?

Notice that in each case the answers both explain the accounting treatment and give the accounting entries. An answer which provided explanation but no accounting entries or vice versa would not satisfy the requirement.

(c)   There would appear to be two possible approaches. One would be to approach the transaction as a secured loan; the other as a leasing arrangement.

Secured loan considerations

The question to be answered is what risks has Timber Products plc borne in this transaction.

It clearly bears the operating risk in the form of maintenance and insurance costs. It needs to be determined whether it has also borne the charge for covering the finance cost of the equipment during construction. Further information is required in considering this transaction to assess whether Extractor-Plus plc is in effect receiving a lender's return. If that were the case, the equipment would appear as an asset in the balance sheet and an amount equal to the cost of the asset as a loan secured on the asset.

Leasing considerations

More information is necessary to establish whether there has been an attempt to word the agreement so that it falls outside the SSAP 21 definition of a finance lease. The additional information would include matters such as the cost of the equipment, the length of the contract, any minimum lease payments particularly in the event of low hourly usage. However, FRS 5 with its substance approach, might influence the accounting treatment.

Did you answer the question?

There is no single right answer to part (c) and so the Examiner is primarily interested in your reasoning. A rambling paragraph would be unlikely to attract as many marks as this answer, which is organised so that the alternative views of the transaction are each considered in a short paragraph.

---

30   (Answer 5 of examination)

Examiner's comments and marking guide

Question 5: part (a)(i) required a memo explaining the objective of a Directors Responsibility Statement and its background.

This part was answered well in general. Some weaker answers confused the Statement with the Directors' Report.

Part (a)(ii) required an explanation of the meaning of the true and fair view and the method by which the Board could confirm its application in a specific situation. Good answers gave a clear definition of true and fair and examples of how the Board could determine that a true and fair view was being given. Marks could have been gained by reference to the fact that accounting principles should be appropriate to the business, accounts should exhibit the qualitative characteristics of financial information and reflect the substance of transactions.

Part (a)(iii) required an explanation of adequate steps to safeguard assets and prevent fraud. This part was reasonably answered. Additional marks could have been gained by considering more than the physical side of safeguarding and maintaining a Fixed Asset Register.

Part (b) required a discussion of Director's proposal that the company should be exempt from the requirement to comply with standards. The quality of answers to this part varied. Credit was given for reasonable points eg, need for comparability, compliance was a requisite for a PLC, discussion of the fact that the information needs of managers/owners of small companies might differ from those of a listed plc.

			Marks	
(a)	(i)	Directors responsibility report background		
		Memo structure	1	
		General understanding	3	
		Development of explanation	3	
			———	
				7/6
	(ii)	Meaning of true and fair:		
		General understanding 1 per point	2	
		Development of explanation	2	
		Board action	2	
			———	
				6/5
	(iii)	Safeguarding assets		
		General understanding 1 per point	3	
		Development of explanation		
		eg, Internal control discussion	3	
			———	
				6/5
(b)		Small company discussion		
		Organisation of discussion	1	
		General awareness of problems	2	
		Development of discussion	3	
			———	
				6/4
				———
				25/20
				———

Step by step answer plan

Step 1 Read the question again and make sure that you focus on precisely what is required. You will need to allocate your time so that you leave about 7 minutes to attempt part (b).

Step 2 Draw up headings for the memo and draft an introductory paragraph.

Step 3 Begin part (a) (i) by explaining the recommendations of Cadbury and the APB. Then explain the reasoning behind the inclusion of the statement.

Step 4 Answer part (a) (ii) by explaining the criteria for determining whether financial statements provide a true and fair view. Then explain the importance of 'substance over form' and UITF 7. Finally explain the Board's responsibility.

Step 5 Approach part (a) (iii) by explaining the background to the requirement and then explain what would constitute adequate steps. Finally, explain the Board's responsibility.

Step 6 Answer part (b), remembering that the requirement is to *discuss*.

Items not required by the Examiner for this question:

- discussion of the Directors' Report in part (a);
- description of the requirements for small company financial statements in part (b).

The examiner's answer

(a)   **Memo to Board of directors**

From: Accountant

Dated: December 1995

Following the enquiry concerning the directors' responsibilities statement that I included in the draft of the 1995 annual accounts, I have set out the following information to explain how the need for the statement has arisen in order for the company to be following best practice.

Did you answer the question?

The headings and the introductory paragraph tell the marker that this answer is in the required format (i.e. a memo).

The background to the inclusion in the annual report of a directors' responsibilities statement

Major changes in corporate governance disclosures were recommended in the report of the Committee on the financial aspects of Corporate Governance (published by the Cadbury Committee in December 1992). In the report, the committee recommended that listed companies should state in their annual report whether they comply with a Code of Best Practice drafted by the committee, giving reasons for non-compliance.

The recommendations included a statement by the directors of their responsibility for preparing the accounts; a report on the effectiveness of their system of internal control; a report explicitly on whether the business is a going concern.

The Auditing Practices Board has included reference to directors' responsibilities in SAS 600 *Auditors' reports on financial statements* with a requirement that where there was not an adequate description of directors' relevant responsibilities, the auditors' report should include such a description (SAS 600.3). The sample wording in Appendix 3 of SAS 600 effectively covers the items in the draft presented to the directors of Daxon plc. The effect of this is that, if the board omit to do so, the statement will be included by the auditors in their report.

However, the essential point is that the primary responsibility for the preparation of financial statements lies with the directors; the auditors' responsibility is to express an opinion on the statements. The responsibilities statement is intended to emphasise this fact.

The requirement to include a statement is to give emphasis to the fact that the financial statements are the responsibility of the directors and, in this way, to reduce the expectation gap.

There is a view that users of the annual report have not distinguished between the directors' responsibilities and the auditors' responsibilities and have assumed that the audit responsibility was far greater than was actually the case.

There is also a view that the inclusion of the statement in the audit report is merely an attempt by the audit profession to transfer responsibility to another party. However, it is important to note that the acknowledgement of directors' responsibilities stemmed from the Cadbury Committee and not merely from the Auditing Practices Board.

Inclusion of a directors responsibilities statement is not mandatory for the company but it was my view that there was merit in bringing to the board's attention the changes that have been occurring in corporate governance and to make Daxon plc's annual report follow best financial reporting practices.

Did you answer the question?

Notice the way in which this answer clearly states the directors' responsibilities. This is the issue that most concerns the readers of the memo.

How the board can determine whether the financial statements give a true and fair view

There has always been a duty on the board to ensure that the financial statements are true and fair. However, it has in the past been the practice to regard this as a matter for the auditor. Inclusion in the directors' responsibility is merely recognition of a long standing duty.

Perhaps it would be helpful to first review the criteria for determining whether financial statements provide a true and fair view which is a step that we have not previously taken. The criteria are:

(i)   They are prepared in accordance with accepted accounting principles.

(ii)   The accounting principles applied are appropriate to the business ie, it is not sufficient to be able to demonstrate that such principles have been applied by other companies and other accounting firms – they also need to be appropriate to the particular company.

The Foreword to Accounting Standards para 16/17 emphasise this approach in stating that compliance with accounting standards will normally be necessary for financial statements to give a true and fair view but that in applying accounting standards it is important to be guided by the spirit and reasoning behind them – the spirit and reasoning being set out in the individual FRSs and are based on the ASB's Statement of Principles for Financial Reporting.

(iii)   They exhibit the qualitative characteristics of financial information set out in Chapter 2 of the Statement of Principles eg, the two primary characteristics relating to content of relevance and reliability, the primary characteristics relating to presentation, such as comparability and understandability.

(iv)   They provide sufficient information for the intended users to be able to comprehend and interpret ie, there is an implication that the financial statements are a reflection of the economic position, regardless of particular accepted accounting policies and rules, which convey the nature of the business to a prospective or current shareholder with no inside knowledge of the company.

This latter criterion is generally referred to as reflecting the substance of transactions.

It is in order to reflect the substance of transactions that there is a requirement that, where the application of existing standards or statutes is not considered by the directors to result in a true and fair view, they are not to be applied. In such a case, there is a requirement to explain the departure. The nature of the disclosure is set out in UITF 7 which effectively requires an explanation as to why the prescribed treatment would not result in a true and fair view.

The board's responsibility is therefore to ensure that the accountant in preparing the accounts has had regard to statutory, mandatory and voluntary pronouncements. The board's responsibility would be discharged by ensuring that the company employs appropriate professional staff and ensuring that their technical knowledge and competence is kept current.

Did you answer the question?

Again, there is a clear statement of the directors' responsibilities. This shows that the memo is directed to the needs of its readers. An explanation which did not relate to this particular situation (an accountant and the Board) would not meet the requirement.

Adequate steps for safeguarding the assets and preventing and detecting fraud

Again, this is a long standing duty.

The Cadbury Committee proposed that this should be explicitly recognised and that the directors should include in their report a statement that there were adequate internal controls in operation designed to protect the assets of the company and prevent and detect material fraud.

This raised the question as to what constituted internal control. The assessment of internal controls has been regularly undertaken by the auditors in order to plan their audit and has had an impact on the nature and scope of their audit tests.

It has never been defined in respect to the directors' responsibilities and a working party was set up which produced draft guidance in a report 'Internal Control and Financial Reporting'. The draft guidance produced an extensive list of elements and features that directors should consider. For example the four elements were the control environment, identification of risks, control priorities and objectives, control activities and monitoring and corrective action. Each element contained a list of features that should be considered. For example, within the control environment element, certain features were specified such as:

–   commitment to truth and fair dealing
–   communication of ethical values
–   independence, integrity and openness at board level
–   appropriate delegation of authority with accountability.

The accountant's draft of the statement presented to the board could reasonably be expected to be extended if the working party proposals were put into effect in that the following report was proposed:

'The company maintains a system of internal financial controls, including suitable monitoring procedures, in order to provide reasonable but not absolute assurance of the maintenance of proper accounting records and the reliability of the financial information used within the business or for publication. The directors are satisfied that these controls operated effectively during the period covered by the financial statements.'

However, there has been disagreement as to the nature of internal control and the extent of the directors acknowledgement of responsibility. The proposals formulated by the working party were watered down by not demanding that directors comment on general controls and removing the requirement to express an opinion on the effectiveness of their company's internal controls. The new draft still requires the annual report to contain statements by the directors that they are responsible for the control system and a description of relevant procedures.

Conclusion

Whilst the company is under no mandatory requirement to include such a statement in its annual report, it could be beneficial for the board to consider the proposals and consider their possible impact on current practices within the company.

Did you answer the question?

The needs of the directors are again addressed by the inclusion of a firm recommendation.

(b)   There has long been an argument that small companies should not be required to apply standards because they are unduly burdensome. However, the view expressed in UK GAAP has much merit in that it approaches the debate from a different aspect. It puts forward the view that it is necessary first to establish a sensible definition for a small company for financial reporting purposes, in contrast to the ASC's definition based on arbitrary size criteria. The definition would not assume that small companies are merely smaller versions of big companies but would relate to the difference in fundamental criteria ie, the composition of its membership and management.

Existing standards cover recognition, measurement and disclosure. The appropriate approach to the question of standards for small companies is not to assess the extent to which the requirements attaching to listed companies should be relaxed but to assess what would be appropriate recognition, measurement and disclosure. This would recognise that the general purpose statements prepared for listed companies are intended for the range of users listed in the statement of principles whereas small companies might be preparing accounts for owner/managers, the bank and the Revenue. In the latter case, none of the users might be interested in information prepared to satisfy the information needs of such a broad spectrum of users.

Did you answer the question?

This part of the answer includes a range of points both for and against a separate regime for small companies, thus meeting the requirement to *discuss*.

Tutorial note

Since this question was originally set, the ASB has issued the Financial Reporting Standard for Smaller Entities (FRSSE). However, Daxon plc would *not* be able to adopt the FRSSE as it is a public company (and therefore not a 'small' company as defined by the Companies Acts).

JUNE 1996 QUESTIONS

Section A - BOTH questions are compulsory and MUST be attempted

31 (Question 1 of examination)

Angol plc acquired 735 million shares of FF1 each in Frank SA on 1 June 1993 when there was a credit balance of FF126 million on reserves. Frank SA acts as a selling agent for Angol plc. The remaining shares in Frank SA are held by French nationals.

The draft profit and loss accounts for the year ended 31 May 1996 were as follows:

70%

	Angol plc £'000	Frank SA FF'000
Operating profit	821,000	588,000
Income from shares in subsidiary	15,125	
Profit on ordinary activities	836,125	588,000
Tax on profit on ordinary activities before taxation	(320,000)	(229,000)
Profit on ordinary activities after tax	516,125	359,000
Dividend		
Paid	-	(185,000)
Proposed	(262,500)	-
	253,625	174,000

The draft balance sheets as at 31 May 1996 were as follows:

	£'000	FF'000
Fixed assets		
Land at cost	630,000	1,218,000
Buildings at depreciated cost	529,200	275,520
Plant and machinery	348,600	111,300
	1,507,800	1,604,820
Investment in subsidiary	147,000	
Current assets		
Stock	168,000	134,400
Debtors	426,300	180,600
Bank	176,400	50,400
	770,700	365,400
Current liabilities		
Creditors	(413,700)	(189,000)
Tax	(320,000)	(229,000)
Proposed dividend	(262,500)	
	(996,200)	(418,000)
Net current liabilities	(225,500)	(52,600)
Total assets less current liabilities	1,429,300	1,552,220

Capital and reserves		
Ordinary shares of £1 and FF1 each	525,000	1,050,000
Reserves	904,300	502,220
	1,429,300	1,552,220

The following information is available:

Goodwill
Goodwill arising on the acquisition of the subsidiary undertaking is amortised through the profit and loss account over three years from the date of acquisition.

Depreciation policy
The group follows a uniform depreciation policy and is writing off buildings over 50 years and plant over 10 years in equal instalments. Full depreciation is charged on additions commencing in the year of purchase.

Fixed assets

Cost:	Angol plc			Frank SA		
	Land £'000	Buildings £'000	Plant £'000	Land FF'000	Buildings FF'000	Plant FF'000
At 1.6.95	630,000	588,000	575,400	1,218,000	504,000	108,150
Additions	-	-	-	-	-	84,000
At 31.5.96	630,000	588,000	575,400	1,218,000	504,000	192,150
Depreciation:						
At 1.6.95		47,040	169,260	-	218,400	61,635
Charge for year		11,760	57,540	-	10,080	19,215
At 31.5.96	-	58,800	226,800	-	228,480	80,850

The additions to plant were made on 1 June 1995. All other fixed assets had been acquired prior to 1 June 1993.

Exchange rates
The rates of exchange were as follows:

Prior to 1 June 1993	FF12	:	£1
1 June 1993	FF10	:	£1
1 June 1995	FF9	:	£1
Average for year	FF8	:	£1
31 May 1996	FF7	:	£1

Assume that closing stock was acquired at the closing rate of exchange.

Audit aspects

In February 1995 the auditors, Risk, Free & Co informed the directors of Angol plc that there were continuing weaknesses in the internal control systems in Frank SA relating to stock; the stock records of physical quantities received and despatched were not kept up to date and the perpetual stocktake procedures were not being consistently applied. Just as for the 1993 and 1994 financial statements, the company agreed to carry out a periodic stocktake at 31 May 1995.

During discussions in July 1995 when finalising the 1995 accounts, the chairman of Angol plc, Mr John Option, informed the audit partner, Miss Free, that there were two major developments planned.

One development was the expansion of operations in France with Frank SA becoming more than simply a selling agent. A capital investment programme had been planned, financed by capital raised through Frank SA over the next three years.

The other development was the rationalisation of stockholding by Angol plc in the UK, to be achieved initially by the rental of additional warehouses near the Channel ports and major cities.

Taking account of the significant changes that were planned for Frank SA, the audit partner reassigned the senior audit manager who had been responsible for the audit of Angol plc for the past four years to assist with the Frank SA audit. The Angol plc audit was managed by a newly joined manager.

At the interim audit in November 1995 the auditors had visited the first new warehouse in Folkestone (a UK port) which had then been operating for two months and recorded the system. Compliance tests were carried out and a note made on the audit file and reported to management that stock records were not up to date. Management had advised verbally that this would be remedied by the appointment of more staff. The matter was discussed by the audit partner and audit manager and it was decided that in the context of the group, the stock at the Folkestone warehouse was not material and that additional compliance and substantive tests would be carried out at the final audit.

On 13 June 1996 Mr Option wrote to Miss Free informing her that stock losses had occurred from the new warehouses due to collusion between the warehouse staff and suppliers. An initial estimate of the losses was £500,000.

He expressed the view that the losses were not detected by Risk, Free & Co because the firm used a manager on the audit who was unfamiliar with the company; he further maintained that the firm had been negligent in failing to detect the errors and fraud during the audit and failing to ensure that the internal control procedures were sound; he requested a reduction in the audit fee.

Required

(a)   Prepare a consolidated profit and loss account for the year ended 31 May 1996 and a consolidated balance sheet as at that date using the temporal method to translate the financial statements of Frank SA.   **(20 marks)**

(b)   [Not reproduced as this part of the question is no longer within the syllabus.]   **(10 marks)**
   (Total 30 marks)

---

32   (Question 2 of examination)

Mike Ried and Jane Thurby were refrigeration engineers who were made redundant in 1993. Whilst working together they had often discussed the idea of setting up on their own. They believed that there was a niche in the market for the manufacture of low temperature thermometers. Following their redundancy, they agreed to attempt to put their idea into practice.

They prepared a business plan which showed that after start up losses the business would be profitable. They estimated that they would need £350,000 to finance the business. They presented their plan to the bank which agreed to provide an overdraft facility of £175,000 for two years on condition that they raised share capital of £175,000.

A company, Thermo Ltd was formed and commenced trading on 1 July 1994. It was financed by the issue of 100,000 shares at par value to Mike and Jane and 75,000 shares at par value to their relatives and friends.

The accounts for the period to 31 March are set out below:

Profit and loss account for the period ending 31 March

	1995 £	1996 £
Sales	304,500	549,500
Cost of sales	(252,787)	(443,170)
Gross profit	51,713	106,330
Administrative expense	(15,100)	(18,050)

Selling expenses		(36,490)	(39,368)
Operating profit		123	48,912
Interest payable		(3,922)	(18,455)
(Loss)/profit before tax		(3,799)	30,457
Taxation		-	(6,637)
(Loss)/profit after tax		(3,799)	23,820

Balance sheets as at 31 March

Fixed assets	1995				1996	
	Cost	Depreciation		Cost	Depreciation	
	£	£	£	£	£	£
Premises	105,000	1,600	103,400	105,000	3,200	101,800
Machinery	87,500	8,750	78,750	122,500	21,000	101,500
Office furniture	3,500	700	2,800	5,250	1,750	3,500
Motor vehicles	21,000	3,937	17,063	21,000	9,187	11,813
			202,013			218,613

Current assets			
Stock	47,775		138,375
Debtors	151,200		190,539
Prepayments			8,750
Cash			1,253
	198,975		338,917

Current liabilities			
Creditors	(93,445)		(125,675)
Accruals	(43,775)		(25,962)
Tax			(5,851)
Overdraft	(74,567)		(188,235)
	211,787		345,723

Net current liabilities	(12,812)	(6,806)
Total assets less current liabilities	189,201	211,807

Provisions for liabilities and charges			
Deferred income: Grants	(18,000)		(16,000)
Deferred tax			(786)
			(16,786)
	171,201		195,021

Capital and reserves		
Share capital	175,000	175,000
Profit and loss account	(3,799)	20,021
	171,201	195,021

Note: Agreed credit terms were 90 days for collection and payment.

In April 1995 Mike and Jane presented their first period's draft accounts to the bank. At the meeting the bank manager produced ratios which he used to analyse the year's results during their discussion.

The ratios prepared by the bank for 1995 were as follows:

Profitability

Gross profit %	17.00%
Operating profit %	0.04%
Profit before tax %	(1.25%)
Profit after tax %	(1.25%)
Return on share capital and reserves	(2.22%)
Net asset turnover	1.78

Liquidity

Current ratio	0.94
Liquid ratio	0.71
Collection period (days)	136
Stock period (days) based on cost of sales	52
Payment period (days) based on purchases	85

Leverage

Total liabilities/tangible net worth	1.24
Bank debt/tangible net worth	0.43
Profit cover for interest	0.03

It was agreed that Mike and Jane would discuss the position with the bank in May 1996. At that meeting they proposed to request a restructuring of the bank facility to take the form of a term loan of £200,000 repayable over three years. They were intending to suggest a repayment schedule of £100,000, £50,000 and £50,000 on 31 March 1997, 31 March 1998 and 31 March 1999 respectively.

They produced projected profit and loss accounts and balance sheets for three years as follows:

	1997 £'000	1998 £'000	1999 £'000
Sales	670	750	960
Cost of sales	(545)	(600)	(760)
Gross profit	125	150	200
Administrative expenses	(18)	(20)	(21)
Selling expenses	(37)	(40)	(42)
Operating profit	70	90	137
Interest payable	(27)	(14)	(5)
Profit before tax	43	76	132
Taxation	(9)	(20)	(33)
Profit after tax	34	56	99

	1997 £'000	£'000	1998 £'000	£'000	1999 £'000	£'000
Fixed assets		230		230		230
Current assets						
Stock	120		170		190	
Debtors	145		126		200	
Prepayments	10		10		10	
	275		306		400	

Current liabilities

Creditors	(140)	(150)	(180)
Accruals	(8)	(9)	(10)
Tax	(4)	(16)	(27)
Overdraft	(5)	(5)	(5)
	(157)	(180)	(222)

Net current assets	118	126	178

Total assets less current liabilities	348	356	408

Less:

Term loan	(100)	(50)	-
Deferred tax	(5)	(9)	(14)
Deferred income	(14)	(12)	(10)
	(119)	(71)	(24)
	229	285	384

Share capital	175	175	175
Profit brought forward	20	54	110
Profit for year	34	56	99
	229	285	384

Mike and Jane have asked you, as their accountant, to assist them in drafting a report to the bank, requesting the restructuring of the bank facility. The report to the bank is to be presented in two sections:

(i)   a review of the company's performance in the two periods: from incorporation to 31 March 1995 and from 1 April 1995 to 31 March 1996, and

(ii)   the case for the request for restructuring of the bank facility, supported by the projected accounts.

Required

(a)   Draft the first section of the report on the company's performance in the two periods from incorporation to 31 March 1996 that Mike and Jane are to present to the bank.   **(9 marks)**

(b)   Draft a report to Mike and Jane commenting on the projected accounts and their request for a restructuring of the bank facility.   **(16 marks)**

(c)   [Not reproduced as this part of the question is no longer within the syllabus.]   **(5 marks)**
                                                                                                          (Total 30 marks)

Section B - TWO questions ONLY to be attempted

---

33   (Question 3 of examination)

Harmonise plc is a plastic toy manufacturer. Its toy sales have been adversely affected by imports and it has been changing towards the supply of plastic office equipment. Profits are expected to continue to fall for the next four years when they are expected to stabilise at the 1999 level. There will be a regular programme of plant renewal.

The following information is available:

Year ended 30 April	Profit before depreciation and tax £	Capital allowances £	Depreciation £
1996	1,250,000	400,000	80,000
1997	1,200,000	80,000	160,000
1998	1,100,000	80,000	240,000
1999	1,000,000	560,000	160,000

Assume a corporation tax rate of 33%. On 1 March 1995 there was a nil balance on the deferred tax account.

Required

(a)　(i)　Prepare the profit and loss and balance sheet extracts for corporation tax and deferred taxation for the four years 1996-1999 using the following methods

　　　　(i)　　Flow-through
　　　　(ii)　　Full provision
　　　　(iii)　　Partial provision

　　　　Notes to the profit and loss account and balance sheet are *not* required.

　　(ii)　[Not reproduced as this part of the question is no longer valid due to technical developments].
　　　　　　　　　　　　　　　　　　　　　　　　　　　　　　　　　　　　(10 marks)

(b)　Discuss arguments for and against each of the three methods in (a) (i) above.　　**(6 marks)**

(c)　Assuming that all of the shares in Harmonise plc were acquired for cash by Grab plc on 1 May 1995, explain the factors that would be taken into account in determining the fair value of deferred tax as at the date of acquisition. Grab plc applies the partial provision method.　　**(4 marks)**
　　　　　　　　　　　　　　　　　　　　　　　　　　　　　　　　　　　(Total 20 marks)

34　　(Question 4 of examination)

Renewal plc was incorporated in 1985 to carry on business as manufacturers of designer jewellery. The company has incurred recent trading losses but has now returned to modest profitability. The directors estimate that raising new capital for additional investment in plant would produce an increase in profit from £1,000,000 to £1,750,000 per year but in order to be able to pay dividends it is necessary to eliminate the debit balance on the profit and loss account.

The balance sheet of Renewal plc as at 31 May 1996 showed:

	£'000	£'000	£'000
Capital and reserves			
Ordinary shares of £1 each - 80p paid up			4,080
8% cumulative preference shares of £1 each			5,440
Profit and loss account balance			(5,046)
Profit attributable to arrears of preference dividends			1,306
			5,780
Fixed assets			
Freehold premises			2,890
Plant and machinery			2,040
Patents			578
Development expenditure			408

Current assets		
Stock	2,108	
Debtors	2,720	
	———	
		4,828
Current liabilities; amounts due in less than one year		
Trade creditors	2,176	
Overdraft	1,768	
Loans from directors	1,020	
	———	
		4,964
Net current liabilities		(136)
		———
		5,780
		———

The directors have formulated the following scheme:

(a)   The unpaid capital on the £1 ordinary shares to be called up.

(b)   The ordinary shareholders to agree to a reduction of 70p on each share held with new shares having a nominal value of 50p and treated as 30p paid up.

(c)   The preference shareholders to agree to the cancellation of their three years' arrears of dividend.

(d)   The preference shareholders to agree to a reduction of 20p on each share held with the new shares having a nominal value of 80p and treated as fully paid up.

(e)   The dividend rate on preference shares to be increased from 8% to 11%.

(f)   The debit balance on the profit and loss account to be eliminated.

(g)   Freehold premises have been professionally valued at £3,800,000.

(h)   Plant is to be written down by £850,000; patents are to be written down to £340,000; development expenditure is to be written off; stock is to be written down by £406,000; a provision for doubtful debts of 10% is to be created.

(i)   New capital to be raised by a rights issue with existing ordinary shareholders subscribing for two shares for every one share held, 30p payable on application, and preference shareholders subscribing for one new 80p preference share for every four preference shares held.

(j)   The directors to agree to £420,000 of their loans to be written off and to accept ordinary shares of 50p each, at a value of 30p (paid up), in settlement of the balance of their loans. These shares are not affected by the rights issue in (i) above.

Required

(a)   (i)   Explain the procedure that a company needs to follow to readjust the rights of members under ss 425 and 426 of the Companies Act 1985.

        (ii)   Advise the directors on an alternative course of action if the ordinary shareholders are not prepared to accept new obligations arising from the proposal to issue partly paid shares.   **(5 marks)**

(b)   Prepare the balance sheet for Renewal plc on the assumption that the directors' scheme has been put into effect.   **(7 marks)**

(c)   Advise the preference shareholders whether they should participate in the scheme.   **(8 marks)**
        (Total 20 marks)

---

35   (Question 5 of examination)

The following questions relate to Finaleyes plc, a car seat manufacturer. The company is pursuing a policy of growth by acquisition and it has targeted a number of specific companies for takeover during the next three years.

For the year ended 30 April 1996 its turnover was £100m; post tax profits £13m applying a tax rate of 33%; net assets £80m and issued share capital £10m in 25p shares. At 30 April 1996 its share price was £6 per share and at 31 May 1996 its share price was £7 per share.

The financial director is reviewing the accounting treatment of various items prior to the signing of the 1996 accounts which is planned for July 1996.

The items are:

(1)   **A share issue**

On 31 January 1996 it was announced that the company was raising £14m before expenses by the issue of shares for cash. The issue took place on 31 May 1996 at market share price.

(2)   **Acquisition of a plant**

On 1 May 1995 the company acquired a factory in Norway for £4m. On 30 April 1996 they obtained professional advice that the building had an expected life of 40 years with no residual value but that the heating systems would require replacing every 15 years at an expected cost of £450,000.

Depreciation on the buildings has been charged following the company's normal accounting policy of using the straight-line method.

A charge of £30,000 has been made to the profit and loss account to create a provision for the replacement of the heating system assuming a 15 year life. The initial reasoning for making the charge for the heating system replacement was that it complied with the ASB definition of a liability ie, 'Liabilities are an entity's obligations to transfer economic benefits as a result of past transactions or events'.

(3)   **Sale and lease back**

At 30 April 1996 the balance sheet included the main offices of the company at a figure of £10m. On 15 May 1996 the company exchanged contracts with the Helpful Friendly Society Ltd for the sale of the main offices for £12m with lease back for an initial period of 20 years at market rentals. The company intended to use the proceeds to invest in office property in Kuala Lumpur. The contract provided that the cash consideration would be paid to Finaleyes plc on 14 June 1996.

(4)   **Stock valuation errors**

The company's policy on stock valuation was to value stock in accordance with SSAP 9 at the lower of cost and net realisable value. The company discovered in May 1996 that there had been an omission for three years to apply this policy to stock held in a warehouse in Cyprus; the provisions required to bring the stock down to net realisable values were £63,000 for 1993, £70,000 for 1994, £105,000 for 1995 and £115,000 for 1996.

The adjustment has been treated as a prior period adjustment and reduced the profit and loss account balance brought forward at 1 May 1995 and the stock by £238,000 being the total of the provisions required for the years ended 30 April 1993 to 1995.

Required

For each of the items (1) to (4) above:

(a)   State your view on the appropriate treatment in the financial statements as at 30 April 1996 giving your reasons; and

(b)   Draft an appropriate note to the accounts and/or state the adjustment that would be made to items in the accounts as required.

Each of the items (1) to (4) carries equal marks.

(20 marks)

ANSWERS TO JUNE 1996 EXAMINATION

31   (Answer 1 of examination)

Examiner's comments and marking guide

Question 1: part (a) of this question required the preparation of consolidated accounts for a UK parent and its 70% owned French subsidiary using the temporal method.

The question was generally well answered and candidates were well prepared for this topic.

Common mistakes and omissions, that meant that candidates did not achieve better marks, included:

- omitting to adjust for depreciation or, where an adjustment was attempted, to calculate it correctly;

- omitting to make any comment or calculation relating to the exchange difference. Marks were awarded to candidates who considered the need and made a reasonable attempt to arrive at an exchange difference;

- errors in the calculation of the minority interest. The errors were varied and included errors of principle such as including a figure in the profit and loss account based on the retained profit in the subsidiary;

- errors in calculating the subsidiary's fixed assets using a translation rate of 12;

- errors in calculating the goodwill or omitting to deal with it in the reserves ie, leaving it as an item in the workings. Marks were gained for a correct calculation but the disclosure mark was missed;

- omitting to calculate the post acquisition reserves of Frank SA and including an incorrect balancing figure in the balance sheet instead.

Overall it seems that this topic is well understood by many of the candidates.

			Marks
(a)	Consolidated profit and loss account		
	Operating profit	2	
	Exchange difference	5	
	Tax	1	
	Minority interest	2	
	Dividend	1	
			11
	Consolidated balance sheet		
	Fixed assets	3	
	Current assets	2	
	Current liabilities	2	
	Share capital	1	
	Reserves	3	
	Minority interest	2	
			13
(b)	Letter - format	2	
	Staff engaged	4	
	Responsibility	4	
	Audit fee	2	
			12
			36

Step by step answer plan

Step 1 Read the question again and make sure that you focus on precisely what is required. The important clue is the words 'selling agent' in the second sentence of the scenario. This indicates that the temporal method is required.

Step 2 Translate the plant and machinery of the subsidiary at 31 May 1996 into sterling. Then translate the rest of the closing balance sheet.

Step 3 Translate the operating profit for the year and then translate the rest of the profit and loss account.

Step 4 Translate the opening balance sheet. This will enable you to calculate the exchange difference in the profit and loss account.

Step 5 Establish the group structure.

Step 6 Calculate the minority interest in the profit and loss account. Then complete the consolidated profit and loss account.

Step 7 Do the main consolidation workings: goodwill, minority interest, retained profits carried forward.

Step 8 Complete the consolidated balance sheet.

The examiner's answer

(a) **Consolidated profit and loss account for the Angol plc Group for the year ended 31 May 1996**

		£'000
Operating profit	W7	867,567
Less: Tax	W8	(348,625)
Profit after tax		518,942
Less: Minority interest	W9	(11,851)
Profit attributable to Angol plc shareholders	N1	507,091
Less: Proposed dividend		(262,500)
		244,591

N1 The profit before dividend dealt with in the accounts of the company is £516,125,000.

Consolidated balance sheet as at 31 May 1996

	Angol plc £'000	*Frank SA* £'000	*Consolidated* £'000
Fixed assets			
Land at cost	630,000	121,800	751,800
Buildings at depreciated cost	529,200	27,552	556,752
Plant and machinery	348,600	11,970	360,570
	1,507,800	161,322	1,669,122
Investment in Frank SA	147,000		
Current assets			
Stock	168,000	19,200	187,200
Debtors	426,300	25,800	452,100
Bank	176,400	7,200	183,600
	770,700	52,200	822,900

		Angol plc £'000	Frank SA £'000	Consolidated £'000
Current liabilities				
Creditors		(413,700)	(27,000)	(440,700)
Tax		(320,000)	(32,714)	(352,714)
Proposed dividend		(262,500)		(262,500)
		(996,200)	(59,714)	(1,055,914)
Net current liabilities		(225,500)	(7,514)	(233,014)
Total assets less current liabilities		1,429,300	153,808	1,436,108
Capital and reserves				
Ordinary shares of £1		525,000		525,000
Reserves	W11	904,300		864,966
Shareholders' funds		1,429,300		1,389,966
Minority interests	W10			46,142
		1,429,300		1,436,108

W1

Translate balance sheet of Frank SA as at 31 May 1996

	FF'000	Rate	£'000
Fixed assets			
Land at cost	1,218,000	10	121,800
Buildings at depreciated cost	275,520	10	27,552
Plant and machinery	111,300	W2	11,970
Current assets			
Stock	134,400	7	19,200
Debtors	180,600	7	25,800
Bank	50,400	7	7,200
	365,400		52,200
Current liabilities			
Creditors	(189,000)	7	(27,000)
Tax	(229,000)	7	(32,714)
	(418,000)		(59,714)
Net current liabilities	(52,600)		(7,514)
	1,552,220		153,808
Capital and reserves			
Ordinary shares of FF1	1,050,000	10	105,000
Reserves at acquisition	126,000	10	12,600
Reserves	376,220	balance	36,208
	1,552,220		153,808

W2

Translating plant

			£'000
Cost:	of existing plant	FF108,150/10	10,815
	of new plant	FF84,000/9	9,333
			20,148
Aggregate depreciation			
	Purchased in year	FF8,400/9	933
	At 1.6.95	FF72,450/10	7,245
			8,178
Net book value		FF111,300	11,970

W3

Translate profit and loss account

	Frank SA FF'000		£'000
Operating profit	588,000	W4	74,139
Tax on profit	(229,000)	W8	(28,625)
Profit after tax	359,000		45,514
Dividend paid	(185,000)	15,125/70 × 100	(21,607)
Retained profit	174,000		23,907

Note that the closing rate is also acceptable for translating the tax figure. This would give a figure of £32,714,285.

W4

Frank SA operating profit translated

			FF'000
Per Frank SA profit and loss account			588,000
Add back depreciation:			
on buildings	[FF504,000/50 years]		10,080
on plant	[FF192,150/10 years]		19,215
			617,295

		£'000	£'000
Translated at average rate	[617,295/8]		77,162
Less depreciation:			
on buildings	[FF10,080/10]	1,008	
on plant existing at			
date of acquisition	[FF10,815/10]	1,082	
acquired on 1.6.95	[FF8,400/9]	933	
			3,023
			74,139

W5

Translate balance sheet of Frank SA as at 1 June 1995

	FF'000	FF'000	Rate	£'000
Fixed assets				
Land at cost		1,218,000	10	121,800
Buildings				
Cost	504,000			
Depreciation	218,400			
		285,600	10	28,560
Plant and machinery				
Cost	108,150			
Depreciation	61,635			
		46,515	10	4,652
		1,550,115		
Net current liabilities [balance]		(171,895)	9	(19,099)
		1,378,220		135,913
Share capital		1,050,000	10	105,000
Reserves:				
at date of acquisition		126,000	10	12,600
post acquisition		202,220	balance	18,313
[1,552,220 – 174,000]		1,378,220		135,913

W6

Exchange difference

Post acquisition reserves at 31.5.96		W1	36,208
Post acquisition reserves at 1.6.95		W5	18,313
Increase			17,895
Retained profit for year		W3	23,907
Exchange loss			(6,012)

W7

Operating profits

		£'000
Angol plc		821,000
Frank SA	W4	74,139
Exchange loss		(6,012)
Goodwill amortisation (64,680 ÷ 3)		(21,560)
		867,567

W8

Tax

	£'000
Angol plc	320,000
Frank SA	28,625
	348,625

W9

Minority interest

	£'000
30% of [£45,514,000 – £6,012,000] =	11,851

W10

Minority interest

Calculate as 30% of £153,808,000 = £46,142,400

W11

Consolidated reserves

	£'000
Angol plc reserves	904,300
Frank SA post acquisition reserves	
70% of £36,208,000	25,346
	929,646
Less goodwill written off W12	64,680
	864,966

W12

Goodwill

	£'000	£'000
Cost of shares in Frank SA		147,000
Less shares		
70% of £105,000,~~000~~	73,500	
pre-acquisition reserves		
70% of £12,600,000	8,820	
		82,320
Goodwill		64,680

---

32   (Answer 2 of examination)

Examiner's comments and marking guide

Question 2: this question related to a private company formed, in July 1994, to exploit a niche in the UK market for a specialised product, financed equally by equity and a bank overdraft. Candidates were required to:

(a)   report on the company's actual performance for the first two periods of trading where there was a loss in the first 9 months and a profit in the second year based on detailed accounts for presentation to the bank which had provided the overdraft; and

(b)   report on projected three years' accounts to 31 March 1999 prepared by the directors for later presentation to the bank to support a request for a switch from an overdraft to a Term Loan of £200,000 repayable over 3 years, with an overdraft retained but at a reduced level of £5,000.

Good answers were in the format of a report to the bank, in appropriate style and included:

proposed restructuring of the finance. This should have been supported by a selection of ratios and cash flow summaries with narrative commentaries and a critical analysis of limitations and deficiencies in the projections.

The critical analysis should have included comments on matters such as:

(i)   changes in rates of sales growth;

(ii)   lack of steady progression in sales and operating margins;

(iii)   excessive optimism in projections for working capital to support the increases in sales;

(iv)   the position re fixed asset investment over the three years;

(v)   no dividend payments for the period;

(vi)   the need for a clear statement of assumptions underlying the sales and expense projections;

(vii)   the absence of cash flow statements for the period linking up with the profit and loss account and balance sheet;

(viii) revision of the projections to a more realistic base.

		Marks
(a)	Report form	2
	Major aspect eg, liquidity	
	three marks per aspect	9
		11
(b)	Report - format	1
	Major aspects eg, sales growth	
	four marks per aspect	12
	Revisions to projections	3
	Conclusion	2
		18
(c)	Audit aspects	
	General introduction	2
	Use in planning	3
	Use as substantive procedure	3
		8
		37

Step by step answer plan

Step 1   Read the question again and make sure that you focus on precisely what is required. This is an 'interpretation' question in two distinct parts. Both parts require a report, but the subject and the recipient is different in each part. In addition, each report is to be based on different information.

Step 2   Begin part (a) by calculating the ratios that the bank will use, based on the 1996 accounts. (The bank has already calculated the ratios for 1995.) Calculate any other useful ratios. Set out the ratios for 1995 and 1996 as an Appendix to the main report.

Step 3   Draw up headings and write an introductory paragraph.

Step 4   Begin to write the main body of the report, covering profitability, liquidity and leverage.

Step 5   Calculate changes in working capital during the year to 31 March 1996. Then discuss cash flows in the period, using this information.

Step 6   Cover any other relevant points and draw a conclusion.

Step 7 Start part (b) by calculating a selection of ratios based on the projections. These will enable you to decide whether: (a) the projections appear realistic; (b) the bank will agree to restructure the loan.

Step 8 Do any other potentially useful calculations (e.g. revision of projections, level of overdraft at period end).

Step 9 Draw up headings and write an introductory paragraph.

Step 10 Write the main body of the report. Cover sales growth, profitability, interest cover and working capital.

Step 11 Conclude the report by making recommendations.

The examiner's answer

(a) **Draft of report on the company's performance in the two periods from incorporation to 31 March 1996**

Date: 14 June 1996
To: Bank
From: Mike Ried and Jane Thurby

Re: Thermo Ltd

This is a report on the performance of Thermo Ltd based on the audited accounts of the company for the nine months period to 31 March 1995 and for the year ended 31 March 1996.

The first period of nine months was a start-up period and the second year will be more indicative of the ratios that can be used for establishing norms for the business and estimating future trends.

Did you answer the question?

The headings and introductory paragraph set out the authors, recipient and terms of reference of the report.

Profitability

Profitability has improved considerably in 1996. The gross profit % is up by two percentage points. The operating profit has increased from the low opening figure of 0.04% to 8.90% due to the improvement in the gross profit percentage and because the fixed cost elements of the administrative and selling expenses have been spread over a greater volume of sales which have increased by 35% in 1996.

The increase in interest charges has meant however that the profit before tax has shown a lower increase of 6.8 percentage points thereby partially diluting the gain from the improved operating.

The company incurred a tax charge in 1996 and achieved a profit after tax rate of 4.3%.

Did you answer the question?

Notice the way in which this answer interprets and makes connections between the ratios rather than merely observing that profitability has improved.

Liquidity

The current ratio has improved from 0.94 to 0.98. However, the liquid ratio has moved in the opposite direction weakening from 0.71 to 0.58 due to the large increase in the inventory period from 52 to 114 days and a more than doubling of the overdraft from £74,567 to £188,235.

This increase in the overdraft means that it has exceeded the limit of £175,000 that was agreed on commencing the business.

The collection period has improved from 136 to 127 days but it is higher than the payment period in both trading periods. The payment periods remained stable at 85 and 86 days and is indicative of reasonable credit taking terms.

If the collection period were reduced to the same level as the payment period the overdraft would be reduced by £61,068 which would have brought the overdraft within agreed limits.

[£190,539 – (£549,500/365 × 86) = £190,539 – £129,471 = £61,068]

Leverage

The bank debt/tangible net assets ratio has worsened from 0.43 to 0.96 which reflects the significant rise in the bank overdraft. However, although the bank has almost as much money in the business as the owners, the profit cover for interest has improved significantly from 0.03 to 2.65.

Did you answer the question?

Notice the way in which the paragraph above attempts to mitigate the effect of potentially damaging information (leverage has worsened) by drawing attention to the improvement in interest cover. This shows that the report is clearly addressing the requirement to report to the bank on the client's behalf.

Cash generation

The 1996 accounts show that with a profit of £30,457 and depreciation of £20,150 the company generated a positive gross cash flow from trading operations of £50,607. Increased capital was required for working capital following the 35% increase in sales and there was an increase in the stock holding period. The working capital increase was £125,525 as follows:

	£
Stock increase	(90,600)
Debtors increase	(39,339)
Prepayments increase	(8,750)
Cash increase	(1,253)
Creditors increase	32,230
Accruals decrease	(17,813)
	(125,525)

This meant that there was a net cash outflow from operations of £74,918 [125,525 – 50,607] which together with the capital investment of £36,750 in machinery and office furniture was financed by an increase in the bank overdraft.

Did you answer the question?

The report must cover cash flows as these will be the prime concern of the bank.

Deferred income

The company received a grant of £20,000 in 1994. This has been credited to income at the rate of £2,000 each financial year and is not a material consideration.

Conclusion

The company has established itself in the market achieving a sales growth of 35%. It has improved the asset turnover rate and is achieving 15.6% return on tangible net assets. Its trading profitability has improved to show 4.3% profit after tax.

The increase in activity and the lengthening of the stockholding period has put pressure on the liquidity and increased the banks' exposure to risk when considered from a capital leverage viewpoint. However, the company is able to service the loan and shows a healthy interest cover of 2.65.

Did you answer the question?

Notice the final paragraph. It mentions the bank's exposure to risk but concludes with a firm positive statement.

For information

Appendix to part (a)

	1995	1996
Profitability		
Sales growth	-	35.34%
[(549,500 – (304,500/9*12))(304,500/9*12)*100]		
Gross profit %	16.98%	19.35%
[51,713/304,500*100][106,330/549,500*100]		
Operating profit %	.04%	8.90%
[123/304,500*100][48,912/549,500*100]		
Profit before tax %	(1.25%)	5.54%
[(3,799)/304,500*100][30,457/549,500*100]		
Profit after tax %	(1.25%)	4.33%
[(3,799)/304,500*100][23,820/549,500*100]		
Return on capital employed	(2.22%)	15.60%
[(3,799)/171,201*100][30,457/195,201*100]		
Net asset turnover	1.78	2.82
[304,500/171,201][549,500/195,201]		
Liquidity		
Current ratio	0.94	0.98
[198,975/211,787][338,917/345,723]		
Liquid ratio	0.71	0.58
[151,200/211,787][200,542/345,723]		
Collection period (days)	136	127
[151,200/(304,500/273)][190,539/(549,500/365)]		
Stock period (days)	52	114
[47,775/(252,787/273)][138,375/(443,170/365)]		
Payment period (days) using purchases		
[93,445/(252,787 + 47,775)*365*9/12]	85	
[125,675/(443,170 – 47,775 + 138,375)*365]		86
Leverage		
Total liabilities/tangible net worth	1.24	1.77
[211,787/(171,201)][345,723/(195,021 + 786)]		
Bank debt/tangible net worth	0.43	0.96
[74,567/171,201][188,235/(195,021 + 786)]		
Long-term debt/tangible net worth		
Profit cover for interest	0.03	2.65
[123/3,922][48,912/18,455]		

(b)   Report on projections

To: Mike and Jane
From:
Date:

Report on projections and restructuring of bank facilities

In accordance with your instructions, we have reviewed the projected accounts for 1997, 1998 and 1999 and your proposals for restructuring the bank facility.

The bank will be viewing the projections to establish whether they are realistic in the light of your 1996 achievement. In particular they will be considering sales growth, operating profit, interest cover, assumptions for working capital changes and the bank's exposure to risk as a result of leverage.

> ### Did you answer the question?
>
> The focus of the report in part (b) is quite different from that of part (a). Whereas the tone of the report in part (a) had to be positive, the report in part (b) must be realistic and must analyse the projections from a critical perspective.

Sales growth

The company is forecasting 21.8%, 11.9% and 28% in 1997, 1998 and 1999. There will need to be a clear explanation of the reason for the change in 1999 eg, change in company policy as regards type and quality of product or geographical area; change in market share. The essential aspect will be to demonstrate that the assumptions are realistic.

Operating profitability

The operating profit is 10.4%, 12.0% and 14.3%. This increase does not arise from improved margins with the gross profit per cent remaining reasonably constant at 19 – 21%. Given that this is a new start-up and a growth business then it could be expected that the benefits of spreading fixed administration and selling costs would continue. However, the assumption that a 75% increase in sales from 1996 to 1999 will only lead to an increase of 17% in the administration costs will need to be explained.

> ### Did you answer the question?
>
> Again, notice that the answer does not simply comment on the figures, but focuses firmly on the questions that the bank will ask.

Interest cover

The interest cover improves from 2.6 to 27.4 as the bank liability is repaid over the three years. This is of course dependent on the company being able to reduce its borrowing.

Working capital

Debtors

The projections show the collection period reducing significantly from 127 days in 1996 to 79 days in 1997, 61 days in 1998 and 76 days in 1999.

We recognise that it is the management's intention to strenuously address this area and this should of course be reflected in the projections. However, the reasonableness of the projected improvement and a reduction of such an amount will be questioned.

Strong evidence would need to be produced that trading conditions can reasonably be assumed to change to this extent or the projections will need to be restated to reflect an approach that is more in line with 1996 performance.

On an initial assumption that the company brings the collection period from 127 days in 1996 down in line with the agreed credit period of 90 days at say 10 days per year the debtors figure would be as follows

	1997	*1998*	*1999*
Sales	£670,000	£750,000	£960,000
Collection period (days)	117	107	97
	£	£	£
Debtors	215,000	220,000	255,000
Debtors in projection	145,000	126,000	200,000
Increased working capital	70,000	94,000	55,000

These revisions will have a material effect on both the amount and the timing of projected borrowing.

> **Did you answer the question?**
>
> The bank will be concerned with movements in working capital because this will affect cash flow. Therefore revised (realistic) projections are an important part of the report.

Stock

The stock period achieved in 1996 was 114 days. The period projected for 1997 is 81 days. Again, accepting that the company will improve the stock period the speed of the change is questionable and will be regarded as too optimistic without strong evidence that it is achievable.

If it were assumed that an improvement of 10 days per year could be achieved the stock levels would be as follows:

	1997	*1998*	*1999*
Cost of sales	£545,000	£600,000	£760,000
Stock period (days)	104	94	90
	£	£	£
Stock	155,000	155,000	187,000
Stock in projections	120,000	170,000	190,000
Increase/(decrease) in working capital	35,000	(15,000)	(3,000)

Payment period

The payment period is projected to remain reasonably constant at 84 days by 1999 [£180,000/(£760,000 − 170,000 + 190,000)*365] which appears reasonable.

Fixed assets

We note that in your projections the fixed assets have not been depreciated. Unless the additions each year equal the depreciation, a depreciation charge needs to be built into the projections.

Revision of projections

The increase in working capital would be reflected in an overdraft figure in the balance sheet. If the revised stock and debtor figures are incorporated, the effect of the difference between the original and revised figures on the projected overdraft would be as follows:

	1997 £'000	*1998* £'000	*1999* £'000
Projected overdraft	(5)	(5)	(50)
Stock (increase)/decrease	(35)	15	3
Debtors increase	(70)	(94)	(55)
Revised overdraft	(110)	(84)	(57)

This indicates that the proposed restructuring in the form of a term loan with a repayment of £100,000 in 1997 will be unachievable and that there would be an overdraft requirement at the end of 1999.

If the revisions are realistic, the company will need to retain an overdraft facility. The revised projections show that there will be £210,000 owing to the bank at 31 May 1997 reducing to £57,000 by the end of 1999.

In our opinion, the projections will need revision before submission to the bank and/or additional supporting information eg, assumptions on administrative expenses and sales growth.

We have approached the review in the same manner as we feel the bank will approach it and raised questions such as they will no doubt raise when you meet.

Please let us know if we can be of further assistance either in revising the projections or at your meeting with the bank.

Did you answer the question?

Notice that the answer does not finish by simply revising the cash flow projections. It states the important fact that the restructuring is unachievable. It then makes firm recommendations.

---

33   (Answer 3 of examination)

Examiner's comments and marking guide

Question 3: (a) (i) required the preparation of Profit and Loss Account and Balance Sheet extracts for Taxation over a period of four years to 1999 based on profits, capital allowances and depreciation figures given, under each of the Nil, Full and Partial Provision methods for Deferred Tax.

The question was popular but candidates struggled with the calculations in this part. Common mistakes were adding back depreciation to profits, using the same figures for both the profit and loss and balance sheet for the Full Provision during the four years, mixing up years and figures for the partial provision, stating that no provision was required for the partial provision.

(a)   (ii)   This part was poorly answered.

(b)   Candidates generally had a good understanding of the arguments for and against all three methods and many candidates scored the majority of their marks on this part.

(c)   This part was poorly answered with answers focusing on the general application of deferred tax, the concept, timing differences etc with no reference to the group situation using acquisition accounting, quasi timing differences, distortion of post acquisition earnings and acquirer's intention.

Overall, candidates were able to explain the three methods for accounting for Deferred Tax but were unable to prepare accurate accounting entries for any of the methods.

			Marks
(a)	(i)	Flow through	2
	(ii)	Full provision	3
	(iii)	Partial provision	4
	(iv)	Debentures	4
			——
			13
(b)		Discuss arguments one mark per point	6
(c)		Fair values	
		Determine on group basis	2
		Existing timing differences	2
		Quasi-timing differences	2
			——
			6
			——
			25
			——

Step by step answer plan

Step 1   Read the question again and make sure that you focus on precisely what is required.

Step 2   Answer part (a) (i).

Step 3   Calculate deferred tax under the full provision method (W1). This will enable you to complete part (a) (ii).

Step 4   Calculate the maximum cumulative reversal. This will enable you to calculate deferred tax under the partial provision method and then to complete part (a) (iii).

Step 5   Jot down arguments for and against each of the three methods. Then write your answer to part (b), taking each method in turn.

Step 6   Re-read requirement (c) to focus on the short scenario. The words 'fair values' and 'acquisition' should be a signal that FRS 7 may be relevant here.

Step 7   Begin part (c) by explaining the general requirements of FRS 7 in relation to deferred tax. Then explain the nature of the deferred tax balances involved: existing balances and timing differences arising as a result of the fair value exercise.

Items not required by the Examiner for this question:

- notes to the accounts in part (a);
- general discussion of the requirements of SSAP 15/FRS 7 without reference to the scenario in part (c).

The examiner's answer

(a)   (i)

Profit and loss account and balance sheet extracts

(i)   **Flow-through method**

	1996 £	1997 £	1998 £	1999 £
Taxable profit	850,000	1,120,000	1,020,000	440,000
Tax at 33%	280,500	369,600	336,600	145,200
Deferred tax	nil	nil	nil	nil
Balance sheet extract				
Provision for liabilities and charges	nil	nil	nil	nil

(ii)   **Full provision method**

	1996 £	1997 £	1998 £	1999 £
Taxable profit	850,000	1,120,000	1,020,000	440,000
Tax at 33%	280,500	369,600	336,600	145,200
Deferred tax W1	105,600	(26,400)	(52,800)	132,000
Balance sheet extract				
Provision for liabilities and charges	105,600	79,200	26,400	158,400

W1 Deferred tax calculations

	1996	1997	1998	1999
Capital allowances	400,000	80,000	80,000	560,000
Depreciation	80,000	160,000	240,000	160,000
	320,000	(80,000)	(160,000)	400,000
Tax at 33%	105,600	(26,400)	(52,800)	132,000

(ii)   **Partial provision method**

£79,200 of the timing difference will reverse in 1997 and 1998.

	1996 £	*1997* £	*1998* £	*1999* £
Taxable profit	850,000	1,120,000	1,020,000	440,000
Tax at 33%	280,500	369,600	336,600	145,200
Deferred tax W1	79,200	(26,400)	(52,800)	
Balance sheet extract				
Provision for liabilities and charges	79,200	52,800	nil	nil

(b)   The following discussion considers the arguments for and against each of the methods.

The flow-through method

This method is based on the principle that only the tax payable in respect of a period should be charged in the profit and loss account of that period. The effect on the balance sheet would be that it would only show the current liability relating to that tax payable.

On grounds of commercial reality, flow-through avoids the need to make assumptions about the future which are uncertain as to outcome; on revenue grounds, recognising income tax when assessed is consistent with the government's policy of assessing tax for the time period in accordance with the fiscal policy of the time. On accounting principle grounds, the flow-through method complies with the matching principle whereby the amount charged in the profit and loss account is based on tax payable in relation to the taxable profit of the accounting period.

The arguments against the method are that the commercial reality is that tax has been deferred and not eliminated and the uncertainties surrounding deferred tax provisioning are similar to many other areas where management exercise judgement. On the question of accounting principle and the matching concept, it is argued that the tax should be matched against the operating results of the accounting period and not the taxable profit. A particular problem is that the EPS is affected by any deferred tax charge. EPS can therefore be distorted by fiscal policy rather than give a fair reflection of operating performance which it is supposed to measure.

Full provision

This method has strong support based on the accounting principles of matching and prudence. The tax charge is matched with the operating results and is prudent because the amount is the full potential tax liability based on the timing differences known at the date of the accounts.

The arguments against the method are largely based on commercial reality in that the result of full provisioning may be to accumulate provisions over time to the extent that they become a material item in the balance sheet without representing a genuine liability of the business. There has been discussion about the advisability of discounting the provision which would reduce its significance in the profit and loss account and balance sheet. However, it could be argued that discounting an accounting allocation is invalid and even if cash flows were identified they would be a subjective estimate of both the amounts and the years of reversals and a subjective choice of the most appropriate discount rate to use.

Even where there has been agreement that full provisioning should be the preferred method, there has been disagreement as to the use of the liability or deferral method. The deferral method places the primary emphasis on the matching concept ie, matching the tax charge in each period with the accounting profit; the liability method places the primary emphasis on maintaining the provision at the best estimate of future tax payable considering the initial charge to be a tentative estimate requiring reassessment over time.

Partial provision

The present approach in the UK is to apply the partial provision method calculating the charge using the liability method.

The arguments in favour of this method are largely based on realism. The tax charge reflects the amount of tax that will become payable based on current knowledge and intention; the provision in the balance sheet is a realistic estimate of the tax liability that will need to be discharged.

The arguments against the method are mainly based on the need to consider the foreseeable future with a prediction of future events. This is subjective and can result in differing treatments of identical situations depending on the business's forecasts of future activity and profitability.

In conclusion, it is unclear whether a decision should be based on commercial reality or accounting principles. There is a conflict between the two which SSAP 15 has attempted to resolve. Similar debates to that in the UK are occurring in other countries and within the IASC. At the moment the UK appears to be out of step with international practice which overwhelmingly uses full provisioning.

Did you answer the question?

Notice how the answer takes each of the three methods in turn and includes arguments both for and against. This meets the requirement to *discuss*. Although this was not explicitly required, the answer concludes with a statement of the current position.

(c)   Assuming that all of the shares in Harmonise plc were acquired for cash by Grab plc on 1 May 1995, explain the factors that would be taken into account in determining the fair value of deferred tax as at the date of acquisition.

Determine on a group basis

FRS 7 provides that deferred tax assets and liabilities recognised in the fair value exercise should be determined on a group basis by considering the enlarged group as a whole. At the end of the accounting period in which the acquisition occurred, the enlarged group's deferred tax provision will be calculated as a single amount, on assumptions applicable to the group and to determine the deferred tax of the acquired company as at the date of acquisition using different assumptions from those applying to the group as a whole would result in the post-acquisition profit and loss account reflecting the change from one set of assumptions to another, rather than any real change in the circumstances of the group.

Existing timing differences

There is no specific guidance given in the standard but the recognition of deferred tax in the context of a fair value exercise falls into two areas. First there will be the existing timing differences within the acquired company which will have been quantified in determining the potential tax liability to deferred tax.

Quasi-timing differences arising from fair value exercise

In addition, the adjustments made as a result of the fair value exercise may lead to quasi-timing differences which will also require provision for deferred tax. Although the difference between the fair values assigned and the tax base values of the assets and liabilities acquired are not in fact strictly timing differences within the SSAP 15 definition, differences between accounting profits and taxable profits will arise in subsequent periods as items pass through the profit and loss account. It is necessary therefore to treat them as timing differences in order to avoid distorting post-acquisition earnings.

The commercial reality is that the partial provisioning method is influenced by management intentions and it is not possible to take a neutral view - the acquirer's intentions will determine the amount and movements on the deferred tax account.

Did you answer the question?

Notice the way in which this answer is organised into short paragraphs, each dealing with one factor.

Tutorial note

Part (a) (ii) of this question has not been reproduced. This asked candidates to calculate the deferred taxation arising from accrued interest on debentures. Following changes in a recent Finance Act, interest is now generally taxed on an accruals basis rather than a cash basis. This means that timing differences no longer arise on accrued interest. Minor changes have also been made to the Examiner's answer to reflect the abolition of ACT.

---

34   (Answer 4 of examination)

Examiner's comments and marking guide

Question 4: part (a) examined knowledge of the statutory procedures applicable when a company wishes to readjust the rights of members and alternative procedures available to the directors. **This was generally well answered.**

Part (b) required the preparation of a balance sheet following the implementation of a scheme. Many candidates scored maximum marks for this section although there was evidence of over-elaboration with some candidates producing both Journal and T Accounts to support the balance sheet entries. Weaker answers were unable to deal with the basic accounting adjustments.

Part (c) carried 8 marks and required the candidates to advise preference shareholders in relation to the scheme outlined in the question. A good answer would have considered the implication of rejecting the scheme as well as the income and capital implications of accepting the scheme.

Answers tended to be either very strong or very poor with very few average answers.

Weaker candidates produced a poorly constructed report, failed to mention either the capital or income implications, failed to calculate the amount available on liquidation, simply stating that there would be no funds available and based their comments on the nominal share capital held by the preference shareholders.

Many candidates recognised that the interest rate paid to preference shareholders had increased, however often did not attempt to calculate the implications of this.

Few candidates attempted to offer a conclusion or give realistic advice to the preference shareholders.

			Marks
(a)	One mark per item up to	6	
		—	
			6
(b)	Share capital	4	
	Reserves	1	
	Fixed assets	1	
	Current assets	3	
	Current liabilities	1	
		—	
			10
(c)	Capital implications	4	
	Income implications	5	
	Advice	1	
		—	
			10
			—
			26
			—

Step by step answer plan

Step 1   Read the question again and make sure that you focus on precisely what is required. The scenario features a capital reconstruction. With this topic, it is particularly important that you read the requirements carefully.

Step 2   Answer part (a) (i), noting that the key words are *explain the procedures*.

Step 3   Answer part (a) (ii) by stating the alternative method and then briefly explaining the procedure. Remember that only 5 marks/8 minutes are available for the whole of part (a).

Step 4 Start part (b) by doing the four main workings: ordinary and preference shares; the balance on capital reserve; and the new bank balance.

Step 5 Complete the balance sheet.

Step 6 Approach part (c) by comparing the position of the preference shareholders under the scheme and under the alternative, voluntary liquidation.

The examiner's answer

(a) (i) Where an arrangement is proposed between a company and its members the court may, on application, order a meeting of the shareholders concerned. If a majority in number and 75% in value agree to the arrangement it becomes binding on the class of shareholders involved and the company, subject to the sanction of the court.

75% must agree

(ii) An alternative method of reconstruction is by voluntary liquidation under ss 110-111 of the Insolvency Act 1986. This requires the shareholders to pass a special resolution putting the company into voluntary liquidation.

The procedure is for the liquidator to sell the business of the old company to a new company and to accept shares in the new company in consideration for the assets. The liquidator distributes the shares in the new company to the shareholders.

Dissenting ordinary shareholders have the right to require the liquidator either to abstain from complying with the resolution or to purchase their shares at an agreed price. This makes the process advantageous for the dissenting shareholders but more difficult for the company.

Did you answer the question?

Notice that this answer does not simply outline the procedure but also points out a potential disadvantage, thus meeting the requirement to *advise*.

(b)

Balance sheet of Renewal plc as at 31 May 1996

		£'000	£'000	£'000
Capital and reserves				
Ordinary shares				
17,300,000 shares of 50p each, 30p paid			W1	5,190
11% cumulative preference shares				
6,800,000 shares of 80p fully paid			W2	5,440
Capital reserve			W3	74
				10,704
Fixed assets				
Freehold premises at valuation				3,800
Plant and machinery	[2,040 – 850]			1,190
Patents	[578 – 238]			340
				5,330
Current assets				
Stock	[2,108 – 406]	1,702		
Debtors	[2,720 – 272]	2,448		
Bank	W4	3,400		
			7,550	

Current liabilities: amounts due in
  less than one year
    Trade creditors   2,176

		2,176
Net current assets		5,374
		10,704

W1   Ordinary shares - 50p shares

	£'000
Opening balance - 5,100,000 shares - 80p paid up	4,080
Balance on 5,100,000 shares - 20p	1,020
	5,100
Less capital reduction 70p per share	(3,570)
Transferred to ordinary shares 50p nominal value	1,530

	£'000
Ordinary shares - 50p shares	
5,100,000 shares - 30p paid up	1,530
New shares 10,200,000 - 30p paid up	3,060
Issued to directors - 2,000,000 - 30p paid up	600
Total 17,300,000 shares of 50p each, 30p paid	5,190

W2   8% Preference shares of £1 each

	£'000
Opening balance - 5,440,000 shares of £1 each	5,440
Less capital reduction - 20p per share	(1,088)
5,440,000 11% preference shares of 80p each	4,352
New shares 1,360,000 - 80p	1,088
New balance	5,440

W3   Capital reduction

	£'000	£'000
Ordinary shares £1 each		3,570
Preference shares £1 each		1,088
Premises		910
Directors' loans		420
Profit attributable to preference dividend arrears		1,306
		7,294
Profit and loss account	5,046	
Plant	850	
Patents	238	
Development expenses	408	
Stock	406	
Debtors	272	
		7,220
Capital reserve		74

W4   Bank

	£'000	£'000
Overdraft per balance sheet		1,768
Less Ordinary shares 80p paid up - balance	1,020	
10,200,000 new ordinary shares of 50p	3,060	
1,360,000 new preference shares	1,088	
		5,168
Closing bank balance		3,400

(c)   **Advise preference shareholders**

Preference shareholders need to consider two aspects of the scheme, namely, the capital and income implications.

Considering the capital implications and basing it on the information on current values implied within the scheme, it would appear that the preference shareholders could receive approximately 80p per share. This means that they have already suffered a reduction in the asset backing for their shares below their nominal value.

	£'000
Fixed assets	5,330
Current assets	4,150
	9,480
Less Current liabilities	4,964
Available for members	4,516

The asset backing has been calculated on the assumption that the values in the scheme could be achieved on a liquidation. In reality they might be substantially lower on a forced sale.

Considering the income implications, it is helpful to consider the position before and after the reduction and reconstruction.

		Income without recon- struction	Income with recon- struction
Total		£1,000,000	£1,750,000
Preference shareholders			
5,440,000 at 8%		435,200	
5,440,000 at 11%			598,400
Ordinary shareholders		564,800	
Directors	2,000,000		133,133
Other ordinary	15,300,000		1,018,467

This shows an increase of £163,200. However, preference shareholders will have put in £1,088,000 additional capital. If the increase is related to that figure it shows a return of approximately 15% on the new funds.

From the preference shareholders point of view the scheme is fair. If they were to be unable to take up the rights issue, the increase in the dividend rate would still leave them in a better position ie, 11% of the reduced capital of £4,352,000 produces £478,720 which exceeds the current dividend of £435,200.

The preference shareholders would not get a better deal in a voluntary liquidation and should accept the scheme.

> **Did you answer the question?**
>
> Notice the approach that the answer takes to evaluating the scheme. It looks at the situation of the preference shareholders in terms of income *and* capital and also considers the consequences were they not able to take up the rights issue. The answer concludes with a firm recommendation, thus meeting the requirement to *advise*.

35   (Answer 5 of examination)

Examiner's comments and marking guide

Question 5: this question examined the implication of post balance sheet events in a variety of practical scenarios. Candidates generally experienced difficulty because, unlike paper 10, the relevant SSAP/FRS was not defined and candidates are required to identify what is relevant to the scenario presented. The question therefore requires careful reading and thought.

Candidates who identified the problem correctly and hence the appropriate SSAP/FRS that was applicable, scored good marks.

Achievement was lower where candidates applied the inappropriate SSAP/FRS eg, in item 1 concentrating on FRS 4 and in item 3 discussing SSAP 21 application in great detail. Candidates also failed to achieve marks where the accounting entries were incorrect eg, in item 4. Many candidates concluded that this item was a prior period adjustment and explained where the £238,000 should be dealt with in the accounts but few realised that it was not the cumulative amount that needed adjusting. Some candidates did state that the closing stock needed reducing by £115,000.

The question had two levels of challenge. The first was to determine the nature of the problem, the second was to explain the appropriate accounting/disclosure treatment. It is important that candidates realise the requirements before selecting and attempting a question.

Generally, there were some excellent answers with candidates performing well and demonstrating a good range of knowledge and skills. Performance could be improved by:

(a)   candidates increasing their technical understanding eg, the basic principles of consolidation;

(b)   improving their skills eg, in report writing; and

(c)   improving their examination technique eg, more careful reading of the question both at a operational level eg, such as to whom a report is being addressed and a more interpretative level eg, such as what is the nature of the problem that is being presented and what is the appropriate SSAP/FRS, accounting treatment or disclosure requirement.

	Marks
Item 1 one mark per point up to	7
Item 2 one mark per point up to	7
Item 3 one mark per point up to	7
Item 4 one mark per point up to	7
	28

Step by step answer plan

Step 1   Read the question again and make sure that you focus on precisely what is required. The fact that the financial director is carrying out a review before the signing of the accounts, plus careful reading of dates should alert you to the possibility that some of the transactions may be post balance sheet events.

Step 2   Taking each item in turn, re-read the description. Determine the nature of the problem (this is not necessarily evident from the title). This will enable you to arrive at the appropriate treatment.

Step 3   Answer part (a), making sure that you explain the reasoning behind your choice of accounting treatment.

Step 4 Calculate the materiality of the item in relation to the financial statements as a whole. This will enable you to determine what level of disclosure is required. Do any rough calculations required and then answer part (b) by presenting the adjustments/disclosure note.

The examiner's answer

(1)

(a) This is a non-adjusting post balance sheet item. Although the decision was made within the financial year ended 30 April 1996 it was not put into effect until the following year ie, the receipt or entitlement to the receipt of cash was not a condition that existed at the date of the balance sheet.

(b) Disclosure is required because it is an event of such materiality that its non-disclosure would affect the ability of the users of the financial statements to reach a proper understanding of the financial position ie, that the share capital has been increased by 5%.

An appropriate note would read:

'On 31 January 1996, it was announced that the company was raising £14m (before expenses) by an issue for cash of 2m new ordinary shares of 25p each (representing 5% of the company's issued capital). The proceeds of the cash placing will assist towards the financing of further identified acquisition opportunities.'

Did you answer the question?

Notice that item (1) is dealt with very briefly and succinctly. There is only one issue involved here; because this is a post balance sheet event FRS 4 is irrelevant.

---

(2)

(a) The main issue is whether a provision can be recognised in respect of the expected future replacement of the heating system at 30 April 1996.

The provision has been recognised on the grounds that the expenditure to replace the heating system complies with the ASB's definition of a liability ie, an obligation to transfer economic benefits as a result of past transactions or events. However, FRS 12 'Provisions, contingent liabilities and contingent assets' now sets out the conditions for recognising a provision in the financial statements. The entity must have a present obligation as a result of a past event; it must be probable that a transfer of economic benefits will be required to settle the obligation; and it must be possible to make a reliable estimate of the amount of the obligation.

It is probable that the expenditure will take place and the expected cost is known, but in practice, the entity will be able to choose whether or not to continue to use the building after fifteen years. Therefore there is no present obligation and the provision cannot be recognised.

Our advice is that replacing the heating system would increase Finaleyes assets, not its liabilities and Finaleyes should depreciate the cost of the new system over its expected life thereby achieving matching. However, the matching will be over the useful life of the heating system not over the useful life of the building.

Did you answer the question?

Note that this answer does not focus on one accounting issue, (e.g. depreciation) but covers all the relevant issues and possible alternative views of the transaction. However, notice also that the answer expresses a view, thus fulfilling the requirement.

(b) Finaleyes should not have depreciated the £4m over 40 years. It should have separated the cost into buildings and plant and machinery and depreciated these separately ie, the heating system over 15 years at £30,000 per annum and the buildings (minus the heating system) over 40 years at £88,750 per annum [(£4m - £450,000)/40 years].

The depreciation charge for the year should be £118,750.

The difference of £11,250 [£100,000 - £88,750] on the buildings' depreciation should be credited to the profit and loss account and debited to the buildings; the provision of £30,000 should be debited and the profit and loss account credited; there should be a charge for depreciation of plant and machinery of £30,000.

(3)   (a)   This is a non-adjusting event. Disclosure is required because it is an event of such materiality that its non-disclosure would affect the ability of the users of the financial statements to reach a proper understanding of the financial position ie, that the company has disposed of net tangible assets representing 12.5% of the net tangible assets.

If the sale had been agreed before the year end on 30 April 1996 with the purchase price determined after the balance sheet date, it would have been treated as an adjusting event.

(b)   An appropriate note would read:

'On 15 May 1996, Finaleyes exchanged contracts with the Helpful Friendly Society Ltd for the sale and leaseback of the main offices of the company. The total consideration was £12m payable in cash and the associated lease is for an initial 20 year term with rentals at market rates. The carrying value of this property at 30 April 1996 was £10m. Completion of the disposal is to take place on 14 June 1996.'

(4)   (a)   The management treatment of the £238,000 as a prior period adjustment is incorrect.

FRS 3 defines a prior period adjustment as 'material adjustments applicable to prior periods arising from changes in accounting policies or from the correction of fundamental errors. They do not include normal recurring adjustments or corrections of estimates made in prior periods'.

In this case, although the reductions in stock value relate to previous years they are not sufficiently material to qualify as a fundamental error. Even if it were a prior period adjustment, it would not be the cumulative figure that needed adjusting as stock errors reverse in the following period.

The reductions have arisen because of a failure to apply an adopted accounting policy correctly and not from a change in an accounting policy.

(b)   The adjustment of £238,000 to the stock and profit and loss account balance brought forward needs to be reversed.

The appropriate accounting treatment is to charge the £115,000 in the 1996 accounts as part of the cost of sales and to disclose £105,000 of this as an exceptional item. £10,000 would have been charged without disclosure in the cost of sales in any event.

Balance sheet stock at 30 April 1996 needs to be reduced by a credit of £115,000.

The £105,000 is classified as exceptional because it is a material item which derives from events that fall within the ordinary activities of the reporting entity and which need to be disclosed by virtue of their size and incidence in order to give a true and fair view.

Did you answer the question?

Notice the way in which this answer does not only state that the treatment is incorrect, but explains why. In part (b) the answer does not only give the figures, but explains how and why the adjustments are made.

(***Tutorial note:*** Since this question was originally set, the ASB has issued FRS 12 *Provisions, contingent liabilities and contingent assets* and FRS 15 *Tangible fixed assets*.

The answer to (2) (a) has been amended to reflect this.)

DECEMBER 1996 QUESTIONS

Section A - BOTH questions are compulsory and MUST be attempted

36 (Question 1 of examination)

Icing Ltd carries on business as a food manufacturer.

Investment in Cake Ltd
On 1 April 1985 it acquired 4m £1 ordinary shares in Cake Ltd at a cost of £4.5m. At the date of acquisition Cake Ltd had an issued capital of 5m £1 ordinary shares and a credit balance on reserves of £1.75m using book values and £1.25m using fair values. It is group policy for subsidiary companies to revalue assets in their own accounts at fair values at the date of acquisition.

Investment in Loaf Ltd
On 1 December 1990 Icing Ltd acquired 336,000 £1 ordinary shares in Loaf Ltd at a cost of £480,000. At the date of acquisition Loaf Ltd had an issued capital of 560,000 £1 ordinary shares and a credit balance on reserves of £70,000 using book values and £80,000 using fair values. The other 224,000 £1 ordinary shares of Loaf Ltd were held by Flour Supplies Ltd which was a major supplier of raw materials to Loaf Ltd.

Until 1993 Loaf Ltd had produced loaves under contract with various supermarkets. In 1993 the company invested in machinery to produce continental style pastries which could be sold at higher gross profit margins. However, trading conditions worsened in 1996 with increased competition from imported frozen products and the directors of Icing Ltd decided to dispose of their holding in Loaf Ltd on a piecemeal basis.

On 31 May 1996 Icing Ltd disposed of 112,000 £1 ordinary shares in Loaf Ltd to the managers of that company for £175,000. At that date the Icing Ltd directors were replaced by Loaf Ltd managers with the exception of the Managing Director of Icing Ltd who was to remain until the final disposal of shares. The Finance Director of Loaf Ltd retired on 31 May 1996 on grounds of ill health and a new Finance Director was appointed on 31 August 1996.

Proposed accounting policy for investment in Loaf Ltd
Icing Ltd proposes to account for its investment in Loaf Ltd as a trade investment in the 1996 accounts and to show the difference on disposal under discontinued operations. The managers of Loaf Ltd were given an option, exercisable by 30 November 1998, to acquire the remainder of the shares held by Icing Ltd. The terms of the option were that the share price would be the higher of three times the profit before tax per share or the price paid by the managers at 31 May 1996. The managers have reached an agreement with the bank that it will not require the overdraft to be reduced pending discussions to raise additional medium term finance in order to reorganise the capital structure of the company. It is group policy to write off goodwill over five years.

Investment in Bun Ltd
On 1 December 1995 Cake Ltd acquired 375,000 £1 ordinary shares in Bun Ltd for £2m. At the date of acquisition Bun Ltd had an issued capital of 500,000 £1 ordinary shares and a credit balance on reserves of £1.5m using book values and £1.2m using fair values.

The draft accounts for Cake Ltd, Bun Ltd and Loaf Ltd for the year ended 30 November 1996 are as follows:

Draft profit and loss accounts for the year ended 30 November 1996

	Cake Ltd £'000	Bun Ltd £'000	Loaf Ltd £'000
Operating profit	2,350	800	24
Dividend from subsidiary undertaking	150		
Profit on ordinary activities before tax	2,500	800	24
Tax on profit on ordinary activities	(1,000)	(300)	(8)
Profit on ordinary activities after tax	1,500	500	16

	£'000	£'000	£'000
Dividends proposed	(1,000)	(200)	
Retained profit for the financial year	500	300	16

Draft balance sheets as at 30 November 1996

	£'000	£'000	£'000
Fixed assets			
Tangible assets	5,550	1,410	1,425
Investment in Bun Ltd.	2,000		
Current assets			
Debtors	1,800	720	300
Bank	300	700	
Current liabilities			
Trade creditors	(1,150)	(630)	(207)
Proposed dividends	(1,000)	(200)	
Bank overdraft			(742)
	7,500	2,000	776
Ordinary shares of £1 each	5,000	500	560
Profit and loss account	2,500	1,500	216
	7,500	2,000	776

At 30 November 1996 the book values are the same as fair values.

Required

(a)   Calculate the amounts that Icing Ltd would include in its consolidated accounts in respect of Cake Ltd and Bun Ltd for the year ended 30 November 1996 for the following:

   (i)   Minority interests for inclusion in the consolidated profit and loss account of the Icing Group

   (ii)   Group profit after tax

   (iii)   Minority interests for inclusion in the consolidated balance sheet

   (iv)   The goodwill or negative goodwill prior to their amortisation.   **(10 marks)**

(b)   Calculate the goodwill figure if Icing Ltd acquired its holding in Cake Ltd by *piecemeal acquisitions* on 1 April 1985 and 1 June 1996 on the following terms:

   On 1 April 1985 it acquired 3m ordinary shares in Cake Ltd at a cost of £3.5m at which date Cake Ltd had an issued capital of 5m ordinary shares and a credit balance on reserves of £1.25m using fair values. On 1 June 1996 it acquired 1m ordinary shares for £1m at which date book values were the same as fair values.

   (4 marks)

(c)   (i)   Calculate the gain/(loss) on sale of the shares in Loaf Ltd both in the accounts of Icing Ltd and in the consolidated accounts for the year ended 30 November 1996. Assume a corporation tax rate of 25%.

   (ii)   Explain how the results of Loaf Ltd will be shown in the consolidated profit and loss account of the Icing Group for the year ended 30 November 1996 assuming that the investment is classified as an associated undertaking after the disposal of shares on 31 May 1996.   **(6 marks)**

(d)   [Not reproduced as this part of the question is no longer within the syllabus.]

   (10 marks)
   (Total: 30 marks)

37   (Question 2 of examination)

Language-ease Ltd is a company incorporated by Peter Wong and Daphne Hillier in 1975 to provide English language teaching to foreign students. Peter and Daphne are the directors and each holds 50% of the issued shares. Since 1975 40 colleges have been opened in city centre locations in the UK and abroad. Each college is owned by a separate company of which Peter and Daphne are the directors and shareholders.

Each college has approximately 400 students for 30 weeks per year. Language-ease Ltd employs staff centrally to market the courses at all of the colleges. Peter and Daphne have appointed a different firm of auditors to audit each separate company and there are different dates for the financial year ends.

In 1990 Student-Food Ltd was incorporated to sell food, mainly in long-life packs priced at approximately £5 per pack, to college students either to eat on the premises or to take away. The directors were Peter Wong's son and Daphne Hillier's sister who had previously taught at a college. Each held 30% of the issued share capital with the remaining shares being held by private business investors.

In some of the colleges, Student-Food Ltd sold to the college and the college itself operated the sales outlet; in the other colleges, Student-Food Ltd operated the sales outlet under a license granted by a college whereby it was permitted to rent space on the college premises for a period of eight years from 1 November 1992 at a rental of £1 per square metre; the market rental was £6.50 per square metre. As at 31 October 1994 the company had fixed assets with a gross cost of £650,000 and a book value of £400,000 consisting of motor vehicles £96,000, storage equipment £200,000 and fixtures and fittings £104,000. The company planned to sell 4 pre-packed units per week to at least 15% of the student population for the year ended 31 October 1995.

In 1995 the company incurred fixed asset expenditure to encourage students to remain on the premises for meals so that the company could achieve its planned sales: by installing a freezer unit costing £5,000 at each college to satisfy health and safety regulations; by installing fittings costing £7,500 per college and storage equipment costing £4,000 per college.

In 1996 it incurred expenditure of £12,500 per college for additional fittings. This fixed asset expenditure was considered to be necessary in order for the company to be able to compete with local city centre restaurants.

The directors considered that the fixed asset expenditure had been successful and they consequently revised their target for 1996 to achieving sales of 4 packs per week to 30% of the student population. On the basis of this estimated increase in turnover, the company undertook further improvements to the college locations. It is company policy not to charge depreciation in the year of acquisition and to charge depreciation in the year of disposal. The bank overdraft and loan increased steadily during 1995 and 1996. Interest of 20% per annum was charged on the bank overdraft. The market rate of interest on loans was 12% per annum.

In 1996 the shareholders decided to dispose of their shares in Student-Food Ltd. The audit of the accounts for the year ended 31 October 1996 was to be completed by January 1997. Extracts from the accounts of Student-Food Ltd for years ended 31 October were as follows:

Profit and Loss Accounts for year ended 31 October

	1994		1995		1996 (draft)	
	£'000	£'000	£'000	£'000	£'000	£'000
Sales		900		1,200		1,240
Gross profit		252		272		320
Less:						
Expenses	66		138		146	
Rent	6		6		6	
Depreciation	60		60		100	
Interest	-		28		84	
		(132)		(232)		(336)
Profit/(Loss) before tax		120		40		(16)

	1994		1995		1996 (draft)
Tax	(28)		(7)		—
	92		33		(16)
Dividends	(48)		(36)		—
	44		(3)		(16)

Balance sheets as at 31 October

	1994		1995		1996 (draft)	
	£'000	£'000	£'000	£'000	£'000	£'000
Ordinary shares of						
£1 each		400		400		400
Profit and loss account		320		317		301
		720		717		701
Loan		—		240		760
		720		957		1,461
Fixed assets		400		1,000		1,400
Current assets						
Stock	240		360		400	
Debtors	160		360		480	
Bank	80		-		-	
	480		720		880	
Current liabilities						
Trade creditors	112		431		518	
Expense creditors	48		29		18	
Bank overdraft	-		303		283	
	160		763		819	
Net current assets/						
(liabilities)		320		(43)		61
		720		957		1,461

Tan, Wether & Co, a firm of Certified Accountants, was informed by a client, Cold Pack Ltd, that the company was having preliminary discussions to acquire the issued share capital of Student-Food Ltd. Cold Pack Ltd has been following a strategy of growth by acquisition. It has been valuing its acquisitions using a Price Earnings multiple of between 10 and 15 applied to earnings after interest. It has been able to improve results by obtaining better terms from suppliers to the acquired companies through centralised purchasing and increasing the gross profit to 42.5% of sales.

On 25 November 1996 Cold Pack Ltd instructed Tan, Wether & Co to prepare a report based on the accounts of Student-Food Ltd for the 3 years ended 31 October 1996 and to prepare a valuation of the business. The valuation was to take into account Cold Pack Ltd's estimate that Student-Food Ltd could maintain its 1996 level of sales and achieve a gross profit of 42.5% under new management.

Joseph Tan, the partner in Tan, Wether & Co responsible for the assignment, has requested Joyce Asprey, a trainee accountant with the firm, to draft a report and a share valuation.

Required

(a)   Assuming that you are Joyce Asprey,

    (i)   Comment on the financial position of Student-Food Ltd as at 31 October 1996 and on the changes that have occurred during the three years to that date for inclusion in a report to Cold Pack Ltd. Please include appropriate financial data; and   **(13 marks)**

    (ii)   Comment on the action that Cold Pack Ltd might need to take to improve the company's profitability.   **(4 marks)**

(b)   Assuming that you are Joseph Tan,

    Prepare an initial valuation of the shares in Student-Food Ltd based on the information available at 25 November 1996;   **(5 marks)**

(c)   [Not reproduced as this part of the question is no longer within the syllabus.]

        (8 marks)
        (Total: 30 marks)

Section B - TWO questions only to be attempted

---

38   (Question 3 of examination)

Shiny Bright plc was incorporated in 1980 to provide cleaning services for hotel, hospital and catering clients; it diversified into hotel ownership in the 1990s. In the early 1990s the company acquired a chain of 20 country hotels from Retort Hotels Ltd, a company then in receivership. 15 of the hotels were located in the South of England and five were located in Ireland. Since 1994 the directors have been preparing to seek a listing on the Alternative Investment Market and part of their strategy has been to dispose of operations that did not achieve an adequate return on capital employed.

At a recent seminar on reporting financial performance attended by the Managing Director, the seminar leader had briefly explained that exceptional items needed to be disclosed by virtue of their size or incidence; emphasised the importance of the operating profit figure and commented that it seemed that the market was often too easily misled by some companies' innovative use of FRS 3's layered approach to the profit and loss account to divert attention from the overall total result for which management was accountable.

When Shiny Bright plc was finalising its accounts for the year ended 31 October 1996 the Managing Director requested the Finance Director to make a brief presentation to the Board explaining exceptional items and innovative uses of the layered approach for the profit and loss account and advising on the accounting treatments that would produce the highest operating profit and on the presentation format that would concentrate attention on the EPS figure that was most favourable to the company.

The operating profit was £4m from continuing operations and £0.1m from its hospital cleaning services, which were discontinued in 1996, before taking account of the following information.

1   The company had acquired a restaurant in Central London for £1m in 1991. It was revalued at £1.5m in 1993. No depreciation had been provided on the property as it was company policy to maintain properties to a high standard.

       The restaurant was sold on 30 September 1996 for £2.5m.

2   All of the hotels acquired from Retort Hotels Ltd which were located in Ireland were sold on 31 August 1996 for £12.5m. They were the only hotels operated by the company in Ireland and the directors decided that they were too distant for them to exercise effective management. They had been acquired for £16m at the date they were purchased from the receiver. No depreciation has been provided by the company.

3   Shiny Bright plc has incurred costs of £1.4m arising from the reorganisation of the hotel administration. This comprised £0.5m for the centralisation of the accounting and booking function, £0.3m for refurbishing the reception area to a common plan, £0.4m for retraining staff and £0.2m for redundancy payments.

---

4   The fixed assets used for cleaning were estimated to have fallen in value by £0.75m following the discovery that cleaning equipment had suffered damage due to staff failing to follow the manufacturers' instructions.

5   There was an item on the agenda for the October 1996 Board meeting proposing the closure in the following financial year of a loss making hotel. The Finance Director had prepared estimates for the following year for this hotel showing turnover £350,000, cost of sales £400,000, write down of equipment £50,000 and redundancy costs £40,000. The proposal was to complete the closure by May 1997.

Required

Assuming that you are the Finance Director, you are required to

(a)   (i)   Explain the terms *size* and *incidence* in relation to exceptional items and the major difficulties in applying these terms.   **(4 marks)**

        (ii)   Explain how companies might be able to make use of FRS 3's layered approach to the profit and loss account to direct attention to a result other than the overall total result for which management was accountable.   **(4 marks)**

(b)   (i)   Describe the accounting treatments in the profit and loss account for the year ended 31 October 1996 that would produce the highest operating profit figure, giving reasons to support your advice in respect of items 1 - 5 above; and

        (ii)   Calculate the operating profit from continuing and discontinued operations for 1996 assuming that your advice was followed; and

        (iii)   Describe the presentation of profit and loss account that would best direct attention to the profit figure most favourable to the company.   **(12 marks)**
                                                                                                                  (Total: 20 marks)

---

39   (Question 4 of examination)

Growmoor plc has carried on business as a food retailer since 1900. It had traded profitably until the late 1980s when it suffered from fierce competition from larger retailers. Its turnover and margins were under severe pressure and its share price fell to an all time low. The directors formulated a strategic plan to grow by acquisition and merger. It has an agreement to be able to borrow funds to finance acquisition at an interest rate of 10% per annum. It is Growmoor plc's policy to amortise goodwill over ten years.

1   *Investment in Smelt plc*

        On 15 June 1994 Growmoor plc had an issued share capital of 1,625,000 ordinary shares of £1 each. On that date it acquired 240,000 of the 1,500,000 issued £1 ordinary shares of Smelt plc for a cash payment of £164,000.

        Growmoor plc makes up its accounts to 31 July. In early 1996 the directors of Growmoor plc and Smelt plc were having discussions with a view to a combination of the two companies.

        The proposal was that:

        (a)   On 1 May 1996 Growmoor plc should acquire 1,200,000 of the issued ordinary shares of Smelt plc which had a market price of £1.30 per share, in exchange for 1,500,000 newly issued ordinary shares in Growmoor plc which had a market price of £1.20p per share. There has been no change in Growmoor plc's share capital since 15 June 1994. The market price of the Smelt plc shares had ranged from £1.20 to £1.50 during the year ended 30 April 1996.

        (b)   It was agreed that the consideration would be increased by 200,000 shares if a contingent liability in Smelt plc in respect of a claim for wrongful dismissal by a former director did not crystallise.

(c)   After the exchange the new board would consist of 6 directors from Growmoor plc and 6 directors from Smelt plc with the Managing Director of Growmoor plc becoming Managing Director of Smelt plc.

(d)   The Growmoor plc head office should be closed and the staff made redundant and the Smelt plc head office should become the head office of the new combination.

(e)   Senior managers of both companies were to re-apply for their posts and be interviewed by an interview panel comprising a director and the personnel managers from each company. The age profile of the two companies differed with the average age of the Growmoor plc managers being 40 and that of Smelt plc being 54 and there was an expectation among the directors of both boards that most of the posts would be filled by Growmoor plc managers.

2   *Investment in Beaten Ltd*

Growmoor plc is planning to acquire all of the 800,000 £1 ordinary shares in Beaten Ltd on 30 June 1996 for a deferred consideration of £500,000 and a contingent consideration payable on 30 June 2000 of 10% of the amount by which profits for the year ended 30 June 2000 exceeded £100,000. Beaten Ltd has suffered trading losses and its directors, who are the major shareholders, support a takeover by Growmoor plc. The fair value of net assets of Beaten Ltd was £685,000 and Growmoor plc expected that re-organisation costs would be £85,000 and future trading losses would be £100,000. Growmoor plc agreed to offer four year service contracts to the directors of Beaten Ltd.

The directors had expected to be able to create a provision for the re-organisation costs and future trading losses but were advised by their Finance Director that FRS 7 required these two items to be treated as post-acquisition items.

Required

(a)   (i)   Explain to the directors of Growmoor plc the extent to which the proposed terms of the combination with Smelt plc satisfied the requirements of the Companies Act 1985 and FRS 6 for the combination to be treated as a merger, and

       (ii)   If the proposed terms fail to satisfy any of the requirements, advise the directors on any changes that could be made so that the combination could be treated as a merger as at 31 July 1996.   **(8 marks)**

(b)   Explain briefly the reasons for the application of the principles of recognition and measurement on an acquisition set out in FRS 7 to provisions for future operating losses and for re-organisation costs.   **(3 marks)**

(c)   (i)   Explain the treatment in the profit and loss account for the year ended 31 July 1996 and the balance sheet as at that date of Growmoor plc on the assumption that the acquisition of Beaten Ltd took place on 30 June 1996 and the consideration for the acquisition was deferred so that £100,000 was payable after one year, £150,000 after two years and the balance after three years. Show your calculations.

       (ii)   Calculate the goodwill to be dealt with in the consolidated accounts for the years ending 31 July 1996 and 1997 explaining clearly the effect of deferred and contingent consideration.

       (iii)   [Not reproduced as this part of the question is no longer valid due to technical developments.]
          (9 marks)
          (Total: 20 marks)

---

40   (Question 5 of examination)

Textures Ltd was incorporated in 1985 to manufacture artificial limbs. Its financial year end is 30 November 1996. It manufactures in the United Kingdom and exports more than 60% of its output. It has a number of foreign subsidiary companies.

It has developed a number of arrangements to support its export sales. These include agreements with Pills Plc, Eduaids Ltd and Bracos and Computer Control Ltd. Information on the agreements is as follows:

1   *Agreement with Pills plc*

An agreement was made in 1992 with Pills Plc, a pharmaceutical company, to jointly fund on a 50:50 basis an entity, Textures & Pills Joint Venture, to operate a marketing office in Asia which would advertise each of the company's products but not trade in the products. Both Textures Ltd and Pills Plc have guaranteed to meet liabilities if the other party fails to meet its share of the costs and risks.

Accounts prepared for Texture & Pills Joint Venture for the year ended 30 November 1996 showed the following:

	£000
Fixed assets	
Premises	300
Current assets	
Bank and cash	30
	330
Capital	
As at 1 December 1995	
Textures Ltd	211
Pills Plc	211
	422
Less: Expenses	92
As at 30 November 1996	330

2   *Agreement with Eduaid Ltd and Bracos*

Textures Ltd entered into an agreement on 1 December 1991 with Eduaids Ltd, a company that manufactured educational equipment, and Bracos, a South American lawyer, to set up under their joint control an unincorporated import undertaking in South America to trade as Eurohelp. Textures Ltd had an effective 30% interest in Eurohelp. The balance sheet of Textures Ltd as at 30 November 1996 showed an investment at cost in Eurohelp of £750,000.

The balance sheet of Eurohelp for the year ended 30 November 1996 showed:

	£'000
Fixed assets	7,500
Net current assets	1,100
	8,600
Capital account	
As at 30 November 1995	6,750
Retained profit for the year	1,850
	8,600

Textures Ltd has used proportional consolidation to account for its interest in Eurohelp since entering into the agreement.

3   *Agreement with Computer Control Ltd*

Textures Ltd entered into an agreement on 1 December 1993 with Computer Control Ltd to jointly control Afrohelp Ltd, a company in which each company held a 50% interest. Afrohelp Ltd assembled mechanical products from Textures Ltd and automated them with control equipment from Computer Control Ltd.

The joint venture has been equity accounted by each investor company. One of the newly appointed non-executive directors has questioned whether the investment in Afrohelp Ltd should be treated as a quasi subsidiary and consolidated.

On 1 November 1996 Textures Ltd sold stock costing £110,000 to Afrohelp Ltd for £162,000. This stock was unsold at 30 November 1996.

Required

(a)   (i)   Explain the advantages of using expanded equity accounting to account for associates in consolidated accounts; and

      (ii)   Discuss the advantages and disadvantages of using proportional consolidation to account for joint ventures.   **(8 marks)**

(b)   (i)   Explain how the joint activity of Textures & Pills Joint Venture would be dealt with in the accounts of Textures Ltd as at 30 November 1996; and

      (ii)   Calculate the retained profit of Eurohelp as at 1 December 1995 that would be included in the consolidated retained profit brought forward in the accounts of Textures Ltd at 30 November 1996 using proportional consolidation.

(4 marks)

(c)   Assuming that you are the Finance Director of Textures Ltd.

      (i)   Advise the non-executive director of the conditions that would need to be satisfied to avoid Afrohelp Ltd being treated as a quasi subsidiary as at 30 November 1996; and

      (ii)   Contrast the treatment of the unrealised gain on the sale of stock to Afrohelp Ltd on consolidating Afrohelp Ltd as an associate compared to as a quasi-subsidiary.   **(8 marks)**
(Total: 20 marks)

ANSWERS TO DECEMBER 1996 EXAMINATION

---

36   (Answer 1 of examination)

Examiner's comments and marking guide

Question 1: Part (a) of this question required the calculation of the minority interest and group profit in the consolidated profit and loss account for a subsidiary and sub-subsidiary and the minority interest and goodwill figures for the consolidated balance sheet.

This part of the question was generally well answered and candidates were well prepared for the topic. Common mistakes were to take the group share of Bun as 75% instead of 60%.

Part (b) of the question examined the ability to calculate reserve on acquisition arising from a piecemeal acquisition.

This part was generally well answered. The most common error was the use of an inappropriate reserve figure on the 1996 acquisition calculation.

Part (c) (i) of the question examined the ability to calculate a gain/loss on disposal in the parent and consolidated accounts. The gain for the parent was correctly calculated by many of the candidates. The common error in the group calculation was to miscalculate the group net assets at point of disposal.

Part (c) (ii) examined understanding of the presentation of Loaf Ltd as a subsidiary for part of year and associate for part of year. This part was generally well answered. A common error was to deal with only one aspect ie, the subsidiary treatment or the associate treatment.

Overall it seems that the accounting aspects of this topic are reasonably well understood by many of the candidates. The audit aspects were poorly answered and candidates need to take greater care to relate their answer to the specific scenario in the question - rote learnt general answers will not be sufficient to achieve a pass mark.

			Marks
(a)	(i)	Profit	1
		Dividend	1
		Minority interest	2
	(ii)	Group interest	2
	(iii)	Ordinary share	1
		Cost of shares	1
		P & L Account	1
	(iv)	Cost of shares	2
		Acquired	2
			13/10
(b)		Cost of investment	1
		Net assets	2
		Group share	1
		Pre-acquisition	1
			5/4
(c)	(i)	Sales proceeds	1
		Cost	1
		Tax	1
	(ii)	Share of net assets	2
		Proportion	1
		Goodwill	2
			8/6

(d)   Entity
             1 per point   8
         Group
             1 per point   6
                                                                                                                                         ──

                                                                                                                                         14/10
                                                                                                                                         ──

                                                                                                                                         40/30
                                                                                                                                         ──

Step by step answer plan

Step 1   Read the question again and make sure that you focus on precisely what is required. This question is unusual in that it does not actually require preparation of consolidated accounts. Instead, it requires calculations of various amounts to be included in the consolidated financial statements. The main complications within the question are a complex group structure in part (a), a piecemeal acquisition in part (b), and a disposal in part (c).

Step 2   Establish the opening and closing group structure.

Step 3   Answer part (a) by calculating each of the figures in turn, showing where the amount or amounts calculated under each part would be included in the consolidated accounts. This part of the question relates to Cake and Bun only.

Step 4   Re-read the short scenario in part (b). This concerns Cake only.

Step 5   Approach the calculation in part (b) in two stages, dealing separately with each acquisition. You will need to calculate Cake's reserves at 1 June 1996 and the accrual for the pre-acquisition dividend before calculating the reserve arising on the second acquisition.

Step 6   Re-read the main scenario relating to Loaf and then start part (c), which concerns Loaf only. Calculate the gain on disposal in the accounts of the parent.

Step 7   You will then be able to calculate the gain on disposal in the accounts of the group, to answer part (c) (i).

Step 8   Answer part (c) (ii) by explaining how the gain on disposal and then the other items in the profit and loss account will be included in the consolidated accounts.

Items not required by the Examiner for this question: workings for Loaf Ltd in part (a).

(Tutorial note: Since this question was originally set, FRS 9 *Associates and joint ventures* has replaced SSAP 1. Minor changes have been made to the wording of the answer to part (c) (ii) to reflect the new presentation requirements. Under FRS 9 associates continue to be consolidated using the equity method.*)*

The examiner's answer

(a)   (i)   Minority interests for the consolidated profit and loss account are as follows

	Cake Ltd £'000		Bun Ltd £'000	CPL £'000
Profit after tax	1,500		500	
Inter company dividends	(150)		-	
	────		────	
	1,350		500	
Minority interest		[100% - (80% × 75%)]		
20% of £1,350,000	270	40% of £500,000	200	470

Note: Minority interest in Bun Ltd is 40% made up as follows:

Shares held by outside shareholders of Bun Ltd	25%
Indirect interest of Cake Ltd's outside shareholders 20% × 75%	15%
	40%

(ii)   Group proportion of profit after tax is as follows:

	Cake Ltd £'000		Bun Ltd £'000	CPL £'000
Profit after tax	1,500		500	
Inter company dividends	(150)		-	
	1,350		500	
Group interest		[100% – 40%]		
80% of £1,350,000	1,080	60% of £500,000	300	1,380

(iii)   Minority interests for the consolidated balance sheet:

	Cake Ltd £'000		Bun Ltd £'000	CBS £'000
Ordinary shares [20%]	1,000	[25%]	125	
Ordinary shares - indirect interest [20% of £375,000]			75	
Cost of shares in Bun Ltd [20% of £2m]	(400)			
P & L Account [20% of £2.5m]	500			
[40% of £1.5m]			600	
	1,100		800	1,900

Shown separately under current liabilities:

	Cake Ltd £'000	Bun Ltd £'000	CBS £'000
Dividends [20% of £1m]	200		200
Creditor [25% of £200,000]		50	50

(iv)   Goodwill on acquisition:

	Cake Ltd £'000	£'000	Bun Ltd £'000	£'000	CBS £'000
Cost of shares		4,500		1,600	
Less: Ordinary shares	5,000		500		
Reserves	1,250		1,200		
	6,250		1,700		
	[80%]	5,000	[60%]	1,020	
Negative goodwill		(500)			(500)
Goodwill				580	580

(b)   Calculation of goodwill following piecemeal acquisition

	(60%)		(20%)		CBS
	£'000	£'000	£'000	£'000	£'000
Cost of investment		3,500		1,000	
Net assets at the date of investment:					
Share capital	5,000		5,000		
Reserves	1,250		2,250		
	6,250		7,250		
Group share (60%/20%)		(3,750)		(1,450)	
Accrual for pre-acquisition dividend $(20\% \times {}^{6}\!/_{12} \times £1,000,000)$				(100)	
Negative goodwill		(250)		(550)	(800)

(c)   (i)   Calculate the gain/(loss) on sale of the shares in Loaf Ltd in both the accounts of Icing Ltd and in the consolidated accounts for the year ended 30 November 1996. Assume a tax rate of 25%.

In parent accounts:	£	£
Sales proceeds		175,000
Less: Cost 112,000/336,000 × £480,000		160,000
		15,000
Less: Tax at 25%		3,750
Gain		11,250
In consolidated accounts:		
Sales proceeds		175,000
Less: Share of net assets at date of disposal		
Share capital	560,000	
Reserve at 1 December 1995 [216,000 - 16,000]	200,000	
In year of disposal [16,000 / 2]	8,000	
	768,000	
Proportion 112,000/560,000 ie, 20%		(153,600)
		21,400
Less: Tax		(3,750)
Gain on disposal		(17,650)

(*Note:* Since all the goodwill purchased on acquiring Loaf Ltd will have been amortised through the consolidated profit and loss account by the disposal date, no further adjustment is required for goodwill in the disposal calculation.)

(ii)   The disclosure treatment of the gain on disposal of £17,650 will be dependent on the classification of the investment. It will be disclosed as a gain on disposal under continuing operations if the investment in Loaf Ltd is classified as an associated undertaking. The reason is that, as an associated undertaking, Loaf Ltd would be contributing to profits on ordinary activities before taxation and to net assets in Icing Ltd's consolidated accounts on an equity accounting basis. Therefore from the group's point of view, the cessation of operation is not complete and no operation has been discontinued.

It will be disclosed as a gain on disposal under discontinued operations only in cases where the former subsidiary becomes merely an investment rather than an associated undertaking and could not be equity accounted for and there are no other subsidiaries within the group involved in the same activity as the subsidiary that has been sold.

The results ie, turnover, cost of sales and expenses should be consolidated for the first six months. In the second six months, the operating profit will be apportioned - £12,000 arising prior to the disposal will be included in operating profit and 40% of £12,000 will be included as income from interests in associated undertakings.

Taxation will include £4,000 within the group tax figure and 40% of £4,000 as share of tax of associated undertaking.

Did you answer the question?

Notice that this answer does not just consider the treatment of the results of Loaf Ltd, but also the disclosure of the profit or loss on disposal. Notice also that the answer is an explanation, not a set of extracts from the financial statements.

---

37   (Answer 2 of examination)

Examiner's comments and marking guide

Question 2: This question concerns a Ltd company formed in 1990 (as an offshoot of an English Language College operating in 40 locations) to sell food, in standard packs, at the colleges - outlets being alternatively operated by the company itself under licence (at low rents) or by the colleges themselves (supplied with packs by the company). The exercise started at 31 December 1994 when the company had completed a successful year. In 1995 based on an optimistic sales forecast of £1.44m the directors embark on capital expenditure spending of £660,000 (for 1995) and £500,000 (for 1996) - the latter to support a revision of targets to 30% student usage (which was never achieved) and resulting in falls in performance indicators and virtual insolvency by the end of 1996. A classic case of excessive optimism and over-trading forcing directors to consider the sale of the company to a competitor company.

Candidates are placed in the position of a trainee accountant acting for the potential buyer and required by the partner to:

(a)   report on the company's financial position and changes occurring over a three year period of trading; and
(b)   prepare a share valuation for the purposes of acquisition; and
(c)   discuss audit procedures and audit significance of related parties.

Part (a) was generally well answered with a standard report in a suitable format with ratios covering core aspects of profitability, liquidity, capital structure/leverage and cash flows placing emphasis on the increase in fixed assets, liquidity problems and high gearing.

Good answers covered aspects such as the effect of the failure to achieve the expansion of sales, identifying the strain on liquidity caused by the lack of a solid capital structure base to support fixed asset investment and working capital expansion and the effect on profitability and falling interest cover. Weaker answers were those that simply calculated a series of ratios with comments such as 'this is increasing' or, frequently, merely drawing an arrow to indicate an increase or decrease! The weaker answers failed to comment on matters such as the absence of correlation between the increase in fixed assets/working capital and sales, non-achievement of sales targets, expansion of fixed assets not properly financed, key reasons for the fall in profitability, effect of depreciation policy, excessive optimism of directors.

Part (b) was poorly answered. Good answers calculated the correct gross profit figure and suggested possible adjustments to the expenses. Many candidates calculated an asset value with no reference that this could be useful as a comparison for the earnings based figure simply giving it as a valuation in its own right with no reference to the policy set out in the question.

There is an improvement in report writing but there is a clear indication that many candidates still need greater practice in answering questions of this nature. The majority obtained virtually all the marks available for the calculation of ratios but it is not sufficient at this level merely to produce a ratio with a brief comment that the ratio has gone up or down with a number of candidates still not even making a narrative comment.

Candidates need additional practice with attention given to establishing such matters as the overall picture, key balance sheet and performance aspects and the relationships between various ratios. This is an important part of the syllabus and requires continuing emphasis on the part of candidates, performance is improving and this improvement needs to be maintained.

			Marks
(a)	(i)	Identifying significant aspect up to 2 per point	6
		Developing aspect up to 2 per point	6
		Supporting data	6
			18/13
	(ii)	1 per point	6/4
(b)		Appropriate method	2
		Data	4
			6/5
(c)	(i)	Procedures	
		1 per point	5
	(ii)	Significance	
		1 per point	5 10/8
			40/30

Step by step answer plan

Step 1 Read the question again and make sure that you focus on precisely what is required. At first sight this appears to be an 'interpretation' question, but note that part (b) requires a share valuation.

In this scenario there is relatively little information in the form of extracts from the accounts, but there is quite a lot of information in the form of narrative about the company's activities, including capital investment and financing.

Step 2 Start by doing the calculations. You will need to calculate some ratios, but you should also compare the narrative part of the scenario with the figures in the profit and loss accounts and balance sheets.

Step 3 The results of your calculations should show you the key areas on which to comment in part (a) and should enable you to produce a rough answer plan. Do not get carried away here, remember that you will need to leave enough time to answer part (b).

Step 4 Approach part (a) (i) by commenting on each of the following areas in turn: financing capital asset expenditure, working capital, turnover and profitability.

Step 5 Finish part (a) (i) by writing a summary.

Step 6 Answer part (a) (ii).

Step 7 Re-read the last three paragraphs of the scenario and the requirement for part (b), to remind yourself of the terms of reference for the share valuation. Then start part (b) by determining which valuation method is appropriate.

Step 8 Perform the share valuation, explaining clearly any assumptions that you make and any areas of uncertainty.

Step 9 Now look back at your answer to ensure that it does actually answer the question as set.

The examiner's answer

(a) (i) Prepare comments on the financial position of Student-Food Ltd as at 31 October 1996 and on the changes that have occurred during the three years to that date for inclusion in a report in Cold Pack Ltd.

The following comments have been drafted:

Financing capital asset expenditure

Student-Food Ltd has achieved sales of £1,240,000 in 1996 which is an increase of 37.8% [(1,240,000 - 900,000)/900,000] over the 1994 figure. However, it has increased its gross cost of fixed assets by £660,000 in 1995 and £500,000 in 1996. This is a 178% [1,160,000/650,000] increase over the 1994 gross cost figure partly due to health and safety considerations and partly due to refurbishment to improve the company's competitiveness with local restaurants. In considering the financial position, it is necessary to identify how the fixed assets were financed. From an inspection of the balance sheets it is clear that the fixed assets acquisitions were largely financed by additional loan capital.

For the purpose of the report a more detailed analysis would be appropriate identifying the extent to which the fixed assets have been financed by internally generated funds, new share capital, long term loans and from changes in working capital.

A statement such as the following could be helpful:

		1995 £'000		1996 £'000
Cost of additional fixed assets		660		500
Financed by:				
Internally generated funds				
- Profit	33		(16)	
Depreciation	60		100	
	93		84	
Less dividends	36		-	
		(57)		(84)
		603		416
New equity capital		-		-
		603		416
Loan capital		(240)		(520)
Reduction/(Increase in working capital)		363		(104)
Stock increase	120		40	
Debtor increase	200		120	
Creditor increase	(300)		(76)	
Bank (increase)/decrease	(383)		20	
		(363)		104

This indicates that 66% of the increase in fixed assets was financed by loan capital [760,000/1,160,000]; 22% by a reduction in working capital [(363,000 - 104,000)/1,160,000]; 12% by internally generated funds [(57,000 + 84,000)/1,160,000]; and nil % by new share capital.

Did you answer the question?

Note that part of the requirement is to comment on the changes that have taken place. By covering the expansion (increase in sales, fixed asset expenditure, lack of proper financing) at the beginning, this answer clearly shows that it is addressing the requirement and that it is identifying the key areas of concern.

Depreciation

The depreciation policy and amounts needs further enquiry. There has been £800,000 expenditure on fittings during 1995 and 1996 and rental agreements having only a further four years to run. *Prima facie* this would indicate that a significantly higher rate of amortisation might be appropriate.

Working capital

The internally generated funds have been insufficient to finance either the fixed assets or the increase in working capital in 1996. The company has become heavily dependent on loans and increases in its creditors.

The stock turnover was:

2.7 in 1994 [(900,000 - 252,000)/240,000];
2.6 times in 1995 [(1,200,000 - 272,000)/360,000]; and
2.3 times in 1996 [(1,240,000 - 320,000)/400,000].

The decrease in the stock turnover could be related to the company failing to meet the increased sales for which it had planned. Although the food packs are stated to be long life, enquiry should be made as to the shelf life of stock and the possibility of stock being out of date and unsaleable. The company sells both direct to students and also to colleges with the debtor figure arising from sales to the colleges. There has been a material change in the percentage of debtors to sales rising from 17.8% in 1994 to 38.7% in 1996. This could simply be a shift to credit sales from cash sales. However, enquiries are necessary to establish how this increase arose. Given the related party relationships it is possible that the company is accommodating the colleges by granting them increasing credit periods or, alternatively, that the colleges are accommodating the company by allowing the company to invoice in order to conceal the increase in stocks and improve the liquidity ratio.

The liquidity ratio [acid test] was:

1.5:1 in 1994 [(160,000 + 80,000)/(112,000 + 48,000)];
0.47:1 [360,000/763,000] in 1995; and
0.59:1 in 1996 [480,000/819,000].

However, if the debtors remained at 17.8% in 1996 as in 1994 the liquidity ratio would have worsened to 0.26:1 [(1,240,000 × 17.8%)/819,000]

The creditors turnover based on cost of sales was:

5.8 in 1994 [(900,000 - 252,000)/112,000];
2.2 times in 1995 [(1,200,000 - 272,000)/431,000]; and
1.8 times in 1996 [(1,240,000 - 320,000)/518,000]

Did you answer the question?

Notice that the Examiner has not simply calculated a series of ratios and made observations on the changes. He makes connections between the ratio analysis and the information in the scenario. He also identifies possible reasons for the changes.

Turnover

The directors planned to sell four £5 packs per week to at least 15% of the students. For 1995, this would have resulted in the sale of 288,000 packs [40 colleges × 400 students × 15% × 4 packs × 30 weeks] and a turnover of £1,440,000. This would have produced an increase in turnover of £540,000 [1,440,000 - 900,000]

Although therefore the actual sales were 33.3% higher than 1994 they were 16.7% under budget [240,000/1,440,000 × 100]. The plan therefore to increase the sales to 30% of the student population in 1996 appeared unrealistic as evidenced by the modest 3% increase actually achieved [40,000/1,200,000 × 100].

Did you answer the question?

Again, the Examiner does not just calculate the standard ratios, but analyses the differences between the sales targets and actual sales.

Profitability

The gross profit % has fallen from 28% in 1994 [252,000/900,000 × 100] to 25.8% in 1996 [320,000/1,240,000 × 100].

Enquiry should be made to obtain the reason for this fall. It was noted that the company experiences competition from local city centre restaurants.

The profit before tax has fallen from a profit of 13.3% in 1994 [120,000/900,000 × 100] to a loss of 1.3% in 1996. Expenses have increased from 7.2% in 1994 [66,000/900,000 × 100] to 11.8% in 1996 [146,000/1,240,000 × 100]. Enquiry should be made to obtain a detailed analysis of the expenses to identify which of the expenses have increased and reasons for the increase.

The rental currently charged is lower than that which would apply in the market. If the market rates were applied the rental charge would be £39,000 per annum - an increase of £33,000 and the profit before tax would have been £87,000 in 1994, £7,000 in 1995 and a loss of £49,000 in 1996.

The bank overdraft carried interest of 20% and on the basis that it arose evenly over the year, the interest charge in 1995 was £24,000 [((303,000/2) × 289/365) × 20%] assuming that the overdraft existed for 289 days in 1995

$$\text{ie } \frac{303}{(80+303)} \times 365 = 289.$$

The loan would therefore appear to carry interest of 3.3% [(28,000 - 24,000)/(240,000/2) × 100].

The bank overdraft carried interest of 20% and on the basis that it arose evenly over the year, the interest charge in 1996 was £59,000 [((303,000 + 283,000)/2) × 20%]. The loans appear to carry interest of 5% [(84,000 - 59,000)/((240,000 + 760,000)/2) × 100].

There is a significant difference in this 5% and the market rate of 12% and enquiry should be made to establish the terms and conditions attaching to loans raised by the company. It could possibly be that loans have been raised at below market rates from related parties.

The worsening operating profit figures are reduced further by interest charges incurred in 1995 and 1996. If the market rate of 12% was applied to the loans, the interest charged would be increased by £10,400 in 1995 [(12% of 120,000) - (4,000)] and £35,000 in 1996 [(12% of 500,000) - (5% of 500,000)].

The effect on the profit before tax figure of commercial rents and interest rates would have been to turn 1995 into a loss of £3,400 and increase the 1996 loss to £84,000.

There is also the question of the adequacy of the depreciation charge made in 1996, in particular, that relating to the fittings but this will clearly be influenced by the length of rental agreements negotiated with the colleges.

Did you answer the question?

Note the way in which the answer addresses the needs of the recipient (the potential acquirer). Cold Pack Ltd are concerned with future profitability, and so the answer analyses the profit figures in detail.

Summary

Although Student-Food Ltd increased its sales by 38.8% from 1994, it failed to achieve its planned sales in 1995 by 16.7% and failed by 13.9% even in 1996 to achieve the sales level planned for 1995. The actual increase achieved in 1995 appears to have misled the directors into assuming that such significant growth would continue. Their planned increase for 1996 was consequently totally over-optimistic.

The company has been unable to finance its sales growth by internally generated funds and is overtrading. It has financed its growth with loans and an increase in current liabilities, thereby incurring interest charges in the profit and loss account which it is unable to fully cover in 1996.

Its gearing in the balance sheet has increased so that loans exceeded shareholders' funds by 1996. The rate of interest charged on the loans is significantly lower than the market rate which might be due to related party relationships.

The company has a liquidity problem and it is in a potentially dangerous financial position.

The company is suffering from falling gross profit margins and falling net profit percentages which means that it will be unable to pay a dividend.

Did you answer the question?

Notice the way in which the summary draws together the key observations and explains their possible implications for a future acquirer.

(ii)   Comment on the action that Cold Pack Ltd might need to take to improve the company's profitability.

Profitability improvement
An analysis is required of the sales and cost of sales to identify whether the fall in gross profit is due to a fall in selling prices and/or an increase in costs.

If there is a fall in selling prices, ascertain whether there has been a general fall in selling prices or whether it relates to any particular sales area e.g. any particular college. Consider pricing and market strategies.

If there is an increase in costs, review purchasing policy and procedures to ascertain the extent to which the company could benefit from centralised buying.

The terms of licensing agreements should be examined and reviewed.

An analysis is required of the expenses by function and an investigation made of significant changes with a view to their reduction.

Where possible, it would be helpful to calculate a return on capital employed for each business segment to establish whether there are any particular segments that are underperforming.

If any segment is underperforming, ascertain whether it is feasible to improve performance to an acceptable level. For example, it might be necessary to improve the location of the outlets or there might be strong local competition which will require combating by advertising or other measures such as staff incentives.

If any segment or location is not able to produce an adequate return on capital employed, it might be necessary to consider closure.

Liquidity - investment in assets
In addition to increasing the operating profit, consideration must be given to substantially increasing the sales or reducing the overall investment in assets.

Monetary asset management needs to be improved.

The stock turnover has fallen since 1994. The rate needs to be increased by reducing stock or increasing sales and enquiries are needed to establish the shelf life of stock. A possible approach would be to decide on the number of days stock to hold at each college taking into account the demand and the shelf life of the stock. Assuming that four weeks supply is to be held in stock - the stock should be reduced to approximately £123,000 [(1,240,000 - 320,000)/30 × 4]. There is also the point to consider that, because sales are not occurring in 22 weeks due to the college year, the timing of the balance sheet date could give unrepresentative figures for current assets and current liabilities.

The debtor position is unclear. There is a significant increase in the period of credit allowed which should be reviewed to secure significant reduction. This is an area that requires further enquiry. Assuming that 50% of the sales are to colleges direct and that 30 days credit is allowed, debtors should be reduced to approximately £83,000 [(1,240,000/2)/30 weeks × 4]. The point made above about the timing of the balance sheet date also applies to debtors.

Credit periods and terms with suppliers should be re-negotiated.

The major expenditure on fixed assets appears to have been on fixtures and fittings. Consequently, it is possible that these may not be capable of being easily reduced or disposed of. However, asset disposals should be considered.

The reduction in current assets would reduce them from £880,000 to £206,000 a saving of £674,000 which would be used to reduce the creditors and overdraft from £819,000 to £145,000.

Finally, budgets and forecasts should be recomputed.

Did you answer the question?

The explicit requirement was to comment on the action that might be needed to improve profitability, but the Examiner also comments on liquidity. This is because the lack of finance indirectly affects profitability, but also because the liquidity problems are so severe that any acquirer would need to deal with them urgently.

(b)   Assuming that you are Joseph Tan, prepare an initial valuation of the shares in Student-Food Ltd based on the information available at 25 November 1996.

Share valuation method
As Cold Pack Ltd is acquiring the whole of the issued share capital of Student-Food Ltd the initial valuation is calculated using the earnings method.

Level of gross profit
The draft accounts for 1996 show loss before tax of £16,000 and it will be necessary to ascertain from Cold Pack Ltd how they propose to bring the company into profit.

Our enquiries appear to indicate that this loss is increased to £84,000 if a market rate is used for the loan interest and rental charges. Enquiries are needed to establish whether the rental and/or loan will continue at the same preferential rate. The question of a possible change in the depreciation charge is to be considered further.

There is information that Cold Pack Ltd will be able to improve gross profit margins by centralising purchasing and obtaining better terms from suppliers. Assuming that the 1996 level of sales will be maintained and that a gross profit of 42.5% is achievable, this would have produced a gross profit in 1996 of £527,000.

Level of trading profit
The trading expenses have been around 12% for the past two years.

Assuming that there is little scope for cost reduction of the expenses of £146,000 and that the depreciation charge should be higher, say, £225,000 ie, 15% of the fixed assets at the end of the year (15% of £1,500,000) the profit after interest will be £55,000.

[527,000 – expenses 146,000 – rental 6,000 – depreciation 225,000 – loan interest 38,000 – bank interest 57,000].

Applying a PE multiple of 10, the shares are valued at £550,000 ie, £1.375 per share.

However, the position would change significantly if the preferential rent and loan interest were not available resulting in a loss of £31,000.

[527,000 – expenses 146,000 – rental 39,000 – depreciation 225,000 – loan interest 91,000 – bank interest 57,000].

Asset backing

The earnings based share valuation should be compared with the asset valuation per share.

Based on the book value of the assets, each share has asset backing of £1.75. Current values eg, insurance values should be obtained immediately from Student-Food Ltd.

Did you answer the question?

The Examiner has not just calculated a figure, but explained the reasoning and assumptions behind the calculation. Notice also that an alternative valuation figure has been calculated.

---

38   (Answer 3 of examination)

Examiner's comments and marking guide

Question 3: Part (a) (i) required an explanation of terms size and incidence in relation to exceptional items. Part (a) (ii) required an explanation as to how companies might be able to make use of the FRS 3's layered approach.

Few candidates seemed to appreciate that management might 'exercise judgement' in the classification of profits, losses, revenue items and costs to their advantage with revenue and profits being classified as continuing while losses and costs are described as discontinued or exceptional. Given this lack of appreciation, weaker answers failed to strike the right balance in approaching part (b).

Part (b) (i) required a description of accounting treatment for 5 transactions to produce the highest operating profit.

This part was poorly answered. Good answers examined each transaction and suggested a treatment aimed at producing the highest operating profit.

Weaker answers produced figures only in (i) and (ii) eg, £3.5m implying that they be included in the profit and loss account but with no clear explanation or suggested treatments such as ignoring the item completely. Some candidates appeared unfamiliar with FRS 3 and answered under previous regulations with a discussion of treatment as extraordinary items.

Part (b) (ii) required a calculation of the profit from continuing and discontinued operations. Marks were awarded for treatment that was congruent with the description in part (b) (i) and reasonable marks were achieved.

(b) This part was poorly answered. Good answers addressed the aspects of columnar presentation that could have an effect on the user's evaluation. Weaker answers omitted to answer this part.

			Marks
(a)	(i)	2 marks per point up to	6
	(ii)	1 mark per point up to	5
			—
			11/8
(b)	(i)	Up to 2 marks per point up to	8
	(ii)	1 mark per point up to	4
	(iii)	2 marks per point up to	4
			—
			16/12
			27/20

Step by step answer plan

Step 1   Read the question again and make sure that you focus on precisely what is required. FRS 3 is the topic being examined, but as usual, you are required to apply your knowledge to a very specific scenario. The focus of the question is on using FRS 3 to give the most favourable presentation of a company's results. Note that you are required to assume the role of the Finance Director addressing the Managing Director.

Step 2   Approach part (a) (i) by dealing with each of the terms in turn. Write short paragraphs on each. Note that the key requirement is to *explain*. Remember that only 4 marks/7 minutes are available.

Step 3   Start part (a) (ii) by stating the relevant requirements of FRS 3. Then develop this by explaining the ways in which these requirements can be used in practice. Again, remember that you only have 7 minutes for this part of the question.

Step 4   Taking each of the five transactions in turn, re-read the description in the scenario to ensure that you have understood the relevant facts. Then describe the way in which the transaction would be treated and explain the reasoning behind this, to complete part (b) (i).

Step 5   Answer part (b) (ii).

Step 6   Approach part (b) (iii) by drawing up an extract from the profit and loss account as it might appear, using the figures calculated in part (b) (ii), together with a brief explanation.

Items not required by the Examiner for this question: general discussion of the requirements of FRS 3 without reference to the scenario.

The examiner's answer

(a)   (i)   *Size*

Size refers to the value of a transaction in monetary terms. It is relevant when assessing effect or significance to the performance of the enterprise

There are two major problems in assessing whether size is significant, namely, the setting of a benchmark and the determination of a base figure.

There are differences of opinion amongst accountants and auditors as to what benchmark to use. Some, for example, assume that if the value exceeds say 10% of a base figure then it is significant. This is not however a universally accepted percentage for determining significance.

There are also differences of opinion over an acceptable base. Some use profit from all activities but there are other acceptable bases eg, profit from continuing activities, profit after tax, related functional expense items or even turnover.

Incidence

This relates to the frequency of occurrence of a transaction with a transaction being exceptional if it is infrequent. This is in practice a most difficult area requiring a review of past experience, an assessment of possible future frequency and a knowledge of management intentions. Incidence changes over time and an item can change from exceptional to ordinary over time.

> **Did you answer the question?**
>
> Notice that this part of the answer is clearly structured, taking each term in turn. Notice also that the Examiner does not simply explain the meaning of the term, but also the difficulties in applying it (thus addressing both parts of the requirement).

(ii)   Explain how companies might be able to make use of FRS 3's layered approach to the profit and loss account to direct attention from the overall total result for which management was accountable.

The summary of FRS 3 states that a layered format is to be used for the profit and loss account to highlight a number of important components of financial performance:

- results of continuing operations (including the results of acquisitions)

- results of discontinued operations

 profits or losses on the sale or termination of an operation, cost of a fundamental re-organisation or restructuring and profits or losses on the disposal of fixed assets

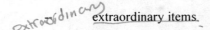 extraordinary items.

It also states that in presenting the profit and loss account the following requirements should be observed.

- The analysis between continuing operations, acquisitions (as a component of continuing operations) and discontinued operations should be disclosed to the level of operating profit. The analysis of turnover and operating profit is the minimum disclosure required in this respect on the face of the profit and loss account.

- All exceptional items, other than those in the item below should be included under the statutory format headings to which they relate. They should be separately disclosed by way of note or, where it is necessary in order that the financial statements give a true and fair view, on the face of the profit and loss account.

- The following items, including provisions in respect of such items, should be shown separately on the face of the profit and loss account after operating profit and before interest:

    - profits or losses on the sale or termination of an operation;
    - costs of a fundamental reorganisation or restructuring; and
    - profits or losses on the disposal of fixed assets.

There is therefore columnar layering with the classification between continuing and discontinued operations and row layering between pre and post operating profit items.

Columnar layering

The classification is important because it provides an indication of future sustainable operating profits. It could therefore be beneficial for loss making operations to be classified as discontinued. Such a treatment would need to satisfy the FRS 3 criteria for discontinued operations. There are opportunities for the exercise of judgement which could influence the classification. These include:

- downsizing

    This falls to be considered within the criteria of material effect on the nature and focus of the reporting entity's operations and represents a material reduction in its operating facilities resulting from either its withdrawal from a particular market (whether class of business or geographical) or from a material reduction in turnover in the reporting entity's continuing markets.

Judgement is required concerning the definition of material.

- partial disposal of non-core business resulting in loss of control

    There are differences of opinion as to whether a partial disposal should be classified as a discontinuance. If approached in the same way as downsizing, a decision to treat as a discontinuance may be supportable.

Row layering

This offers an opportunity to influence the operating profit figure by attempting to structure transactions to satisfy the criteria for disclosure as exceptional items after operating profit. In addition these exceptional costs are themselves required to be separated under continuing and discontinued headings.

The decision as to what constitutes a fundamental reorganisation or restructuring is a highly subjective and judgmental exercise.

Did you answer the question?

This part of the answer needs to begin by describing the requirements of FRS 3, but only in sufficient detail to enable the Examiner to explain how they can be applied in practice. Notice the way in which the Examiner focuses on 'layering' and explains *both* columnar layering and row layering.

(b)   (i)   **1   Profit on disposal of a fixed asset**

Profit on disposal of fixed assets is required under FRS 3 to be disclosed on the face of the profit and loss account after operating profit. The profit is required to be based on the carrying value of the asset i.e. £1.5m resulting in a profit of £1m to be disclosed in the profit and loss account. The £500,000 that had been credited to the Revaluation Reserve will be transferred to the profit and loss reserve as a transfer on realisation.

In order to bring the profit on sale into the operating profit the company could consider reclassifying the fixed asset as a current asset in anticipation of sale. In making this decision attention should be given to FRS 5 para k which states that where the nature of any recognised asset or liability differs from that usually found under the relevant balance sheet heading, the difference should be explained. The effect of this is that there should be a time delay between the asset being used and being sold. It should also be remembered that such an accounting treatment could be considered by the Financial Reporting Review Panel.

2   Loss on the sale of an operation

The hotels acquired from Retort Hotels Ltd which were located in Ireland were sold on 31 August 1996 for £12.5m. They had been valued at £16m at the date they were purchased from the receiver. No depreciation has been provided by the company.

The loss satisfies FRS 3 para 20 for the treatment as an exceptional loss to be disclosed after operating profit either as a loss on disposal of an asset or as a loss on sale of an operation.

If the company is able to support the judgement that the sale has a material effect on the nature and focus of the reporting entity's operations and represents a material reduction in its operating facilities resulting from its withdrawal from a particular geographical market then it can classify the loss under the discontinued heading.

It could support such a judgement in Shiny Bright plc based on the fact that the company has changed the positioning of its services by withdrawal from a geographical area, namely, withdrawal from Ireland and the amounts appear material.

The other criteria relating to discontinuance appear to have been satisfied.

3   Cost of fundamental re-organisation

Shiny Bright plc has incurred costs of £1.1m arising from the reorganisation of the hotel administration. This comprised £0.5m for the centralisation of the accounting and booking function, £0.4m for retraining staff and £0.2m for redundancy payments. The refurbishment costs have been treated as fixed assets.

If the company is able to support a judgement that the re-organisation is fundamental then the costs will be treated as exceptional and reported after the operating profit.

It might be able to argue that the centralisation of the booking system had a material effect on the nature and focus of the reporting entity's operations which justified treating it as a fundamental re-organisation.

Failing this, the costs will be shown as an increase in the administrative expenses under continuing operations.

4 Permanent diminution in asset values

The fixed assets used for cleaning were estimated to have fallen by £0.75m following the discovery that cleaning equipment had suffered damage due to staff failing to follow the manufacturers instructions.

This cost is an exceptional operating expense which is required to be analysed under the statutory format heading to which it relates i.e. the whole amount would be allocated to cost of sales.

5 Decision to close the loss making hotel

Although there is a proposal on the agenda, it has not yet been accepted by the Board.

If the proposal is accepted at the October 1996 Board meeting it will be necessary to consider whether it can be classified as discontinued. The fact that the completion of the sale is not expected until May 1997 means that the sale cannot be treated under the discontinued heading in the 1996 accounts. It would however be necessary to consider the creation of a provision for loss on operations to be discontinued in the 1996 accounts. This would be disclosed after the operating profit but it would reduce the EPS figure for 1996.

It would be preferable therefore to delay the decision to close until after the accounts for 1996 have been signed. This would also avoid it being treated as a post balance sheet event in the 1996 accounts. If this route is followed it would be advisable to delete it from the agenda and not to minute the decision at this point.

Did you answer the question?

The Examiner assumes the role of a Finance Director advising a Managing Director. The content of the answer reflects this by advising treatments which would be as advantageous as possible, yet which would still comply with FRS 3. Notice that for each item there is a suggested treatment, with appropriate figures *and* an explanation.

(ii)   Revised operating profit

	Continuing operations £m	Discontinued operations £m	Total £m
As stated in question	4.0	0.1	4.1
1. Restaurant sale treated as operating profit	1.0		1.0
4. Cost of sales increased	(0.75)		(0.75)
Revised figure	4.25	0.1	4.35
Exceptional items			
3. Cost of fundamental reorganisation	(1.1)		(1.1)
2. Loss on sale		(3.5)	(3.5)
	3.15	(3.4)	(0.25)

(iii)   Describe the presentation of profit and loss account that would concentrate attention on the profit figure most favourable to the company.

The company is required to disclose the EPS as calculated under FRS 14. However, it is also permitted to disclose additional EPS figures and the format used by Imperial Chemical Industries plc (1992) attempts to focus the reader's attention on the profit before exceptional items using the layout:

	Continuing operations Before exceptional items	Discontinued operations	Exceptional items	Total
	£m	£m	£m	£m
As stated in question	4.0	0.1		4.1
4. Cost of sales increased			(0.75)	(0.75)
Exceptional items				
1. Restaurant sale treated as operating profit			1.0	1.0
3. Cost of fundamental reorganisation			(1.1)	(1.1)
2. Loss on sale			(3.5)	(3.5)
	4.0	0.1	(4.35)	(0.25)

There is therefore a certain amount of flexibility in the layout of the profit and loss account which could assist the company to direct the readers' attention.

The company could produce an EPS figure based on the profit from continuing operations. However, where it does this, FRS 3 insists that the reason is given and a reconciliation to the FRS 14 EPS figure is given on an item by item basis.

There are alternative presentations that could be used, such as that proposed by the Institute of Investment and Management Research but provided companies give an explanation and a reconciliation to the FRS 14 defined EPS figure, they are able to tell their own story.

Did you answer the question?

Notice that the Examiner gives an illustrative example, even though this was not explicitly required. A narrative description by itself would not have been as clear. Other illustrative examples (adapted from other financial statements or invented) would have been possible here.

---

39   (Answer 4 of examination)

Examiner's comments and marking guide

Question 4: Part (a) of the question examined a knowledge of the criteria under FRS 6 and its application to the scenario of Growmoor and Beaten.

Most candidates were familiar with all the criteria and produced excellent answers applying the criteria to the facts of the case. The decisions were accepted as judgements and marks were awarded for reasonable evaluations eg, that Growmoor was too dominant because of effective control by their management.

Part (b) required an explanation of the reasons for FRS 7 provisions relating to provisions. This part was well answered.

Part (c) (i) required an explanation for deferred consideration. There were some very good answers with an understanding of the need to discount, supported by a figure of £402,685, and a split of the figure into creditors within 1 year and more than 1 year. Few, however, either explained or calculated the figure for finance cost. Marks were awarded for calculation or explanation in this part.

Part (c) (ii) required a calculation of goodwill and explanation of the effect of deferred and contingent consideration. There were several answers that calculated a goodwill figure, either £282,315 or £185,000, and marks were awarded for goodwill congruent with (c) (i). Good answers referred to contingent consideration and the wisdom of not providing for it until the position could be seen more clearly.

Generally candidates appeared well prepared for this question and overall it was well answered.

			Marks
(a)	1 mark per comment on Criterion	5	
	Up to 4 for development	4	
	Advising on changes	2	
			11/8
(b)	Up to 2 marks per point up to	5	
			5/3
(c) (i)	Balance sheet treatment	2	
	Profit and loss account treatment	2	
(ii)	Calculation	1	
	Deferred consideration	1	
	Contingent consideration	1	
(iii)	1 mark per point up to	4	
			11/9
			27/20

Step by step answer plan

Step 1 Read the question again and make sure that you focus on precisely what is required. The requirements indicate that FRS 6 and FRS 7 are being examined. The scenario describes two combinations and you should be clear that the first (Smelt) is the subject of part (a) and that the second (Beaten) is the subject of part (c).

Step 2 Approach part (a) (i) by taking each of the FRS 6 criteria and the Companies Act criteria in turn. Explain whether the combination meets each of the criteria.

Step 3 Answer part (a) (ii) by considering the way in which the terms could be changed so that the combination satisfied the criteria and explain the reasons for the changes.

Step 4 Answer part (b), noting that the key requirement words are *explain briefly the reasons*.

Step 5 Re-read the details of the acquisition of Beaten and requirement (c) (i) and make sure that you understand the information and the assumptions that you are required to make.

Step 6 Briefly state the relevant requirement of FRS 7 and calculate the liability for deferred consideration that will appear in the balance sheet and the finance cost that will appear in the profit and loss account. Explain your calculations.

Step 7 Calculate the goodwill arising and then explain the effect of the deferred and contingent consideration to complete part (c) (ii).

Items not required by the Examiner for this question: statement of the requirements of FRS 6 and FRS 7 without reference to the scenario.

The examiner's answer

(a) (i) FRS 6 requires that to determine whether a business combination meets the definition of a merger, it should be assessed against certain specified criteria; failure to meet any of these criteria indicates that the definition was not met and thus that merger accounting is not to be used for the combination.

This entails considering the following 5 criteria:

Criterion 1: No party to the combination is portrayed as either acquirer or acquired, either by its own board or management or by that of another party to the combination.

Para 61 of FRS 6 elaborates on this stating that where the terms of a share-for-share exchange indicate that one party has paid a premium over the market value of the shares acquired, this is evidence that that party has taken the role of acquirer unless there is a clear explanation for this apparent premium other than its being a premium paid to acquire control.

This is relevant in the present situation where the value of the Growmoor plc shares issued as consideration was [1,500,000 × £1.20p] £1,800,000 to acquire Smelt plc shares valued at £1,560,000 resulting in a premium of £240,000.

This indicates *prima facie* that it was an acquisition. However, the exchange price was within the range [£1.20 - £1.50] of market prices for Smelt plc during the previous year. This could well be a clear explanation for this apparent premium other than its being a premium paid to acquire control.

The circumstances surrounding the transaction also support the view that this is a merger. For example, the closure and redundancy programme applied to Growmoor plc and not to Smelt plc.

Criterion 2: All parties to the combination, as represented by the boards of directors or their appointees, participate in establishing the management structure for the combined entity and in selecting the management personnel, and such decisions are made on the basis of a consensus between the parties rather than by an exercise in voting.

The need for re-application for posts and appearance before an interview panel indicates that there will be a consensus decision on appropriate personnel which would satisfy Criterion 2 even though the final result might be that the posts are largely filled by Growmoor plc managers.

Criterion 3: The relative sizes of the combining entities are not so disparate that one party dominates the combined entity by virtue of its relative size.

This requires a consideration of the proportion of the equity of the combined entity attributable to the shareholders of each of the combining parties to test if one is more than 50% larger than the other. This 50% is a rebuttable presumption. In this case, Growmoor plc shareholders hold 1,625,000 shares and Smelt plc 1,500,000 shares. This indicates that the criterion is satisfied even though the 1,500,000 shares are in consideration of only 80% of Smelt plc's capital.

Criterion 4: Under the terms of the combination or related arrangements, the consideration received by equity shareholders in relation to their shareholding comprises primarily equity shares in the combined entity; and any non-equity consideration, or equity shares carrying substantially reduced voting or distribution rights, represents an immaterial proportion of the fair value of the consideration received by the equity shareholders. Where one of the combining entities has, within the period of two years before the combination, acquired equity shares in another of the combining entities, the consideration for this acquisition should be taken into account in determining whether this criterion has been met.

This indicates that the cash payment made on 15 June 1994 should be taken into account being less than two years before the combination on 1 May 1996. Appendix 1 of FRS 6 refers to the Companies Act requirements for a transaction to be treated as a merger. This includes the provision that the fair value of any consideration other than the issue of equity shares given pursuant to the arrangement by the parent company did not exceed 10% of the nominal value of the equity shares issued.

The transaction does not comply with this requirement and would be required to be treated as an acquisition.

Criterion 5: No equity shareholders of any of the combining entities retain any material interest in the future performance of only part of the combined entity.

This criterion is concerned with situations where the allocation depended to any material extent on the post-combination performance of the business. In the present case, the allocation is dependent on the determination of the eventual value of a specific liability as opposed to the future operating performance and the criterion is satisfied.

> **Did you answer the question?**
>
> This part of the answer does not simply state the FRS 6 criteria, but applies them to the combination, explaining the way in which they are applied.

(ii) Change of terms

The Companies Act requirement is not met because the cash payment of £164,000 in 1994 is more than 10% of the nominal value of the shares issued which was £1,500,000.

The company has acquired 16% of the shares of Smelt plc in 1994 and 80% in 1995. The company could require the holders of the remaining 4% to sell their shares on the same terms as those offered to the holder of the 80% but, even if it did this, the new shares issued as consideration would be 1,575,000 and the Companies Act requirement would still not be satisfied with the cash payment of £164,000 being 10.4%.

A further, and more common, possibility is that Growmoor plc could make a small bonus issue, say 1 for 10, prior to the exchange thus increasing the nominal value of the equity given from £1,500,000 to £1,650,000. The cash payment of £164,000 is then reduced to less than 10% of the nominal value.

(b) The following reasons could be put forward for the approach taken by the ASB in formulating the FRS 7 requirements concerning provisions on acquisition.

The practice of companies creating provisions or accruals for future operating losses and/or reorganisation costs expected to be incurred as a result of an acquisition was abused. Companies created provisions which gave rise to a larger goodwill figure that could be written off immediately against reserves and a provision against which expenses could be charged in subsequent accounting periods resulting in a higher profit figure. The effect of this was to prevent the accounts showing a true and fair view of the substance of commercial activities that had taken place in an accounting period.

(c) (i) FRS 7 para 77 states that when settlement of cash consideration is deferred, fair values are obtained by discounting to their present value the amounts expected to be payable in the future.

The appropriate discount rate is the rate at which the acquirer could obtain a similar borrowing, taking into account its credit standing and any security given.

For the Beaten Ltd acquisition the appropriate rate is 10% as stated in the question.

Treatment in the balance sheet of Growmoor plc as at 31 July 1996

The discounted deferred consideration payable is a form of debt instrument. It is this amount that will appear as the investment's cost in the acquiring company's balance sheet i.e. £402,685. The same amount would appear as a creditor for the deferred consideration. [100,000 × .9090 + 150,000 × .8264 + 250,000 × .7513]. The liability would be split into £90,900 payable within 1 year and £311,785 payable in more than one year.

Treatment in the profit and loss account of Growmoor plc for the year ended 31 July 1996

Because the deferred consideration is a form of debt instrument, the difference of £97,315 between the discounted amount of the payments and the total cash amount [500,000 - 402,685] is treated as a finance cost to be charged as an interest expense in Growmoor plc's profit and loss account over the period the liability is outstanding so that the annual cost gives a constant rate on the liability's carrying amount. The finance cost charged in the accounts to 31 July 1996 is £3,355 representing 1 month's charge on £402,685 at 10% finance charge.

> **Did you answer the question?**
>
> Notice that this answer does not only calculate the amounts to be included in the accounts, but explains the reasoning behind the calculations.

(ii)   *Goodwill calculation*

Goodwill is calculated as at the date of acquisition based on the discounted amount of the cash payments. This results in a negative goodwill figure of £282,315 [402,685 - 685,000].

Effect of deferred consideration

There is no adjustment to this figure on the stage payments of the consideration. Growmoor plc has obtained the benefit of deferring the payment of the consideration and the cost of this benefit is charged in the profit and loss account over the period of the deferral.

Effect of contingent consideration

The terms of the agreement are such that it is impossible to say whether and how much additional consideration will be paid and the appropriate treatment is to deal with the matter by disclosure rather than provision.

Enquiries would be needed to establish whether the service agreement with the directors of Beaten Ltd constitutes a payment for the business acquired or an expense for services. If the substance of the agreement is payment for the business acquired the payments would be accounted for as a part of the purchase consideration and, as they are quantified, they would be included within the goodwill calculation.

40   (Answer 5 of examination)

Examiner's comments and marking guide

Question 5: Part (a) (i) required an explanation of the advantages of using expanded equity accounting to account for associates. Good answers identified aspects such as the impact on assessment of gearing and off balance sheet considerations. Many merely stated that it gave more information with no indication of what the information consisted of or how it affected the valuation of the group's financial position.

It appeared that the term 'expanded' was not familiar to many candidates.

(a) (ii) required a discussion of proportional consolidation. Answers varied widely. Good answers gave a full discussion of advantages and disadvantages.

Part (b) required an explanation for the accounting treatment of the Joint Venture in the accounts of Textures Ltd and a calculation of retained profit for inclusion in the consolidated accounts. This part was generally poorly answered.

Part (c) (i) required advising the non-executive director of the conditions necessary to avoid Afrohelp being treated as a quasi-subsidiary. Good answers referred to control, made suggestions for adjusting the holding eg, making a downward alteration to the shareholding to ensure treatment using equity accounting and referred to making sure that Textures Ltd had no or little influence via Board appointments or otherwise. A number of candidates summarised FRS 2 provisions for 'exemption from consolidation' to cover the situation. Answers indicated that in general the concept of quasi-subsidiaries and the regulations surrounding off balance sheet situations are not well understood and require further attention in preparing for the examination.

Part (c) (ii) required candidates to contrast the treatment of unrealised gains on the sale of stock to a quasi-subsidiary and an associated company. This was generally well answered although there was some uncertainty in weaker answers about the treatment where there is an Associate, with some stating no adjustment was required, others partial and others full adjustment.

				Marks
(a)	(i)	1 mark per point	5	
	(ii)	Advantages	4	
		Disadvantages	4	
			——	
				13/8
(b)	(i)	1 mark per point	2	

	(ii)	Calculation		3
				⎯
				5/4
(c)	(i)	1 per point to	5	
	(ii)	1 per item up to	4	
			⎯	
				9/8
				⎯
				27/20
				⎯

Step by step answer plan

Step 1   Read the question again and make sure that you focus on precisely what is required. The scenario describes several joint ventures, but although the requirements of FRS 9 are relevant, the question also covers proportional consolidation and quasi-subsidiaries. You will need to read the requirements carefully as some of them specify the accounting treatment to be used or explained.

Step 2   Approach part (a) (i) by briefly stating the current position (under equity accounting) and then explaining the additional information that would be disclosed under the expanded equity method (basically the gross equity method under FRS 9).

Step 3   Answer part (a) (ii) by writing short paragraphs on the advantages of proportional consolidation and then on its disadvantages.

Step 4   Re-read the scenario for the agreement with Pills plc, and make sure that you have understood the nature of the agreement. Then answer part (b) (i). Remember that you only have 4 marks/7 minutes for the whole of part (b).

Step 5   Re-read the scenario for the agreement with Eduaids Ltd and Bracos and make sure that you have understood the nature of the agreement. Then answer part (b) (ii).

Step 6   Re-read the scenario for the agreement with Computer Control Ltd and make sure that you have understood the information. Then answer part (c) (i) by explaining the principles of a joint venture (the conditions which would need to be satisfied).

Step 7   Answer part (c) (ii).

Items not required by the Examiner for this question:

- general discussion of the requirements of FRS 9 without reference to the scenario;
- detailed FRS 2 definition of a subsidiary in part (c) (i) (see Examiner's comments).

The examiner's answer

(a)   (i)   *Explain the advantages of using expanded equity accounting to account for associates in consolidated accounts*

FRS 9 requires information, usually by way of note, to show the group's share of net assets as at the balance sheet date other than goodwill stated where possible after attributing fair values at the time of acquisition; the group's share of any goodwill in the associate's books and the premium or discount on the acquisition of the associate.

The aim of the expanded equity method is to provide an analysis of the net asset figure. At its simplest it could show the totals for fixed and current assets, current liabilities and loans.

Problem of significant debt - debt: equity ratio

There is a problem, where the equity method is used, when there is a significant level of debt in an associate. It has been argued that expanded equity information allows a user to calculate the correct debt: equity ratio. Without the expanded equity information the debt: equity ratio would be understated when there was a significant debt in the associate.

The existence of such loans have been a form of Off Balance Sheet financing as far as the Group were concerned.

Problem of significant debt - ROCE

In so far as the value of the associate in the consolidated balance sheet is represented by the investor's share of the net assets of the associate, the investor's share of any debt is not separately included in the balance sheet. This means that the existence of significant debt reduces the net assets and produces a higher ROCE. This can be adjusted for if expanded equity information is disclosed.

The amount of detail is of course debatable and there will be a compromise between providing a complete balance sheet of the associate to providing selected key totals.

Treatment of assets that are not controlled by parent company

The expanded equity method allows a user to understand the assets that underlie the investment in associates. The method does not require consolidation on a line by line basis which would involve the aggregation of assets that were not under the control of the parent company management. The expanded equity method therefore overcomes the disadvantages of the one line equity method whilst still distinguishing between assets under the control of the group and those held through strategic alliances.

Did you answer the question?

Notice the way in which this part of the answer is structured, with one short paragraph for each problem of equity accounting overcome by the 'expanded' (gross) method.

(ii)   Discuss the advantages and disadvantages of using proportional consolidation to account for joint ventures.

The discussion could include advantages and disadvantages such as the following:

Advantages

- Proportional consolidation includes the investor's share of its joint activity assets and liabilities under each format heading, not merely summary or net amounts. This gives an indication of the size of, and liabilities related to, the investor's interests in its joint venture. Including the investor's share of both assets and liabilities also helps users to take account of the structure and financing of the group and its joint ventures. In total the information provided is useful in assessing the investor's past performance and future prospects

- The best way to present an investor's interest in the results and assets of its joint venture is to treat it as having sole control over its proportionate share of these even though, in fact, it shares control over the whole.

- Joint activities amounting to a sharing of facilities are proportionally consolidated and consistency would require the same treatment for all joint ventures with each participant accounting for its share of the results, assets and liabilities directly in its individual financial statements.

Disadvantages

- Unless a clear distinction is maintained between assets and liabilities that are, directly or indirectly, within the control of the investor and those that are not, the performance and resources of the group are obscured and the usefulness of financial statements that aggregate consolidated amounts with proportionally consolidated amounts on a line-by-line basis is questionable.

- the results, assets and liabilities do not satisfy the criteria set out in the Statement of Principles eg, assets require the ability to control rights or other access to benefits and in a joint venture the control does not exist. The investor should account for what it does control which is the net investment.

- including fractions of underlying items could make understanding of the financial statements difficult.

Did you answer the question?

Again, notice the structure. The answer deals with the advantages and then with the disadvantages, giving roughly equal weight to each.

(b) (i) *Textures & Pills Joint Venture would be dealt with in the accounts of Textures Ltd as at 30 November 1996 as follows:*

This joint activity amounts only to a sharing of facilities with the joint venturers deriving their benefit from services rather than by receiving a share in the profits of trading from the joint activity.

This means that each of the joint venturers should account for their share of the costs, assets and liabilities arising from those activities in their individual financial statements.

For Textures Ltd there would be assets in its balance sheet comprising premises £150,000 and Bank £15,000 and an expense charge to the profit and loss account of £46,000.

(ii) The retained profit of Eurohelp that appears in the consolidated profit and loss account as at 30 November 1996 as a brought forward figure is calculated as follows:

	£'000
Net assets at 1 December 1995 were	6,750
Capital introduced was	
£750,000/30 × 100	2,500
Accumulated profit at 1 December 1995	4,250
Attributable to Textures Ltd - 30%	1,275

(c) (i) Advise the non-executive director of the conditions that would need to be satisfied to avoid Afrohelp Ltd being treated as a quasi subsidiary as at 30 November 1996.

Where there is a 50:50 situation, the joint venture can still be 'off balance sheet', in so far as the disclosure is restricted to that required by the gross equity method, for both investor companies provided the two companies are genuine equals in terms of ability to control the venture and their interests in its underlying assets and its profits.

This would initially seem to be the situation with Computer Control Ltd because each is a trading company and it is not a situation where one is a trading company and the other a financial institution which would bring it within the FRS 5 *Reporting the Substance of Transactions* classification of a quasi subsidiary.

However, there are other criteria and it would be necessary to confirm that:

- the risks and rewards of ownership of the Afrohelp Ltd assets are to be shared equally between its two shareholders; and

- one company does not exert dominant influence over Afrohelp Ltd which would create a subsidiary relationship;

- profits and losses are to be shared equally between Textures Ltd and Computer Control Ltd with no arrangement for differential dividend rights or payments such as management charges that had the effect of stripping out the profits in favour of one of the investor companies.

Did you answer the question?

This answer does not simply repeat the definitions of joint venture, subsidiary and quasi-subsidiary. Instead, it *advises* on the aspects of the agreement that would influence its accounting treatment in practice.

(ii)   Contrast the treatment of the unrealised gain on sale of equipment to Afrohelp Ltd on the consolidation of Afrohelp as an associate compared to as a quasi-subsidiary.

Treatment if an associate

The gain of £26,000 [50% of (£162,000 - £110,000)] that cannot be treated as realised should be deducted from the net assets of Afrohelp Ltd.

Treatment as a quasi-subsidiary

If Afrohelp Ltd results are consolidated turnover would be reduced by £162,000; cost of sales by £110,000; stock would be reduced by £52,000 thus eliminating the whole of the unrealised gain.

Tutorial note

At the time this question was originally set, there was no accounting standard which dealt with joint ventures. The ASB has now issued FRS 9 *Associates and joint ventures*. Minor changes have been made to the question and answer as a result. The question contained no specific requirement to apply FRS 9. However, there are several points to note:

1   Despite the fact that there is a separate entity, Textures & Pills Joint Venture is effectively a joint arrangement under FRS 9, rather than a joint venture. This is because it is a sharing of facilities. Textures Ltd would account for its own assets, liabilities and cash flows. The answer to part (b) (i) would be unchanged.

2   It is unclear whether Eurohelp is a joint arrangement or a joint venture under FRS 9 although the fact that there are retained profits suggests that the undertaking is trading on its own and is therefore a joint venture. Under the Companies Act, unincorporated joint ventures can be proportionally consolidated (which is the treatment followed in the answer). Under FRS 9 (assuming that Eurohelp meets the definition of a joint venture), the gross equity method would be used. The retained profit of Eurohelp included in the consolidated profit and loss account would be 30% × (6,750 – 2,500) and the answer to part (b) (ii) would be unchanged.

3   The status of Afrohelp Ltd is unclear. If it were a joint venture under FRS 9 it would be included in the consolidated financial statements using the gross equity method and the answer to part (c) (ii) would be unchanged.

The original answer has also been amended slightly to reflect the introduction of FRS 10 *'Goodwill and intangible assets'*.

1997 PILOT PAPER

41 (Question 1 of pilot paper)

Section A - BOTH questions are compulsory and MUST be attempted

1. Walsh, a public limited company, acquired 80% of the ordinary share capital of Marsh, a public limited company, on 1 April 1993 when the retained earnings of Marsh were £350 million (credit). The cost of the shares of Marsh was £544 million and the share capital acquired by Walsh was 120 million of the £1 ordinary shares. On 1 July 1996 Walsh sold 20 million shares of £1 of Marsh for £350 million. There has been no change in the ordinary share capital of Marsh since 1 April 1993.

On 1 April 1996 Walsh acquired 85% of the 200 million ordinary shares of £1 of Short, a public limited company at a cost of £900 million.

The draft profit and loss accounts for the year ended 31 December 1996 are:

	Walsh plc £m	Marsh plc £m	Short plc £m
Turnover	10,000	8,000	2,000
Cost of sales	(7,000)	(5,500)	(800)
Gross profit	3,000	2,500	1,200
Administrative expenses	(880)	(570)	(180)
Distribution costs	(1,310)	(830)	(240)
Operating profit	810	1,100	780
Interest payable	(7)	-	(4)
Bank interest receivable	5	-	-
Profit on ordinary activities before taxation	808	1,100	776
Tax on profit	(250)	(350)	(200)
Profit on ordinary activities after taxation	558	750	576
Dividends	(85)	-	-
Retained profit for year	473	750	576
Profit and loss reserve at 1 January 1996	1,500	1,650	675

The following information is relevant to the preparation of the group accounts.

(i) Goodwill is amortised through the profit and loss account over three years, with a full year's charge in the year of acquisition and no charge in the year of disposal.

(ii) The sale of the shares in Marsh plc has not been accounted for in the accounting records of Walsh plc (ignore the taxation aspects of the sale).

(iii) Short plc sold goods to Walsh plc to the selling value of £80 million on 1 August 1996 at cost plus 20%. Walsh plc had sold £62 million of these goods at the year end.

(iv)   Assume that the fair values of the net assets of the subsidiary companies were the same as the book values at the date of acquisition.

(v)   Assume that profits accrue evenly and that there are no other reserves than the profit and loss reserve.

The principal auditors audit only the holding company and Marsh plc as Short plc was only acquired during the current year and the annual general meeting of Short plc has not yet been held. The directors of Walsh plc have expressed a strong wish that the principal auditors should also audit Short plc. The principal auditors have been in office for many years and at present the audit fee of the Walsh Group plc constitutes approximately 7% of their gross practice income.

Required:

(a)   Prepare a consolidated profit and loss account for the Walsh Group plc for the year ended 31 December 1996 in accordance with the Companies Acts, FRS 2 'Accounting for Subsidiary Undertakings', FRS 3 'Reporting Financial Performance'. Earnings per share and the notes to the accounts are not required.

(15 marks)

(b)   Calculate the balance on the group profit and loss reserve at 31 December 1996.

(5 marks)

(c)   [Not reproduced as this part of the question is no longer within the syllabus.]

(4 marks)

(d)   [Not reproduced as this part of the question is no longer within the syllabus.]

(6 marks)
(Total: 30 marks)

(All calculations should be to the nearest million pounds.)

---

42   (Question 2 of pilot paper)

2   The following draft financial statements relate to the Hebden Group plc.

Draft group profit and loss account for the year ended 31 July 1996

	£m	£m
Turnover		5,845
Cost of sales		(2,160)
Gross profit		3,685
Distribution costs	510	
Administrative expenses	210	(720)
Operating profit group		2,965
Share of operating profit of associates		990
		3,955
Profit on disposal of tangible fixed assets		300
Income from investments		80
Interest payable		(300)
Profit on ordinary activities before taxation		4,035
Tax on profit on ordinary activities		(1,345)
Profit on ordinary activities after tax		2,690
Minority Interests - equity		(200)
Profit attributable to members of parent company		2,490

Dividends paid and proposed (800)

1,690

Draft group balance sheet as at 31 July 1996

	1996 £m	1995 £m
Fixed assets		
Intangible assets	200	-
Tangible assets	7,750	5,000
Investment in associated undertaking	2,200	2,000
Other fixed asset investments	820	820
	10,970	7,820
Current assets		
Stocks	3,950	2,000
Debtors	3,700	2,550
Cash at bank and in hand	9,030	3,640
	16,680	8,190
Creditors: Amounts falling due within one year	(3,084)	(1,854)
Net current assets	13,596	6,336
Total assets less current liabilities	24,566	14,156
Creditors: Amounts falling due after more than one year	(4,340)	(1,340)
Provision for liabilities and charges		
Deferred taxation	(60)	(26)
Minority interests - equity	(230)	-
	19,936	12,790
Capital and reserves		
Called up share capital	7,880	4,000
Share premium account	5,766	4,190
Profit and loss account	6,290	4,600
Total shareholders funds - equity	19,936	12,790

The following information is relevant to Hebden Group plc.

(a) The Hebden Group plc has two wholly owned subsidiaries. In addition it acquired a 75% interest in Hendry Ltd on 1 August 1995. It also holds a 40% interest in Sullivan Ltd which it acquired several years ago. Goodwill arising on acquisitions has been capitalised as an intangible fixed asset. No amortisation was charged during the year ended 31 July 1996.

(b) The following balance sheet recorded at fair values refers to Hendry Ltd at the date of acquisition.

Balance Sheet at 1 August 1995

	£m	£m
Plant and machinery		330
Current assets		
Stocks	64	
Debtors	56	
Cash at bank and in hand	224	
	344	
Creditors		
Amounts falling due after more than one year		
(including Corporation tax £34m)	(170)	
		174
		504
Called up share capital		100
Profit and loss account		404
		504

The consideration for the purchase of the shares of Hendry comprised 440 million ordinary shares of £1 of Hebden plc at a value of £550 million and a balance of £28 million was paid in cash.

(c)   The taxation charge in the profit and loss account is made up of the following items:

	£m
Corporation tax	782
Deferred taxation	208
Tax attributable to associated undertakings	355
	1,345

(d)   The tangible fixed assets of the Hebden Group plc comprise the following:

	Buildings	Plant and Machinery	Total
	£m	£m	£m
1 August 1995 cost or valuation	5,100	2,800	7,900
Additions	-	4,200	4,200
Disposals	-	(1,000)	(1,000)
At 31 July 1996	5,100	6,000	11,100
Depreciation			
At 1 August 1995	700	2,200	2,900
Provided during year	250	400	650
Disposals		(200)	(200)
At 31 July 1996	950	2,400	3,350
Net Book Value at 31 July 1996	4,150	3,600	7,750
Net Book Value at 1 August 1995	4,400	600	5,000

Included in additions of plant and machinery are items totalling £1,700m acquired under finance leases. The plant and machinery disposed of resulted in a profit of £300m. Because of the nature of the industry the finance leases are normally quite short term.

(e)   Creditors: amounts falling due within one year comprise the following items:

	1996 £m	1995 £m
Trade creditors	1,000	560
Obligations under finance leases	480	400
Corporation tax	924	434
Dividends	600	400
Accrued interest and finance charges	80	60
	3,084	1,854

The interest paid on the finance lease rental payments in the year was calculated by the accountant to be £100m.

(f)   Creditors: amounts falling due after more than one year included the following items:

	1996 £m	1995 £m
Obligations under finance leases	1,434	1,340
6% Debentures repayable 1.8.2005	2,906	-
	4,340	1,340

There had been an issue of debentures on 1 August 1995. The debentures of face value of £3,000 million had been issued at a discount of £100m effectively increasing the yield on the loan to 6.2% approximately.

Required:

(a)   Prepare a group cash flow statement for the Hebden Group plc for the year ended 31 July 1996 in accordance with the requirements of FRS 1 (Revised) 'Cash Flow Statements'. Your answer should only include the following notes:

   (i)   A reconciliation of operating profit to net cash flow from operating activities.
   (ii)   A reconciliation of net cash flow to movement in net debt/net funds.
   (iii)   An analysis of movements in net debt/net funds.

(25 marks)

(b)   [Not reproduced as this part of the question is no longer within the syllabus.]

(5 marks)
(Total: 30 marks)

Section B - TWO questions ONLY to be attempted

---

43   (Question 3 of pilot paper)

---

3   In 1996 the Accounting Standards Board (ASB) issued a Discussion Paper on 'Earnings per Share' which was essentially an exposure draft on the same subject published by the International Accounting Standards Committee (IASC) (E52 'Earnings per Share' published by IASC). The ASB has now issued FRS 14 'Earnings per share', which replaces SSAP 3.

(a)   Both SSAP 3 'Earnings per share' and FRS 14 state that only those financial instruments that would dilute basic EPS should be taken into account when calculating diluted EPS. FRS 14 additionally states that the order in which potential ordinary shares are considered can affect the dilution of basic EPS and that the sequence of each issue of shares should be considered from the most to the least dilutionary in order to determine whether potential ordinary shares are anti dilutive.

(b)   FRS 14 requires a new method of calculation to deal with the dilutive effects of share options and warrants. The assumed proceeds should be considered to have been received from the issue of shares at fair value. The difference between the actual number of shares issued and the number that would have been issued at fair value to generate the proceeds is treated as the amount of the dilution.

Required:

(a)   Explain why the ASB has started to issue Exposure Drafts of the IASC as Discussion Papers (students should refer to Earnings per Share in their answer).

(3 marks)

(b)   Discuss why there is a need to disclose diluted earnings per share.

(3 marks)

(c)   Calculate the diluted EPS according to FRS 14 given the following information.

X plc - Accounting Data Year Ended 31 May 1997

Net profit after tax and minority interest	£18,160,000
Ordinary shares of £1 (fully paid)	£40,000,000
Average fair value for year of ordinary shares	£1.50

(1)   Share Options have been granted to directors giving them the right to subscribe for ordinary shares between 1998 and 2000 at £1.20 per share. The options outstanding at 31 May 1997 were 2,000,000 in number.

(2)   The company has £20 million of 6% convertible loan stock in issue. The terms of conversion of the loan stock per £200 nominal value of loan stock at the date of issue (1 May 1996) were

Conversion Date	Number of Shares
31 May 1997	24
31 May 1998	23
31 May 1999	22

No loan stock has as yet been converted. The loan stock had been issued at a discount of 1% and the company has complied with FRS 4 'Capital Instruments' as regards the treatment of the discount.

(3)   There are 1,600,000 convertible preference shares in issue. The cumulative dividend is 10p per share and each preference share can convert into two ordinary shares. The preference shares can be converted in 1999.

(4)   Assume a corporation tax rate of 33%.

(5)   The price of 2.5% Consolidated Stock on 1 June 1996 for the purpose of this question is to be taken as £25.

(9 marks)

(d)   [Not reproduced as this part of the question is no longer valid due to technical developments.]

(5 marks)
(Total: 20 marks)

---

44   (Question 4 of pilot paper)

---

4   The basic accounting objective of SSAP 24 'Accounting for Pension Costs' is that the employer should recognise the cost of providing pensions on a systematic and rational basis over the period during which the employer receives the benefit from employees' services. Accounting for defined benefit schemes achieves this objective by applying actuarial valuation methods and assumptions. The standard's measurement rules state

that the basic charge for the pension cost should be the 'regular cost' but with adjustments for the effects of the variations from that cost which may arise from time to time.

Required:

(a)   Explain what is meant by the term 'regular cost' in relation to accounting for pension costs.

(3 marks)

(b)   Describe four categories of variations from regular pension cost which might arise under a defined benefit scheme. An example of each category of variation should be given.

(4 marks)

(c)   The actuarial valuation of the defined benefit pension scheme of Ceepay plc at 31 March 1996 showed a surplus of £36 million. The actuary suggested that the surplus should be eliminated by taking a contribution holiday for four years and then paying reduced contributions for eight years. The regular pension cost is £5 million and the average remaining service life of the employees in the pension scheme is 12 years at 31 March 1996 (ignore interest).

   (i)   Explain how the actuary's suggestions would affect the funding of the scheme and the amount charged in the profit and loss account over the 12 year period.

   (ii)   Explain how the above treatment would vary if £6 million of the surplus was due to a redundancy scheme associated with the closure of a business segment in the current year.

(8 marks)

(d)   Discuss the view that one of the central problems of pension accounting is the difference in approach taken by actuaries and accountants.

(5 marks)
(Total: 20 marks)

---

45   (Question 5 of pilot paper)

5   FRS 5 'Reporting the Substance of Transactions' requires an entity's financial statements to report the substance of transactions in to which it has entered. Once a transaction's commercial purpose has been established, it is necessary under FRS 5 to decide whether the transaction gives rise to new assets or liabilities, or changes the company's existing assets or liabilities.

Required:

(a)   Explain briefly how an asset or liability is identified under FRS 5.   (4 marks)

(b)   Explain and comment briefly on the principles behind

   (i)   the recognition of an asset or liability in an entity's balance sheet.
   (ii)   the complete derecognition of an asset.   (5 marks)

(c)   Mortgage Lend Ltd, a subsidiary of Lendco plc, has sold a portfolio of mortgages to Borrow Ltd. Borrow Ltd has financed this purchase by issuing floating rate loan notes that are secured on all of the assets of Borrow Ltd. Borrow Ltd was set up for the purpose of this transaction and has issued a small amount of equity share capital.

Discuss the criteria which would determine how the above transaction would be treated in the financial statements of:

   (i)   Borrow Ltd
   (ii)   Mortgage Lend Ltd
   (iii)   Lendco Group plc

(Students should discuss whether the transaction should be treated as a linked or separate transaction or derecognised in the financial statements of the companies.)   (11 marks)
(Total: 20 marks)

ANSWERS TO 1997 PILOT PAPER

41   (Answer 1 of pilot paper)

Marking guide

		Marks
(a)	Turnover - split	2
	Cost of sales	2
	Distribution costs	1
	Administrative costs	1
	Operating profit split	2
	Profit on disposal of shares	3
	Interest payable	1
	Bank Interest receivable	1
	Tax	1
	Minority Interests	3
	Dividends	1
		—
	Available	18
		—
	Maximum	15
		—
(b)	1 mark per figure excluding	5
	opening balance	
(c)	Subjective assessment	4
(d)	Independence	
	- dependence	1
	- objectivity	1
	- size of group	1
	- close relationship	1
	- loss of client	1
	- public perception	1
	- fee income	1
	- review machinery	1
	- independent partner	1
		—
	Available	9
		—
	Maximum	6
	Available	36
		—
	Maximum	30
		—

Step by step answer plan

Step 1   Read the question again and make sure that you focus on precisely what is required. This is a group accounts question and the main complications are a mid-year acquisition and a disposal.

Step 2   Establish the group structure after the disposal. You will need to know whether Marsh ceases to be a subsidiary in order to prepare the profit and loss account. Calculate the proportion of Short's profit that will be included in the results for the year.

Step 3   Calculate the inter-company unrealised profit. Then set up a columnar working and use this to add together the individual profit and loss accounts, line by line, as far as gross profit. Draw up the consolidated profit and loss account as far as gross profit.

Step 4	Calculate the goodwill arising on the acquisition of Short (see Tutorial Note). This will enable you to calculate the amortisation charge for the year. Then calculate the gain or loss on disposal of the shares in Marsh.
Step 5	Complete the consolidated profit and loss account as far as profit on ordinary activities after taxation.
Step 6	Calculate minority interests and then complete the consolidated profit and loss account down to retained profit for the year. This completes part (a).
Step 7	Calculate the goodwill arising on the acquisition of Marsh. You should then be able to calculate the consolidated profit and loss account reserve at 31 December 1996 to answer part (b).

Items not required by the Examiner for this question:

- earnings per share calculation;
- notes to the accounts.

The examiner's answer

(a)

Walsh Group
Group Profit and Loss Account for the Year Ended 31 December 1996

	£m	£m
Turnover		
Continuing operations		
Ongoing	18,000	
Acquisitions	1,420	
		19,420
Cost of sales		(13,023)
Gross profit		6,397
Distribution costs	2,320	
Administrative expenses	1,596	
		(3,916)
Operating profit		
Continuing operations		
Ongoing	1,899	
Acquisitions	582	
		2,481
Profit on disposal of shares in subsidiary		60
Bank interest receivable		5
Interest payable		(10)
Profit on ordinary activities before tax		2,536
Tax on profit on ordinary activities		(750)
Profit on ordinary activities after taxation		1,786
Minority interests - equity		(264)
Profit attributable to members of the parent company		1,522
Dividends		(85)
Retained profit for the year		1,437

(b)

Profit and loss reserve as at 31 December 1996

	£m
Walsh plc balance at 1 January 1996	1,500
Post acquisition reserves of Marsh plc	
80% × (1,650 - 350)	1,040
Retained profit for year	1,437
	3,977

Less Goodwill adjustments

Goodwill - Marsh plc	
(544 - 80% (150 + 350))	(144)
Group profit and loss reserve at 31 December 1996	3,833

Alternative calculation

Walsh retained profits	1,973
Profit on sale of shares in Walsh plc accounts	
$(350 - \frac{20}{120} \times 544)$	259
Marsh retained profits	1,367
$\frac{100}{150} \times (2400 - 350)$	
Short retained profits	
$85\% \times \left[(\frac{9}{12} \text{ of } 576) - 3 \right]$	365
Less goodwill amortised	
Marsh $\frac{100}{120} \times 144$	(120)
Short	(11)
	3,833

Workings (all in £ million)

	Walsh plc	Marsh plc	Goodwill	Sub Total	Short plc	InterCo	InterCo profit	Sub Total	Grand Total
Turnover	10,000	8,000	-	18,000	1,500	(80)	-	1,420	19,420
Cost of sales	(7,000)	(5,500)	-	(12,500)	(600)	80	(3)	(523)	(13,023)
Gross profit	3,000	2,500	-	5,500	900	-	(3)	897	6,397
Admin expenses	(880)	(570)	(11)	(1,461)	(135)	-	-	(135)	(1,596)
Distribution costs	(1,310)	(830)	-	(2,140)	(180)			(180)	(2,320)
Operating profit	810	1,100	(11)	1,899	585	-	(3)	582	2,481

Did you answer the question?

This is the best form of profit and loss account working where there are changes to the group during the year. This working has been drawn up so that it produces sub-totals for continuing operations and acquisitions, as required by the question.

Profit on sale of shares in Marsh plc

Proceeds of sale		
less net assets sold - Marsh plc		350
Net assets at 31 December 1996		
Ordinary share capital	150	
Profit and Loss Reserve (750 + 1,650)	2,400	
	2,550	
Less six months profit	(375)	
Net assets at 1 July 1996	2,175	
Net assets disposed of $\frac{20}{150} \times 2{,}175$		(290)
		60

(*Note:* No adjustment for goodwill is required since all the goodwill relating to Marsh plc has already been charged through the consolidated profit and loss account.)

Minority interests

Marsh plc

$20\% \times 750 \times 6/12$	75
$33\frac{1}{3}\% \times 750 \times 6/12$	125
	200

Short plc

15% of $\left[(\frac{9}{12} \text{ of } 576) - 3 \right]$	64
(The £3 million is the unrealised profit)	
	264

Tutorial note

This question and answer have been amended to reflect the issue of FRS 10 *Goodwill and intangible assets*. Goodwill on the acquisition of Short plc is calculated as follows:

		£m	£m
Cost of investment			900
Less:	Share capital	200	
	Profit and loss account reserve b/f	675	
	Profit 1.1.96 - 31.3.96 ($^3/_{12} \times 576$)	144	
		1,019	
Group share (85%)			(866)
			34
Amortisation (34 ÷ 3)			11

42   (Answer 2 of pilot paper)

Marking guide

		Marks
(a)	Net cash inflow from operating activities	1
	Interest paid	2
	Dividends from associates	2
	Dividends from investments	1
	Dividends to minority	2
	Dividends paid	1
	Taxation	2
	Payments for fixed assets	1
	Receipts from sale of fixed assets	1
	Purchase of subsidiary	2
	Issue of share capital	1
	Long-term loans	2
	Finance leases	2
	Presentation of cash flow statement	3
	Reconciliation to net cash inflow	3
	Analysis of changes in financing	2
	Analysis of net cash flow due to subsidiary	1
	Available	29
	Maximum	25
(b)	Analytical review	
	Truth and fairness	1
	Going concern	1
	Consistency	1
	Comparison	1
	Poor audit evidence	2
	Further investigation	1
	Available	8
	Maximum	5
	Available	37
	Maximum	30

(*Note:* This marking guide is based on the original version of the question, which required slightly different notes to the cash flow statement.)

Step by step answer plan

Step 1   Read the question again and make sure that you focus on precisely what is required.

Step 2   Complete the reconciliation of operating profit to net cash flow from operating activities.

Step 3   Calculate the cash flows from: dividends received from associates; dividends paid to minority interests; tax paid; payments for tangible fixed assets.

Step 4	Complete the cash flow statement as far as net cash flow before financing
Step 5	Calculate the cash flows from the issue of share capital, the issue of loans and the finance leases.
Step 6	Complete the financing section. Add up the statement and complete the totals.
Step 7	Complete the analysis note. Then use this to complete the reconciliation of net cash flow to movements in net debt/funds.

Items not required by the Examiner for this question: notes to the cash flow statement other than those specified in the requirement.

The examiner's answer

(a)

Hebden Group plc
Group statement of cash flows for the year ended 31 July 1996

Reconciliation of operating profit to net cash flow from operating activities

	£m
Operating profit	2,965
Depreciation charges	650
Increase in stocks (3,950-2,000-64)	(1,886)
Increase in debtors (3,700-2,550-56)	(1,094)
Increase in creditors (1,000-560-(170-34))	304
Net cash inflow from operating activities	939

Cash flow statement

	£m
Net cash inflow from operating activities	939
Dividends received from associates	435
Returns on investments and servicing of finance	
Interest paid (300 - discount 6 - 80 + 60 - 100)	(174)
Interest element of finance lease rental payments	(100)
Dividends from fixed asset investments	80
Dividends paid to minority interests	(96)
Net cash outflow from returns on investments and servicing of finance	(290)
Taxation	
Corporation tax paid	(500)
Capital expenditure	
Payments to acquire tangible fixed assets	(2,170)
Receipts from sale of tangible fixed assets	1,100
Net cash outflow from capital expenditure	(1,070)
Acquisitions and disposals	
Purchase of subsidiary undertaking	(28)
Cash at bank and in hand acquired	224
Net cash inflow from acquisitions and disposals	196

Equity dividends paid	(600)
Net cash outflow before financing	(890)
Financing	
Issue of ordinary share capital	4,906
New long-term loans	2,900
Repayments of capital element of finance lease rentals	(1,526)
Net cash inflow from financing	6,280
Increase in cash	5,390

Reconciliation of net cash flow to movement in net funds (Note)

	£m
Increase in cash in the period	5,390
Cash outflow from lease financing	1,526
Cash inflow from new long term loans	(2,900)
Change in net funds resulting from cash flows	4,016
Accrued interest on loans	(6)
New finance leases	(1,700)
Movement in net funds in the period	2,310
Net funds at 1 August 1995	1,900
Net funds at 31 July 1996	4,210

Note to the group cash flow statement

Analysis of changes in net funds

	At 1 Aug 1995 £m	Cash flows £m	Other changes £m	At 31 July 1996 £m
Cash at bank and in hand	3,640	5,390		9,030
Debentures	–	(2,900)	(6)	(2,906)
Obligations under finance leases	(1,740)	1,526	(1,700)	(1,914)
Total	1,900	4,016	(1,706)	4,210

Workings (all in £m)

(1)	Dividends from associated undertakings	
	Opening balance 1 August 1995	2,000
	add share of profit	990
	less taxation	(355)
	less closing balance 31 July 1996	(2,200)
	Cash inflow	435

(2)   Dividends paid to minority interest
      Opening balance 1 August 1995   -
      add profit for year   200
      Acquisition of Hendry Ltd   126
      (504 × 25%)
      less closing balance   (230)
                                                         ─────
                                                           96
                                                         ─────

(3)   *Taxation paid*
      Opening balances 1 August 1995
      Corporation tax   434
      Deferred tax   26
                                                         ─────
                                                                        460
      Profit and loss account (782 + 208)   990
      Tax on acquisition of Hendry Ltd   34

      less closing balances

      Corporation tax   924
      Deferred tax   60
                                                         ─────
                                                                       (984)
                                                                      ─────
      Cash outflow   500
                                                                      ─────

(4)   Payments for tangible fixed assets
      Acquisitions in period   4,200
      less arising from acquisition   (330)
      leased assets   (1,700)
                                                       ───────
      Cash outflow   2,170
                                                       ───────

(5)   Purchase of subsidiary
      Cash acquired from acquisition   224
      less cash in consideration   (28)
                                                        ──────
      Cash inflow   196
                                                        ──────

(6)   Issue of ordinary share capital
      Balance 31 July 1996 -   ordinary shares   7,880
                                  share premium   5,766
      Non cash consideration -   ordinary shares   (440)
                                  share premium   (110)
      less opening balance 1 August 1995
                                  ordinary shares   (4,000)
                                  share premium   (4,190)
                                                       ───────
                                                         4,906
                                                       ───────

(7)   New long-term loans
      Balance 31 July 1996   2,906
      less finance cost - discount   (6)
      (6.2% - 6%) × 3,000   ─────
      Cash inflow   2,900
                                                        ─────

(8)	Repayments of capital lease rentals	
	Balance 1 August 1995 (1,340 + 400)	1,740
	New lease commitments	1,700
	less closing balance 31 July 1996 (1,434 + 480)	(1,914)
		1,526

Tutorial note

This question and answer have both been updated to reflect the changes introduced by FRS 1 (Revised) and FRS 10.

---

43   (Answer 3 of pilot paper)

Tutorial note

This question was originally based on the proposals in a Discussion Paper 'Earnings per share', which has since been developed into FRS 14. Minor amendments have been made to both the question and the answer as a result.

Part (c) of the original question required the calculation of diluted EPS according to both the Discussion Paper/FRS 14 and SSAP 3. The marking guide has been amended accordingly. The calculations according to SSAP 3 have been reproduced for information, as they illustrate the differences between the two standards.

Part (d) of the original question required a discussion of the results of the two calculations and comments on the acceptability of the possible revisions to SSAP 3.

Marking guide

(a)	International developments	1
	IOSCO	1
	Form views	1
	Consistency	1
	Internationally acceptable EPS	1
	Available	5
	Maximum	3
(b)	Impact of future dilution	1
	Low interest rate instrument	1
	Finance of acquisition	1
	Illusory growth	1
	Real growth	1
	Available	5
	Maximum	3
(c)	Options	3
	Convertible preference shares	3
	Convertible loan stock	3
	Maximum	9
(d)	Subjective	5
	Available	26
	Maximum	20

Step by step answer plan

Step 1   Read the question again and make sure that you focus on precisely what is required. It is designed to test your understanding of the ASB's recent FRS on earnings per share.

Step 2   Answer part (a), remembering that the key requirement words are *explain why*.

Step 3   Approach part (b) by explaining what the diluted EPS attempts to show. Give some examples of situations in which diluted EPS provides useful information.

Step 4   Re-read the scenario in part (c) to ensure that you focus on the information given.

Step 5   Calculate the number of shares deemed to be issued for no consideration when the options are taken up (Working 1). Then calculate the earnings per incremental share arising on each of the three types of potentially dilutive share. This determines the order in which the securities are included in the calculation per the Discussion Paper/FRS 14. (See Tutorial Notes.)

Step 6   Calculate the diluted EPS per the Discussion Paper/FRS 14.

Items not required by the Examiner for this question: detailed requirements of the Discussion Paper/FRS 14.

The examiner's answer

3   (a)   The Accounting Standards Board (ASB) has recognised the importance of international developments in accounting standards to companies raising capital overseas. The International Organisation of Securities Commissions (IOSCO) may recognise International Accounting Standards as a basis for listing by foreign companies on world-wide stock markets. The ASB therefore plans to include on its agenda most of the issues that are the subjects of standards being developed by the International Accounting Standards Committee. This approach means that the ASB can form views on a subject so that it can exert influence on the IAS being developed. It also ensures that future FRSs are as consistent as possible with international accounting requirements.

Earnings per share is a widely quoted statistic in financial analysis and the ASB is supporting the attempt to reach agreement on an internationally acceptable level of computation and disclosure. The publication of the Discussion Paper allows the financial community to express views on international developments at an early stage. The ASB will, in the light of comments made, be able to put forward proposals to the IASC which may result in a FRED/FRS which is internationally acceptable.

(b)   Diluted earnings per share is an attempt to show the effect of a future issue of dividend earning shares. The future dilution will affect shareholders who should be informed of the impact on EPS. This is particularly important where the financial instruments giving rise to the dilution carrying a low interest rate in compensation for the future rights they give. (Disclosure of these rights is required under FRS 4 'Capital Instruments'). Where a company finances an acquisition through the use of convertible loan stock or preference shares, the securities often carry a low interest or dividend coupon due to the conversion privilege. Therefore, it is possible to achieve illusory growth in basic EPS as consolidated earnings will be boosted without any increase in ordinary share capital (assuming that the post tax finance cost is covered and current profits are maintained). Diluted earnings per share will however show the 'real' growth in EPS for existing shareholders since the 'cost' i.e. conversion privilege of using convertible finance is reflected in the calculation of EPS.

> **Did you answer the question?**
>
> Notice the way in which this answer does not only state why diluted earnings per share must be disclosed, but also illustrates the explanation with examples of situations in which disclosure provides useful information.

(c)   **Diluted earnings per share - FRS 14**

	000 Ordinary shares	£'000 Net profit	EPS	Status
Net profit after tax & Minority Interests		18,160		
less preference dividend		(160)		
	40,000	18,000	45p	
Options (Working 1)	400			
	40,400	18,000	44.6p	dilutive
Convertible preference shares	3,200	160		
	43,600	18,160	41.7p	dilutive
Convertible loan stock				
Interest (6% × 20 million × .67)		804		
Discount		200		
Shares converted				
$\frac{20 \text{ million}}{200} \times 23$	2,300			
	45,900	19,164	41.8p	Anti-dilutive

Since the convertible loan stock increases diluted earnings per share, they are anti-dilutive and are ignored in the calculation of diluted earnings per share. Diluted EPS is therefore 41.7p per FRS 14.

SSAP 3 - Diluted earnings per share (for information only)

	000 Ordinary shares	£'000 Net profit	Incremental EPS	EPS
	40,000	18,000		45p
Options	2,000			
Assumed yield on Consolidated				
Stock £2.4 million × $\frac{2.5}{25}$		240		
less taxation		(79)	8p	
	42,000	18,161		43.2
Convertible preference shares	3,200	160	5p	
	45,200	18,321		40.5
Convertible loan stock	2,300	804	35p	
	47,500	19,125		40.3p

Under SSAP 3 all of the transactions are deemed to be dilutive as each adjustment has a dilutive effect being less than 45p per share.

Workings

1.	Fair value of one ordinary share	£1.50
	Number of options	2,000,000
	Exercise price	£1.20
	Proceeds from exercise of options	£2,400,000
	Number of shares assumed to be issued at fair value	1,600,000
	Number of shares issued for no consideration (2 million - 1.6 million)	400,000

(Tutorial note: The order in which dilutive securities are included in the EPS calculation is determined as follows:

	Increase in earnings £'000	Increase in no of ordinary shares 000	Earnings per incremental share
Options	NIL	400	NIL
Convertible loan stock	1,004	2,300	44p
Convertible preference shares	160	3,200	5p

The options are the most dilutive and the convertible loan stock is the least dilutive. The most dilutive must be included in the calculation first, so the order is: options, convertible preference shares, convertible loan stock.*)

44   (Answer 4 of pilot paper)

Marking guide

					Marks
(a)	Subjective assessment				3
(b)	1 mark for each point				4
(c)	(i)	calculation		2	
		discussion		2	
	(ii)	calculation		3	
		discussion		2	
	Available				9
	Maximum				8
(d)	Subjective assessment				5
	Available				21
	Maximum				20

Step by step answer plan

Step 1   Read the question again and make sure that you focus on precisely what is required.

Step 2   Answer part (a).

Step 3   Approach part (b) by writing a brief paragraph on each of the four variations. In each paragraph, write one sentence describing the variation and another sentence describing the example. Remember that only 1 mark is available for each variation.

Step 4   Re-read the short scenario in part (c) to focus on the facts given. Approach part (c) (i) by calculating the charge to the profit and loss account and explaining the reasoning behind the calculation.

Step 5   Answer part (c) (ii) by calculating the revised profit and loss account charge and explaining the reasoning behind the calculation.

Step 6   Approach part (d) by discussing the approaches and concerns of actuaries and accountants in dealing with pension costs. Remember to write a brief conclusion.

Items not required by the Examiner for this question: restatement of the requirements of SSAP 24.

The examiner's answer

(a)   Regular cost is the consistent ongoing cost recognised under the actuarial method. It is the amount which the actuary regards as sufficient contribution to provide pensions to be given in respect of future service. The presumption is that the present actuarial assumptions about the future will be borne out in practice and there are no future changes to the terms of the scheme. The amount will depend upon the particular method which the actuary uses to attribute cost to the individual years.

(b)   SSAP 24 'Accounting for Pension Costs' identifies four types of variation from regular cost. These types of variation can be categorised into those variations which relate to the actuarial process and those which relate to changes in the scheme itself. The following variations can occur.

    (i)   Surpluses or deficiencies which have arisen because actuarial assumptions made at the time of a previous valuation have been proven to be inaccurate because of past experience. For example the anticipated income from the schemes investments may have exceeded the anticipated rate of return.

    (ii)   The effects on the value of accrued benefits due to changes in method or assumptions in the future rather than to the period since the last valuation. For example, a change in the rate of predicted salary inflation which will have the effect of increasing the future pension cost of the scheme.

    (iii)   Retrospective changes in the conditions or benefits of the scheme. For example, the rights of existing members of the scheme may be improved.

    (iv)   Increases to pensions currently being paid or to deferred pensions for which there is no current provision, (except where these increases are of a discretionary or ex gratia nature). For example where the rights of retired employees are improved.

Did you answer the question?

Notice that the answer addresses both parts of the requirement; four variations and an example of each.

(c)   (i)   The actuarial valuation has showed a surplus of £36 million. Thus the regular cost of £5 million will be adjusted to take account of this variation. There is a difference between the funding objective for a pension scheme and the accounting objective. The actuary has recommended that a contribution holiday be taken for four years followed by reduced contributions for eight years. Thus there will be no funding for four years for the scheme and then for the next eight years there will be funding of £3 million.

        12 years × £5m = £60m

$$\frac{£60m - £36 \text{ million}}{8} \qquad \text{ie, £3 million}$$

        However the charge in the profit and loss account will vary from the funded amount. The charge will be the regular cost minus the surplus spread over the remaining service life of the employees,

$$\text{ie, £5million} - \frac{36 \text{ million}}{12} \quad \text{ie, } \underline{£2 \text{ million}}$$

        The difference between the amounts funded and the amounts charged in the profit and loss account will be shown as a provision in the balance sheet over the 12 year period.

    (ii)   If the actuary has advised the company that £6 million of the surplus was due to a redundancy scheme occurring in the current year, then this variation from regular cost ought to be recognised immediately. The remaining £30 million would be effectively amortised over the remaining working life of the employees. Thus the amount of the annual funding would remain the same as the surplus for whatever reason is still in existence. However the amount charged in the profit and loss account will vary as follows. The profit and loss account will be credited with £6 million in year 1 and debited with the regular cost minus the surplus (net of the exceptional surplus of £6 million) spread over the remaining service life of the employees i.e. £5 million $- \frac{(36-6)}{12}$ million ie, $\underline{£2.5 \text{ million}}$.

From year 2 until year 12, the profit and loss account will be charged with £2.5 million. Again the difference between the amounts funded and amounts charged in the profit and loss account will be shown as a provision in the balance sheet.

Did you answer the question?

Note that the Examiner does not just do the calculations, but explains the reasoning behind them. Both calculations and explanations are necessary to gain maximum marks.

(d)   It can be argued that accounting for pension costs is more dependent upon the actuaries assessment of the funding of a scheme rather than the accountants view of the allocation of the costs of a pension scheme. Actuaries often use great flexibility and subjectivity in their judgements. Their assumptions address such issues as probable returns on pension fund assets, mortality rates, average retirement age and the numbers of potential employees who will leave before retirement age. It is unlikely that actuaries will ever standardise these assumptions as circumstances will differ from company to company. Obviously therefore this element of choice in their assumptions can cause variations in their conclusions regarding the adequacy of the pension contributions. Also there is no particular method of attributing pension costs to years of employment which best applies the matching concept. There are two main methods used by actuaries and these are the accrued benefits methods and the projected benefits methods.

Accountants however, are looking to treat pension costs consistently from period to period and to allocate the cost of retirement benefits over the working life of the employee. They are concerned with recognition and measurement issues. For example accountants are concerned with the measurement methods and assumptions which are most appropriate for estimating the obligation for pensions and the periodic pension cost. Accountants are also concerned with the disclosure and reporting of pension costs. Thus it can be seen that the objectives of the actuary and the accountant are different but perhaps more importantly is the fact that the accounting for pension costs is fundamentally dependent upon the subjective assessment and judgement of the actuaries. Whatever accounting process is determined by the standard setting bodies, actuarial judgement will essentially determine the periodic pension cost.

Did you answer the question?

Notice that this answer discusses both actuaries and accountants and that it contains a brief conclusion.

---

45   (Answer 5 of pilot paper)

Marking guide

			Marks
(a)	Subjective assessment		4
			—
(b)	Recognition	3	
	Derecognition	2	
		—	
			5
			—
(c)	Borrow Ltd	3	
	Mortgage Lend Ltd	5	
	Lendco Group plc	4	
		—	
	Available		12
			—
	Maximum		11
			—
	Available		21
			—
	Maximum		20
			—

Step by step answer plan

Step 1   Read the question again and make sure that you focus on precisely what is required. From the introductory paragraph it is clear that this question is mainly about substance over form.

Step 2   Answer part (a), remembering that the key requirement word is *explain*.

Step 3   Approach part (b) by stating the relevant requirements of FRS 5 and then commenting on them, with examples. Remember that only 5 marks/8 minutes are available for this part of the question.

Step 4   Re-read the short scenario in part (c) to focus on the information given. Analyse the transaction from the viewpoint of Borrow Ltd, Mortgage Lend Ltd and Lendco Group plc in turn to answer parts (i), (ii) and (iii). Discuss the extent to which each experiences the risks and benefits associated with the mortgages. This will indicate which accounting treatments may be appropriate.

The examiner's answer

(a)   Once a transaction's commercial purpose has been determined, it is necessary to ascertain whether a new asset or liability has arisen or whether the entity's existing assets or liabilities have changed. Assets are defined in FRS 5 'Reporting the substance of transactions' as 'Rights or other access to future economic benefits controlled by an entity as a result of past transactions or events'.

The control over the rights to economic benefits should entail the right to obtain the future economic benefits relating to the asset and the ability to restrict the ability of others to access those benefits. Management of the assets is not the same as control. Management of the assets is the ability to direct the use of the asset as a fund manager may do. However, the fund manager will not gain the economic benefits from those assets. Evidence of whether an entity is exposed to the risks associated with the asset is taken as evidence that the entity has access to the asset's future economic benefits. Therefore if the entity controls the rights to the economic benefits an asset may arise.

Liabilities are defined as 'an entity's obligations to transfer economic benefits as a result of past transactions or events'. If an outflow of resources arises as a result of an obligation then a liability will arise. If the entity is unable to avoid the outflow of funds either legally or commercially, then such an obligation will exist. Where this obligation is contingent upon the outcome of a future uncertain event, a liability will not necessarily be recognised. Such an obligation will be accounted for under FRS 12 and a liability will arise where the future event confirms a loss already estimated with reasonable accuracy at the time of the financial statements.

Did you answer the question?

Note that the Examiner does not simply state the relevant requirements of FRS 5, but explains them.

(b)   (i)   Once an asset or liability has been identified, it should be recognised in the entity's balance sheet if there is sufficient evidence of the item's existence and the item can be measured with sufficient reliability at a monetary amount. The problem with those principles is that conventional accounting recognises most transactions when they are performed. For example when goods are physically sold under a contract. However one interpretation of the recognition criteria might be that an asset is created when a contract (for example) for the sale of goods has been entered into. The assets created are the sale proceeds and the liability is the right to the goods by a third party. However, this interpretation of the recognition criteria would create a radical change in practice.

(ii)   Where a transaction transfers all the significant benefits and risks relating to an asset, the asset should cease to be recognised. 'Significant' should not be judged in relation to all possible benefits and risks that could occur but only those which are likely to occur in practice. The importance of the risk retained by the transferor of the asset must be assessed in the context of the total risk which relates to that asset.

If a high quality asset is sold, for example debtors, and the seller agrees to compensate the buyer for any subsequent loss of up to 5% of the assets value, then if the risk of bad debts is very low, then effectively all the risk may be being retained by the seller, in which case the transaction may not be a sale.

FRS 5 addresses the issue of derecognition only in relation to assets and not liabilities.

Did you answer the question?

Again, notice that the Examiner does not merely state the requirements of FRS 5, but illustrates and comments on them.

(c)   Securitisation of assets is often used by originators of mortgage loans to package assets together to sell to a sparsely capitalised vehicle or company. As securitisation makes use of the Special Purpose Vehicles (SPV), it is necessary to consider the accounting treatment in three sets of financial statements, the originator's, the SPV's and the originator group's financial statements.

(i)   **Borrow Ltd**

The financial statements of Borrow Ltd (the SPV) are perhaps the easiest to deal with. Borrow Ltd will treat the transaction as a separate presentation assuming the company has access to all of the future benefits and risks related to the securitised assets and the loan noteholders have recourse to all the assets of Borrow Ltd including assets other than the mortgages. For example the cash balance of Borrow Ltd.

Borrow Ltd is exposed to the inherent risks of collecting the cash from the mortgagors. Hence derecognition would not be appropriate. Because Borrow Ltd's exposure to loss does not appear to be limited, the use of the linked presentation will also not be appropriate.

(ii)   **Mortgage Lend Ltd**

In the financial statements of Mortgage Lend Ltd there are again three possible accounting treatments:

(i)   derecognition
(ii)   linked presentation
(iii)   separate presentation.

If the transaction is to be derecognised then the price of the sale of the mortgages should have been determined at an arm's length, for a single, non-returnable fixed sum and there should be no recourse to Mortgage Lend Ltd for losses. If these conditions are met then the mortgages will be taken off the balance sheet of Mortgage Lend Ltd and the value of the mortgage will be offset against the proceeds with the difference taken to the profit and loss account. If significant benefits or risks are retained by Mortgage Lend Ltd then derecognition cannot be utilised. However in such a situation a linked presentation might apply.

It is common in securitisation schemes for the originator of the scheme (Mortgage Lend Ltd) to retain some benefits relating to the securitised assets. This benefit may be in the form of earning income from the management of the mortgages. However the linked presentation is only appropriate where the risk exposure is limited to a fixed monetary amount and the conditions under FRS 5 for a linked presentation are met. Indicators which may point to a linked presentation are that the transaction price is not at arm's length and the right of the originator to further sums other than the non-returnable proceeds. Where a linked presentation is applied the mortgages will remain on the assets side of the balance sheet. Extensive disclosure requirements apply in this situation.

If the conditions for derecognition or linked presentation do not apply then a separate presentation is required. This means that the mortgages will remain on the balance sheet of Mortgage Lend Ltd and the proceeds will be shown as a loan in creditors.

(iii)   **Lendco Group plc**

In the context of the Lendco Group plc, the important consideration is the nature of the relationship between Borrow Ltd and the group. If Borrow Ltd is owned by an independent third party which has made a large investment and has the benefits and risks of Borrow Ltd's net assets, derecognition may be appropriate. If Borrow Ltd is essentially a quasi-subsidiary of Mortgage Lend Ltd and the conditions for a linked presentation are met from a group perspective, then the latter presentation will be effected even if separate presentation has been used in Borrow Ltd's financial statements.

If Borrow Ltd is a subsidiary of Mortgage Lend Ltd, then separate presentations may be appropriate in the group accounts and Borrow Ltd should be consolidated in the normal way unless the linked presentation is possible in the subsidiary. It is normal in securitisation schemes for the SPV to fall within the definition of a quasi-subsidiary.

Did you answer the question?

The requirement for this part of the question was to *discuss*. The Examiner addresses this by looking at alternative possibilities (e.g. 'If Borrow Ltd is a subsidiary....then separate presentations may be appropriate...'). Notice how the answer to part (ii) discusses the three possible accounting treatments in turn.

JUNE 1997 QUESTIONS

Section A - BOTH questions are compulsory and MUST be attempted

46 (Question 1 of examination)

1 The following financial statements relate to A plc, B plc, C Ltd and D Ltd for the year ended 31 May 1997.

	A plc £m	B plc £m	C Ltd £m	D Ltd £m
Fixed assets:				
Tangible fixed assets	3,500	550	60	90
Investment in B	900			
Investment in C		90		
Investment in D	50			
	4,450	640		
Net current assets	1,830	400	70	60
Creditors falling due after 1 year	130	30	10	5
	6,150	1,010	120	145
Capital and reserves				
Called up share capital of £1	1,350	100	30	20
Share premium account	1,550	100	10	20
Profit and loss account	3,250	810	80	105
	6,150	1,010	120	145

Profit and loss accounts for the year ended 31 May 1997

	A plc £m	B plc £m	C Ltd £m	D Ltd £m
Turnover	8,000	3,000	325	530
Cost of sales	5,000	2,000	195	320
Gross profit	3,000	1,000	130	210
Administrative and distribution costs	2,000	400	35	125
Income from group companies	13	4	-	
Operating profit before taxation	1,013	604	95	85
Taxation	300	200	40	25
Profit on ordinary activities after tax	713	404	55	60
Dividends paid	30	10	5	5
Retained profit for year	683	394	50	55

(i) The directors of A plc decided to reconstruct the group at 31 May 1997. Under the scheme the existing group of companies was split into two separate groups in order to separate their different trades. A plc has disposed of its shareholding in B plc to another company E plc. In return the shares in E plc were distributed to the shareholders in A plc. No profit or loss arose on the disposal of the shares in B plc as the 'demerger' simply involved a distribution to the shareholders of A plc of the shares of E plc.

(ii)   After the 'demerger', there were two separate groups controlled by A plc and E plc. A plc and D Ltd formed one group. E plc and the B group plc formed another group. E plc issued 300 million ordinary shares of £1 in exchange for A plc's investment in B plc. The transaction took place on 31 May 1997.

(iii)   The following information relates to the dates of acquisition of the investments in group companies:

Holding company	*Co. Acquired*	*% Acquired*	*Dates*	*£m Share premium account*	*£m Profit/Loss account*
A plc	B plc	100	1.1.94	100	250
A plc	D Ltd	60	1.5.95	20	90
B plc	C Ltd	80	1.6.95	10	60

(iv)   The group's policy is not to amortise goodwill arising on acquisition of a subsidiary unless annual impairment reviews show that a write-down is necessary. No fair value adjustments have been required.

(v)   Dividends paid by group companies have been accounted for by the recipient companies. A group plc has decided to show the effect of the distribution of the shares in E plc and the demerger of B group plc in its profit and loss account and not as a movement on reserves.

(vi)   The group is to take advantage of the provisions of the Companies Act 1985 regarding group reconstruction relief and the transaction qualifies as a merger.

(vii)   The auditors of A group plc have also been asked to audit E group plc.

Required:

(a)   Prepare the consolidated balance sheet of the B group plc as at 31 May 1997.

(5 marks)

(b)   Prepare the consolidated profit and loss account and balance sheet of A Group plc for the year ended 31 May 1997 after accounting for the demerger.

(14 marks)

(Candidates should prepare the financial statements in accordance with FRS 3 'Reporting Financial Performance').

(c)   Show the share capital and reserves of E Group plc at 31 May 1997.

(2 marks)

(d)   [Not reproduced as this part of the question is no longer within the syllabus.]

(6 marks)

(e)   [Not reproduced as this part of the question is no longer within the syllabus.]

(3 marks)
(Total: 30 marks)

47	**(Question 2 of examination)**

2   Morgan plc is considering the acquisition of one of two companies. Their investment advisers have prepared a report on the acquisition of the companies, one of which is situated in the United Kingdom, UK Group plc, the other is situated overseas. The overseas company, Overseas Group Inc prepares its financial statements in accordance with local accounting standards. The following financial ratios had been prepared for discussion at a board meeting of Morgan plc based on the financial statements for the year ending 31 May 1997.

	UK Group plc	Overseas Group Inc
Current ratio - $\dfrac{\text{Current assets}}{\text{Current liabilities}}$	1.75 to 1	1.2 to 1
Stock turnover - $\dfrac{\text{Cost of goods sold}}{\text{Closing stock}}$	6.5 times	2.6 times
Debtors collection period - $\dfrac{\text{Closing debtors}}{\text{Sales per day}}$	41.7 days	85.5 days
Interest cover - $\dfrac{\text{Earnings before interest and tax}}{\text{Interest charges}}$	6 times	1.8 times
Profit margin - $\dfrac{\text{Net profit before tax}}{\text{Sales}}$	5.4%	0.6%
Return on total assets - $\dfrac{\text{Earnings before interest and tax}}{\text{Total assets}}$	7.4%	0.8%
Return on net worth - $\dfrac{\text{Net profit before tax}}{\substack{\text{Shareholders funds} \\ \text{(including minority interests)}}}$	12.2%	1.6%
Gearing ratio - $\dfrac{\text{Total long - term debt}}{\text{Total assets}}$	27.7%	43.3%
Price earnings ratio - $\dfrac{\text{Market price per share}}{\text{Earnings per share}}$	15	81.6

The financial statements of Overseas Group Inc are as follows:

Consolidated profit and loss account for year ending 31 May 1997

	$'000
Sales	132,495
Operating costs (see below)	(130,655)
Operating profit	1,840
Interest	(1,020)
Profit before tax	820
Income taxes	(200)
Profit after tax	620
Minority interests	(80)
Net profit for the year before extraordinary item	540
Extraordinary profit	72
Taxation	(18)
	54
Net profit	594

Note:

Operating costs comprise cost of goods sold of $110,100,000 and other expenses of $20,555,000.

Consolidated balance sheet at 31 May 1997

	$'000
Assets	
Current assets	
Cash and deposits	22,230
Debtors	31,050
Stock	42,020
	95,300
Long-term assets	135,200
Total assets	230,500
Liabilities and shareholders equity	
Current liabilities	79,400
Long-term liabilities	99,700
Minority interests in subsidiaries	8,200
Shareholders equity	
Ordinary shares	30,000
Retained earnings	13,200
	43,200
Total liabilities and shareholders equity	230,500

At the board meeting the financial director questioned the validity of the financial ratios in view of the differences in the accounting practices of the UK and Overseas countries. She requested that the ratios be recalculated on a common basis using UK Generally Accepted Accounting Practice. The following information is relevant to these calculations.

(i)   Overseas Inc had purchased a 60% holding in a subsidiary on 1 June 1996. For accounting purposes the purchase consideration was taken as $10 million to be satisfied by the issue of 8 million ordinary shares of $1 and $2 million in cash. Overseas Inc's shares were valued at $2 each on 1 June 1996. If the subsidiary makes profits in excess of the profit for the year ended 31 May 1997 in the financial year to 31 May 1998, then a further cash sum of $200,000 is payable on 1 June 1998. Preliminary indications suggest that the subsidiary will exceed this target profit.

(ii)   Overseas Inc had taken account of the above transaction by proportionately reducing the fixed assets of the subsidiary by the negative goodwill figure of $2 million which was calculated by using the book value of the net assets acquired of $20 million. The fair value of the net assets of the subsidiary at the date of acquisition was $25 million. The difference between the book value and fair value of the assets comprised the increase in the value of buildings which are depreciated at 2% per annum on cost. No adjustment to the depreciation charge is required for the treatment of negative goodwill. The current borrowing cost in the overseas country is 10%. UK plc capitalises goodwill and amortises it through the profit and loss account over five years.

(iii)   Overseas Inc had capitalised the costs of developing computer software products totalling $1 million incurred in 1997. The product's first revenues were received in the year to 31 May 1997 and were expected to have an economic life of four years. Overseas Inc amortises such costs based on the economic life of the product. UK plc charges all such costs in the year in which they are incurred.

(iv)   Overseas Inc has a share option scheme under which options are granted to certain directors. On 1 December 1996 100,000 ordinary shares were allotted for $175,000 upon the exercise of options. The company had accounted for the full market price of $250,000 of the shares with the discount on the share price being treated by Overseas Inc as directors' remuneration. Additionally the company had included an employee share ownership trust in its balance sheet at a cost of $7 million. The assets of the trust had been deducted from the reserves of Overseas Inc.

(v)   The share capital of UK plc is 50 million ordinary shares of £1 and of Overseas Inc 30 million shares of $1 at 31 May 1997. The earnings per share calculation used in the Price Earnings ratio calculations had utilised the above share capital figures. The market price of Overseas Inc's shares at 31 May 1997 was $1.47.

(vi)   The extraordinary item in the profit and loss account of Overseas Inc is the profit on the repayment of long-term debt in the accounts of a subsidiary.

(vii)   Part of the stock of Overseas Inc has been valued at market value. Overseas Inc does not trade in commodities but purchases precious metals which it uses in the production process. The stock of these precious metals and related values are as follows:

	Market value $'000	Cost $'000
Year end 31 May 1996	30,000	21,000
Year end 31 May 1997	10,000	7,500

There is no tax impact of any change in policy regarding stock. Because of the poor quality of the initial report by the investment analyst, the financial director has asked the auditor to prepare another report on the potential acquisition taking into account the above factors.

Required:

(a)   Recalculate the financial ratios of Overseas Inc so that they can be compared to UK plc's ratios. (Candidates should describe the reasons for the adjustments to the financial statements of Overseas Inc.)

(16 marks)

(b)   Discuss the implications of the revision of the financial ratios on the decision to acquire UK plc or Overseas Inc.

(5 marks)

(c)   Explain what considerations other than differences in accounting practice should be taken into account when analysing the financial ratios of an overseas company, such as Overseas Inc.

(5 marks)

(d)   [Not reproduced as this part of the question is no longer within the syllabus.]

(4 marks)
(Total: 30 marks)

(All workings should be to the nearest thousand units of currency.)

Section B - TWO questions ONLY to be attempted

48   (Question 3 of examination)

3   Financial Reporting Standard (FRS) 10 addresses the accounting for goodwill and intangible assets. Accounting for goodwill has been a contentious issue in the UK for several years and FRS 10 'Goodwill and Intangible Assets' attempts to eliminate the problems associated with SSAP 22 'Accounting for Goodwill'.

Required:

(a)   Describe the requirements of FRS 10 regarding the initial recognition and measurement of goodwill and intangible assets.

(6 marks)

(b)   Explain the approach set out by FRS 10 for the amortisation of positive goodwill and intangible assets.

(5 marks)

(c)   Territory plc acquired 80% of the ordinary share capital of Yukon plc on 31 May 1996. The balance sheet of Yukon plc at 31 May 1996 was:

Yukon plc - balance sheet at 31 May 1996

	£'000
Fixed assets	
Intangible assets	6,020
Tangible assets	38,300
	44,320
Current assets	
Stocks	21,600
Debtors	23,200
Cash	8,800
	53,600
Creditors: amounts falling due within one year	24,000
Net current assets	29,600
Total assets less current liabilities	73,920
Creditors: amounts falling due after more than one year	12,100
Provision for liabilities and charges	886
Accruals and deferred income	
Deferred government grants	2,700
	58,234
Capital reserves	
Called up share capital	10,000
(Ordinary shares of £1)	
Share premium account	5,570
Profit and loss account	42,664
	58,234

Additional information relating to the above balance sheet

(i)   The intangible assets of Yukon plc were brand names currently utilised by the company. The directors felt that they were worth £7 million but there was no readily ascertainable market value at the balance sheet date, nor any information to verify the directors' estimated value.

(ii)   The provisional market value of the land and buildings was £20 million at 31 May 1996. This valuation had again been determined by the directors. A valuers report received on 30 November 1996 stated the market value of land and buildings to be £23 million as at 31 May 1996. The depreciated replacement cost of the remainder of the tangible fixed assets was £18 million at 31 May 1996, net of government grants.

(iii)   The replacement cost of stocks was estimated at £25 million and its net realisable value was deemed to be £20 million. Debtors and Creditors due within one year are stated at the amounts expected to be received and paid.

(iv)   Creditors amounts falling due after more than one year was a long-term loan with a bank. The initial loan on 1 June 1995 was £11 million at a fixed interest rate of 10% per annum. The total amount of the interest is to be paid at the end of the loan period on 31 May 1999. The current bank lending rate is 7% per annum.

(v)   The provision for liabilities and charges relates to costs of reorganisation of Yukon plc. This provision had been set up by the directors of Yukon plc prior to the offer by Territory plc and the reorganisation would have taken place even if Territory plc had not purchased the shares of Yukon plc. Additionally Territory plc wishes to set up a provision for future losses of £10 million which it feels will be incurred by rationalising the group.

(vi)   The offer made to all of the shareholders of Yukon plc was 2.5 £1 ordinary shares of Territory plc at the market price of £2.25 per share plus £1 cash, per Yukon plc ordinary share.

(vii)   Goodwill is to be dealt with in accordance with FRS 10. The estimated useful economic life is deemed to be 10 years. The directors of Yukon plc informed Territory plc that as at 31 May 1997, the brand names were worthless as the products to which they related had recently been withdrawn from sale because they were deemed to be a health hazard.

(viii)   A full year's charge for amortisation of goodwill is included in the group profit and loss account of Territory plc in the year of purchase.

Required:

Calculate the amortisation of goodwill in the Group Profit and Loss Account of Territory plc for accounting periods ending on 31 May 1996 and 31 May 1997.

(9 marks)
(Total: 20 marks)

49   (Question 4 of examination)

4   Marsh plc acquired the whole of the share capital of the Brenel Group plc on 1 January 1996. Marsh plc acquired Brenel with the intention of disposing of one of its business segments and accounted for it accordingly in its financial statements for the year ending 31 May 1996. Unfortunately Marsh plc did not receive any offers for the business segment and decided on 31 May 1997 that it would not sell the business.

Additionally the employees of the Brenel Group plc were all members of a defined contribution pension scheme. From 1 June 1996 it was decided that this pension scheme should be converted into a defined benefit scheme identical to Marsh but separate from the one operated by Marsh plc. On the conversion of the scheme on 1 June 1996 the actuarial valuation showed a surplus of £40 million which has not been accounted for. The average remaining service lives of the employees of Brenel plc is 10 years and the regular cost under the new scheme is deemed to be £35 million per year. The actuary also valued the pension scheme of Marsh plc and a cumulative surplus of £50 million arose as at 1 June 1996. However, in the balance sheet of Marsh plc at 31 May 1996, there was a deferred pension provision of £14 million which represented the unamortised surplus from the previous actuarial valuation on 1 June 1993. The remaining service lives of the employees of Marsh plc were 10 years in 1993 and 1996, and the actuary recommended a standard contribution of £25 million in 1993 and in 1996.

Finally, the two companies have bank overdrafts and deposits with the same banking group. They signed an agreement to allow the bank to offset in net settlement debit and credit balances with the bank. The two companies however, do not have this facility of offset of overdrafts and deposits.

Required:

(a)   Discuss the accounting treatment in the financial statements of Marsh plc of:

   (i)   the business segment of Brenel Group plc

(6 marks)

   (ii)   the pension scheme

(5 marks)

   (iii)   the bank overdrafts and deposits

(5 marks)

(b)   the conversion of the pension scheme in the financial statements of Brenel Group plc

(4 marks)
(Total: 20 marks)

(Ignore the effects of interest and the time value of money in any calculations.)

50   (Question 5 of examination)

5   The Companies Act 1985 and the Stock Exchange Listing rules contain requirements for disclosure of some related party transactions. The Accounting Standards Board has however, published FRS 8 'Related Party Disclosures' in order to give users of financial information a more detailed insight into transactions. FRS 8 adopted the proposals of FRED 8 'Related Party Disclosures' with a few amendments which came about as a result of comments made on the exposure draft. Without disclosure to the contrary, there is a general presumption that transactions reflected in financial statements have been conducted on an arms length basis between independent parties. However this presumption is not justified when related party transactions exist because the requisite conditions of competitive, free market dealings may not exist.

Required:

(a)   (i)   Explain the reasons why the ASB felt that FRS 8 'Related Party Disclosures' was required when disclosure of such transactions was already deemed necessary under the Companies Act 1985 and the Stock Exchange Listing Rules.

(6 marks)

(ii)   Explain the reasons why the ASB feel that it is important to obtain comment on Financial Reporting Exposure Drafts prior to their acceptance as Financial Reporting Standards.

(3 marks)

(b)   Maxpool plc, a listed company, owned 60% of the shares in Ching Ltd. Bay plc, a listed company, owned the remaining 40% of the £1 ordinary shares in Ching Ltd. The holdings of shares were acquired on 1 January 1996. Ching Ltd sold a factory outlet site to Bay at a price determined by an independent surveyor on 30 November 1996. On 1 March 1997 Maxpool plc purchased a further 30% of the £1 ordinary shares of Ching Ltd from Bay plc and purchased 25% of the ordinary shares of £1 of Bay plc. On 30 June 1997 Ching Ltd sold the whole of its fleet of vehicles to Bay plc at a price determined by a vehicle auctioneer.

Explain the implications of the above transactions for the determination of related party relationships and disclosure of such transactions in the financial statements of Maxpool Group plc, Ching Ltd and Bay plc for the years ending 31 December 1996 and 31 December 1997.

(11 marks)
(Total: 20 marks)

ANSWERS TO JUNE 1997 EXAMINATION

46 (Answer 1 of examination)

Examiner's comments and marking guide

Question 1: This question sought to examine the principles of group accounting through the medium of a demerger. The nature of the demerger was set out in the question and if candidates followed the logical order of the requirements and understood the basis of group accounting they generally performed very well. Surprisingly the audit elements of the questions were often the weakest part of candidates' answers. It is important for candidates to answer all parts of all questions. Part C of the question required candidates to explain the key areas of audit risk in a demerger. Several candidates simply described the main element of audit risk without making reference to a demerger.

Although many candidates may not have accounted for a demerger prior to the examination, the majority of marks were allocated to fundamental group accounting techniques and as long as candidates did not panic and applied themselves, the marks they achieved were generally very good.

			Marks
(a)	Balance sheet of B Group plc		5
		Available/Maximum	5
(b)	Profit and Loss account		8
	Balance sheet		6
		Available/Maximum	14
(c)	Ordinary shares		1
	Profit/Loss account		1
		Available/Maximum	2
(d)	1 mark per point up to max		6
(e)	Minimal work		1
	Ethical issues		1
	Risk profile		1
	Discussion with directors		1
		Available	4
		Maximum	3
		Available	31
		Maximum	30

Step by step answer plan

Step 1 Read the question again and make sure that you focus on precisely what is required. The information in point (i) of the scenario indicates that the main complication is a demerger and from the details of the dates of acquisition in point (iii) you should be able to tell that this is a complex group structure.

Step 2 Establish the group structure before and after the demerger.

Step 3 Start part (a) by doing the main consolidation workings for the balance sheet: goodwill, minority interests and consolidated reserves. Then complete the balance sheet.

Step 4   Begin part (b) by completing the consolidated profit and loss account as far as operating profit. Then calculate the goodwill on discontinued operations. This will enable you to complete the profit and loss account as far as profit on ordinary activities after taxation.

Step 5   Calculate the minority interest in the profit and loss account. Then calculate the dividend in specie (from the balance sheet in part (a)) and complete the consolidated profit and loss account down to retained profit for the financial year.

Step 6   Do the main consolidation workings for the balance sheet: goodwill, minority interests and consolidated reserves. Then complete the consolidated balance sheet.

Step 7   Calculate the consolidated profit and loss account balance of the E Group. This will enable you to show the share capital and reserves to answer part (c).

Items not required by the Examiner for this question:

- consolidated profit and loss account and balance sheet of the E Group;
- notes to the consolidated financial statements.

The examiner's answer

(a)   **Consolidated balance sheet of B Group plc at 31 May 1997**

	£m
Intangible assets: goodwill	10
Tangible assets	610
Net current assets	470
Creditors due after one year	(40)
Minority interest	(24)
	1,026
Called up share capital	100
Share premium account	100
Profit and loss account	826
	1,026

WORKINGS (all in £ million)

Adj a/c

Inv in C	90	Share capital C	24
		Share premium C	8
		Profit/Loss a/c	48
		Goodwill	10
	90		90

Minority interest

Bal	24	Share Capital	6
		C Res	18
	24		24

Group Res

Goodwill amortisation	-	Bal	810
Bal c/d	826	C Res	16
	826		826

Share premium

	Bal	100

C Reserves

Adj a/c - Sh premium	8	Bal P/L a/c	80
- P/L a/c	48	Sh Premium	10
Minority Int	18		
20% of (80 + 10)			
Group res	16		
	90		90

(b)

A Group plc
Consolidated profit and loss account for the year ended 31 May 1997

	£m Continuing operations	£m Discontinued operations	£m Total
Turnover	8,530	3,325	11,855
Cost of sales	(5,320)	(2,195)	(7,515)
Gross profit	3,210	1,130	4,340
Net operating expenses	(2,125)	(435)	(2,560)
Operating profit	1,085	695	1,780
Goodwill on discontinued operations		(460)	(460)
Profit on ordinary activities before taxation	1,085	235	1,320
Taxation			(565)
Profit on ordinary activities after taxation			755
Minority interests			(35)
Profit for financial year			720
Dividends			(1,046)
Retained loss for financial year			(326)

Did you answer the question?

Notice that this profit and loss account follows Example Format 2 of FRS 3. Although this gives more information than is strictly required, using this format saves time here because it replaces the columnar working that might otherwise be necessary.

A Group plc (after demerger)
Consolidated balance sheet at 31 May 1997

	£m
Intangible assets: negative goodwill	(28)
Tangible assets	3,590
Net current assets	1,890
Creditors due after one year	(135)
Minority interest	(58)
	5,259
Called up share capital	1,350
Share premium account	1,550
Profit and loss account	2,359
	5,259

WORKINGS (all in £ million)

Adj a/c

Inv in D	50	Share capital D	12
		Share premium D	12
		Profit/Loss a/c D	54
		Negative goodwill	(28)
	50		50

D Res

Adj a/c	12	Share premium	20
MI	8	Profit and loss account	105
Adj a/c	54		
MI	42		
Group Res	9		
	125		125

Minority interest

Bal	58	Share cap	8
		Sh premium	8
		Profit/Loss a/c D	42
	58		58

Group res

Demerger of B	900	Bal	3,250
Bal	2,359	D Res	9
	3,259		3,259

Minority Interest - A Group Profit/Loss account

Minority interest in D 40% of 60	24
Minority interest in C 20% of 55	11
	35

Goodwill

Cost of investment - B plc		900
Net assets acquired - B plc (100 + 100 + 250)		(450)
		450
Goodwill on acquisition of C		10
Goodwill on discontinued operations		460

Demerged assets

DR Profit/loss a/c (dividend in specie)   1,016

CR Separable net assets of B group plc (1,026 – 10)
BEFORE demerger   1,016

There will be no profit or loss on the demerger of B group plc as the demerger involves simply a distribution of assets effectively to existing shareholders in the form of a dividend in specie.

Dividends -	dividend paid	30
	- dividend in specie	1,016
		1,046

Consolidated reserves (for information only)

At 1 June 1996	2,685
Loss for period	(326)
at 31 May 1997	2,359

Opening balance on reserves

A	(3,250 – 683)	2,567
B	(810 – 394 – 250)	166
C	80% of (80 – 50 – 60)	(24)
D	60% of (105 – 55 – 90)	(24)
		2,685

(c)   E Group plc
      Share Capital and Reserves at 31 May 1997

	£m
Ordinary shares of £1	300
Profit and loss account	716
	1,016

Profit and loss account		
B Group's Profit and loss account (826 – 10)		816
Less difference on consolidation		
E's share capital	300	
B's share capital	(100)	
B's share premium	(100)	
		100
		716

(Tutorial note: It would be possible to present the consolidation workings in part (a) and (b) as schedules rather than as T accounts. The workings below follow the approach described in the Textbook and the Lynchpin.

Part (a)

	£m	£m
Goodwill		
Cost of investment		90
Less: Share of net assets acquired:		
Share capital	30	
Share premium	10	
Profit and loss account	60	
	100	
Group share (80%)		(80)
		10
Minority interest		
Share capital	30	
Share premium	10	
Profit and loss account	80	
	120	
MI share (20%)		24
Group profit and loss account		
B plc		810
C Ltd:		
At year-end	80	
At acquisition	(60)	
	20	
Group share (80%)		16
Less: goodwill amortisation to date		(-)
		826

Part (b)

	£m	£m
Goodwill		
Cost of investment		50
Less: Share of net assets acquired:		
Share capital	20	
Share premium	20	
Profit and loss account	90	
	130	
Group share (60%)		(78)
		(28)
Minority interest		
Share capital	20	
Share premium	20	
Profit and loss account	105	
	145	
MI share (40%)		58
Group profit and loss account		
A plc		3,250
D Ltd:		
At year-end	105	
At acquisition	(90)	
	15	

Group share (60%)   9
Less: demerger (cost of investment in B plc)   (900)
                                                         ──────
                                                          2,359

---

47 (Answer 2 of examination)

Examiner's comments and marking guide

Question 2: This question sought to examine candidates on their knowledge of accounting standards by requiring them to adjust a set of overseas accounts and bring them into compliance with local accounting standards. A similar but simpler question was asked at paper 10 in a recent diet and therefore the nature of the question should not have been too surprising for candidates. The main criticism of the performance of candidates was their inability to plan their answers. In order for the answers to be accurate, it was necessary for candidates to reconstruct the profit and loss account and balance sheet of the overseas company to bring it into line with local standards and then to recompile the financial ratios. Very few candidates actually attempted the question in this manner. Marks were given for the calculation of the ratios even if they were not totally accurate. Similarly marks were given for the discussion of ratios calculated by candidates again even if the candidates were discussing inaccurate ratios.

Part (c) required an explanation of the factors to be taken into account when analysing overseas financial statements. This part of the question was quite well answered by candidates although part (d) on the potential liability of the auditor for the report to be prepared was poorly answered with candidates simply writing the first thing they thought of concerning the legal liability of the auditor.

		Marks
(a)	Purchase of subsidiary	6
	Computer software	2
	Share options	2
	ESOT	2
	Stock	2
	Extraordinary item	2
	Recalculation of ratios	5
		──
	Available	21
	Maximum	16
		──
(b)	Subjective assessment	5
(c)	Subjective assessment	5
(d)	Subjective assessment	4
		──
	Available	35
	Maximum	30
		──

Step by step answer plan

Step 1 Read the question again and make sure that you focus on precisely what is required. At first sight this appears to be an 'interpretation' question, but on reading the requirements you should notice that only 5 marks are in fact available for this. Most of the marks are for adjustment of overseas financial statements. Reading the scenario should tell you that several topics are being examined incidentally to the main requirement: deferred consideration, goodwill, development costs, share options and ESOPs, and stock valuation.

Step 2 Set up a columnar working to adjust the financial statements (see answer).

Step 3 Take each of the points in the scenario in turn. Do any calculations required and determine the adjustment(s). Enter the adjustments on the main working schedule. Then write a short paragraph explaining the reason for the adjustment (i.e. the requirement of UK GAAP) and showing the calculations.

Step 4 Complete the main working schedule by extending the totals across. Add up the schedule. Then compute the revised EPS figure (which you will need to calculate the revised P/E ratio).

Step 5 Recalculate the ratios to complete part (a). Set out the results of your calculations using the UK Group plc ratios from the question as comparative figures, if time allows. This will make it easier for you to compare the two sets of ratios in part (b).

Step 6 Answer part (b) by commenting on the changes and by comparing the two sets of ratios.

Step 7 Approach part (c) by jotting down as many considerations as possible. Then write your answer by explaining each consideration in a paragraph.

Items not required by the Examiner for this question:

- revised accounts for publication in part (a)
- discussion of accounting policy differences in part (c).

The examiner's answer

(a)   Revised Financial Ratios of Overseas Group Inc

			UK group plc from question
Current ratio	$\dfrac{92,800}{79,400}$	1.17 to 1	1.75 to 1
Stock turnover	$\dfrac{(110,100-6,000)}{39,520}$	2.62 times	6.5 times
Average collection period unchanged		85.5 days	41.7 days
Interest cover	$\dfrac{7,052}{1,036}$	6.81 times	6 times
Profit margin	$\dfrac{6,016\times100}{132,495}=$	4.5%	5.4%
Return on total assets	$\dfrac{7,052\times100}{243,682}=$	2.9%	7.4%
Return on net worth	$\dfrac{6,016\times100}{64,401}=$	9.3%	12.2%
Gearing ratio	$\dfrac{99,881}{243,682}=$	41.0%	27.7%
Price earnings ratio	$\dfrac{147}{19.1}=$	7.7	15

Earnings per share calculation

		Weighted	Total
Shares issued 1.6.96 - purchase of subsidiary	8,000	1	8,000
Shares issued - options	100	6/12	50
Balance	21,900		21,900
	30,000		29,950

Earnings per share $\dfrac{5,710}{29,950}$ ie, 19.1c

WORKINGS (all in $000)

Overseas Group Inc
Summarised Financial Statements
Period ending 31 May 1997

Balance sheet

		Purchase of subsidiary	Software	Share option	ESOT	Stock and extraordinary item	Total
Fixed assets	135,200	9,432	(750)		7,000		150,882
Current assets							
Stock	42,020					(2,500)	39,520
Debtors	31,050						31,050
Cash	22,230						22,230
	95,300						92,800
Current liabilities	(79,400)						(79,400)
Long term debt	(99,700)	(165) (16)					(99,881)
Shareholders funds	51,400						64,401
Share capital	30,000						30,000
Other reserves inc		(40)					
minority interest	20,806	10,000		(75)	7,000	(9,000)	28,691
Profit for year	594	(60) (16)	(750)	75		6,500	5,710
	51,400	(633)					64,401

Profit and loss account

		Purchase of subsidiary	Software	Share option	ESOT	Stock and extraordinary item	Total
Profit before interest and tax	1,840	(100) (633)	(750)	75		120 6,500	7,052
Interest	(1,020)	(16)					(1,036)
Profit before tax	820						6,016
Tax	(200)					(30)	(230)
Profit/loss for year before minority interests	620						5,786
Minority interests	(80)	40				(36)	(76)
Earnings available for ordinary shareholders	540						5,710

Extraordinary item	54	(54)	
Net profit	594		5,710
EPS	1.8c		19.1c

Computer software

In the UK the development costs of computer software products are expensed in the year in which they are incurred hence fixed assets will be reduced by the costs not yet written off and profit will be reduced also.

Share options and ESOT

Under FRS 4 the share options should be recorded at their discounted price ie, the net proceeds received. Hence the discount on the market price has to be adjusted to allow for UK GAAP.

DR Other reserves (Share premium a/c)	75
CR Profit/loss account	75
Market price	250
Proceeds	(175)
Directors remuneration to be eliminated	75

In the UK UITF 13 states that ESOT's should be recorded as fixed asset investments and not deducted from shareholders funds.

Purchase of subsidiary

Purchase consideration

8 million ordinary shares of $1 - value $2	16,000
Cash	2,000
Deferred consideration (200 discounted for two years)	165
	18,165
less fair value of assets acquired 60% of 25,000	15,000
Goodwill	3,165
Less: Amortisation (3,165 ÷ 5)	(633)
	2,532

So therefore the negative goodwill of 2,000 should be added back to fixed assets. The adjustments required in the financial statements of Overseas Group Inc are therefore:

Fixed assets - negative goodwill added back	2,000
- revaluation	5,000
increase depreciation	(100)
- goodwill	2,532
	9,432

Profit and loss account

There will be a charge for depreciation on the increased value of the fixed asset ($100) and this will affect the minority interest (40% of 100 ie, 40). Also there will be a notional charge of (10% of 165 for the interest on the long term loan ie, 16) and the amortisation charge for the year of 633.

Other reserves

Share premium	8,000
Minority interest 40% of 5,000	2,000
	10,000

Extraordinary item

The extraordinary profit of $54 would be treated as normal profit under FRS 3 'Reporting Financial Performance'. Therefore it should be included in the pre tax and pre minority interest calculation of profit. Therefore as the holding company's share of this item is $54, the minority's share must be $36 ($\frac{40}{60} \times 54$), thus the pre tax and pre minority interest value of this item will be:

	HC	*MI*	*Total*
Extraordinary profit	72	48	120
Tax	18	12	30
	54	36	90

Stock

Closing stock adjustment	(2,500)
Opening stock adjustment	9,000
Net profit increase	6,500

The policy of 'marking to market' value has developed in the UK where commodities are being dealt with on a recognised market and dealing in such commodities is the company's principal activity. In this case however in order to ensure consistency, the stock should be valued at the lower of cost and net realisable value. The latter value can be equated in this case to market value.

The result of this adjustment will be as follows:

DR	Opening reserves	9,000
CR	Cost of sales	6,500
	Closing stock	2,500

Did you answer the question?

Notice that this answer does not only show the calculations, but explains the reasons for them. (See the requirement.)

(b)   The revision of the financial ratios for the differing accounting policies has enhanced those ratios determined by the pre tax profitability of the company. There has been little change in the liquidity ratios which seem to indicate that the UK Group plc is more liquid and solvent than the Overseas Group Inc. The interest cover ratio has been significantly improved. The profit margin, return on total assets and return on net worth ratios were quite poor compared to UK group plc prior to the revision and therefore the improvement in these ratios may have a major impact on the decision to purchase one of the companies.

Overseas Group Inc is significantly higher geared than UK Group plc although the adjustment for differing accounting practices has in fact slightly reduced the level of gearing of Overseas Group Inc. The PE ratios of the two companies are significantly different. The adjustments have affected the PE ratio of Overseas Group Inc to the extent that it has been significantly reduced.

Overall it would appear that the UK group is more liquid, more profitable and has a lower gearing ratio. However, although one might automatically advise Morgan plc to acquire UK Group plc there are other factors which ought to be taken into account when analysing such ratios. These factors are set out in part (c) of the answers.

Did you answer the question?

Notice the way in which this part of the answer does not simply compare the two sets of ratios, but concentrates on the implications of the revisions to the Overseas Group ratios. It also draws a (necessarily) tentative conclusion.

(c)   Financial ratios may be appropriate measures of risk efficiency and profitability in a UK context but they may be misinterpreted when applied to an international situation because an investor may not understand the foreign environment and business conditions. Restatement of foreign companies financial statements for UK GAAP does have some effect on observed ratio differences as is evidenced by part (a) and (b) of this answer.

However, in many cases these accounting effects only explain a minor portion of the reasons for difference in ratios. Highly geared companies may be the norm in the country concerned. The relationship between the banks/loan creditors may be quite close even to the extent of the bank holding shares in the company. In this situation a bank would be loathe to impose financial penalties for slow payment of a debt. A key bank official may be on the board of directors to provide assistance in financial matters. The nature of business finance may therefore be quite different with long-term debt being more like an equity shareholding.

If this is the case then interest is essentially a dividend and lower interest coverage ratios will not therefore be viewed with as much concern. Institutional and cultural factors can cause liquidity ratios to differ without necessarily changing the basic financial risk being measured. The low current ratio of Overseas Group plc may indicate a weak short-term debt paying ability. However, if short-term interest rates are more attractive than long-term interest rates and short-term debts are rolled over by banks into long-term loans, then such a low current ratio does not indicate corporate illiquidity. In the UK, the use of short-term debt to finance long-term assets is frowned upon but this may be the norm in the overseas country.

Debtors collection periods may also reflect differences in business customs. Repayment terms may be longer for several reasons. For example economic downturns may result, not in tighter credit controls being exercised but exactly the opposite may occur in order to ensure more business stability. Lower stock turnover statistics may be indicative of employment policy rather than obsolete stock or slow sales. During slack periods, companies may prefer to continue production rather than make workers redundant. Short-term profitability may not be the main concern of corporate shareholders. If banks, customers and suppliers own shares in the company they will be more interested in strengthening the business rather than short-term stock market profits. If management are more secure in their employment, then short-term profits will not be as important to them. Companies such as Overseas Inc may wish to increase their market share on the basis that profits will come in the long-term. In order to do this, profit margins may suffer due to intense price competition. Hence this may be the reason for Overseas Inc's profitability ratios. Thus it is important that financial analysts not only understand major differences in accounting principles between the UK and other countries but also national business and financial customs. Additionally appropriate country and industry ratio aggregates may give analysts useful standards against which to compare and interpret ratios on a global basis.

Did you answer the question?

Note that the Examiner has not discussed accounting policy differences, which the question stated explicitly were not required. Instead, the answer describes and explains economic and cultural considerations, with examples.

---

48   (Answer 3 of examination)

(*Note:* At the time that this question was originally set, FRS 10 had not been issued. Minor amendments have been made to the question and answer to reflect the change from FRED 12).

Examiner's comments and marking guide

Question 3: This question examined FRED 12 'Goodwill and intangible assets'. Parts (a) and (b) sought to test candidates' basic knowledge of the FRED by requiring an outline of the proposed rules for the recognition, measurement and amortisation of goodwill and intangible assets. These parts were generally answered satisfactorily. Part (c) required the calculation of goodwill on the acquisition of a subsidiary utilising FRS 7 and FRED 12. Candidates performed quite well on this part of the question although very few successfully completed it. If candidates incorporated the valuation of the land and buildings into the financial statements for the year ending the 31 May 1996, then the marks were given for this. Treatments of the valuation could still have been treated as an adjusting post balance sheet event. Generally the question was well answered.

			Marks
(a)	1 mark per part except (iv)		5
	answer iv		2
			—
		Available	7
		Maximum	6
			—
(b)	Proposed approach		2
	Amortisation - 20 years		1
	If exceed 20 years		1
	If less than 20 years		1
	Discussion of significance of value		
	and capability of measurement		1
	Impairment/useful life review		1
	Residual value		1
			—
		Available	8
		Maximum	5
			—
(c)	Intangible assets		1
	Land and buildings		1
	Stocks		1
	Creditors more than 1 year		2
	Provisions		1
	Government Grants		1
	Purchase consideration		1
	Charge to profit and loss account	1996	1
		1997	4
			—
		Available	13
		Maximum	9
			—
		Available	28
		Maximum	20
			—

Step by step answer plan

Step 1   Read the question again and make sure that you focus on precisely what is required. The introductory paragraph shows that this question is about goodwill and the changes introduced by FRS 10. The scenario in part (c) contains details of asset values relating to an acquired company. This indicates that FRS 7 is also being examined.

Step 2   Answer part (a) by stating the relevant requirements of FRS 10.

Step 3   The key requirement words in part (b) are *explain the approach*. Explain the requirements of FRS 10 and the reasoning behind them.

Step 4   Re-read the scenario and requirement for part (c) to focus on the information given.

Step 5   Restate the balance sheet of Yukon at 31 May 1996, incorporating fair values. Calculate the fair value of the consideration. You will then be able to calculate the goodwill on the acquisition and the amortisation charge for the year.

Step 6   Start from the net book value of the goodwill at 1 June 1996 and adjust this for the changes in fair value of tangible and intangible assets. Then calculate the charge to the profit and loss account for 1997 and the adjustment to the fair value of goodwill.

The examiner's answer

(a)   FRS 10 'Goodwill and Intangible Assets' sets out the following recommendations for the initial recognition and measurement of goodwill and intangible assets.

   (i)   Positive purchased goodwill should be capitalised and shown as an asset on the balance sheet. Negative purchased goodwill should be disclosed separately on the balance sheet, immediately below the goodwill heading.

   (ii)   Internally generated goodwill should not be recognised.

   (iii)   An intangible asset purchased separately from a company should be capitalised at its cost.

   (iv)   An intangible asset acquired as part of the acquisition of a business should be recognised separately from goodwill if its value can be reliably measured. The intangible asset should be measured at its fair value, subject to the constraint that, unless the asset has a readily ascertainable market value, the fair value should be limited to an amount that does not create or increase any negative goodwill arising on the acquisition.

   (v)   If its value cannot be measured reliably, an intangible asset acquired on the acquisition of a business should be subsumed within the value of goodwill.

   (vi)   An internally developed intangible asset may be recognised only if it has a readily ascertainable market value.

(b)   The required approach seeks to charge goodwill to the profit and loss account only to the extent that the carrying value of goodwill is not supported by the current value of the goodwill within the acquired business. Amortisation is a practical means of recognising the reduction in value of goodwill that has a limited useful economic life. The useful economic life of purchased goodwill is the period over which the value of an acquired business is expected to exceed the values of its identifiable assets and liabilities.

There is a rebuttable presumption in FRS 10 that the useful economic life of purchased goodwill and intangible assets are limited and do not exceed 20 years. If there are valid grounds for the life of the asset to exceed 20 years (for example where the benefit of the intangible asset is achieved through renewable legal rights), then the longer period may be used but the tone of FRS 10 indicates that a 20 year life should normally be considered to be the maximum life. However there may be grounds for rebutting that presumption and treating the asset's life as indefinite.

Where the useful economic life of goodwill or an intangible asset is believed to be 20 years or less, the carrying value should be amortised in the profit and loss account over the estimated useful economic life. If the useful economic life is believed to exceed 20 years but the value is insignificant and is not capable of future measurement, then a deemed economic life of 20 years should be used. If the economic life of goodwill or an intangible asset is believed to exceed 20 years and the value is significant and expected to be capable of future continued measurement, then:

(i)   If the useful economic life can be estimated, then the goodwill or the intangible asset should be amortised in the profit and loss account over that life.

(ii)   If the useful economic life is indefinite, the goodwill or intangible asset should not be amortised.

The goodwill or intangible asset should be reviewed for impairment each period. In amortising an intangible asset, a residual value may be assumed only if such a value can be measured reliably. No residual value may be assumed for goodwill. A straight line method should be used unless inappropriate. The useful economic lives of goodwill and intangible assets should be reviewed at the end of each reporting period and revised if necessary.

Did you answer the question?

Here, the Examiner does not just state the requirements of FRS 10. The requirement was to *explain the approach*, so the answer explains the reasoning behind the general approach (amortisation) and then the specific proposals.

(c)   **Fair values of net assets acquired at 31 May 1996 by Territory plc**

	£'000
Intangible assets (subsumed within goodwill)	
Land and buildings	20,000
Other tangible fixed assets	18,000
Stocks	20,000
Debtors	23,200
Cash	8,800
Creditors due within 1 year	(24,000)
Creditors due more than 1 year	(13,147)
Provisions for liabilities and charges	(886)
Fair value	51,967
Purchase consideration	
25 million × 2.25 per share	56,250
Cash	10,000
	66,250
Goodwill (66,250 – 51,967) × 80%	11,426

Charge to profit and loss account

Year to 31 May 1996	$\dfrac{11,426}{10 \text{ years}}$	1,143

	£'000
Year to 31 May 1997	
Net book value at 1 June 1996	10,283
Adjustment for fair value	
of tangible asset (3,000 × .8 × .9)	(2,160)
Intangible assets written off (6,020 × .8 × .9)	(4,334)
	3,789
Amortisation (÷9)	421
Write off of intangible assets	4,334
Charge to profit/loss account	4,755

Adjustment for fair value
- goodwill (2,400 – 2,160)   (240) CREDIT

Where an impairment in value arises, such as in the case of the intangible asset, the loss should be charged in the profit and loss account. The fair value adjustment is in relation to the revision of the value of the land and buildings.

Notes:

(i)   FRS 7 'Fair values in acquisition accounting' allows adjustments to fair values up to the accounts for a full financial year following an acquisition. Therefore as a valuation of land and buildings by an independent valuer was received within this period, then this value £23 million will be taken into account for the fair value exercise in the accounts for the year ended 31 May 1997.

(ii)   Where an intangible asset cannot be measured reliably on acquisition, its value should be subsumed within purchased goodwill.

(iii)   Stocks are stated for fair value purposes at current replacement cost. However the fair value should not exceed the recoverable amount which is its net realisable value ie, £20 million.

(iv)   Creditors: amounts falling due more than one year.

Amount due on 31 May 1999
£11 million × 1.464   £16,105,100

Fair value 31 May 1996   £13,146,559

$$\left(\frac{£16,105,100}{1.07^3} \right)$$

Current market interest rates should be taken into account when calculating the fair value of the long-term loan.

(v)   As the reorganisation of Yukon plc would have taken place irrespective of the acquisition, the provision is included in the fair value exercise. The provision for future losses however is deemed to be post acquisition.

(vi)   The deferred government grants will be ignored as the fair value of the assets to which they relate has already been included in the fair value exercise.

---

49   (Answer 4 of examination)

Examiner's comments and marking guide

Question 4: This question was poorly answered. It sought to examine pension accounting, the right of offset of bank balances and the disposal of a business segment. The latter two elements of the question were quite well answered but pension accounting still appears to be a problem area for candidates. Candidates need to adopt a more discursive style in answering questions as many answers are restricted to a factual level without any opinions being expressed. Candidates receive credit for their own views on a subject as often there is no 'correct' answer to an accounting problem but simply a range of views within the current regulations. Questions of this nature will be infrequent in future as questions in section B will generally be topic based.

			Marks
(a)	(i)	Recognised as single identifiable asset	1
		Fair value estimated net proceeds	1
		Identification of purchaser/being sought	1
		Disposal within one year	1
		Reason - distortion of continuing activities	1
		Inconsistent with FRS 7 approach	1
		If not sold - consolidated	1

Fair values		1
Prior period adjustment		1
Disclosure		1
	Available	10
	Maximum	6

(ii)	Spread over expected remaining service lives		1
	Inevitably unamortised balance		1
	Total surplus of £64 million		1
	New variation - £30 million		1
	Combine surpluses		1
	Amortise old surplus over remaining life		1
	Amortise new surplus over 10 years		1
		Available	7
		Maximum	5

(iii)	FRS 5 - accounted individually		1
	Netting off - where not really separate		1
	assets and liabilities		
	Owe/due from same third party		1
	legal right		
	Determinable monetary amounts		1
	Reporting entity can insist on net settlement		1
	Insist on net settlement beyond doubt		1
	Bank can insist so therefore no offset		2
		Available	8
		Maximum	5

(b)	Winding up and being set up	1
	Transfer of assets to new scheme	1
	Spread surplus	1
	Employers liability changed	1
	SSAP 24 allows departure	2
	where discontinuance	
	Immediate recognition of surplus	1
	Accounting for surplus	2
	Available	9
	Maximum	4
	Available	34
	Maximum	20

Step by step answer plan

Step 1   Read the question again and make sure that you focus on precisely what is required. The scenario describes four separate accounting problems. It is particularly important to read the requirements carefully; you are required to consider how three of them might be treated in the accounts of the parent company (Marsh) and to consider the treatment of the fourth in the accounts of the subsidiary (Brenel Group).

Step 2   Approach the question by considering each of the four transactions in turn. For each transaction:

- look carefully at the transaction and consider all the possibilities (jot down ideas);
- do any calculations required (this applies to (a) (ii) and to (b));
- consider what other information you might need to determine a correct accounting treatment.

Remember that you only have about 10 minutes to answer part (a) (i), 8 minutes for parts (a) (ii) and (iii) and 7 minutes to answer part (b).

Step 3   Write your answer, remembering that the key requirement word is to *discuss*.

Items not required by the Examiner for this question: restatement of the requirements of FRSs/SSAPs/Companies Act without reference to the scenario.

The examiner's answer

(a)   (i)   Where a business segment is acquired and held for resale, FRS 7 'Fair values in acquisition accounting' requires that the segment should be recognised in the balance sheet as a single identifiable current asset. A single fair value would be given to this asset and the actual net realised value will normally provide the most reliable fair value at the date of acquisition. Its value in the financial statements of Marsh plc for the year ending 31 May 1996 would be an estimate of the estimated net proceeds of sale provided that a purchaser has been identified or is being sought and disposal is reasonably expected to occur within one year of acquisition. The reason for this treatment is that the consolidation of the results and net assets of such a business segment would distort the view of the group's continuing activities. However, the general approach of FRS 7 and the fair value exercise is that the values should not reflect the acquirers intentions in the future and the above treatment is inconsistent with this approach.

The standard requires that if the segment is not sold within approximately one year, then it should be consolidated with fair values attributed to the net assets and goodwill as at the date of acquisition. In the case of March plc it decided on 31 May 1997 in any event that it would not sell the segment. Although FRS 7 does not explicitly say so it could be argued that a prior period adjustment would be necessary in order to deal with the change in accounting policy and the segment would be stated at fair value as at the date of acquisition. Thus it would be consolidated in the financial statements for the year ended 31 May 1997 and the comparative figures for the year ended 31 May 1996 would be restated on a comparable basis.

(ii)   Most variations from regular pension costs are spread over the expected remaining service lives of the current employees in the scheme. (SSAP 24 'Accounting for pension costs'.) This spreading of costs will invariably mean that an unamortised balance will remain from the last valuation which has not yet been charged or credited to the profit and loss account. It would appear that in the case of Marsh plc that there is a cumulative surplus of £50 million which will go to reduce the pension cost even further. At present prior to taking into account the surplus on the new actuarial valuation, there is an unamortised surplus of £14 million which relates to the valuation as at 1 June 1993. It might appear therefore that there is a total surplus of £64 million to be taken into account. However, based upon the valuation on 1 June 1993, it would appear that the anticipated surplus as at 1 June 1996 would have been £20 million as the recommended contributions have been maintained by the company since 1993.

Annual amortisation $\dfrac{\text{£14 million}}{7 \text{ years}} = \text{£2 million}$

Estimated remaining service life at 1 June 1993   <u>10 years</u>

Surplus at 1 June 1993   <u>£20 million</u>

Therefore the new variation which has arisen as a result of the actuarial valuation is (£50 − £20) million ie, £30 million. There are two methods to account for the surpluses.

The surpluses (£30 million and the unamortised balance of £14 million) can be combined and written off over 10 years or the original amortisation period (a further seven years) can be maintained for the original variation and the new variation written off over 10 years.

(iii) FRS 5 ' Reporting the substance of transactions' makes it clear that assets and liabilities should be accounted for individually rather than netted off. Netting off is allowed by the standard only where the debit and credit balances are not really separate assets and liabilities. This could be where the amounts are due to and from the same third party and where there is a legal right of set off. The detailed criteria for offset set out in FRS 5 are:

(i) the parties owe each other determinable monetary amounts.

(ii) the reporting entity has the ability to insist on net settlement, which can be enforced in all situations of default by the other party.

(iii) the reporting entity's ability to insist on net settlement is assured beyond doubt.

Consequently for the bank balances and overdrafts to be offset, there should be no possibility that the companies could, in any circumstances be required to repay the overdraft and be unable to obtain access to their deposits. Therefore where the bank can insist on a net settlement but the company cannot, the balances will not be able to be offset in the financial statements.

(b) In the case of the change of pension scheme from a defined contribution to defined benefit scheme in the financial statements of Brenel plc essentially the former is being wound up and the latter is being set up. The accrued liability for the old scheme has been settled by transferring the assets to the new scheme. SSAP 24 'Accounting for Pension Costs' would normally spread a surplus in a defined benefit scheme over the expected remaining service lives of the employees. This treatment may be appropriate when employees are transferred from one defined benefit scheme to another but in this case the nature of the employers liability has changed fundamentally from a service cost of the contributions only to a cost to be determined by actuarial valuation. SSAP 24 allows a departure from the spreading principle in limited circumstances. These circumstances include reductions in employees relating to the sale or termination of an operation and other significant reductions in employer numbers. It can be argued that the reason for the allowed alternative treatment is because part of the scheme has in effect been discontinued. The corresponding surplus is recognised in the profit and loss account.

Effectively the defined contribution scheme has been terminated and therefore the surplus relating to the settlement of the scheme should be recognised immediately with a pension asset being shown in the balance sheet of Brenel plc.

The regular cost of the pension scheme of £35 million would be charged in the profit and loss account and credited against the pension asset in balance sheet. In the year to 31 May 1998 the pension asset will be used up and cash contributions will commence. (There will be a cash contribution of £35 million - (£40 – £35) million ie, £30 million).

Did you answer the question?

Notice the way in which the Examiner approaches each part of the question. The requirement is to *discuss*, and this is addressed by explaining all the possibilities and factors which might influence an accounting treatment, as well as relevant requirements of FRSs/SSAPs. Simply stating one accounting treatment would not be sufficient here. (See the Examiner's Comments.)

---

50   (Answer 5 of examination)

Examiner's comments and marking guide

Question 5: This question was poorly answered by candidates. The question required an understanding of FRS 8 'Related party disclosures' and the purpose of obtaining comment on FREDs. Part (a) required candidates to discuss the purpose of FRS 8 and this section was quite well answered. However when candidates were asked to apply the standard to a given set of facts, they were generally unable to do so in a coherent and analytical way. A question applying FRS 8 has not been set before and there are few examples of its practical application in textbooks. However it is important that when a new standard is issued candidates do not wait for an examination question to appear before studying the practical application of a standard. Paper 13 requires a detailed knowledge of a standard not a cursory overview.

(a)	(i)	Greater disclosure	1
		Failed companies	1
		Onus on auditors	1
		Wider perspective	1
		Definitions different	1
		Comprehensive	1
		International consistency	1
		Not adequate safeguarding users	1

| | | Available | 8 |
| | | Maximum | 6 |

	(ii)	Insight into views	1
		Alternative solutions	1
		Conflicts with practice	1
		Consistency	1

| | | Available | 4 |
| | | Maximum | 3 |

| (b) | Year to 31 December 1996 | 6 |
| | Year to 31 December 1997 | 6 |

| | | Available | 12 |
| | | Maximum | 11 |

| | | Available | 24 |
| | | Maximum | 20 |

Step by step answer plan

Step 1   Read the question again and make sure that you focus on precisely what is required. The introductory paragraph clearly indicates that FRS 8 is being examined, but as usual, the requirements are very specific and it is important to read them carefully.

Step 2   Approach part (a) (i) by explaining the significance of related party relationships and the ways in which FRS 8 goes further than the statutory and Stock Exchange requirements.

Step 3   Answer part (a) (ii), remembering that the key requirement words are *explain the reasons*.

Step 4   Re-read the short scenario and the requirement in part (c) to focus on the facts given.

Step 5   Answer part (c) by considering each of the three companies in turn. Determine whether each company was a related party of the other two during each of the two years. This will enable you to decide on the disclosures needed in each case.

Items not required by the Examiner for this question: general discussion of the requirements of FRS 8 without reference to the scenario.

The examiner's answer

(a)   (i)   There are extensive Companies Act and Stock Exchange requirements regarding the disclosure of transactions with related parties. However, these provisions, such as the disclosure of transactions with directors and the disclosure of group companies are designed to highlight the stewardship nature of the director's work and not necessarily the users' perspective. As a result the need for greater disclosure was recognised by the ASB.

There are many transactions carried out by companies that are not on commercial terms and DTI reports on failed companies have highlighted the need to disclose such transactions. One of the first major cases in the UK involving related party transactions investigated by the DTI was that of

Pergamon Press Ltd in 1969 where the chairman was Robert Maxwell. Further, the publishing of an FRS on related party transactions places a greater onus on auditors to identify related party transactions and to prevent the deliberate concealment of such transactions by the directors. (The Auditing Practices Board has also responded by providing guidance to auditors in SAS 460 'Related Parties'). The ASB felt that a much wider perspective was required as regards related party transactions and FRS 8 concentrates on the relevance of information to users of financial statements.

The amount of the disclosure required extends existing requirements. The definition of a related party is different in FRS 8 to that in the Stock Exchange's listing rules. The specific disclosures relevant to related parties required by the Stock Exchange relate only to the directors and shareholders of the company.

FRS 8's definition is much more comprehensive dealing with the wider issues of control, common control, influence and common influence. Further, FRS 8 states that all material related party transactions ought to be disclosed and this brings the standard broadly in line with International Accounting Standard 24. The ASB felt that it was important to provide an appropriate standard which would ensure consistency with international practice in this area. In the absence of contrary information, users will assume that all transactions have been undertaken at arms length. Where related party relationships exist this assumption is not justified because free market dealings have not occurred. Such transactions between these parties are susceptible to alteration or may not have occurred if the relationship did not exist or may be on terms different from those with an unrelated party.

Thus the ASB felt that existing legislation and rules did not adequately safeguard users of financial statements in these areas and require disclosure of such related party transactions.

Did you answer the question?

This part of the answer does not simply state the requirements of the Companies Act and FRS 8. Instead, it explains the ways in which FRS 8 differs from and goes further than previous requirements.

(ii)   It is important to gain comment on any accounting issue as it gives the Accounting Standards Board an insight into the views of preparers and users of financial statements as well as occasionally the views of academics. The ASB is keen to hear views on possible alternative solutions to issues and the needs of users of financial statements. Further it is important to obtain information on how the proposed standard conflicts or is consistent with existing practice in a particular area.

Additionally, comments on the consistency of the proposed treatment with current requirements and practices that are applied around the world to these accounting issues and the reasons for these requirements and practices, are most helpful to the ASB. Also the consistency of the proposed treatment with existing UK pronouncements, statute and the Statement of Principles will have been considered by the ASB but occasionally anomalies will arise and constructive comment in this area will be of use.

(b)   For the financial year ending 31 December 1996, the following related party disclosures would be made. Bay plc is an investor owning more than 20% of Ching Ltd and therefore is a related party of this company. Thus details of the transaction will have to be included in both sets of financial statements. Disclosures will include any elements of the transactions necessary for an understanding of the financial statements. As the factory outlet site was sold to a major investor, it is important that the financial statements note that the price was determined by an independent surveyor.

Maxpool plc and Bay plc both have an investment in Ching Ltd but this fact does not by itself make these companies related parties. There would appear to be no related party relationship between them and therefore there will be no disclosure in Maxpool plc's financial statements. Maxpool Group plc may be a related party of Bay plc only if they fall within the definition of FRS 8 paragraph 2.5(a) which states that such a relationship exists where there is the necessary control or influence by one party. This influence may be for example where Bay plc persuaded Maxpool plc to sell the factory at below market value.

The question of one party having subordinated its interests is unlikely as the value of the factory outlet site was determined independently and therefore in this situation no disclosure would be made in the group financial statements under FRS 8. However, as Maxpool plc is a listed company, the transaction may require disclosure under the Stock Exchange rules. The disclosure will depend upon the size of the transaction in relation to specified criteria laid down by the Stock Exchange. For listed companies and their subsidiaries transactions with related parties include shareholders holding 10% or more of the voting rights.

During the financial year to 31 December 1997, there were significant changes in the shareholdings within the group. As a result the following related party relationships exist under FRS 8:

(i)   Maxpool plc is presumed to be a related party of Bay plc as Maxpool plc has a holding of more than 20% (FRS 8 paragraph 2.5c).

(ii)   Maxpool plc is a related party of Ching Ltd but any transactions between the two companies are exempted from disclosure under FRS 8 as Maxpool plc holds a 90% stake in Ching Ltd (FRS 8 paragraph 3c).

(iii)   Bay plc is not necessarily a related party of Ching Ltd as there is no presumption that 10% shareholders have the requisite level of influence. Additionally although Maxpool plc controls Ching Ltd and has influence over Bay plc, FRS 8 indicates that the relationship between Bay and Ching would not normally justify being treated as related parties of each other. However, one would have to see if one party has subordinated its interests to the other before being definite about this relationship. In this instance, as regards the disclosure of the purchase of the vehicles by Bay plc, it appears that under FRS 8 that Bay and Ching are not related parties and therefore no disclosure would be required in the financial statements of either company.

Although Bay plc is not a related party of Ching Ltd it is an associate of Maxpool plc and by definition is a related party of Maxpool plc. Thus, Maxpool plc will have to disclose details of the transaction between a group member and Bay plc in the group financial statements. Financial statements should disclosure material transactions undertaken by the reporting entity (Maxpool group) with a related party (FRS 8 paragraph 6).

As Bay plc is a listed company, the Stock Exchange rules include as related parties shareholders holding 10% or more of the voting rights. Thus the transaction between Bay and Ching may need disclosure under the listing rules.

Did you answer the question?

Notice the way in which this answer does not simply state what disclosures would be required, but explains why.

DECEMBER 1997 QUESTIONS

Section A – This ONE question is compulsory and MUST be attempted

51   (Question 1 of examination)

The following draft financial statements relate to the Baron Group plc.

Draft Group Profit and Loss Account for the Year Ended
30 November 1997

	£m	£m
Turnover		
Continuing operations	4,458	
Discontinued operations	1,263	
		5,721
Cost of sales		(4,560)
Gross profit		1,161
Distribution costs	309	
Administration expenses	285	
		(594)
		567
Income from interests in joint venture		75
Defence costs of take-over bid		(20)
Operating profit		
Continuing operations	438	
Discontinued operations	184	
		622
Loss on disposal of tangible fixed assets	(7)	
Loss on disposal of discontinued operations (note a)	(25)	(32)
Interest receivable	27	
Interest payable	(19)	8
Profit on ordinary activities before taxation		598
Tax on profit on ordinary activities (note c)		(191)
Profit on ordinary activities after taxation		407
Minority interests — equity		(75)
Profit attributable to members of the parent company		332
Dividends — ordinary dividend		(130)
Retained profit for the year		202

Group Statement of Total Recognised Gains and Losses for the
Year Ended 30 November 1997

	£m
Profit attributable to members of the parent company	332
Deficit on revaluation of land and buildings	(30)
Deficit on revaluation of land and buildings in joint venture	(15)
Gain on revaluation of loan	28
Total recognised gains and losses relating to the year	315

Draft Group Balance Sheet as at 30 November 1997

	1997 £m	1996 £m
Fixed assets		
Intangible assets	60	144
Tangible fixed assets (note d)	1,415	1,800
Investments (notes b and e)	600	-
	2,075	1,944
Current assets		
Stocks	720	680
Short term investments (note e)	152	44
Debtors (note f)	680	540
Cash at bank and in hand	24	133
	1,576	1,397
Creditors:		
Amounts falling due within one year (note g)	(1,601)	(1,223)
Net current assets	(25)	174
Total assets less current liabilities	2,050	2,118
Creditors: amounts falling due after more than one year	(186)	(214)
Provision for liabilities and charges - bid defence costs	(30)	(15)
Minority interests - equity	(330)	(570)
	1,504	1,319
Capital and reserves		
Called up share capital	440	440
Share premium account	101	101
Revaluation reserve	33	50
Profit and loss account	930	728
Total shareholders' funds - equity	1,504	1,319

The following information is relevant to the Baron Group plc.

(a)   The group disposed of a major subsidiary Piece plc on 1 September 1997. Baron held an 80% interest in the subsidiary at the date of disposal. Piece plc's results are classified as discontinued in the profit and loss account.

The group required the subsidiary Piece plc to prepare an interim balance sheet at the date of the disposal and this is as follows:

Tangible fixed assets (depreciation 30)	310
Current assets	
Stocks	60
Debtors	50
Cash at bank and in hand	130
	240
Creditors: amounts falling due within one year (including corporation tax - £25m)	(130)
	110
	420

Called up share capital	100
Profit and loss account	320
	420

The consolidated carrying values of all the assets and liabilities at that date are as above. The depreciation charge in the profit and loss account for the period was £9 million. The carrying amount relating to goodwill in the group accounts arising on the acquisition of Piece plc was £64 million at 1 December 1996. The loss on sale of discontinued operations in the group accounts comprises:

Sale proceeds	375
Net assets sold (80% × £420m)	(336)
Goodwill	(64)
	(25)

The consideration for the sale of Piece plc was 200 million ordinary shares of £1 in Meal plc, the acquiring company, at a value of £300 million and £75 million in cash. The group's policy is to amortise goodwill arising on acquisition but not in the year of sale of a subsidiary. The amortisation for the year was £20 million on other intangible assets.

(b)   During the year, Baron plc had transferred several of its tangible assets to a newly created company, Kevla Ltd which is owned jointly by three parties. The total investment at the date of transfer in the joint venture by Baron plc was £225 million at carrying value comprising £200 million in tangible fixed assets and £25 million in cash. In the draft accounts the group has used equity accounting for the joint venture in Kevla Ltd. No dividends have been received from Kevla Ltd but the land and buildings transferred have been revalued at the year end.

(c)   The taxation charge in the profit and loss account is made up of the following items:

	£m
Corporation tax	171
Tax attributable to joint venture	20 → Reduce income from J.V.
	191

(d)   The movement on tangible fixed assets of the Baron Group plc during the year was as follows:

	£m
Cost or valuation 1 December 1996	2,100
Additions	380
Revaluation	(30) → LOSS, STRGL
Disposals and transfers	(680)
At 30 November 1997	1,770
Depreciation	
1 December 1996	300
Provided during year	150
Disposals and transfers	(95)
At 30 November 1997	355
Carrying value at 30 November 1997	1,415
Carrying value at 1 December 1996	1,800

(e)   The investments included under fixed assets comprised the joint venture in Kevla Ltd (£265 million), the shares in Meal plc (£300 million), and investments in corporate bonds (£35 million). The bonds had been purchased in November 1997 and were deemed to be highly liquid, although Baron plc intended to hold them for the longer term as their maturity date is 1 January 1999.

The short term investments comprised the following items:

	1997	1996
		£'m
Government securities (Repayable 1 April 1998)	51	23
Cash on seven day deposit	101	21
	152	44

→ manag of liquid
as not within 24 hrs

(f)   A prepayment of £20 million has been included in debtors against an exceptional pension liability which will fall due in the following financial year. Interest receivable included in debtors was £5 million at 30 November 1997 (£4 million at 30 November 1996).

(g)   Creditors: amounts falling due within one year comprise the following items:

	1997 £m	1996 £m
Trade creditors	1,300	973
Corporation tax	181	150
Dividends	80	70
Accrued interest	40	30
	1,601	1,223

Required:

(a)   Prepare a group cash flow statement using the 'indirect method' for the Baron Group plc for the year ended 30 November 1997 in accordance with the requirements of FRS 1 (Revised 1996) 'Cash Flow Statements' and FRS 9 'Associates and Joint Ventures'. Your answer should include the following:

(i)   Reconciliation of operating profit to operating cash flows.
(ii)   An analysis of cash flows for any headings netted in the cash flow statement.

(Candidates should distinguish net cash flows from continuing and discontinued operations.)   **(26 marks)**

The notes regarding the sale of the subsidiary and a reconciliation of net cash flow to movement in net debt are not required.

(b)   Explain why the Accounting Standards Board feel that cash flow statements should focus on cash rather than a broader measure such as 'net debt'.   **(4 marks)**
    (Total: 30 marks)

Section B — TWO questions ONLY to be attempted

52   (Question 2 of examination)

SSAP 20 'Foreign Currency Translation' states that the method used to translate financial statements for consolidation purposes should reflect the financial and other operational relationships which exist between an investing company and its foreign enterprises. A key element in determining this relationship is the dependency of the trade of the foreign enterprise on the economic environment of the investing company's currency rather than that of its own reporting currency. Thus it is important to determine the dominant or functional currency in order to determine whether the temporal method should be utilised.

However, where the foreign enterprise operates in a country with a high rate of inflation, the translation process may not be sufficient to present fairly the financial position of the foreign enterprise. Some adjustment for inflation should be undertaken to the local currency financial statements before translation. UITF 9 'Accounting for operations in hyper-inflationary economies' deals with this issue.

Required:

(a)   Explain the factors which should be taken into account in determining the dominant or functional currency and how these factors influence the choice of method to be used to translate the financial statements of a foreign enterprise.

(10 marks)

(b)   Discuss the reasons why adjustments for hyper-inflation in the financial statements of foreign enterprises are felt necessary before their translation.

(5 marks)

(c)   On 30 November 1993, Gold plc, a UK company, set up a subsidiary in an overseas country where the local currency is effados. The principal assets of this subsidiary were a chain of hotels. The value of the hotels on this date was 20 million effados. The rate of inflation for the period 30 November 1993 to 30 November 1997 has been significantly high. The following information is relevant to the economy of the overseas country:

	Effados in exchange for £UK	Effados in exchange for $US	Consumer Price Index in overseas country	Exchange Rate UK£ to US$
30 November 1993	1.34	0.93	100	£0.69 to $1
30 November 1997	17.87	11.91	3,254	£0.66 to $1

There is no depreciation charged in the financial statements as the hotels are maintained to a high standard.

Required:

(i)   Calculate the value at which the hotels would be included in the group financial statements of Gold plc on the following dates and using the methods outlined below.

   (1)   At 30 November 1993 and 30 November 1997 using the closing rate/net investment method.
   (2)   At 30 November 1997 after adjusting for current price levels.
   (3)   At 30 November 1997 after remeasuring using the dollar as the stable currency.   **(5 marks)**

   (Methods (2) and (3) are those outlined in UITF 9 'Accounting for operations in hyper-inflationary economies').

(ii)   Discuss the results of the valuations of the hotels commenting on the validity of the different bases outlined above.

(5 marks)

(Total: 25 marks)

---

53   (Question 3 of examination)

A merger is 'a business combination that results in the creation of a new reporting entity formed from the combining parties, in which the combining entities come together in a partnership for the mutual sharing of the risks and benefits of the combined entity, and in which no party to the combination in substance obtains control over any other, or is otherwise seen to be dominant...' FRS 6 'Acquisitions and Mergers'. The continuity of ownership, control and the sharing of risks and benefits in the combined entity are seen as crucial to a combination being accounted for as a merger. There are certain criteria under FRS 6 which can be verified and substantiated in order to determine whether there is continuity of ownership. Similarly there are certain criteria in FRS 6 which could be said to be circumstantial or implied evidence of a merger and which cannot be exactly determined. This type of evidence is somewhat subjective. Finally FRS 6 has invoked certain criteria which attempt to prevent a company creating the superficial or cosmetic appearance of the occurrence of a merger.

Required:

(a)   Analyse and describe the criteria that a business combination must meet under FRS 6 for it to be accounted for as a merger under the following classes:

   (i)   verifiable and substantive signs of a merger
   (ii)   implied or circumstantial evidence of a merger
   (iii)   terms which prevent superficial mergers (anti avoidance criteria).   **(9 marks)**

(b)   The following abridged financial statements relate to Merge plc and Acquire plc for the year ended 30 November 1997.

Profit and Loss Account Year Ended 30 November 1997

	Merge plc £000	Acquire plc £000
Turnover	21,285	18,000
Cost of sales	(16,950)	(14,450)
Gross profit	4,335	3,550
Distribution and administrative expenses	(3,310)	(2,730)
Operating profit	1,025	820
Income from investments	200	100
Profit before taxation	1,225	920
Taxation	(365)	(274)
Dividends	(208)	(148)
Retained profit for year	652	498

Balance Sheet at 30 November 1997

	Merge plc	Acquire plc
Fixed assets	4,099	3,590
(including cost of investment in Acquire plc)		
Current assets	5,530	4,350
Creditors: Amounts falling due within one year	(2,502)	(2,530)
Net current assets	3,028	1,820
Total assets less current liabilities	7,127	5,410
Capital and reserves		
Called up share capital -		
ordinary shares of £1	2,500	1,250
Share premium account	400	250
Revaluation reserve	75	185
Other reserves	100	-
Profit and loss account	4,052	3,725
	7,127	5,410

(i)   During the year the entire share capital of Acquire plc was acquired following a recommended offer by merchant bankers on 30 April 1997. Ordinary shares were issued to those shareholders of Acquire plc who accepted the offer and at the same time £36,000 was paid in cash to shareholders who took the cash alternative. The offer was made on the basis of six shares in Merge plc for every five shares in Acquire plc. A fully underwritten cash alternative of £2.25 per share was offered to the shareholders of Acquire plc. The offer became unconditional on 31 May 1997 when the market value of shares in Merge plc was £2.50 per share. On 31 August 1997 Merge plc compulsorily acquired 8,000 shares of Acquire plc for cash from shareholders who had not accepted the initial offer under the Companies Act 1985. The above transactions had been incorporated in the financial records of Merge plc at their nominal value.

(ii)   Merge plc incurred £156,000 of expenses in connection with the acquisition of Acquire plc. This figure included issue costs of shares of £58,000 and has been included in administrative expenses.

(iii) Acquire plc paid dividends of £48,000 on 31 March 1997 and has proposed a final dividend of £100,000. Merge plc's dividends are all proposed. The proposed dividend of Acquire plc has been taken into account in Merge plc's financial statements.

(iv)   The acquisition fulfils all of the criteria in the Companies Acts and FRS 6 for merger accounting except for the criteria relating to the purchase consideration which has not been tested.

(v)   There is no group election for tax purposes in force.

Required:

Prepare the group profit and loss account for the year ended 30 November 1997 and the balance sheet as at 30 November 1997 for the Merge Group plc.

(16 marks)

(Total: 25 marks)

---

54   (Question 4 of examination)

The Accounting Standards Board (ASB) currently faces a dilemma. IAS 12 (revised), 'Income Taxes' published by the International Accounting Standards Committee (IASC) recommends measures which significantly differ from current UK practice set out in SSAP 15 'Accounting for Deferred Tax'. IAS 12 requires an enterprise to provide for deferred tax in full for all deferred tax liabilities with only limited exceptions whereas SSAP 15 utilises the partial provision approach. The dilemma facing the ASB is whether to adopt the principles of IAS 12 (revised) and face criticism from many UK companies who agree with the partial provision approach. FRED 19 'Deferred Tax' indicates that the ASB wish to eliminate the partial provision method.

The different approaches are particularly significant when acquiring subsidiaries because of the fair value adjustments and also when dealing with revaluations of fixed assets as the IAS requires companies to provide for deferred tax on these amounts.

Required:

(a)   Explain the main reasons why SSAP 15 has been criticised.

(8 marks)

(b)   Discuss the arguments in favour of and against providing for deferred tax on:
         (i)   fair value adjustments on the acquisition of a subsidiary
         (ii)   revaluations of fixed assets. *⌐ Notional no tax implication ∴ No DT.*

(7 marks)

(c)   XL plc has the following net assets at 30 November 1997. *If more than Cost then could make a gain and hence capital gains tax.*

	£'000	Tax value (WDV) £'000
Fixed assets		
Buildings	33,500	7,500
Plant and equipment	52,000	13,000
Investments	66,000	66,000
	151,500	86,500
Current assets	15,000	15,000
Creditors: Amounts falling due within one year		
Creditors	13,500	(13,500)
Liability for health care benefits	300	-
	(13,800)	
Net current assets	1,200	1,500
Provision for deferred tax	(9,010)	(9,010)
	143,690	78,990

XL plc has acquired 100% of the shares of BZ Ltd on 30 November 1997. The following statement of net assets relates to BZ Ltd on 30 November 1997.

	Fair value £'000	Carrying value £'000	Tax value £'000
Buildings	500	300	100
Plant and equipment	40	30	15
Stock	124	114	114
Debtors	110	110	110
Retirement benefit liability	(60)	(60)	-
Creditors	(105)	(105)	(105)
	609	389	234

There is currently no deferred tax provision in the accounts of BZ Ltd. In order to achieve a measure of consistency XL plc decided that it would revalue its land and buildings to £50 million and the plant and equipment to £60 million. The company did not feel it necessary to revalue the investments. The liabilities for retirement benefits and healthcare costs are anticipated to remain at their current amounts for the foreseeable future.

The land and buildings of XL plc had originally cost £45 million and the plant and equipment £70 million. The company has no intention of selling any of its fixed assets other than the land and buildings which it may sell and lease back. XL plc currently utilises the full provision method to account for deferred taxation. The projected depreciation charges and tax allowances of XL plc and BZ Ltd are as follows for the years ending 30 November:

	1998 £'000	1999 £'000	2000 £'000
Depreciation (Buildings, plant and equipment)			
XL plc	7,010	8,400	7,560
BZ Ltd	30	32	34
Tax allowances			
XL plc	8,000	4,500	3,000
BZ Ltd	40	36	30

The corporation tax rate had changed from 35% to 30% in the current year. Ignore any indexation allowance or rollover relief and assume that XL plc and BZ Ltd are in the same tax jurisdiction.

Required:

Calculate the deferred tax expense for XL plc which would appear in the group financial statements at 30 November 1997 using:

(i)   the full provision method incorporating the effects of the revaluation of assets in XL plc and the acquisition of BZ Ltd. *— fair Value*

(ii)   the partial provision method. *— Book Value*

(10 marks)
(Total: 25 marks)

(Candidates should not answer in accordance with IAS 12 (Revised) 'Income Taxes').

Section C — ONE question ONLY to be attempted

55   (Question 5 of examination)

Political commentators have pointed out in recent years instances of where the auditor may appear not to be independent. An example of this lack of independence could be deemed to be the situation where the accounting firm provides audit services and other services such as consultancy advice to a client. In these circumstances objectivity may be threatened by undue dependence on a client. However an issue which may well gain in prominence is that of the hiring by audit clients of personnel who were formerly employed by their independent auditors.

Where an audit partner or other senior audit staff are employed by a client on leaving the audit firm, there is an element of risk that the objectivity of future audits may be impaired. There may be a public perception that the auditor of a company cannot be independent, where former employees of the audit firm are employed in senior positions.

Required:

(a)   Discuss the advantages to a client of their auditor moving to undertake employment as a senior executive in their company.   **(6 marks)**

(b)   Discuss the ethical problems associated with a former audit partner becoming the financial director of the audit firms principal client.   **(6 marks)**

(c)   Describe the current ethical guidance designed to deal with the problems associated with the auditor accepting a senior position with the firm's principal client, discussing any additional safeguards which could be introduced.   **(8 marks)**
    (Total: 20 marks)

---

56   (Question 6 of examination)

It is perhaps one of the ironies of English law that the possibility of creating a partnership under which some of the partners enjoyed limited liability was introduced in the same year (1907) that statutory provision was made for the incorporation of a business in a simple and inexpensive form. This contribution to commercial law has until recently proved to be substantially irrelevant, with very few businesses taking advantage of the Limited Partnerships Act (1907).

However, Limited Liability Partnerships (LLP) are now being considered by firms of auditors. The government in the United Kingdom is considering suggestions to change the rules relating to Limited Liability Partnerships in order to facilitate the change to this business form for audit firms. If this change of legislation is not forthcoming, audit firms have stated that they may consider registering in another jurisdiction which will enact the legislation. This latter possibility has led some commentators to suggest that audit firms are holding the UK government to ransom.

Required:

(a)   Discuss how the partnership status of a firm of auditors can maintain audit service quality.   **(5 marks)**

(b)   Discuss the reasons why audit firms may wish to change their legal form to Limited Liability Partnerships and the changes in the current law relating to Limited Liability Partnerships which are sought by them.
    (7 marks)

(c)   Discuss the current reaction in the UK by the public and the government to the audit firms moves to limit their liability.   **(8 marks)**
    (Total: 20 marks)

ANSWERS TO DECEMBER 1997 EXAMINATION

51   (Answer 1 of examination)

Examiner's comments and marking guide

Question 1: This question required candidates to prepare a group cash flow statement for a year in which there was a disposal of a subsidiary and an investment in a joint venture. There was a considerable amount of information in the question for candidates to assimilate and it was quite pleasing to see the majority of candidates performed well on this question. The average mark for this question was quite high. Perhaps the least well answered part of the question was the purchase of the joint venture and treatment of continuing and discontinued operations (in the UK). This was the first time that FRS 1 (revised) had been examined in the UK and candidates seemed to be familiar with its layout and principles.

		Marks
(a)	Cash flow from operating activities	10
	Returns on investments and servicing of finance	3
	Taxation	2
	Capital expenditure	3
	Acquisitions and disposals	3
	Equity dividends	2
	Management of liquid resources	3
	Exceptional cash outflows	2
	Presentation	5
	Available	33
	Maximum	26
(b)	1 mark per point	4
	Available	37
	Maximum	30

Step by step answer plan

Step 1 Read the question again and make sure that you focus on precisely what is required. As is usual with questions on group cash flow statements, there is a lot of information to deal with. Reading this information should alert you to the main complications; a disposal of a subsidiary and the acquisition of a joint venture. Although most of the available marks are for the preparation of the cash flow statement, you should ensure that you leave enough time to answer part (b) and gain valuable (and easy) marks.

Step 2 Calculate operating profit and the movement in debtors. You should then be able to complete the reconciliation of operating profit to operating cash flows. Remember that you must analyse the components of the reconciliation between continuing and discontinued operations.

Step 3 Prepare workings for dividends received from minority interest; taxation paid; cash received from sale of tangible fixed assets and equity dividends paid. Use either schedules or T accounts.

Step 4 Complete Note 2 (gross cash flows) for returns on investments, capital expenditure, acquisitions and disposals and management of liquid resources.

Step 5 Draw up the cash flow statement itself and add it up.

Step 6 Answer part (b). This should take approximately seven minutes.

Items not required by the Examiner for this question:

- reconciliation of net cash flow to movement in net debt
- note analysing sale of subisidiary

The examiner's answer

(a)

Baron Group plc Cash Flow Statement for the year ended 30 November 1997

	£m
Cash flow from operating activities (note 1)	875
Returns on investments and servicing of finance (note 2)	(214)
Taxation (working 5)	(115)
Capital expenditure (note 2)	(312)
Acquisitions and disposals (note 2)	(80)
Equity dividends paid (working 2)	(120)
Cash inflow before use of liquid resources and financing	34
Management of liquid resources (note 2)	(143)
Decrease in cash in the period	(109)

Note 1: Reconciliation of Operating Profit to Operating Cash flows

	Continuing £m	Discontinued £m	Total £m
Operating profit (working 1)	383	184	567
Depreciation charges	141	9	150
Goodwill	20		20
Increase in stocks	(40)	(60)	(100)
Increase in debtors (working 4)	(119)	(50)	(169)
Increase in creditors	327	105	432
Net cash inflow from continuing operating activities	712		
Net cash inflow in respect of discontinued activities		188	
Net cash inflow from operating activities			900
Bid defence cash outflow	(5)		(5)
Pension prepayment	(20)		(20)
	687	188	875

Note 2: Analysis of cash flows for headings netted in the cash flow statement

	£m	£m
Returns on investments and servicing of finance		
Interest received (4 + 27 – 5)	26	
Interest paid (30 + 19 – 40)	(9)	
Minority interest – equity dividend (working 2)	(231)	
Net cash outflow for returns on investments and servicing of finance		(214)
Capital expenditure		
Purchase of tangible fixed assets	(380)	
Sale of tangible fixed assets (working 3)	68	
Net cash outflow for capital expenditure		(312)

Acquisitions and disposals		
Purchase of interest in joint venture	(25)	
Cash disposed of with subsidiary	(130)	
Disposal proceeds of subsidiary	75	
Net cash outflow for acquisitions and disposals		(80)
Management of liquid resources		
Purchase of corporate bonds	(35)	
Purchase of government securities	(28)	
Cash deposited on seven day deposit	(80)	
		(143)

WORKINGS

Working 1

Operating profit — continuing activities	438
less income from joint venture*	(75)
add bid defence costs	20
Per cash flow statement	383

---

*Tutorial note

FRS 9 requires that the share of a joint venture's operating profit should not be included in the group operating profit.

Working 2

Minority interest - opening balance	570	
- Sale of Piece plc (20% of 420)	(84)	
Profit for year	75	
- Closing balance	(330)	
Minority interest - equity dividend		231
Dividends paid to equity (130 + 70 – 80)		120

Working 3

Cost/valuation - disposals	680	
Depreciation	(95)	
Carrying value		585
Less: Subsidiary disposed of		(310)
		275
Less: Transfer to joint venture		(200)
Carrying value disposed of		75
Loss on disposal		(7)
Cash proceeds		68

Working 4

Debtors

Debtors - 30.11.97	680
Less: Prepayment - pension	(20)
Less: Interest receivable	(5)
	655

Debtors - 30.11.96	540
Less: Interest receivable	(4)
	536
Increase in debtors	119

Working 5

Taxation on profit	191
Tax on subsidiary disposed of	(25)
Opening balance on taxation account	150
Closing balance on taxation account	(181)
Taxation on joint venture	(20)
	115

Working 6

Intangible assets - opening balance	144
Written off to profit/loss account on disposal	(64)
Amortisation for year	(20)
Closing balance 30.11.97	60

(b) FRS 1 (Revised 1996) focuses on cash rather than an alternative measure such as net debt for the following reasons.

(i) The cash flow statement highlights the significant components of cash which is useful for informational purposes.

(ii) Certain cash flow movements would not be captured by a broader measure. If two transactions fell within that broader measure then they would not be reported individually.

(iii) Comparison of the cash flow performances of different entities is facilitated.

(iv) Internationally the focus of such statements is cash and therefore international comparability is made easier.

The standard does in fact recognise that movements in net debt can give useful information and requires an analysis of the movement in net debt or net funds in the period. This is particularly important in the UK where management, shareholders and investment analysts pay close attention to measures of indebtedness, such as the gearing ratio.

Did you answer the question?

Notice how this answer makes four concise points, each worth one mark. Each point explains a different reason for focusing on cash.

Tutorial note

The examiner's answer to part (a) of this question has been amended to reflect the changes to cash flow statements required by FRS 9.

---

52   (Answer 2 of examination)

Examiner's comments and marking guide

Question 2: Many holding companies have to deal with subsidiaries who are trading in the emerging economies such as Russia, China, Eastern Europe etc. One of the problems that these companies have to deal with in some of these economies is hyper inflation, thus this question took this scenario and developed it. The first factor to be determined is the relationship with the subsidiary and this will determine the accounting treatment (part (a)). Secondly, the reasons why adjustments need to be made for hyper inflation were examined in the question (part (b)) and finally the application of such adjustments was required in part (c). Candidates answered this question quite well. The weakest parts were the remeasurement of an asset using the dollar as a stable currency and the discussion of the results of calculations made.

This type of question is topical nationally and internationally and examined the basic requirements of SSAP 20, the reasons why accounts need to be changed for inflation, simple calculations utilising a UITF pronouncement and a discussion of a simple set of statistics. The aim of the question was to put inflation in the context of practical issues facing multinational companies and candidates responded well to the question.

		Marks
(a)	Discussion of functional currency re closing rate method	5
	Discussion re temporal method	5
	General characteristics	3
	Available	13
	Maximum	10
(b)	Profits	2
	Exchange loss	1
	Performance	1
	Assessment re local currency and impact of inflation	1
	Devaluation	1
	Emerging economies	1
	Available	7
	Maximum	5
(c)	No inflation adj	1
	Price adj	2
	Stable currency	2
	Explanation	7
	Available	12
	Maximum	10
	Available	32
	Maximum	25

Step by step answer plan

Step 1 Read the question again and make sure that you focus on precisely what is required. The opening paragraph is simply there to set the scene. There is very little information to deal with; most of the question is discursive. Therefore it is particularly important to read the actual requirements carefully.

Step 2 Answer part (a), which should take approximately 18 minutes. Note that the key requirement word is *explain*. Review your answer very quickly to ensure that you have answered the question as set.

Step 3 Approach part (b) by explaining the effect of high inflation and the advantages of adjusting the financial statements. This part of the question should take approximately 9 minutes.

Step 4 Answer part (c)(i) by doing each of the three calculations in turn.

Step 5 Answer part (c)(ii) by commenting on the three calculations. This part of the question should take approximately 9 minutes.

Items not required by the Examiner for this question: general discussion of the requirements of SSAP 20 and UITF Abstract 9 without reference to the specific requirements of the question.

The examiner's answer

(a)   For most investments in foreign enterprises from the UK, the foreign companies will normally be separate or quasi independent entities. The normal operations will be based in local currency and are likely to be at least partly financed locally and are unlikely to be totally dependent upon the reporting currency of the holding company. The foreign enterprise will probably be managed in such a way as to maximise the local currency profits attributable to the holding company.

If as described above, the foreign entity's operations are relatively self contained and integrated within a foreign country, its functional or dominant currency would ordinarily be its local one and therefore the closing rate method would be used to preserve the financial statement ratios.

The financial statements expressed in local currency will be the best indicator of the performance of the foreign enterprise. Thus in order to preserve the inter relationships of the items in the financial statements denominated in local currency, a single rate of exchange ought to be used when translating them into the holding company's currency. If however the trade of the foreign enterprise is more dependent on the economic environment of the investing company's currency and is merely an extension of the holding company's operations, then its functional or dominant currency would be that of the holding company. In this case the temporal method should be used as this method reflects the transaction as if they had been carried out by the investing company itself.

No single factor would indicate when the temporal method should be used but the following factors should be taken into account:

(i)   The extent to which the cash flows of the enterprise have an impact on those of the investing company.

(ii)   The extent to which the functioning of the enterprise is dependent directly upon the investing company.

(iii)   The currency in which the majority of the trading transactions are denominated.

(iv)   The major currency to which the operation is exposed in its financing structure.

It is possible to summarise the factors which might determine the functional currency into:

(i)   Cash flow indicators.
(ii)   Sales price and market indicators - is the price and market determined locally?
(iii)   Expense indicators - local costs or imported labour/parts.
(iv)   Financing indicators - locally or from parent company.
(v)   Intercompany transactions - low volume or high volume of transactions.

The functional currency determines the translation method used. As the two main methods are so diverse in their application and effect on the financial statements, this decision is the key feature as the disposition of exchange gains and losses is determined by it.

> ### Did you answer the question?
>
> Care must be taken here as this is *not* the usual question about the choice of translation method. You are required to explain the factors determining the *functional currency* as well as how *these factors* influence the choice of method. An answer which simply explained how to choose a translation method would not attract full marks. Notice the way in which the penultimate paragraph specifically addresses the requirement.

(b)   Failure to adjust for hyper-inflation before translating the financial statements of a foreign enterprise can cause significant distortion in the group accounts. Profits may be inflated either from high interest income on deposits in a rapidly depreciating currency or from trading at unrealistic levels of profitability. Additionally a significant exchange loss may be taken to reserves.

More generally, adjusting for hyper-inflation enables management to gauge better the performance of the subsidiary's financial assets within the environment in which the subsidiaries assets are domiciled. Financial statements can be assessed in terms of local currency as well as the impact of inflation on these results.

Additionally if devaluation of a currency occurs, the full effects of the devaluation and the hyper-inflation can be assessed.

Foreign currency translation methods under SSAP 20 ignore the effects of hyper-inflation in the consolidation process. With many of the emerging economies suffering from high inflation, it is important that local currency financial statements are adjusted to reflect current price levels.

Did you answer the question?

The requirement is to discuss *the reasons*, therefore the answer briefly covers several points, rather than, for example, describing the effects of inflation in detail.

(c)   (i)   1

	Value E million	Exchange rate	£ million
30 November 1993	20	1.34	14.93
30 November 1997	20	17.87	1.12

Therefore on 30 November 1993, the value of the hotels would be £14.93 million but would drop to £1.12 million on 30 November 1997.

2

	Value E million	Index	Exchange rate £	£ million
30 November 1997	20	$\times \dfrac{3,254}{100}$	17.87	= 36.42

Therefore the value of the hotels would be £36.42 million after adjusting for current price levels.

3

	Value E million	Dollar rate	Value $ million	Pound rate per $	Value £ million
30 November 1997	20	0.93	21.51	0.66	14.2

The asset is remeasured using the historical rate of exchange for US dollars at 30 November 1993. The original cost of the asset is therefore $21.51 million. This is then translated into sterling at the US dollar exchange rate at 30 November 1997 ie, £14.2 million.

(ii)   Part (1) of the answer illustrates the disappearing assets' problem associated with foreign enterprises in hyper-inflationary economies. The value of the hotels has dropped due to exchange rate movements and not necessarily due to local factors. In the country concerned the value may have increased. This point is illustrated in answer (2) where on adjustment for the consumer price index, it appears that the asset may be worth substantially more than on acquisition.

Answer (3) utilises a method which uses the movement between the original currency of record and a stable currency as a surrogate for an inflation index. However, if one looks at the underlying principles of methods (2) and (3) it can be argued that the translation of an inflation adjusted foreign currency amount could result in a double charge for inflation as exchange rates also reflect the increase in inflation in a country. Additionally historical amounts translated into a stable currency are seldom perfectly negatively correlated with price level changes whereas balance sheet amounts may be adjusted for inflation effects. Thus all three methods have underlying faults not least of which being that they produce significantly different valuations. UITF 9 does however state that if either of methods (2) and (3) are inappropriate, then alternative methods to eliminate the distortions should be adopted.

Method (3) treats the investment in property as if it were a dollar monetary investment. The effect therefore is that the value of the hotel is based on the movement of the dollar/pound sterling exchange rate which may not be affected by the pound/effados rate and the value of the property.

Did you answer the question?

This answer does not just compare the results of the three calculations, but also discusses the validity of the different approaches to adjusting for the effects of inflation.

---

53   (Answer 3 of examination)

Examiner's comments and marking guide

Question 3: It is a common misconception that UK companies do not use merger accounting. Smith Kline Beecham use this method of accounting in their financial statements, for example. Part (a) of the question in the UK required candidates to analyse the current criteria for merger accounting under FRS 6 into various categories. Candidates found the analysis quite difficult but were not unduly penalised if they wrongly classified items.

Part (b) of the question required the preparation of a group balance sheet and profit and loss account using merger accounting. The basic principles were generally understood by candidates but the treatment of the share premium account of the subsidiary and reserve movements were not well understood by candidates. Overall, however, the question was well answered by candidates.

		Marks
(a)	Verifiable signs	4
	Implied evidence	3
	Anti avoidance	3
		——
	Available	10
		——
	Maximum	9
(b)	Verification of use of merger accounting	5
	Turnover/cost of sales	1
	Distribution and admin expenses	1
	Reorganisation expenses	1
	Income	1
	Tax	1
	Dividends	1
	Fixed assets	1
	Net current assets	1
	Share premium	1
	Revaluation reserve	1
	Other reserves	1
	Profit/loss account	1
		——
	Available	17
		——
	Maximum	16
		——
	Available	27
		——
	Maximum	25

Step by step answer plan

Step 1   Read the question again and make sure that you focus on precisely what is required. The introductory paragraph helps to explain the requirement of part (a), which is discursive. Part (b) requires the preparation of consolidated accounts. It should be clear that you will be required to determine whether the combination meets the CA 85 criteria for merger accounting and to use the appropriate method.

Step 2   Taking each of the three classes of criteria in turn, answer part (a), noting that the key requirement words are *analyse* and *describe*. Ensure that you allocate your time; this part should take no more than 16 minutes.

Step 3   Re-read the scenario in part (b). Then calculate the non-equity proportion of the consideration for the purchase of Acquire. This tells you whether to use acquisition or merger accounting.

Step 4   Do any consolidation workings that are necessary.

Step 5   Prepare the consolidated accounts.

The examiner's answer

(a)   FRS 6 requires that to determine whether a business combination meets the definition of a merger it should be assessed against five criteria. If one analyses these criteria, it can be seen that it is possible to categorise these criteria into the three elements set out in the question.

Verifiable signs of a merger

FRS 6 states that an essential feature of a merger is a genuine combining of interests. No one party should have a dominant role as an acquirer or subservient role of being acquired. Therefore no acquirer should be identifiable. For example, where one party has paid a premium over the market value of the shares acquired, this is evidence of that party having taken the role of an acquirer.

The consideration received by equity shareholders of each party to the combination should comprise primarily equity shares in the combined entity. All but an immaterial proportion of the fair value of the consideration must be in the form of equity shares. FRS 6 utilises company legislation to state that the value of consideration other than equity shares should not exceed 10% of the nominal value of the shares issued. A business combination may not be accounted for as a merger if a material part of the consideration is in the form of shares with substantially reduced rights. This latter offer would be contrary to the mutual sharing of the risks and rewards of the combined entity.

The above criteria are verifiable and show substantive signs of continuity of ownership.

Implied evidence of a merger

An essential feature of a merger is that all parties to the merger are involved in determining the management structure of the combined entity and reach consensus on the appropriate structure and personnel. If one party dominates this process, possibly by the exercise of majority voting rights, then it is not a genuine pooling of interests. Where the senior management structure and personnel are essentially those of one of the combining parties, then the criterion will not have been met unless all parties to the merger have genuinely participated in the decision.

Where one party is substantially larger than the other parties, this will not be consistent with the equal partnership view of a merger. A party would be presumed to dominate if it is more than 50% larger than each of the other parties to the combination (by reference to ownership interests). This presumption may be rebutted if it can be clearly shown that there is no such dominance.

The circumstances surrounding the transaction may provide evidence as to the role of the parties to the combination. Certain characteristics although not conclusive would need to be considered. For example, the plans for the entity's future operations and the proposed corporate image.

Anti-avoidance terms

FRS 6 utilises general anti-avoidance provisions. All arrangements made in conjunction with the combination must be taken into account. Equity shareholders will be considered to have disposed of their shareholding for cash where they have been able to exchange or redeem the shares for cash or other non-equity consideration. For example a vendor placing is treated as giving rise to non-equity consideration. Also if one entity has acquired an interest in exchange for non-equity consideration or equity shares with reduced rights within two years of the combination, then such consideration is deemed to be part of the total consideration for the use of determining the non-equity consideration.

Finally, merger accounting cannot be used where one party has been created as a result of divestment from a larger party as the divested business will not be sufficiently independent until it has established a track record of its own. FRS 6 does not quantify divestment time limits.

Did you answer the question?

This answer does not simply restate the conditions for merger accounting but analyses them into three classes, as required.

(b)

Merge Group plc
Profit and Loss Account for the Year Ended 30 November 1997

	£'000
Turnover	39,285
Cost of sales	(31,400)
	7,885
Distribution and administration expenses	(5,884)
Operating profit	2,001
Reorganisation expenses of merger	(156)
Income from investments	200
Profit before taxation	2,045
Taxation	(639)
	1,406
Dividends	
Pre-merger dividend	(48)
Proposed dividend	(208)
Retained profit for year	1,150

Merge Group plc
Balance Sheet at 30 November 1997

	£'000
Fixed assets	6,164
Current assets	9,780
Creditors: Amounts falling due within one year	(4,932)
Net current assets	4,848
Total assets less current liabilities	11,012
Called up share capital	2,500
Share premium account	342
Revaluation reserve	260
Other reserves	75
Profit and loss account	7,835
	11,012

WORKINGS

Purchase consideration	Nominal value £'000	Fair value £'000
Shares issued	1,471	3,678
Cash - initial offer	36	36
Compulsorily acquired	18	18
(8,000 × 2.25)		
	1,525	3,732

Shares issued

Share capital - Acquire plc	1,250
Less: Shares - cash equivalent taken £54,000 divided by £2.25	(24)
	1,226
× factor 6:5	1,471

The Companies Act 1985 requires that non-equity consideration should not exceed 10% of the nominal amount of shares issued. FRS 6 requires that all but an immaterial portion of the fair value of the consideration should be in the form of equity shares. The above cash consideration is 3.5% of the nominal value of shares issued and 1.4% of the fair value of the consideration. Therefore the criteria are both met for merger accounting.

Distribution and administrative expenses	£'000
Per question (3,310 and 2,730)	6,040
Less: Expenses	(156)
	5,884

Income from investments	
Per question (200 + 100)	300
Less: Inter company dividend	(100)
	200

Taxation	
Per question (365 + 274)	639

Dividends

The pre-merger dividends of the parent and subsidiary are shown in the profit and loss account but after the date of the merger only those of the parent are shown.

Current assets and creditors	
Current assets per question (5,530 + 4,350)	9,880
Less: Inter co div	(100)
	9,780
Creditors per question (2,502 + 2,530)	5,032
Less: Inter co div	(100)
	4,932

Fixed assets	
Balance per question (4,099 + 3,590)	7,689
Less: Cost of investment in Acquire plc	(1,525)
	6,164

Share premium account - Merge plc	
Balance per question	400
Less: Issue costs	(58)
	342

Profit and loss account	
Balance per question (4,052 + 3,725)	7,777
Add: Issue costs to share premium	58
	7,835

Equity elimination

Cost of investment	1,525
Less: Share capital - Acquire plc	(1,250)
Share premium account - Acquire plc	(250)
To other reserves	25

Other reserves

Balance per question	100
less equity elimination	(25)
Other reserves	75

54   (Answer 4 of examination)

Examiner's comments and marking guide

Question 4: The UK faces a problem over accounting for deferred taxation as it is out of line with methods used internationally. The question required a critique of the partial provision method and a discussion of the provision for deferred tax on revaluations of assets and business combinations. The latter items are key areas identified by the UK discussion paper on taxation. Candidates generally answered part (a) of the question quite well on the problems with the partial provision method but did not seem to understand the arguments for and against deferred tax on fair value adjustments and revaluations. The final part of the question in the UK required calculation of the deferred tax expense using the full and partial provision methods. The answers were of mixed quality with some students being able to compute the expense utilising the partial provision and vice versa. This part of the question essentially compared the balance sheet approach to calculating deferred tax with the profit and loss account approach.

		Marks
(a)	2 marks per point	8
(b)	Fair value adjustments	4
	Revaluation	3
	Available/Maximum	7
(c)	Full provision	6
	Partial provision	4
	Available/Maximum	10
	Available/Maximum	25

Step by step answer plan

Step 1   Read the question again and make sure that you focus on precisely what is required. The question is about current developments in accounting for deferred tax and as usual, the requirements are very specific.

Step 2   Answer part (a) by making a number of points.

Step 3   Approach part (b) by taking each situation in turn. Ensure that you argue both for and against providing deferred tax and make as many points as you can.

Step 4   Re-read the scenario for part (c). Then calculate the deferred tax expense under full provision.

Step 5   Start part (c)(ii) by calculating the timing differences for the group at 30.11.97. Then work out the maximum reversal to give the profit and loss amount under partial provision. Adjust this for the revaluation of land and buildings to give the final answer.

Items not required by the Examiner for this question:

* general discussion/explanation of full provision and partial provision without reference to the specific requirements of the question (part (a))

* notes to the financial statements (part (c))

* deferred tax balance under full provision (it has to be calculated to arrive at the expense under partial provision) (part (c))

The examiner's answer

(a) The main reasons for the criticism of SSAP 15 'Accounting for Deferred Tax' are as follows:

(i) The recognition rule of SSAP 15 is different from that of other standards. Deferred tax assets and liabilities are only recognised when they will not be replaced by equivalent assets and liabilities. If this rule were applied to current assets such as stock or debtors then a significant part of such assets may not be recognised in the financial statements as in many companies these values remain static with a hard core of the asset remaining. This problem led to the issue of an amendment to SSAP 15 in 1992 in respect of post retirement benefits.

(ii) SSAP 15 is dependent upon future events and the intentions of management. It is thought this may be contrary to the Statement of Principles which defines assets and liabilities in relation to past events and states that management's intentions alone do not give rise to assets and liabilities.

(iii) There have been variations in practice in the application of SSAP 15. There are variations in practice over fair value adjustments made in acquisition accounting as some companies provide for deferred tax on such adjustments and others do not. Similarly there is no specific guidance given in SSAP 15 as regards the effects of revaluation on the calculation of deferred tax relating to timing differences between the depreciation charged in the financial statements and tax allowances.

(iv) The partial provision method is not internationally acceptable. It is required only in a small number of countries and the global trend is towards full provision particularly where there is a conceptual framework similar to the Statement of Principles.

Did you answer the question?

This answer consists of a number of short paragraphs. Each paragraph explains a reason why SSAP 15 has been criticised. There are only 8 marks/14 minutes available, so this approach will attract more marks than exploring one or two criticisms in depth.

(b) (i) *Fair value adjustments*

The issue is whether fair value adjustments in acquisition accounting give rise to deferred tax if the full provision method is used. At present fair value adjustments are not timing differences in SSAP 15 but permanent differences. It is felt that deferred tax should not be provided on fair value adjustments because these adjustments are made as a consolidation entry only. They are not taxable or tax deductible and do not affect the tax burden of the company.

It is argued that providing for deferred tax on fair value adjustments is not an allocation of an expense but a smoothing device. Finally the difference between the carrying value of the net assets acquired and their fair value is goodwill and therefore no deferred tax is required. The arguments in favour of deferred tax are conceptual by nature. If the net assets of the acquired company are shown in the group accounts at fair value, then this will affect the post acquisition earnings of the group. For example, an increase in the stock value by £10,000 will result in profit being reduced by £10,000 in the post acquisition period. Therefore it seems consistent to exclude the tax on these profits from the post acquisition period also.

Additionally since an acquisition gives rise to no tax effect, the effective tax rate in the profit and loss account should not be distorted as a result of the acquisition. Providing for deferred tax ensures that distortion does not occur.

Some commentators feel that deferred tax should be provided on assets purchased in an acquisition as a 'valuation' adjustment. If the asset had been purchased in an arm's-length transaction for example stocks, then this cost would have been totally tax deductible. As this is not the case then the asset is worth less to the company because it is not tax deductible. Therefore deferred tax should be provided as an adjustment to reflect the reduction in the true value of the asset.

(ii)   *Revaluations of fixed assets*

The revaluation of a fixed asset can be seen as creating a further timing difference because it reflects an adjustment of depreciation which is itself a timing difference. An alternative view is that it is a permanent difference as it has no equivalent within the tax computation. The revaluation is not seen as a reversal of previous depreciation, simply that the remaining life of the asset will be measured at a different amount. The additional depreciation charge has no tax equivalent and it would be incorrect to make any tax adjustments in respect of this amount. If however the revaluation takes the asset value above its original cost, then a chargeable gain may arise and a provision for tax should be considered if disposal is likely.

As with fair value adjustments, it can be argued that deferred tax is a valuation adjustment and whilst a revaluation does not directly give rise to a tax liability, the tax status of the asset is inferior to an equivalent asset at historical cost and therefore provision for deferred tax should be made in order to reflect the true after tax cost of the asset. The revalued asset would not attract the same tax allowances as an asset purchased for the same amount and therefore if deferred tax was not provided it would distort the post revaluation effective tax rate. (This would only be the case if the asset is the type which is deductible for tax purposes. Rollover relief postpones rather than extinguishes any tax liability and therefore should not affect the recognition of deferred tax.)

Did you answer the question?

Notice the way in which this answer examines several arguments for and against providing deferred tax in each situation. This meets the requirement to *discuss*.

(c)   (i)   **Full provision**

	Valuation £'000	Tax value £'000	Temporary difference £'000
XL plc			
Buildings	50,000	7,500	42,500
Plant and equipment	60,000	13,000	47,000
Health care benefits	(300)	-	(300)
	109,700	20,500	89,200
BZ Ltd			
Buildings	500	100	400
Plant and equipment	40	15	25
Stock	124	114	10
Retirement benefit	(60)	-	(60)
	604	229	375
Total	110,304	20,729	89,575
Deferred tax liability	89,935 at 30%		26,980
Deferred tax asset	(360) at 30%		(108)
	89,575 at 30%		26,872

less opening deferred tax liability	(9,010)
Adjustment due to change in tax rate	

$$9,010 \times \frac{100}{35} \times 5\%$$ 1,287

Deferred tax expense for year	19,149

The deferred tax expense relating to the revaluation of assets would not be shown in the group profit and loss account as it relates to items credited to equity.

(ii)   Partial provision

Group Position Based on Carrying Values Before Any Fair Value Adjustments or Revaluation

	£'000
Balance at 30.11.97	
Buildings XL plc	33,500
BZ Ltd	300
Plant and equipment	
XL plc	52,000
BZ Ltd	30
	85,830
Tax values at 30.11.97	
Buildings XL plc	7,500
BZ Ltd	100
Plant and equipment	
XL plc	13,000
BZ Ltd	15
	20,615
Timing differences	65,215

Timing differences	30.11.97 £'000	30.11.98 £'000	30.11.99 £'000	30.11.2000 £'000
Depreciation		(7,040)	(8,432)	(7,594)
Tax allowances		8,040	4,536	3,030
	65,215	1,000	(3,896)	(4,564)
Cumulative	65,215	66,215	62,319	57,755

Maximum reversal 65,215 - 57,755	=		7,460
Provision required 7,460 at 30%	=		2,238

Therefore there will be a release of the existing provision if deferred tax were calculated using the partial provision method. However because the land and buildings had originally cost £45 million and the revaluation takes the value above this amount an additional provision of £50 - 45 million at 30% ie, £1.5 million needs to be provided.

Thus the deferred tax provision will be reduced to:

£'000

2,238 Timing differences
1,500 Tax on revaluation—chargeable gain
——
3,738

The deferred tax released to the profit and loss account will be (9,010 − 3,738) ie, **£5,272,000**

There will be no deferred tax consequences of the retirement benefit liability or healthcare costs under the partial provision method as it is anticipated that there will be no movement in the balance sheet amount.

(Tutorial note: This question and answer were set before the issue of FRED 19 *Deferred Tax.* FRED 19 is based on the proposals in the ASB's Discussion paper 'Accounting for Tax' which was mentioned in the original question.*)*

---

55   (Answer 5 of examination)

Examiner's comments and marking guide

Question 5: This question dealt with the ethical problems and advantages to the client of an auditor moving to a client company. The question was quite well answered although some candidates simply wrote all they knew about independence without relating their answer to the case in point.

		Marks
(a)	Familiarity with clients accounting and business environment	1
	Reduction of 'settling in' time	1
	Wide and varied experience	1
	Up to date	1
	Close professional relationship	1
	Cost saving	1
	Lower risk of poor selection	1
		—
	Available	7
		—
	Maximum	6
		—
(b)	Public perception	1
	Knowledge of audit personnel	1
	Adjust to new positions	1
	Influence	1
	Significant connections	1
	Disproportionate reliance	1
	Participation in audit of partner about to join	1
	Knowledge of audit strategy	1
	Principal client and influence	1
		—
	Available	9
		—
	Maximum	6
		—
(c)	Objectivity	1
	Seen to be independent	1
	Close personal relationship	1
	Safeguards - review by partner	1
	Independent review by partner	1
	Undue dependence	1
	Not prohibited	1
	Close connected does not deal with situation	1
	Officer/employee within two years	1
	Rules - suggestions	3
		—
	Available	12
		—
	Maximum	8
		—

Available   28

Maximum   20

The examiner's answer

(a)   The auditor is very familiar with the clients accounting system and the business environment in which the client is trading. Thus if the client hires the auditor as a senior member of its management team, it will be relatively easy for the former auditor to quickly become integrated with the rest of the management team. The time required for the former auditor to familiarise himself with the new environment should be dramatically reduced from that normally required.

Auditors gain a wide and varied experience through exposure to different accounting systems and having to solve differing accounting issues. The auditor is invariably up to date on the latest accounting techniques and thought. As a consequence auditors who have these qualities are sought after by client companies.

Auditors and the key client personnel often develop a close professional relationship and become familiar with the quality of each others work. Thus it is perhaps understandable that if a client recognises in an auditor the qualities required to undertake a senior executive role in the company, then it is likely that the auditor may be approached.

If the auditor accepts a senior position with a client, then the client will save money through not having to utilise expensive recruitment consultants to find the ideal candidate. Additionally, the risk of the client selecting the wrong person for the position is reduced by employing an employee of the audit firm who will be well known to the client.

(b)   In a situation where a former audit partner becomes the financial director of the firm's principal client, several ethical problems may arise. The public will perceive perhaps that there is a lack of independence between the two parties even though in reality it is likely that objectivity will be maintained. The former partner in the audit firm will know the members of the audit team and may have had a close professional relationship with them. It may therefore be difficult for both parties to adjust to their new positions and the new interactions between them. The public could question the ability of the audit personnel to deal with a situation where an ex audit partner is accountable to audit personnel who were formerly his subordinates. A measure of influence over the audit personnel may still exist.

Additionally disproportionate reliance may be placed upon the ex audit partners representations. The audit team may feel that greater reliance can be placed upon the ex audit partners assertions. However the audit team should not place undue reliance upon any audit evidence from the ex audit partner and should evaluate the audit risk as they would with any audit client. If disagreement occurs between the parties, any agreement reached over the matter may be perceived as being a compromise between two formerly related parties and not an independently determined solution.

The ex audit partner will know quite intimately the audit strategy and procedures which will be applied to his company. In theory, the ex audit partner could conceivably conceal certain matters from the audit firm. This possibility should be taken into account by the audit firm when designing their audit programme. Threats to the firm's objectivity may be apparent where there remains significant connections between the director and the former audit firm. For example, if the director receives retirement or other benefits from the audit firm.

Additionally, the firms objectivity may be threatened because of participation in the conduct of an audit by a partner who is about to join a client. If the client is the audit firms' principal client, there will be additional pressures placed upon the audit firm. The audit firm whilst remaining objective will not wish to adversely affect their relationship with the client and coupled with the influence which the ex audit partner will undoubtedly have within the audit firm, it is a situation where the general public would find it difficult to accept auditor independence and objectivity.

(c)   Under the current rules of professional conduct, a member's objectivity must be beyond question if he (or she) is to report as an auditor. That objectivity can only be assured if the member is and is seen to be independent. The rules additionally state that a member's objectivity may be threatened or appear to be threatened as a consequence of a close personal relationship. Where an officer of a company is closely connected with a partner or staff member of the audit firm, safeguards should be set up in the practice to ensure objectivity.

These safeguards include the setting up of review machinery whereby the audit firm can satisfy itself that each engagement may be continued or accepted and to identify situations where independence may be at risk. Where additional safeguards are recommended, the audit should only be continued or accepted when an independent review has been undertaken by a partner unconnected with the engagement or by an independent firm of auditors.

Additionally, the current rules of professional conduct state that objectivity may be threatened by undue dependence on an audit client. Factors to be taken into account here include the size and nature of the practice and client, and its relationship with the client. The weight of factors such as the desire not to lose a principal client are difficult to assess.

It can be seen that the current ACCA ethical rules do not specifically prohibit an audit firm continuing to act as auditor to a client where an ex-partner or employee is in a senior position. Obviously if a junior member of the audit firm joined a client, it is unlikely that objectivity would be compromised but in this situation the audit firm would have to set up review procedures in order to determine whether they could act. The definition of 'closely connected' does not deal with this situation. Additionally, the rules state that a member should not take part in the audit of a company if that member has been an officer or employee of that company within the previous two years.

There are no current rules concerning the appointment of a former auditor as an officer of the company. The audit firm will have to determine itself whether objectivity is threatened or seen to be threatened. Perhaps rules ought to be introduced concerning audit partners who have been offered positions or are in discussions over positions with clients whereby they are removed from that audit until the outcome of the employment offer has been determined. Also where audit partners have accepted positions with clients then this fact could be disclosed in financial statements, or auditors could be required to wait for a period before accepting such an appointment or it could simply be prohibited.

56   (Answer 6 of examination)

Examiner's comments and marking guide

Question 6: The UK question dealt with audit service quality and the phenomenon of limited liability partnerships. Candidates seemed to be familiar with the area because of its topical interest and produced quite good answers. However, candidates did not answer part (c) very well. In this part, the question of public reaction to limited liability partnership and the image created by the profession of moves in this direction was to be discussed and unfortunately there were several candidates who simply rewrote their answers to part (b).

Generally the auditing questions were answered well. Candidates' average marks were relatively higher on these questions. It appears that some candidates wrote extensively on questions 5 and 6 without regard to time. It is important to realise that each part of a question has a maximum mark and the time allocated to a question part must be just as strict as to a whole question.

		Marks
(a)	Quality not visible	1
	Monitoring	1
	Joint and several liability	1
	Unlimited liability	1
	Avoid litigation	1
	Profit share	1
	Cannot transfer partnership share	1
	Available	7
	Maximum	5
(b)	Limited liability companies	1
	Disclosure of profit	1
	Subject to tax rules	1
	Litigation	1

Cap on legal liability	1
Duty of care to whom?	1
Personal liability unrealistic	1
Multi service providers	1
Protection for auditor	1
Partners not directly involved	1
Specialist form	1
Some of partners limited liability	1
At least one general partner	1
Cannot participate in management	1
Provides capital in return for share of profits	1
Little use to audit profession	1
Still joint and several liability	1
Change law accordingly	1

	Available	18

(Note: there are many facets to this answer hence the available marks are high) Maximum   7

(c)   Subjective assessment   8

	Available	33
	Maximum	20

The examiner's answer

(a)   The quality of an audit is difficult to assess by third parties as audit quality is not always visible to clients and the public. The assurance of the quality of the audit therefore is left up to the auditors to monitor. Monitoring of the audit work is implemented by partners within a firm and by national monitoring units (for example in the UK the Joint Monitoring Unit (JMU)). Mutual monitoring is more important and more likely to be encouraged under a partnership than a limited liability entity because of the legal nature of a partnership. As partners are jointly and severally liable, there is an incentive for partners to monitor each others and other professional staff's work.

Thus a partnership which gives unlimited liability to its partners acts as a bond to induce partners to monitor each others work. Poor quality work is discouraged by the fact that only partners share in the profits. Thus there is an incentive to ensure audit quality and thus avoid litigation and the poor image that this portrays. Each partners profit share will be negotiated annually based on the performance of that partner and if partners do not provide clients with a quality service then this profit share will be reduced.

Partners cannot transfer their share of the partnership without the consent of other partners. This restraint fosters a common interest in the well-being of the partnership and is more likely to induce the mutual monitoring of work and ensure the quality of audit services for the public.

(b)   Audit firms have the right to form limited liability companies which would give partners a measure of protection from negligence claims. However auditors would have to disclose their profitability and net assets to the public and be subject to corporation tax rules. Thus some audit firms have changed their views recently and have decided that limited liability partnerships are perhaps the most suitable constitution for their firms.

Because of the constant threat of litigation and the possibility of large negligence settlements, auditors are seeking a cap on their legal liability and the right to negotiate their liability with directors. Additionally the persons to whom the auditor owes a duty of care are not clear cut and tends to alter depending upon court decisions. Auditors wish to know to whom they are liable and for what amount. Legal liability partnerships can at least help in quantifying the firms legal liability.

Auditors believe that the need for all partners to be personally liable is unrealistic in a world where Big Six partnerships are now akin to major corporations. Big Six firms of auditors have built themselves into powerful multi-service providers and their constitution is not suitable for this type of business.

A case can be put forward for a degree of protection for auditors against negligence claims and it perhaps makes sense that partners not directly involved in the audit should be given a measure of protection. Legal liability partnerships could give this protection.

Limited liability partnerships are a specialist form of partnership. They are governed by the Limited Partnerships Act 1907 and also by general partnership law. Under this law some of the partners are allowed limited liability. However, a limited partnership must consist of a combination of limited partners with at least one general partner. The limited partners liability is limited to the capital they have made available to the partnership but they lose their limited liability if they participate in the management of the partnership. The limited partners' function therefore is to provide capital in return for a share of the profits.

It is obvious therefore that this form of partnership is of little use to audit firms as only general partners are allowed to participate in the management of a limited partnership. Thus there is no advantage to large firms of auditors to form limited partnerships as those partners who run the firm will still have joint and several liability. The audit profession has realised that the nature of this vehicle, the limited liability partnership, will have to be altered by law in order to suit their requirements.

Current proposals at the time of writing by the profession which are to be enacted in Jersey are that the LLP should provide a surety on registration of £5 million and a legal action against the auditor will be able to recover the net assets of the partnership, the £5 million bond and the assets of the negligent partners.

(c)   The audit profession in the form of the Big Six firms is very powerful and profitable. They provide many services to clients and this diversification has established them as some of the UK's most successful businesses. However, despite their size, the major accounting firms published no meaningful information about their affairs. The government gave auditors in 1989 the right to form limited liability companies but this form of constitution requires disclosure of information to the public and a change in the nature of the tax assessment procedures. The public perception therefore could easily be that audit firms wish to remain silent on their affairs and in order to achieve this the firms are prepared to leave the UK and locate in another jurisdiction (Jersey). Jersey, at the time of writing, has agreed to enact new legislation in order that the audit firms may form an acceptable type of limited liability partnership.

Jersey legislation cannot affect consumer rights and common law in England. It could be argued that by threatening to register in Jersey, the audit firms are forcing the UK government into setting up similar legislation. The Minister for Deregulation in the UK has stated that the government does not want to see 'the wholesale export of partnerships, whether they are accounting, actuarial or whatever, so we are considering what needs to be done. There is a case for some protection against suits, and a degree of protection may be sensible for partners not directly involved in the action'.

At a time when the Scott and Nolan reports are calling for greater transparency in business life, the audit firms desire to maintain secrecy may appear to the public to be contrary to current business practice. Audit firms are verifying financial statements and looking at accountability but it may seem to the public that they are not accountable themselves. It would appear strange that audit firms who enjoy a monopolistic position in the UK should wish to operate from another jurisdiction. The image of the audit profession has not been enhanced by this proposed move and it may appear to be motivated by self interest.

The Big Six accountancy firms filed a standard set of contract terms with the Office of Fair Trading and the European Commission that attempts to cap the liability for due diligence work to the value of a deal or £25 million whichever is the lower. The reaction of many venture capitalists at whom these terms are aimed is that the Big Six firms are trying to dictate and impose a set of terms and conditions on their clients and is as such anti competitive. The Department of Trade and Industry have published a White Paper (March 1997) which proposes certain restrictions on UK limited liability partnerships.

JUNE 1998 QUESTIONS

Section A – This ONE question is compulsory and MUST be attempted

57   (Question 1 of examination)

XY, a public limited company, owns 80% of AG, a public limited company which is situated in a foreign country. The currency of this country is the Kram (KR). XY acquired AG on 30 April 1996 for £220 million when the retained profits of AG were KR 610 million. AG has not issued any share capital since acquisition. The following financial statements relate to XY and AG:

Balance sheets at 31 December 1997

	XY £ million	AG KR million
Fixed assets		
Tangible assets	945	1,890
Investment in AG	270 *so diff*	-
Net current assets	735	645
Creditors: falling due after one year	(375)	(1,115)
	1,575	1,420
Share capital	330	240
Share premium	350	80
Profit and loss account	895	1,100
	1,575	1,420

Profit and loss account – year ended 31 December 1997

	XY £ million	AG KR million
Turnover	1,650	3,060
Cost of sales	(945)	(2,550)
Gross profit	705	510
Administrative and distribution costs	(420)	(51)
Income from AG	8	-
Interest payable	(22)	(102)
Operating profit before taxation	271	357
Taxation	(79)	(153)
Profit on ordinary activities after tax	192	204
Dividends paid	(20)	(52)
Retained profit for year	172	152

(i)   During the year AG sold goods to XY for KR 104 million. The subsidiary made a profit of KR 26 million on the transaction. The exchange rate ruling at the date of the transaction was £1 = KR 5.2. All of the goods remained unsold at the year end of 31 December 1997. XY had paid for the goods on receipt and there were no inter company current balances outstanding at 31 December 1997. At 31 December 1996 there were goods sold by AG to XY held in the stock of XY. These goods amounted to £6 million on which AG made a profit of £2 million.

(ii) A loan of £50 million in sterling was raised by AG from XY on 31 May 1997. The loan is interest free and is repayable in 2007. The loan to the subsidiary was translated at the temporal rate in the subsidiary's financial statements and had been included in the investment in AG figure in the balance sheet of XY. An amount of KR 65 million had been paid to XY by AG on 31 December 1997 in part settlement of the loan. This amount had not been received by XY and was not included in its financial statements.

(iii) The fair value of the net assets of AG at the date of acquisition was KR 1,040 million. Goodwill on consolidation is to be amortised on a straight line basis over three years and is to be calculated using historical cost goodwill. Goodwill is treated as a sterling asset which does not fluctuate with changes in the exchange rate. The increase in the fair value of AG over carrying value is attributable to tangible fixed assets which are depreciated over five years on the straight line basis. Tangible and intangible assets are depreciated without time apportionment in the year of acquisition and the fair value adjustment was not incorporated into the books of AG.

(iv) AG paid the dividend for the year ended 31 December 1997 on 30 June 1997. No more dividends were paid or proposed by AG during the year.

(v) The following exchange rates are relevant to the financial statements:

KRAMS to the £

30 April 1996	4.0
31 December 1996	4.6
1 January 1997	4.7
31 May 1997	5.3
30 June 1997	5.2
31 December 1997	5
Weighted Average 1997	5.1

(vi) The group policy is to use the closing rate/net investment method and translate the profit and loss account at the weighted average rate.

Required:

(a) Prepare a consolidated profit and loss account for the year ended 31 December 1997 and a balance sheet as at that date for the XY group. (All calculations should be to one place of decimals).

(21 marks)

(b) Prepare a statement of the movement in consolidated reserves for the financial year ending 31 December 1997.

(4 marks)

(c) Discuss why SSAP 20 'Foreign Currency Translation' fails to deal adequately with accounting for foreign currency translation.

(5 marks)

(Total: 30 marks)

Section B - TWO questions ONLY to be attempted

---

58 (Question 2 of examination)

There has been widespread debate for several years concerning the declining value of traditional methods of measuring corporate performance and the ability to predict corporate failure. Earnings per share, return on capital employed and other investment ratios are seemingly out of step with the needs of investors. The analysis of financial ratios is to a large extent concerned with the efficiency and effectiveness of management's use of resources and also with the financial stability of the company. Researchers have developed models which attempt to predict business failure. Altman's 'Z score', and Argenti's failure model are examples of such research.

However many analysts feel that financial statements require several adjustments before any meaningful evaluation of corporate performance can be made. Analysts often make amendments to corporate profit and net assets before calculating even the most basic of ratios because of their disapproval of certain generally accepted accounting principles and in an attempt to obtain comparability.

Required:

(a)   Evaluate the usefulness of traditional accounting ratios, calculated by reference to published financial statements, in providing adequate information for analysts and investors.   **(8 marks)**

(b)   Discuss the value and usefulness of the corporate failure prediction models such as those developed by Altman and Argenti.   **(8 marks)**

(c)   Describe, with reasons, an accounting adjustment which analysts might wish to make to financial statements before evaluating corporate performance in the case of each of the following elements:

    (i)   [Not reproduced as no longer valid due to technical developments.]
    (ii)   Deferred Taxation
    (iii)   Depreciation   **(9 marks)**
                                                      (Total: 25 marks)

---

59   (Question 3 of examination)

— ASB SOP.

(a)   The development of conceptual frameworks for financial reporting by accounting standard setters could fundamentally change the way in which financial contracts such as leases are accounted for.   These frameworks identify the basic elements of financial statements as assets, liabilities, equity, gains and losses *CHP 4* and set down their recognition rules.   In analysing the definitions of assets and liabilities one could conclude that most leases, including non-cancellable operating leases, qualify for recognition as assets and liabilities because the lessee is likely to enjoy the future economic benefit embodied in the leased asset and will have an unavoidable obligation to transfer economic benefits to the lessor.   Because of the problems of accounting for leases, there have been calls for the capitalisation of all non-cancellable operating leases so that the only problem would be the definition of the term 'non-cancellable'.

Required:

    (i)   Explain how leases are accounted for in the books of the lessee under SSAP 21 'Accounting for leases and hire purchase contracts'.   **(7 marks)**

    (ii)   Discuss the current problems relating to the recognition and classification of leases in corporate financial statements. (Candidates should give examples where necessary.)

                                                                 (8 marks)

(b)   (i)   During the financial year to 31 May 1998, AB plc disposed of electrical distribution systems from its electrical power plants to CD plc for a consideration of £198m.   At the same time AB plc entered into a long-term distribution agreement with CD plc whereby the assets were leased back under a 10-year operating lease.   The fair value of the assets sold was £98m and the carrying value based on the depreciated historic cost of the assets was £33m.   The lease rental payments were £24m per annum which represented twice the normal payment for leasing this type of asset.   **(5 marks)**

    (ii)   Additionally on 1 June 1997, AB plc sold plant with a book value of £100m to EF plc when there was a balance on the revaluation reserve of £30m which related to the plant.   The fair value and selling price of the plant at that date was £152m.   The plant was immediately leased back over a lease term of four years which is the asset's remaining useful life.   The residual value at the end of the lease period is estimated to be a negligible amount.   AB plc can purchase the plant at the end of the lease for a nominal sum of £1.   The lease is non-cancellable and requires equal rental payments of £43.5m at the commencement of each financial year.   AB plc has to pay all of the costs of maintaining and insuring the plant.   The implicit interest rate in the lease is 10% per annum.   The plant is depreciated on a straight line basis. (The present value of an ordinary annuity of £1 per period for three years at 10% interest is £2.49.)   **(5 marks)**

HP.

Required:

    Show and explain how the above transactions should be dealt with in the financial statements of AB plc for the year ending 31 May 1998 in accordance with SSAP 21 'Accounting for leases and hire purchase contracts' and FRS 5 'Reporting the substance of transactions'.   **(Total: 25 marks)**

---

60 (Question 4 of examination)

(a) The administrative and legislative burdens which have been imposed on small companies have been the subject of debate for several years. The application of accounting standards to small companies has been the subject of considerable research. It is the view of some accountants that accounting standards should apply to all financial statements whilst others feel that small companies should have a completely different set of accounting standards. In response to the continuing debate in this area, the Accounting Standards Board has issued a Financial Reporting Standard 'Financial Reporting Standard for Smaller Entities'.

Required:

Discuss the main issues in the development of an accounting framework for small companies with reference to the Financial Reporting Standard 'Financial Reporting Standard for Smaller Entities'. **(6 marks)**

(b) The directors of the Old Parcels Limited, an unlisted company, have drawn up their financial statements in accordance with the Financial Reporting Standard 'Financial Reporting Standard for Smaller Entities' (FRSSE) for the year ended 31 May 1998. All exemptions from compliance with accounting standards given to small companies by the FRSSE have been utilised by the company. They have been approached by a publicly quoted company, New Parcels plc, with a view to selling the whole of the share capital of Old Parcels Ltd to this company. New Parcels plc is in the same industry as Old Parcels Ltd and has a Price Earnings ratio of 14. The shares in Old Parcels Ltd are held by one family who have agreed to sell all of the shares to New Parcels plc subject to an independently agreed valuation of the shares. Following the purchase of the shares, the two companies are to be joined together to form a single company.

Financial Information — Old Parcels Ltd
Balance Sheet at 31 May 1998

	£'000
Fixed Assets	
Intangible asset	12
Tangible assets	278
	290
Current Assets	835
Creditors: amounts falling due within one year	(365)
Net Current Assets	470
Total Assets less Current liabilities	760
Creditors: amounts falling due after more than one year	(119)
Provisions for liabilities and charges	(12)
	629
Capital and Reserves	
Share capital	204
Profit and Loss Account	425
	629

Profits and Dividends 1994 to 1999

Year ended 31 May	Profit/(Loss) on ordinary activities after tax (£)	Dividends (include Pref Dividend) declared (£)	Preference Share Redemption-Additional finance cost (£)
1994	60,000	6,000	-
1995	66,000	6,500	-

1996	75,000	8,000	510
1997	45,000	2,100	554
1998	(30,000)	Nil	603
1999 (projected)	35,000	6,200	654

The profit/loss amounts are before dividend payments.

(1)   The intangible asset is a license to distribute a product and is estimated to generate net income before tax in the future of £10,000 per annum for the period of the license which expires on 31 May 2000. The carrying value in the balance sheet represents the original cost of £20,000 less amortisation and it is estimated that the market value of the license is £15,000.

(2)   The tangible fixed assets were revalued on 31 May 1997 by an independent valuer. The assets are depreciated at 10% per annum. The directors estimate that the market price of the fixed assets has increased by approximately 5% of their current carrying value during the year and that the net realisable value of the assets is £250,000.

(3)   The company has an employee share ownership scheme which is run by trustees with rules which prevent transfer of the schemes assets to the company. The assets of the scheme amount to £150,000 at 31 May 1998 and have not been included in the balance sheet. The costs of the scheme have been charged to the profit and loss account for the year.

(4)   The current assets and liabilities are felt to be worth their balance sheet amounts. The creditors falling due after more than one year are 6% Debentures which are repayable at a premium of 25% on 31 May 1999. The original debenture loan was £100,000. Interest is payable on 31 May of each year and the finance cost has been allocated at a constant rate on the carrying amount.

(5)   The provision for liabilities and charges in the accounts of Old Parcels Ltd represents the provision for deferred taxation calculated using the partial provision method. The basis of the calculation is the crystallisation of the accumulated net deferred timing differences of £52,000. There is no provision in the financial statements of New Parcels plc as their timing differences are anticipated to rise by £70,000 per annum from 31 May 1998 until the millennium.

(6)   The share capital comprises the following elements:

	£
30,000 7% cumulative redeemable preference shares of £1	33,767
170,000 ordinary shares of £1	170,000
	203,767

There are one year's arrears of preference dividends at 31 May 1998 included in the above figure for preference shares and the shares are redeemable at 31 May 2000 at a premium of 10%. There were no issue costs or premiums paid on the original issue of the preference shares on 1 June 1995. The share capital is owned by the directors of Old Parcels Ltd. Share options have been granted to certain senior employees and these will be exercised in the event of a sale or stock market flotation of the company if it is financially beneficial. There are options outstanding at 31 May 1998 to subscribe for 30,000 shares at £1 per share.

(7)   The company operates a computer system which will require adjustment for the effects of the new millennium. The costs of a new system would be £100,000 and the cost of adjusting the existing system would be £30,000 as at 31 May 1998.

(8)   During the current financial year, the company discontinued part of its business activities. The operating loss after tax of these activities was £6,000 and the loss on the disposal of the sale of the operation was £3,000. This part of the business normally contributed 20% of the annual post tax profit or loss of Old Parcels Ltd.

(9)   The appropriate discount rate to be used in any calculations is a rate of 8% per annum. Corporation Tax is 23%. Assume any future dividend payments are made at the year end.

Required:

Calculate and discuss the range of share values which may be placed on the ordinary shares of Old Parcels Ltd utilising the following methods of valuation:

(i)   Net assets valuation (going concern basis)   **(11 marks)**
(ii)   Earnings based valuation   **(8 marks)**
                                                                   (Total: 25 marks)

Section C — ONE question ONLY to be attempted

61   (Question 5 of examination)

Audit practitioners have recently initiated substantive changes in the audit approach. It appears to be the strategy that audit firms are moving away from the audit of financial statements and more to the provision of assurances on financial data, systems and controls in those systems. Auditors are focusing on providing 'business assurance' and 'business risk' which gives clients wider assurance than the traditional audit has offered. Auditors are reviewing the business from a process standpoint utilising benchmarking, performance measurements and best control practices as the key criteria. It seems that the audit is moving more to the analysis of business risk and the alignment of the audit much more to the management perspective.

A wide range of risk assessment services is now part of the audit service which clients can subscribe to. The provision of internal audit services is becoming an increasingly larger part of the 'business assurance' service offered by auditors. It seems that the audit is becoming a management consultancy exercise with internal audit, external audit and consultancy assignments being seen as complementary services.

Required:

(a)   Discuss the implications of the external auditor providing an internal audit service to a client, explaining the current ethical guidance on the provision of other services to clients.   **(10 marks)**

(b)   Explain the principal effects of the external auditor providing wider assurance to the client.   **(6 marks)**

(c)   Critically evaluate the move by large auditing firms to providing 'business risk and assurance' services rather than the traditional audit assurance for investors and creditors.   **(4 marks)**
                                                       (Total: 20 marks)

62   (Question 6 of examination)

The objective of a system of corporate governance is to secure the effective, sound and efficient operation of companies. This objective transcends any legislation or voluntary code. Good corporate governance embraces not only making the company prosper but also doing business in a legal and ethical manner. A key element of corporate governance is the audit committee. The audit committee is a committee of the board of directors and is of a voluntary nature regulated by voluntary codes. The Cadbury and Greenbury codes set out the voluntary codes governing corporate governance and therefore audit committees.

Required:

(a)   Explain how an audit committee could improve the effectiveness of the external auditor's work.   **(10 marks)**

(b)   Discuss the problems of ensuring the 'independence' of the members of the audit committee.   **(5 marks)**

(c)   Discuss the view that the role of the audit committee should not be left to voluntary codes of practice but should be regulated by statute.   **(5 marks)**
                                                       (Total: 20 marks)

ANSWERS TO JUNE 1998 EXAMINATION

---

57 (Answer 1 of examination)

Examiner's comments and marking guide

Question 1: This question required candidates to prepare a consolidated set of financial statements for a group with a foreign subsidiary. The question required candidates to make fair value, cash-in-transit, depreciation, and inter company adjustments. Candidates performed quite well on this quite difficult question which looked at the issues in a very practical way. Part (b) of the question required a statement of the movement in consolidated reserves. As many candidates did not successfully complete part (a) of the question, there were very few correct answers to this part of the question. However, candidates were given credit for answers to part (b) which were based on their calculations in part (a).

Part (c) required candidates to discuss the problems with the current accounting standard on foreign currency translation. This required an appreciation of the current issues in translating foreign currency based accounts. This type of issue is covered extensively by such publications as UK GAAP which is a recommended text. Candidates did not answer this section very well in the main.

		Marks
(a)	Translation of subsidiary's balance sheet	3
	Consolidated balance sheet workings	8
	Presentation of consolidated balance sheet/Profit/loss account	3
	Translation of subsidiary's profit/loss account	2
	Consolidated profit/loss account	10
	Available	26
	Maximum	21
(b)	Total exchange difference and movement on reserves	4
(c)	1 mark per valid point raised	5
	Available	35
	Maximum	30

Step by step answer plan

Step 1 Read the question again and make sure that you focus on precisely what is required. Most of the available marks are for preparing consolidated accounts including a foreign subsidiary. Note that the closing rate method should be used and that there are several inter-group transactions.

Step 2 Translate the profit and loss account and balance sheet of AG into sterling.

Step 3 Set up a columnar working for the consolidated balance sheet (see working (iii)).

Step 4 Deal with the fair value adjustment and the adjustments for the inter-group transactions.

Step 5 You should then be able to do the main balance sheet consolidation workings: goodwill; minority interests; consolidated reserves.

Step 6 Complete the consolidated balance sheet working and draw up the final version of the consolidated balance sheet.

Step 7   Set up a columnar working for the consolidated profit and loss account (see working (v)) and complete it as far as profit after tax.

Step 8   Calculate minority interest and complete the working. Draw up the final version of the consolidated profit and loss account.

Step 9   Start part (b) by translating the opening balance sheet of AG into sterling. You should then be able to work out opening consolidated reserves.

Step 10   Add the profit for the year and calculate the exchange differences to arrive at closing consolidated reserves.

Step 11   Answer part (c), making as many points as possible.

The examiner's answer

(a)

Consolidated Balance Sheet at 31 December 1997
XY Group

	£m
Tangible fixed assets	1,340
Goodwill	4
Net current assets	872
Long-term creditors	(558)
Minority interests	(60)
	1,598
Share capital	330
Share premium	350
Reserves	918
	1,598

It is acceptable to show the consolidated balance sheet/profit and loss account as per working (iii)/(v) although candidates will not gain maximum marks for presentation.

Workings

(i)   *Translation of subsidiary's balance sheet*

	KR	rate	£m
Net assets	1,420	5	284
Share capital	240	4	60
Share premium	80	4	20
Pre acquisition reserves	610	4	152.5
Post acquisition reserves	490	Balance	51.5
	1,420		284

(ii)   *Consolidated balance sheet workings*

£m

Group

	Total	Preacq	Postacq	MI
Share capital	60	48		12
Share premium	20	16		4
Reserves at acquisition	152.5	122		30.5
Reserves since acquisition	51.5		41.2	10.3
Revaluation	27.5	22		5.5
Cost of investment (270-50)		220		
		——		
Goodwill		12	(8)	
		——	——	——
			33.2	62.3
			——	——

(Revaluation = 1040 – (240 + 80 + 610) divided by 4 = £27.5m)

(iii)   *Consolidated balance sheet*

XY Group at 31 December 1997

	XY	AG	Fair Value Adj	Inter Co	Cash in Trans	Depr	Trans Gains/ Losses	Total
Tangible fixed assets	945	378	27.5			(11)		1,339.5
Goodwill (working (ii))								4
Loan to AG	50			(37)	(13)			-
Net current assets	735	129		(5)	13			872
Long-term creditors	375	223		(40)				(558)
Minority interest (working (ii))		62.3		(1)		(2.2)	0.6	(59.7)
								1,597.8
								——
Share capital	330							330
Share premium	350							350
Reserves (working (ii))	895	33.2		(4)		(8.8)	2.4	917.8
								——
								1,597.8

Consolidated profit and loss account for the year ended 31 December 1997
XY Group

	£m
Turnover	2,230
Cost of sales (including extra depreciation)	(1,434)
Gross profit	796
Administrative and distribution expenses	(430)
Exchange gains	3
Amortisation of goodwill	(4)
Interest payable	(42)
	——
Profit before tax on ordinary activities	323
Taxation	(109)
	——
Profit after tax on ordinary activities	214

Minority interest	(7)
Dividends	(20)
	187

Workings

(iv) *Translation of subsidiary AG's Profit and Loss account*

	KR	Rate	£m
Turnover	3,060		600
Cost of sales	(2,550)		(500)
Administrative and distribution costs	(51)	5.1	(10)
Interest payable	(102)		(20)
Taxation	(153)		(30)
Dividends	(52)	5.2	(10)
	152		30

(v)

Consolidated Profit and Loss Account
XY Group for year ended 31 December 1997

	XY	AG	Inter Co	Minority Interest	Goodwill	Con
Turnover	1,650	600	(20)			2,230
Cost of sales	(945)	(500)	20			(1,428)
Stock adj			(3)			
Gross profit	705	100	(3)			802
Administrative & distribution exp	(420)	(10)				(430)
Exchange gain		3				3
Additional depreciation		(5.5)				(5.5)
Goodwill amortisation					(4)	(4)
Interest payable	(22)	(20)				(42)
Taxation	(79)	(30)				(109)
	184	37.5	(3)		(4)	214.5
Minority interest (37.5 – 3) × 20%)				(6.9)		(6.9)
Inter group div	8	(8)				
Dividends paid	(20)					(20)
	172	29.5	(3)	(6.9)	(4)	187.6

The inter group dividend has been translated at the same rate as that of the holding company in order to eliminate it on consolidation. If the weighted average rate is used, then exchange differences will arise.

(vi) *Total exchange difference on translation of subsidiary*

	KR	Rate	£m
AG – net assets at 31 December 1996	1,268	4.6	275.7
Share capital	240		60
Share premium	80	4	20
Pre acquisition reserves	610		152.5
Post acquisition reserves	338	Balance	43.2
	1,268		275.7

	£m
Post acquisition reserves at 31 December 1996	(43.2)
Post acquisition reserves at 31 December 1997	51.5
	8.3
Retained profit (working (iv))	(30)
Exchange difference – loss	(21.7)

Movement on reserves 80% of £21.7m ie, <u>£17.4m</u>

(vii)   *Exchange difference – analysis*

	£m
Equity interest at 31 December 1996	275.7
Loss on retranslation at closing rate	(22.1)
$(1,268 \div 4.6 - 1,268 \div 5)$	
Equity interest at 31 December 1996	253.6
restated at closing rate (5 KR = £1)	
Retained profit for year (working (iv))	30
Exchange difference – profit and loss at weighted average rate	0.4
compared with closing rate $\dfrac{152}{5} - 30$	
	284

Total exchange difference $(22.1 - 0.4) \times 80\% = £17.4m$

Explanatory notes

(i)   Where the weighted average rate is used to translate the results of foreign subsidiaries then the rate ruling on the date of the transaction is used to eliminate inter company profit in stock. In this case £20m (104 KR divided by 5.2) has to be eliminated from turnover and purchases and additionally £2m has to be eliminated from opening stock and £5m from closing stock giving a net adjustment of £3m. The amount of profit to be eliminated is the amount of profit in the holding company's financial statements.

(ii)   The loan from XY to AG is not a permanent loan as it is intended that it will be repaid. Evidence of this is the fact that an amount of KR 65 million has been repaid at the year end. As a result the loan should be restated at the closing rate and the resulting exchange differences taken to the profit and loss account.

	KR
Loan	265
Less paid 31 December	(65)
	200
translated at closing rate	£40m
(KR5 = £1)	

The loan in the parent company's books is £50m.
The cash in transit is KR 65 million divided by 5 ie, £13m.
Therefore there is an exchange gain of £40m - £37m ie, **£3 million** in the books of AG

(iii)   *Goodwill – historical cost rate*

This method regards goodwill as the excess of the price paid over the fair value of the net assets of the subsidiary expressed in the foreign currency translated into the holding company's currency at the date of acquisition. The asset is not deemed to fluctuate with changes in the exchange rate. Although not specifically dealt with by SSAP 20, it would appear by inference to be the method adopted by the standard. Under this method the fair value of the net assets of AG has been translated into sterling at the date of acquisition and therefore as the revaluation has not been incorporated into the records of AG, there is no requirement to retranslate the fair value of the net assets of AG at subsequent year ends.

Calculation (see also working (ii))

	£m
XY - investment	220
less	
AG (80%)	
Share capital (£1 = KR 4.0)	(48)
Share premium (£1 = KR 4.0)	(16)
Pre acquisition reserves (£1 = KR 4.0)	(122)
Revaluation (£1 = KR 4.0)	(22)
Goodwill	12
Goodwill amortisation 1996	4
Goodwill amortisation 1997	4
Balance in consolidated balance sheet	4

(iv) *Tangible fixed assets*

The tangible assets in the consolidated balance sheet will be stated as follows:

	KR	Rate	£m
Balance per AG accounts	1,890	5	378
Increase to fair value (KR (1,040 − (240 + 80 + 610)))	110	4	27.5
Less: Increase in depreciation (2 years)	(44)	4	(11)
			394.5
XY's tangible assets			945
			1,339.5

(v) *Net current assets*

	£m
XY	735
AG (645 divided by 5)	129
Less: Inter company profit in stock	(5)
Cash in transit	13
	872

(vi) *Long-term creditors*

	£m
XY	375
AG	223
	598
Less: Inter company loan (explanatory note (ii))	(40)
	558

(vii)   *Minority interest*

	£m
Balance per working (ii)	62.3
Less inter company profit in stock	(1)
Additional depreciation on fair value	(2.2)
Add gain on exchange on loan (20% × 3)	0.6
	59.7

(b)   **Movement on consolidated reserves**

	£m XY	£m AG	£m Total
Profit and loss account at 1 January 1997	723	34.6	757.6
		(80% of 43.2)	
Adjustments: Fair value depreciation (80% × 5.5)			(4.4)
Inter company profit on opening stock (80% × 2)			(1.6)
Goodwill written off			(4)
Retained profit for year			187.6
Exchange loss (working (vi))			(17.4)
Profit and loss account at 31 December 1997			917.8

(c)   SSAP 20 'Foreign currency translation' fails to deal adequately with certain issues relating to overseas transactions. The following issues are a cause for concern as they can lead to subjective judgement being used in the preparation of financial statements.

(i)   The basic requirement of SSAP20 is that transactions should be recorded at the rate ruling at the date the transaction occurred but there is little guidance as to what that date should be. For example should this date be the order date, the shipping date, the date of receipt, or the date of the invoice.

(ii)   Average rates can be used if rates do not fluctuate significantly. However little guidance is given on the calculation and use of the average rate. For example over what period should average rates be calculated? Should average rates be used for large transactions where the exchange rate is known?

(iii)   A problem arises where there are two or more exchange rates for a currency or there has been a suspension of an exchange rate. SSAP20 does not give guidance on these matters. Fundamental accounting concepts such as prudence and conservatism would prevail in these circumstances.

(iv)   There are certain areas where SSAP20 does not give definitive guidance on the accounting treatment of certain items.

(a)   Not all items neatly fall into monetary or non monetary categories for translation purposes and problems arise where this distinction is not clear: for example debt securities held as investments.

(b)   Little reference is made in SSAP20 to hedge accounting and forward contracts. The only specific reference to hedge accounting is to borrowings in a foreign currency used as a hedge against foreign currency equity investments. Similarly forward contracts are only mentioned briefly. These complex areas are partially dealt with in a standard on financial instruments and derivatives (FRS 13 'Derivatives and other financial instruments: Disclosures').

(c)   SSAP20 does not specifically deal with cumulative exchange differences and the net investment in a foreign subsidiary when all or part of it is sold. There are problems over which method should be used to calculate goodwill on consolidation, ie, the historical rate or current rate. Additionally the rate to be used when eliminating inter group profits could be either the closing rate or average rate.

In conclusion, there is concern over the inadequacy of present accounting rules in this area. Hedge accounting has not been effectively dealt with by the ASB and there is an urgent need to deal with the problem areas of SSAP20 as the volume and complexity of overseas transactions significantly increase.

Did you answer the question?

This answer covers a range of shortcomings of SSAP 20, rather than concentrating on one or two (meeting the requirement to *discuss why*). The Examiner has said that you should aim at one point per mark as a rough guide. There are 5 marks, so there should be at least five separate points.

---

58   (Answer 2 of examination)

Examiner's comments and marking guide

Question 2: This question required candidates to discuss the usefulness of accounting ratios and corporate failure prediction models in evaluating corporate performance. In addition, candidates had to discuss adjustments which analysts might wish to make to financial statements in respect of goodwill, deferred taxation and depreciation.

Generally this question was answered quite well. The main problem with some answers was that candidates simply listed ratios (in part a) and discussed them rather than taking a macro approach and looking at the general usefulness of ratios as a decision making tool.

		Marks
(a)	Subjective assessment	8
(b)	Subjective assessment	8
(c)	1 mark per adjustment	3
	2 marks for reasons per adjustment	6
	Available/maximum	9
	Available	25
	Maximum	25

Step by step answer plan

Step 1   Read the question again and make sure that you focus on precisely what is required. Ensure that you allocate your time between the three sections.

Step 2   Approach part (a) by describing the limitations of ratio analysis and its usefulness.

Step 3   Answer part (b) by briefly describing the models and then evaluate their usefulness and limitations.

Step 4   Answer part (c) by taking each situation in turn, explaining the problem and then describing the possible adjustment(s).

The examiner's answer

(a)   Ratio analysis can be a useful way of interpreting financial information but its predictive powers should not be overestimated. Ratios calculated from historical cost accounts do not reflect the current values of assets or the current costs of operations and as a consequence if users wish to predict a company's future performance, they are restricted in their analysis by the provision of historical cost information in corporate financial statements. Comparison of ratios between companies is very difficult. Companies are inherently different in structure and use different accounting policies and although these may be disclosed in financial statements, it is difficult sometimes to adjust the accounts for these differing policies as the information required to carry out the adjustment may not be disclosed.

The environment within which the company operates may change. If the rate of inflation changes or the business environment changes, then performance over time using ratio analysis may be distorted.

The potential usefulness of many ratios both as an indicator of current performance and as a guide to future performance would appear to require that the constituent elements of the profit and loss account and balance sheet should be expressed in comparable prices. The use of profitability ratios is limited if the numerator is expressed in current prices (for example turnover) and the denominator is based upon historical values (for example capital employed). An organisation showing a satisfactory gross profit percentage may not be generating sufficient funds to replace stock at current prices or to meet its operating costs, and ratio analysis based on published data would not pick up this weakness.

Return on capital employed is a key investment ratio but the figure for capital employed is based upon the historical value of capital provided. The real cost of the shareholders' investment in the company is the opportunity cost of their investment which is the amount sacrificed by not selling their shares (ie, market price). Similarly the return to ordinary shareholders is dependent upon dividends received and expected to be received. Neither of these components are used in the calculation of return on capital employed traditionally used by users of financial statements.

Traditional ratio analysis is dependent upon items included in the financial statements. Companies, despite the introduction of FRS5 'Reporting the substance of transactions', still leave assets and liabilities 'off the balance sheet'. The accounting for pension costs and leases are still areas where traditional accounting rules allow companies to leave assets and liabilities off the balance sheet. In many cases, the balance sheet is a repository for elements not charged in the profit and loss account under accrual accounting. Thus certain items in the balance sheet are 'sunk costs'. For example research and development expenditure. Companies still use creativity in formulation of financial statements and directors still believe that capital markets are 'fooled' by 'creative' accounting practices. If the remuneration of managers (including share options) is linked to profit and if their value in the labour market is enhanced by running a 'profitable' company, then management may attempt to influence the accounting treatments adopted by the company. Although analysts are aware of the above facts, it is not always easy to adjust financial statements for them. Thus the effectiveness of ratio analysis is reduced.

These limitations do not necessarily mean that ratio analysis should be discarded as an interpretative mechanism. If the cost of providing such information was greater than its usefulness then understandably ratio analysis would not be used. Financial statements are part of conventional accrual accounting and are subject to the preferences, judgements and objectives of management. Analysts need to be aware of these limitations. Ratio analysis is part of the process of information gathering for decision making and is not an absolute performance measure in itself.

Did you answer the question?

The requirement was to *evaluate the usefulness* of ratio analysis, not simply to state its limitations. This answer necessarily concentrates on the limitations, but the concluding paragraph 'balances' the answer by stating that ratio analysis is useful, subject to these. Because of the requirement to *evaluate*, some description is needed. A list of 'bullet points' would not fully address the requirement.

(b) Empirical studies have been undertaken to determine the extent to which financial ratios can be used to predict corporate failure. The ability to predict corporate failure is important from the investors viewpoint and from a social perspective, and an early warning system would allow investors and management to take preventative action. Both univariate and multivariate (Altman) approaches have been used to predict corporate failure and essentially these analyses are capable of saying whether a company exhibits characteristics similar to companies which have failed in the past without being able to determine whether a particular company is going to fail.

Altman (1968/1983) determined multiple predictors of business failure using multiple discriminant analysis for the development of a linear function which purported to predict corporate failure. The 'Z' score selected five (out of 22 utilised in the research) financial ratios for his final discriminant function. The ratios and weighting were derived from an empirical study of US companies. The effectiveness of the 'Z' score in predicting corporate failure declined when used on data other than that used in the empirical study.

Argenti developed a failure model only partly based on financial information and developed the failure model to include such variates as the nature of management, response to change, the accounting systems and financial problems and mistakes.

All models which predict corporate failure from financial statements suffer from the underlying weakness of a lack of comparability of financial statements. Also managers may start creative accounting practices when they realise that their company is having problems. It is unlikely that corporate failure can be predicted on the basis of a univariate or multivariate model alone. There are several other factors such as those outlined by Argenti that one has to take into account.

The accounting ratios used by researchers are based on historic information but ideally prospective information is likely to be more useful in predicting corporate failure. Historic information is often published too late to be of use in determining the going concern status of companies and contains information which has 'mixed values' inasmuch that some items will be at net replacement cost, others will be at historic cost and some items at current value.

The underlying theory behind the models is suspect and little attempt has been made to explain the logic of the models. As a result confidence in the models varies and their ability to predict corporate failure has been undermined. The ability of the models to predict the time-scale of the failure has been criticised. The models were developed in the 1960s, 70s and 80s when business transactions and the sophistication of accounting techniques were different to those of the current generation of companies. Therefore, the application of 'Z' scores to the current business environment may be unrealistic. Additionally these models do not take account of inflation in their calculations.

Despite the criticisms of multivariate analyses they are used by banks to analyse credit risk, by companies to monitor credit worthiness and audit firms in their analytical review procedures. However, they are not used in isolation but are utilised alongside other information about a company.

Did you answer the question?

As in part (a), this answer makes a number of points in a descriptive way, meeting the requirement to *discuss the value*. The Altman and Argenti models are only described in so far as is necessary to explain their advantages and limitations; the answer avoids lengthy description and explanation for its own sake.

(c)   Financial analysts may undertake several adjustments to financial statements. The reasons for this may vary from the fact that the basis of several balance sheet items is the subjective assessment of the directors to the fact that balance sheet write-offs reduce the carrying value of net assets to 'unrealistic' levels. Three such adjustments may be:

(i)   [Answer not included since no longer valid.]

(ii)   Deferred taxation: current accounting standards (SSAP15) require that tax deferred or accelerated by the effect of timing differences should be accounted for to the extent that it is probable that a liability or asset will crystallise. The crystallisation of the liability is to some degree subjective being based upon future projections of, for example, capital expenditure. Analysts could adjust the financial statements for deferred taxation because of this subjectivity in two possible ways:

-        utilise the flow through method whereby only committed taxation liabilities are accounted for

-        utilise the full provision method whereby all potential taxation liabilities are accounted for

The impact of these two methods will be to affect reported liabilities, profitability and the gearing of the company. Analysts would tend to discount deferred taxation calculated on the 'partial provision' method.

(iii)   Depreciation; analysts often review the depreciation rates of capital intensive businesses as the profitability of such businesses is affected by accelerated depreciation rates. Such depreciation rates cause a concave decline in net asset values whereas often the asset values decline in convex terms. Analysts therefore often add back depreciation, thus charging it at a slower rate. Differences in depreciation methods and revaluations of assets also cause distortions in the ratios. Many analysts are looking to adjust accounts in order that they might arrive at 'economic' value and profit.

> **Did you answer the question?**
>
> In each case the answer does not simply describe the adjustment, but gives the reasons for it.

Tutorial note

Part (c)(i) concerned goodwill. When this question was originally set, SSAP 22 was still in force. Under SSAP 22, purchased goodwill could be written off against reserves and analysts often made adjustments to the financial statements to bring it back onto the balance sheet. FRS 10 has now prohibited this treatment and this part of the question and answer has therefore been deleted.

---

59   (Answer 3 of examination)

Examiner's comments and marking guide

Question 3: This question dealt with the subject of leases. Part (a) of the question required candidates to simply state how leases are dealt with in the accounting records of the lessee. This part of the question was quite straight forward but many candidates did not deal with the recognition issues relating to leases.

Part (a) (i) required candidates to discuss the current problems relating to the recognition and classification of leases. These issues are important locally and internationally and are currently being discussed by standard setters world wide. Candidates did not answer this part of the question very well. It is important that candidates are aware of current issues relating to the core parts of the syllabus. Current issues do not exclusively mean exposure drafts or discussion papers but issues relating to current standards possibly not under review by the standard setting bodies. Part (b) required an explanation of how certain sale and lease back transactions should be dealt with. Many candidates did not discuss the various elements of the question in sufficient detail relying on a numerical answer to the question. If the question requires an explanation of the figures in it, it is essential that candidates discuss the results of their calculations.

				Marks
(a)	(i)	Finance lease		5
		Operating lease		2
				7
	(ii)	Subjective assessment		8
(b)		Operating lease		5
		Finance lease		5
		Overall discussion		4
			Available	14
			Maximum	10
			Available	29
			Maximum	25

Step by step answer plan

Step 1   Read the question again and make sure that you focus on precisely what is required. The introductory paragraph should alert you not only to the fact that the question is about leases, but that classification is a major issue.

Step 2   Answer part (a)(i). Note that the requirement word is *explain*, not simply state. You should spend no more than 12 minutes on this part.

Step 3 Approach part (a)(ii) by writing short paragraphs, covering as many points as possible, and giving examples.

Step 4 Re-read part (b)(i) and decide whether the agreement is a finance lease or an operating lease. Then consider the requirements of both SSAP 21 and FRS 5 and write your answer.

Step 5 Deal with the agreement in (b)(ii) in the same way.

The examiner's answer

(a) (i) SSAP 21 'Accounting for leases and hire purchase contracts' requires a distinction to be made between finance leases and operating leases. A finance lease is defined as one that 'transfers substantially all of the risks and rewards of ownership of an asset to the lessee', whilst an operating lease 'is a lease other than a finance lease'. A finance lease should be capitalised in the financial statements at the present value of the minimum lease payments utilising the lease term and the interest rate implicit in the lease contract. Any residual payments guaranteed by the lessee should also be taken into account. The capitalised asset is then depreciated on a basis similar to owned assets. For finance leases the depreciation should be calculated over the lease term if this is shorter than its useful life.

The interest and principal components of the periodic lease payments must be identified, allocated to accounting periods and the lease liability reduced accordingly. The finance charge is calculated as the difference between the undiscounted total of the minimum lease payments and the value given to the fixed asset in the financial statements. The discount element will be the finance charge. The lease obligation will be the present value of the minimum lease payments and the double entry will be completed by capitalising the fixed asset. Finance charges must produce a constant periodic rate of charge.

Operating lease rentals are charged to the profit and loss account on a straight-line basis over the lease term irrespective of when payments are due. This reflects the pattern of benefits derived from the leased asset.

The classification of leases can therefore have significant financial reporting consequences.

> **Did you answer the question?**
>
> This answer explains the treatment of leases, but does not go into lengthy detail, as there are only 7 marks available.

(ii) Current accounting standards do not deal adequately with leases. They do not require the rights and obligations arising under operating leases to be recognised in the lessee's financial statements. However addressing the situation presents a problem for standard setters. When the current standard on leasing (SSAP21) was developed, the principles as regards recognition of assets were left largely intact with those transactions which were essentially purchase agreements appearing on the balance sheet. The principle which was generated from the standard was one of the transfer of the risks and rewards of ownership. Those leases which transferred the benefits and risks of ownership were classified as finance leases and accounted for as assets and liabilities. All other leasing transactions were classified as operating leases. SSAP21 contains specific guidance regarding lease accounting and one would look to the standard as the primary source of authoritative guidance although the general principles of FRS5 are also relevant in ensuring that leases are classified as finance or operating in accordance with their substance.

Where a lease contract secures SUBSTANTIALLY all of the risks and rewards of ownership to a lessee, a recognisable asset and liability exists. 'Substantially', however has been judged against quantitative rather than qualitative criteria. If the lease is non-cancellable and the present value of the minimum lease payments is equal to or greater than 90 per cent of the fair value of the leased asset then the lease is normally classified as a finance lease.

The quantitative criteria have been perceived as the effective rules rather than the qualitative criteria set out in SSAP21 and FRS5. The standards have been thwarted by the fact that many lease arrangements have been designed to fail the specific quantitative tests for classification as a finance lease by the smallest of margins. Even where the substance of a lease contract can be objectively assessed, different weightings can be given to different factors by different accountants thus causing failure in the classification of a finance lease. For example the relative responsibilities of the lessor and lessee for maintenance, insurance, and bearing of losses can be blurred.

Long-term financing leases can be packaged as operating leases to secure the benefits of off balance sheet finance. The problem which arises is that substantially the same leasing arrangement will be accounted for in a substantially different way depending upon the satisfaction of the quantitative criteria and the perception of the relevant risks and rewards criteria. The following examples set out the ways in which contracts which in substance are finance leases may be classified as operating leases:

(i)   The criterion that the present value of the minimum lease payments must be less than 90 per cent of the fair value of the asset for a lease to be classified as an operating lease may be satisfied by the use of contingent rentals which are not included in the present value calculation. Alternatively the present value of minimum lease payments may be reduced by lessening the guaranteed residual value or capping the lessee's liability at an amount less than the residual value.

(ii)   The interest rate implicit in the lease may be impossible to calculate. Normally the lessee would then estimate the rate which would be paid on a similar lease. This estimated rate might then bring the present value below the 90% threshold.

(iii)   Leases of land and buildings are classified as operating or finance leases in the same way as other assets. As land has normally an indefinable useful life, and if the title is not expected to pass to the lessee, then the lessee does not receive substantially all of the risks and rewards of ownership. Thus such a lease will normally be an operating lease. Some leases however may have the characteristics of a finance lease (for example a lease of a building with a short useful life). However, even in these cases companies will allocate as large a value as possible to the land so that it will automatically be classified as an operating lease.

It is worth noting that although some lease contracts do not satisfy the quantitative criteria for classification as a finance lease, they often do not change the substance of the lease agreement which may include certain criteria regarding the rights and obligations of the lessee which in themselves will determine the fact that it is a finance lease.

The various methods employed to avoid the standards can be seen as a shortcoming of the current rules. The arbitrary criteria used to determine 'de facto' ownership are easily circumvented and the difficulty of establishing the substance of leases raises serious questions about the adequacy of the arbitrary separation of leases into finance and operating leases. A major deficiency of the current accounting standards is the non-recognition in lessee's balance sheets of material assets and liabilities arising from operating leases.

Did you answer the question?

Notice that this answer makes a variety of points (the key requirement word is *discuss*) and includes examples, as requested.

(b)   (i)   *Electrical distribution system*

Where a lessee enters into a sale and leaseback transaction which results in an operating lease then the original asset should be treated as being sold and the operating lease should be accounted for under SSAP21. If the transaction is at fair value then immediate recognition of the profit or loss on the sale of the asset should occur. However where the transaction is above fair value, the following should happen:

(i)   the profit based on fair value should be recognised immediately (£98m − £33m, ie, £65m)

(ii)   the balance of the sales value over the fair value should be deferred and amortised over the shorter of the lease term and the period to the next lease rental review (£198m − £98m, ie, £100m divided by 10 years = £10m per annum)

If the sales value is not the fair value, then the operating lease rentals (£24m) are likely to have been adjusted for the excess price paid for the assets. In the case of AB plc the sales value is more than double the fair value of the asset and FRS5 may dictate that the substance of the transaction is essentially that of the sale of an asset and also a loan which equates to the deferred income element. Thus part of the commitments under the distribution agreement may in fact be more in the way of a financing cost (£12m). The company may therefore show the excess over the fair value as a loan (£100m) and part of the costs of the operating lease will essentially be a repayment of capital and interest on this amount.

(ii)   *Sale and leaseback of plant*

The sale and leaseback of the plant appears to result in the creation of a finance lease as the present value of the minimum lease payments is greater than 90% of the fair value of the plant and AB plc has to pay all of the costs of maintaining and insuring the plant. Additionally the lease runs for the remaining useful life of the plant after which it can be purchased by AB plc for a nominal amount, ie, the lease contains a bargain purchase option. (£43.5m + £43.5m × 2.49 = £151.82m: fair value £152m).

FRS5 states that the asset remains in the lessee's balance sheet at the carrying value and the sale proceeds (£152m) are shown as a creditor (Application Note B4 and B20). The creditor balance represents the finance lease liability and as the payments are made, they are treated partly as repayment of that creditor and partly as a finance charge against income. The revaluation reserve (£30m) will continue to be treated as before and if it is being transferred to the profit and loss reserve, this will now be over the lease term/assets life of four years.

Did you answer the question?

The answer does not only describe the accounting treatment in each case, but explains the reasoning behind it.

---

60   (Answer 4 of examination)

Examiner's comments and marking guide

Question 4: This question was based upon the issues involved in developing an accounting framework for small companies. In the UK, the ASB have developed the 'FRSSE' and the IASC are currently considering whether 'one standard fits all' is the correct approach to take in the case of smaller entities. In many countries, IAS's are the only standards available to large and small companies alike and therefore an accounting framework for small companies is very much an issue internationally. Candidates generally answered this part of the question reasonably well without discussing the recognition and measurement issues at any length.

Part (b) required candidates to value the shares of a company utilising an assets approach and an earnings approach. The valuation of the shares required a knowledge of current accounting standards and the application of common sense. The question was quite challenging as candidates would have seen this type of question before but previous questions have not used the current range of accounting standards available for the valuation of shares.

The solution to the question depended upon several assumptions and therefore alternative solutions were possible. However, again candidates often failed to discuss the nature of their calculations and simply produced a detailed calculation of the share valuation. Generally this question was not popular and candidates did not perform very well on this question.

			Marks
(a)	Subjective assessment		6
(b)	Assets valuation -	intangible	2
		tangible	2
		ESOP	1
		CA/CL	1
		Debentures/preference shares	5

	Deferred tax	2
	Millennium cost	1
	Share options	2
Earnings method -	P/E ratio	6
	discussion	3

Available	25
Maximum	19
Available	31
Maximum	25

(**Step by step answer plan**)

Step 1 Read the question again and make sure that you focus on precisely what is required. Although at first sight the question appears to be about the FRSSE, most of the available marks are for performing a share valuation of a private company.

Step 2 Approach part (a) by using the introductory paragraph as a source of ideas. Write a number of short paragraphs, each covering one point. You should not spend more than about 11 minutes on this part.

Step 3 Start part (b)(i) by using the information in the scenario to value the assets of Old Parcels, then calculate a price per ordinary share. Remember to explain the reasoning behind your calculations and any assumptions that you make.

Step 4 Do part (b)(ii) in a similar way, estimate annual earnings, then use this to calculate possible prices per share.

Step 5 Write a brief conclusion.

Items not required by the Examiner for this question: detailed requirements of the FRSSE.

(**The examiner's answer**)

(a) The main aim of developing an accounting framework for small companies is to provide users with a reporting framework which generates reliable, relevant and useful information. It is important that the accounting standards which are used by small companies are of value to them and therefore it is necessary to determine which companies are to be within the definition of a small company. Very few accounting issues need to be addressed by a small company simply because of its size. The criteria for a small company need not be determined by reference to size but would be more meaningful if the definition were based on the relationship between the shareholders and management. Small companies could be defined by reference to the ownership and management of the company. It is inaccurate to assume that small companies are simply smaller versions of large public companies.

The basis for developing an accounting framework for small companies ought to be based around the issues of recognition, measurement and disclosure. The question to be answered is whether alternative standards should be developed in recognising, measuring and disclosing transactions of small companies.

The objectives of financial reporting differ between large companies and owner managed companies. The nature of accountability is different between large and small companies and thus there is a major distinction between the objectives of financial reporting for the two types of company. The needs of users of financial statements should determine the nature of those statements. It is intellectually and commercially sound to develop an accounting framework on the basis of the objectives of the financial statements.

The ASB has developed an accounting standard 'Financial Reporting Standard for Smaller Entities' (FRSSE) which uses size criteria to determine the nature of a small company.

It is often stated that the purpose of producing an accounting framework for smaller companies is to reduce the administrative burden on those companies. In reality the financial statements are produced by external accountants and thus the production of such a framework on the pretext of reducing the administrative costs is an unrealistic objective. Additionally many of these accounting standards will have a negligible impact on a small company and those standards which are selected for application to small companies may apply to some and not to others. It might appear that an approach which takes existing accounting standards and eliminates those which are thought not to be applicable to small companies is going to result in a framework which is simply a hybrid version of the large company's regulatory system.

The FRSSE in the UK has been received with mixed feelings as it aims to simplify and reduce the financial reporting requirements of small companies. It selects certain elements of certain accounting standards as a basis of reporting for small companies and exempts entities from compliance with the other extant accounting standards and UITF Abstracts. It applies the size criteria set out in the Companies Acts for a small company and utilises the same measurement bases as for large companies. Measurement requirements of a complex nature have been omitted but small companies do undertake complex transactions and in these cases they are referred to the full standard. It is not surprising that this accounting standard will in fact increase the amount of work involved in preparing financial statements in the short term whilst companies change the nature of the information disclosed and become expert in the application of the standard.

Did you answer the question?

This answer covers several issues: criteria for determining 'small'; objectives of the FRSSE; usefulness of the FRSSE. An answer which only covered one of these would not attract full marks.

(b)   When valuing the shares of an unlisted company, it is unlikely that one value will be used in isolation. The more common methods include a dividend yield basis, the present value of future dividends, the earnings basis, the accounting rate of return, the net assets basis, the use of the Capital Asset Pricing Model, the super-profits method and the present value of future maintainable earnings. The dividend bases are only really applicable to preference shares or the sale of a small number of shares. In general all of the methods set out above will provide a guide to a share price but the final price will be negotiated between the parties after taking into account intangible factors such as personal circumstances, business consideration and the market for the shares.

Net Assets Basis of Valuation

The valuation of the ordinary shares can depend upon how the ownership of the ordinary shares is dispersed, the holding of the shares being sold and the use to which the assets are to be put after the sale. As the whole of the capital of the family is being sold and the companies are to merge, a dividend yield basis is not realistic.

Asset valuation (Going concern basis)

	Valuation (£'000)
Intangible asset - licence (note (i))	15
Tangible assets (278 × 1.05) (note (ii))	292
Current assets	835
Creditors due within one year	(365)
Creditors: falling due after more than one year (note (iv))	(121)
Preference shares (note (iv))	(34)
Deferred taxation (note (v))	-
Other items not in balance sheet	
Millennium costs (note (vi))	(30)
Inflow of cash for share issue (note (vii))	30
Total net asset value	622
Shares in issue	170,000
Options	30,000
	200,000
Price per ordinary share	£3.11

Notes on asset valuation

As the company is being sold as a going concern, this basis has been used to calculate the value of the net assets.

(i)   The intangible asset has an estimated market value of £15,000. If the intangible asset is valued on an income basis then its valuation is £10,000 per annum discounted for two years at a rate of 8%, ie, £17,832. As the income stream is perhaps more subjective than a current market valuation the latter value has been taken in the answer.

(ii)   As the assets are being valued on a going concern basis, the net realisable value of the tangible fixed assets has not been used as a valuation method. An estimate of current value has been made utilising the information concerning the increase in the value of the assets. Taxation has been ignored as there is no intention to sell the assets.

(iii) The FRSSE does not deal with UITF13 'Accounting for employee share ownership plan trusts' and therefore the company is currently in compliance with the standard by not including the assets of the ESOP in the valuation of the assets of Old Parcels Ltd. As the assets of the trust cannot be transferred to the company they are not included in the asset valuation.

(iv)   The company has complied with the FRSSE regarding FRS 4 'Capital Instruments'. However, the 'true' value of the debenture liability could be calculated as the net present value of the future interest payments and redemption cost.

	£
Loan interest payable 31 May 1999	6,000
Loan and premium payable 31 May 1999 on redemption	125,000
	131,000
Discounted at 8% per annum	121,296

Similarly, the preference shares might be valued at their net present value.

	Dividend	Redemption amount	Discount factor	Present value £
31 May 1999	4,200	-	8%	3,889
31 May 2000	2,100	33,000	8%	30,093
				33,982

(v)   Deferred taxation has been eliminated from the asset value as it is highly subjective and also the timing differences of New Parcels plc in the event of a takeover will eliminate the need for a provision for deferred taxation as they are in excess of the fall in the net cumulative timing differences of Old Parcels Ltd.

(vi)   The cost of converting the computer to allow for the millennium could be taken into account or ignored depending upon the use to which New Parcels plc would put the existing system. The shareholders of Old Parcels Ltd would not be happy with a calculation which takes into account the renewal of the system.

(vii) It is assumed that the holders of the share options would exercise them as the option price will be well below the offer price.

Earnings method of valuation

The price earnings ratio is the market value of a share divided by the earnings per share. Therefore, the market value of a share can be assessed by multiplying the P/E ratio by the earnings per share.

The FRSSE does not require companies to disclose the results of discontinued operations but obviously they will be included in the Profit or Loss for the year. The results from discontinued operations ought to be excluded from any profit calculation.

	£'000
Profits (1994-98)	216
Less: Discontinued activities (20% of 216)	(43)
Preference dividends 3 years × 7% × £30,000	(6.3)
Preference share appropriation (510 + 554 + 603)	(1.7)
Net profits available to ordinary shareholders	165
Average profits (divided by 5)	33

The average profits for the last five years are £33,000 and the projected profits are £35,000 − £2,100 (preference dividend) − £654 (preference share appropriation) ie, **£32,246**. Therefore the figure of £33,000 seems to be a reasonable one to use in the earnings based calculation of the price of the ordinary shares. New Parcels plc has a P/E ratio of 14 but because any growth in the profits is uncertain and because Old Parcels Ltd is an unquoted company, a lower P/E ratio may be more suitable for the valuation of Old Parcels Ltd's shares. However because additional capital will be provided by the holders of share options, future profits may result from this inflow, therefore, the discount applied to the P/E ratio need not be too severe.

$$\text{Market value per share} = \frac{\text{P/E ratio} \times \text{Earnings}}{\text{Number of shares}}$$

$$= \frac{10 \text{ (say)} \times 33,000}{200,000}$$

Market price per share is **£1.65**

If the P/E ratio of New Parcels is applied to the earnings of Old Parcels Ltd then the price per share is

$$\frac{14 \times 33,000}{200,000} \text{ ie, } \textbf{£2.31}$$

If one assumes that Old Parcels Ltd has future maintainable earnings of £33,000 at a discount rate of 8%, then a value can be placed on the shares of

$$\frac{£33,000}{8\%} \text{ ie, £412,500 or } \textbf{£2.06} \text{ per share}$$

Conclusion

It would appear that the owners of the ordinary shares of Old Parcels Ltd would require a price for their shares of around £3.11 but New Parcels may attempt to acquire the ordinary shares for between £1.65 and £2.31 per share. The above answers are a basis for valuing the shares of Old Parcels Ltd, candidates will be given due credit for alternative assumptions and solutions.

61 (Answer 5 of examination)

Examiner's comments and marking guide

Question 5: This question was the first of the auditing questions and dealt with the provision of internal audit services to clients by the auditors and business assurance and risk services. The question was not popular with candidates and this may be indicative of a lack of reading of the accountancy press. The question could have been answered by utilising basic auditing knowledge and did not need an in-depth knowledge of the services currently performed by auditors. However, if candidates do not read current professional literature then they will find this type of question quite difficult because of their lack of familiarity with the subject.

Candidates did not answer this question very well at all.

			Marks
(a)	Current guidance		4
	Ethical considerations		8
	(2 marks per point)		
	Conclusion		1
		Available	13
		Maximum	10
(b)	Explanation of effects a - d		4
	e		2
		Available/Maximum	6
(c)	Evaluation of the move - subjective		4
		Available	23
		Maximum	20

Step by step answer plan

Step 1   Read the question again and make sure that you focus on precisely what is required.

Step 2   Part (a) requires a 'discussion' ie, more than just a series of bullet points. The current ethical guidance does not prohibit the external auditor from providing an internal audit service, but you must point out what the guidance does state eg, not to perform management functions.

Step 3   Part (b) concerns the possibility of the external auditor providing a wider assurance than the traditional audit offers. If the auditor is to carry out more work, audit costs will rise and the client will have to pay for it. Try and make 6 separate points to earn the 6 marks available.

Step 4   part (c) is only worth 4 marks, so there is no need to write too much in your answers. Stick to important areas such as materiality levels and the independence of the external auditor.

The examiner's answer

(a)   Current ACCA guidance on the provision of other services to audit clients states that objectivity may be threatened by the provision to an audit client of services other than audit. There is no objection in principle to a practice providing additional services to a client but care must be taken not to perform management functions or make management decisions. In many cases, particularly small clients, a range of accountancy services are provided. However in the case of a listed or public interest company an auditor should not participate in the preparation of the company's accounting records, save in relation to assistance of a mechanical nature or in an emergency. Additionally the guidance says that if preparation of accounting records is carried out for a client, the client must accept responsibility for the records and the practice should always make appropriate audit tests. Thus there is no specific guidance which prevents an auditor undertaking the internal audit function.

The provision of internal audit services by the external auditors does however create certain ethical conflicts. For example the following dilemmas could occur:

    (a)   Is it possible for an external auditor to report independently upon an internal control system which has been developed by an internal audit department made up of employees of the audit practice?

    (b)   Will an external audit firm test in depth the work performed by the internal auditor or a system of control which has been verified by an internal audit department within which there are colleagues of the external auditor?

    (c)   The internal audit programme may be designed to reduce the work of the external auditor rather than the reduction of 'business risk'.

(d)   The internal audit department may be deemed to be part of the management structure of the company depending upon the status of the department within the company. If this is the case then the ethical guidance offered by the Code of Conduct of the ACCA has been breached.

(e)   Many large firms of auditors have increased their fee income by large amounts by providing internal audit services. (In the UK, Price Waterhouse increased fee income by 100% and Ernst and Young by 260%.) There has been massive growth in this area and as a result external auditors are becoming quite dependent upon internal audit income. This increases the dependency upon the client and reduces the independent status of the external auditor.

(f)   The risk profile of the client company immediately changes. The external auditor will sense that there is an immediate reduction in the audit risk because there will be a presumption that control risk has been reduced because of the involvement of the audit firm in internal audit. However the external auditor should review audit risk from an independent viewpoint and this is impossible given the above scenario.

It is interesting that views are split over the restriction of internal audit activity by external audit. Rules are laid down by the Bank of England and the Building Societies Commission in the UK which prevent the same firm performing both internal and external audit service in the financial services sector. However the AICPA in the USA takes a relaxed view, surprisingly, by allowing the provision of both audit services as long as the strategic and management controls are retained by the client. The latter regulatory control however is somewhat subjective in its application.

(b)   Ultimately it is the management of an organisation who are responsible for the control of business risk. Business risk is the threat that an event or action will adversely affect an organisation's ability to achieve its business objectives and execute its strategies successfully. The risk may be any adverse impact on business activities and could include the products of the organisation, processing, business interruption, regulatory non-compliance and even the effect of adverse publicity.

The immediate effects of the external auditor providing assurance as to the business risk of a client are as follows:

(a)   the external auditor will become legally liable for a wider range of assurances

(b)   the resources required to provide a business assurance service are quite large. Therefore auditors must ensure that they have the prerequisite skills

(c)   the audit cost to the client may rise. If, however, the audit costs remain the same, and there will be market pressure for this to be the case, then these value added services may be at the expense of traditional audit assurance for investors and creditors

(d)   Auditors are operating in a buyers' market and competition to provide audit services is intense. These current developments are seen by many as a marketing exercise. The problem which arises is that the expectations of audit clients are raised and this may create a greater 'expectations gap' than the one which already exists

(e)   if wider assurance is being given to audit clients, this may mean that current audit reports become inappropriate for reporting purposes. However, it is unlikely that audit reports will change because most users of financial statements are familiar with the level of assurance being given in such reports and auditors do not wish to increase their liability, holding themselves out in writing to be giving 'business assurance'. The audit report will remain familiar but may be based on less auditor contact with the basic controls and transactions of the business.

(c)   Several large audit firms are stating that auditing is currently undergoing a revolutionary change because of major changes in information technology and the desire from companies for wider assurance than the traditional audit. The audit is seen by some as developing into a super-efficient 'factory approach' with 'back-office' processing centres handling basic audit work thus leaving the auditor more time to concentrate on the client with the focus on the management perspective. The audit is being repackaged by these firms into a much more 'desirable' commodity. Auditors will be carrying out the work where they feel that the risks are and that seems to mean looking at the business as a whole. Basic auditing work will be forgone as it is perceived as adding little to the audit.

However, in an increasingly litigious society, auditors should be providing more basic assurance from the audit based on lower materiality thresholds and a grounded knowledge by the auditor of systems and controls.

It appears that the external auditors will be placing great emphasis on the role of the audit committee and internal audit in providing basic assurance in those areas. If internal audit services are being provided by the external auditor then less audit work will be carried out by the audit firm in their capacity as external auditors. It appears that the new audit approach is simply a repackaging of audit and consultancy work with the former being undertaken by the audit firm in the guise of an internal auditor and the latter under the cover of the external audit banner. In any event total fee income for audit firms seems set to rise but it is dangerous to pretend that the external audit is basically a consultancy exercise as traditional audit assurance will be lost.

---

62   (Answer 6 of examination)

Examiner's comments and marking guide

Question 6: This question proved very popular with candidates and was answered very well. The question dealt with audit committees and their relationship with the auditor and the company. It also dealt with the regulation of such committees. Candidates had obviously prepared quite well for this question, although yet again in part (c) where discussion of the regulation of audit committees was required there were many weak answers because it required an amount of original thought.

Marks

(a)	Assurance	1
	External audit independence	1
	Selection	1
	Terms and scope	1
	Management letter	1
	Improve internal controls	1
	Specialists	1
	Duplication	1
	Impact of new standards	1
	Timing of reports	1
	Contentious issues	1
	Problem areas	1
	Performance of auditor	1
	Enhances quality	1
	Restrictions	1
	Sundry points (1 each)	5
	Available	20
	Maximum	10
(b)	Explanation of problem	2
	Other directorships	1
	Several capacities	1
	Workings of board	1
	Share holdings/pensions	1
	Conclusion	1
	Available	7
	Maximum	5
(c)	Prescription v market forces	2
	Inconsistency	1
	Publication of reports	1
	Disproportional significance	1
	Single model	1
	Smaller companies	1
	Conclusion/overview	1

	Available	8
	Maximum	5
	Available	35
	Maximum	20

Step by step answer plan

Step 1 Read the question again and make sure that you focus on precisely what is required. This looks a fairly friendly question on audit committees.

Step 2 Don't just write all that you can think of about audit committees in part (a). The question is specific – explain how the committee can help the auditor. One approach would be to describe a list of the typical duties of the audit committee, and explain how each can help the auditor to be effective.

Step 3 The Combined Code on corporate governance envisages an audit committee of at least three non-executive directors. How can these persons be 'independent' if they are paid directors of the company? Answer part (b) accordingly.

Step 4 There is no single correct answer to part (c). Try and make points both for and against statutory regulation of audit committees in your answer.

The examiner's answer

(a) An audit committee can improve the effectiveness of the external auditor's work by increasing the assurance that the external auditors can derive from systems of corporate governance and internal financial controls. The committee will be involved in ensuring that the external auditor is independent and will participate in the selection of the auditor by recommending certain firms who have a knowledge of their industry and reviewing the source and rationale for selecting certain firms of auditors. Additionally the terms and scope of the external audit and corporate governance engagement will be discussed as will the management letter and its effect on the current years audit.

The committee will encourage discussions with the external auditor as to how internal controls might be improved, and the rationale as to the use of specialist departments of the audit firm and specialist advisors. A meeting of internal auditors, external auditors and the audit committee will review the audit plan with a view to minimising duplication of work, the impact of new auditing standards and providing value for money for the company. The timing and nature of reports from the external auditors will be reviewed as to their effectiveness and any contentious accounting issues discussed. Any problems with the directors statements of compliance with the Cadbury Code, the going concern statement or the statement on internal control will be discussed at an early stage of the audit and generally the audit committee will make suggestions as to the problem areas which the audit can address. The external audit partner and the chairman of the audit committee will discuss differences of opinion and attitudes of committee members and feedback on the performance of the auditors. The opening up of communication channels between the external auditor and the audit committee and two-way discussions enhances the quality of the audit and adds value to the audit process.

The audit committee will further discuss with the internal and external auditor the intended scope of their work with a view to satisfying itself that no unjustified restrictions have been imposed by executive management. Additionally the following duties of the audit committee may assist in the external audit process.

(i) dealing with difficulties in the performance of the audit such as non availability of client personnel;
(ii) reviewing the findings of the internal and external auditors;
(iii) reviewing the company's financial statements and annual report prior to the submission to the board;
(iv) reviewing public announcements that have a financial impact;
(v) reviewing and monitoring compliance with the corporate code of conduct, and legal and statutory requirements.

Audit committees are seen as valuable not only for overseeing the external reporting process and external audit but as a means of ensuring responsible corporate governance. They are an aid in ensuring the professional independence of auditors and the efficiency and effectiveness of the audit and the system of corporate governance.

(b)   The members of the audit committee normally comprise non-executive directors (NED) and although they should be independent of the company and declare any interests in the company, the absence of regulations in this area means that independence is often hard to achieve. For example the NED's often sit on committees of several companies and there are no regulations as regards conflicts of interest in this area. Additionally the company pays the NED's salaries and this fact ensures that independence is difficult to achieve under a voluntary code.

The NED's often sit not only on the audit committee but also on several other board committees making strategic contributions to the running of the business. They have to balance their role as audit committee member and the monitoring of executive directors and management with their role as corporate strategist. They are acting in several capacities and therefore their source of influence is somewhat diffuse and because of the complexity of the NED's role it is difficult to imagine that they can act independently when it comes to exercising their corporate governance role. The ability of NED's to bring independent judgement to the audit committee will depend on the workings of the board and its committees. NED's may have previous executive involvement with the company and have participation in share option schemes. If NED's have shareholdings in the company, this is inconsistent with the exercise of independent judgement as is the provision of a pension scheme for the NED's. It is extremely difficult for a NED to exercise independent judgement when they have an interest in the company, are appointed by the company and are remunerated by the company.

(c)   If the audit committee is not governed by statute then several issues arise. One of the problems of allowing self regulation in the area of corporate governance and audit committees is that if prescriptive approaches are advocated, they may not receive the support of key industry groups and in the absence of major corporate failure or fraud, governments may be reluctant to impose regulations on industry as it may be seen to be a further burden to management.

Without statutory regulation, there will be inconsistency of practice and standards between audit committees. Members of audit committees may find it difficult to criticise management. The form of the annual report of the audit committee may not be consistent without some form of statutory regulation. Shareholders are poorly informed about the working of the audit committee and there would seem to be substantial benefits from making publication of the report of the audit committee a statutory requirement. Greater transparency and disclosure can be uncomfortable for companies but the current reliance on voluntary practices creates a market risk which can be alleviated through changes in statute and disclosure practices.

However the prescriptive approach to the formation of an audit committee may result in disproportionate significance being given to its role and may impact on corporate performance and long-term potential. Problems would also arise if a single model audit committee were imposed on a wide range of companies of different sizes and financial profiles, and different internal structures. Many smaller companies would not see the benefits of appointing an audit committee and they may feel that statutory regulation is counter productive, with the costs outweighing any benefits. However it is important that some form of monitoring report is made to shareholders even in the case of small publicly quoted companies.

If audit committees are unregulated then there is little formal requirement for adherence to professional values of competence, independence or effective reporting to shareholders. The identity and experience of the audit committees' members becomes an important issue in these circumstances. Accountancy bodies will find it difficult to set standards for NED's on audit committees where such persons are non-accountants, and the problems of independence of NED's set out in part (b) of the answer may dictate that some form of statutory regulation may be required.

DECEMBER 1998 QUESTIONS

Section A – This ONE question is compulsory and MUST be attempted

63   (Question 1 of examination)

Wright, a public limited company, acquired 80% of the ordinary share capital of Berg, a public limited company, on 1 July 1996 when the retained earnings of Berg were £300 million. The cost of the shares was £600 million and the share capital and share premium account of Berg at that date were respectively £250 million and £50 million. The fair values of the net assets of Berg at the date of acquisition were equivalent to their book values. Wright sold half of its holding of the shares in Berg on 1 July 1998 for £350 million.

On 1 April 1998, Wright acquired 80% of the ordinary share capital of £500 million of Chang, a public limited company, at a cost of £700 million.

The draft profit and loss accounts for the year ended 31 December 1998 are:

	Wright plc £m	Berg plc £m	Chang plc £m
Turnover	18,000	1,200	1,600
Cost of sales	(12,000)	(840)	(1,020)
Gross profit	6,000	360	580
Distribution costs	(1,800)	(120)	(140)
Administrative expenses	(180)	(12)	(12)
Operating profit	4,020	228	428
Interest payable	(30)	(8)	(4)
Bank interest receivable	15	10	20
Dividends receivable (all inter company)	112	–	–
Profit on ordinary activities before taxation	4,117	230	444
Tax on profit on ordinary activities	(1,320)	(74)	(80)
Profit on ordinary activities after tax	2,797	156	364
Dividends – proposed	(200)	(80)	(100)
Retained profit for the year	2,597	76	264
Profit and loss reserve at 1.1.98	8,500	324	249

The following information is relevant to the preparation of the group accounts:

(i)   During the period Wright plc closed down 15 of its 100 retail outlets because they were unprofitable and inefficient. These outlets contributed 5% of the turnover and operating costs of Wright plc. The costs of this downsizing included in cost of sales amounted to £14 million.

(ii)   The net assets of Chang acquired on 1 April 1998 and their fair values were as follows:

	Carrying value £m	Fair value adjustment £m	Fair values £m
Tangible fixed assets	500	(30)	470
Stock and work-in-progress	240	(40)	200
Provision for re-organisation	(30)	(20)	(50)
Other net assets	130		130
	840	(90)	750

The provision for reorganisation of £30 million relates to the reorganisation of the retail outlets of Chang which had been committed and provided for on 31 December 1997 and a further post acquisition provision of £20 million is required which relates to the reorganisation of the remaining retail outlets as a result of the acquisition. The reduction in the stock value relates to a change in the accounting policy for stocks in order to bring it into line with that of Wright. The required change in the closing stock value of Chang to ensure uniform group accounting policies is a decrease of £30 million. The stock of Chang at 1 January 1998 was £150 million and at 31 December 1998 was £350 million.

(iii)   Berg sold goods to Wright on 1 September 1998 which had a selling value of £60 million. The profit made by Berg on these goods was £6 million and Wright had sold half of these goods by the year end.

(iv)   Goodwill arising on the acquisition of subsidiaries is amortised through the profit and loss account in cost of sales over four years with a full year's charge being made in the year of acquisition. Depreciation is charged on all group fixed assets at 20% per annum on the carrying value. The depreciation policy of Chang has been the same as the group's policy for several years. The fair value adjustments had not been incorporated into Chang's accounting records.

(v)   The sale of the shares in Berg has not been accounted for by Wright, although the dividends receivable reflect the change in Wright's shareholding. Assume that profits accrue evenly and that there are no other expenses or share capital in issue other than those stated in the question. Taxation on any capital gain is to be ignored.

Required:

(a)   Prepare a consolidated profit and loss account for the Wright Group plc for the year ended 31 December 1998 in accordance with the Companies Acts and UK Accounting Standards. (The amount of the consolidated profit dealt with in the holding company's accounts is not required.)

(25 marks)

(b)   Show the composition of the balance on the group profit and loss reserve at 31 December 1998.

(5 marks)
(Total: 30 marks)

Section B – TWO questions ONLY to be attempted

64   (Question 2 of examination)

There are several measurement systems which can be used in accounting. The most important single characteristic which distinguishes them is whether they are based on historical cost or current value. A further related issue is that of general price changes which affect the significance of reported profits and the ownership interest. It is often stated that a measurement system based on current values is superior to one based on historical cost and that accounting practice should develop by greater utilisation of current values. Current value systems can utilise replacement cost accounting and net realisable value techniques which use entry and exit values respectively. If general inflation is a problem, it is possible to eliminate the effect by producing a 'real terms' measure of total gains and losses, where a current value system of accounting is adjusted for the effects of changes in current purchasing power (CPP).

Required:

(a)   Describe the problems associated with replacement cost accounting and net realisable value accounting when used as an alternative to historical cost accounting. **(7 marks)**

(b)   The following summary financial statements relate to AB, a public limited company, for its first year of trading to 30 November 1998:

Profit and loss account

	£m
Turnover	4,500
Cost of sales (including depreciation)	(3,000)
Gross profit	1,500
Distribution and administrative expenses	(500)
Profit before taxation	1,000
Taxation	(300)
Profit after taxation	700

Balance sheet

	£m
Fixed assets (net of depreciation £600m)	2,000
Current assets	
Stock	1,200
Debtors	2,400
Cash	300
	3,900
Creditors: amounts falling due within one year	(1,200)
Net current assets	2,700
Creditors: amounts falling due after more than one year	(1,500)
	3,200
Capital and reserves	
Share capital	2,500
Reserves	700
	3,200

The company has decided to adjust its financial statements for the impact of changing prices and has generated the following information to assist in these adjustments for the period.

		£m
Turnover	– amount in terms of current purchasing power (CPP)	4,950
Cost of sales	– cost of goods sold in terms of CPP	3,300
	– current cost of goods sold	3,750
Distribution & administrative expenses	– historical cost in terms of CPP	550
Depreciation	– cost of depreciation in terms of CPP	660
	– current cost depreciation	720
Gain on loan (CPP)		20
Monetary working capital adjustment		400
Gearing adjustment		423
Stock – current value		1,600
– in terms of CPP		1,320
Fixed Assets – current value (replacement cost)		3,120
– in terms of CPP before depreciation		2,860

Assume a rate of inflation of 20% per annum

Prepare a balance sheet as at 30 November 1998 and a profit and loss account for the year ended 30 November 1998 showing the impact of changing prices for each of the following models:

(i)   Current purchasing power accounting (CPP)   **(7 marks)**

(ii)   Current cost accounting incorporating a gearing adjustment.   **(6 marks)**

(c)   Describe the principal features of a 'Real Terms' system of accounting for inflation by reference to the financial statements of AB in part (b) of this question.   **(5 marks)**

                                                                                     (Total: 25 marks)

---

65   (Question 3 of examination)

XYZ Ltd is a well established family company with 85% of its ordinary shares and 50% of its preference share capital held by family members. The following summarised balance sheet and fair value table refers to XYZ Ltd at 30 November 1998.

	Carrying value £m	Fair value £m
Fixed assets		
Intangible assets	15	-
Tangible assets	45	40
	60	40
Current assets	55	50
Creditors: Amounts falling due within one year	(47)	(56)
Net current assets	8	(6)
Creditors: Amounts falling due after more than one year	(38)	(39)
(£35m of 8% unsecured debenture stock 1999 redeemable at a premium of 10%)		
	30	(5)
Capital and reserves		
Called up share capital – £1 ordinary shares	40	40
10% Preference shares of £1 (£10m – par value) redeemable at a premium of 5%	11	12
Profit and loss account	(21)	(57)
	30	(5)

XYZ Ltd had incurred losses for several years. In 1998 the family had sold a 5% holding in the ordinary shares to PQ plc and a further 10% holding to outside interests. Prior to this event, all the ordinary shares were held by the family. PQ plc have indicated to XYZ that they wish to increase their interest in XYZ Ltd.

XYZ Ltd has projected that it will make profits before interest and taxation in the year to 30 November 1999 of £8 million and that this will increase by 25% per annum. The directors of XYZ Ltd have decided to reconstruct the capital of the company and have suggested the following scheme of reconstruction.

(i)   The ordinary shares of £1 are to be reduced to 20p shares. Additionally 20 million ordinary shares of 20p are to be issued for cash. PQ plc will subscribe for 15 million of these shares and the family shareholders will purchase the balance.

(ii)   The holders of the ordinary shares not held by the family or PQ plc will be offered one new 7% convertible cumulative preference share of £1 for every two ordinary shares that they own and their shares will be cancelled.

(iii) A merchant bank has agreed to subscribe in cash for £25 million of new 8% (secured on tangible assets) loan stock and PQ plc and the family shareholders will subscribe equally in cash for £25 million of new unsecured 10% loan stock. Both issues are at par value.

(iv) The existing preference shares held by the family will be cancelled and the balance not held by the family will be repaid along with the 8% debentures on the following terms:

> Arrears of accrued preference dividends included in creditors to be cancelled (2 years).
> 10% preference shares repaid at £0.80 per share.
> Debenture stock repaid at par (there is no accrued interest).

(v) The assets and liabilities are to be shown at fair value in the reconstructed balance sheet and the directors' loans of £8 million included in short-term creditors are to be written off.

(vi) PQ plc is to pay a non-equity capital contribution to shareholders funds of £10 million to XYZ Ltd in order to bolster its liquid funds.

(vii) The bank overdraft included in current liabilities currently stands at £5 million.

(viii) The procedures under the Companies Act 1985 have been followed as regards the varying of shareholders rights.

(ix) Assume corporation tax at 30%.

Required:

(a) Prepare a balance sheet for XYZ Ltd after the implementation of the scheme on the assumption that the proposed scheme was accepted. **(15 marks)**

(b) Discuss the fairness of the above scheme to the parties concerned and the likelihood of the scheme being accepted. **(10 marks)**
(Candidates should include relevant financial computations.)

(Total: 25 marks)

---

66 (Question 4 of examination)

SSAP 12 'Accounting for Depreciation' required that where there has been a permanent diminution in the value of a fixed asset, the carrying amount should be written down to the recoverable amount. The phrase 'recoverable amount' was defined in SSAP 12 as 'the greater of the net realisable value of an asset and, where appropriate, the amount recoverable from its further use'. The issues of how one identifies an impaired asset, the measurement of an asset when impairment has occurred and the recognition of impairment losses were not adequately dealt with by the standard. As a result a new financial reporting standard, FRS 11 'Impairment of Fixed Assets and Goodwill' was issued by the Accounting Standards Board in order to address the above issues.

Required:

(a) (i) Describe the circumstances which indicate that an impairment loss relating to a fixed asset may have occurred. **(7 marks)**

(ii) Explain how Financial Reporting Standard 11 deals with the recognition and measurement of the impairment of fixed assets. **(7 marks)**

(b) AB, a public limited company has decided to comply with FRS 11, as regards the impairment of its fixed assets. The following information is relevant to the impairment review:

(i) Certain items of machinery appeared to have suffered a permanent diminution in value. The product produced by the machines was being sold below its cost and this occurrence had affected the value of the productive machinery. The carrying value at historical cost of these machines was £290,000 and their net realisable value was estimated at £120,000. The anticipated net cash inflows from the machines were £100,000 per annum for the next three years. A market discount rate of 10% per annum is to be used in any present value computations. **(4 marks)**

(ii)   AB acquired a car taxi business on 1 January 1998 for £230,000. The values of the assets of the business at that date based on net realisable values were as follows:

		£000
Vehicles		120
Intangible assets (taxi licence)		30
Debtors		10
Cash		50
Creditors		(20)
		190

On 1 February 1998, the taxi company had three of its vehicles stolen. The net realisable value (NRV) of these vehicles was £30,000 and because of non-disclosure of certain risks to the insurance company, the vehicles were uninsured. As a result of this event, AB wishes to recognise an impairment loss of £45,000 (inclusive of the loss of the stolen vehicles) due to the decline in the value in use of the income generating unit, that is the taxi business. On 1 March 1998 a rival taxi company commenced business in the same area. It is anticipated that the business revenue will be reduced by 25% and that a further impairment loss has occurred due to a decline in the present value in use of the business which is calculated at £150,000. The NRV of the taxi licence has fallen to £25,000 as a result of the rival taxi operator. The net realisable values of the other assets have remained the same as at 1 January 1998 throughout the period.   **(7 marks)**

Required:

Describe how AB should treat the above impairments of assets in its financial statements. (In part (b) (ii) candidates should show the treatment of the impairment loss at 1 February 1998 and 1 March 1998)

Please note that the mark allocation is shown after paragraphs (b) (i) and (b) (ii) above.

(Total: 25 marks)

Section C – ONE question ONLY to be attempted

67   (Question 5 of examination)

The increase in the size of audit firms has been a source of concern to regulators and clients alike. Some audit firms feel that mergers between the largest firms of auditors are necessary in order to meet the global demand for their services. However, their clients are concerned that such mergers will create a monopolistic market for audit services which will not be in their best interests.

Required:

(a)   Explain the reasons why the largest audit firms might wish to merge their practices.   **(10 marks)**

(b)   Discuss the potential problems created by mergers of the largest firms of auditors.   **(10 marks)**
(Total: 20 marks)

68   (Question 6 of examination)

(a)   It can be argued that integrity, objectivity and independence are important at both the individual practitioner level and also at the national professional body level. At the practitioner level, one is concerned with the conduct and attitudes of the individual accountant whilst at the national level, the image and integrity of the profession are of paramount importance.

Required:

Explain the role that practitioners play in the maintenance of professional integrity, objectivity and independence.   **(7 marks)**

(b)   The following notes relate to the personal files of two student accountants undertaking training in an accounting firm:

File Note 1

The student was asked by an audit senior whether she had taken her ACCA professional examinations – Module F in June 1998. She replied that she had not taken the examinations but was planning to take the examinations in December 1998. The student in fact did take the examinations in June 1998 but did not wish to disclose the fact in case she failed the examinations and lost her reputation as having passed the examinations at the first attempt. The audit senior has formally complained about the conduct of the student. The student subsequently passed the June examinations.

                                                                             (7 marks)

File Note 2

The student has consistently completed his assigned tasks below the budgeted hours allocated to those audit tasks. The audit senior has no tangible proof that the tasks have not been carried out but suspects that this may be the case or alternatively time spent on the audit work is not being recorded. The audit senior has reported his suspicions to the audit partner.

                                                                             (6 marks)

Required:

Discuss the implications of the above file notes and how each of the matters should be dealt with by the audit partner.

Please note that the mark allocation is shown after File Notes 1 and 2 above   **(Total: 20 marks)**

ANSWERS TO DECEMBER 1998 EXAMINATION

63 (Answer 1 of examination)

Examiner's comments and marking guide

Question 1: the question sought to test candidates' knowledge of a consolidated profit and loss account. The main elements of the question involved consolidating a subsidiary which became an associate in the year, consolidating a subsidiary acquired in the year, dealing with a downsizing and provisioning and accounting for the sale of shares in a subsidiary.

Many candidates treated the downsizing as a discontinuance and as such the format of their answer was significantly different from that of the model answer. Candidates are not unduly penalised for this as their mistake is only a single error and does not affect other elements of the question. Another common mistake was not accounting for the associated undertaking for the last half of the financial year. Additionally many UK candidates did not apply FRS 9 'Associates and Joint Ventures' in answering the question.

The question required candidates to calculate the profit on the sale of shares in the subsidiary but many candidates forgot to accrue the profit for the half year to the date of sale and many did not understand the nature of the calculation.

Part (b) of the question required candidates to show the composition of the balance of the group profit and loss account at the period end. Very few candidates produced accurate answers mainly because of errors in part (a) of the question. However marks were awarded for the way in which the balance on the reserve had been generated.

The question was generally answered quite well with candidates scoring good marks.

		Marks
(a)	Turnover	2
	Cost of Sales – Goodwill	3
	– Fixed assets	1
	– Restructuring	1
	– Stock/remainder	4
	Distribution and administrative costs	1
	Associated company	4
	Interest/bank interest	1
	Exceptional items	2
	Taxation	1
	Associated company tax	1
	Profit on disposal	3
	Minority interests	2
	Dividend	1
	Layout – acquisitions etc	3
	Explanation of discontinuance	2
		—
	Available	32
		—
	Maximum	25
		—
(b)	Wright's reserves	2
	Berg's reserves	2
	Profit for period	2
	Goodwill written off	2
		—
	Available	8
		—
	Maximum	5
		—

(Alternative calculation 2 marks per element except Wright's retained profit and profit on sale of shares – 1 mark)

Available	40
Maximum	30

Step by step answer plan

Step 1 Read the question again and make sure that you focus on precisely what is required. This question requires the preparation of a consolidated profit and loss account. The opening paragraphs tell you that there has been an acquisition and a disposal during the year and you should notice that Berg plc is a subsidiary for the first half of the year and an associate for the second half of the year. The additional notes tell you that there are further complications: a restructuring; fair value adjustments; and intra group sales.

Step 2 Start part (a) by drawing up the group structure, paying particular attention to the dates on which changes took place. Then draw up a columnar profit and loss account working (W1).

Step 3 Deal with the depreciation adjustment (W2) and the stock adjustment (W3). Calculate goodwill on acquisition of both subsidiaries and the amortisation charge for the year (W4 and W8). You should now be able to complete the profit and loss account working as far as gross profit.

Step 4 Calculate the profit on disposal of shares in Berg plc (W5) and the amounts to be included in the profit and loss account in respect of the associate (W7). Then complete the profit and loss account working as far as profit after tax.

Step 5 Calculate minority interests (W6). Then complete the profit and loss account working. Draw up the consolidated profit and loss account.

Step 6 Calculate the balance on group reserves (part (b)).

Items not required by the Examiner for this question:

- notes to the consolidated profit and loss account

The examiner's answer

(a)

Wright Group plc
Group profit and loss account for the year ended 31 December 1998

	£m	£m	£m
Turnover			
Continuing operations			
Ongoing		18,600	
Acquisition – Chang plc		1,200	
			19,800
Cost of sales			(13,232)
Gross profit			6,568
Distribution costs		1,965	
Administrative expenses		195	
			(2,160)

Operating profit		
Continuing operations		
Ongoing	4,112	
Acquisitions	296	4,408
Profit on disposal of shares in subsidiary	47	
Costs of restructuring	(34)	13
		4,421
Share of operating profit in associate		37
Bank interest receivable – group	35	
– associates	2	37
Interest payable – group	37	
– associates	2	(39)
		(2)
Profit on ordinary activities		4,456
*Tax on profit on ordinary activities		(1,432)
Profit on ordinary activities after taxation		3,024
Minority interests – equity		(61)
Profit attributable to members of the parent company		2,963
Dividends		(200)
Retained profit for the year		2,763
*Tax relates to the following:		
Parent and Subsidiaries		1,417
Associate		15
		1,432

(b)   **Balance on Wright Group reserves 31 December 1998**

	£m
Wright's reserves – 1.1.98	8,500
Berg's reserves– 1.1.98 (324 – 300) × 80%	19
Profit for period	2,763
Goodwill written off	(60)
Balance at 31.12.98	11,222
Alternative calculation	
Wright's retained profits	11,097
Profit on sale of shares (in Wright's accounts)	50
Berg's retained profits (40% × (400 – 300 – 38))	39
Chang's retained profits	102
Goodwill written off (60 + 44 – 38)	(66)
	11,222

Did you answer the question?

Notice that part (b) is presented as a calculation, showing the composition of the balance. Two possible presentations are shown.

Workings

1

	Wright	Berg (1/2)	Chang (3/4)	Ass Co	Goodwill	Adj	Total
Turnover	18,000	600	1,200				19,800
Cost of sales	12,000	420	795		36		13,251
Fixed assets dep'n			(5)				(5)
Restructuring costs	(14)						(14)
	11,986	420	790		36		13,232
Distribution costs	1,800	60	105				1,965
Admin. expenses	180	6	9				195
Associated Co				(45)	8		(37)
Interest payable	30	4	3	2			39
Bank interest receivable	(15)	(5)	(15)	(2)			(37)
Exceptional item	14		20				34
Taxation	1,320	37	60				1,417
Associates taxation				15			15
	3,329	102	182	(30)	8		3,591
Profit for period	2,685	78	228	30	(44)		2,977
Profit on disposal	50					(3)	47
Inter group div	112	(32)	(80)				-
Minority interests		(15)	(46)				(61)
Dividend	(200)						(200)
	2,647	31	102	30	(44)	(3)	2,763

2   The depreciation on the fixed assets of Chang needs adjustment for the revaluation adjustment This amounts to £30m × 20% × 9/12, ie, £4.5 million.

Downsizing can only be classified under discontinued operations where there is a material effect on the nature and focus of the operations. Therefore the main effect of this restructuring is to show the costs (£14m) as a non-operating exceptional item and to eliminate them from the cost of sales. Therefore the total adjustment to cost of sales is £18.5m.

3   *Chang plc stock* – the cost of sales of Chang will be calculated as follows:

	£m
Stock at acquisition (240 – 40)	200
Purchases 3/4 × (1,020 – 150 + 350)	915
less closing stock (350 – 30)	(320)
	795

4   *Goodwill*

	£m
Chang plc	
Purchase consideration	700
less net assets acquired 80% × (750 + 20)	(616)
Goodwill	84
Charge for year ÷ 4	21

The post acquisition provision of £20 million will be eliminated from the goodwill calculation and charged to post acquisition profits. It is assumed that this provision will be accrued for in the group profit and loss account and included as a non-operating exceptional item.

5   *Profit on sale of shares of Berg*

	£m	£m
Proceeds of sale		350
Less net assets sold		
Equity share capital	250	
Share premium	50	
Retained profit (b/f)	324	
add 1/2 year profit	78	
	702 × 40%	(280.8)
		69.2
Goodwill relating to disposal not written off (60 − 15) × 40/80		(22.5)
Profit on sale of shares		46.7

Alternative calculation

		£m
Proceeds		350
Cost of inv. (40/80 of 600)		(300)
Profit in Wright's account		50
less		
Opening reserves	324	
Profit for six months	78	
less profits at acquisition	(300)	
	102 × 40%	(40.8)
		9.2
add goodwill written off (120 × 40/80 − 22.5)		37.5
		46.7

6   *Minority interest*

	£m
Berg – 20% × 78	15.6
Chang – 20% × 228	45.6
	61.2

7   *Associated Company profit*

	£m
Operating profit for the year - Berg	228
Operating profit for the half year	114
Less: Inter company profit	(3)
	111
Operating profit relating to associate (40%)	44.4
Less: Goodwill	(7.5)
	36.9
Less: Interest payable (4 × .4)	(1.6)

Add: Bank interest receivable (5 × .4)	2.0	
Less: Tax on profit (74 × 40% × 1/2)	(14.8)	
	22.5	

The inter company sales of £60 million would not affect the turnover in the group profit and loss account as they occurred when Berg was an associate. The goodwill charged on associates would be disclosed.

8   *Berg*

	£m	£m
Purchase consideration		600
Less net assets acquired		
Share capital	250	
Share premium	50	
Retained earnings	300	
	600 × 80%	(480)
Goodwill		120
Less: Written off (two years)		(60)
Balance at 1.1.98		60
Less: Written off 1998		
Goodwill		(15)
(as an associate) 1.7.98 – 31.12.98		(7.5)
Less: Written off on sale of shares		(22.5)
		15

The charge for goodwill amortisation in the consolidated profit and loss account in cost of sales is Berg £15m and Chang (working 4) £21m ie, £36m.

9   It is assumed that the exceptional item is material and that the costs of restructuring would be shown in the financial statements.

64   (Answer 2 of examination)

Examiner's comments and marking guide

Question 2: The question sought to test candidates' knowledge of different measurement systems with particular reference to replacement cost accounting (RCA), and net realisable value (NRV) accounting techniques. It also required candidates to restate a set of historical cost accounts using Current (General) purchasing power accounting (CPP/GPP) and Current cost accounting (CCA). Additionally candidates required a knowledge of 'real terms' accounting. This question was poorly answered by candidates throughout all of the parts of the question. The question itself was very straightforward with very little in the way of complex calculations or analytical thinking. It required a basic understanding of the problems of RCA and NRV accounting and a similar understanding of the basic principles of CPP (GPP) and CCA. No calculations of the adjustments required under CCA were required of candidates. Candidates who understood CPP and CCA scored very well on this question but these individuals were few and far between.

This area is a core part of the syllabus and will be examined on an irregular basis in Section B of the paper. It is important for tutors and candidates to realise that the whole syllabus is examinable and will be examined over a period of time.

		Marks
(a)	Subjective	7
(b)	CPP	7

	CCA	6
(c)	Real terms	5
	Available/Maximum	25

Step by step answer plan

Step 1   Read the question again and make sure that you focus on precisely what is required. It is particularly important that you read the requirements carefully and that you allocate your time between the three parts of the question.

Step 2   Answer part (a) by writing brief paragraphs on the disadvantages of replacement cost accounting and then on the disadvantages of net realisable value accounting. Remember that there are only 7 marks available and therefore this should take no longer than 12 minutes.

Step 3   Prepare the CPP balance sheet and then calculate the loss on net monetary items (W2). Then prepare the CPP profit and loss account.

Step 4   Calculate the current cost operating adjustments (W1) and then prepare the CCA accounts. This completes part (b).

Step 5   Start part (c) by briefly explaining the 'real terms' system. Then calculate the real holding gains (W4) and the 'real terms' capital maintenance adjustment (W3).

Step 6   Present the relevant extracts from the profit and loss account and the balance sheet under the 'real terms' system, with any explanatory notes that are necessary.

Items not required by the Examiner for this question:

* detailed explanations of CPP and CCA accounting.

The examiner's answer

(a)   Replacement cost accounting is often thought to be more relevant to investors than historical cost accounting. However there are disadvantages with this form of accounting:

1   Replacement cost accounting (RCA) is often criticised on the grounds that the measurements can be subjective. Indices are often used in the measurement of assets and these values may be unreliable.

2   This system is based on the assumption that the firm is a going concern and that reliable entry price data is available and can be readily obtained. This may be a problem during a period of technological change as the replacement cost may relate to a new generation of asset rather than the existing asset.

3   RCA does not take account of changes in the general price level and gains and losses on holding monetary assets and liabilities.

4   There is a problem in correctly specifying what 'replacement cost' price actually means. The question arises as to the purpose of holding the assets as this will determine its value. There are alternative interpretations of 'replacement cost'. For example it can mean the used value or the reproduction cost or the cost of an equivalent asset.

Similarly there are significant disadvantages with a net realisable value method of valuation:

1   This system is only relevant for assets that are expected to be sold and for which a second-hand market exists. It will be more difficult to determine an exit value for specialised equipment with little or no alternative use.

2   The exit price has little relevance for assets that the firm expects to use. The disclosure of the cash value is not likely to be relevant to a user interested in the profitability of the company.

3   It is difficult to value certain assets/liabilities at their exit value. There is a problem of valuing intangibles and goodwill, and also of the valuation of liabilities. The problem arises as to whether liabilities should be valued at their contractual amounts or at amounts required to fund the liabilities.

4   There is a contradiction between the realisation principle and the established assumption that the company is a going concern.

5   As with RCA an exit based system does not take into account changes in the general price level.

Did you answer the question?

The requirement is to *describe*. This means that simply listing the disadvantages as 'bullet points' will not be sufficient.

(b)

Profit and loss accounts

	CPP £m	CCA £m
Turnover	4,950	4,500
Cost of sales	(3,300)	(3,000)
Gross profit	1,650	1,500
Distribution and administrative expenses	(550)	(500)
Current cost operating adjustment (W1)		(1,150)
Loss on net monetary items (W2)	(280)	
Operating profit (loss)	820	(150)
Gearing adjustment		423
Profit before taxation	820	273
Taxation	(300)	(300)
Profit/(loss) after taxation	520	(27)

Balance sheets

	CPP	CCA
Fixed assets (net of depreciation)	2,200	2,400
Current assets and liabilities		
Stock	1,320	1,600
Debtors	2,400	2,400
Cash	300	300
Creditors: amounts falling due in one year	(1,200)	(1,200)
Net current assets	2,820	3,100
Creditors: amounts falling due after one year	(1,500)	(1,500)
	3,520	4,000
Capital and reserves		
Share capital	3,000	2,500
Reserves – Profit/(loss)	520	(27)
Capital maintenance		1,527
	3,520	4,000

Note that there are alternative presentations of the above information.

WORKINGS

1   **Current cost operating adjustments**

	£m
Monetary working capital adjustment	400
Depreciation adjustment	120
Cost of sales adjustment (3,750 – 3,000 – 120)	630
	1,150

2   **Capital maintenance**

	£m	£m
CPP – Loss on short-term monetary items		
Bank movements		
Capital		(500)
Fixed assets (2,860 – 2,600)		260
Turnover (4,950 – 4,500)		(450)
Distribution costs (550 – 500)		50
Purchases		360
Loan raised		(20)
		(300)

Purchases = COS (3,300 – 3,000) + stock (1,320 – 1,200) – depreciation (660 – 600) ie, 360

	£m
Loss on short-term monetary items	(300)
Gain on long-term monetary items	20
	(280)

CCA		
Current cost adjustment		
MWCA	400	
COSA	630	
Gearing	(423)	
		607
Fixed assets		520
Stock		400
		1,527

(c)   If general inflation is a significant factor in an economy, it may be suitable to adjust a current value system for the effects of inflation in order to produce a 'real terms' system. This system can be presented in several ways. Normally the total real gains are determined by utilising CPP accounting. This essentially takes account of the increase in asset values and deducts a charge for general inflation.

Working 4 shows this calculation which results in a real holding gain of £560m. The profit for the year would be adjusted for this amount. Additionally current cost adjustments would be dealt with in the financial statements as well as a computation of the amount required to maintain the capital of the company. The profit for the period could be calculated as follows:

	£m
Operating loss – CCA	(150)
Real holding gains	560
Taxation	(300)
Profit	110

The balance sheet could be shown as follows:

	£m	
Net assets – CCA		4,000
		─────
Share capital		3,000
Profit		110
Capital maintenance (working 3)		890
		─────
		4,000

Did you answer the question?

The requirement is quite clear that you are required to illustrate your answer using AB, in other words, with figures. A description of the 'real terms' system on its own would not earn maximum marks.

WORKINGS

		£m	£m
3	**Real terms CCA**		
	Current cost reserve (above without gearing adj.)		1,950
	(1,527 + 423)		
	Real holding gains		(560)
	Capital maintenance		(500)
			─────
			890
4	**Real holding gains adjustment**		
	Stock – current value	1,600	
	– CPP	1,320	
		─────	
			280
	Fixed assets – current value	3,120	
	– CPP	2,860	
		─────	
			260
	Gain on monetary items		20
			─────
			560

---

65   (Answer 3 of examination)

Examiner's comments and marking guide

Question 3: This question required candidates to implement and comment on the fairness of a scheme of reconstruction. The question again was quite straightforward and candidates performed quite well in part (a) where a balance sheet had to be produced after the implementation of the scheme. However, part (b) was poorly answered. This part of the question required candidates to comment on the fairness of the scheme of reconstruction. Very little meaningful comment was forthcoming from many candidates. Many candidates showed several computations in part (b) but failed to discuss these computations in any depth or in some cases at all. The aim of part (b) of the question was to examine whether candidates had the necessary experience and knowledge to explain the impact of a reconstruction scheme on the parties involved and unfortunately in many cases this ability was lacking.

		Marks
(a)	Balance sheet – Capital reduction account	7
	Ordinary shares	3
	Cash	4
	Creditors – short term	2
	Creditors – long term	1
	Fixed assets	1
	Current assets	1
	Preference shares	1

Capital contribution		1
	Available	21
	Maximum	15

(b)
Preference shareholders		2
Unsecured debenture stock (8%)		2
Minority interest		4
Majority shareholding		5
Merchant bank		1
Finance		1
	Available	15
	Maximum	10
	Available	36
	Maximum	25

Step by step answer plan

Step 1 Read the question again and make sure that you focus on precisely what is required. It is important to note that there are two requirements: you are required to comment on the reconstruction scheme as well as to prepare a balance sheet after it has been implemented.

Step 2 Complete the main workings: capital reduction (reconstruction account); ordinary share capital; redeemable preference shares; and cash. These may either be presented as in the Examiner's Answer, or as 'T' accounts.

Step 3 Draw up the balance sheet to complete part (a), which should have taken about 25 minutes in total.

Step 4 Approach part (b) by writing about each of the affected parties in turn. Remember to present your calculations as part of your answer, rather than as workings (the question specifically asks for this).

The examiner's answer

(a)

XYZ Ltd
Balance sheet after reconstruction

	£m	£m
Fixed assets		40
Current assets	70	
Creditors: amounts falling due within one year	(41)	
Net current assets		29
Creditors: amounts falling due after more than one year		(50)
		19
Capital and reserves		
Called up share capital		11.2
7% convertible preference shares		2
Capital contribution	10	
Less capital reserve	(4.2)	
		5.8
		19

WORKINGS

(i)   **Capital reduction**

	£m
Ordinary shares of £1	32
Preference shares dividend arrears	2
Outside shareholders holding of ordinary shares	0.8
Directors' loans	8
Family preference shares	5.5
Preference shares redeemed – balance	1.5
Debentures redeemed balance	3
	——
	52.8
Less:	
Outside shareholders holding converted to preference shares (4m × .5)	(2)
Net assets written down – intangible	(15)
– tangible	(5)
– current assets	(5)
Increase in creditors	(9)
Profit and loss account	(21)
	——
	57
	——
Balance	(4.2)
	——

(ii)   **Ordinary shares**

Opening balance	40
Less:	
Reduction to 20p shares	(32)
Outside shareholders offered preference shares	(0.8)
Add: Shares issued for cash	4
	——
	11.2
	——

(iii)   **Redeemable preference shares**

	£m
Opening balance	11
Less:	
Capital reduction – family shares	(5.5)
Preference shares redeemed – cash	(4)
Outside preference shares cap. reduction	(1.5)
	——
Closing balance	0
	——

(iv)   **Cash/(overdraft)**

Opening balance	(5)
Cash from ordinary shares	4
Loan stock proceeds – bank	25
– family	25
Capital contribution – PQ plc	10
	——
	59
Less: Preference shares (5m at 80p)	(4)
Debenture stock at par	(35)
	——
	20
	——

(v)   **Creditors: amounts falling due within one year**

Balance	47
Fair value adjustment	9
Directors' loans	(8)
Bank overdraft	(5)
Arrears of preference dividend	(2)
	41

(b)   The proposed capital reduction scheme has differing impacts depending upon the nature of the relationship with XYZ Ltd.

Preference shareholders (outside)

At present the preference shareholders are not receiving payment of dividends although if the profit forecast is accurate, then dividends may become payable in several years time. There is no asset backing for the preference shareholders as the creditors will require payment before any excess is paid to the preference shareholders and given the fair values of the assets, this seems to be unlikely. Thus a payment of 50p per share seems to be quite acceptable in the light of the above comments.

8% Unsecured debenture stock

The future cover for debenture interest will be $\dfrac{\pounds 8\,\text{million}}{\pounds 2.8\,\text{million}} = 2.86$

This cover is reasonably satisfactory but is dependent upon future profits being earned. Similarly the asset cover for the debentures is quite poor as the debentures are unsecured and would rank alongside the other creditors in the event of liquidation.

	HC £m	Fair value £m
Total assets (excluding intangible)	100	90
Total liabilities	85	95
Cover	1.25	0.95

Thus when the asset cover is based on fair values there is sufficient assets to cover the debentures and creditors. Additionally some of the short-term creditors (tax, VAT, wages) may rank for priority of repayment before the debenture holders. Thus an offer of redemption at par value without any premium would seem to be acceptable.

Minority interest (10%) – ordinary shares

There will be no asset backing for the ordinary shares and possible future earnings without the reconstruction scheme would be:

	£m
Profit before tax and interest	8
less debenture interest	(2.8)
	5.2
less taxation (at 30%)	(1.6)
	3.6
less preference dividend	1.0
	2.6
Earnings per share (shares 40 million)	6.5p

However the debit balance on the profit and loss account will have to be eliminated before any dividends are paid and together with the lack of asset backing, the minority interest are unlikely to object to the scheme especially as there are conversion rights attached to the preference shares and the fact that the preference shares are cumulative.

Majority shareholding

These persons are subscribing the additional risk capital. The control of the company is likely to change.

	Before scheme		After scheme	
	Shares *(m)*	*%*	*Shares* *(m)*	*%*
Family	34	85	7.8	70
PQ plc	2	5	3.4	30
Others	4	10	–	
	40	100	11.2	100

Although the family still maintains control, PQ plc now has a substantial interest in the company and is likely to want representation on the board of directors. Additionally the family is loaning the company £12.5 million without any security and similarly PQ plc is giving the company a capital contribution of £10 million and loaning the company £12.5 million without security. The family and PQ are receiving a higher rate of interest than the merchant bank on the debentures because of a lack of security of the loan.

The forecast profit for the future based upon the projected profit would be

	1999 £'000	2000 £'000	2001 £'000
Profit before interest and tax	8,000	10,000	12,500
Less: Debenture interest (2,500 + 2,000)	(4,500)	(4,500)	(4,500)
	3,500	5,500	8,000
Less: Taxation 30%	(1,050)	(1,650)	(2,400)
	2,450	3,850	5,600
Less: Preference dividend	(140)	(140)	(140)
Available for ordinary shareholders	2,310	3,710	5,460
Capital invested	11,200		
Returns on capital invested	20.6%	33.1%	48.8%

Thus if the projected profit is accurate, then the return on capital invested is good. PQ plc must presumably be looking to take over the company, particularly as it has been prepared to make a capital contribution without any interest. (In PQ plc's books this contribution will be included in the cost of the investment in XYZ Ltd.) It appears therefore that the scheme will be acceptable to all parties including the merchant bank which is providing a secured loan. The scheme also provides sufficient working capital for the maintenance of operations.

Did you answer the question?

The answer makes as many relevant points as possible, thus meeting the key requirement to *discuss*. Notice the way in which the answer is structured. It takes each party to the scheme in turn, discusses whether the scheme is fair to them and then reaches a conclusion as to whether it will be accepted. In this way it addresses both parts of the requirement.

---

66   (Answer 4 of examination)

Examiner's comments and marking guide

Question 4: This question required candidates to discuss the impairment of assets in terms of the indicators of an impairment loss and the recognition and measurement of the impairment loss under FRS 11. The final part of the question required candidates to apply the principles of part (a) to two small cases.

Candidates performed very well on this question and scored heavily, particularly on parts (a) and (bi). However, answers to part (bii) were not as good with candidates not realising that the carrying amount of the assets should not be reduced below their net realisable value.

Overall the question was well answered.

			Marks
(a)	(i)	1 mark per circumstance up to maximum	7
	(ii)	Definition of recoverable amount	1
		Proposed approach	1
		Procedural aspect of impairment loss	7
			—
		Available	9
			—
		Maximum	7
			—
(b)	(i)	Impairment review	1
		Comparison with recoverable amount	1
		Calculation of NPV	1
		Discussion of impairment	2
	(ii)	As at 1.2.98	4
		As at 1.3.98	4
			—
			13
			—
		Maximum	11
			—
		Available	29
			—
		Maximum	25
			—

Step by step answer plan

Step 1 Read the question again and make sure that you focus on precisely what is required. The style is fairly typical of this Examiner's questions on current or recent developments: a discursive section followed by a practical section in which you are required to apply the requirements of FRS 11. Each section is split into two so that there are four parts to answer in all. Therefore it is very important to allocate your time.

Step 2 Complete part (a)(i) by restating the appropriate part of FRS 11. This should take about 12 minutes.

Step 3 Answer part (a)(ii) by explaining how impairment is measured and then how it is recognised. (This is the logical order in which to tackle the two aspects of the requirement, even though the question says 'recognition and measurement'.) This section should also take about 12 minutes.

Step 4 Calculate the impairment loss and then explain your calculation to answer part (b)(i). This should take about 7 minutes.

Step 5 Start part (b)(ii) by allocating the impairment loss at 1 February 1998 and then allocate the impairment loss at 1 March 1998. Then briefly explain your allocation to complete the question.

Items not required by the Examiner for this question: general discussion of FRS 11 not related to the specific requirements of the question.

The examiner's answer

(a)   (i)   A review for impairment of a fixed asset should be carried out if events or changes in circumstance indicate that the carrying amount may not be recoverable. In identifying whether an impairment of a tangible fixed asset may have occurred an enterprise should consider the following indications:

-     there has been a significant decrease in the market value of the asset in excess of the normal process of depreciation

-     there has been a significant adverse change in either the business or the market in which the asset is involved.   This will include changes in the technological, economic or legal environment in which the enterprise operates and changes in market interest rates or other market rates of return

-     there has been a significant adverse change in the manner in which the asset has been used

-     evidence is available that indicates that the economic performance of the asset will be worse than expected

-     the asset has suffered considerable physical change, or obsolescence or physical damage

-     there has been an accumulation of costs significantly in excess of those originally expected in the acquisition or construction of an asset so that it may affect profitability

-     the management is committed to a significant reorganisation programme or redundancy of key employees

-     where an asset is valued in terms of value in use and the actual cash flows are less than the estimated cash flows before discounting

-     there has been a significant adverse change in any value indicator used to measure the fair value of the fixed asset or acquisition

-     a current period operating loss and net cash outflow combined with similar past and predicted occurrences

---

Did you answer the question?

The key requirement word is *describe* and so the answer must be more than simply a list of 'bullet points'.

(ii)   FRS 11 'Impairment of Fixed Assets and Goodwill' says that if there is an indication of impairment, then a review must be undertaken to confirm this fact and establish the extent of the impairment. The Statement of Principles states that an asset should not be valued at an amount greater than its cost or recoverable amount in a historical cost system. The recoverable amount is defined as the higher of net realisable value (if known and based on market value) and value in use (net present value of future cash flows). The above rule applies, also, to assets which have been revalued to replacement cost. The FRS 11 approach is to compare the carrying value of the asset with its recoverable amount. If the NRV or value in use exceeds the carrying value then no write down is necessary and there is no need to estimate the other amount. If the recoverable amount is lower than the carrying value, the asset is impaired. Impairment is measured on a post-tax basis.

If no reliable estimate of NRV can be made, the recoverable amount is determined by value in use alone. If the NRV is lower than the carrying amount, one should consider whether the value in use is lower still. If it is not then the recoverable amount is based on value in use not NRV.

Impairment can often be tested only for groups of assets because the cash flows used for the calculation do not arise from the use of a single asset. In these cases impairment is measured for the smallest income generating unit that produces independent income streams. To the extent that the carrying amount exceeds the value in use of the income generating unit, the unit is impaired and in the absence of impairment of specific assets, the impairment should be allocated first to goodwill, then to capitalised intangible assets and finally to tangible assets in the unit.

The consideration of past impairment losses should be recognised when the recoverable amount of a tangible fixed asset has increased because of a change in economic conditions. There must be a demonstrable reversal of the economic event which caused the impairment and this must not have originally been foreseen.

Impairment losses are recognised in the profit and loss account unless they arise on revalued assets. In the latter case they are recognised in the statement of total recognised gains and losses until the carrying value falls below depreciated historical cost. If the impairment is due to a reduction in the service potential of the asset, it is recognised in the profit and loss account. Impairments below depreciated historical cost are recognised in the profit and loss account. Where an impairment loss on a fixed asset is recognised, the remaining useful economic life should be reviewed and revised if necessary. A reversal of an impairment loss should be recognised in the profit and loss account but in the case of a revalued asset only to the extent that the original impairment loss was so recognised.

Did you answer the question?

The key requirement word here is *explain*. Simply restating the requirements of FRS 11 would not earn maximum marks.

(b)   (i)   AB will have undertaken an impairment review because of the effect of the stock losses and the problems associated with the taxi business. FRS 11 first requires an assessment of whether there was a reliable estimate of NRV and value in use. The next step would be to determine whether the value in use is less than or equal to the NRV. In this case NRV is substantially less than the carrying value (NRV £120,000, carrying value £290,000). The FRS then requires management to compare NRV with the value in use. The value in use is £248,600 (£100,000 for three years discounted at 10% per annum). As value in use is not lower than NRV, the recoverable amount will be based on value in use.

It would appear therefore that in this case the management of AB would write down the asset to its net present value of £248,600 and recognise the loss in the profit and loss account.

(ii)   AB will recognise the impairment losses relating to the taxi business in the following way. (Impairment losses should be recognised if the recoverable amount of the income generating unit is less than the carrying value of the items of that unit.)

At 1 February 1998

	1.1.98 £000	Impairment loss £000	1.2.98 £000
Goodwill	40	(15)	25
Intangible assets	30		30
Vehicles	120	(30)	90
Sundry net assets	40		40
	230	(45)	185

An impairment loss of £30,000 is recognised first for the stolen vehicles and the balance (£15,000) is attributed to goodwill.

At 1 March 1998

	1.2.98 £'000	Impairment loss £'000	1.3.98 £'000
Goodwill	25	(25)	
Intangible assets	30	(5)	25
Vehicles	90		90
Sundry net assets	40		40
	185	(30)	155

AB recognises a further impairment loss of £30,000 although the value in use of the business is lower (£150,000), the carrying amounts of the individual assets are not reduced below their net realisable value.

Any impairment loss should usually be allocated in priority to those assets which have the most subjective valuations. Thus impairment identified in this way should usually be allocated firstly to goodwill, thereafter to intangible assets for which there is no active market and finally to any tangible assets in the unit. However, in doing this no asset should be written down to below its net realisable value.

(Tutorial Note: Since this question was originally set, SSAP 12 has been superseded by FRS 15 *Tangible fixed assets.* As a result, one sentence has been deleted from the answer to part (b)(i); the rest of the answer is still valid.*)*

67 (Answer 5 of examination)

Examiner's comments and marking guide

Question 5: This question dealt with the recent mergers of the large firms of accountants requiring candidates to discuss the reasons for these mergers and the potential problems created by these mergers.

Candidates' answers to this question were excellent. The question gave candidates the opportunity to deal with a topical issue and they dealt with it remarkably well. The main problem was that many candidates merely listed points and often these points were not even in a coherent sentence. Candidates who answer questions requiring discussion of a topic by utilising a list of points can expect to lose a small amount of marks because they were ignoring the rubric of the question.

		Marks
(a)	Global market	1
	Multinational companies	1
	Cover and skills	1
	Organic growth	1
	Consultancy	1
	Investment	1
	Acquisitions	1
	Corporate finance	1
	Legal liability	2
	Independence	2
	Available	12
	Maximum	10
(b)	Restriction in choice/audit concentration	2
	Conflicts of interest	2
	Consultancy	2
	Limiting liability	1
	Self regulation	1
	Overlap of services	1
	Regulators	2
	Compatibility	1
	Realignment	1
	Redundancy	1
	Available	14
	Maximum	10
	Available	26
	Maximum	20

Step by step answer plan

Step 1   Read the question again and make sure that you focus on precisely what is required.

Step 2   Answer part (a) from the point of view of audit firms wishing to merge. Write in short paragraphs, each paragraph making a different point.

Step 3   In part (b) you can identify problems encountered by each of the parties involved; firms, clients, regulators. Three points for each of these three parties should be enough to earn the 10 marks available.

The examiner's answer

(a)   The largest firms of auditors compete for client services on a global scale and look to increase their share of this global market. Therefore a merger between two firms would create an audit firm whose sheer size would increase its world-wide reach so that it could provide multinational companies with a wide range of professional services in all parts of the world. A merger between such firms would also give the firm a more comprehensive cover in terms of the expertise available. One firm may have skills in telecommunications and the other in the media and entertainment sectors, for example.

Organic growth is extremely difficult for large firms of auditors and therefore mergers seem inevitable if they are to expand their business. A key component of the accountants' business is the management consultancy sector and it is the need to globalise these services which can lead to mergers. Consultancy work accounts for a significant proportion of the firms' total revenue and is growing faster than the rate of audit work. In order to compete in this expanding market, audit firms need to be competitive and size appears to enhance their competitiveness.

Mergers increase the size of the funds available for investment. Whilst traditional audit and accountancy work requires mainly intellectual capital, the new range of consultancy services offered are more capital intensive. Similarly mergers allow the firm to make acquisitions of other consultancy companies. Although the audit market is dominated by a small number of firms, the accountants have to compete with many organisations when offering consultancy services. In the area of corporate financial advice, the market place is dominated by merchant banks. A merger of large audit firms would threaten this domination.

By increasing their size, auditors are more likely to be able to sustain the impact of large legal liability claims against them. Insurance companies do not completely indemnify audit firms against damages awarded against them. Thus the smaller the audit firm the larger the impact on individual partners of the damages not covered by insurance companies.

It is possible to argue that mergers could enhance the independence of auditors. Directors essentially appoint and remunerate the auditor albeit by recommendation to the Annual General Meeting and formal approval by the shareholders. The influence that a major client may have on an audit firm is diminished by an increase in the size of the audit firm. The merger between Price Waterhouse and Coopers and Lybrand has resulted in an entity which audits a large proportion of the FTSE 100 companies in the UK. The loss of one of these audit clients would not affect the credibility and income of the combined firm quite as much as if one of the two merging parties lost such a client. Thus the influence of the directors is diminished and independence enhanced.

(b)   Although there are many auditing firms throughout the world, the reduction in the number of major audit firms will restrict the choice of auditors for the multinational companies and a concentration of the audit market will occur. Conflicts of interest could therefore arise where a large firm of auditors was servicing too many competing clients. In an environment where auditors are now assessing 'business risk' it seems that independence is going to be compromised where auditors assess the risk by reference to an industrial sector where they may audit a significant number of the companies in that sector.

The provision of consultancy and other services to clients has been seen as endangering the independence of auditors' opinions. The creation of larger audit practices will encourage public debate about the merits of allowing giant audit firms to sell other services to their audit clients. As audit firms become larger the risk of the abuse of their position becomes greater.

Auditors throughout the world have been campaigning for the limitation of their liability by legislative change. The growth of audit firms into entities which are large by world corporate standards weakens the arguments for limiting auditors liability as it might appear that the current liability position may be acting as a measure of control over these audit giants. Self regulation of the accounting profession may appear to third parties to mean domination by a small number of firms. A merger of audit firms strengthens the hands of the critics of self regulation and is perhaps more likely to lead to government intervention in the audit process.

The merger of audit firms will lead to an overlap of the services provided by the merging firms and possible duplication of resources which in turn would lead to redundancies. A merger between two major international firms will always lead to scrutiny by the regulators of the United States, United Kingdom and the European Union. If it is accepted by two of these bodies and not by the other one, then the country(ies) concerned will be isolated in its (their) attitude to such a merger. Such isolation would be untenable in the 'global' economy and thus it is likely that if such mergers are acceptable to most regulators, the other regulators will follow suit. For example the Price Waterhouse/Coopers and Lybrand merger resulted in a firm which is second largest in the US and which in Europe would have 21% of the accountancy market. In these terms one could argue that the merger was bound to be accepted by the US and the EU, and that therefore the UK had to concur with their judgement.

When large audit firms merge, their practices are not necessarily compatible or their partners totally in agreement with the merger. The senior partners determine the nature of the merger and it is voted upon by the remainder of the partners. In the case of the Price Waterhouse/Coopers and Lybrand merger, 8,500 partners had to vote to accept the proposal and disagreement led to several partners resigning and forming new practices, or joining rival audit firms.

Mergers can result in a realignment of clients. Many companies receive tax advice from one firm and audit services from another firm. If a merger means that these firms are the same entity then the client may go elsewhere for one of the services. Also clients may not like the audit concentration in one sector and may change auditors.

68 (Answer 6 of examination)

Examiner's comments and marking guide

Question 6: This question dealt with ethics and in particular in part (a) with integrity, objectivity and independence. Part (b) of the question dealt with the unethical practices of candidates. The question was answered quite well. However, in part (a), several candidates ignored the requirements of the question and merely listed the rules of independence without any discussion of integrity and objectivity. The question required an overview of the role of practitioners in maintaining the professional code of conduct. Some candidates simply ignored this and listed pages of their books by rote. A candidate cannot hope to gain marks if the nature of the question is ignored. In part (b), two cases of possible unethical behaviour were cited and candidates had to comment on them. Many candidates did not see the ethical dilemmas involved and seemed to think that there were administrative rather than ethical problems (part bii). It was a little disappointing to find so many candidates who could not identify the ethical problem.

Overall, however, candidates performed reasonably well on the question.

			Marks
(a)		Subjective	7
(b)	(i)	Integrity	1
		Trust	1
		Professionalism	1
		Credibility	1
		Informed practice if failed	1
		Pressures	1
		Knowingly falsified	1
		Truthfulness	1
		Action	2
			—
		Available	10
			—
		Maximum	7

(ii)	Serious	1
	Falsification of records – implications	1
	Time budgets etc	1
	Audit risk	1
	Litigation	1
	Evidence	1
	Reperformance	1
	Discipline – firm	1
	– ACCA	1
	Conclusion	1

Available	10
Maximum	6
Available	27
Maximum	20

Step by step answer plan

Step 1   Read the question again and make sure that you focus on precisely what is required.

Step 2   In part (a), try and deal separately with each of integrity, objectivity and independence. They are not the same as each other. Concentrate on actions that individual practitioners can take.

Step 3   There are two requirements in part (b) for each of the scenarios: discuss the situation and how the audit partner should proceed. This part is clearly dealing with the topic of integrity, and may offer some points that could be made in part (a) on integrity. Since the requirement is to 'discuss', you should offer a number of possible alternatives in your answer to part (b), rather than being too specific.

The examiner's answer

(a)   Practitioners should behave with integrity in all professional relationships and should not subject themselves to influences which may affect their objectivity. Practitioner independence relates to individual accountants in the performance of their work and is concerned with integrity, refusal to have their opinion influenced and freedom from self interest. The individual practitioner has the responsibility of maintaining a state of mind which results in independent actions. There are specific areas where they must maintain their independence.

The auditor must not be influenced or succumb to pressures concerning the work to be performed or techniques to be utilised. Auditors must develop their own audit programmes and must not be pressurised by management or anyone else into modifying their work. Their work should only be reviewed by their professional peers and not by management. The auditor must not be restricted in his work and no source of information should be unavailable to the auditor. Access to the books and records and transactional data should not be denied the auditor.

The practitioner should be free from any pressures to suppress facts revealed by the audit work. There should be no undue influence on his reporting or judgement, and there should be no sense of obligation to anyone other than to the statutory duties placed on the auditor. Such pressures may be in the form of fee dependence where a practitioner is dependent on the income from one particular client.

Professional independence relates to both individuals and the profession as a whole. Both parties are important constituents if the image of the profession is to be maintained and the public assured of the integrity of the profession.

(b)   (i)   It is important that all students act with integrity at all times and can be trusted by clients and other members of the audit firm. One way of looking at the incident is to say that the student lied about her examinations and therefore cannot be trusted to act in a professional manner, and should be disciplined accordingly either by the audit firm or by the ACCA. Her credibility with the audit senior has been tarnished and the question arises as to whether the student would have informed the practice about the examinations she had taken if she had failed. If this attitude is taken then the student may be asked to leave and the ACCA informed of the student's conduct.

A more lenient view might be that the student was succumbing to the pressures of the accounting world and it was her inexperience which caused her to react in this way and she should be cautioned and her future conduct scrutinised. However, the student knowingly falsified information; she had a premeditated plan and chose to lie to her seniors about a matter which could influence her career. Such an action would undermine her integrity and the matter should be dealt with in the same manner as any breach of integrity. A fundamental principle of the rules of professional conduct is the fact that students should behave with integrity in all professional business and personal financial relationships. Integrity implies not merely honesty but fair dealing and truthfulness.

In this case the audit partner may consider a complaint to the ACCA if the audit senior has formally complained to the partner.

(ii)   This accusation about the student is in many ways more serious than the first one. If the student is falsifying records then this has major implications for the firm and the student. Falsification of time records will affect the time budgets, the audit fee and future audits. Falsification of audit work will increase the audit risk and potentially lead to litigation against the audit firm. However, before any action can be taken, evidence as to the truthfulness of the accusation must be gathered. Audit tasks must be reperformed by the audit senior and hours spent on these audit tasks carefully analysed, scrutinised and compared with the norm for the tasks completed. Suspicions are not sufficient grounds for disciplinary action against the student. If the suspicions are proven and time is not being recorded, then the audit firm's internal disciplinary system should be adequate to deal with the problem. If audit tasks are not being performed as stated, then the ACCA may be informed and appropriate disciplinary action taken. It is unlikely that the audit firm would wish to continue employing the student. The image of the profession can only be maintained if students and members of professional bodies act with integrity.

JUNE 1999 QUESTIONS

69   (Question 1 of examination)

Section A – This ONE question is compulsory and MUST be attempted

X, a public limited company, acquired 100 million ordinary shares of £1 in Y, a public limited company on 1 April 1996 when the accumulated reserves were £120 million. Y acquired 45 million ordinary shares of £1 in Z, a public limited company, on 1 April 1994 when the accumulated reserves were £10 million. On 1 April 1994 there were no material differences between the carrying values and the fair values of Z. On 1 April 1996, the accumulated reserves of Z were £20 million.

Y acquired 30% of the ordinary shares of W, a limited company, on 1 April 1996 for £50 million when the accumulated reserves of W were £7 million. Y exercises significant influence over W and there were no material differences between the carrying values and the fair values of W at that date.

There had been no share issues since 1 April 1994 by any of the group companies. The following balance sheets relate to the group companies as at 31 March 1999.

	X £m	Y £m	Z £m	W £m
Fixed assets - tangible	900	100	30	40
- intangible		30		
Investment in Y	320			
Investment in Z		90		
Investment in W		50		
Net Current Assets	640	360	75	73
Creditors: amounts falling due after one year	(200)	(150)	(15)	(10)
	1,660	480	90	103
Share Capital	360	150	50	80
Share Premium	250	120	10	6
Accumulated reserves	1,050	210	30	17
	1,660	480	90	103

(i)   The following fair value table sets out the carrying values and fair values of certain assets and liabilities of the group companies together with any accounting policy adjustments required to ensure consistent group policies at 1 April 1996.

	Carrying value		Accounting policy adj.		Fair value adj.		New carrying value	
	Y £m	Z £m	Y £m	Z £m	Y £m	Z £m	Y £m	Z £m
Tangible fixed assets	90	20			30	10	120	30
Intangible fixed assets	30		(30)				-	
Stocks	20	12	2		(8)	(5)	14	7
Provision for bad debts	(15)				(9)		(24)	

These values had not been incorporated into the financial records. Group companies have consistent accounting policies as at 31 March 1999.

(ii) During the year ended 31 March 1999, Z had sold goods to X and Y. At 31 March 1999, there were £44 million of these goods in the stock of X and £16 million in the stock of Y. Z had made a profit of 25% on selling price on the goods.

(iii) On 1 June 1996, an amount of £36 million was received by Y from an arbitration award against Q. This receipt was secured as a result of an action against Q prior to Y's acquisition by X but was not included in the assets of Y at 1 April 1996.

(iv) The group charges depreciation on all tangible fixed assets on the straight line basis at 10% per annum and formerly wrote-off goodwill immediately to reserves. However it has decided to utilise the transitional provisions of FRS 10 'Goodwill and Intangible Assets' and reinstate and capitalise the goodwill and amortise it over 11 years from the date of acquisition.

Required:

(a) Prepare a consolidated balance sheet as at 31 March 1999 for the X group. **(26 marks)**

(b) Describe the transitional provisions of FRS 10 relating to the reinstatement of goodwill which has previously been written off to reserves. **(4 marks)**

(All calculations should be rounded to the nearest £ million). **(Total: 30 marks)**

Section B – TWO questions ONLY to be attempted

70 (Question 2 of examination)

(a) For enterprises that are engaged in different businesses with differing risks and opportunities, the usefulness of financial information concerning these enterprises is greatly enhanced if it is supplemented by information on individual business segments. It is recognised that there are two main approaches to segmental reporting. The 'risk and returns' approach where segments are identified on the basis of different risks and returns arising from different lines of business and geographical areas, and the 'managerial' approach whereby segments are identified corresponding to the enterprises' internal organisation structure.

Required:

(i) Explain why the information content of financial statements is improved by the inclusion of segmental data on individual business segments. **(5 marks)**

(ii) Discuss the advantages and disadvantages of analysing segmental data using

the 'risk and returns' approach **(4 marks)**

the 'managerial' approach. **(3 marks)**

(b) AZ, a public limited company, operates in the global marketplace.

(i) The major revenue-earning asset is a fleet of aircraft which are registered in the UK and its other main source of revenue comes from the sale of holidays. The directors are unsure as to how business segments are identified. **(3 marks)**

(ii) The company also owns a small aircraft manufacturing plant which supplies aircraft to its domestic airline and to third parties. The preferred method for determining transfer prices for these aircraft between the group companies is market price, but where the aircraft is of a specialised nature with no equivalent market price the companies fix the price by negotiation. **(2 marks)**

(iii)   The company has incurred an exceptional loss on the sale of several aircraft to a foreign government. This loss occurred due to a fixed price contract signed several years ago for the sale of secondhand aircraft and resulted through the fluctuation of the exchange rates between the two countries.   **(3 marks)**

(iv)   During the year the company discontinued its holiday business due to competition in the sector.   **(2 marks)**

(v)   The company owns 40% of the ordinary shares of Eurocat Ltd, a specialist aircraft engine producer with operations in China and Russia. The investment is accounted for by the equity method and it is proposed to exclude the company's results from segment assets and revenue.   **(3 marks)**

Required:

Discuss the implications of each of the above points for the determination of the segmental information required to be prepared and disclosed under SSAP 25 'Segmental Reporting' and FRS 3 'Reporting Financial Performance'.

Please note that the mark allocation is shown after each paragraph in part (b).

(Total: 25 marks)

---

71   (Question 3 of examination)

(a)   FRS 9 'Associates and Joint Ventures' deals not only with the accounting treatment of associated companies and joint venture operations but covers certain types of joint business arrangements not carried on through a separate entity. The main changes made by FRS 9 are to restrict the circumstances in which equity accounting can be applied and to provide detailed rules for accounting for joint ventures.

Required:

(i)   Explain the criteria which distinguish an associate from an ordinary fixed asset investment.
                                                                                (6 marks)

(ii)   Explain the principal difference between a joint venture and a 'joint arrangement' and the impact that this classification has upon the accounting for such relationships.   **(4 marks)**

(b)   The following financial statements relate to Baden, a public limited company.

**Profit and loss account
for year ended 31 December 1998**

	£m	£m
Turnover		212
Cost of sales		(170)
Gross profit		42
Distribution costs	17	
Administrative costs	8	
		(25)
		17

Other operating income		12
Operating profit		29
Exceptional item		(10)
Interest payable		(4)
Profit on ordinary activities before tax		15
Taxation on profit on ordinary activities		(3)
		12
Ordinary dividend - paid		(4)
Retained profit for year		8

Balance Sheet at 31 December 1998

	£m	£m
Fixed assets - tangible	30	
goodwill	7	
		37
Current assets	31	
Creditors: amounts falling due within one year	(12)	
Net current assets		19
Total assets less current liabilities		56
Creditors: amounts falling due after more than one year		(10)
		46
Capital and Reserves		
Called up share capital –		
Ordinary shares of £1		10
Share premium account		4
Profit and loss account		32
		46

(i)   Cable, a public limited company, acquired 30% of the ordinary share capital of Baden at a cost of £14 million on 1 January 1997. The share capital of Baden has not changed since acquisition when the profit and loss reserve of Baden was £9 million.

(ii)   At 1 January 1997 the following fair values were attributed to the net assets of Baden but not incorporated in its accounting records.

	£m
	£m
Tangible fixed assets	30 (carrying value £20m)
Goodwill (estimate)	10
Current assets	31
Creditors: amounts falling due within one year	20
Creditors: amounts falling after more than one year	8

(iii) Guy, an associated company of Cable, also holds a 25% interest in the ordinary share capital of Baden. This was acquired on 1 January 1998.

(iv) During the year to 31 December 1998, Baden sold goods to Cable to the value of £35 million. The inventory of Cable at 31 December 1998 included goods purchased from Baden on which the company made a profit of £10 million.

(v) The policy of all companies in the Cable Group is to amortise goodwill over four years and to depreciate tangible fixed assets at 20% per annum on the straight line basis.

(vi) Baden does not represent a material part of the group and is significantly less than the 15% additional disclosure threshold required under FRS 9 'Associates and Joint Ventures'.

Required:

(i) Show how the investment in Baden would be stated in the consolidated balance sheet and profit and loss account of the Cable Group under FRS 9 'Associates and Joint Ventures', for the year ended 31 December 1998 on the assumption that Baden is an associate. **(9 marks)**

(ii) Show how the treatment of Baden would change if Baden was classified as an investment in a joint venture. **(6 marks)**
(Total: 25 marks)

72 (Question 4 of examination)

Earnings per share is one of the most quoted statistics in financial analysis, coming into prominence because of the widespread use of the price earnings ratio as an investment decision making yardstick. In 1972 SSAP3 'Earnings per share' was issued and revised in 1974, and the standard as amended was operating reasonably effectively. In fact the Accounting Standards Board (ASB) has stated that a review of earnings per share would not normally have been given priority at this stage of the Board's programme. However, in June 1997 FRED16 'Earnings Per Share' was issued which proposed amendments to SSAP3 and subsequently in October 1998 FRS 14 'Earnings Per Share' was published.

Required:

(a) (i) Describe the main changes to SSAP3 which have occurred as a result of FRS 14 and the main reasons for those changes. **(6 marks)**

(ii) Explain why there is a need to disclose diluted earnings per share in financial statements. **(5 marks)**

(b) The following financial statement extracts for the year ending 31 May 1999 [20 x 9] relate to Mayes, a public limited company.

	£'000	£'000
Operating profit		
Continuing operations	26,700	
Discontinued operations	(1,120)	
	——	25,580
Continuing operations		
Profit on disposal of tangible fixed assets		2,500
Discontinued operations		
(Loss) on sale of operations		(5,080)
		——
		23,000

Fully diluted ignore

Interest payable	(2,100)
Profit on ordinary activities before taxation	20,900
Tax on profit on ordinary activities	(7,500)
Profit on ordinary activities after tax	13,400
Minority interest – equity	(540)
Profit attributable to members of parent company	12,860

Dividends:

Preference dividend on non-equity shares	210	
Ordinary dividend on equity shares	300	
	—	(510)
Other appropriations – non equity shares (note iii)		(80)
Retained profit for year		12,270

Capital as at 31 May 1999 £'000

End ∴
work backwards.

Allotted, called up and fully paid ordinary shares of £1 each	12,500
7% convertible cumulative redeemable preference shares of £1	3,000 ←
	15,500

Additional Information

7 mths

(i)   On 1 January 1999, 3·6 million ordinary shares were issued at £2·50 in consideration of the acquisition of June Ltd for £9 million. These shares do not rank for dividend in the current period. Additionally the company purchased and cancelled £2·4 million of its own £1 ordinary shares on 1 April 1999. On 1 July 1999, the company made a bonus issue of 1 for 5 ordinary shares before the financial statements were issued for the year ended 31 May 1999.

(ii)   The company has a share option scheme under which certain directors can subscribe for the company's shares. The following details relate to the scheme.

Options outstanding 31 May 1998:
(i) 1·2 million ordinary shares at £2 each
(ii) 2 million ordinary shares at £3 each
both sets of options are exercisable before 31 May 2000.

Options granted during year 31 May 1999
(i) One million ordinary shares at £4 each exercisable before 31 May 2002, granted 1 June 1998.

During the year to 31 May 1999, the options relating to the 1·2 million ordinary shares (at a price of £2) were exercised on 1 March 1999.

The average fair value of one ordinary share during the year was £5.

(iii)   The 7% convertible cumulative redeemable preference shares are convertible at the option of the shareholder or the company on 1 July 2000, 2001, 2002 on the basis of <u>two ordinary shares for every three preference shares</u>. The preference share dividends are not in arrears. The shares are redeemable at the option of the shareholder on 1 July 2000, 2001, 2002 at £1·50 per share. The <u>'other appropriations – non equity shares' item charged against the profits relates to the amortisation</u> of the redemption premium and issue costs on the preference shares.

(iv)   Mayes issued £6 million of 6% convertible bonds on 1 June 1998 to finance the acquisition of Space Ltd. Each bond is convertible into 2 ordinary shares of £1. Assume a corporation tax rate of 35%.

(v)   The interest payable relates entirely to continuing operations and the taxation charge relating to discontinued operations is assessed at £100,000 despite the accounting losses. The loss on discontinued operations relating to the minority interest is £600,000.

Required:

Calculate the basic and diluted earnings per share for the year ended 31 May 1999 for Mayes plc utilising FRS 14 'Earnings per Share'.   **(14 marks)**

(Candidates should show a calculation of whether potential ordinary shares are dilutive or anti-dilutive).   **(Total: 25 marks)**

73	**(Question 5 of examination)**

Section C – ONE question ONLY to be attempted

The senior partner of JLPN, a firm of auditors, has issued an 'Audit Risk Alert' letter to all partners dealing with key areas of concern which should be given due consideration by his firm when auditing public companies. The letter outlines certain trends in audit reporting that, if not scrutinised by the auditors, could lead to a loss of reliability and transparency in the financial statements. The following three key concerns were outlined in the letter:

(a)   Audit committees play a very important role together with the financial director and auditor in achieving high quality financial control and auditing. Recently the efforts of certain audit committees have been questioned in the press.

(b)   The Stock Exchange had reported cases of inappropriate revenue recognition practices including:

(i)   accelerating revenue prior to the delivery of the product to the customer's site, or prior to the completion of the terms of the sales arrangement.

(ii)   recognition of revenue when customers have unilateral cancellation or termination provisions, other than the normal customary product return provisions.

(c)   It had been reported that the management of companies had intentionally violated UK Generally Accepted Accounting Practice by immaterial amounts. The reason for this had been the sensitivity of reported earnings per share in a market place where missing the market's expectation of earnings per share by a small amount could have significant consequences.

Required:

(a)   Explain the importance of the role of an 'Audit Risk Alert' letter to a firm of auditors.

    (5 marks)

(b)   Discuss the way in which the auditor should deal with each of the key concerns outlined in the letter in order to ensure that audit risk is kept to an acceptable level.

Please note that the three key concerns (a), (b) and (c), carry five marks each.   **(15 marks)**
    (Total: 20 marks)

---

74   (Question 6 of examination)

Many computer systems are not programmed to deal with the start of the new century and may encounter processing inaccuracies or even failure in certain circumstances (often called the Year 2000 Issue). Awareness of the potential operational difficulties is widespread in the business community and auditors have an important part to play in raising the awareness of companies to the problem and ensuring appropriate action is taken. However, it is possible that an 'expectation gap' may arise between the perceived responsibilities of management and the auditor in relation to this issue.

Required:

(a)   Explain how the 'Year 2000 Issue' affects the business risk of an entity.   **(7 marks)**

(b)   Discuss the responsibilities of the auditors and directors in relation to the 'Year 2000 Issue'.

(8 marks)

(c)   Discuss how an 'expectation gap' between the responsibilities of the auditor and management may be avoided over this issue.

(5 marks)
(Total: 20 marks)

JUNE 1999 ANSWERS

69   (Answer 1 of examination)

(**Examiner's comments and marking guide**)

Question 1: This question sought to test candidates' knowledge of complex groups. The question dealt with sub-subsidiaries, associates, inter group profit elimination, the treatment of contingencies, fair value adjustments and the write off of goodwill.

The question was quite complex and required a good understanding of acquisition accounting. The published answer is shown in tabular form but 'T' accounts or any other form of answer was acceptable. However, many candidates produced very poor quality workings, which were difficult to follow. The actual numbers in candidates' answers often did not correspond to the model answer, and markers in these circumstances followed the process carried out by candidates. However, if the workings cannot be deciphered, then the markers have extreme difficulty in allocating marks to numbers whose source is difficult to derive. Candidates found the fair value and accounting policy adjustments quite difficult and often calculated the realised profit incorrectly. Additionally the relative shareholdings of the group and minority interest were calculated incorrectly. It is important with this type of question to spend time clarifying the group structure and relationships before commencing the question.

The question asked in part (b) varied according to the particular variant that was being taken. It dealt with accounting practice or policy relating to goodwill. Many candidates simply ignored this part of the question or wrote an answer to the question they would have liked to have been asked. It is important to answer such questions and make the answer relevant. Five marks are a significant amount of marks to lose in this examination.

			Marks
(a)	Tangible fixed assets		3
	Investment		2
	Goodwill		6
	Net current assets		5
	Long term liabilities		1
	Reserves		5
	Minority interest		8
		Available	30
		Maximum	26
(b)	Subjective assessment		4
		Available	34
		Maximum	30

(**Step by step answer plan**)

Step 1   Read the question again and make sure that you focus on precisely what is required. This question features a complex group: the main complications are an associate owned by a subsidiary and fair value adjustments at acquisition.

Step 2   Establish the group structure.

Step 3   Deal with the fair value adjustments and then calculate goodwill.

Step 4   Adjust for the intra group sale and then calculate minority interests.

Step 5 Calculate the interest in associated undertaking and the amount to be included in consolidated reserves in respect of the associate. You should then be able to calculate consolidated reserves.

Step 6 Draw up the consolidated balance sheet, remembering to adjust tangible fixed assets to fair value and stocks for the unrealised profit on the intra group sale. This completes part (a).

Step 7 Answer part (b).

Items not required by the Examiner for this question: description of aspects of FRS 10 other than transitional arrangements in part (b).

The examiner's answer

(a)

X Group
Balance Sheet as at 31 March 1999

	£m
Tangible fixed assets	1,058
Investment	47
Goodwill	40
Net current assets	1,060
Creditors due more than one year	(365)
	1,840
Share capital	360
Share premium	250
Reserves	1,071
Minority interest	159
	1,840

Consolidation Schedule (£m)

Working	Total	Adj	Goodwill (Cost of Control)	M.I.	Cd. Res.	B/S
(1) Tangible fixed assets	1,030	40	(26)	(14)		
	(12)		4	8	1,058	
Intangible fixed assets	30		20	10		–
Inv in W	50	(3)		1	2	47
Inv in Y	320		320			
Inv in Z	90		60	30		
(2) Net C.A.	1,075	(15)		6	9	1,060
(3)			7		(7)	
(4)			(24)		24	
			6		(6)	
Creditors: due more 1 yr.	(365)					(365)
Share capital – X	360					360
– Y	150		(100)	(50)		
– Z	50		(30)	(20)		
Share premium – X	250					250
– Y	120		(80)	(40)		
– Z	10		(6)	(4)		

Profit/loss a/c	– X	1,050			(1,050)
	– Y	210	(80)	(70)	(60)
	– Z	30	(12)	(12)	(6)
			55		(1,086)
Goodwill write off (3/11)			(15)		15
			40	(159)	(1,071)

The holding of X in Y and Z is as follows:

		Y	Z
	X	2/3	6/10 (2/3 of 90%)
	MI	1/3	4/10

Goodwill is calculated at 1 April 1996 when X gained control of Y and hence Z.

Workings

1   **Tangible fixed assets**

	X £m	MI £m	Total £m
Fair value adj. – Y	20	10	30
Fair value adj. – Z	6	4	10
	26	14	40

Depreciation – additional depreciation of $40 \times 10\% \times 3$ years needs to charged ie £12m. This will be split between the consolidated reserves and the minority interest as follows.

	X £m	MI £m	Total £m
Y 1/3 : 2/3	6	3	9
Z 4/10 : 6/10	2	1	3
	8	4	12

Accounting entries	£m
DR Fixed assets	40
CR Cost of control	26
Minority interest	14
DR Consolidated reserves	8
Minority interest	4
CR Depreciation	12

2   **Stocks – Inter company profit and fair values**

		Cd res £m	MI £m	Total £m
Inter co. profit				
Sales to X	44			
Sales to Y	16 ⁄			
	$60 \times 25\%$ ⁄	9	6	15

Profit will be eliminated by reference to the relative shareholdings of X and the minority interest in Z (4/10).

DR	Consolidated reserves	9
	Minority Interest	6
CR	Stock	15

Fair value and change in accounting policy

On acquisition of Y net decrease is £6m
X's share of this decrease is 2/3 ie £4m
On acquisition of Z net decrease is £5m
X's share of this decrease is 6/10 ie £3m

| DR | Cost of control | £7m |
| CR | Consolidated reserves | £7m |

3   Arbitration receipts

The amount of £36m received on 1 June 1996 is an amount which relates to the preacquisition period and as such was the crystallisation of a contingent asset as at 1 April 1996. Therefore it should be included in the fair value exercise. The group's share of the debtor is 2/3 of £36m ie £24m.

	£m
DR Consolidated reserves	24
CR Cost of control	24

4   Provision for bad debts

The increase in the provision on acquisition is £9m

	£m
DR Cost of control	6
CR Post acquisition profits	6

The increase in the provision moves profits from the post acquisition period into the pre-acquisition period (£9m × $^2/_3$).

5   The associated company of Y is also deemed to be an associate of X and therefore is equity accounted. In practice the group would be consolidated using the indirect method and W would be equity accounted in the group accounts of Y. Therefore in the group accounts of X, using the direct method, W should be equity accounted. The investment in W will be debited with 30% (£17m - £7m) ie £3m and the consolidated reserves and minority interest credited with £2m and £1m respectively. The goodwill arising on acquisition will be

	£m
Cost of investment	50
Net assets acquired 30% of (80 + 6 + 7)	(28)
	—
Goodwill	22
	—

Therefore goodwill would be amortised over eleven years with three years having elapsed.

Goodwill written off associate 3/11 × 22 = £6m.

Thus the total adjustment to the investment in W would be (in £m).

		Investment		MI	$C^D Res$
Post acquisition Reserves	DR	3	CR	1	2
Goodwill	CR	(6)	DR	(2)	(4)
		—		—	—
		(3)		(1)	(2)
		—		—	—

(b)   There is no requirement in FRS 10 to reinstate goodwill which has previously been written off to reserves although an entity can do so if it wishes. The option to reinstate applies to all 'old ' goodwill or all 'old' post-FRS 7 goodwill. The rule prevents companies choosing which goodwill to reinstate. Any impairment of goodwill must be determined and the notes to the financial statements should disclose the original cost of goodwill and any amortisation or impairment. Goodwill should be reinstated at its net book value or original carrying value less impairment. The reinstatements are to be accounted for by way of a prior year adjustment and in the year of adjustment the comparative figures will also be affected.

Did you answer the question?

Only 4 marks are available for part (b) and therefore it is not necessary to do more than state the relevant requirements of FRS 10.

(Tutorial Note: The Examiner's Answer presents the workings in a columnar format, but it would be possible to present the main consolidation workings as schedules. The workings below follow the approach described in the Textbook and the Lynchpin.

Goodwill

	£m	£m	£m
In Y			
Cost of investment			320
Less: share of net assets acquired:			
Share capital		150	
Share premium		120	
Reserves	120		
Adjustments $(30 - 8 - 9 - 30 + 2 + 36)$	21		
		141	
		411	
Group share (2/3)			(274)
			46
In Z			
Cost of investment $(2/3 \times 90)$			60
Less: share of net assets acquired:			
Share capital		50	
Share premium		10	
Reserves	20		
Adjustments $(10 - 5)$	5		
		25	
		85	
Group share (60%)			(51)
			9
Total goodwill			
Y			46
Z			9
			55
Less amortisation $(55 \times 3/11)$			(15)
			40

Minority interest

	£m	£m	£m
In Y			
Share capital		150	
Share premium		120	
Reserves	210		
Fair value adjustments (30 – 30)	–		
Additional depreciation	(9)		
		201	
W (50 – 47)		(3)	
		468	
MI share (1/3)			156
In Z			
Share capital		50	
Share premium		10	
Reserves	30		
Fair value adjustment	10		
Additional depreciation	(3)		
Provision for unrealised profit	(15)		
		22	
		82	
MI share (40%)			33
Less: cost of investment (1/3 × 90)			(30)
			159

Group reserves

	£m	£m
X		1,050
Y:		
At year-end	201	
At acquisition	(141)	
	60	
Group share (2/3)		40
Z:		
At year-end	22	
At acquisition	(25)	
	(3)	
Group share (60%)		(2)
W:		
At year-end	17	
At acquisition	(10)	
	7	
Group share (30%)		2
Less: amortisation of goodwill		
Group	15	
W (2/3 × 22 × 3/11)	4	
		(19)
		1,071

---

70 (Answer 2 of examination)

Examiner's comments and marking guide

Question 2: This question was designed to test candidates knowledge of segmental reporting by asking in part (a) about the importance of segmental data and the advantages and disadvantages of the managerial approach and the risk and return approach to analysing segmental data. This question was not popular with UK variant students but was popular with other variants. Generally candidates answered this part of the question very well, particularly part (a)(ii).

Part (b) of the question required candidates to discuss the implications of certain events for the determination of segmental information to be provided in the financial statements. UK variant candidates were asked to consider not only SSAP 25 but also FRS 3 in their answers. These candidates focused heavily on FRS 3 and often did not give SSAP 25 due consideration.

Many candidates did not answer all sections of part (b), which is poor examination technique. Marks can only be obtained if attempts at a question are made and it is a better policy to write an answer, which may be relevant than make no attempt at all. Most candidates who attempted all parts of this question achieved a pass standard.

			Marks
(a)	(i)	Subjective assessment	5
	(ii)	Approach in financial statements	1
		Reconciliation	1
		Consistent	1
		Comparability	1
		Fluctuations	1
		Affects assessment	1
		Subjective	1
		Valuable information	1
		Cost effective	1
		Reflect classifications	1
		Sensitive	1
		Quality of information	1
		Variability	1
			—
		Available	13
			—
		Maximum	7
			—
(b)		Definition of segment	4
		intersegment pricing	2
		exceptional items	3
		discontinued operations	3
		associate	3
			—
		Available	15
			—
		Maximum	13
			—
		Available	33
			—
		Maximum	25
			—

Step by step answer plan

Step 1 Read the question again and make sure that you focus on precisely what is required. The introductory paragraph 'sets the scene' and explains the terminology used in part (a)(ii). This question is split into no less than eight sub-sections, each with a precise mark allocation, and so it is essential that you read each requirement carefully and allocate your time.

Step 2 Answer part (a)(i), remembering that the key requirement words are *explain why*. This part of the question should take no more than 9 minutes.

Step 3 Approach part (a)(ii) by considering each of the two approaches in turn, making as many points as possible in the time allowed. This part of the question should take no more than 12 minutes.

Step 4 Answer part (b), remembering that you must not get carried away on any of the points to the exclusion of the others.

Items not required by the Examiner for this question: general description of the requirements of SSAP 25/FRS 3

The examiner's answer

(a) (i) Many companies and groups of companies conduct their business in several industrial sectors and in a number of different countries. Such companies also may manufacture in one country and supply goods to customers in another country. These different parts of the business will be subject to different risks determined by the business environment in which they are operating. Additionally each segment may have a different growth potential because of the region of the world in which it is trading and may have different regional problems to deal with. For example, there may be high inflation in that part of the world, or currency problems. There is greater awareness of cultural and environmental differences between countries by investors and therefore geographical knowledge of business operations is increasingly important.

The provision of segmental information will enable users to better understand the company's past performance and to make more informed judgements about the company as a whole. If users are to be able to assess the performance of a company and attempt to predict likely future results, then disaggregation of the data in the financial statements is necessary. It is important that users are aware of the impact that changes in significant components of the business may have on the business as a whole. Several companies are currently demerging their activities and as a result of this, the provision of segmental information becomes increasingly important. The computation of key accounting ratios for the different segments is important information for potential investors in the demerged activities.

Did you answer the question?

The answer concentrates on the information that segmental disclosures give to users and why it is useful, rather than restating the disclosure requirements of SSAP 25.

(ii) If a company analyses its segmental information using the 'risk and returns' approach then this will reflect the approach taken in the financial statements for external reporting. If information is analysed segmentally on any other basis than that required for external reporting, then there will be difficulty in reconciling the segmental information to the financial statements. Segmental reporting on the risks and returns basis will produce information which is more consistent over time and comparable between companies, although the use of directors judgement in segmental analysis affects comparability. The greater consistency of this method occurs because the managerial method is subject to fluctuations due to the changing allocation of managers to the task of producing segmental information. This method assists in the assessment of profitability, and returns and the risks of the component parts of the enterprise. The determination of business segments under this method had been somewhat subjective and it is thought segments based on an existing internal structure should be somewhat less subjective. In any event knowledge of the internal structure of a company is valuable information in itself and may enhance a user's ability to predict the actions of the management.

Utilising the managerial approach will be more cost effective as the incremental cost of providing segmental information will be low. If segmental information is reported on the same basis as for internal decision making, then this will reflect the classifications used by managers to discuss the progress of the business. However, the information produced by this form of classification is more likely to be sensitive because of the strategic way in which business is organised. Also segments with different risks and returns will be combined thus affecting the quality of the financial information produced. If the managerial approach is adopted, the definition of a segment will be determined solely by management which means that the nature of the information disclosed will be highly variable.

Did you answer the question?

The answer gives both advantages and disadvantages of *each* method, thus meeting the requirement to *discuss*.

(b)   (i)   SSAP 25 states that the definition of a segment should be made by the management of the company and gives guidance but only in general terms. SSAP25 states that the directors should have regard to the main purpose of presenting segmental information and the need of information to users.   There is no single set of factors which are universally applicable although the standard sets out the factors to be taken into account (for example these factors may be the nature of and markets for the products). Once the features of a segment have been distinguished it has to be significant to warrant separate disclosure and a 10 per cent threshold as regards third party turnover, results and net assets is set out in SSAP25. Thus the directors of AZ will take into account the above and perhaps may look to how the company is organised into divisions or subsidiaries, and may look to the management accounts for guidance.

In the case of an airline, the segments may be determined by the destination of the aircraft, or the location in which the sale was made. The geographical analysis of the net assets may be difficult as the aircraft will be deployed across the world-wide route network. Companies which operate in global markets will have difficulty in analysing their operations geographically.

(ii)   Turnover for each segment should be split under SSAP25 between sales to external customers and sales to other segments.   Thus the sales of aircraft to its domestic airline should be disclosed. However, the basis of inter segment sales is not required to be disclosed by SSAP25 and therefore the fact that the companies can negotiate a price for the aircraft with the possibility of resultant creativity in the intersegmental analysis need not be disclosed.

(iii) SSAP25 requires the results of the segments to be analysed before accounting for 'taxation, minority interests and extraordinary items'.   The standard was issued before FRS 3 'Reporting Financial Performance' and the resultant impact on the categorisation of exceptional and extraordinary items. Exceptional items are not specifically dealt with in SSAP25 but by implication should be included in the analysed results.   However, because specific guidance is not given some companies do not disclose the segments to which the exceptional items belong.   In this case the nature of the exceptional item will be disclosed in the financial statements so that whatever the policy chosen by the directors, users should be able to allocate the loss to a particular segment.

(iv)   FRS 3 requires the disclosure of the impact of a discontinuance on a major business segment where this is material.   Many companies in the UK do not give comprehensive segmental analysis of discontinuance but show discontinued operations as a residual category, analysing only results from continuing operations into segments which was not the purpose of FRS 3. It is however, normally self evident in the financial statements as to what the discontinued operations relate to. It is likely that the holiday company would have been disclosed separately in the segmental analysis and also in the financial statements as it would be classified as a discontinued activity under FRS 3.

(v)   The standard requires groups to give segmental disclosure of the profit/loss before tax, minority interests and extraordinary items of associates and the groups share of the net assets. The results of the associate need only be disclosed if the associate forms a material part of the groups results or assets. (Materiality has a 20% threshold in the context). If publication of the information is thought to be prejudicial to the business of the associate then segmental information need not be disclosed. Additionally where the holding company is unable to obtain the information concerning the associate it need not be disclosed. Thus Eurocat Ltd. may feel that the publication of information about its business (specialist aircraft engines) is prejudicial and may either request non publication or refuse to supply information on the above grounds then the standard has not been contravened.

Did you answer the question?

The mark requirement for each point indicates the level of detail required.

71	**(Answer 3 of examination)**

Examiner's comments and marking guide

Question 3: This question sought to test candidates on accounting for associates. Part (a) of the question simply required candidates to describe the difference between an associate and an ordinary non-current asset investment, and to describe the different classifications of 'joint ventures'. Generally candidates performed well on this part of the question, as it did not require any other skills than those involved in rote learning. Many candidates had obviously learned the various classifications in a significant amount of detail and scored very heavily.

Part (b) required the application of the accounting standards dealt with in part (a) (FRS 9 for the UK stream).

This part of the question was not particularly well answered as it required detailed knowledge of the accounting for associates and joint ventures. It appears that there is a lack of detailed knowledge on accounting for associates as candidates found difficulty in dealing with goodwill, post acquisition profits and the elimination of inter company profits.

				Marks
(a)	(i)	Passive role		1
		Accounting policies		1
		Significant influence		2
		Dividend policy		2
		Board representation		1
			Available	7
			Maximum	6
	(ii)	Entity		1
		Not carry on trade		1
		Indicators		2
		Accounting		2
			Available	6
			Maximum	4
(b)	(i)	Fair value		1
		Cost of investment/investment		4
		Goodwill		1
		Profit/loss account		4
			Available	10
			Maximum	9
	(ii)	Profit/Loss account		3
		Balance sheet		3
			Available/Maximum	6
			Available	29
			Maximum	25

Step by step answer plan

Step 1 Read the question again and make sure that you focus on precisely what is required. This question is clearly examining the requirements of FRS 9 and consists of a fairly straightforward discursive part (a) followed by part (b) in which you are required to apply your knowledge of the standard.

Step 2 Answer part (a)(i) by explaining the FRS 9 definition of an associate.

Step 3 Answer part (a)(ii) by restating and explaining the relevant requirements of FRS 9.

Step 4 Start part (b)(i) by dealing with the fair value adjustments, then calculate goodwill. You should then be able to calculate the amount at which the investment in Baden will be included in the consolidated balance sheet.

Step 5 Calculate the amounts to be included in the consolidated profit and loss account.

Step 6 Calculate the group's share of turnover, gross assets and gross liabilities to answer part (b)(ii).

Items not required by the Examiner for this question: additional disclosures for material associates and joint ventures (see point (vi) in question).

The examiner's answer

(a) (i) The principal difference between an associate and an ordinary fixed asset investment is that in the latter case the investor takes on a relatively passive role whereas an associate is a medium through which an investor conducts its business. Thus an associate will normally implement accounting policies that are consistent with those of the investor. The investor must be able to exercise a significant influence over the investee and maintain a participating interest, which is an interest in shares held on a long term basis for the purpose of securing a contribution to the investor's activities by the exercise of control or influence.

FRS 9 'Associates and Joint Ventures' states that a holding of 20% or more of the voting rights suggests but does not ensure that the investor exercises significant influence. The FRS also suggests that the attitude towards the investee's dividend policy may indicate the status of the investment. In the case of an ordinary fixed asset investment, the investor may press for a high dividend but in the case of an associate the investor will be more interested in reinvestment of cash flows and less with dividend. FRS 9 indicates that associate status is achieved where the investor has board representation or equivalent participation in the decision making process combined with at least 20% voting rights. Additionally the investor must not merely have the ability to exercise significant influence but must actively exercise it.

(ii) A joint venture must be an 'entity' whereas a joint arrangement is not. An entity is essentially a body corporate, partnership or incorporated association carrying on a trade or business of its own and where all significant matters of operating and financial policy are predetermined by the participants. For example several oil companies may own a pipeline, the throughput of which is sold separately by the companies rather than the joint venture. FRS 9 states that there are indicators of a joint arrangement and these are:

(a) the participants derive their benefit from products or services taken in kind rather than by receiving a share in the trading results.

(b) each participant's share of output or result is determined by its supply of key inputs to the production process.

A joint arrangement is accounted for by each participant accounting for their own 'assets, liabilities and cash flows' within the arrangement. In many cases this will generate the same numbers that would have been obtained using proportional consolidation. FRS 9 states that this is not proportional consolidation but a reporting entity recording its own transactions, and therefore requires such arrangements to be accounted for at the individual entity level and on consolidation.

Did you answer the question?

Notice the way in which the answer does not simply restate the definitions and requirements of FRS 9 but *explains* them.

(b)   (i)   In the consolidated balance sheet, the group's share of the net assets will be shown as a single line under FRS 9 'Associates and Joint Ventures'.

At 1 January 1997 – fair value of assets.

	£m
Tangible fixed assets	30
Current assets	31
Creditors – within one year	(20)
Creditors – more than one year	(8)
Fair value of net assets	33
Shareholding 30% – value of assets purchased	9.9
Cost of investment	14
Goodwill	4.1

In calculating goodwill FRS 9 (para 31) states that 'any goodwill carried in the balance sheet of the investee should not be included in the calculations'.

At 31 December 1998 – Balance Sheet amount

	£m
Cost of investment	14
Post acquisition profits 30% of (32 – 9 – URP 10)	3.9
Less	
Goodwill written off (2 years)	(2)
Increased depreciation of tangible fixed assets due to fair values	
$2 \times 20\% \times (30 - 20) \times 30\%$	(1.2)
Investment in associate	14.7

Alternative presentation

		£m
Net assets 30% x (46 – URP 10)		10·8
Fair value increase (net assets 31/12/98)	46	
less profit 1997 + 1998	23	
Net assets at acquisition	23	
Fair value	33	
Increase in fair value	$10 \times 30\%$	3
		13·8
Goodwill		4·1
		17·9
less goodwill written off		(2)
Depreciation		(1·2)
Investment in associate		14·7

FRS 9 states that goodwill should be treated in accordance with FRS 10 'Goodwill and Intangible Assets' that inter company profit should be eliminated and that depreciation should be based on fair values.

The investment in the associate should be included as a fixed asset investment and goodwill of £2·1million should be included in the carrying amount and disclosed separately.

The following amounts would be shown in the consolidated profit and loss account.

Profit and Loss account for year ended 31 December 1998

	£m
Share of operating profit in associate	4·1
[(30% of 29) – goodwill 1– interco. profit 3 – depreciation 0·6]	
Exceptional item – associate	(3)
Interest payable – associate	(1·2)
*Taxation on profit on ordinary activities	
*Tax relates to the following:	
Associate	(0·9)

Note: that the amount of goodwill written off will be disclosed.
The investors share of group turnover may be shown as a memorandum item in the profit and loss account..

Note: any interest held by associates or joint ventures are ignored (such as those held by Guy).

The intercompany profit on stock will be treated as follows:

(i)   in the consolidated profit and loss account, the profit will be eliminated from the share of the associates profit as the associate recorded the profit.

(ii)   in the consolidated balance sheet the profit will be eliminated from stock as this is the asset subject to the transaction which is held by the holding company.

(b)   (ii)   Joint ventures are accounted for under FRS 9 using the 'gross' equity method.   This is the same as the equity method for associates but with two exceptions

(a)   In the consolidated profit and loss account the group's share of turnover must be shown, but as a memorandum item separate from group turnover.

	£m
Turnover: group and share of joint ventures	y + 53.1
$(212 - 35) \times 30\%$	
Less share of joint ventures turnover	(53.1)
	____
Where y = group turnover	y
	____

(b)   In the consolidated balance sheet, the share of net assets of joint ventures must be sub analysed into the group's share of assets and liabilities and included as a fixed asset investment.   Any goodwill (£2·1 million) should be disclosed separately.

Investment in joint ventures	
Share of gross assets (working 1)	21·3
Share of gross liabilities (30% of 12 + 10).	(6·6)
	____
	14·7
	____

Groups may give memorandum information on the face of the consolidated profit and loss account and balance sheet of the amount of each line item.

Working 1.

Fixed assets	37		
Current assets (31–10)	21		
	——		
	58 × 30%	17·4	
Increase in fair value		3	
Goodwill		4·1	
less goodwill write off		(2)	
Depreciation		(1·2)	
		——	
		21·3	

---

72   (Answer 4 of examination)

Examiner's comments and marking guide

Question 4: This question dealt with Earnings Per Share (EPS). It has been the subject of a recent accounting standard and thus warranted examination in paper 13. Part (a) sought to establish whether candidates know why changes to an existing standard were required (UK). Additionally the question required candidates to discuss why diluted earnings per share should be disclosed in financial statements. Most candidates answered this part of the question quite well and the answers were quite encouraging.

Part (b) of the question required the calculations of basic and diluted earnings per share. The question was quite complex requiring knowledge of the impact of bonus issues, share option schemes, and other capital instruments. Additionally, the question required candidates to rank the dilutive elements ignoring any antidilutive elements. The importance of utilising net profit from continuing operations in these computations was lost on many candidates. However, overall the results on this question were quite good.

			Marks
(a)	International comparability		2
	Shares in basic EPS		2
	Bonus issues		1
	Diluted EPS		2
	Disclosure		2
	Outside scope of IAS		1
			——
		Available	10
			——
		Maximum	6
			——
(b)	Future issues		1
	Forecast		1
	Illusion of growth		1
	True growth		1
	Variability		1
	Theoretical Measure		1
	Warning device		1
			——
		Available	7
			——
		Maximum	5
			——
(c)	Basic earnings		3
	Basic per share		5
	Calculation		1
	Dilution v antidilution		6
	Earnings – dilution		2

Calculation   1

Available	18
Maximum	14
Available	35
Maximum	25

Step by step answer plan

Step 1 Read the question again and make sure that you focus on precisely what is required. Again, it is in a style typical of the current Examiner: a discursive part followed by a requirement to apply FRS 14 to the calculation of basic and diluted earnings per share. You should have noted that as well as several actual share issues during the year there is more than one type of potential ordinary (ie, dilutive) share. Over half the available marks are for the calculations in part (b), therefore you must be careful not to spend too much time on part (a).

Step 2 Answer part (a)(i), remembering that the requirement word is *describe*.

Step 3 Approach part (a)(ii) by briefly describing situations in which the disclosure of basic earnings per share is inadequate and then explain how disclosing diluted earnings per share is useful.

Step 4 Re-read the scenario in part (b) to ensure that you focus on the information given.

Step 5 Calculate basic earnings. Then calculate the weighted average number of shares in issue. This will enable you to arrive at basic earnings per share.

Step 6 Calculate the earnings per incremental share arising on each of the three types of potentially dilutive share. This determines the order in which the securities are included in the calculation (See Tutorial Note).

Step 7 Calculate earnings from continuing operations. You should then be able to calculate which potential ordinary shares are dilutive. This working will also give you the number of potential ordinary shares.

Step 8 Adjust basic earnings and then calculate diluted earnings per share.

Items not required by the Examiner for this question: disclosure notes relating to the calculations in part (b).

The examiner's answer

(a)   (i)   The ASB decided to review SSAP3 because there were international discussions and developments in this area. Thus in the interests of comparability, it was decided to review SSAP3 in the light of the IASC Standard (IAS33). The ASB felt that there was little merit in making unnecessary changes to the IASC requirements and amendments to SSAP3 were framed with this in mind.

The determination of the shares to be included in the calculation of basic EPS needed to be widened as under SSAP3 only those shares ranking for dividend in the period were included whilst all ordinary shares are included in the calculation under FRS 14. Greater guidance was required as to when shares are to be included in the calculation and this is now given. For example ordinary shares issued as a result of the conversion of a debt instrument to ordinary shares are included as of the date interest ceases to accrue. Additionally the treatment of bonus issues, share splits etc. occurring after the year end but before the issue of the accounts required consistent application. Such issues are adjusted retrospectively.

More specific guidance was required on the calculation of diluted EPS, including the sequence in which potential ordinary shares should be considered. There was some concern over the method used to take into account the impact of options and warrants and the use of implied earnings in the calculation. The Treasury Stock method was used in the USA and internationally, in order to achieve international comparability. This method has essentially been introduced into FRS 14.

Also with the growth in the variety of financial instruments more specific guidance was required in certain areas. For example in the area of contingently issuable shares.

The ASB wished to update the disclosure requirements of SSAP3 and to this end decided that if the basic EPS is a loss per share then it should be disclosed. Exemption from disclosure on the grounds of materiality (dilution less than 5%) has been dropped as has the 'nil' basis of EPS which was deemed not to be as important as the net basis and could be calculated by reference to the financial statements in any event.

Following the decision to revise EPS in line with the international standard, the Board looked to see if any additional guidance was required on matters outside the scope of the IAS. The ASB concluded that further guidance in respect of financial statistics that appear in historical summaries was required.

Did you answer the question?

Notice that the answer does not simply state the main changes from SSAP 3, but gives the reasons why the changes were necessary.

(ii)   Basic EPS takes account only of those shares which are in issue (FRS 14) and does not take account of obligations that could dilute the EPS in future. The company could have convertible stock, options or warrants to subscribe for shares. Additionally, a company could have entered into deferred consideration agreements under which additional shares may be issued at a future date. Investors are not only interested in past performance but also with forecasting future earnings per share. Thus it is important to disclose the effect of any dilution in the future. Many companies use convertible stocks to achieve the illusion of growth in basic EPS. Where convertible loan stock or shares are used to finance expansion, the securities normally carry a low rate of interest due to the fact that they can be converted into shares. If current performance is sustained and the incremental finance cost is covered, then EPS can be increased. Diluted EPS, however, will reveal the true growth in earnings as an attempt is made to show the true cost of using convertible stock to finance growth in earnings.

The disclosure is intended to help users assess the potential variability of future EPS and the risk attaching to it. It can function as an indicator to users that the current level of basic EPS may not be sustainable in future. However, it is also felt that the objectives of the basic and diluted EPS should be the same and act as a performance measure. The diluted EPS is a theoretical measure of the effect of dilution on basic EPS and analysts do not use this measure as much as basic EPS because of its hypothetical nature. However, the diluted EPS can serve as a warning device to equity shareholders that future earnings will be affected by diluting factors.

(b)   **Earnings per share – basic**

	£'000
Profit attributable to the members of the parent company.	12,860
less preference dividend	(210)
other appropriations	(80)
Earnings – basic	12,570

Weighted average number of shares. (000)

	Shares		Weight	No.
1 June 1998	10,100	×	1	10,100
1 January 1999 – issued	3,600	×	5/12	1,500
1 March 1999 – options	1,200	×	3/12	300
1 April 1999 – purchased	(2,400)	×	2/12	(400)
31 May 1999	12,500			11,500

Bonus issue 1 July 1999 1 for 5	2,300
Number of shares	13,800

Basic Earnings Per Share $\dfrac{12,570}{13,800}$ $= 91\text{p}$

FRS 14 states that the shares used in the basic EPS calculation should be based on the weighted average number of equity shares in issue, unlike SSAP3 which requires only those ranking for dividend to be included. FRS 14 also states that a bonus issue should be taken into account in calculating basic EPS if the issue was before the publication of the financial statements.

Diluted Earnings per Share.

Computation of whether potential ordinary shares are dilutive or antidilutive.

	£'000 Net profit from continuing operations	Ordinary Shares (000)	Per share pence
Net profit from continuing operations	18,270	13,800	132
Options			
$1,200 \times \dfrac{5-2}{5} \times 9/12$		540	
$2,000 \times \dfrac{5-3}{5}$		800	
$1,000 \times \dfrac{5-4}{5}$		200	
	18,270	15,340	119 Dilutive
6% Bonds			
$(6\% \times 6,000 \times .65)$	234	12,000	
	18,504	27,340	67.7 Dilutive
Convertible Redeemable	210		
Preference Shares	80	2,000	
	18,794	29,340	64.1 Dilutive

Therefore all adjustments are dilutive and should be taken into account. FRS 14 states that potential ordinary shares which increase earnings per share from continuing operations are deemed to be anti-dilutive and are ignored in calculating diluted EPS. However in this case all dilutive elements would be taken into account.

Diluted Earnings Per Share Calculation.

	£'000
Profit/Earnings – basic	12,570
6% Bonds – interest	234
Convertible preference shares	290
Earnings -- diluted EPS	13,094
Ordinary shares	29,340
Diluted Earnings per Share	44·6p

Working

Net Profit from continuing operations.

	£'000
Operating Profit – continuing operations	26,700
Profit on fixed assets	2,500
Interest payable	(2,100)
Taxation (7,500 – 100)	(7,400)
Minority Interest (540 + 600)	(1,140)
Dividends – preference	(210)
Other appropriations	(80)
Net profit from continuing operations	18,270

(Tutorial Note: The order in which dilutive securities are included in the EPS calculation is determined as follows:

	Increase in earnings	Increase in no of ordinary shares	Earnings per incremental share
	£'000	000	
Options	NIL	1,540	NIL
Convertible preference shares	290	2,000	14.5p
6% convertible bonds	234	12,000	1.9p

Options are always more dilutive than other securities because there is no increase in earnings. The order in which the securities must be included in the calculation is: options, convertible bonds, convertible preference shares.*)*

73 (Answer 5 of examination)

Examiner's comments and marking guide

Question 5: This question was not very popular. The reason for this fact was the popularity of question 6, not the degree of difficulty of this question. Those candidates who answered the question performed quite well. The question required in part, an explanation of the importance of an 'Audit Risk Alert' letter. This term is not widely used but the nature of the letter was explained in the preamble to the question. Part (b) required a discussion of three key concerns to a fictional firm of auditors and how the auditors should reduce the audit risk surrounding these concerns. Candidates are not required to have detailed knowledge of auditing standards when answering this type of question but are required to demonstrate that they understand the underlying problem and how to deal in general terms with that problem. Answers to this part of the question were generally quite good.

		Marks
(a)	Subjective	5
(b)	Audit Committee	5
	Revenue Recognition	5
	GAAP violations	5
	Available/Maximum	20

Step by step answer plan

Step 1 Read the question again and make sure that you focus on precisely what is required.

Step 2 Part (a) is only worth 5 marks, so don't get carried away and write too much. Stick to mainstream auditing ideas: the management of audit risk, the gathering of audit evidence, quality control in the course of the audit.

Step 3 part (b) offers 5 marks for each of the three scenarios described. For each scenario, describe how the problem might affect audit risk. For example, an ineffective audit committee might increase the control risk component of audit risk.

The examiner's answer

(a) The audit risk alert letter is a memorandum letter sent by the senior partner to his fellow partners detailing key areas of concern which may have emerged through dealings with the large public companies, the Stock Exchange or the regulatory authorities. The form of the letter will vary from firm to firm but the content of the letter highlights trends which, if left unaddressed, may threaten the quality of the financial statements and hence the audit.

The importance of the role of the letter is as follows:

(i) it ensures that key areas of audit risk are reviewed.

(ii) it ensures that trends in financial reporting ranging from inappropriate management of earnings to fraud, and inappropriate application of GAAP are highlighted to auditors.

(iii) it assists in achieving high quality and integrity in the audit process.

(iv) it reduces the risk of audit failure and litigation.

(v) it helps prevent the erosion of investor confidence which may occur if investors believe that financial information is a product of manipulation.

(b) **Audit Committees**

Audit Committees play an important role in achieving high quality internal controls and financial reporting by public companies. If the efforts of audit committees are put into question then the auditor should review the role of the audit committee in the organisation. The audit committee should fulfil its responsibility to the Board of Directors for overseeing the integrity and quality of the accounting process. The auditor should determine whether the audit committee receives the information necessary to carry out its responsibilities and determine whether the audit committee is informed of such things as:

(i) changes in accounting policies
(ii) adjustments proposed by the auditor
(iii) disagreements with management
(iv) difficulties encountered in performing the audit

The auditor should review the independence of the audit committee. Although the committee can never be truly independent, the auditor should review the procedures for appointment of its members and the influence of management on its workings and report. The audit committee must be in a position to independently ask management and the auditor the necessary questions about selection of accounting procedures, disclosure requirements, the impact of transactions of the auditor's independence, internal controls and any other significant financial reporting issue. If this process is not occurring the auditor should make the necessary recommendations.

Accelerating Revenue

Auditors should be well aware of the company's revenue recognition policy for each type of material transaction. However, the auditor should be aware of the possibility of unusual or complex transactions. If the latter is the case then the auditor should make enquiries of company personnel who have the appropriate level of expertise and utilise appropriate acceptable accounting practices. Revenue should not be recognised until it is realised or realisable and earned. The practices set out are inappropriate revenue recognition procedures. Revenue should not be accelerated prior to the delivery of a product unless a persuasive evidence of an arrangement exists and the risks of ownership have passed to the buyer with the seller not retaining any specific performance obligation. The price should be fixed or determinable and collectibility probable. This latter condition would preclude revenue recognition where customers can cancel or terminate agreements.

The auditor should be satisfied that inappropriate revenue recognition policies have not been used in formulating the financial statement by performing relevant substantive testing procedures including cut-off tests.

Intentional immaterial GAAP violations

Auditors set familiar materiality levels prior to the commencement of the audit and revise them during the audit. However the traditional measures of materiality may need revision by the auditor, especially where missing the market's expectation of earnings per share by a small amount can have significant consequences.

Qualitative factors must be taken into account as well as quantitative factors in determining materiality. Percentage tests are not always conclusive and trends of earnings may be as important as selective percentages.

It is important that all known errors are recorded, especially intentional errors, and where qualitative information significantly alters the apparent significance of a matter, the item should be disclosed. The auditor should ensure that all staff are trained not purely in quantitative measures of materiality and when considering materiality all accounting regulations and practice should be taken into account. It is important that audit staff have the degree of technical training and proficiency in the determination of materiality.

All errors, intentional or otherwise, should be collated and then considered for adjustment in the financial statements. If management are intentionally violating GAAP, then the auditor should question the integrity of management and consider whether the firm wishes to continue to act as auditors.

---

74   (Answer 6 of examination)

Examiner's comments and marking guide

Question 6: This question was attempted by the majority of candidates and was answered very well. The question required an explanation of the effect of the 'year 2000 issue' on the business risk of an entity, the responsibilities of the auditors and directors and a discussion of any possible 'expectation gap' over the responsibilities of the auditor and management as regards this issue. Parts (a) and (b) were answered exceptionally well but part (c) was not quite as well answered with candidates often ignoring the question and simply writing the same points that had been made earlier in the question. Perhaps the main fault with answers generally was the tendency of candidates to discuss what the Year 2000 issue actually was rather than discussing the effect on the business risk. However, overall the answers were very good.

		Marks
(a)	Subjective assessment	7
(b)	Auditor's responsibilities	4
	Directors' responsibilities	4
(c)	Subjective assessment	5
		—
	Available/Maximum	20
		—

Step by step answer plan

Step 1 Read the question again and make sure that you focus on precisely what is required. The Y2k issue has received considerable publicity in recent months, so candidates are expected to be familiar with what it is.

Step 2 'Business risk in the context of part (a) can be thought of as the possibility that events or actions will adversely affect an organisation's ability to achieve its business objectives and execute its strategies successfully. Given that the Y2k issue is explained in the question, you should be able to identify the issue's impact on business risk.

[Step 3] Explain each of the auditors' and the directors' responsibilities in part (b). Although it is the directors' responsibility to maintain satisfactory systems, the auditor will have responsibilities too eg, to consider going concern.

[Step 4] The expectation gap in part (c) might arise in the minds of management or shareholders. It is safest to consider both possibilities in your answer.

The examiner's answer

(a) The 'Year 2000 Issue' has the potential to be a major problem for many businesses and is a business and therefore audit risk on a large scale. Some businesses will suffer major additional costs of modification or disruption of computer systems. It is important that directors and auditors review the impact on the business and plan to address anticipated problems which could include the impact on the financial statements. All aspects of the computer environment could be affected including any application software developed by the IT department or user departments, packaged software, the utilisation of computer service organisations and any embedded systems.

Additionally the problems encountered by other businesses may have an effect on the audit client and therefore the organisation should identify the nature of the risk, consider the scale and nature of the problem and how to achieve the optimal solution. If this identification process has not been undertaken the business risk will be high.

The scale of the programming problem is quite immense and as a result many organisations have decided to replace existing systems with new ones and that in itself increases the risk because of the problems associated with the implementation of new computer systems.

The 'Year 2000 Issue' could affect the going concern status of the entity. Systems failures may be so serious that it may jeopardise the entity's ability to continue in business. Additionally customer and suppliers may stop doing business with the entity because of their own problems and this may have a significant impact on the cash flow of the entity. If third parties are concerned over whether the entity's directors are taking appropriate action to mitigate the impact of the 'Year 2000 Issue', then they may threaten to cease doing business with the entity or demand accelerated loan payments or other such actions. Finally the Year 2000 remediation costs may be of such magnitude as to cause financing difficulties or violate loan covenants. Thus the issue could have serious repercussions on the business risk of the entity and therefore early identification of the scale of the problem is required.

(b) In principle there is no increased audit responsibility but auditors need to be fully aware of the impact of the Issue on the entity. The financial statements of any organisation could be affected materially either because of impairment of assets, increased costs incurred, or because of going concern issues. The auditor needs to be fully aware of the impact of the Issue on the financial statements and going concern. The directors are solely responsible for analysing the impact of the Issue on the business and developing plans to mitigate the effects. Additionally the directors should assess the impact on the going concern basis and the need for related disclosures in order that the financial statements might show a true and fair view. Also the directors need to consider any need for disclosures in the annual report as a result of the requirements of UITF Abstract 20.

The auditors should inform the directors that their own responsibilities are not affected and that they will consider the Issue as part of their existing responsibilities. Auditors will have no obligation to third parties to provide assurances as to the entity's Year 2000 compliance other than their normal reporting responsibilities. The auditor will assess the reliability of information supporting any management assertion with the objective of high level enquiry sufficient to meet reasonable expectations of what a professional auditor's responsibility is with regards to this issue. If the auditor is confident in management's information then there will be no requirement to make further enquiries although the Issue would be taken into consideration in all aspects of audit testing.

The auditor may wish specific representations from management on the Issue and be satisfied that the directors have considered it at board level and taken responsibility for the effects on the financial statements and other published information.

(c) Expectation gaps arise where there is a misunderstanding between two parties and inevitably this increases risk. It is important that management and directors are quite clear as to their responsibilities for the Issue. A written record of the respective responsibilities of the auditor and the directors would be good practice, although this might not be effected through the engagement letter as it might indicate some new responsibility.

The objective would be to clarify what comes within the scope of the audit and what is outside, and it is possible that separate terms of engagement may arise in order that the auditor might provide advice or even possible assurance as to the potential impact of the Issue.

Audit reporting should be used to close the gap rather than perpetuate misunderstanding. Where enquiries have been made by the auditor and issues have arisen, then these issues should be reported to management for corrective action even if there is no immediate financial statement impact. The scope of the Year 2000 enquiries could be explained to management and the fact that silence by the auditors does not necessarily mean assurance. It is important that rigorous enquiries are made by the auditor as to the impact of the Issue and that directors understand the importance that these enquiries have appropriate answers and have considered the reporting requirements.

Did you answer the question?

Notice how the answer provided is in the form of proper paragraphs rather than lists of points. This is because the instructions are to 'explain' and 'discuss' rather than 'list' or 'itemise'.

DECEMBER 1999 QUESTIONS

75 (Question 1 of examination)

Section A – This ONE question is COMPULSORY and MUST be attempted

A, a public limited company, has acquired shareholdings in two companies, X and Y, both themselves public limited companies. The following table shows the way in which the current shareholdings in these companies have been acquired:

X plc

Date	Holding Acquired	Fair Value of total net assets £m	Purchase Consideration £m
31.8.97	10%	30	5
31.10.98	45%	52	25
31.10.99	10%	60	8
	65%		

(handwritten: 55% ; 30)

Y plc

31 October 1998	60%	70	54

The following balance sheets relate to A, X and Y as at 31 October 1999: *(handwritten: 2nd Acq'n Included)*

	A £m	X £m	Y £m
Tangible fixed assets	108	50	60
Cost of investments	92		
Net current assets	26	25	15
Long-term liabilities	(6)	(35)	(10)
	220	40	65
Share capital – ordinary shares of £1	80	10	30
Share premium			10
Retained profits brought forward	100	20	15
Profit for year	40	10	10
	220	40	65

(i) Goodwill arising on acquisition is amortised through the profit and loss account over four years with a full year's charge in the year of acquisition. The increase in the fair values is attributable to net current assets.

(ii) A owned 12 million ordinary shares of £1 in Y at 31 October 1998. On 31 October 1999, Y issued 10 million ordinary shares of £1 to third parties for a consideration of £20 million.

(handwritten notes: 60% to 40%, dilution, Sub to ass.)

2 million Profit.

(iii) A had sold £10 million of goods to Y on 31 August 1999, making a profit of 25 per cent on cost. All of these goods remained in the stock of Y at 31 October 1999. X had sold a piece of land to A for £28 million during the year to 31 October 1999. The land was purchased originally from Y on 1 January 1999 for £20 million at a profit of £5 million. A had not paid the liability to X as at 31 October 1999.

(iv) A purchased a five per cent holding on 1 October 1999 in an overseas company for 42 million krona when the exchange rate was 3·5 krona = £1. This investment is included in tangible fixed assets. It partially financed the investment by borrowing 21 million krona on the same date. This loan is included in long-term liabilities. The company has not repaid any of the loan as at 31 October 1999 and no adjustments for the change in the exchange rate have been made. The exchange rate at 31 October 1999 is 3 krona = £1. The company wishes to maximise its reported earnings.

(v) X commenced on 1 November 1997 manufacturing product Z, and gives a warranty on this product at the time of sale to its customers. Under the terms of the warranty, X undertakes to repair or replace items that fail to perform satisfactorily for two years from the date of sale. The current policy of the company is to charge the cost of claims under the warranty against the profit and loss account in the year in which the claims are settled and this policy has been used to arrive at the fair values of X's net assets. It is estimated that the claims would amount to approximately 5% of sales in a year. Sales of product Z to third parties were £300 million for the year to 31 October 1998 and £200 million for the year to 31 October 1999. The charges against profits for the claims were £3 million in 1998 and £5 million in 1999. Assume that there is no inflationary adjustment to be made on the provisions.

1998 12 M.
1999 5 M

↳ constructive provision.

Required:

(a) Calculate the goodwill arising on the purchase of X and Y which would be shown in the group financial statements for the year ended 31 October 1998. **(5 marks)**

(b) Prepare the consolidated balance sheet for the A group as at 31 October 1999. **(25 marks)**

(Total: 30 marks)

Section B – TWO questions ONLY to be attempted

---

76 (Question 2 of examination)

Related party relationships and transactions are a normal feature of business. Enterprises often carry on their business activities through subsidiaries and associates and it is inevitable that transactions will occur between group companies. Until relatively recently the disclosure of related party relationships and transactions has been regarded as an area which has a relatively low priority. However, recent financial scandals have emphasised the importance of an accounting standard in this area.

Required:

(a) (i) Explain why the disclosure of related party relationships and transactions is an important issue. **(6 marks)**

(ii) Discuss the view that small companies should be exempt from the disclosure of related party relationships and transactions on the grounds of their size. **(4 marks)**

(b) Discuss whether the following events would require disclosure in the financial statements of the RP Group plc under FRS 8 'Related Party Disclosures'.

RP Group plc, merchant bankers, has a number of subsidiaries, associates and joint ventures in its group structure. During the financial year to 31 October 1999, the following events occurred:

(i)   The company agreed to finance a management buyout of a group company, AB, a limited company. In addition to providing loan finance, the company has retained a twenty-five per cent equity holding in the company and has a main board director on the board of AB. RP received management fees, interest payments and dividends from AB.   **(6 marks)**

(ii)   On 1 July 1999, RP sold a wholly owned subsidiary, X, a limited company, to Z, a public limited company. During the year RP supplied X with second hand office equipment and X leased its factory from RP. The transactions were all contracted for at market rates.

(4 marks)

(iii)   The pension scheme of the group is managed by another merchant bank. An investment manager of the group pension scheme is also a non-executive director of the RP Group and received an annual fee for his services of £25,000 which is not material in the group context. The company pays £16m per annum into the scheme and occasionally transfers assets into the scheme. In 1999, fixed assets of £10m were transferred into the scheme and a recharge of administrative costs of £3m was made.   **(5 marks)**
(Total: 25 marks)

---

77   (Question 3 of examination)

Standard setters have been struggling for several years with the practical issues of the disclosure, recognition and measurement of financial instruments. The ASB has issued a Discussion Paper on 'Derivatives and Other Financial Instruments' and Financial Reporting Standard 13 on the disclosure of such instruments. The dynamic nature of international financial markets has resulted in the widespread use of a variety of financial instruments but present accounting rules in this area do not ensure that the financial statements portray effectively the impact and risks of the instruments currently being used.

Required:

(a)   (i)   Discuss the concerns about the accounting practices used for financial instruments which led to demands for an accounting standard.   **(7 marks)**

        (ii)   Explain why regulations dealing with disclosure alone cannot solve the problem of accounting for financial instruments.   **(4 marks)**

(b)   (i)   Discuss three ways in which gains and losses on financial instruments might be recorded in the financial statements commenting on the relative merits of each method.   **(8 marks)**

        (ii)   AX, a public limited company, issued a three year £30 million 5% debenture at par on 1 December 1998 when the market rate of interest was 5%. Interest is paid annually on 30 November each year. Market rates of interest on debentures of equivalent term and risk are 6% and 4% at the end of the financial years to 30 November 1999 and 30 November 2000. (Assume that the changes in interest rates took place on 30 November each year.)

                Show the effect on 'profit' for the three years to 30 November 2001 if the debenture and the interest charge were valued on a fair value basis.   **(6 marks)**
(Total: 25 marks)

---

78   (Question 4 of examination)

Provisions are particular kinds of liabilities. It therefore follows that provisions should be recognised when the definition of a liability has been met. The key requirement of a liability is a present obligation and thus

---

this requirement is critical also in the context of the recognition of a provision. However, although accounting for provisions is an important topic for standard setters, it is only recently that guidance has been issued on provisioning in financial statements. In the UK, the Accounting Standards Board has recently issued FRS 12: 'Provisions, Contingent Liabilities and Contingent Assets'.

Required:

(a) (i) Explain why there was a need for more detailed guidance on accounting for provisions in the UK.

(7 marks)

(ii) Explain the circumstances under which a provision should be recognised in the financial statements according to FRS 12: 'Provisions, Contingent Liabilities and Contingent Assets'.

(6 marks)

(b) Discuss whether the following provisions have been accounted for correctly under FRS 12: 'Provisions, Contingent Liabilities and Contingent Assets'.

World Wide Nuclear Fuels plc disclosed the following information in its financial statements for the year ending 30 November 1999:

Provisions and long-term commitments

(i) Provision for decommissioning the Group's radioactive facilities is made over their useful life and covers complete demolition of the facility within fifty years of it being taken out of service together with any associated waste disposal. The provision is based on future prices and is discounted using a current market rate of interest.

Provision for decommissioning costs

	£m
Balance at 1.12.98	675
Adjustment arising from change in price levels charged to reserves	33
Charged in the year to profit and loss account	125
Adjustment due to change in knowledge (charged to reserves)	27
Balance at 30.11.99	860

There are still decommissioning costs of £1,231m (undiscounted) to be provided for in respect of the group's radioactive facilities as the company's policy is to build up the required provision over the life of the facility.

Assume that adjustments to the provision due to change in knowledge about the accuracy of the provision do not give rise to future economic benefits.

(7 marks)

(ii) The company purchased an oil company during the year. As part of the sale agreement, oil has to be supplied for a five year period to the company's former holding company at an uneconomic rate. As a result a provision for future operating losses has been set up of £135m which relates solely to the uneconomic supply of oil. Additionally the oil company is exposed to environmental liabilities arising out of its past obligations, principally in respect of remedial work to soil and ground water systems, although currently there is no legal obligation to carry out the work. Liabilities for environmental costs are provided for when the Group determines a formal plan of action on the closure of an inactive site and when expenditure on remedial work is probable and the cost can be measured with reasonable certainty. However in this case, it has been decided to provide for £120m in respect of the environmental liability on the acquisition of the oil company. World Wide

Nuclear Fuels has a reputation for ensuring that the environment is preserved and protected from the effects of its business activities.

(5 marks)

(Total: 25 marks)

Section C – ONE question ONLY to be attempted

79	**(Question 5 of examination)**

The traditional audit approach has been influenced by the notion that auditing is a process of risk assessment and management. A key element of any assessment of risk is the materiality of the item being assessed. As the way the auditor conducts the audit changes, it is becoming increasingly apparent that the traditional approach to the determination of the materiality of an item has to change and a wider concept of materiality has to be promoted.

Required:

(a) (i) Explain the traditional approach to determining whether an item is material and the problems associated with the definition of materiality. **(6 marks)**

(ii) Explain the recent developments which have made it increasingly difficult to determine the materiality of items to be disclosed in financial statements. **(8 marks)**

(b) Discuss the criteria which would determine whether the following sale of an asset would be deemed to be material and require disclosure in the financial statements:

AB, a public limited company, manufactures engineering parts, and is preparing its financial statements for the year ending 30 November 1999.

AB has sold a piece of land to one of its directors who retired on 30 November 1999. The selling price of the land was £500,000 and the company made a profit of £200,000 on the transaction. If the land price index rises more than 50 per cent in the next two years then a further £100,000 becomes payable by the director. The company does not normally sell land and this transaction is the first of its kind in the company records. The director was earning £400,000 per annum at the time of her retirement.

The company normally makes profits of between £40m and £50m but the current year's operating profits have dropped to £3m. The net assets of the company are £400m and the carrying value of land and buildings in the balance sheet is £100m. **(6 marks)**

(Total: 20 marks)

80	**(Question 6 of examination)**

BG are a multinational firm of accountants. Their managing partner has been requested to appear in court in connection with one of their largest clients, BV, a public limited company. BG carry out the audit and tax work for BV. BV is being investigated for a possible tax fraud, which was linked to the establishment of a secret fund designed to make political contributions. The funds were maintained in an overseas bank, TBL, which was also a client of the audit firm. The existence of the fund had been discovered by the managing partner during the audit of the overseas bank.

The judge had ordered that the audit and tax working papers of BV be submitted to the court. However, the managing partner of BG had refused to submit the tax working papers of BV and copies of letters between BV and their solicitors on the grounds that they contained confidential information that would be damaging to their client.

The manager in charge of the tax affairs of BV was disturbed by the partner's actions and felt that they were ethically wrong as the tax working papers proved that BV was guilty of fraud and he had refused to carry on acting for BV. He decided that he was going to submit the tax working papers to the court without the partner's due authority.

Required:

(a)   Explain how the audit firm should have dealt with the discovery of the existence of the 'secret fund'.

(6 marks)

(b)   Discuss whether the managing partner of BG was justified on the grounds of confidentiality in not providing the court with all the working papers of BV plc.

(7 marks)

(c)   Discuss the position of the tax manager if he submits the tax working papers to the court against the partner's wishes.

(7 marks)

(Total: 20 marks)

DECEMBER 1999 ANSWERS

---

75   (Answer 1 of examination)

(a)   A acquired a controlling interest in X in two stages and FRS 2 'Accounting for subsidiary undertakings' recommends that goodwill be computed in a single computation by reference to the fair value of the net assets of the subsidiary when it becomes part of the group. This complies with the Companies Act 1985 (Sch4A paragraph 9).

X plc

Date	Holding	Net Assets £m	Consideration £m
31.8.97	10%		5
31.10.98	45%	52	25
		52	
less provision for warranty ((5% of 300)–3)		(12)	
	55%	40	30

Goodwill = £30 million – (55% of 40 million)
= £8 million

Y plc

Purchase consideration	54	
Fair value of assets acquired (60% of 70)		(42)
Goodwill	12	
Total Goodwill (8 + 12 =)	20	
Amortisation	5	
Goodwill	15	

(b)   Where a group increases its interest in an undertaking that is already a subsidiary, the subsidiary's assets should be revalued to fair value on consolidation. Goodwill arising on the increased interest in the company should be calculated by reference to those values.

A Group
Consolidated Balance Sheet as at 31 October 1999

Tangible fixed assets	150
Associated company	51·2
Goodwill	7·4
Net current assets (26 + 25 + 20)	71
Long-term liabilities (6 + 35 + 1)	(42)
Provision for warranties	(17)
	220.6
Share Capital	80
Retained Profits	128·35
Minority Interest	12·25
	220.6

Workings (£m)

Consolidation of A and X including previous years' balances for illustration
Cost of Control

Cost of Investment	30	Share Capital – X	5·5
Provision	6·6	Reserves	11
		Revaluation (55% 52 – 30)	12·1
		Goodwill	8
	36·6		36·6

Goodwill	8	Transfer to grp. res	2
		Balance c/d (31.10.98)	6
	8		8

Balance b/d	6	Share Capital from MI	1
Cost of investment (10%)	8	Reserves from MI	2
Provision	1·7	X – profit for 1999	1
(10% of 5 + 1·2 MI)		Minority Interest revaluation	2·2
Inter company profit	0·8	Revaluation	(0·2)
		Goodwill c/d	10·5
	16·5		16·5

Goodwill b/d	10·5	Goodwill written off (2 + 1·1)	3·1
		Balance	7·4
	10·5		10·5

Inter group profit X

X has made a profit on the sale of land to A and it needs to be eliminated

DR	Minority Interests 35% of 8	2·8
	Group Reserves 55% of 8	4·4
	Cost of Control 10% of 8	0·8
CR	Tangible fixed assets	8

Group Reserves

Goodwill	X 1998 2	Balance (31.10.98)	100
X 1999	3·1	Profit for year	40
Y (1998/99)	6	X Reserves	5·5
Provision (55% 5)	2·75	Exchange gain	1
Revaluation Reserves	1·1	Associated Co – post acqn profit	4
Inter group profit – X	4·4		
– Y (2 + 0·8)	2·8		
Balance	128·35		
	150·5		150·5

Minority Interest

Provision	5·4	Share Capital	4·5
Balance c/d	18	X Reserves	9
		Revaluation (45% 52 – 30)	9·9
	23·4		23·4

To Cost of Control – Share Capital (10% of 10)	1	Balance (31.10.98)	18
To Cost of Control – Reserves (10% of 20)	2	X Reserves	3·5
To Cost of Control – Revaluation (10% of 22)	2·2	Provision – Cost of Control	1·2
Provision (35% 5)	1·75		
Revaluation Reserves	0·7		
Inter group profit	2·8		
Balance	12·25		
	22·7		22·7

X Reserves

Cost of Control (55% of 20)	11	Balance (31.10.98)	20
Minority Interest (45% of 20)	9		
	20		20
To Cost of Control (10% of 10)	1	Profit for 1999	10
Minority Interest	3·5		
Group Reserves	5·5		
	10		10

Group Revaluation Reserves

Cost of Control	12·1	Revaluation of X (31.10.98)	22
Minority Interest	9·9		
	22		22
Revaluation deficit (60 – (52 + 10))	2	Minority Interest (35% 2)	0·7
		Cost of Control (10% 2)	0·2
		Group Reserves (55% 2)	1·1
	2		2

Provision for Warranties

Balance c/f	17	Balance	12
		Additional provision (5% of 200) – 5	5
	17		17

Overseas Investment

Equity shares recorded at $\dfrac{42m}{3.5} = £12m$

Loan recorded at $\dfrac{21m}{3.5} = £6m$

Loan retranslated at 31.10.99 $\dfrac{21m}{3} = £7m$

Equity shares retranslated at 31.10.99 $\dfrac{42m}{3} = £14m$

Therefore there is an exchange gain of £2m on the investment and an exchange loss on the loan of £1m. The exchange gain and loss can be taken to reserves under SSAP20 'Foreign Currency Translation'.

Y Deemed Disposal

A owns 12 million ordinary shares of £1 of Y and this amounted to a 60% holding on 1.11.98. However Y has issued a further 10 million ordinary shares of £1 to third parties. Thus A's holding is now

$$\frac{12 \text{ million}}{20 \text{ million} + 10 \text{ million}} \text{ ie } \underline{40\%}.$$

Thus it would appear that Y is now an associated company.

	£m
Cost of investment	54
Add post acquisition profit (10 × 40%)	4
less – intercompany profit in stock (2 × 40%)	(0·8)
Less goodwill 12 ÷ 4 × 2 years	(6)
Associated Company	51·2

Tangible Fixed Assets

	£m
A	108
X	50
Inter group profit – X	(8)
Inter group profit – Y	(2)
(land £5m × 40%)	
Foreign currency gain	2
	150

Note: not all of the inter group profit arising on transactions with the associate Y has been eliminated. Only the investors share has been eliminated. FRS 9 'Associates and Joint Ventures' states that profits on inter company trading should be made in the balance sheet against the carrying amount of the asset if it is still held by the group.

Provision for warranty	£m	£m Expense	£m Provn
1998 5% × 300	= 15	(3)	12
1999 5% × 200	= 10	(5)	5
			17

Pre acqn 12 × 55%	=	6·6
Pre acqn 17 × 10%	=	1·7
Post acqn 5 × 55%	=	2·75
Minority 17 × 35%	=	5·95

(5·4 − 1·2 + 1·75)

Proof of Minority Interest and goodwill on purchase of 10% holding in X on 31.10.99

		£m
Minority Interest:	Share of net assets $60 \times 35\%$	21
	Provision (above)	(5·95)
	Inter company	(2·8)
		12·25
Goodwill (10% purchase)	Cost of acqn	8
	Share of net assets	
	$(60 - 17 - 8) \times 10\%$	(3·5)
Goodwill		4·5

---

76   (Answer 2 of examination)

(a)   (i)   Related party relationships are part of the normal business process. Entities operate the separate parts of their business through subsidiaries and associates and acquire interests in other enterprises for investment or commercial reasons. Thus control or significant influence can be exercised over the investee by the investing company. These relationships can have a significant effect on the financial position and operating results of the company and lead to transactions which would not normally be undertaken. For example, a company may sell a large proportion of its production to its parent company because it cannot and could not find a market elsewhere. Additionally the transactions may be effected at prices which would not be acceptable to unrelated parties.

Even if there are no transactions between the related parties it is still possible for the operating results and financial position of an enterprise to be affected by the relationship. A recently acquired subsidiary can be forced to finish a relationship with a company in order to benefit group companies. Transactions may be entered into on terms different from those applicable to an unrelated party. For example, a holding company may lease equipment to a subsidiary on terms unrelated to market rates for equivalent leases.

In the absence of contrary information, it is assumed that the financial statements of an entity reflect transactions carried out on an arm's length basis and that the entity has independent discretionary power over its actions and pursues its activities independently. If these assumptions are not justified because of related party transactions, then disclosure of this fact should be made. Even if transactions are at arm's length, the disclosure of related party transactions is useful because it is likely that future transactions may be affected by such relationships. The main issues in determining such disclosures are the identification of related parties, the types of transactions and arrangements and the information to be disclosed.

(ii)   The disclosure of related party information is as important to the user of the accounts of small companies as it is to the user of larger entities. If the transaction involves individuals who have an interest in the small company then it may have greater significance because of the disproportionate influence that this individual may have. The directors may also be the shareholders and this degree of control may affect the nature of certain transactions with the company. It is argued that the confidential nature of such disclosures would affect a small company but these disclosures are likely to be excluded from abbreviated accounts made available to the public. In any event if these disclosures are so significant then it can be argued that they ought to be disclosed.

It is possible that the costs of providing the information to be disclosed could outweigh the benefits of reporting it. However, this point of view is difficult to evaluate but the value of appropriate related party disclosures is particularly important and relevant information in small company accounts since transactions with related parties are more likely to be material. The Financial Reporting Standard for Smaller Entities (FRSSE) requires disclosure of material transactions with related parties including personal guarantees given by directors in respect of borrowings by the reporting entity. There are exemptions from disclosure if the reporting entity applies the FRSSE and these include non disclosure of pension contributions paid to a pension fund and transactions with certain parties such as providers of finance, and government departments.

It is felt by some that the Companies Acts requirements in this area were sufficient to enable adequate disclosure. However the Companies Acts gave a certain amount of information as regards the disclosure of directors and other officers transactions but these requirements only give limited assurance and therefore FRS 8 and the FRSSE requirements were required in order to extend the disclosure and produce a comprehensive set of regulations in the area.

(b)　(i)　FRS 8 does not require disclosure of the relationship and transactions between the reporting entity and providers of finance in the normal course of their business even though they may influence decisions. Thus as RP is a merchant bank, there are no requirements to disclose transactions between RP and AB because of this relationship. However, RP has a twenty-five per cent equity interest in AB. FRS 8 states that in order to avoid any doubt there are certain relationships that are deemed to be related parties. One of these relationships is that of investor and associate. Thus under FRS 9 'Associates and Joint Ventures' the entity has to have a participating interest and be able to exercise significant influence over the operating and financial policies of the company in order for associate status to exist. In order to exercise significant influence the company must actively be involved and be influential. Thus the equity holding in AB may not necessarily mean that AB is an associate especially as the remaining seventy-five per cent of the shares are held by the management of AB who are likely to control decisions on strategic issues. Also merchant banks often do not regard companies in which they have invested as associates but as investments and such 'portfolio investors' are acknowledged in FRS 9. FRS 9 says that if the business of the investor is to provide capital to the entity accompanied by advice and guidance then the holding should be accounted for as an investment rather than an associate.

However, FRS 8 presumes that a person owning or able to exercise control over twenty per cent or more of the voting rights of the reporting entity is a related party. An investor with a twenty-five per cent equity holding and a director on the board would be expected to have influence over the financial and operating policies in such a way as to inhibit the pursuit of their separate interests. If it can be shown that such influence does not exist, then there is no related party relationship. The two entities are not related parties simply because they have a main board director on the board of AB (directors in common do not make the companies related parties FRS 8). Thus it is apparent that the establishment of a related party relationship in this case involves consideration of several issues.

If, however, it is deemed that they are related parties then all material transactions will require disclosure including the management fees, interest, dividends and the terms of the loan.

(ii)　No disclosure is required in consolidated accounts of intragroup transactions and balances eliminated on consolidation. Thus transactions between related parties will be disclosed to the extent that they were undertaken when X was not part of the group. Disclosure has to be made of transactions between related parties if they were related at any time during the financial period. Thus any transactions between RP and X during the period 1 July 1999 to 31 October 1999 will be disclosed but transactions prior to 1 July 1999 would have been eliminated on consolidation. There is no related party relationship between RP and Z, as it is simply a business transaction unless there has been a subordinating of interests when entering into the transaction due to influence or control.

(iii)　Pension schemes for the benefit of employees of the reporting entity are related parties of the entity. This requirement of FRS 8 was inevitable after the problems associated with the Maxwell affair. Contributions paid to the pension scheme are exempt from the disclosure under FRS 8 but it is the other transactions with RP which must be disclosed. Thus the transfers of fixed assets (£10m) and the recharge of administrative costs (£3m) must be disclosed. The pension scheme's investment managers would not normally be considered a related party of the reporting sponsoring company and it does not follow that related parties of the pension scheme are also the company's related parties. There would however be a related party relationship if it can be demonstrated that the investment manager can 'influence the financial and operating policies' of RP through his position as non-executive director of that company. Directors under FRS 8 are deemed to be related parties. The fact that the investment manager is paid £25,000 as a fee and this is not material to the group does not mean that it should not be disclosed. Materiality is defined in the context of its significance to the other related party which in this instance is the investment manager. It is likely that the fee will be material in this respect.

77   (Answer 3 of examination)

(a)   (i)   In recent years   the growth and complexity of financial instruments has been quite significant. Companies use a range of instruments to transform and manage their financial risk. However, accounting standards have not developed at the same rate as the growth in the instruments. The main concern of standard setters is that many derivatives are not recognised on the balance sheet. The main reason for this is the use of the historical cost concept in financial statements together with the fact that many derivatives have a nil cost. However, derivatives may be substantial assets and liabilities and may expose the entity to significant risk. Additionally many companies measure financial assets at amortised cost even though there are reliable quoted market prices that differ from amortised cost and the assets are readily saleable.

At present unrealised gains and losses arising from changes in the value of many financial instruments are often ignored. Unrealised losses are recognised if the instrument is valued on the basis of the lower of cost or market value but ignored if the instrument is classed as a hedge. The danger is that such unrealised losses are overlooked. Additionally companies can choose when they recognise profits on instruments in order that they can smooth profits. This applies both to derivatives and non-derivatives.

The use of hedge accounting currently causes significant problems. The practical problem with hedge accounting is translating business decisions into an accounting transaction that satisfies the hedging criteria. Hedge accounting relies on management intent and the result of this is that identical instruments can be accounted for differently depending upon the intentions of management in relation to them. Hedge accounting is often used for hedges of uncontracted future transactions and in these circumstances can be used to justify deferring almost any gain or loss on the derivative.

Circumstances can change quickly in the financial markets and the resultant effect on a company's derivatives can quickly transform the risk profile of a company. The present accounting framework does not adequately make this movement in the position and risk apparent to users of financial statements.

(ii)   Disclosure of the risk of an entity in relation to financial instruments is an important element of accounting for financial instruments and the ASB has developed FRS 13 'Derivatives and Other Financial Instruments: Disclosures' to deal with this issue. However disclosure requirements alone are not sufficient to deal with the problem. Recognition and measurement issues need to be dealt with. Many derivatives are kept off the balance sheet with unrealised gains and losses being ignored. Hedge accounting problems cannot be dealt with purely by requiring narrative disclosures of the hedging instrument or of any deferred or unrecognised gain or loss. It is important that some consensus is achieved over the possible measurement bases which can be used. The use of current values for financial instruments requires agreement as it is a critical measurement issue. For example, could current values be used for derivatives but not for non-derivatives. There are issues of impairment of financial instruments and the recognition of such instruments which need to be dealt with in a standard. Most issues in accounting are dealt with by standards focusing on measurement, recognition and disclosure issues. A financial instrument is no exception in this regard and it is such an important issue that disclosure alone could never effectively deal with the issues satisfactorily.

(b)   (i)   There are four alternative ways in which gains and losses on financial instruments can be reported:

(i)   all gains and losses in the profit and loss account

(ii)   certain gains and losses in the profit and loss account and others in the statement of total recognised gains and losses (STRGL)

(iii)   some gains and losses could be recorded within assets and liabilities or as a separate component of shareholders funds and transferred to the profit and loss account in a future period once they are realised

(iv)   Some gains and losses could be held temporarily in equity via the STRGL, and recycled to the profit and loss account once they are realised.

Method (i)

The main arguments for reporting all changes in value in the profit and loss account are that all gains and losses represent the performance of management who are responsible for the decision to buy or hold certain instruments. Additionally if all changes in value are recorded in the profit and loss account it restricts abuses and the manipulation of profits although decisions will have to be made about how the gains and losses are reported. For example should the interest expense be shown separately from other changes in value. However if unrealised gains and losses on fixed rate debt were recorded in the profit and loss account it might imply that such debt carried risk and companies might fear that the reporting of gains and losses on this debt in this manner might be misunderstood. Additionally such gains and losses are of a different character to trading profits and losses but would be amalgamated with the latter in the profit and loss account.

Method (ii)

The advantage of this approach is that the different types of gains and losses would be reported separately. Gains and losses on long-term instruments could be reported in the STRGL and those on short term investment in the profit and loss account. The profit and loss account could be protected from volatile movements if this method were adopted. The main problem however is drawing a distinction between those gains and losses to be reported in the profit and loss account and those to be reported in the STRGL. There are principles and a code of practice to be developed. The question is simply about which performance statement they should be shown in and the rationale for such a distinction.

Method (iii)

Under this method, gains and losses are deferred until a future period when the gain or loss is transferred to the profit and loss account. This 'recycling' could occur on realisation or at a constant rate over the remaining life of the instrument. This approach would avoid the volatility which would result from recording all changes in value in the profit and loss account. If the gains and losses were transferred on realisation then present practice would not be significantly altered. However, gains and losses would not be reported in the year in which they occurred but are deferred and this gives opportunities for abuse. Also the balance sheet will record amounts which are meaningless. The deferred debits and credits are not assets and liabilities and the alternative of showing the items as a component of shareholders funds amounts to reserve accounting and is difficult to justify in principle.

Method (iv)

This is a similar method to (iii) above. Certain gains and losses are recorded in STRGL and are transferred to the profit and loss account at a later date perhaps when realised or at a constant rate over the life of the instrument. All gains and losses would be recorded in the year they occur. However, under this method the reported figures can be meaningless as a loss can be reported in two performance statements at different times. The STRGL becomes an account which temporarily holds gains and losses that have not been reported in the profit and loss account and this conflicts with the rationale for the current usage of the statement. Also the approach conflicts with FRS 3 'Reporting Financial Performance'. It might appear that the best solution is method (ii) as it enables separate reporting of different gains and losses.

(Candidates need only discuss three of the above four methods.)

(ii) **AX plc**

	1999 £'000	2000 £'000	2001 £'000
Historical cost interest 5%	1,500	1,500	1,500
Adjustment to fair value for market rate of interest	-	267	(288)
Effective interest cost	1,500	1,767	1,212
(Gain)/Loss due to change in fair value	(550)	571	-
Net charge to 'profit'	950	2,338	1,212

Fair value of debenture at 30 November 1999

	£m	Disct at 6%
Interest payable 30.11.2000	1·5	1,415,094
Interest and capital payable 30.11.2001	31·5	28,034,887
		29,449,981

Gain on fair valuation is £30m–£29·45m =   £550,000

Fair value of debenture at 30 November 2000

	£m	Disct at 4%
Interest and capital payable 30.11.2001	31·5	£30,288,461

Loss/(Gain) due to change in fair value   £30,288,461 – (266,999 + 29,449,981)
                                             i.e. £571,481

Interest adjustment
1999 – No adjustment
2000 – 6% of £29,449,981 = £1,766,999
2001 – 4% of £30,288,461 = £1,211,538

---

78   (Answer 4 of examination)

(a)   (i)   A provision for a liability or charge is defined in the Companies Act as 'any amount retained as reasonably necessary for the purposes of providing for any liability or loss which is likely to be incurred, or certain to be incurred but uncertain as to the amount or as to the date on which it will arise'. However, the ASB is anxious to ensure that only those amounts that meet its definition of liabilities are reported in the balance sheet. Thus the ASB proposes to edit the Act's definition to 'liabilities in respect of which the amount or timing of the expenditure that will be undertaken is uncertain', as the Companies Act definition is more discretionary than that in FRS 12. The Board is keen to prevent companies from providing for future operating losses as in the ASB's opinion they should be accounted for in the future.

It is often quite difficult to differentiate between provisions and liabilities and reclassification from one category to another is not uncommon. The importance of the distinction is that provisions are subject to disclosure requirements which do not apply to other creditors. For example the Companies Act requires disclosure of the movement on a provision in the year but not creditors. However even such disclosure does not solve the difficulty with provisioning as quite often the largest disclosed balance is 'other provisions' with no information being disclosed in the financial statements.

The transparency of disclosure is possibly the most important issue in accounting for provisions. Once a provision has been established it is possible to bypass the profit and loss account with expenditure that is charged to it. Some of the provisions that have been set up in this manner have been very large. Planned expenditures for several years may be aggregated into one large provision that is reported as an exceptional item. The user of financial statements may then add the provision back to income in the year and fail to take account of charges made to that provision in future years. (This is often referred to as 'big bath accounting'.)

There has been concern that the basis on which provisions have been recognised has not been clear. In some cases the recognition of provisions has been based on management's intentions rather than on the basis of a present obligation. Thus management have been able to exercise discretion over the timing of recognition of provisions with the following effects:

(i)   inconsistency between the accounting for provisions between different companies
(ii)   the smoothing of earnings by management
(iii)   the impairment of the balance sheet as a useful statement.

It is important that provisions are recognised and measured on a consistent basis and that sufficient information is disclosed in the notes to the financial statements to enable users to understand their nature, timing and amount.

(ii)   FRS 12 utilises the ASB's 'Statement of Principles for Financial Reporting' and concludes that provisions are an element of the liabilities and not a separate element of the financial statements. Provisions should be recognised when and only when:

(i)   an enterprise has a present legal or constructive obligation as a result of past events

(ii)   it is probable that a transfer of economic benefits will be required to settle the obligation

(iii)   a reliable estimate of the amount required to settle the obligation can be made. A reliable estimate can always be made if there is a reasonable range of possible outcomes.

An obligation exists when the entity has no realistic alternative to making a transfer of economic benefits. This is the case only where the obligation can be enforced by law or in the case of constructive obligation (see below). No provision is recognised for costs that need to be incurred to operate in the future. The only liabilities recognised are those that exist at the balance sheet date. The obligations must have arisen from past events and must exist independently from the company's future actions. If the company can avoid the expenditure by its future actions then no provision is recognised. These rules are designed to allow a provision to escape recognition only in rare cases. In these rare cases there is an obligation if having taken into account all available evidence, it is more likely than not that a present obligation exists at the balance sheet date.

It is not necessary to know the identity of the party to whom the obligation is owed in order for an obligation to exist but in principle there must be another party. The mere intention or necessity to incur expenditure is not enough to create an obligation. Where there are a number of similar obligations, the whole class of obligations must be considered when determining whether economic benefits will be transferred.

There is a need to provide for legal obligations although there is the important issue of timing and the identification of the past event which triggers the recognition. However FRS 12 also deals with the concept of 'constructive obligation'. For example where a retail store gives refunds to dissatisfied customers even though there is no legal obligation to do so in order that it will preserve its reputation. Therefore, an entity may be committed to certain expenditure because any alternative would be too onerous to contemplate. The determination of a constructive obligation is extremely difficult and is a somewhat subjective concept.

An event may give rise to an obligation at a later date because of changes in the law or because of a constructive obligation. Provision will be made when the law is virtually certain to be enacted or the entity publicly accepts responsibility for the event in a way which creates a constructive obligation.

The rules for recognition are expanded to deal explicitly with certain specific cases:

(i)   no provision should be recognised for future operating losses

(ii)   a present obligation for restructuring only exists and thus a provision recognised when a constructive obligation to restructure exists at the balance sheet date and the criteria for recognition laid out in FRS 12 are satisfied.

(iii)   If an entity has a contract that is onerous, the present obligation under the contract should be recognised and measured as a provision.

FRS 12 essentially looks at the problem of provisions from a balance sheet perspective choosing to concentrate on liability recognition rather than the recognition of an expense.

(b)   (i)   FRS 12 has a significant impact on decommissioning activities. It appears that the company is building up the required provision over the useful life of the radioactive facility often called the 'units of production' method. However FRS 12 requires the full liability to be established as soon as the obligation exists to the extent of the damage already done or goods and services received. The provision should be capitalised as an asset if the expenditure provides access to future economic benefits. If this is not the case, then the provision should be charged immediately to the profit and loss account. The asset so created will be written off over the life of the facility. Thus the decommissioning costs of £1,231m (undiscounted) not yet provided for will have to be brought onto the balance sheet at its discounted amount and a corresponding asset created.

The current practice adopted by the company as regards the discounting of the provision is inconsistent. The provision is based on future cash flows but the discount rate is based upon current market rates of interest. FRS 12 states that companies may use current prices discounted by a real interest rate or future prices discounted by a nominal rate. The company is currently utilising a mix of these practices. FRS 12 states that a risk free rate should be used where a prudent estimate of future cash flows already reflects risk. (The government bond rate is recommended.)

The company currently makes a reserve adjustment for changes in price levels. However this adjustment should have two elements and be charged to the profit and loss account. The first element would be the current adjustment on the total provision for changes in the discount rate and the second element would be an element representing the unwinding of the discount. Thus the profit and loss account would be charged with the amortisation of the asset created by the setting up of the provision, and also with an adjustment for the change in price levels and the unwinding of the discount. FRS 12 requires this latter amount to be shown as a financial item adjacent to but separate from 'interest'.

It appears that any subsequent amendment of the provision should be recognised in the profit and loss account if it does not give rise to future economic benefits (paragraph 66). However the company appears to be treating the adjustment of £27m as a movement on reserves. This would not be allowed under FRS 12.

(ii)   One of the quite explicit rules of FRS 12 is that no provision should be made for future operating losses. However, if the company has entered into an onerous contract then a provision will be required. An onerous contract is one entered into with another party under which the unavoidable costs of fulfilling the contract exceed the revenues to be received and where the entity would have to pay compensation to the other party if the contract was not fulfilled. Thus it appears that the contract should be loss-making by nature. Thus in this case the provision of £135m would remain in the financial statements and would affect the fair value exercise and the computation of goodwill.

Provisions for environmental liabilities should be recognised when the entity becomes obliged (legally or constructively) to rectify environmental damage or perform restorative work on the environment. A provision should only be made where the company has no real option but to carry out remedial work. The mere existence of environmental contamination caused by the company's activities does not in itself give rise to an obligation. Thus in this case there is no current obligation. However it can be argued that there is a 'constructive obligation' to provide for the remedial work because the conduct of the company has created a valid expectation that the company will clean up the environment. Thus there is no easy solution to the problem as it will be determined by the subjective assessment of the directors and auditors as to whether there is a 'constructive obligation'. It is a difficult concept and one which will result in different interpretations. If one takes example 2B in FRS 12 as a guide then a provision should be made.

79   (Answer 5 of examination)

(a)   (i)   The approach to materiality is that an item is material if its omission or misstatement would influence the decision of the addressee of the auditor's report. Materiality is considered in the context of the individual primary statement in the financial statements or the individual line elements. Materiality involves both qualitative and quantitative judgement. Additionally auditors should assess the materiality of the total of all uncorrected misstatements. Thus the materiality may be determined by considerations such as legal and regulatory requirements, the degree of accuracy required in certain disclosures (directors emoluments), inaccurate descriptions of an accounting policy, and the impact on the view given by financial statements of relatively small errors.

The problem with materiality is that it is difficult to mathematically define a materiality level. In the US, the Securities and Exchange Commission reputedly requires adjustment for an error of 10% or more and does not require adjustment for an error of 5% or less. Between 5% and 10% is a matter of professional judgement. The materiality decision will always depend on the professional judgement of the auditor and the nature of the company being audited. This creates the possibility of inconsistencies between the materiality thresholds of different auditors. A rigid materiality model which could be used to determine adjustment thresholds, would be unrealistic and unworkable. Additionally it is impossible to know who the 'addressee' of the auditor's report actually is and whether the item would affect their decision. The addressee could be a sophisticated analyst who looks at the financial statements in detail, or an individual shareholder who does little more than glance at the financial statements.

(ii) The purpose of the information in financial statements is to assist users in making economic decisions and recent developments in corporate governance and accounting standards have enabled them to analyse corporate performance on a better informed basis. However, the complexity of recent accounting standards, the pronouncements of the Financial Reporting Review Panel, and developments in corporate governance have made it more difficult to determine the materiality of an item, and also where certain disclosures should be made. The question arises as to whether these disclosures are to be made in the audited financial statements or should they be disclosed perhaps in the Operating and Financial Review. Recently a wider concept of materiality has been developed. Accounting standards have created a broader definition of materiality. There is no accepted definition of what constitutes the user of financial statements for the purpose of defining whether the decision of a user could be affected. FRS 8 'Related Party Disclosures' intimates that a material transaction would influence the decisions made by users of general purpose financial statements whereas SAS220 'Materiality and the Audit' refers to a narrower definition of user. According to SAS220 the user is the addressee of the audit report. This inconsistency in definition could lead to differing decisions by auditors as regards the materiality of an item.

In recent accounting standards there is an increasing reliance on disclosures containing detailed explanations and it is difficult for auditors to determine the extent of the content of such disclosures in terms of their materiality to users. For example, FRS 3 'Reporting Financial Performance' requires the provision of an 'adequate' explanation of exceptional items to enable their nature to be understood. The problem is the determination of the 'adequacy' and relevance of the information being disclosed.

The problem of accounting for derivatives and financial instruments has been dealt with currently by requiring narrative disclosures (FRS 13). An explanation of the major financial risks faced by certain entities and the management of those risks is required by the standard. The decision as to the materiality of the information to be disclosed in this area is a difficult decision faced by auditors.

There has been a dramatic increase in the regulations which often govern a company. The auditor faces a sometimes difficult decision as to whether the breach of a regulation affects the truth and fairness of the financial statements, whether the relevant regulators need informing or whether it is related to the reporting on the standard of corporate governance. This decision can have a material impact upon the information to be disclosed in financial statements.

The London Stock Exchange's combined code on corporate governance extends the directors review to non-financial controls and the report specifically states that the review should encompass compliance with laws and regulations as well as minimising the risk of fraud. If there has been a material failure of such controls, explanation is required in the annual report. Frauds are rarely disclosed in annual reports and therefore the auditor has to determine whether this information is relevant to user needs and hence requires disclosure.

Thus accounting standards have modified the definition of materiality. Whether a material misstatement or omission of information has occurred is extremely difficult to determine given the proliferation of standards, regulations and corporate governance requirements. Materiality has become a difficult concept to articulate and traditional views which explain it in terms of simply the potential impact of the error or omission to total in financial statements are outdated. The auditor is faced with more qualitative judgements concerning materiality than was previously the case, particularly as the 'standard user' of financial statements is indefinable and the fact that shareholders have very different expectations.

(b) There are several criteria which must be considered when determining whether the sale of the land is deemed to be material:

(i) size – the size of the profit (£200,000) made on the sale of land is quite small in relation to the normal profit of the company (£40m–£50m). However current years profits have dropped to £3m with the result that the profit made on the sale of the land is 6·7% of the years operating profit. This could be argued as being immaterial especially as the 'normal profits' are so large. Additionally the net assets, and land and buildings valuations are respectively £400m and £100m which would indicate that the profit as a percentage of these values is immaterial.

(ii)   exceptional item – profits and losses on the sale of fixed assets should be shown as a non-operating exceptional item under FRS 3 'Reporting Financial Performance'. The profit made on the sale of the land is 6·7% of the operating profit and as discussed above this could be deemed to be immaterial and therefore not required to be disclosed. However size is only one criterion to be considered. The nature and incidence of transactions should also be taken into account according to the standard.

(iii)   contingent on an event or condition – the profit on the sale of the land is not fixed as a further amount may become payable if the land price index moves in the next two years. Thus there is a possibility that a further amount may become payable. It is unlikely that such an occurrence would be remote as such a provision would not be placed in a contract if there was no possibility of it occurring. FRS 12 'Provisions, Contingent Liabilities and Contingent Assets' requires disclosures of contingent assets when an inflow of economic benefits is probable. The determination of the probability of the event occurring is based on the subjective judgement of the client and auditor, as is the materiality of the additional amount which may become payable.

(iv)   nature and incidence of the transaction – it could be argued that because the transaction is unusual in terms of its nature and incidence then it should be disclosed. The company does not normally sell land and therefore it is an exceptional transaction. Additionally the transaction involves a retiring director who during the year was a related party. It is debatable whether the transaction is material to AB but it is certainly material to the director. Materiality in the context of FRS 8 is defined in terms of the influence on decisions of users and therefore any transaction of a sensitive nature could be deemed to be material. Thus size criteria are not as important under this standard and given the borderline nature of the other criteria, this item would be deemed to be material when one considers collectively all the criteria outlined above.

---

80   (Answer 6 of examination)

(a)   The existence of the secret fund designed to make political contributions came to light because of audit work carried out at a mutual client company, that is, the overseas bank. The audit firm has acquired information which discredits the information given to it by BV, the public limited company. The audit firm may at this point have considered whether it wished to continue to act for BV. In this case the audit firm would not be able to reveal its findings to BV as it would be deemed to be a breach of confidence to reveal this information without the permission of the overseas bank. It would be difficult to obtain such permission from the bank without a breach of confidence in respect of BV.

The existence of the fund should be substantiated by reference to the books and records of BV plc and if this had proved to be impossible the consent of BV should have been received to obtain direct confirmation from the overseas bank of the existence of the fund. If permission is refused, then the auditors should consider qualifying the audit report or resigning. It would appear from the case study that neither of these options appeared necessary.

(b)   Confidentiality of information is implied in all contracts with clients. Thus as a general rule auditors should not disclose to other persons information about a client against the client's wishes. It is in the public interest that this confidential relationship is maintained, as without confidentiality clients may be reluctant to seek advice from auditors. Generally where an auditor becomes aware that the client has committed an unlawful act, the auditor is under no legal obligation to disclose the information other than to the directors. However, it may be deemed to be in the 'public interest' that a disclosure is made and legal advice should be taken before making such disclosure. In the UK, the 'Public Interest Disclosure Act 1998' will offer protection to auditors who disclose information in the public interest.

Thus it could be argued, on the basis of the above information, that the managing partner was within his rights to refuse to submit the tax working papers and correspondence between the client and their solicitors. However, auditors must disclose information if compelled by the process of law and a court order constitutes such a due process. It is in the managing partner's own interest to disclose the information as suspicions as to collusion between the partner and the client may be aroused in the event of non-disclosure. Similarly a criminal charge may be brought against the partner for contempt of court with a prison sentence possibly resulting. Thus the managing partner ought to disclose the information to the court both as it is obligatory under the law and as it is in his own interest.

(c)   The position of the tax manager if he submits the tax working papers is as follows. The manager has decided that the managing partner has not followed the ethical guidance of the ACCA. In the event of taxation offences, the auditor should in the case of past accounts have advised full disclosure to the Inland Revenue, or if this was not forthcoming, should have resigned and informed the Inland Revenue that they were no longer prepared to report on the financial and other documents in the same terms as previously.

Additionally they should inform the Inland Revenue when they have ceased to act for BV. The auditor is under no duty to indicate in what way the financial statements are defective.

However, the tax manager has no authority to send the tax working papers to the court as the court has ordered the partners of the firm to make these papers available. It is a breach of his professional confidence. Additionally, the gesture is futile, as the managing partner will be forced by law to make the papers available. The tax manager will have created a confrontational situation and will be branded a 'whistle blower'. However, it appears that under the 'Public Interest Disclosure Act 1998' some measure of protection may be given to the tax manager. Where an employee discloses a criminal offence in good faith and without personal gain, then legal protection is given to that employee. For example, there is a right not to suffer a detriment, for example, a demotion. A dismissal for making a protected disclosure is deemed to be unfair dismissal.

However, the disclosure of the offence is protected but the release of the tax working papers without due sanction cannot be condoned. The tax manager should have allowed the judicial process to deal with this situation.

Marking Scheme

				Marks
1	(a)		Calculation of goodwill of X	4
			Calculation of goodwill of Y	1
				—
			Available/Maximum	5
				—
	(b)		Tangible fixed assets – inter co. profit	1
			– foreign investment	2
			Associate Company – deemed disposal	4
			Goodwill	4
			Net Current Assets	1
			Long-term liabilities – provision	2
			– overseas loan	1
			Revaluation Reserves	2
			Group Reserves	5
			X Reserves	2
			Minority Interest	4
				—
			Available	28
				—
			Maximum	25
				—
			Available	33
				—
			Maximum	30
				—
2	(a)	(i)	Normal business relationship	1
			Control and influence	1
			Significant effect on financial position and lead to transactions	2
			No transactions	1
			Different terms	1
			Assumption of arm's length	2
			Disclosure	2
				—
			Available	10
				—
			Maximum	6
				—
		(ii)	Equal importance	1
			Greater significance	1
			Directors/shareholders	1
			Confidential nature	1
			Cost/Benefits	1
			FRSSE	1
			Materiality	1
			Companies Acts	1
				—
			Available	8
				—
			Maximum	4
				—
	(b)	(i)	Providers of finance	1
			Equity interest	1
			Associate discussion	3
			Exercise control over 20%	1
			No influence	1
			Common director	1
			Disclose material transactions	1
				—
			Available	9
				—

				Maximum 6

(ii)	Intergroup eliminations		1
	X not part of group		1
	Any time in financial year		1
	Disclosure 1/7 to 31.10.99		1
	RP and Z not related parties unless subordinating Interest		1
			Available 5
			Maximum 4
(iii)	Pension scheme – related party		1
	Contributions v transactions		2
	Investment manager		3
	Materiality		1
			Available 7
			Maximum 5
			Available 39
			Maximum 25

3	(a)	(i)	Growth and complexity	1
			Standards not developed	1
			Non recognition	1
			Historical cost	1
			Risk of derivatives	1
			Unrealised gains and losses	1
			Hedge accounting	3
			Smooth profits	1
			Circumstances change quickly	1
				Available 11
				Maximum 7
		(ii)	Recognition and measurement	2
			Off balance sheet	1
			Hedge accounting problems	1
			Consensus over measurement	1
			Current values	1
			Derecognition	1
				Available 7
				Maximum 4
	(b)	(i)	3 marks per method	Maximum 8
		(ii)	1999	2
			2000	3
			2001	1
				Available/Maximum 6
				Available 32

Maximum 25

4	(a)	(i)	Subjective	7
		(ii)	Liability	1
			Legal/constructive obligation	2
			Reasonable estimate	1
			No alternative	1
			Recognition	1
			Do not need to know identity	1
			Onerous contracts	1

Available 8

Maximum 6

	(b)	(i)	Full liability	2
			Accounting	3
			Discounting	2
			Price level adjustment and interest	2
			Amendment of provision	1

Available 10

Maximum 7

		(ii)	No provision for future losses	1
			Onerous contract	2
			Provision stays	1
			Environment costs – obligation	2
			Mere existence	1

Available 7

Maximum 5

Available 32

Maximum 25

5	(a)	(i)	Subjective assessment	6
		(ii)	Developments in standards and corporate governance	2
			FRRP	1
			Disclosure – where to disclose	2
			User of financial statements	1
			Extent of disclosure	2
			Exceptional item	1
			Financial Instruments or similar example	1
			Regulations	2
			London Stock Exchange	1
			Traditional views outdated	1
			Conclusion	2

Available 16

Maximum 8

(b)   Subjective   6
                                                                                           ___
                                                                            Available 28

                                                                            Maximum 20
                                                                                           ___

6   (a)   Mutual client company   1
               Discredits information   1
               Continue to act   1
               Breach of confidence to reveal   3
               Refer to books and records of BV   1
               Consent of BV   1
               Qualify/resign   1
                                                                                           ___
                                                                            Available 9

                                                                            Maximum 6
                                                                                           ___

       (b)   General discussion of confidentiality   3
               Specific discussion of case   4
                                                                                           ___
                                                                    Available/Maximum 7
                                                                                           ___

       (c)   Tax affairs   2
               Confrontation pointless   1
               Not legally obligated   1
               No authority   1
               Public Interest Disclosure Act   2
               Conclusion   2
                                                                                           ___
                                                                            Available 9

                                                                            Maximum 7
                                                                                           ___
                                                                            Available 25

                                                                            Maximum 20
                                                                                           ___

ACCA
AT FOULKS LYNCH

HOTLINES
Telephone: 00 44 (0) 20 8844 0667
Enquiries: 00 44 (0) 20 8831 9990
Fax: 00 44 (0) 20 8831 9991

AT FOULKS LYNCH LTD
Number 4, The Griffin Centre
Staines Road, Feltham
Middlesex TW14 0HS

Examination Date:
☐ June 2000
☐ December 2000

	Publications				Distance Learning	Open Learning
	Textbooks (Pub'd July 99)	**Revision Series** (Pub'd Feb 2000)	**Lynchpins** Pub'd Feb 2000	**Tracks** (Audio Tapes)	**Include helpline & marking** (except for overseas Open Learning)	
Module A – Foundation Stage						
1 Accounting Framework	£18.95 [UK] [IAS]	£10.95 [UK] [IAS]	£5.95 [UK] [IAS]	£10.95	£85 [UK] [IAS]	£89
2 Legal Framework	£18.95	£10.95	£5.95	£10.95	£85	£89
Module B						
3 Management Information	£18.95	£10.95	£5.95	£10.95	£85	£89
4 Organisational Framework	£18.95	£10.95	£5.95	£10.95	£85	£89
Module C – Certificate Stage						
5 Information Analysis	£18.95	£10.95	£5.95	£10.95	£85	£89
6 Audit Framework	£18.95 [UK] [IAS]	£10.95 [UK] [IAS]	£5.95 [UK] [IAS]	£10.95	£85 [UK] [IAS]	£89
Module D						
7 Tax Framework FA99 - D/J00	£18.95	£10.95	£5.95	*£10.95	£85	£89
8 Managerial Finance	£18.95	£10.95	£5.95	£10.95	£85	£89
Module E – Professional Stage						
9 ICDM	£18.95	£10.95	£5.95	£10.95	£85	£89
10 Accounting & Audit Practice	£22.95 [UK] [IAS] (£23.95)	£10.95 [UK] [IAS]	£5.95 [UK] [IAS]	£10.95	£85 [UK] [IAS]	£89
11 Tax Planning FA99 - J/D00	£18.95	£10.95	£5.95	*£10.95	£85	£89
Module F						
12 Management & Strategy	£18.95	£10.95	£5.95	£10.95	£85	£89
13 Financial Rep Environment	£20.95 [UK] [IAS]	£10.95 [UK] [IAS]	£5.95 [UK] [IAS]	£10.95	£85 [UK] [IAS]	£89
14 Financial Strategy	£19.95	£10.95	£5.95	£10.95	£85	£89
			P7 & 11 Pub'd 7/99	*Available Feb 2000		

P & P + Delivery						
UK Mainland	£2.00/book	£1.00/book	£1.00/book	£1.00/tape	£5.00/subject	£5.00/subject
NI, ROI & EU Countries	£5.00/book	£3.00/book	£3.00/book	£1.00/tape	£15.00/subject	£15.00/subject
Rest of world standard air service	£10.00/book	£8.00/book	£8.00/book	£2.00/tape	£25.00/subject	£25.00/subject
Rest of world courier service†	£22.00/book	£20.00/book	Not applicable	Not applicable	£47.00/subject	£47.00/subject

SINGLE ITEM SUPPLEMENT FOR TEXTBOOKS AND REVISION SERIES:
If you only order 1 item, INCREASE postage costs by £2.50 for UK, NI & EU Countries or by £15.00 for Rest of World Services

TOTAL						
Sub Total £						
Post & Packing £						
Total £						

†*Telephone number essential for this service*   *Payments in Sterling in London* | Order Total   £ |

DELIVERY DETAILS
☐ Mr ☐ Miss ☐ Mrs ☐ Ms Other
Initials   Surname
Address
....
....
....
                    Postcode
Telephone   Deliver to home ☐
Company name
Address
....
....
                    Postcode
Telephone   Fax
Monthly report to go to employer ☐   Deliver to work ☐

PAYMENT
1 I enclose Cheque/PO/Bankers Draft for £_____
   Please make cheques payable to AT Foulks Lynch Ltd.

2 Charge Mastercard/Visa/Switch A/C No:

Valid from: |__|__|__| Expiry Date: |__|__|__|
Issue No: (Switch only) |__|__|
Signature   Date

DECLARATION
I agree to pay as indicated on this form and understand that
AT Foulks Lynch Terms and Conditions apply (available on
request). I understand that AT Foulks Lynch Ltd are not liable
for non-delivery if the rest of world standard air service is used.

Signature   Date

Please Allow:	UK mainland	- 5-10 w/days
	NI, ROI & EU Countries	- 1-3 weeks
	Rest of world standard air service	- 6 weeks
	Rest of world courier service	- 10 w/days

Notes: All delivery times subject to stock availability. Signature required on receipt (except rest of world standard air service). Please give both addresses for Distance Learning students where possible.

Form effective December 99   *All details correct at time of printing*   *Source: ACRS00*